The Arthurian Texts of the Percy Folio

EXETER MEDIEVAL TEXTS AND STUDIES

Series Editors: Richard Dance and Eddie Jones

Emeritus Editors:
M.J. Swanton (founder)
Marion Glasscoe
Vincent Gillespie

The Arthurian Texts of the Percy Folio

Edited by
John Withrington

with the assistance of
Gillian Rogers

LIVERPOOL UNIVERSITY PRESS

First published in 2023 by
Liverpool University Press
4 Cambridge Street
Liverpool
L69 7ZU

Copyright © 2023 John Withrington

John Withrington has asserted the right to be identified as the author of this book in accordance with the Copyright, Designs and Patents Act 1988.

All rights reserved. No part of this book may be reproduced, stored in a retrieval system, or transmitted, in any form or by any means, electronic, mechanical, photocopying, recording, or otherwise, without the prior written permission of the publisher.

British Library Cataloguing-in-Publication data
A British Library CIP record is available

ISBN 978-1-83764-509-1

Typeset by Carnegie Book Production, Lancaster
Printed and bound by CPI Group (UK) Ltd, Croydon CR0 4YY

For Roz, Laura, and Sophie,
and in memory of my parents

also in memory of the late
Dr W. R. J. Barron

The Turke & Gowin

Listen lords great & small
what adventures did befall
in England where hath beene
of knights that hold the round table
w{th} sword dought{y} & fittable
of kempys truth & boun{e}
all England both east & west
lords & ladyes of the best
they busked made them bowne
& Ken the king sate in seate
lords served him at his meate
into the hall a buzuw' there come

He was not hyg but he was broad
& like a turke he was made
both legg & thye
& said is there any will as a brother
give a buffett & take another
or if any soe hardy bee
& on spake S{r} Key that raked h{t}
& said man thou seemst not soe wise
if thou be not afrayd
for there be one h{er} w{th}in this hall
w{th} a buffett will gar y{ou} fall
& make y{ou} to the ground

And thou be not soe stalworth of hands
I shall bring thee to the ground
it dare I safely sweare
then spake S{r} Gawaine that worthy knight
saith to y{ou} Kay thou speakst not right
leave w{th} thy answere
What & that man wants of his will
Gawaine worshipp wow to deo yitt
if thou shold him forsake
Then spake the turke w{th} words thraw
w{th} some the better of y{o}r tow
to Gowin e s{r}

*kempys i.e.
warriors.

*barne i.e.
homo.

*i.e.
stout.

*brem i.e. fierce

Contents

Acknowledgements and Contributors	ix
List of Abbreviations	xi
Preface	xv
Notes to Preface	xvi

INTRODUCTION

The Manuscript — 1
  Discovery of the Manuscript — 1
  Contents and Date — 1
  The Scribe/Compiler at Work — 3
  The Scribe/Compiler: Background and Identity — 4
  The Scribe/Compiler: Sources and Composition — 7
  Percy's Annotations — 8
  Notes — 9

The Arthurian Texts of the Percy Folio — 13
  Assembling the *Reliques* — 14
  'This vague and indiscriminating name' — 15
  A Matter of Taste — 17
  'This tale grew in the telling' — 20
  Conclusion — 24
  Notes — 25

The Arthurian Background — 32
  King Arthur as Historical Figure — 32
  Enlisting the Arthurian Legend — 33
  The Arthurian Legend in Literature and Prophecy — 35
  Percy and the Arthurian Legend — 37
  Notes — 39

Previous Editions and Methodology Adopted for this Edition — 44

Appendix: Extract from letter by Thomas Percy to Thomas Warton, 28 May 1761 — 46

THE TEXTS — 49
  King Arthur and King Cornwall — 51
  Sir Lancelott of Dulake — 71
  The Turke & Gowin — 78

The Marriage of Sir Gawaine	99
Sir Lambewell	114
Merline	141
Kinge Arthurs Death	210
The Grene Knyght	224
Boy and Mantle	247
Libius Disconius	259
Carle off Carlile	331

BIBLIOGRAPHY 353

INDEX 368

Acknowledgements and Contributors

Acknowledgements
The British Library for permission to print the texts from the Percy Folio MS, and for the reproduction of f. 17v; the late Dr W. R. J. Barron, the 'prime mover' of this project; Professor Nick Groom, for his co-operation, guidance, encouragement, support, and comments; The Vinaver Trust of the British Branch of the International Arthurian Society, for offering to underwrite the book in its first manifestation; Professor P. J. C. Field for his encouragement and suggestions; Professor Ad Putter for his generous comments in respect of the Introduction; Professor Felicity Riddy, as one of the original editors alongside Elizabeth Williams, for helping to shape and clarify the project in its early stages; and colleagues at the University of Exeter Press and latterly Liverpool University Press for their patience and keeping the faith through many years. Finally, during the years I have been involved with this project, for my wife Roz, whose patience and encouragement have meant so much. Above all, for Gillian Rogers, one of the original editors for this project, whose vision, enthusiasm, and keen eye helped bring this book to fruition.

The Contributors
Elizabeth Darović (*MER*) earned her MA from King's College London, and her MA Ed. in Secondary English Education from DePaul University, Chicago.

Maldwyn Mills (*LD*) The late Maldwyn Mills was Professor of Medieval English at the University of Aberystwyth and wrote extensively on Middle English romances and Chaucer. His edition of *Lybeaus Desconus* for the Early English Text Society was published in 1969. He also edited *Six Middle English Romances* (1973), *Ywain and Gawain, Sir Percyvell of Gales*, and *The Anturs of Arther* (1992).

Raluca Radulescu (*BM, SLDL*) is Professor of Medieval Literature and founding Director of the Centre for Arthurian Studies at Bangor University. She is Vice-President of the International Arthurian Society. Her two monographs discuss Arthurian and non-Arthurian romance and culture (*The Gentry Context for Malory's 'Morte Darthur'*, 2003; *Romance and Its Contexts in Late Medieval England: Politics, Piety and Penitence*, 2013). Collections of essays she has co-edited have focused on chronicles and genealogies, heraldry, popular romance, manuscript miscellanies, and editing. Her *Routledge Companion to Medieval English Literature* was published in 2023. The *Cambridge History of Arthurian Literature and Culture*, co-edited with Prof. Andrew Lynch, is forthcoming in 2024.

Gillian Rogers (*CARLE, KAKC, MER, TG*) was formerly the English Faculty Librarian in the University of Cambridge. Her PhD dissertation for the University of Wales – 'Themes and Variations: Studies in some English Gawain-Poems' – was awarded in 1978. She has published articles on the Percy Folio MS, *Golagros and Gawain*, *The Grene Knyght*, and edited the chapter on 'Folk Romance' in *The Arthur of the English* (1999).

Diane Speed AM (*GK*) has a BA Hons, MA Hons, and MTh Hons from the University of Sydney, and a PhD from the University of London. She is Professor Emerita and former Dean and CEO of the Sydney College of Divinity, having spent many years as a medievalist in the University of Sydney. Her research interests include biblical literature, romance, hagiography, and exempla, with current projects narrative theology, neo-Gothic church windows, and the *Otuel* romances. Her book *Medieval English Romances*, which includes an edition of *The Grene Knyght*, was first published in 1987, with a 3rd edition in 1993. The *Anglo-Latin Gesta Romanorum*, of which she is part-editor, appeared in 2019.

Marian Trudgill (*KAD*). After graduating from the University of Wales in 1995, Dr Trudgill pursued her interest in medieval literature as a postgraduate and tutor at the University of Bristol, where she completed her MA and PhD. Her research interests include chivalry, medieval romance, Arthurian legend, and the role of aristocratic women in the twelfth century.

Elizabeth Williams (*LAMBE*). The late Elizabeth Williams taught at Leeds University until her retirement in 1981, her chief interests being medieval romances with folk- and fairy-tale elements, and the interaction between oral and literary narrative. One of the original editors for this project, her edition of *Sir Launfal* appeared in *Leeds Studies in English* in 1984.

John Withrington (*INTRODUCTION, CARLE, KAKC, LAMBE, LD, MER, KAD, MSG, TG*) studied at the universities of Cambridge, Leicester, and York, where his DPhil was on late medieval attitudes to the death and supposed return of King Arthur. His publications include the first critical edition of *The Wedding of Sir Gawain and Dame Ragnell* (1991) and co-authorship with Professor P. J. C. Field of the chapter on the 'Wife of Bath's Tale' for *Sources and Analogues of the Canterbury Tales* (2005). A former Honorary Research Fellow of the University of Exeter, prior to retirement he was Head of the university's International Office.

List of Abbreviations

1794 *Reliques*	Thomas Percy, *Reliques of Ancient English Poetry: Consisting of Old Heroic Ballads, Songs, and other Pieces of our earlier Poets, Together with some few of later Date*, 4th ed., 3 vols (London: Printed by John Nichols, for F. and C. Rivington, 1794)
AE	W. R. J. Barron (ed.), *The Arthur of the English: The Arthurian Legend in Medieval English Life and Literature*, Arthurian Literature in the Middle Ages 2 (Cardiff: University of Wales Press, 1999)
AM	*Arthour and Merlin*
AMA	*Alliterative Morte Arthure*
BI	*Le Bel Inconnu*
BL	British Library, London
BM	*Boy and Mantle*
Bodl.	Bodleian Library, Oxford
Carelyle	*Carle of Carelyle*
CARLE	*Carle off Carlile*
Child	Francis James Child (ed.), *The English and Scottish Popular Ballads*, 5 vols (Boston: Houghton, Mifflin, 1882–98; repr. Cambridge: Cambridge University Press, 2014, online 2014)
Collection	Anon., *A Collection of Old Ballads. Corrected from the best and most Ancient Copies Extant. With Introductions Historical, Critical, or Humorous. Illustrated with Copper Plates*, 3 vols (London: J. Roberts and D. Leach, 1723–25)
DSL	*Dictionaries of the Scots Language*, https://dsl.ac.uk
EETS	Early English Text Society
ESTC	English Short Title Catalogue (citation number)
FLOR	John Gower, 'The Tale of Florent', *Confessio Amantis*
GK	*The Grene Knyght*
Groom, 1996	Nick Groom (ed.), Thomas Percy, '*Reliques of Ancient English Poetry*', With a New Introduction by Nick Groom, 3 vols; facsimile of the 1765 edition (London: Routledge/Thoemmes Press, 1996)
Groom, 1999	*The Making of Percy's* Reliques (Oxford: Clarendon Press, 1999)
Hahn	Thomas Hahn (ed.), *Sir Gawain: Eleven Romances and Tales* (Kalamazoo, MI: Medieval Institute Publications, 1995), https://d.lib.rochester.edu/teams/publication/hahn-sir-gawain

HF	John W. Hales and Frederick J. Furnivall (eds), *Bishop Percy's Folio Manuscript: Ballads and Romances*, 3 vols (London: Trübner, 1867–68)
HRB	Michael D. Reeve (ed.) and Neil Wright (trans.), *Geoffrey of Monmouth: The History of the Kings of Britain. An Edition and Translation of the* De gestis Britonum [*Historia Regum Brittanniae*], Arthurian Studies 69 (Woodbridge: Boydell Press, 2007)
KAD	*Kinge Arthurs Death*
KAKC	*King Arthur and King Cornwall*
LAMBE	*Sir Lambewell*
LD	*Libius Disconius*
Letters	*The Percy Letters* vol. I, *The Correspondence of Thomas Percy & Edmond Malone*, ed. Arthur Tillotson (Baton Rouge: Louisiana State University Press, 1944); vol. II, *The Correspondence of Thomas Percy & Richard Farmer*, ed. Cleanth Brooks (Baton Rouge: Louisiana State University Press, 1946); vol. III, *The Correspondence of Thomas Percy & Thomas Warton*, ed. M. G. Robinson and Leah Dennis (Baton Rouge: Louisiana State University Press, 1951); vol. IV, *The Correspondence of Thomas Percy & David Dalrymple, Lord Hailes*, ed. A. F. Falconer (Baton Rouge: Louisiana State University Press, 1954); vol. V, *The Correspondence of Thomas Percy & Evan Evans*, ed. Aneirin Lewis (Baton Rouge: Louisiana State University Press, 1957); vol. VI, *The Correspondence of Thomas Percy & George Paton*, ed. A. F. Falconer (New Haven, CT: Yale University Press, 1961); gen. eds Cleanth Brooks and A. F. Falconer; vol. VII, *The Correspondence of Thomas Percy & William Shenstone*, ed. Cleanth Brooks (New Haven, CT: Yale University Press, 1977); vol. VIII, *The Correspondence of Thomas Percy & John Pinkerton*, ed. Harriet Harvey Wood (New Haven, CT: Yale University Press, 1985); vol. IX, *The Correspondence of Thomas Percy & Robert Anderson*, ed. W. E. K. Anderson (New Haven, CT: Yale University Press, 1988)
LH	left-hand
LMD	H. Oskar Sommer (ed.), *Le Morte Darthur by Syr Thomas Malory, reprinted and ed. H. Oskar Sommer* (London: David Nutt, 1889–91), https://quod.lib.umich.edu/cgi/t/text/text-idx?c=cme;idno=MaloryWks2[1]
Madden	Sir Frederic Madden (ed.), *Syr Gawayne: A Collection of Ancient Romance-Poems, by Scotish and English Authors, Relating to that Celebrated Knight of the Round Table, with an Introduction, Notes, and a Glossary* (London: Richard and John Taylor, 1839), https://archive.org/details/syrgawaynecoll6100madduoft/page/n5/mode/2up
ME	Middle English

---

[1] Percy and his predecessors would have known *LMD* through the version first printed by Caxton in July 1485. Sommer's edition has been selected as providing the most scholarly and accessible edition of the Caxton text.

MED	*Middle English Dictionary*, https://quod.lib.umich.edu/m/middle-english-dictionary/dictionary
MER	*Merline*
MSG	*The Marriage of Sir Gawaine*
NLS	National Library of Scotland, Edinburgh
NLW	National Library of Wales, Aberystwyth
OED	*Oxford English Dictionary*, https://www.oed.com
P	Thomas Percy
PF	Percy Folio manuscript (BL MS Add. 27879)
Reliques	Thomas Percy, *Reliques of Ancient English Poetry: Consisting of Old Heroic Ballads, Songs, and other Pieces of our earlier Poets* (*Chiefly of the Lyric Kind.*) *Together with some few of later Date*, 3 vols (London: J. Dodsley, 1765)
RH	right-hand
SGGK	*Sir Gawain and the Green Knight*
SLDL	*Sir Lancelott of Dulake*
TG	*The Turke & Gowin*
TR	*Thomas the Rymer*
WBT	'The Wife of Bath's Tale'
WSG	*The Wedding of Sir Gawain and Dame Ragnell*

Preface

British Library MS Add. 27879, known as the Percy Folio (PF), is a collection compiled between 1640 and 1650 by an unknown enthusiast with a keen interest in ballad and romance material. Rescued from a friend's fire by the antiquarian clergyman Thomas Percy in about 1753, the manuscript formed a key inspiration for his publication in 1765 of *Reliques of Ancient English Poetry: Consisting of Old Heroic Ballads, Songs, and other Pieces of our earlier Poets* (*Chiefly of the Lyric Kind.*) *Together with some few of later Date*. Notwithstanding that the 11 Arthurian texts in the PF constitute a relatively small proportion of the total content, and the PF itself only contributed about a quarter of the works ultimately published in the *Reliques*, such was the appeal of this work that subsequent editions appeared in 1767, 1775, and 1794.[1] The ballads printed by Percy, including those that were imaginatively reconstructed and rewritten by him, were the subject of intense scholarly and public interest, and their influence was far reaching. James Beattie's poem *The Minstrel* was published in 1771, a work which, alongside Gray's *Elegy*, was 'among the most popular compositions of the later eighteenth century';[2] it has been suggested that *The Marriage of Sir Gawaine* proved influential in the composition of Coleridge's *Christabel*;[3] Wordsworth's 'Essay, Supplementary to the Preface' of his *Poems* (1815) acknowledged the importance of the *Reliques* in the development of English poetry; while Percy's romantic idealization of such ballads as reflecting a bygone Golden Age of Minstrelsy proved to be a direct inspiration for Sir Walter Scott, who at the age of 13 lost himself in its pages.[4] Scott's interest in balladry and medieval texts, including Malory's *Le Morte Darthur*, led to a number of highly successful period novels which contributed to the renewed interest in Arthurian material in the nineteenth century.[5] In short, the PF was to play a crucial role in the publication of the *Reliques* – a work that proved to be the 'seminal, epoch-making work of English Romanticism'[6] – and the subsequent Arthurian revival.

Two ballads from the PF were to play a key role in the publication of the *Reliques*, bringing to the attention of the general public seemingly ancient texts on an Arthurian theme. *The Marriage of Sir Gawaine* and *Boy and Mantle* were displayed from the outset by Percy as the jewels in the minstrelsy crown.[7] When Percy carefully approached for the first time the celebrated critic and future Poet Laureate Thomas Warton, he was extravagant not just in his praise for Warton and for the importance of the PF but claimed that Chaucer had drawn on *The Marriage of Sir Gawaine* itself for the 'Wife of Bath's Tale' (see Appendix, pp. 46–47 below). Having bestowed apparent legitimacy and credibility upon ballad and collection, these two Arthurian pieces, his 'best materials at hand',[8] were to have been published in the opening volume of the *Reliques*. Percy's late decision to dedicate his work to Elizabeth Percy, Countess of Northumberland, resulted in a reversal of the volume order: instead of these pieces opening the *Reliques*, volume 1 commenced with 'Chevy Chase', a ballad featuring the Northumberland Percys of old, and volume 3 was subtitled 'Ballads on King Arthur, etc.', with an essay from Percy on the chivalric tradition, followed by 'The Boy and the Mantle', 'The Marriage of Sir Gawaine', 'King Ryence's Challenge' (not to be found in the PF), 'King Arthur's death. A Fragment' and 'The Legend of King Arthur'.[9] While Percy was subsequently to disown the very work that had brought him such fame, the *Reliques* conferred upon the ballads, Arthurian and otherwise, a historical pedigree and canonical respectability for texts which otherwise, quite literally, would have burned in obscurity: 'in the history of Arthurian literature, the *Reliques* occupies a special place as having made possible through its ... Arthurian pieces a wide familiarity with some elements of the traditional story'.[10]

This book draws together for the first time critical editions of all 11 Arthurian texts to be found in the Percy Folio, with transcriptions taken directly from BL MS Add. 27879. The aim has been to appeal to the general reader as well as to the scholar, and to provide context as well as reliable transcriptions. The texts are prefaced by a discussion of the Percy Folio, its history and ownership, their place within a ballad tradition, attitudes to King Arthur up to the time of the *Reliques*' publication, and Percy's interest in and knowledge of Arthurian legend. Previous editions and the methodology adopted for this edition are given, and the book concludes with a bibliography. Each text is prefaced by a Headnote with references and suggestions for further reading, and accompanied by Explanatory Notes and Textual Notes, including transcripts of Percy's own annotations.

Notes to Preface

[1] While the 4th edition is dated 1794, it actually appeared in the following year.

[2] Kathryn Sutherland, 'The Native Poet: The Influence of Percy's Minstrel from Beattie to Wordsworth', *Review of English Studies* 33(132) (1982), p. 414.

[3] Donald Reuel Tuttle, '*Christabel* Sources in Percy's *Reliques* and the Gothic Romance', *PMLA* 53(2) (1938), p. 446.

[4] For the influence of the *Reliques* on, e.g., Scott's *Minstrelsy of the Scottish Border* (1802) and *Sir Tristrem* (1809), see Arthur Johnston, *Enchanted Ground: The Study of Medieval Romance in the Eighteenth Century* (London: Athlone Press, 1964), pp. 177–94. Scott's reverence for the *Reliques* led to him being introduced to Percy by Robert Anderson (*Letters*, IX, 29). Percy approved of Scott's proposal to collect Scottish ballad material, and Scott sought Percy's help for more information about the medieval romance 'Eger and Greme'. The response to Scott, via Anderson, included the request by Percy that any reference to him be not 'by my professional Title, but only as the Possessor of the old folio MS, or the original Editor of the Reliques of ancient English Poetry' (*Letters*, IX, 29, 43, 45).

[5] Scott owned a copy of Stansby's 1634 edition of *Le Morte Darthur*, and at one stage planned to publish an edition of his own (Johnston, 1964, 190–91).

[6] Groom, 1999, 3.

[7] In the Percy Folio (PF), the ballad's title is 'Boy and Mantle'. For the *Reliques*, Percy allocated the title 'The Boy and the Mantle'.

[8] Groom, 1996, I, 28.

[9] 'Kinge Arthurs Death' in the Percy Folio was published by Percy in two parts, i.e., 'King Arthur's death. A Fragment' and 'The Legend of King Arthur'. For a discussion of the decision to dedicate the *Reliques* to the Countess of Northumberland, and its impact upon the shape and production of the *Reliques*, see Groom, 1999, 219–25.

[10] James Douglas Merriman, *The Flower of Kings: A Study of the Arthurian Legend in England between 1485 and 1835* (Lawrence: University Press of Kansas, 1973), p. 94.

Introduction: The Manuscript

Discovery of the Manuscript

In a note dated 7 November 1769, written on the inside cover of the PF, Percy recounted the discovery of the manuscript at the home of his friend, Humphrey Pitt: 'I saw it lying dirty on the floor under a Bureau in ye Parlour: being used by the Maids to light the fire'.[1] Immediately before this comment is a separate, undated, note by Percy, where he records that the discovery took place when he was 'very young' (although a date of around 1753 has been suggested as a possibility),[2] but by late 1757 Percy was sharing his find with various friends, including William Shenstone, to whom he wrote in November, advertising his previous contacts with Samuel Johnson. The following month Percy embarked on a compilation of an index for the MS (Groom, 1999, 121).

However, Percy's account invites further consideration. In 1967, Leslie Shepard reported that a copy of the 1775 *Reliques* in his possession included an inscription by previous owner William Yonge, in which Yonge stated that he had seen the MS in Pitt's office in 'about the year 1757', and 'soon became an eager reader'.[3] Yonge was an old man by the time he wrote this in 1826, so the year in question may not be accurate, but as Shepard suggests, 'it is also quite possible that Percy had already rescued the MS *before* Yonge saw it and did not collect it until a later date'.[4] Percy, of course, volunteered nothing to clarify the circumstances of the manuscript's discovery and its background, his protective secrecy constituting an open invitation for others to speculate on the manuscript's contents.[5]

Contents and Date

BL MS Add. 27879 in its present mutilated state comprises 527 pages, containing 195 verse items covering a range of subjects, from short lyrics to long medieval romance, from political songs to tales of heroes such as King Arthur.[6] Certain groups can be identified, for example ballads of Robin Hood, medieval romance, Cavalier poetry and the humorous and historical, while chronologically speaking pieces range from 'The Siege of Roune' (*c*.1420) to 'Newarke' (1645). The PF is a collection that very much reflects the highly personal interests of its compiler/scribe, who were most likely one and the same person.

I

The MS is written on folios folded lengthwise, measuring approximately 390 mm × 140 mm. Following the partial destruction in Pitt's household, further loss was incurred when Percy sent the MS to the binders, who pared the margins, thereby losing lines at the tops and bottoms of the leaves and some parts of Percy's side-glosses. The first extant 28 leaves were folded across, presumably to make it easy for Sir Humphrey Pitt's housemaids to tear the pages for the fire. Furnivall intervened to prevent further tears at the end of the MS, reinforcing the early pages by patching them with pieces of gummed paper, and employing a binder to 'put a stiff guard of pasteboard behind these half pages, to carry their weight' (HF, I, xxiv).[7] Following acquisition of the MS by the British Museum in 1868, the 28 half-leaves were remounted in a pattern that disturbed the logical sequence, i.e., alternately two top-mounted and two bottom-mounted. (The 29th leaf is intact but torn across: one-half of which was incorrectly incorporated as part of *Sir Lambewell* (*LAMBE*).) These repairs, probably undertaken in 1954 in an attempt to prevent further splitting of the fragile pages, were complemented by the removal of the gutters, with each leaf gauzed and mounted in a paper frame.

The condition of the MS is generally poor: it suffered further deterioration since HF's edition of 1867–68, some of the readings having been lost. There is frequent bleed-through, with blots obscuring letters and sometimes whole words; holes have been caused by the acidic nature of the ink used; there is crumbling of the edges, particularly at the bottom right corner of the leaves; and some water damage is evident. The numbering system adopted is initially confused, a situation not helped by the probable lack of some seven opening leaves, with a continuous sequence of pagination only commencing on the verso of the current fifth half-leaf. It is not apparent whether this pagination is the work of the original scribe.

Date

Watermarks of the 'Norman pot' variety imply a date towards the middle of the seventeenth century (Rogers, 1991, 41–42). St Clair-Kendall remarked on the scribe's early use of facile/rapid Elizabethan secretary with hybrid-italic for headings, and that standard secretary miniscule continues to appear later in the MS. Noting that 'Elizabethan Secretary had become unusual by the end of the third decade of the 17th century ... and flourished until about the end of the 1630s', she proposed a date for the hand of between 1630 and before 1650 (St Clair-Kendall, 2007, 9).

More robust evidence for dating, however, is offered by a cluster of Royalist political songs and Cavalier lyrics, implying a particular burst of activity on the part of the scribe. 'The Tribe off Banburye' alludes to an incident in the English Civil War in 1642; Richard Lovelace's poem 'To Althea from Prison' – which has the title 'When loue with unconfined' in the MS – was probably written about the same time: textual variations imply that the MS version was indebted to a manuscript copy of the text written on or after 1642, as opposed to its publication seven years later. 'The Kinge enioies his righ[ts againe]' is thought to have been written by Martin Parker sometime after July 1643, and the poem 'Newarke' commemorates the third and final siege of this Royalist town: St Clair-Kendall argues for a date for its composition of November 1645, the town eventually surrendering on 8 May the following year.[8] Elsewhere, 'The Aegiptian Quene', usually called 'Mark Anthony' and previously ascribed to John Cleveland, dates to *c*.1639 and was published in 1647.[9] Six MSS were in circulation before that time, so it is likely that, as with Lovelace's poem, the scribe took his version from a manuscript text as opposed to one in print. Taking into account the Royalist texts, the scribal hand, and watermarks, St Clair-Kendall concluded that given the absence of a reference to the death of Charles I 'the compilation of the *Percy Folio* can be dated with reasonable certainty as having taken place on various occasions between 1640 and 1648' (2007, 13).

The Scribe/Compiler at Work
Transcription and Dialect

The PF is the work of one hand throughout, mixing secretary with italic. The delivery is confident and emphatic, but untidy, and on occasions it is difficult to distinguish between certain letters, particularly *e* and *o*, and *a* and *u*. The letters most influenced by an italic style are *h* (particularly in combination with an initial *th-* formation, often in the same sentence as the more frequently used secretary *h* in that formation); in the characteristic form of *–ght* for *–gth* (as in 'strenght'), where the scribe normally uses the secretary *h*; and *e*, where the italic form, resembling a Greek ε, is only used when the word begins with that letter. Minims are frequently either one too many or one too few, while flamboyant descenders often intrude so far that they obscure letters in the line below. Characteristic is a seemingly random doubling of consonants, the addition of a final *–e*, and otiose ampersands at the beginning of lines.[10] Along with other scribes of the time, virtually no punctuation is employed, apart from colons separating the words of some titles, which were possibly intended as ornamentation, a form of the hash-sign to signify a refrain, and a somewhat random use of the medial punctus and virgule at the ends of some lines. This latter combination was normally used as a full-stop, although the punctus was usually on the line, not above it. The virgule, a diagonal slash /, was commonly used before 1580 but less frequently after the end of the century. While the usual order would have been to employ in sequence a virgule and medial dot, the PF scribe frequently reverses the order, possibly due to a lack of familiarity with early practice.[11]

The text displays signs of a northern dialect – 'thoust' ('thou shalt'), 'youst' ('you will'), and 'unbethought' ('umbethought'), as well as the use of 'ist' for 'I will', 'clemmed', 'be-happened', 'neshe' – some of which were noted by Furnivall (HF, I, xiii), who believed that this indicated a Lancashire provenance. It is possible, however, that dialectal features may simply reflect the faithful copying of the source text in question.

Presentation

There are no gaps in the sequence of texts, implying that the scribe had the leisure both to make up a gathering in advance and to allow the ink to dry on a recto before continuing on the verso. Catchwords on both recto and verso would have helped him to keep the pages in order. Pages normally begin in a small, reasonably neat, script, which gets larger and more sprawling as the page progresses; gaps between the lines are more spaced-out and have a tendency to slope down to the right. Most lines start with a lower-case letter. The first word of each text is written in large italics, extending down over two lines, necessitating indentation. The longer items, particularly the romances, are divided into parts – seemingly the scribe's own divisions – while the stanzaic texts have the opening stanza bracketed in the left margin at the start of each new Part. The scribe occasionally writes proper names in larger italics, which might indicate that he was working from a text, be that manuscript or print, which differentiated names in this fashion. On occasions he provides his own title to an item, usually the first line, rather than use the title by which a text is popularly known. For example, Cobbett's 'The Distracted Puritan' is called 'O Noble Festus'.[12]

The scribe seems to have worked out his layout over the first few leaves, containing the mutilated 'Robin Hood' ballads.[13] The thick black ruled left margins are there from the beginning, as are the thinner right-hand ones, which the scribe often ignored. He made some attempt to indicate stanza divisions by leaving gaps but is inconsistent in his approach: most stanzas are also marked off freehand in short dark-brown or black lines across the left margins, although it is not clear whether the scribe or Percy was responsible. (Percy was, however, responsible for much of the stanza-numbering in the longer items, mostly in fives, and not always accurately. Many of the later texts are unnumbered.)[14] Titles are written in italics, using the Greek ε, and become larger and more flamboyant as the manuscript progresses. Beginning with 'Musleboorrowe [*sic*] Ffeild', all subsequent titles have emphatic ruled lines above and below them.

The Scribe/Compiler: Background and Identity

Nothing definite is known about the scribe/compiler, although certain assumptions can be made – for example, that the individual was male, and quite likely Catholic with Royalist sympathies, given the burst of such materials transcribed, seemingly in relatively short order. He must have been reasonably well educated: the satirical poem 'To Oxfforde', on the visit of James I to Oxford (HF, III, 315–18) could indicate at least a nodding acquaintance with that institution, and a grammar school background is implied, given that his Latin was good.[15] We can assume that he was reasonably well off, given his access to the required amount of paper, ink, and quills, and that he seemingly had the leisure to travel, search out, and copy those pieces that intrigued him. The conundrum is that the very eclectic nature of the PF makes it difficult to conclude much more than this. Literary value does not appear to have been a major criterion for textual inclusion (the ballad 'Thomas, Lord Cromwell' is not even complete),[16] and it seems likely that the major driver was simply what caught his eye, or what reflected an antiquarian's desire to preserve, a trait he shared with Percy himself. The manuscript bears accordingly the hallmarks of a collection written for personal enjoyment by an individual who not only valued his work but took pride in what he wrote: pains are taken to correct written errors, sometimes seemingly immediately, sometimes going back over what had been written, with carets and on occasion pi-symbols being employed to signal omissions. It is equally possible that the care demonstrated in the copying may have been motivated in part by a desire on the part of the scribe/compiler to share his book of treasures, although no evidence of annotation by a diligent reader other than Percy is evident.

The Stanley Connection

Furnivall remarked upon the 'strong local feeling shown by the copier in favour of Lancashire and Cheshire and the Stanleys' (HF, I, xiii), although it does not necessarily follow that the Lancashire dialect he identified means that the scribe was himself from that county.[17] The two ballads on the battle of Flodden in 1513 ('Fflodden ffeilde', 'Scotish ffeilde'), and three on the battle of Bosworth in 1485 ('The Rose of Englande', 'Bosworthe ffeilde', 'Ladye Bessiye'), are at the heart of an apparent Stanley connection. (The two latter texts even have two stanzas in common: lines 589–96 and 1043–50 respectively are almost identical.) These Stanley-themed texts are scattered throughout the manuscript, but the connection does not end there. In lines 328–30 of *The Turke & Gowin* (*TG*) the disenchanted Turk is made King of Man by Arthur, and the castle of Hutton at line 493 in *The Grene Knight* (*GK*) could well be Hooton in Cheshire, a Stanley stronghold.[18] Paradoxically, two additional texts offer less than heroic portraits of the Stanley family. In 'Sir John Butler', Lady Butler asks for the death of her brother Stanley in revenge for her husband's murder (HF, III, 205), while in 'Panders come awaye', Venetia Stanley, the wife of Sir Kenelm Digby and the granddaughter, both of the Earl of Derby and of the 7th Earl of Northumberland, is listed as one of the prostitutes of London.[19]

There is no way of knowing whether the scribe's apparently close interest in the Stanleys was due to a connection involving family, friends, historical interest, or simply a reflection of his broad tastes. The inclusion of both flattering and unflattering texts in respect of the Stanleys must remain a puzzle.

Thomas Blount

Percy's note at the beginning of the manuscript, dated 7 November 1769, records Pitt's belief that the Herefordshire antiquary Thomas Blount (1618–79) was the scribe. Pitt's view was based on the fact that the manuscript had been part of Blount's library, which had been passed down to his great-nephew, Edward Blount, the Shifnal apothecary, in 1737 or 1738.

Blount was called to the Bar in 1648, aged 30. Unable to follow this profession given his firm Catholicism, as a result he was free to follow his own interests, which covered the legal, historical, antiquarian, and literary. At first sight, the timing of this self-imposed leisure might be thought to fit the assumed date of the production of the PF, i.e., between 1640 and 1648. However, a number of issues make Blount's authorship unlikely. The editor of Blount's letters, Theo Bongaerts, pointed out that 'Not a single specimen of Blount's handwriting has been found in the "Folio MS", when compared with Blount's handwriting in his letters and his *History of Herefordshire*'.[20] The examples analysed by Bongaerts were all from the 1670s, i.e., some 20 years or so after composition of the PF, but one feature in particular differs radically from our scribe's practice, namely the 'r', which more resembles a 'w', as was common in secretary hand: in contrast, the PF scribe almost invariably uses the italic form. Not only would it be unusual for a man under 30 to be employing a hand that was already going out of fashion, but the assumed Lancashire dialect of the PF does not sit comfortably in the case of a man born in Worcestershire, and who hailed from Hertfordshire. Percy himself recognized this contradiction, but his reflection that Blount 'may however have spent much of his time in Cheshire or Lancashire' (note on the inside cover of the PF), does not convince.

Blount's Catholicism and Royalist sympathies match in part the apparent taste of the PF compiler (for example, in 1660 Blount published both a list of notable Catholics killed in the Civil War and an account of the escape of Charles II after the battle of Worcester), but the overlap is not complete. If Blount were the scribe/compiler one might expect the PF's broad range of subject material to be reflected in his later publications – in particular, an interest in ballad material. Not only is such evidence lacking, but Blount himself seemed to have been less than enamoured of a genre that not only inspired much balladry, but which directly contributed material to the manuscript in question. Blount's address to the Reader on his sources for *Glossographia*, a dictionary of difficult words published in 1656, explains that he has 'avoided Poetical Stories, as much as I could, since they are not necessary to be understood by the Generality', later defining Romance as 'a feigned History, either in Verse or in Prose in the Vulgar Language … but we now give the name *Romance* most commonly to a feigned History writ in Prose'. It seems unlikely that the author of the *Glossographia* is the same person as the diligent enthusiast who copied out the 2,241 lines of *Libius Disconius* (*LD*) and transcribed, or indeed even listened to, some of the more ribald material in the PF.

Tantalizingly enigmatic is the inscription in the left-hand margin of f. 140r, 'my sweet brother sweet Cous' Edward Revell' Booke Elizabeth Revell', which implies either that Elizabeth believed that the book belonged to her kinsman or, less likely, that he was the actual scribe/compiler. The hand appears to be later than that of Blount's, which makes the latter interpretation unlikely, but the inscription seemingly calls into question ownership of the manuscript after Thomas Blount, given that the PF passed down through generations of the Blount family. Perhaps Edward Revell borrowed the manuscript and Elizabeth wrote in it, assuming it to be his. There is the name 'Henery', upside down and presumably a pen-trial, on the verso of the leaf in question.

The only other clue to ownership or audience is an annotation on f. 188v. Someone has written a copy of Rochester's song, 'I promised Sylvia' and, after a space, the first lines of Congreve's 'I tell thee Charmion', from his play *Love for Love*, which was first produced in 1695. It seems probable that these two entries, seemingly in the same hand, were copied into the manuscript around the same time. While tempting to view this as evidence that the annotation was made by an enthusiastic owner in the closing years of the seventeenth century, the incomplete nature of the annotation could simply be a personal recollection from a later date. The only other intrusive script, apart from Percy's, occurs on f. 39r, where someone has attempted to imitate the title 'Scotish ffeilde', managing only the word 'Scotish'. Unless a connection is discovered between Blount, a branch of the Revell family, and the unknown scribe of f. 188v, it is unlikely that the ownership history of this manuscript will ever be solved.

The Scribe/Compiler: Sources and Composition
Furnivall's belief 'That much, if not all, of the MS. was written from dictation' (HF, I, xiii) or the possibility of transcription from a performance, is not borne out by the evidence. What might seem at first to be auditory errors – e.g., 'there' for 'their', 'way' for 'weigh', 'buy' for 'by', 'rought' for 'wrought', 'knight' for 'night', 'wright' for 'right', 'ishulese' for 'issueless' – is easily explained as arising from haste or simple homophonic slips. Another sign of copying rather than hearing is the scribe's occasional confusion of the long-tailed *s* with *f*, as at *MER*, 1426, which has 'saine' for the preferable 'frayne', found in MS Lincoln Inn Hale 150 (see note to line 1426 on p. 199, below).[21] Nevertheless, it is likely that at least some of the PF's contents may have been derived at first or second hand from oral sources: for example, the nonsensical 'imuptelasze' for 'immortalize' ('Hero & Leander'), 'amorus tresses', for 'amber tresses', and 'Iove with euers races' for 'Jove with embraces' in 'The Aegyptian Quene'. It is more than likely that some of the scribe's material was known to him as song.

The scribe/compiler relied on both printed and manuscript sources for his collection. Donatelli identifies a number of printed broadsides, probably dating from 1608 onwards, while Rogers notes that of the PF's seven medieval romances, five have survived in printed and manuscript form, and concludes that the PF *Sir Triamore* was derived from print.[22] A clear debt is also owed to Thomas Deloney's 1604 collection *The Garland of Good Will* (13 items) and the 1602 *Strange Histories* (two items). Self-evidently, had the scribe/compiler gained access to a major collection of broadsides, such as was granted to Percy in the case of the collection by Samuel Pepys (1633–1703), that would have proven a veritable treasure trove of material. Access to a manuscript collection of ballad material, such as that owned by Captain Cox (see below) would also have provided a ready source for the scribe/compiler. But it is also possible that the scribe/compiler was not alone in his interests and was able to draw on a network of like-minded gentlemen who had libraries containing manuscript and printed sources that they were willing to allow him to consult or borrow. Indeed, exploitation of such a network could explain in part the startling variety of material to be found in the PF. In such circumstances it would be reasonable to assume that the scribe/compiler was not without texts of his own to offer up for sharing.[23] Particularly long texts, such as *Merline*, might have necessitated either frequent visits by the scribe/compiler or, as Percy himself employed, extended borrowing.

As for the sequence of transcriptions, given that the PF does not contain gaps, it is likely that the scribe/compiler simply copied out texts as he found them: that would also account for the fairly random groupings throughout the entire manuscript. Particularly interesting was his decision to copy these texts onto 'tall' folio gatherings, presumably collated in advance of any anticipated copying. Andrew Taylor has effectively demolished the theory that such 'holster' manuscripts were the stock in trade of travelling minstrels, but his observation that the 'long, narrow format is well suited to writing a long, single column of text, which can be easily scanned and cuts down on the number of times the pages have to be turned' would fit well with a compiler keen to add pieces to his collection in the most economical and portable way possible.[24] The central folding across many of the leaves, with wear on the outer sheets evident in the early part of the PF, certainly points to gatherings that were taken 'on the road'. The lack of such wear towards the end of the PF coincides with an increase in the number of texts taken from printed material (St Clair-Kendall, 2007, 13). It may well be that, by this stage, the scribe/compiler had access to a large collection of printed texts that afforded him the leisure of working from home.

In short, the PF has the hallmarks of a highly personal collection, built up over a relatively short space of time: St Clair-Kendall (2007, 9) estimates that 'ten years would be a generous estimate'. There is no indication that the scribe/compiler intended to produce a 'fair copy', and it seems likely that he stitched quires together as he went along, possibly protecting them beforehand with a wrapper of some sort. Percy himself said that he found the manuscript 'unbound and sadly torn' (HF, I, lxxiv). We do not know, of course, its state prior to being used to light a fire: whether the scribe/compiler considered his work unfinished, or whether age, infirmity, or worse prevented its completion is unlikely ever to be known.

Percy's Annotations

Percy's scribbles and annotations are extensive, and while to a modern eye they may appear the defacement of a sacred text, his comments reflect nonetheless not just a wide range of reading acquired from an early age,[25] but for the most part, learned and thoughtful observations. For much of his life Percy's correspondence abounds with a restless inquisitiveness, displaying an almost ruthless engagement in his search for material and opinion. He was frank, however, that his initial treatment of the PF had been less than respectful. Writing on the inside cover of the PF he confessed:

> When I first got possession of this MS. I was very young, and being in no Degree an Antiquary, I had not then learnt to reverence it; which must be my excuse for the scribble which I then spread over some parts of its Margin. and in one or two instances for even taking out the Leaves to save the trouble of transcribing. I have since been more careful.[26]

Percy's 'confession' could imply that his annotations were, at least to begin with, merely idle musings as opposed to antiquarian research, but his diligence and learning remain impressive. Authorities frequently cited include the Reverend Edward Lye, 'my near Neighbour and intimate Friend' (*Letters*, VII, 10), who had offered to assist Percy in the compilation of a glossary for what would become the *Reliques* (I, xiii), and who in 1743 had published the *Etymologicum Anglicanum*, the etymological dictionary of the English language by Franciscus Junius. Other sources included the 'Scottish Chaucerian', Gavin Douglas, author of the *Eneados*, a translation of the *Aeneid* that was of great interest to literary scholars and etymologists alike. From the outset, Percy's extravagant claims for the PF had rested upon *The Marriage of Sir Gawaine* (*MSG*) being a direct inspiration for Chaucer, and while there is no mention of an edition of Chaucer in Sotheby's 1969 sale catalogue of the remainder of Percy's library, the items subsequently being purchased by the Queen's University in Belfast, it is possible that Percy's reference copy was Urry's edition of 1721, given that this name appears so frequently in Percy's glosses.

Notes

[1] The note is reproduced at HF, I, lxxiv.
[2] Bertram H. Davis, *Thomas Percy: A Scholar-Cleric in the Age of Johnson* (Philadelphia: University of Pennsylvania Press, 1989), p. 24. Percy would have been aged 24 in April 1753.
[3] Leslie Shepard, 'The Finding of the Percy Folio Manuscript: A Claim of Prior Discovery', *Notes & Queries* 212 (1967), pp. 415–16.
[4] Groom (1999, p. 39n52) notes that Armagh Public Library possesses a seventeenth-century commonplace book (MS G.V.21), possibly once belonging to Percy, which has an enigmatic note on its cover by an unidentified owner recording that 'This book was found in the same basket with the celebrated MSS from which the principal writing of the *Reliques* of ancient English poetry was extracted'.
[5] For a sceptical view of Percy's account of the discovery, see Nicola McDonald, 'A Polemical Introduction', in Nicola McDonald (ed.), *Pulp Fictions of Medieval England: Essays in Popular Romance* (Manchester: Manchester University Press, 2004), p. 5: 'whether or not Percy's narrative is true – it bears … [a] striking resemblance to a number of stories concerning the rescue of early manuscripts circulating at the time'. The PF appears in Percy's left hand in a painting by Sir Joshua Reynolds in 1773. Although an engraving of the painting was made two years later, the original was lost in the fire of 1780, which also destroyed part of Percy's library (see Bertram H. Davis, 'Thomas Percy, the Reynolds Portrait, and the Northumberland House Fire', *Review of English Studies* NS 33(129) (1982), pp. 23–33).
[6] S. G. St Clair-Kendall ('Narrative Form and Mediaeval Continuity in the Percy Folio Manuscript: A Study of Selected Poems', PhD thesis, 2 vols, University of Sydney, 1988; rev. 2007 (paginated continuously), 14–17) lists all 195 items, noting that the total would have been 196 had Percy not torn out 'King Estmere' when he sent it to the printers for inclusion in the *Reliques*. Her observation on p. 17 that of these items some 88 (i.e., 45 per cent) are either unique to the PF or unique variants of existing texts, testifies to the manuscript's importance. The conclusion by Furnivall that the *Reliques* contained 176 pieces, of which only 45 were drawn from the PF (John W. Hales and Frederick J. Furnivall (eds), *Bishop Percy's Folio Manuscript: Ballads and Romances*, 3 vols (London: Trübner & Co., 1867–68), I, xxii), was challenged by Albert B. Friedman ('Percy's Folio Manuscript Revalued', *Journal of English and Germanic Philology*, 53 (1954), p. 525). In 1867, HF published an additional volume of texts from the PF, entitled *Loose and Humorous Songs*, remarking primly that 'We have not written Introductions to every one of these pieces, as to the Ballads and Romances of the MS. Let it be enough that they are put in type … Some of these songs the Editors would have been glad had it not fallen to their lot to put forth' (pp. iv–v).

7 Furnivall's comment that 'a few bits more of eaten-through, ink-saturated patches have been broken away by the frequent turning over of the leaves' (HF, I, xxiv) indicates that some readings, now lost, were probably available to him. For a detailed description of the MS, see Gillian Rogers, 'The Percy Folio Manuscript Revisited', in Maldwyn Mills, Jennifer Fellows, and Carol M. Meale (eds), *Romance in Medieval England* (Cambridge: D. S. Brewer, 1991), pp. 41–44 and St Clair-Kendall, 2007, 5–8. The Rev. T. F. Dibdin saw the MS in 1815 – i.e., some 50 years before Hales and Furnivall – and reproduced, in full, Percy's account of his discovery of the MS and his regret at its treatment by his hands. Dibdin recorded that the MS was 'a narrow, half-bound book, with blue-paper sides, and brown leather back. It is 15 inches and five eighths in length, by about 5 and six eighths in width', calling it 'something like a tradesman's day-book'. T. F. Dibdin, *The Bibliographical Decameron; or, Ten Days Pleasant Discourse upon Illuminated Manuscripts, and Subjects Connected with Early Engravings, Typography, and Bibliography*, 3 vols (London: Shakespeare Press, 1817), III, 338, 340.

8 St Clair-Kendall, 2007, 12. The ascription to Cleveland as author of 'Newarke' seems to rest largely on Percy's fanciful notion that, since Cleveland was Judge Advocate of the town at the time of the siege, it was probably written to 'Chear the Garrison' (quoted by HF, II, 33).

9 *The Poems of John Cleveland*, ed. Brian Morris and Eleanor Withington (Oxford: Clarendon Press, 1967), xxxv, 133. The dating of the Civil War texts from the PF is taken from St Clair-Kendall, 2007, 8–13.

10 Joseph Donatelli, 'The Percy Folio Manuscript: A Seventeenth-Century Context for Medieval Poetry', in P. Beal and J. Griffiths (eds), *English Manuscript Studies, 1100–1700*, vol. 4 (Toronto: University of Toronto Press, 1993), p. 120. The scribe also uses an upright 'pi' symbol on a number of occasions to indicate an error of omission, e.g., at line 685 of *Merline*.

11 For example, medial dots followed by a virgule occur in *TG* at the ends of lines 152, 153, 195, and 225.

12 'The number of available tunes was not especially large, but buyers were sometimes perplexed by the name given on the broadside. A writer customarily named his tune after the first line or title of his own ballad' (Hyder E. Rollins, 'The Black-Letter Broadside Ballad', *PMLA* 34(2) (1919), p. 313). 'A new issue of a ballad might be arranged with a different text or a different tune or different woodcuts – or all three at the same time'. Patricia Fumerton, 'Remembering by Dismembering: Databases, Archiving, and the Recollection of Seventeenth-Century Broadside Ballads', in Patricia Fumerton, Anita Guerrini, and Kris McAbee (eds), *Ballads and Broadsides in Britain, 1500–1800* (Farnham: Ashgate 2010), p. 17.

13 According to St Clair-Kendall (2007, 8), the PF was originally composed of gatherings of 16, and 'it seems likely that folios 1–10 are the eighth to final leaves surviving from a gathering of 16, of which the first seven are missing'.

14 Donatelli (1993, 118) remarks on the scribe's various use of 'partes' and 'fitts' to divide his texts. The six divisions of 'Eglamore' appear to be idiosyncratic, while in *Libius Disconius* (*LD*) announcements of Parts 7 and 8 appear in the middle of stanzas (after lines 1546 and 1857). Rollins thought it likely that 'the custom of dividing a ballad into two parts, usually with separate headings, came from a purpose to make people pay before they heard all the ballad. Presumably only one part was publicly sung' (Rollins, 1919, 316).

15 St Clair-Kendall (2007, 23) notes that the scribe appears unfamiliar with French or classic Arthurian literature, e.g., the copying of the tautological title 'Sir Lancelott of Dulake'. In 'When Scortching Phœbus', the phrases 'toujours bon temps' and 'par meilleur chance' are transcribed respectively as 'to laur bonne tannce' and 'par melio shannce'.

16 Priscilla Bawcutt ('*Sir Lamwell* in Scotland', in Rhiannon Purdie and Nicola Royan (eds), *The Scots and Medieval Arthurian Legend*, Arthurian Studies LXI (Cambridge: D. S. Brewer, 2005), p. 91) notes that the owner of a Scottish analogue to *LAMBE* may have cut short his text because an English print of 'Sir Lamwell' was only on short-term loan. The scribe of the Percy Folio may have had the same experience.

17 'Given the lack of evidence for direct Stanley patronage, it is safer to think of the poems as Stanleyite (rather than Stanley) in origin and message' (Aisling Byrne and Victoria Flood, 'The Romance of the Stanleys: Regional and National Imaginings in the Percy Folio', *Viator* 46(1)

(2015), p. 328. Byrne and Flood draw attention to the fact that all bar one of the Stanleyite ballads from the period appear in the PF). The ballad 'Childe Waters' also has a marginal Stanley association, in that Child Waters offers Ellen 'Cheshire & Lancashire both'. For 'Lady Bessiye', see Helen Cooper, 'Romance after Bosworth', in Evelyn Mullally and John Thompson (eds), *The Court and Cultural Diversity: Selected Papers from the Eighth Triennial Meeting of the International Courtly Literature Society* (Cambridge: D. S. Brewer, 1997), pp. 153–57. For a discussion of Stanley material, including that to be found in the PF, see Robert W. Barrett, Jr, *Against All England: Regional Identity and Cheshire Writing, 1195–1656* (Notre Dame, IN: University of Notre Dame Press, 2009), pp. 171–97.

[18] Sir John Stanley saw military service with the Grand Turk and was made King of Man in 1405, and as ruler of Man was an independent signatory to an Anglo-French treaty signed in 1414. See David Lawton, 'History and Legend: The Exile and the Turk', in Patricia Clare Ingham and Michelle R. Warren (eds), *Postcolonial Moves: Medieval through Modern* (Basingstoke: Palgrave Macmillan, 2003), p. 188; Byrne and Flood, 2015, 343. Lines 47–48 of 'Fflodden ffeilde' have the king call for 'the King of Man,/the Honnorable Thomas Erle of Darbye' (HF, I, 320. The reference is to Edward Stanley). See also David Lawton, '*Scottish Field*: Alliterative Verse and Stanley Encomium in the Percy Folio', *Leeds Studies in English* NS 10 (1978), pp. 42–57.

[19] Venetia's name was sufficiently well known in the taverns of London for this popular ballad to include the lines, 'Gallants, come not near to brave VENETIA stanley!/her Lord hath placed her there, that will maintain her ma[nly]/without ffeare' (John W. Hales and F. J. Furnivall (eds), *Bishop Percy's Folio Manuscript: Loose and Humorous Songs* (London: Trübner & Co, 1867), 105, lines 32–34). See also Joe Moschenska, 'A New Plot', *Times Literary Supplement*, 18 March 2016.

[20] Theo Bongaerts (ed.), *Correspondence of Thomas Blount (1618–1679): A Recusant Antiquary; His Letters to Anthony Wood and Other Restoration Antiquaries* (Amsterdam: Holland University Press, 1978), p. 16.

[21] 'The scribe shows himself capable time and time again of writing nonsense in one place while recording the same word correctly elsewhere, be it a few lines or a hundred folios later' (Donatelli, 1993, 127).

[22] Donatelli, 1993, 122–24; Rogers, 1991, 45, 48. Donatelli notes that sources for the romances could have included manuscript copies of printed texts. See Rogers, 1991, 45–54, for a detailed discussion of the compiler's indebtedness to script and print in the case of romances found in the PF.

[23] Samuel Moore has shown that a network of landed gentry in fifteenth-century East Anglia actively commissioned new literature, observing that 'the number of possible readers of a new book was increased by its chance of passing from the hands of the patron for whom it was written into those of friends who would cause it to be copied (Samuel Moore, 'Patrons of Letters in Norfolk and Suffolk, *c*.1450', *PMLA* 27(2) (1912), pp. 188–90). Lawton (1978, 42) argues for a coterie of Lancashire and Cheshire gentry in the first half of the sixteenth century who had access to Middle English alliterative texts, including those with an Arthurian flavour. While Lawton does not go so far as to suggest that such texts were freely exchanged, Moore's observation that the spirit of emulation would thrive among patrons who knew each other would equally apply. It is wholly plausible that the PF scribe was also able to draw upon a network of like-minded individuals of a similar class.

[24] Andrew Taylor, 'The Myth of the Minstrel Manuscript', *Speculum* 66 (1991), p. 57. Taylor adds that the format was so convenient it was often used for Tudor prompt books, and books of this kind 'were prepared in advance and sold as blank copybooks' (p. 58). One such example, Cambridge, Trinity College MS 0.9.38, dates from *c*.1450 and was used for keeping accounts. Interestingly, this MS also contains an Arthurian-related piece, i.e., an epitaph for Joseph of Arimathea, commemorating his supposed burial at Glastonbury. See John Withrington, 'The Arthurian Epitaph in Malory's "Morte Darthur"', in Richard Barber (ed.), *Arthurian Literature* 7 (Cambridge: D. S. Brewer, 1987), pp. 103–44. London, Lincoln's Inn MS 150, dating to the first quarter of the fifteenth century, and containing *Merlyn*, a close analogue of *MER*, is also in the same format. See Simon Horobin and Alison Wiggins, 'Reconsidering Lincoln's Inn MS 150', *Medium Aevum* 77(1) (2008), pp. 31–32.

[25] By the age of 17, Percy had already assembled a personal library of almost 300 books, and ten years later he took some 455 volumes with him to the vicarage at Easton Maudit (Groom, 1999, 5). Soon after his death in 1811, and with the exception of some 220 items retained by the family, most of his library (some 1,719 bound volumes and 1,300 pamphlets) was sold to the Earl of Caledon (Margaret M. Smith (ed.), *Index of English Literary Manuscripts*, vol. 3, *1700–1800. Part 2: John Gay–Ambrose Philips, with a First-Line Index to Parts 1 and 2* (London: Mansell, 1989), p. 264). For Percy's education, see J. F. A. Mason, 'Bishop Percy's Account of His Own Education', *Notes & Queries* 204 (1959), pp. 404–8.

[26] HF, I, lxxiv. For the inclusion of 'King Estmere' in the *Reliques*, Percy simply tore out the relevant leaves and sent them to the printer, thus also losing the conclusion to the preceding 'Durham Fielde'. Curiously, Percy's reference to tearing out leaves occurs immediately *before* his account of his discovery of the MS itself, an account dated 7 November 1769, implying that it was probably written sometime between late 1764 and late 1769. Given Percy's obsessive attitude towards the MS, and his refusal to let others see it – to the extent that Ritson publicly doubted its very existence – it is fascinating that Percy felt obliged to 'confess' to this act of vandalism in what was a highly private and personal possession.

The Arthurian Texts of the Percy Folio

For Percy, the discovery of the contents of his precious manuscript meant more than a simple collection of old ballads. They revealed an insight into a glorious past, apparent evidence of the part played by minstrels in civilizing and enriching a nation's culture. Jealously guarding the manuscript from prying eyes, Percy was to make extravagant claims for the value and significance of the damaged treasure in his possession. In his Preface to the first edition of the *Reliques*, Percy reported that the greater part [*sic*] of the material published had been

> extracted from an ancient folio manuscript, in the Editor's possession, which contains near 200 poems, songs, and metrical romances. This MS. was written about the middle of the last century, but contains compositions of all times and dates, from the ages prior to Chaucer, to the conclusion of the reign of Charles I.[1]

From the outset, Percy was keen to emphasize the credentials of his manuscript in terms of the Arthurian material it contained. On 24 November 1757, he wrote to William Shenstone, informing him that his manuscript had been seen by Johnson, who wished to see it printed, and that it contained 'many old Romantic and Historical Ballads: upon King Arthur and the Knights of his round Table: Merlin &c …' (*Letters*, VII, 4). On 28 May 1761, he wrote to Warton observing that 'the Old Ballads about King Arthur and his Knights seem to have been as current among our plain but martial Ancestors, as the *Rhapsodies* of Homer were among his countrymen' (*Letters*, III, 3). However, Arthurian pieces accounted for only 11 of the PF's items, and of those 11, seven pieces did not find their way into the *Reliques*. While in comparison the folk heroes Guy of Warwick and Robin Hood only mustered three and seven appearances respectively in Percy's manuscript,[2] both figures enjoyed considerable popularity in the time before the PF was written. For example, the legend of Guy of Warwick dates back to the mid-thirteenth century: as well as surviving in English in six medieval manuscripts, seven editions appeared in print between *c*.1497 and *c*.1609, and a ?1560 copy was among a number of romances Percy borrowed from Garrick in 1761 and 1763.[3] Ballads of Robin Hood were particularly popular: the Bodleian Library's website 'Broadside Ballads Online' lists some 52 broadsides associated with this figure from between 1450 and 1750.[4]

Nonetheless, there are tantalizing hints that Arthurian ballads and performances enjoyed a degree of popularity before the composition of the PF. For example, 'The

Jeaste of Syr Gawayne' has survived in four sixteenth-century copies, and while 'Sir Lamwell' has come down to us in two texts, also from the same period, all are in an incomplete state.[5] The lost ballad 'Vortiger' was entered into the Stationers' Register in 1589 and the lost play *Vortigerne* performed at the Rose Theatre in 1593, while Thomas Deloney's ballad of Lancelot seems to have enjoyed popularity from *c.*1595 onwards.[6] Nevertheless it seems that by the time the *Reliques* was published in 1765, Arthurian heroes had proven less durable than others. The burlesque 'St George for England', which according to Percy was taken by him from a 1612 black-letter copy found in the Pepys collection (*Reliques*, III, 286), openly questions why people should celebrate Arthur and his knights over England's patron saint.[7]

Notwithstanding the relatively small contribution made by Arthurian texts in the PF to Percy's *Reliques*, this material was to play an important role, structurally and in terms of the work's reception, in respect of attitudes to popular ballads and Arthurian literature. Percy's valorization of *MSG* from May 1761 onwards bestowed upon the Arthurian texts in the Percy Folio a weight beyond their numbers. The remainder of this section looks at the reception of the *Reliques* and its intended audience, and the place of some of the Arthurian texts in the PF as part of a ballad and performance tradition.

Assembling the *Reliques*

By the time the *Reliques* was published in 1765, the Reverend Thomas Percy had already proven himself an industrious scholar of broad tastes. Four years previously he had published *Hao Kiou Choaan*, a rendition in English of a Portuguese translation of a Chinese novel, with *Miscellaneous Pieces Relating to the Chinese* appearing the following year, while 1763 saw the publication of translations of Icelandic texts (*Five Pieces of Runic Poetry*), a translation of *The Song of Solomon*, and a key to the New Testament.[8]

However, it was the rescue of an old manuscript containing ballad material that, almost literally, fired Percy's imagination. As well as consulting and purchasing ballads in his quest,[9] Percy assiduously cultivated – some might say exploited – various connections in order to further his research and cause. William Shenstone encouraged the idea of a published collection of ballads, and provided detailed advice in the form of what material might be considered appropriate for inclusion, although his influence was to wane. Percy also persuaded Samuel Johnson to write the Preface for the first edition of the *Reliques*, and corresponded with the Oxford Professor of Poetry Thomas Warton, Shakespearean scholar Richard Farmer, and a number of notable and less notable figures in his search for material and inspiration. Publication of the *Reliques* turned out to be a frantic affair as Percy strove desperately to marshal his material in order to meet printing deadlines, but the end result was a literary best-seller.[10] Central to Percy's thesis was that the materials he had gathered – and indeed edited and on occasion augmented – were part of a noble and long-standing tradition. Minstrels were the natural successors to the bards of old: uniting poetry and music they had 'got their livelihood by singing verses to the harp, at the houses of the great' (*Reliques*, I, xvi). Percy explained that minstrels continued until the reign of Queen Elizabeth I, after which time the 'genuine old Minstrelsy' became extinct, and ballads began to be collected at first into 'Garlands', and then specifically written for inclusion in such collections. Percy hence romanticized the origin of ballads such as those he had chosen to print ('I have no doubt but most of the old heroic ballads in this collection were produced by this order of men' (*Reliques*, I, xvi)), attributing a northern origin to the minstrels who had inspired such verse. These ballads accordingly represented evidence of a long-standing literary tradition, and thus showed 'the gradation of our language, exhibit the progress of popular opinions, display the peculiar manners and customs of former ages, or throw light on our earlier classical poets' (*Reliques*, I, ix). The *Reliques* provided readers with a tangible link to a shared and noble past, but Percy's fascination with, and admiration for, these texts and what he believed they proved about an ancient tradition of minstrelsy, were to prove a mixed blessing. Having achieved a degree of public respectability through his association with the Northumberland Percys (the *Reliques* was dedicated to the Countess of Northumberland), and having been made Bishop of Dromore in 1782, Percy began to feel ashamed of his work. In Groom's words, the *Reliques* became 'a folly, a bastard offspring he could barely admit his own'.[11] Distancing himself from his most popular published work, and refusing to allow others to examine his precious manuscript, Percy found himself the frequent target of Joseph Ritson, a man with a sharp eye and a critical tongue: as well as Percy no less a figure than Warton had found himself the object of Ritson's contempt,[12] while Percy's reticence allowed Ritson openly to doubt the very existence of Percy's manuscript.[13] Gleefully noting that Percy had published the fourth edition of the *Reliques* not under his own name but under that of his namesake, his nephew, Ritson was unsparing in his sarcasm. The MS was obviously imperfect, but fortunately Percy had been able to turn a parcel of rags into an elegant new suit; there was 'scarcely one single poem, song or ballad, fairly or honestly printed'; Percy had inserted 'his own fabrications for the sake of provideing more refine'd entertainment for readers of taste'.[14] To force home the point Ritson printed together *The Marriage of Sir Gawaine* as it appeared in the fourth edition ('The Original') and the version as it appeared in the 1775 reprint of the first edition ('The Improvement' [*sic*]). An Arthurian ballad that had once been the centrepiece of Percy's claims for a minstrelsy tradition, a text that had even supposedly been used by Chaucer as a source for his 'Canterbury Tales', now proved to be a double-edged sword. Ritson's accusations of duplicity and amateur intervention were to colour appreciation of Percy's contribution to the ballad tradition for many years to come.[15]

'This vague and indiscriminating name'

Percy's industrious investigation in the course of his research for the *Reliques* had resulted in him unearthing a substantial number of texts upon which he could draw.

However, not all of the Arthurian pieces within the PF were destined for inclusion in a collection of ballads that supposedly contained echoes of the heroic and noble bards and minstrels of old. In his essay 'On the Ancient Metrical Romances, &c.', which appeared at the beginning of volume III of the *Reliques*, Percy lavished praise on *Libius Disconius* for its epic style, but as a lengthy 'romance' it was clearly not fit for inclusion. Also excluded were *King Arthur and King Cornwall* (*KAKC*) and *Sir Lambewell*, both of which Percy annotated as being 'ballads'; the 'poem' *Merline* (*MER*); the 'adventure' *The Grene Knyght*; the 'song' *The Carle off Carlisle* (*CARLE*); and *The Turke & Gowin*.

What is striking is the terminology Percy employed in each case. *A Collection of Old Ballads* (1723–25, also the working title initially adopted for the *Reliques*) provided Percy with a structure for his own published collection;[16] but while the anonymous author of the *Collection* referred to his material as 'songs' (p. vi), curiously enough its publication, and that of Percy's *Reliques* some 40 years later, did not lead to an agreed understanding of what the word 'ballad' actually meant. Nathan Bailey's *An Universal Etymological English Dictionary* had defined the word as meaning 'a Song commonly sung up and down the Streets' (Groom, 1999, 23 and n., citing the 9th edition of 1740). Johnson, who owned and annotated a copy of Bailey's work, simply defined it in his magisterial *A Dictionary of the English Language* (1755–56) as a 'song', illustrating that definition with Isaac Watt's remark '*Ballad*, once signified a solemn and sacred song, as well as trivial, when Solomon's Song was called the *ballad of ballads*; but now it is applied to nothing but trifling verse'; while in the very year of the *Reliques*' publication the word was defined by Thomas Dyche as 'a song, but now commonly applied to the meaner sort, that are sung in the streets by the vulgar'.[17] Shenstone, however, was clear:

> do you make any Distinction betwixt a Ballad, and a Song ... ? With the common people, I believe, a Song becomes a ballad as it grows in years; as they think an old serpent becomes a Dragon ... For my own part, I ... am apt to consider a Ballad as containing some little story, either real or invented.[18]

In 1781, Thomas Warton himself was to profess the very word ambiguous:

> The title of BALLET was often applied to poems of considerable length ... A romance, or History, versified, so as to form a book or pamphlet, was sometimes called a ballad ... Sometimes a Ballad is a work in prose ... A play or interlude was sometimes called a ballet ... Religious subjects were frequently called by this vague and indiscriminating name.[19]

What is undeniable, however, is the widespread circulation that ballads enjoyed before the publication of the *Reliques* in 1765. The ability of presses to print large numbers of ballads and broadsides has led one historian to estimate that in the latter half of the sixteenth century, 'before the seventeenth-century heyday of the broadside ballad – thousands of ballads were printed and likely millions of copies circulated'.[20] Nor was a lack of basic literate skills an obstacle to their popularity or enjoyment: 'as Nicholas Bownd observed in the 1590s, there were many who "though they cannot reade themselues, nor any of theirs, yet will haue many ballades set vp in their houses, so that they might learne them as they shall haue occasion"' (Fox, 2002, 38).[21] Paula McDowell notes that the lapse in 1695 of the Printing or Licensing Act of 1662 effectively ended 'prepublication censorship and ... restrictions on the number of presses, printers and apprentices ... by 1705 there were between sixty-five and seventy printing houses in London alone'.[22] Percy himself, an assiduous collector of ballad material – 'I am a collector of ballads in all languages'[23] – was able to access some 1,800 broadsides in the Pepys collection when he visited Cambridge in 1761, and also relied upon ballads that he bought himself: for example, over 300 survive from those he purchased from the printer Cluer Dicey. Ballads were sold by the bundle and freely purchased, exchanged, adapted, recycled, and dispensed with – Percy himself complained on 11 September 1773 that three volumes of ballads bought by a friend 'consisted of loose detached ballads collected into Vol^s – Such as are still sold on stalls; not one in a hundred of them fit to be republished; and the best among them, were the same as what I had selected out of Pepys' Collection'.[24] Some 25 years after the approximate date the PF was written, the dramatist Wycherley could have one of his characters say, 'Pray, have you any ballads? Give me sixpenny worth'. Indeed, one of the most extraordinary things about the *Reliques* is that so many ballads survived that Percy could freely choose which texts to publish.[25]

A Matter of Taste
While Percy was well read in romances, the challenge was to select the right sort of material for publication. The *Collection* and similar works, such as Allan Ramsay's *The Tea-Table Miscellany* (1723–37) and *The Ever Green* (1724), had proven popular and were drawn on by Percy. However, the appearance in 1760 of *Fragments of Ancient Poetry* – supposedly translations of poems by the blind Highland poet Ossian, a bard living in the third century, although in fact a work of complete fiction – had an enormous impact in the following years.[26] For Percy, the argument that an illiterate society relied upon oral transmission for its key texts found a ready echo in his own belief that some of the tales in his manuscript also owed their origin to the bards and minstrels of yesteryear.[27] Such examples might be unpolished, but they retained nevertheless a 'pleasing simplicity' (*Reliques*, I, x).

But while inclusion of 'old heroic ballads' had their place in the *Reliques*, ballads of a common sort were a different matter. The author of the *Collection* had written in his Preface that there was 'something I hope to hit every Taste ... There are many who perhaps will think it ridiculous enough to enter seriously into a Dissertation upon Ballads',[28] while Ramsay had solemnly stated in the Preface to *The Tea-Table Miscellany* that he had 'kept out all smut and ribaldry'.[29] On 8 September 1763, Percy wrote to David Dalrymple, Lord Hailes, explaining that his manuscript contained 'an infinite farrago of ancient Songs, Ballads, Metrical Romances, Legends in verse and poems of the low and popular kind' (*Letters*, IV, 54); texts of a low and popular kind would never do, but for Shenstone, pearls of historical insight that might be uncovered were not as important as the literary shell: 'mere *Historical, without poetical* Merit, is not a sufficient recommendation. And there are many Pieces in this Collection that falsify history, almost in yᵉ same Degree that they discredit Poetry – written perhaps by the same rank of Men that produce our modern half-penny ballads' (*Letters*, VII, 177). Writing to Percy on 3 February 1762, Shenstone stressed the value of the MS as raw material to be refined for people of taste:

> For my own part, I ever considered your old MSS. as the noblest treasure in a *Poet's hands*; even as pure gold in Dust or Ingots, which the Owner might either mint himself, or dispose of in the shape he found it, for the Benefit of other *Artists* – Remember I use the word *Artists* – for if you publish these old pieces *un-improved only*, I consider them as not every one's money, but as a prize merely for either *virtuosoes*; or else the *manufacturers* in this kind of ware. (*Letters*, VII, 136)

Such ballads required a virtuous setting: Shenstone's Billet 2 to Percy noted that 'Many of R. Hood's ball: are in yᵉ true ballad-stile; and only deficient in their moral'.[30] Hence, when it came to publishing the *Reliques*, in Groom's elegant phrase, Percy found himself 'pulled in opposite directions: towards scholarly precision by his antiquarian associates, and towards polite, elegant revision (and marketability) by Shenstone and the Dodsleys'.[31] Why then did Percy choose the Arthurian texts he did from the PF? An influential factor for Percy was surely recognition of the reception of Richard Hurd's *Letters on Chivalry and Romance*, published in 1762, the same year as Warton's second edition of *Observations on the 'Faerie Queene'*. Hurd's vision of chivalric romance in medieval times, as well as his comments on the role of Arthur in Spenser's work and his opinion that the *Faerie Queene* was not so much a classic poem as Gothic, prompted Percy to consider the readership of the planned *Reliques*. On 8 September 1763, he wrote to Hailes concerning various texts in the PF: 'Mʳ Hurd's Letters of Chivalry (which you must have seen) may perhaps dispose the public to give a favourable reception to a few of the best of these ancient Romances'.[32]

While not described by Percy as a 'romance', *MSG*, with its supposed Chaucerian connection and Arthurian context, helped nonetheless to bestow credibility by association on the *Reliques* as a whole. Another ballad, supporting a seemingly ancient pedigree, was *Boy and Mantle* (*BM*). To be sure, the latter required some bowdlerization before publication,[33] but given that the trial of the horn was an episode in common with *Le Morte Darthur*, which Percy believed to be itself 'translated out of French in the time of K. Edw. IV, and first printed anno 1484' (*Reliques*, III, 2), that too may have helped shape and define both Percy's thesis on minstrelsy and the appeal of the *Reliques* to its audience. Other Arthurian texts helping to underpin this ancient edifice were *Sir Lancelott of Dulake* (*SLDL*), a ballad that matched Percy's criteria, since it had been published in Deloney's *The Garland of Good Will*, complete with the name of the tune to which it was to be sung; the Arthurian 'King Ryence's Challenge' (not to be found in the PF but featuring as part of a court entertainment for Elizabeth I in 1575); and *Kinge Arthur's Death* (*KAD*), supposedly taken from Malory's *Le Morte Darthur*. Of the 'many [sic] Songs and Romances about King Arthur and his Knights' to be found in the PF, Percy simply deemed some 'very imperfect' (*Reliques*, III, xix), and hence not suitable for inclusion.[34]

In his discussion of medieval poetry and romance, Derek Pearsall has remarked on 'the prevailing image, which has survived any number of scholarly knocks … of the "minstrel" reciting to a public audience', a standpoint which remains persistent and 'peculiarly tenacious'.[35] Percy's vision of minstrels reciting or singing romances or ballads to a public audience may be a sentimentalized fiction and part of that long-standing interpretation, but, as Radulescu notes, 'the common critical assumption about ballads is that they emerged at the end of the Middle Ages as a combination of ancient metrical romance and the mainstream of folksong, thus giving birth to what many have called the 'debased' versions of romances'.[36] For Fowler, the fifteenth century was a turning point, when 'the metrical romance tradition of the later Middle Ages joined the mainstream of folksong to create a type of narrative song which we now call the ballad'.[37]

One of the problems with Fowler's explanation, as Friedman observed, is that it reinforces the view that romances degenerated into a debased form of minstrelsy that ultimately led to the emergence of ballads 'on the lips of the peasants once the minstrels left the scene'.[38] Indeed, appreciation of medieval culture as a whole, of which romance is part, has often been viewed 'as if it were governed by some social analogue of gravity, always moving downward from the privileged to the masses', Carl Lindahl noting that 'the elite world is one of writing, so the folk world must be exclusively oral'.[39] Percy himself was of the view that ballads had suffered a process of decline since their glory days. Minstrels, he explained, continued up to the reign of Elizabeth I, 'in whose time they had 'lost much of their dignity; and were sinking into contempt and neglect' (*Reliques*, I, xix).[40] While Caxton had been the first to print prose books of chivalry, 'As the old Minstrelsy wore out, prose books of Chivalry became more admired … [and] … the most popular metrical Romances began to be reduced into prose' (*Reliques*, III, vii). But it is important to recognize that Percy was highly selective in the material he chose to include in the *Reliques*. His statement that it contained '*Old Heroic Ballads, Songs, and other Pieces of our earlier Poets (Chiefly of the Lyric Kind)*', bestowed gravitas and respectability upon the texts he selected for publication, texts which fell into the narrow categories and themes he chose to highlight. In the course of his research, Percy would have come across ballads covering the full spectrum of human behaviour, including those serving as vehicles for political dissent, others which revelled in the violent and scurrilous, those supposedly featuring the last words of the condemned on the scaffold … all in all a bewildering flood of texts which freely borrowed words, illustrations, tunes, and lyrics from each other.[41] From this maelstrom, Percy's selectivity enabled him to recast, intellectualize, contextualize, and valorize his chosen material, enabling an audience of taste to reflect from a safe distance on the 'barbarous productions of unpolished ages' (*Reliques*, I, vi). Having rescued these relics of the past and thus restored them to an appreciative present, the priority for Percy was not just to separate the wheat from the chaff, but to ensure that the end product was suitable for purchase by an appropriate and appreciative audience: 'for Percy, and for virtually all learned ballad collectors after him, redefining balladry as a fit object of study meant separating scholarly collections from mere vendible commodities'.[42]

'This tale grew in the telling'

Percy's decision to open the first volume of his *Reliques* with 'The Ancient Ballad of Chevy Chase', with its story of the rivalry between the Percy and Douglas families, was a shrewd choice: not only was the *Reliques* dedicated to Elizabeth Percy, Countess of Northumberland, but Percy could claim 'Chevy Chase' as a prime example of an ancient and popular ballad ('I flatter myself, I have here recovered the genuine antique poem' (*Reliques*, I, 2)). However, while one legacy of Percy's thesis may have been to encourage a binary approach to the evolution of ballads, whereby oral and written pathways rarely intersect, 'Chevy Chase' is an example of just how porous are the walls between such pathways. The first recorded version of this ballad is to be found in Bodleian Library MS Ashmole 48, a notebook containing songs and ballads compiled between 1557 and 1565, and by this time the text

> was already the product of a long series of interactions between oral, manuscript, and print culture. What probably began in manuscript form passed into oral circulation and eventually into print. From print it passed back again into manuscript and lived on in the mouths of minstrels and their audience.[43]

While *LD* and *MER* will have survived as a result of manual transmission (i.e., copies made by hand, most likely from a private collection, and possibly collated with one or more versions in script or print), *Sir Triamore* is based upon a printed copy, with other texts – e.g., the PF romances *Eger and Grime* and *Guy and Colebrand* – being shaped by the process of memorial, as opposed to oral, transmission.[44]

Hence the recycling of ballad material was achieved not just by the transfer of texts and pictures through the equivalent of cutting and pasting, but also by means of a direct response on the part of the consumer or audience, be that in the form of the act of transcription or the result of performance.[45] Of the PF, it has been argued that 'there is very little evidence for an oral or musical context in the Percy Folio manuscript itself; moreover any traces of these contexts are found not in the traditional ballads or medieval romances, but rather in the contemporary pieces' (Donatelli, 1993, 130). However, Putter notes not just that 'throughout the medieval and early modern period, romances were transmitted orally and indeed musically', but that the music for *Eger and Grime* still survives (Putter, 2011, 349, 346). Of 162 texts within the PF, St Clair-Kendall found 'either the actual tune to which it was sung; a reference to it in connection with an air which apparently no longer exists; or a reference to it as a sung piece but with no notification of any special music' (St Clair-Kendall, 2007, 23). It is important accordingly to remember that the singing of a ballad was not a solitary activity; in *The Compleat Angler* – its publication date of 1653 puts it within a handful of years of the PF's likely date of completion – Izaak Walton's Piscator suggests to his friends that they 'tel tales, or sing Ballads, or make a Catch, or find some harmless sport to content us'.[46] A ballad could develop over time through a myriad of interchanges and audiences.

As well as the communal practice of sharing ballads through singing, it is worth noting that up to and beyond the publication of the *Reliques* there would have been a tradition of dramatic performance that included Arthurian themes. Contemporaneous with Caxton's reference to Arthur in the Preface to the *Le Morte Darthur* as one of the Worthies is the king's appearance in Bodl. MS Tanner 407, a commonplace book from Norfolk dating from the late fifteenth century. The manuscript contains stanzas spoken by Three Worthies, commencing with Arthur, which 'appear to be a fragment of a pageant of the Nine Worthies'. This fragment is succeeded by a separate piece, featuring speeches by all Nine, which seem 'well-suited to performance in a village community ... It is probable that his pageant was recorded as a guild entertainment'.[47] Of Richard Lloyd's verse *The Nine Worthies* (1584), a work that informed *KAD*, Millican has argued that Arthur speaks 'in the manner of the mystery plays', and that 'the condition of Lloyd's verses in the Folio Manuscript ... points definitely to folk transmission from the printed pages of 1584 to the manuscript in Humphrey Pitts's sitting room'.[48] These brief references point to the possibility that the story of Arthur as a folk hero may have continued in the popular imagination in dramatic and balladic form up to the date of the Percy Folio itself. The similarities between mummings and early medieval liturgical drama suggest that community-based performances, with audience engagement, could have helped preserve a tradition of dynamic Arthurian texts, which, like ballads, were enjoyed by many. In his discussion of the role played by the figure of the Turk in medieval times, David Lawton looks at the late fifteenth-century English drama *The Croxton Play of the Sacrament*, through mummings (where St George's adversary is sometimes known as the Turkey Knight), to *TG*. While the Revesby Mummers' Play, first recorded in 1779, does not feature Arthurian characters, the fact that it has been dated to 'not before 1750' demonstrates that this particular form of folk entertainment was being enjoyed at most just 15 years before the publication of the *Reliques*.[49] Echoes of such themes are found to this day in the form of Morris dancing.

A degree of continuity between medieval Arthurian-based performance and the Arthurian texts in the PF cannot be proved, but *MSG* – one of only three known analogues to Chaucer's 'Wife of Bath's Tale', and closely related to *The Wedding of Sir Gawain and Dame Ragnell* (*WSG*) – is a reminder that this ballad, like all ballads, was meant to be enjoyed as performance. While the relationship between *WSG* and *MSG* remains uncertain, we are presented with two versions of the same story: the manuscript containing *WSG* dates towards the close of the fifteenth century, while the PF, which contains the unique copy of *MSG*, was written in the 1640s.[50] *MSG* played a key role in the formation of the *Reliques* and the credibility of Percy's thesis concerning the historical role of minstrels; but another reason for its survival and inclusion was surely its simple entertainment value.[51] As Nicola McDonald reminds us of 'popular' medieval romance in general, such romance is 'popular' in that it has the capacity 'to attract a large and heterogeneous ... audience, as well as ... its ability to provide that audience with enormous enjoyment' (McDonald, 2004, 2): this particular brand of 'unadulterated good fun' surely explains in part the longevity of the material Percy found included in his manuscript. Laughter is the sole preserve of neither the courtly nor the common.

WSG, which exists uniquely in Bodl. MS Rawlinson C.86, has survived in what is obviously a seriously corrupted state: its rhyme scheme has collapsed, there are puzzling readings, attempts have made to 'improve' the text, including the interpolation of material from 'The Wife of Bath's Tale' ... and yet even so, its appeal remains apparent.[52] Putter argues that two texts in the PF – *Eger and Grime* and *Guy of Warwick* – demonstrate strong evidence of oral transmission, and points out that in cases of scribal reproduction, 'errors tend to be due to misreading of the written exemplar (eye-skip, mistaken anticipation)', whereas in oral transmission, errors and variations tend to be due to memory loops and miscues (Putter, 2011, 347). *WSG* certainly has its fair share of scribal errors, but it is worth bearing in mind that attempts to 'improve' the text could be the result of oral transmission, or even changes made as a result of performance, as opposed to being due wholly to authorial confusion or careless copying.

Linda Marie Zaerr has also argued persuasively the case that medieval romances were meant to be heard, her experience in presenting *WSG* for performance shedding light on how romances (and hence ballads) may have been received, recorded, and transmitted. In short, how these related strands of the Loathly Lady legend may have 'grown in the telling', from the time of Chaucer to the time that *MSG* was written down in the Percy Folio.[53] Zaerr's experimentation and improvisation readily explain how *WSG* might have developed organically between transcriptions – indeed, even changed between performances. With a performance, be that through recitation or staged, there is always the potential for the excitement of the unknown: if popular romance has been looked down on because of a 'reliance on stereotypes, formulae and conventional plot structures, and its particular brand of unadulterated good fun' (McDonald, 2004, 2), the recognition/reiteration/frustration of that expectation can add to the popularity and longevity of the text in question, be that Arthurian romance or popular ballad.

Percy himself was very much aware of the way Arthurian characters in the PF conformed to stereotype. As he remarked to Warton on 28 May 1761, Gawaine 'is always drawn courteous and gentle', Kay is 'rugged and brutal', and Guenever 'light and inconstant' (*Letters*, III, 3). The texts in the PF largely reflect these characterizations: hence the courteous Gawaine appears as the central character in *MSG*, *TG*, *GK*, and *CARLE*, while playing a minor albeit positive role in *LAMBE*.[54] Kay is 'crabbed' in both *CARLE* and *LAMBE*, a boastful braggart in *TG*, and in *MSG* says he would rather die than marry the Loathly Lady. Guinevere is the unfaithful and disloyal wife in *LAMBE*, and subject to humiliating criticism in *BM*. Arthur himself fares poorly in the PF. While a degree of dignity is to be expected in the two ballads owing their origins in part to *Le Morte Darthur* (i.e., *KAD* and *Sir Lancelott of Dulake* (*SLDL*)), in *LAMBE* he condemns to death the eponymous hero on Guinevere's word alone, in *BM* he is the hapless cuckold, he is a guest at dinner in *CARLE*, and he simply makes an appearance in *KAKC*, *TG*, *GK*, and *LD*. However, Arthur's characterization in *MSG* (and indeed *WSG*) is a different matter altogether: portrayed as timid, helpless, and weak, the potential for humour, particularly when reciting or performing the ballad, is self-evident.[55] It was a dramatic opportunity exploited by Shakespeare in *The Second Part of King Henry IV*: Falstaff enters, singing the first two lines of a ballad, probably by Deloney, which later makes its appearance in the Percy Folio as *SLDL*. Falstaff fails to complete the opening line, omitting the last word in favour of the instruction 'Empty the jourdan'. The comic potential offered by this juxtapositional interplay of speech and slapstick, of Arthurian romance and vulgar reality, is obvious. It is hard to believe that this same potential was lost on the readers and performers of the Arthurian ballads in the PF.

It has been observed that 'key to modern scholarship's ambivalence about the kind of pleasure that popular romance generates is the assumption that it is passive, a pleasure that comes from … consumption' (McDonald, 2004, 12). The presence of pious tags and phrases in romance has often been taken as evidence of such passivity: such formulae can be seen as a clichéd address on the part of the author/narrator, or even simple padding. However, Roger Dalrymple's discussion of the proclivity of Middle English romances 'to employ *periphrastic* rather than name-based forms' when it comes to naming God offers a more nuanced approach,[56] one which emphasizes the participatory relationship between author/narrator and audience. Such formulae, he argues, may possess not just a 'devotional resonance' while fulfilling a mnemonic function, but serve also to engage, bind, and encourage interaction between the participants. This symbiotic relationship may be established, for example, at the very beginning of a text with a traditional opening prayer, whereby 'audience/readership, narrator and fictional character are united under a single frame of reference. From the initial prayers onwards, pious tags are employed to anchor response to narrative and to foster a participatory dynamic between audience, narrator, and text' (Dalrymple, 2000, 29). This relationship may be reinforced symmetrically through the use of prayers to close the text in question, building upon a 'shared devotional perspective'.[57] While Dalrymple does not consider how the performance of such texts may result in their organic development, he draws attention to the fact that romances such as those involving Guy of Warwick and King Arthur enjoyed new audiences in broadside form and beyond:

> The survival of pious formulae in such a context [might] well reflect their curious status as both oral and written invocation. The Percy Folio romances certainly offer evidence of the conflation of the two modes as the conventional formulae are invoked in apposition to more exclamatory, less ceremonial oath phrases. (2000, 143)[58]

How might a participatory experience help shape and develop texts such as those which appear in the PF itself? Zaerr's experience in performing *WSG* illustrates how performance can both entertain and shape a narrative, how material can 'grow in the telling'. Music can be used as a leitmotif for a specific character; a nod and a wink to the audience; a change in voice register or tone – all such actions and feedback may determine the popularity and fate of romance or ballad: 'The more listeners involved in an oral performance, the better the chance that the performer will be heard again – but also the greater the chance of variety in the interpretation' (Lindahl, 1995, 67). It is not too far-fetched to see *WSG*'s occasionally chaotic state – and that of *MSG* and other Arthurian texts of the PF – not as the result of careless textual transmission and intervention, nor arising from a single author determined to deliver a new 'mirror for princes', let alone a crusading feminist viewpoint, but reflecting instead a proactive response to audience feedback by a series of authors/scribes/performers looking to realize the text's entertainment potential.[59] Whether recited or sung, Hahn's observation about English medieval Gawaine romances is as true of the ballads and broadsheets enjoyed in Percy's time and the variants in between:

> [T]he broad support for these stories among late medieval people reflects a deep enjoyment in listening or reading as a social (rather than solitary) event. The circumstances of public performance make 'audience' itself perhaps too confining a term, since listeners must have taken some active part in such readings ... or become storytellers in their own right on other occasions. Performance artists must have given boisterous and flamboyantly histrionic recitals, impersonating roles through change of voice or gesture, playing the melodramatic sentimentality and violence to the upmost, priming and inciting their listeners' responses ... it was clearly as popular performance art, with strong elements of mimicry and burlesque, that ... [Gawaine romances] ... brought pleasure to the majority of their earliest listeners.[60]

Conclusion

Romances such as *LAMBE*, *LD*, and *MER* did not fit with Percy's intentions for the *Reliques*, whereas his extravagant claims for *MSG* and *BM* bestowed upon the texts and *Reliques* alike both antiquity and respectability. The example of *WSG*, the cousin of *MSG*, hints at the important role that performance could have played in the popularity and survival of some of the Arthurian texts that found their way into the Percy Folio.

Stung by criticism and the feeling in later life that the material was not in keeping with the sobriety required of a churchman, Percy was to disown the very work that had made his name: having once pronounced his work 'a strange collection of trash', for the 1794 fourth edition of the *Reliques* he took the extraordinary step of disowning his work altogether by having the book published under the name of his nephew, also called Thomas Percy, writing that 'I am so little interested about the amusements of my youth, that, had it not been for the benefit of my nephew, I could contentedly have let the "Reliques of Ancient Poetry" remain unpublished'.[61]

Having put away childish things, and by being highly selective in the ballads he chose to print, elevating them to the status of tasteful literature worthy of attention while attempting to recreate and improve the texts concerned, Percy left himself open to the charge of exaggerating and undermining the very texts he had commended. In a further irony, by fixing protean ballads in the medium of print, Percy had condemned these texts to literary permafrost: frozen in time they were now incapable of growing in the telling, becoming instead specimens for veneration. The caustic and highly personal attacks of Ritson, who mocked not just Percy's literary skill but his scholastic integrity, undoubtedly left their mark, as Percy wearily revealed in a letter written on 4 April 1801, just ten years before he died:

> [Y]ou will see the defective and incorrect state of the old text in the ancient folio MS. and the irresistible demand on the Editor of the 'Reliques' to attempt some of those conjectural emendations which have been blamed by one or two rigid critics, but without which the collection would not have deserved a moment's attention.[62]

It has perhaps become too easy to see Percy as an individual better suited to the world of *The Dunciad* than a man whose diligent research rescued and popularized ballad material, and who paved the way for future generations to enjoy, and be inspired by, Arthurian romance in general.[63] We have seen how popular the ballad was in the heyday of its printed existence in the seventeenth century, and how performance may well have shaped and preserved for posterity some of the Arthurian ballads that Percy either considered or actually used in the *Reliques*. In seeking to reconstruct and recreate material that he found in his manuscript, drawing upon his own extensive research and the advice of leading literary figures of his time, Percy was in fact doing no more than working within the ballad tradition. Without his enthusiasm, and a legacy that was to lead to his ballads being revered by Scott amongst others, it is quite possible that the Arthurian revival in the nineteenth century would have looked very different. In a subject that enjoys a number of ironies it is perhaps the very last irony that, notwithstanding a final repudiation and a reputation that has been less than kind, Thomas Percy reveals himself to have been just one in a long line of ballad makers.

Notes

[1] Thomas Percy, *Reliques of Ancient English Poetry: Consisting of Old Heroic Ballads, Songs, and other Pieces of our earlier Poets (Chiefly of the Lyric Kind.) Together with some few of later Date*, 3 vols (London: J. Dodsley, 1765), I, ix. All quotations by volume and page number are from the 1765 edition of the *Reliques* unless stated otherwise.

[2] In 1559, John Bale noted that the popular fifteenth-century poet John Lydgate had composed pieces entitled 'Guy of Warwick' and 'Guy of Colbrand'. See Henry Noble MacCracken (ed.), *The Minor Poems of John Lydgate. Part I. The Lydgate Canon, Religious Poems*, EETS ES 107 (London: Oxford University Press, 1911; repr. 2006), p. xxxvii. Lydgate was drawing on the legend, as opposed to being the original author of these stories.

[3] 'Most significant among the Garrick volumes borrowed were not plays at all, but two volumes of sixteenth-century romances' (Groom, 1999, 152). *Guy* is the first item listed under 'Mr Garrick. Old Plays. K. vol. 9' on f. 103v of Bodl. MS Percy c.9. I am grateful to the Bodleian Library for supplying me with a facsimile of this manuscript. For a discussion of manuscripts and early printed books featuring Guy, see Alison Eve Wiggins, '*Guy of Warwick*: Study and Transcription', PhD thesis, University of Sheffield, 2000, pp. 96–195.

[4] See http://ballads.bodleian.ox.ac.uk/search/subject/Robin%20Hood%20%28legendary%20character%29/ (accessed July 2023). This website lists no Arthurian broadsides for the period.

Of 'Robin Hood and the Pindar of Wakefield', Percy himself notes (I, 181) that in Shakespeare's *2 Henry IV*, Silence 'hums a scrap' from this ballad, which 'may be found on every stall, and therefore is not here reprinted'. 'Robin Hoode' appears as the third item listed under 'Old Plays K. vol. 10' on f. 103v of Bodl. MS Percy c.9.

5   *The Jeaste* survives in MS Bodl. Douce 261 (c.1564), and three fragmentary prints, i.e., London, Lambeth Palace Library (?1528); London, Westminster Abbey (c.1530–32); and BL MS Harley 5927, Arts 32 (?1540). See 'The Jeaste of Sir Gawain', in Rhiannon Purdie, *Anglicising Romance: Tail-Rhyme and Genre in Medieval English Literature* (Cambridge: D. S. Brewer, 2008), pp. 206–7, and p. 346 below. For the sixteenth-century prints of 'Sir Lamwell', see pp. 114–19, below.

6   Nastali and Boardman note that Deloney's ballad, 'The Noble Acts of King Arthur and the Knights of the Round Table; with the Valiant Atchievements of Sir Lancelot du Lake', was in circulation prior to 1600, and was probably in early editions of Deloney's ballad collection, *The Garland of Good Will* (1604). The earliest extant version is a broadside printed c.1615 (Daniel P. Nastali and Phillip C. Boardman, *The Arthurian Annals: The Tradition in English from 1250 to 2000*, 2 vols (Oxford: Oxford University Press, 2004), I, 25).

7   See Roger Simpson, 'St George and the Pendragon', in Richard Utz and Tom Shippey (eds), *Medievalism in the Modern World: Essays in Honour of Leslie J. Workman* (Turnhout: Brepols, 1982), pp. 131–53. As well as referring to Spenser's use of the legend of St George in his preface to 'The Birth of St George' (III, 213), Percy credits Richard Johnson – author of *The Nine Worthies of London* and *A crown garland of goulden roses*, amongst other works – as the author of this ballad.

8   In April 1768, Percy was to write to John Bowle, calling Spanish literature 'his favourite subject'. Daniel Eisenberg (ed.), *Thomas Percy & John Bowle. Cervantine Correspondence* (Exeter: Short Run Press, 1987), p. 12. In 1770 Percy published a translation of Mallet's *Introduction à l'histoire de Dannemarc* and a version of the *Prose Edda*.

9   Percy lists some of his sources in his Preface to the *Reliques*, including the ballad collection in the Pepys Library in Cambridge, the Wood Collection in Oxford, the archives of the Antiquarian Society in London, and the British Museum.

10 For an excellent summary of Percy's life, the formation of the *Reliques*, and its place in literary history, see Groom, 1996, I, 1–67.

11 Groom, 1999, 8. In December 1781, Percy was to look back wistfully on his time in Northamptonshire, 'where for many years I led a life of rural leisure, most agreeably devoted to literary amusements' (*Letters*, VIII, 41), but by January 1783 he was earnestly asking Pinkerton to refer to him only as the editor of the *Reliques*, i.e., omitting his clerical title. Whereas previously Percy had signed his letters with his own name, the following month he was signing as 'Tho: Dromore' (*Letters*, VIII, 44, 46). Percy's marriage, however, may have put the brake on his earlier frenetic research. Writing to his cousin, William Cleiveland, on 20 October 1759, Percy confided, 'Nothing I find can spoil Correspondence like Matrimony: Time has been when I thought myself extremely obliged to anyone that would but receive my Letters: but since I have worn the silken yoke my itch of scribbling is a good deal abated' (BL MS Add. 32333, f. 23r). Percy had married Anne Gutteridge earlier that year.

12 Of Warton's supposed debt to Percy regarding the ballad 'Richard of Almaigne', Ritson thundered, 'YOU, Mr. Warton, have followed him with a most literal and servile exactness ... you might have escaped undetected ... but, unluckyly, his lordships accuracy, being much of a piece with your own, suffered him to omit a complete stanza' (Joseph Ritson, *Observations on the Three First Volumes of the History of English Poetry*, 3 vols (London: J. Stockdale & R. Faulder, 1782), I, 5).

13 Among Ritson's works was the posthumously published *Life of King Arthur*. Having gone insane and made a bonfire of his manuscripts in his own room, Ritson died in 1803.

14 Joseph Ritson, *Ancient Engleish Metrical Romanceës*, 3 vols (London: G. & W. Nicol, 1802), I, cix. As early as 3 January 1783, Percy had signalled a supposed interest on the part of his 'very poetical nephew' in providing a supplement to the *Reliques*. This sentiment was repeated to Pinkerton on 12 March 1785, when Percy wrote that *GK* would be a fit inclusion in such a collection (*Letters*, VIII, 43, 53).

[15] Of 'The Child of Ell', Hales and Furnivall memorably remarked that the text had been 'buried in a heap of "polished" verses composed by Percy ... [who] ... was unhappily moved to try his hand at its completion. A wax-doll-maker might as well try to restore Milo's Venus' (HF, I, 132).

[16] The first two volumes of *A Collection of Old Ballads. Corrected from the best and most Ancient Copies Extant. With Introductions Historical, Critical, or Humorous. Illustrated with Copper Plates* were printed in London by J. Roberts and D. Leach in 1723, with a third following in 1725. For a discussion of the influence of the *Collection* on Percy, see Groom (1999, 135–42) and Paula McDowell, '"The Art of Printing was Fatal": Print Commerce and the Idea of Oral Tradition in Long Eighteenth-Century Ballad Discourse', in Fumerton, Guerrini, and McAbee, 2010, pp. 41–46. McDowell draws attention to the Frontispiece of volume I, with its busts of ancient and modern poets – Homer is described as a 'blind ballad singer' – but notes that the author makes no great claims for the value of his material.

[17] Samuel Johnson, *A Dictionary of the English Language* (London: J. & P. Knapton, 1755), p. 196; Thomas Dyche, *A New General English Dictionary*, rev. William Pardon (London: Catherine & Richard Ware, 1765), quoted by Groom (1999, 23).

[18] Letter to Percy dated 24 April 1761 (*Letters*, VII, 94). It was a theme to which Shenstone returned a number of times in his 'billets', i.e., slips of paper containing comments sent to Percy concerning the suitability of various ballads for inclusion: 'I think you are right in admitting what I call *Songs*, as well as *Ballads*' (Billet 2); 'The distinction betwixt *songs* and *Ballads* is by no means accurate; but may serve to afford some sort of *Hint* to Mr Percy' (Billet 3); 'N.B. *Ballads* in general suit my Idea of yr Collection, better than *Songs*' (Billet 7) (*Letters*, VII, 178, 180, 191).

[19] Thomas Warton, *The History of English Poetry from the Close of the Eleventh to the Commencement of the Eighteenth Century*, 4 vols (London: J. Dodsley et al., 1781), III, 423.

[20] Patricia Fumerton and Anita Guerrini, 'Introduction: Straws in the Wind', citing Tessa Watt, in Fumerton, Guerrini, and McAbee, 2010, 2. That 'only 65 per cent of the sixteenth-century ballads which have come down to us appear in the Stationers' register' implies a substantial trade in unlicensed material (Adam Fox, *Oral and Literate Culture in England, 1500–1700* (Oxford: Clarendon Press, 2000), p. 3). I am grateful to Prof. Ad Putter for drawing my attention to Fox's book.

[21] 'By 1700 it may reasonably be assumed that England was a society in which at least half the adult population could read print' (Fox, 2000, 19).

[22] Paula McDowell, 'Mediating Media Past and Present: Towards a Genealogy of "Print Culture" and "Oral Tradition"', in Clifford Siskin and William Warner (eds), *This is Enlightenment* (Chicago: University of Chicago Press, 2010), p. 234. McDowell's observation is a reminder that the PF scribe/compiler need not have relied entirely on the London market for his material.

[23] Letter to Lord Hailes, 28 February 1764 (*Letters*, IV, 70).

[24] Letter to George Paton, 11 September 1773 (*Letters*, VI, 69).

[25] For a discussion of the circulation of ballads and recycling of material, see Patricia Fumerton, 'Remembering by Dismembering: Databases, Archiving, and the Recollection of Seventeenth-Century Broadside Ballads', in Fumerton, Guerrini, and McAbee, 2010, pp. 13–34. Fumerton draws attention to the quote from Wycherley's *The Country Wife* (1675) on p. 16.

[26] *Fragments of Ancient Poetry, collected in the Highlands of Scotland, and translated from the Galic or Erse Language* was the creation of the 24-year-old James McPherson. Percy expressed admiration for these works in the 1767 2nd edition of the *Reliques* (I, xlv). Johnson was one of the sceptics regarding Ossian's existence.

[27] Bards and minstrels 'contributed to soften the roughness of a martial and unlettered people by their songs and by their music' (I, ix). Since 'the civilising of nations has begun from the South: the North would therefore be the last civilised'; the very lack of sophistication was a mark of authenticity, the northern dialect of many of the old ballads being 'extremely incorrect' (I, xxi, xxii).

[28] *Collection*, II, vj. The frontispiece for volume II shows a crowd of people clamouring to buy ballads in the street. The Preface concludes with the intention that the third and final volume of the series would include 'a very fine Collection of old Drinking Songs', but in the Preface to

the succeeding volume the author confesses that 'private business' had obliged him to defer that promise.

29 Allan Ramsay, *The Tea-Table Miscellany: or, a Collection of Choice Songs, Scots and English*, 4 vols (London: A. Millar, 1740), I, ix. Ramsay would have been in sympathy with the vicar in the 1949 film *Kind Hearts and Coronets*, who pronounces, 'I always say that my West Window has all the exuberance of Chaucer without, happily, any of the concomitant crudities of his period'.

30 *Letters*, VII, 175. Shenstone added of the ballads 'Gilderoy' and 'Bonny Dundee' that they were agreeable, 'particularly the Last, if their Moral do not exclude them'. Of 'Sir Lancelott of Dulake', he dismissively remarked that it was 'poor, but may-be curious'.

31 Groom, 1999, 9. Warton endeavoured to square this circle in his *History of English Poetry* (1774–81), hoping both to 'merit the thanks of the antiquarian' as well as to 'gratify the reader of taste' (cited by Donatelli, who adds: 'The antiquary did not have to be persuaded of the merits of the subject, but a general readership had to be encouraged to appreciate its value'. Joseph M. P. Donatelli, 'The Medieval Fictions of Thomas Warton and Thomas Percy', *University of Toronto Quarterly* 60(4) (1991), p. 437).

32 *Letters*, IV, 56. Percy had written to Farmer on the subject on 9 September 1762: 'I am glad to find a taste for the Old Romances begins to revive (not among the common Readers, where it would do hurt, but) amongst our Critics and Poets. Mr Hurd's Letters place them in a very respectable light'(*Letters*, II, 7). He had been less effusive when writing to Shenstone on 17 June 1762: 'Have you seen Hurd's new Letters on Chivalry? He is clever, but he is a Coxcomb' (*Letters*, VII, 157).

33 Lines 71–72 of 'Boy and Mantle' record that when Kay's lady tried on the garment, 'Then was shee bare/All above the Buttocckes'. The equivalent line in the *Reliques* reads, 'Then was she bare/ Before all the rout'. Such sensitivity did not extend, however, to lines 147–48 of the original ('Shee is a bitch & a witch/& a whore bold!'), which remained essentially unchanged in the printed version.

34 *King Arthur and King Cornwall* was singled out as an 'imperfect text', although this argument did not prevent Percy from printing his own reconstruction of *MSG*. Percy was to call *MSG* itself 'so imperfect a Fragment', and hence not fit for publication, in his preface to the ballad in the so-called Sheet B, i.e., an early cancelled sheet, ultimately not included for publication in the *Reliques*. Percy's explanation at that point was that the 'curiosity of the subject' warranted inclusion. See Groom, I, 1996, 393–401 for the complete text.

35 Derek Pearsall, 'Middle English Romance and its Audiences', in M.-J. Arn, H. Wirtjes, and H. Jansen (eds), *Historical & Editorial Studies in Medieval & Early Modern English, for Johan Gerritsen* (Groningen: Wolters-Noordhoff, 1985), pp. 38–39.

36 Raluca L. Radulescu, 'Ballad and Popular Romance in the Percy Folio', in Keith Busby and Roger Dalrymple (eds), *Arthurian Literature* 23 (Cambridge: D. S. Brewer, 2006), p. 71.

37 David C. Fowler, *A Literary History of the Popular Ballad* (Durham, NC: Duke University Press, 1968), p. 18.

38 Albert B. Friedman, Review of David C. Fowler's *A Literary History of the Popular Ballad*, *Speculum* 45(1) (1970), p. 128. The futility of trying to force a ballad into a particular category is well illustrated by *BM*. Radulescu observes that 'on the one hand "Boy and Mantle"'s typical ballad form has led to a classification in this genre; on the other, its Arthurian content helped to place it in the romance category' (Radulescu, 2006, 76).

39 Carl Lindahl, 'The Oral Undertones of Late Medieval Romance', in W. F. H. Nicolaisen (ed.), *Oral Tradition in the Middle Ages* (Binghampton, NY: Medieval & Renaissance Texts & Studies, 1995), p. 60.

40 As for Percy's claim that by this stage minstrels had lost their dignity, Ritson observed that 'it is pretty clear they never had any to lose' (Joseph Ritson, 'Observations on the Ancient English Minstrels', in *Ancient Songs, from the Reign of King Henry the Third, to the Revolution* (London: J. Johnson, 1790), p. x). Ad Putter notes that 'One misconception is that minstrels (*qua* storytellers) were becoming extinct in the later Middle Ages. It is true that, in aristocratic (and later civic) contexts, the term "minstrel" began to designate professional musicians rather than storytellers – but, in other spheres of life, storytellers (variously referred to as minstrels, harpers, rhymers)

[41] See Groom, I, 1996, 7–9; Groom, 1999, 44ff.; and Fumerton, 2010, 16 and 25–26.

[42] McDowell, 2010, 46. Of Percy's role as a medium, McDonald observes that he promoted the Middle Ages 'as an age of romance, wild with imagination but, in perfect antithesis to his own eminently tasteful time, irredeemably barbarous; at the same time he promotes himself as someone able to know the difference' (McDonald, 2004, 7).

[43] Fox, 2000, 3. On p. 5, Fox adds, 'It is difficult to know whether to describe such a ballad as the product of oral, scribal, or print culture'. For an excellent discussion of this interface, see Fox, 2000, 1–10. Bodl. MS Ashmole 48, 'an ordinary commonplace book copied largely from broadsides', includes five pieces by the minstrel Richard Sheale. For a discussion of the MS and Sheale's career, see Tessa Watt, *Cheap Print and Popular Piety, 1550–1640* (Cambridge: Cambridge University Press, 1991), pp. 16–21.

[44] 'Comparison of the printed versions with the Percy Folio makes it abundantly clear that the Percy Folio text had passed through at least one stage of memorial transmission before the scribe committed the text to paper', while 'a comparison of the Percy version with other versions of *Guy of Warwick* shows that the Percy Folio text had been reconstituted from memory at some stage in its textual history' (Putter, 2011, 347–48). For a discussion of the transmission of the PF's *Guy and Colebrand*, see Demelza Jayne Curnow, 'Five Case Studies on the Transmission of Popular Middle English Verse Romances', PhD thesis, University of Bristol, 2002, pp. 196–214. I am grateful to Prof. Putter for bringing this work to my attention.

[45] Of the number of ballads that have survived, Friedman observed that '"Oral transmission" is not an excrescent characteristic of the ballad; it is of the essence', adding that 'The popular ballads were not only preserved orally but are created or recreated by an oral process as well. The recorded ballads, certainly those few examples written down before field collections were made, are lucky accidents, radically altered in many cases in the act of getting embalmed on paper' (Friedman, 1970, 128).

[46] Quoted by Andrew Taylor, 'Performing the Percy Folio', in Jacqueline Jenkins and Julie Sanders (eds), *Editing, Performance, Texts: New Practices in Medieval and Early Modern English Drama* (London: Palgrave Macmillan, 2014), p. 84.

[47] Cameron Louis (ed.), *The Commonplace Book of Robert Reynes of Acle: An Edition of Tanner MS 407*, Garland Medieval Texts 1 (New York: Garland, 1980), pp. 432, 437.

[48] Charles Bowie Millican, 'The Original of the Ballad "Kinge: Arthurs Death" in the Percy Folio MS', *PMLA* 46(4) (1931), pp. 1020, 1023. Millican prints in full on pp. 1023–24 the Arthurian section.

[49] Lawton, 2003, 183–90. See also Esha Niyogi De, 'From Theater to Ritual: A Study of the Revesby Mummers Play', in Nicolaisen, 1995, 115–27; and Michael J. Preston, 'The Revesby Sword Play', *Journal of American Folklore* 85(335) (1972), p. 56. One of the mummings written by the prolific and popular poet John Lydgate is that of St George, written at the request of the armourers of London, and which survives in Cambridge, Trinity College MS R.3.20, compiled in the early 1430s. East Anglia seems to have been particularly interested in drama of this kind: Croxley is located in the region, and the MS containing the N-town plays, BL MS Cotton Vespasian D.8, was probably written in the region too. Lydgate lived at Bury St Edmunds, and 'it would have been hard for him to be unaware of the region's performance traditions' (Claire Sponsler (ed.), John Lydgate, *Mummings and Entertainments* (Kalamazoo, MI: Medieval Institute Publications, 2010), p. 5. See also Claire Sponsler, *The Queen's Dumb Shows: John Lydgate and the Making of Early Theater* (Philadelphia: University of Pennsylvania Press, 2014)).

[50] For the dating of *WSG*, see John Withrington, '*The Weddynge of Sir Gawen and Dame Ragnell* and *The Marriage of Sir Gawaine*', *AE*, 209–10. See pp. 99–113, below for a discussion of the relationship between *MSG* and *WSG*.

[51] So entertaining, in fact, that *MSG* inspired 'The Marriage of Sir Gawaine: An Opera'. Published in the May and July editions of the *European Magazine* in 1782, the work was 'Dedicated to those who love Antiquity for its nonsense more than for its sense'. The longevity of the Loathly Lady story is reflected in more modern retellings, e.g., the children's book *Sir Gawain and the Loathly*

Lady, by Selina Hastings, with illustrations by Juan Wijngaard (London: Walker Books, 1985). In 2015, *The Wedding of Sir Gawain and Dame Ragnelle*, 'an Arthurian comedy with a feminist twist!', was performed at the National Opera Center in New York, www.martinhennessy.net/the-wedding-of-sir-gawain-and-dame-ragnelle (accessed July 2023).

52 Coincidentally, the Rawlinson MS contains both *MSG* and a copy of *Sir Landevale*, a precursor to *LAMBE*.

53 Linda Marie Zaerr, '*The Weddynge of Sir Gawen and Dame Ragnell*: Performance and Intertextuality in Middle English Popular Romance', in Evelyn Birge Vitz et al. (eds), *Performing Medieval Narrative* (Cambridge: D. S. Brewer, 2005), pp. 193–208. For a performance by Zaerr, see https://vimeo.com/arthurperform (accessed July 2023). The phrase, 'this tale grew in the telling', is from the Foreword of J. R. R. Tolkien's *The Lord of the Rings*.

54 Gawaine may also have played a larger role in the missing parts of *KAKC*, while his substitution for Lancelot in *LD* (lines 1163–64) would indicate a deliberate attempt to raise his profile.

55 Percy himself seems to have been almost embarrassed by *MSG*'s lack of reverence towards the king, claiming in Sheet B that 'if the reader is offended to find the British hero, king ARTHUR, make so shabby an appearance in this and the preceding ballad, we can assure him, that most of the old romances writers, &c. take the same liberties with his character' (quoted by Groom (1996, I, 393)).

56 Roger Dalrymple, *Language and Piety in Middle English Romance* (Cambridge: D. S. Brewer, 2000), p. x. I am grateful to Prof. Vincent Gillespie for drawing my attention to this book.

57 Dalrymple, 2000, 31. See, for example, *MER*, 1–4 and 2375–79, below, for an example of such symmetry.

58 Dalrymple discussed the use of oaths on pp. 5–10, and again on p. 87, as part of his excellent analysis of the stanzaic *Morte Arthur*.

59 Of *WSG*, Chaucer's 'Wife of Bath's Tale', and Gower's 'Tale of Florent', Lindahl writes that 'the shared plot of these three tales can be made the property of any late medieval class or value system. I am convinced that all three versions were orally performed, probably frequently' (Lindahl, 1995, 75). This does not, of course, take into account the darker side of *WSG*, with its reference to an imprisoned author. For an interpretation of *WSG* as a humourless pristine text by a single author, see S. Elizabeth Passmore and Susan B. Carter (eds), *The English 'Loathly Lady' Tales: Boundaries, Traditions, Motifs* (Kalamazoo, MI: Medieval Institute Publications, 2007).

60 Thomas Hahn (ed.), *Sir Gawain: Eleven Romances and Tales* (Kalamazoo: Western Michigan University, 1995), pp. 21–22. Downloadable from https://d.lib.rochester.edu/teams/publication/hahn-sir-gawain (accessed July 2023). Of the 61 Middle English verse romance texts listed by Zaerr as mentioning 'minstrels', 14 are Arthurian, including some featured in the PF (Linda Marie Zaerr, *Performance and the Middle English Romance* (Cambridge: D. S. Brewer, 2012), pp. 181–233).

61 Letter to Rev. Dr Birch, dated 2 February 1765; letter to Charles Rivington of 13 June 1794, printed by John Nichols in *Illustrations of the Literary History of the Eighteenth Century: Consisting of Authentic Memoirs and Original Letters of Eminent Persons, and Intended as a Sequel to the 'Literary Anecdotes'*, 8 vols (London: John Nichols and Son, 1817–58), VII, 577; VIII, 309. Percy had previously anticipated that his nephew would one day be editing a collection that included the poetry of Surrey and Wyatt: a warehouse fire in February 1808 destroyed the printed edition of a project nurtured by Percy for 45 years (*Letters*, IX, 25, 18; II, 175–200). Notwithstanding his apparent indifference, Percy was still working on the *Reliques* after 1794 (Prof. Nick Groom: private communication).

62 Letter to Robert Jamieson (Nichols, *Illustrations*, VIII, 341). Percy's lasting bitterness towards Ritson is evident in his correspondence. In July 1792, he wrote to John Pinkerton, presumably hoping that Pinkerton would take his side, vowing of Ritson that 'the MS shall never be exposed to his Sight in my Life time', presumably in response to a letter, now lost, in which Pinkerton suggested that in order to counter Ritson's criticisms, the PF should be made public (*Letters*, VIII, 88). On 4 September 1794, Pinkerton again wrote to Percy, pointing out that there are two sides to every argument: 'you must contend against hundreds on the opposite side. For a part Ritson's book may be referred to', adding 'Sometimes I have found brevity look like harshness ... and I am

sorry even to object to any of your opinions' (*Letters*, VIII, 97–98). This letter effectively severed the relationship between the two men. In a letter dated 4 January 1808, Percy wrote to Robert Anderson, referring to Ritson as 'that poor, Miserable Maniac' (*Letters*, IX, 264–65). Five years after Ritson's death it is evident that the wounds were still raw.

[63] In 1807, just 13 years after the fourth edition of the *Reliques*, selections from Percy's work were already being bowdlerized for a more genteel audience, an anonymous lady being of the view that many of the ballads were unfit for the youth of her day. (See Katie Garner, 'Gendering Percy's *Reliques*: Ancient Ballads and the Making of Women's Arthurian Writing', in Karl Fugelso (ed.), *Corporate Medievalism II*, Studies in Medievalism 22 (Cambridge: Boydell & Brewer, D. S. Brewer, 2013), pp. 45–67.) Having published *The Boy's King Arthur* in 1880, Sidney Lanier's *The Boy's Percy, being Old Ballads of War, Adventure and Love* (1882) included *MSG* from the *Reliques*. However, Lanier deleted lines 105–8, where Gawain kisses his new bride in bed 'lying upon the sheete'. The accompanying illustration shows the married couple chastely greeting each other across the room, a crumpled sheet to one side being the only concession to the original text.

The Arthurian Background

James Douglas Merriman's study of the Arthurian story between 1485 and 1835 calls the seventeenth and early eighteenth centuries 'The Death of a Legend'.[1] The year after his victory on Bosworth Field in 1485, the future Henry VII named his son 'Arthur', with the implication that, having united the Houses of York and Lancaster by marriage, the Tudor dynasty would be the start of a new Arthurian Age.[2] And yet by the time Percy published his *Reliques* in 1765, King Arthur's very existence was open to question, while the great king's standing in literature was such that he was to play a less than heroic role in Fielding's 1730 farcical burlesque *The Tragedy of Tragedies; or the Life and Death of Tom Thumb the Great*.

King Arthur as Historical Figure

In his Preface to Malory's *Le Morte Darthur* (*LMD*, printed in the same year as Bosworth Field), Caxton claimed that he was encouraged by a 'noble gentleman' to print the history of King Arthur and his knights. Whether Caxton's apparent doubt about Arthur's existence – 'divers men hold opinion that there was no such Arthur, and that all such books as be made of him be but feigned and fables' – was the result of genuine uncertainty, or a shrewd marketing ploy,[3] the Preface seemingly shows him convinced by evidence of various sorts, from references to Arthur in the chronicle *Polychronicon*,[4] and the presence of various Arthurian artefacts apparently still extant (for example, Gawaine's skull and Craddock's mantle at Dover Castle). Increasingly, however, succeeding generations came to view with more caution the existence and legacy of this most famous king, the first major challenge to the historical portrayal of Arthur, as set out in Geoffrey of Monmouth's *Historia Regum Britanniae* (*HRB*, completed by 1139), coming with Polydore Vergil's *Anglica Historia*. This history, written at the request of Henry VII but not published until 1534, criticizes Geoffrey for openly inventing details about Arthur, as well as embroidering the prophecies of Merlin. Robert Fabyan's *The Newe Cryoncles of Englande and Fraunce* (1516) takes a similarly sceptical view of Geoffrey, a position shared by John Rastell in his history, *The Pastyme of People*, published in 1529. John Hardyng's verse chronicle, published by Richard Grafton in two editions in 1543, adopted a more enthusiastic and uncritical view of Arthur,[5] while John Leland's *Assertio Inclytissimi Arturii Regis Britanniae*, published in Latin in 1544, vigorously defended the historicity of Arthur, reaching a wider audience with its translation into English by Richard Robinson in 1582.[6]

John Bale's *Illustrium Maioris Britanniae Scriptorum* (1548), an ambitious work providing biographical notes of authors over the previous five centuries and expanded as *Illustrium Maioris Brytanniae* (1557, with volume 2, *Scriptorum Illustrium Maioris Brytanniae*, following in 1559), identified Malory as the author of *LMD*, but Bale had no doubts that the fantastic elements of the story obscured a real truth: 'his work abounds in old wives' tales which need to be expurgated lest the historical veracity of the work be compromised'.[7] John Harington, in his 1591 verse translation of Ariosto's *Orlando Furioso*, expressed his belief in the historical existence of both Arthur and Merlin, while *The Birth, Life and Death of honourable Arthur King of Brittaine* (1601) by Robert Chester sets out to refute 'in this doubtfull age of opinions, a controuersie of that esteemed Prince of Brittaine', and repeats Caxton's assertion that Gawaine's skull and Cradock's mantle are still to be found.[8] William Camden's influential *Britain, or, a Chorographicall Description of the Flourishing Kingdomes, England, Scotland, and Ireland* took a sceptical view of *HRB*, with John Speed's *The History of Great Britaine* (1611) musing that the more fantastic accounts surrounding Arthur had contributed to doubts about his very existence.[9]

John Milton, who abandoned the idea of a poetic Arthuriad in favour of *Paradise Lost*, had commenced work c.1649 on his own *History of Britain*. This unfinished text, published in 1670, adopts a particularly sceptical tone when it comes to King Arthur, Milton writing, 'But who Arthur was, and whether every any such reign'd in Britain, hath bin doubted heretofore, and may again with good reason', adding that 'he who can accept of Legends for good story, may quickly swell a volume with trash'.[10] William Dugdale's *Monasticon Anglicanum* (1655) mentions Arthur only in the context of his connection with Glastonbury, but by the close of the seventeenth century the diplomat and essayist Sir William Temple, a man whose prose style was admired by Johnson, could lament that any historical argument for King Arthur's existence had been left open to doubt.

> [T]his whole Story is left so uncertain or obscure by those poor Writers, who have pretended to leave the Tales, rather than the History of those times behind them, that it remains in doubt, whether to consider them as a part of the Story of that, or the Fables of succeeding Ages. Whatever there was of plain Stuff, the Embroidery of it ... seems to have been introduced by that Vein of the Spanish Romances, which many Ages after filled the World with so much of that idle Trash.[11]

Three years before the publication of Percy's *Reliques*, the Scottish philosopher David Hume could observe in his *History of England*, 'This is that Arthur so much celebrated in the songs of Thaliessin, and the other British bards, and whose military atchievements have been blended with so many fables, as to give occasion for entertaining a doubt of his real existence'.[12]

Enlisting the Arthurian Legend
The Heirs of King Arthur

The Round Table at Winchester, most likely made in 1289 on the occasion of a tournament held in the reign of that notable Arthurian enthusiast, Edward I,[13] was restored in 1516, in time for Henry VIII to display to the visiting Emperor Charles V.[14] Henry returned to the Arthurian theme on the occasion of Charles's visit to London in 1522, when Arthur appeared in one of a series of pageants, a child flattering the emperor as 'resemblyng hym in noblenes to the seyd Arthur' (Biddle, 2000, 427). But Arthur's role as a cheerleader for the Tudor dynasty proved to be more incidental than central. The extravagant and flattering pageant staged for Elizabeth I at Kenilworth Castle in 1575 featured an Arthurian theme, with the Lady of the Lake pronouncing that she had kept the castle since the time of Arthur, while welcoming Elizabeth to the proceedings. This was a spectacular event, the occasion being recorded by Robert Laneham, who was particularly taken by the performance and learning of one Captain Cox: 'an od man … and hardy az Gawin', with all sorts of material 'at hiz fingers endz', e.g., 'king Arthurz book … Sir Lamwell … Syr Gawyn … with many moe then I rehearz heere'. Laneham adds, 'what a bunch of ballets & songs, all auncient'.[15] Percy approvingly pointed to the Arthurian entertainment at Kenilworth as evidence of a hierarchical minstrel tradition ('From the expression of SQUIRE MINSTREL … we may conclude there were other inferior orders'), and solemnly quoted verbatim the eccentric dress and performance of the minstrel concerned: 'A pair of pumps on his feet, with a cross cut at his toes for corns … a scutcheon … of the ancient arms of Islington … and after a little warbling on his HARP … came forth with a solemn song, warranted for story out of King Arthur's acts'.[16] However, the dress and fastidious manner of the minstrel, and in particular the response of those present at the time, indicates that this performance was not so much about replicating a minstrel tradition as gently satirizing the ridiculous. In short, Percy did not get the joke.[17]

In 1592, Elizabeth was treated to a further spectacle with an Arthurian theme, this time in the tiltyard at Whitehall, when the Queen's Champion, the Earl of Cumberland, gave a speech as a knight of Pendragon Castle. The most celebrated use of the Arthurian myth in Elizabethan times, however, was surely in Spenser's *The Faerie Queene* of 1590; and yet, as Warton observed in 1762, Arthur himself plays a subsidiary, almost incidental role: 'The poet ought to have made his ARTHUR the principal agent in the redress of each particular wrong … At present he is only a subordinate, or rather accessory character'.[18] The accession of James I as successor to Elizabeth breathed some life into the creative use of the Arthurian legend, Thomas Campion's *Masque at Lord Hays Marriage* (1607) arguing, for example, that Merlin's prophecy of Arthur's return had been fulfilled when James assumed the crown. Ben Jonson's *The Speeches at Prince Henries Barriers*, a masque performed in January 1610 to celebrate the investiture of the young Prince of Wales, featured Arthur as the star Arcturus, and Henry himself appeared as the knight Meliadus.[19] But the value of the Arthurian legend as myth and metaphor in the context of the royal house was diminishing: 'as the Stuart sun waned, so did interest in Arthur, and during the Commonwealth he was all but forgotten' (Merriman, 1973, 51).

Arthur as Exemplum

Caxton advocated in his Preface to *LMD* that his readers should 'do after the good and leave the evil, and it shall bring you to good fame and renown'. However, succeeding generations were not always ready to accept that the Arthurian story provided an appropriate moral compass.[20] Nevertheless, both king and legend served for a period of time as a lesson for princes and people alike. Two early poetic examples – *Sir Gawain and the Green Knight* (c.1400) and the *Awntyrs off Arthure* (c.1400) – drew upon the English stereotype of Gawaine as the model of courtesy, a characterization that persisted up to and including the ballads that Percy found in his Folio.

As a noble figure worthy of emulation, Arthur often appears as a member of the Nine Worthies – three groups of three heroes, drawn from the Bible (Joshua, David, and Judas Maccabeus), classical times (Hector, Alexander the Great, and Julius Caesar), and the ranks of notable Christians (Arthur, Charlemagne, and Godfrey of Bouillon). The topos first featured in Jacques de Longuyon's *Les vouex du paon* (c.1312), and these figures were celebrated as late as 1584, in Richard Lloyd's *The Nine Worthies*, itself a source of inspiration for *KAD*.[21] Arthur's rise and fall as one of the Nine Worthies was seen by many in the Middle Ages as an example of how even the most famous and noble of men was still subject to fate and fortune.[22] Arthur also featured alongside other famous figures in history, literature, and the Bible as part of the 'mirror for princes' homiletic tradition, a notable example of which was the *Fall of Princes* (c.1438), a work of 36,365 lines by the prolific and highly popular John Lydgate, the excerpted Arthurian section of this monumental work enjoying a degree of currency in the late fifteenth century.[23] Some hundred years after the *Fall* was written these extracts were popular enough for John Bale, the first to attempt a compilation of the Lydgate canon, to include 'Arthur' and 'The Round Table' as separate works. It is possible that excerpts of Lydgate's *Fall of Princes*, circulating under that name and referencing Arthur, inspired ballad-makers for some considerable time thereafter: the PF itself contains a ballad in the *ubi sunt* tradition called 'The Fall of Princes', which includes the lament

> Where is King Arthur the venturer, with his Knights bold?
> or Sir Tristeram, that treasure of curtesye?
> or Sir Gawaine the good, with his helmett made of gold?
> or Sir Lancelott dulake, a Knight of Chiualrye? (HF, III, 168–73; lines 73–76)

The Arthurian Legend in Literature and Prophecy

While one might have expected the publication of Caxton's *LMD* to be the start of a continuous interest in King Arthur lasting to the present day, the truth is that awareness of Arthurian romance by Percy's time was not a result of unbroken popularity of this prose text. Malory's work was reprinted by Wynkyn de Worde in 1498 and 1529 and by Copland in 1557, with further editions published by East in 1578 and Stansby in 1634. Between January 1752 and December 1754, Warton had spent considerable time in the Bodleian Library in Oxford in pursuit of his interest in English literary history. Included in the works he consulted was Stansby's *LMD* (Johnston, 1964, 115), and recognition of Malory's work by the general public as well as by Percy was increased by his references both within *Observations on the Faerie Queene* and in the later *The History of English Poetry*.[24] Nevertheless, notwithstanding Warton's recognition of Spenser's debt to Malory and an appreciation of *LMD*, it was not until 1816 that *LMD* again appeared in print.[25]

While 1588 saw the first known Arthurian drama in England (Thomas Hughes's *The Misfortunes of Arthur*),[26] as we have seen, there was also a tradition of a less than heroic portrayal of the Arthurian world. Contemporary with Shakespeare, Richard Johnson's humorous *The Most Pleasant History of Tom a Lincolne* (1599, with a sequel in 1607) features the adventures, sexual and otherwise, of Arthur's illegitimate son Tom: Arthur himself is anything but the chivalrous hero of old.[27] Rowley's *The Birth of Merlin*[28] and Johnson's *The History of Tom Thumb* (1621, probably a prose retelling of a late sixteenth-century ballad which charts the story of the diminutive knight of Arthur's court),[29] both mine the legend for its comic potential. The reverential use of the legend by Dryden in his masque *King Arthur: or the British Worthy* (1691), with music by Henry Purcell, might well have signalled a new age of creative genius in respect of the Arthurian legend, instead of which Sir Richard Blackmore published *Prince ARTHUR. An Heroick POEM. In Ten Books* (1695), followed by *King ARTHUR. An Heroick POEM. In Twelve Books* (1697). Whereas Milton decided against the idea of an epic Arthuriad, Blackmore suffered no such self-doubt, using the Arthurian legend and classical literature to compose lengthy paeons in praise of William III. Mercilessly satirized by Pope in both *Peri Bathos: Or the Art of Sinking in Poetry* (1728) and *The Dunciad* (first published 1728, where he is described as the 'everlasting Blackmore' who manages to put his entire audience to sleep), Blackmore's contributions seemingly laid to rest forever the prospect of a worthy Arthurian epic. Henry Fielding's comic and parodic burlesque *Tom Thumb* (1730), a work rewritten by its author the following year as *The Tragedy of Tragedies*, may have been aimed at the hyperbole of Restoration tragedies (Merriman, 1973, 77), but the collateral damage to the sobriety of the Arthurian legend was clear. King Arthur proclaims 'To-day it is our Pleasure to be drunk,/And this our Queen shall be as drunk as We';[30] Arthur's wife, Dollallola [sic], falls for Tom Thumb, and as part of the bloodbath that concludes the play, the diminutive Tom is devoured by a cow.

Finally, a popular use of the Arthurian legend was prophecies derived from, or inspired by, Geoffrey of Monmouth's early twelfth-century *Prophetia Merlini*. Incorporated into *HRB*, these supposed prophecies by Merlin provided a ready inspiration for centuries thereafter, political ballads and Merlinic prophecies flourishing during particularly troubled times. For example, the emergence of the popular 'The Cock of the North' prophecy was associated with the Percy family's rebellion of the early fifteenth century, while PF's 'The Rose of Englande', possibly written before 1495, 'owes an important debt to political prophecy of a distinctly Galfridian character, with strong Arthurian resonances' (Byrne and Flood, 2015, 336).[31] Nevertheless, although political ballads and subversive prophecies were to appear during the English Civil War, and while almanacs and astrologers continued to draw on Merlin's name for mass market appeal,[32] Swift's harsh satire of John Partridge's *Merlinus Liberatus* (1689–1707) 'failed to destroy the astrologer's reputation among the commonalty … the rapid decline in the numbers of such publications during the century suggests that … the skepticism of the age of Reason had begun to do its work' (Merriman, 1973, 79).[33]

Percy and the Arthurian Legend

In addition to the PF, Percy drew upon a wide range of sources for the *Reliques* – in 1761 he visited Cambridge to examine Samuel Pepys's collection of some 1,800 broadsides, while among Percy's own collection were numerous works bought from Cluer Dicey[34] – but it would seem that Arthurian material did not feature prominently in his searches. While Percy was not an Arthurian scholar by nature, he found the legend and literature intriguing,[35] his curiosity driving him to explore the subject in terms of both its origins and its representation in different languages. For example, at some stage between 1764 and 1766, Percy borrowed manuscripts of the prose *Tristan* (NLS MS Adv.19.1.3.) and Chrétien de Troyes's *Perceval* (NLS MS Adv.19.1.5.),[36] while of Arthur's mysterious disappearance after the battle against Mordred, Percy noted next to line 231 of *KAD* that 'This is the tradition alluded to by Don Quixote'.[37] On 25 July 1762, Percy's interest in this legend led him to write to the Welsh clergyman Evan Evans, asking him for any information about the death of Arthur in Welsh histories;[38] and yet, for a man who believed in the legacy offered by seemingly ancient ballads, Percy was curiously dismissive at times of chronicle material. Of Robert of Gloucester's history he scathingly remarked to Shenstone in October 1762 that the 'rhimes are to the last degree mean and contemptible', the language such that it 'serves as a veil to hide the poverty and barrenness of his thoughts' (*Letters*, VII, 163), while in a letter to Hailes dated 8 September 1763, Percy wrote,

> The antiquaries who have republished the productions of our old English poets, have generally been men totally void of all taste and feeling, and therefore have always fastidiously rejected these old poetical Romances', adding that all the while 'they have been careful to grab up every petty fragment of Robert of Gloucester, Gower, Lydgate, Harding, and other wretched Rhymists. (*Letters*, IV, 56)

Especially interesting from an Arthurian point of view is Percy's first extant letter to William Shenstone – dated 24 November 1757 – in which Percy carefully drew attention to the existence of the PF, describing it as 'a very curious old MS Collection of ancient Ballads many of which I believe were never printed'. The closing lines of the postscript to his letter add of the PF that 'It contains many old Romantic and Historical Ballads: upon King Arthur and the Knights of his round Table: Merlin &c., &c. &c.'.[39] Percy's elevation of the relatively few Arthurian pieces was equally to the fore when he wrote for the first time to Thomas Warton, Professor of

Poetry at Oxford University.[40] Percy opens his letter by stating his admiration, and that of Shenstone, for Warton's *Observations on the Faerie Queene*, remarking that Warton had clearly demonstrated Spenser's reliance upon *LMD*.[41] He then states that he can prove 'that the Author of *Mort. Arthur* (however he came by them in French) only drew up a prose narrative of, and threw together into a regular story the Subject of a hundred Old Ballads'. Having thus gained Warton's attention, he refers to the PF, and boldly states that the ballads contained therein are 'of very remote antiquity. They are many of them earlier than Chaucer, a plain proof of which is, their being expressly quoted, or particularly alluded to, by him', adding of *MSG*, 'I am of opinion that he borrowed his *wife of Bath's Tale* from it'.[42] Enclosed with the letter to Warton were transcripts of *BM* and *MSG*.[43] The Arthurian bait was taken, and Warton was on board: 'Percy would introduce himself to his readers in the same way as he had won the support of his different collaborators: with the ballad fables of the Matter of Britain' (Groom, 1999, 186). Indeed, *BM* was to make more than one appearance in the cause. While it had opened the third volume of the *Reliques*, for readers who had 'no relish for antiquity', a 'more modern copy' was provided at the close. 'Revised and altered by a modern hand' (*Reliques*, III, 314),[44] Percy took the opportunity at this point to draw the attention of the reader to Warton's observation that the ballad was taken from 'an old French piece intitled LE COURT MANTEL', reaffirming his belief in the primacy of British material over works from across the Channel: "tis most likely that all the old stories concerning K. Arthur are originally of British growth, and that what the French and other southern nations have of this kind were at first exported from this island' (*Reliques*, III, 314).

Percy would have been delighted to receive Warton's highly positive response of 19 June, and the willingness of this literary giant to engage in ongoing correspondence; not only did Warton wish him 'Success in your intended publication', but he agreed with Percy that Spenser 'certainly had the *Boy and the Mantle*' in view when writing the *Faerie Queen*: Percy's credentials, his access to an unparalleled scholarly resource, and an endorsement of the worth of his MS were all secure.[45] In July 1761, Warton wrote back to Percy, thanking him for sending the two Arthurian transcripts, and mused on the origins of 'King Ryence's Challenge'. Percy's belief that this ballad was composed for the Kenilworth festivities, and certainly not older than the time of Queen Elizabeth, was taken up by Warton in his letter of 23 November 1761. Warton reported that he had collated the ballad with a copy found in the 1634 edition of *LMD*, concluding that the ballad 'is not very old', but acknowledged his error in previously thinking that it was an integral part of *LMD*.[46] As a result, while Percy included this ballad alongside the Arthurian texts that opened volume III of the *Reliques*, he was clear why: 'This song is more modern than many of those which follow it, but is placed here for the sake of the subject' (*Reliques*, III, 25). The importance of Arthurian material for the *Reliques* had once again reasserted itself.

The fruitful cooperation with Warton continued. On 28 February 1762, Percy wrote to Warton, informing him that he had come across a French translation of the Spanish romance *The History of Tirante the White*, which included a description of the San Greal (*Letters*, III, 31–32). Accompanying the letter was Sheet B, containing *BM* and *MSG*. As a result, when it came to the sequence of ballads to be printed in the *Reliques*, 'the order was determined by Percy's best materials at hand – the same ballads with which he had introduced himself to Warton the year before' (Groom, 1996, I, 28). Percy's subsequent decision to dedicate his work to the Countess of Northumberland led once more to *MSG* being pressed into service: Sheet B was entirely reset by Percy as he looked to his own genius to recreate a complete text of the ballad, a phoenix-like version arising from the ashes of antiquity. The end result, as Groom says, was to establish 'almost at the outset of printing that the anthology would consist of polished verses rather than antiquarian detritus ... Printing was already under way before Percy decided to retire the Folio MS from the *Reliques*, and from that moment it was paraded more as a token reference than as an absolute textual authority' (Groom, 1999, 226–27).

Two Arthurian texts had played a crucial role in bringing together a collection of ballads that went through four editions in some 30 years, a collection which was to serve as an inspiration for generations to come. Opening as they did the third volume of the *Reliques*, a volume entitled 'Ballads on King Arthur, etc.', *BM* and *MSG* carried a weight far beyond their brief lines. The enduring irony is that Ritson's caustic criticism resulted in Percy having to publish *MSG*, for the fourth edition of the *Reliques*, not as it should have been, but as it was in his once precious manuscript. Percy's legacy as a scholar, antiquarian, and visionary was thus tainted by a reputation for amateur vainglory from which it has never truly recovered.

Notes

[1] Merriman, 1973, 49–80.

[2] Born and baptized in Winchester, a location traditionally identified as the site of Camelot, the heir to the throne was made Duke of Cornwall (presumably in recognition of Tintagel being identified by Geoffrey of Monmouth in the *Historia Regum Britanniae* as the birthplace of King Arthur), and was greeted by his namesake at a pageant in Coventry in 1498. For Henry VII's accession and the Tudors' use of an Arthurian theme, see Sydney Anglo, 'The *British History* in Early Tudor Propaganda', *Bulletin of the John Rylands Library* 44(1) (1961), pp. 28–33. Anglo cautions, however, that such events 'cannot be adduced as evidence for a continuous cult of King Arthur by the Early Tudors' (30). Helen Cooper adds that 'Arthur, however, was simply too far distant to be of much help in legitimising the Tudor usurpation' (Cooper, 1996, 150). Prince Arthur died in 1502.

[3] Russell Rutter has suggested that such an approach might have provided 'just the tang of excitement needed to make someone buy a large and costly book' (Russell Rutter, 'William Caxton and Literary Patronage', *Studies in Philology* 84 (1987), p. 468). Even so, Caxton was careful not to confirm one way or another his personal views on Arthur's very existence: 'but for to give faith and belief that all is true that is contained herein, ye be at your liberty'. For a less cynical interpretation, Richard Barber has suggested that Caxton may have been approached by those genuinely interested in a printed book featuring the story of King Arthur: 'Malory the political fugitive and prisoner may well have been better known to his contemporaries as Malory the courtier' (Richard Barber, 'Malory's *Le Morte Darthur* and Court Culture under Edward IV',

in James P. Carley and Felicity Riddy (eds), *Arthurian Literature* 12 (Cambridge: D. S. Brewer, 1993), p. 155).

4   Ranulph Higden's fourteenth-century chronicle was translated from Latin into English by John Trevisa, and published by Caxton in 1480.

5   Hardyng's chronicle is preserved in two different versions. The first, seemingly presented to Henry VI in 1457, is found uniquely in BL MS Lansdowne 204. Hardyng's subsequent revision of his chronicle, itself likely to have been known to Malory, is found in 12 manuscripts and various fragments, and formed the basis for Grafton's editions of 1543. Grafton's *An Abridgement of the Chronicles of England* (1562, with five revised editions up to 1572) was followed in 1569 by a version recommending the Arthurian reader to follow Leland for more information.

6   For Robinson's translation, see William Edward Mead (ed.), *The Famous Historie of Chinon of England by Christopher Middleton*, EETS OS 165 (London: Oxford University Press, 1925). John Stow's *The Chronicles of England, from Brut vnto this present yeare of Christ. 1580* went so far as to present as fact the story of Arthur, even providing a date for his death of 21 May 542. Adam Fox notes the indignation of at least one resident of Elizabethan England at the way Arthur was abused by featuring in 'monkish verses' and 'vile painting in an alehouse' (Fox, 2000, 34).

7   Quoted in translation by Marylyn Parins (ed.), *Sir Thomas Malory: The Critical Heritage* (London: Routledge, 1987), p. 55. A similar view was expressed by William Warner in *Albion's England* (1586): while happy to recognize Arthur as a historical figure, as for the more fantastic elements, 'I credite not' (quoted by Merriman, 1973, 38).

8   *Robert Chester's 'Love's Martyr, Or, Rosalins Complaint' With Its Supplement, 'Diverse Poeticall Essaies on the Turtle and the Phoenix'*, ed. Alexander Balloch Grosart (London: Trübner, 1878; repr. Cambridge: Cambridge University Press, 2014), p. 42.

9   The title of Camden's work is that of the translation from Latin published in 1610, the original having been published in 1586 and reaching five editions by 1607.

10 John Milton, *The history of Britain, that part especially now call'd England from the first traditional beginning, continu'd to the Norman conquest* (London: James Allestry, 1670), pp. 122–23, https://quod.lib.umich.edu/e/eebo/A50902.0001.001?view=toc (accessed July 2023). See also Helen Cooper, 'Milton's King Arthur', *Review of English Studies* 65(269) (2014), pp. 252–65.

11 Sir William Temple, *An Introduction to the History of England* (London: Richard Simpson, Ralph Simpson, 1695), pp. 51–52.

12 David Hume, *The History of England, from the Invasion of Julius Cæsar to the Revolution in 1688 in Six Volumes* (London: A. Millar, 1762), I, 17.

13 The Round Table was noted by Caxton as further evidence of Arthur's historicity. Its status as a symbol of royal authority most likely led to it being used for target practice, probably by Parliamentarian forces, following the fall of the city in 1642 during the English Civil War (Martin Biddle, *King Arthur's Round Table: An Archaeological Investigation* (Woodbridge: Boydell, 2000), pp. 390, 142).

14 'The emperor cannot have failed to remark in King Arthur the likeness of his bearded host' (Biddle, 2000, 432).

15 F. J. Furnivall (ed.), *Robert Laneham's Letter: Describing a Part of the Entertainment unto Queen Elizabeth at the Castle of Kenilworth in 1575* (London: Chatto & Windus, 1907), pp. 28–30. The list of pieces Cox supposedly had access to is extensive: 'and a hundred more, he hath, fair wrapt vp in Parchment, and bound with a whipcord'. Rather than carrying a minstrel book, Andrew Taylor believes that material used by Cox would have been 'a fistful of songs and ballads accumulated slowly over the years, copied down on different sheets and scraps of paper or parchment … simply piled together and placed in a leather wrapper' (Andrew Taylor, 'The Myth of the Minstrel Manuscript', *Speculum* 66 (1991), p. 73).

16 *Reliques*, I, xx–xxi. In Elizabeth's time, Islington enjoyed a mixed reputation. 'In 1548 there were 440 communicants in Islington, where the small village with its hamlets was known principally for its inns, which often harboured recusants and fugitives, and for fields which were used for illicit prayer meetings, counterfeiting coins, training militia, fighting duels, and archery and other sport' (T. F. T. Baker (ed.), *A History of the County of Middlesex*, Victoria History of the Counties of England (gen. ed. C. R. Elrington), vol. 8, *Islington and Stoke Newington Parishes* (London:

Oxford University Press for the Institute of Historical Research, 1985), p. 9). Nearby fields were often used for secret gatherings: c.1558 about 40 men and women were arrested at a prayer meeting, 13 of whom were burnt at the stake. Of the ballad, 'The Bailiff's Daughter of Islington', Percy assumed that 'ISLINGTON in Norfolk is probably the place here meant' (*Reliques*, III, 344).

[17] See Furnivall, 1907, 41 for the response of the audience at the time. The humorous nature of the event is reinforced by the probability that the author of the *Letter* was one William Patten, who satirically ascribed the narration of the events to the real Robert Langham. See David Scott, 'William Patten and the Authorship of "Robert Laneham's Letter" (1575)', *English Literary Renaissance* 7(3) (1977), pp. 297–306.

[18] Thomas Warton, *Observations on the Fairie Queene of Spenser* (London: R. and J. Dodsley, 1754), https://quod.lib.umich.edu/e/ecco/004884515.0001.000?view=toc (accessed July 2023), p. 5. *The Faerie Queene* was never completed, the first three books being published in 1590, and the second three in 1596.

[19] Association of Arthur with the star Arcturus goes back at least to 1380, appearing as it does in Chaucer's translation of Boethius' *De consolatione philosophiae*. The heir to James I, as with Henry VII's son Prince Arthur, did not survive to take the throne, Prince Henry dying in 1612 at the age of 18.

[20] Notably Roger Ascham, tutor to the future Elizabeth I, who famously denounced *LMD* in *The Scholemaster* (1570): 'the whole pleasure of which booke standeth in two speciall poyntes, in open mans slaughter, and bold bawdrye: In which booke those be counted the noblest Knightes, that do kill most men without any quarell, and commit fowlest aduoulteries by sutlest shiftes' (quoted by Parins (1987, 57)).

[21] Richard Lloyd, *A brief discourse of the most renowned actes and right valiant conquests of those puissant princes, called the nine worthies wherein is declared their seuverall proportions and dispositions, and what armes euerie one gaue, as also in what time ech of them liued, and how at the length they ended their liues* (London: R. Warde, 1584).

[22] The alliterative *Morte Arthure* (c.1400) unusually combines Arthur's status as a Worthy with his presence on the Wheel of Fortune.

[23] See Withrington, 1987, 124–33 for the popularity of the Arthurian story in the *Fall of Princes* and Malory's possible debt to Lydgate. Such was its popularity that the *Fall* was printed in 1494, 1527, and 1554 (twice). One of the most popular extracts from the *Fall*, albeit not Arthurian, is found in NLW MS Brogyntyn 1.8, which contains the unique text of 'Syre Gawene and the Carle of Carelyle'. Harvard, bMS Eng. 893 (18), a collection of Percy's 'Refatimentos', has been described as 'possibly a projected publication' by Percy: item PeT 130 comprises 12 pieces, including *KAKC*, 'The Sequel of St George' and 'The churl & the bird' (Smith, 1989, 282). The latter is presumably the highly popular poem by Lydgate, which formed part of Captain Cox's repertoire alongside Lydgate's 'Stans puer ad mensam'.

[24] See David Fairer, 'The Origins of Warton's *History of English Poetry*', *Review of English Studies* NS 32(125) (1981), pp. 37–63. Texts consulted by Warton between 1752 and 1754 included the romances 'Syr Bevis of Hampton', 'Syr Degore', 'Syr Tryamore', and the popular ballad 'Adam Bell, Clim of the Clough, and William of Cloudesle' (David Nichol Smith notes that it was in Warton's *Observations* 'that Malory makes his entrance into literary criticism'. David Nichol Smith, 'Warton's History of English Poetry', *Proceedings of the British Academy* 15 (1929), p. 76).

[25] Bishop William Nicolson discusses *LMD* in his *English Historical Library* (1696–99), and it is possible that Percy knew of Nicolson's work: the parallels between the two men are striking. In 1681, Nicolson was made a prebend of Carlisle Cathedral, archdeacon the following year, and in 1702, Bishop of Carlisle (Percy was made Dean of Carlisle in 1778). In 1718, Nicolson became Bishop of Derry (Percy was made Bishop of Dromore, also in Ireland, in 1782).

[26] Presented before Elizabeth by the Gentlemen of Gray's Inn, this Senecan play eschews the fantastic and takes a historical view of the Arthurian legend in a performance that is 'more an exercise in learned ingenuity than a dramatic presentation of human passion' (Merriman, 1973, 45–46). For a discussion of the play and its Anglo-Scottish context, see Andrew King, 'Dead Butchers and Fiend-like Queens: Literary and Political History in *The Misfortunes of Arthur* and

Macbeth', in Rhiannon Purdie and Nicola Royan (eds), *The Scots and Medieval Arthurian Legend*, Arthurian Studies LXI (Cambridge: D. S. Brewer, 2005), pp. 121–34.

[27] The earliest extant copy of this work in two parts is the sixth edition of 1631: a thirteenth edition had been reached by 1704, with Part I having been adapted for the stage (Nastali and Boardman, 2004, I, 26–27). A manuscript *Tom a Lincoln*, dated to between 1611 and 1619 and probably by or for law students, is discussed by Elisabeth Michelsson in *Appropriating King Arthur: The Arthurian Legend in English Drama and Entertainments, 1485–1625* (Uppsala: Uppsala University, 1999), pp. 244–75.

[28] The surviving print of 1662 credits the Jacobean playwright William Rowley as author, but improbably claims that the play was written in collaboration with Shakespeare.

[29] The full title is *The History of Tom Thumbe, the Little, for his Small Stature Surnamed, King Arthur's Dwarfe: Whose Life and Adventures Containe Many Strange and Wonderful Accidents, Published for the Delight of Merry Timespenders*.

[30] *The Tragedy of Tragedies; or the Life and Death of Tom Thumb the Great. As it is Acted at the Theatre in the Hay-Market. With the Annotations of H. Scriblerus Secundus* (London: J. Roberts, 1731; facsimile repr. London: Scolar Press, 1973), p. 7.

[31] For 'The Cock of the North', see J. R. Lumby (ed.), *Bernardus de Cura Rei Famuliaris, with Some Early Scottish Prophecies*, EETS OS 42 (London: Oxford University Press, 1870) and chap. 4 of Victoria Flood's, *Prophecy, Politics and Place in Medieval England: From Geoffrey of Monmouth to Thomas of Erceldoune* (Cambridge: D. S. Brewer, 2016). Nastali and Boardman (2004, I, 16–17) list several other Arthurian-based prophecies for the year 1530, alongside 'The Cock of the North'.

[32] In 1642, it was remarked that halter and ballad makers were 'two principal trades of late: ballads being sold by whole hundreds in the city, and halters sent by whole barrels full to Berwick, to hang up the rebels with' ('The Scots Scouts' Discoveries', cited by Rollins, 1919, 261). For the role of ballads in rumour and prophecy in Tudor and Stuart England, see Fox, 2000, 335ff. The first edition of William Lilley's almanac, *Merlinus Anglicus Junior* (1644), sold out within a week. The series continued to be published until 1763 (Nastali and Boardman, 2004, I, 35).

[33] In March 1785, Percy wrote to John Pinkerton, informing him that he had secured a letter written by Partridge following Swift's satirical criticisms (*Letters*, VIII, 53–54).

[34] Of ballads bought from Dicey, over 300 remain, although Percy's black-letter collection was destroyed in a fire in 1780. Groom estimates that in the first five years of the 1760s Percy had borrowed over 1,000 books (Groom, 1999, 147–48, 154).

[35] Writing to Percy in January 1764, the poet James Grainger reminisced how they had both shared 'the amusement that Arthur's Court used to do at your fireside' (Nichols, *Illustrations*, VII, 285). Tantalizingly, Bodl. MS Percy c.9, Percy's own record of books borrowed and returned, notes on f. 96r that he borrowed via Dodsley a 'Romance of King Arthur'. (The item is deleted and overwritten with the words 'Spelman's Glossary (cost me 1–6)', part of a series of updates dated 9 April 1765.)

[36] Roger Middleton, 'Chrétien de Troyes at Auction: Nicolas-Joseph Foucault and Other Eighteenth-Century Collectors', in Peter Damian-Grint (ed.), *Medievalism and 'manière gothique' in Enlightenment France* (Oxford: Voltaire Foundation, 2008), pp. 261–83. Middleton (278) notes that the modern title page of the *Perceval* is in Percy's own hand, and it is to this manuscript that Percy refers as being in his possession in the 1767 edition of the *Reliques* (III, ix, n. d). Middleton concludes that it was most likely not until 1808 that both manuscripts ended up in the Advocates Library in Edinburgh.

[37] As early as 28 February 1762, Percy was reporting to Warton that he had made 'a Collection of most of the old Spanish Romances, so finely ridicul'd in Don Quixote' (*Letters*, III, 31). Percy's correspondence with John Bowle, the first scholarly editor of Cervantes's *Don Quixote*, began in 1767. On 22 June 1771, Percy wrote to Bowle to say that he had recently acquired a copy of the French *San Graal*, and thought it likely that it contained the legend that Arthur had been turned into a crow, a legend also mentioned in *Don Quixote*. On 28 July 1772, Bowle wrote to update Percy on the *Espejo de Cavallerias* – 'This Historian is Merlins Genealogist' – and on 17 August 1778, Bowle wrote again to say that his friend, Mr Dillon, was exploring the royal library in

[38] Madrid to seek out other possible references to legends of Arthur's survival as a crow (Eisenberg, 1987, 19, 22, 54).

[38] 'Please to inform me what the earliest Welsh Historians have delivered concerning the Death of Arthur' (*Letters*, V, 28). Percy first wrote to Evans in 1761, Evans being the 'friend' who informed him of the Welsh analogues of *BM* (*Reliques*, III, 323). Percy owed to Evans the explanation that Carlisle was 'probably a corruption of CAER-LEON', Evans making this point as one of over a dozen commentaries on Arthurian names and places in a letter dated 8 March 1764 (*Letters*, V, 68–70). Evans's *Some Specimens of the Poetry of the Antient Welsh Bards*, a collection of Welsh poetry with his own translations into English, was published in the same year, and features a number of references to Arthur. Percy alluded to this publication in the second edition of the *Reliques* (I, xlv).

[39] *Letters*, VII, 3–4. Percy sent transcripts of *BM* and the fragmentary *MSG* to Shenstone on 4 February 1759, but his reliance on, and use for, Shenstone as a guide for the production of the *Reliques* waned to the extent that on 16 May 1762 Shenstone wrote, in some exasperation, 'You will think it proper to insert something that comprizes the actions of this great Champion *Guy*, as well as those of King *Arthur*; and yet there is evidently not a single particle of poetic Merit in *either* of the Ballads', warning Percy that, 'Once for all, it is extremely certain that an *Over* proportion of *this Kind* of *Ballast*, will sink your vessel to the Bottom of the Sea' (*Letters*, VII, 150). Shenstone died in February the following year.

[40] An extract from this letter is to be found as the Appendix to this Introduction.

[41] Percy's familiarity with *LMD* itself is not clear, but in his opening comments to *BM* in the *Reliques* he dated the first printing to 1484 [*sic*]. His reference in the opening comments to *SLDL* to an edition of *LMD* from 1634 shows that he was aware of Stansby's print of that year.

[42] Percy was less emphatic when it came to annotating the PF itself. In the RH margin, against the title of *MSG*, he wrote: 'This is upon th[e] same Subject as the Wife of Bath's Tale in Chaucer. from which Chaucer very probably took the Story'.

[43] In a letter to Evans of 23 November 1761 – a letter 'remarkably similar to his first to Warton' (Groom, 1999, 161) – Percy also enclosed transcripts of *BM* and *MSG*, repeating his assertion of the latter that it was 'certainly more ancient than the time of Chaucer, who took his *Wife of Bath's Tale* from *it*'. He continued, 'I cannot help thinking many of these pieces about *K. Arthur*, translations from the Ancient British Tongue' (*Letters*, V, 22). In January 1764, Evans reported that the story of the boy and the mantle was to be found in old Welsh texts, but it was not until Percy's reply the following month that Percy actually revealed to Evans the existence of the PF, stating his opinion that the basis for old British Romances was not translations from French, as Warton believed, but rather 'imitations from the Welsh' (*Letters*, V, 62).

[44] The 'modern hand' was Shenstone. Groom (1999, 225) notes that even after Shenstone's death, 'Percy could not resist meddling': in printing the *Reliques*, Percy decided to omit the last stanza of Shenstone's version.

[45] *Letters*, III, 10. Indeed, for his second edition of his *Observations*, in 1762, Warton credited Percy – albeit as an 'ingenious correspondent' – for bringing *BM* to his attention.

[46] 'My mistake in quoting it as a ballad in M. Arthur, arose from my finding it written into the Bodleian copy, in the place, as I imagined, of a Leaf torn out' (*Letters*, III, 29).

Previous Editions and Methodology Adopted for this Edition

The only complete edition of the PF, and the standard work of reference, remains that published in 1867–68 by John W. Hales and Frederick J. Furnivall (HF), dedicated to the pioneering American scholar of ballads, F. J. Child. After much reluctance on the part of the Percy family, the decision to release the MS was secured by the offer of £100 on the part of HF, supplemented by a further £50 from Child. Granted a period of six months in which to copy, edit, and print their findings, an extension to 13 months was granted, at which point the MS was returned to the family, who later sold it to the British Museum. It was evidently a traumatic experience for the editors, so much so that Furnivall wearily recorded that all these trials and setbacks had 'dulled one's pleasure in the book' (HF, I, x). The accumulation of so much debt in order to ensure the printing of the MS must also have dulled Furnivall's satisfaction in the completion of this monumental task.

Furnivall wrote that 'To tell the truth, and tell the whole truth, of a text or MS. is an editor's first duty' (HF, I, xx). The approach in this book has been to go back to the PF and produce as accurately as possible the Arthurian texts as they were recorded in the mid-seventeenth century, suitably presented for a modern audience. Inevitably, this has meant on occasion having to rely on the transcriptions provided by HF, given the deterioration of the MS over the past 150 years, but such debts are recorded in the Textual Notes, and references to subsequent editions of each text can be found in the corresponding Headnote.

In respect of the PF's marginal glosses, Percy tends spontaneously to react to the text in front of him, his usual slanted cursive hand sometimes changing to a more 'upright' hand with separated letters for emphasis, although this practice is far from consistent. Such inconsistency extends to Percy's use of punctuation: the distinction between commas and full points is often far from clear. Punctuative marks are frequently absent altogether. The matter is further complicated in that Hales and Furnivall were seemingly able to see some textual readings now lost, and were also inconsistent in their editorial practice when it came to italicization and punctuation. Given that the intention of this book is to produce texts that sit comfortably with both the scholar and the general reader, the decision has been taken to forego italics altogether in Percy's marginal comments, although Percy's occasional underlining of his comments has been retained. Punctation within Percy's comments follows the MS reading as closely as possible, but, as with HF, may be augmented or revised for the benefit of the modern reader.

The following editorial conventions have therefore been adopted.

- modern punctuation and modernization where appropriate: for example, letters *u* to *v* and *i* to *j*; 'wil be' for 'wilbe', 'by-dene', 'iwis', 'ifere', and 'i.e.' throughout;
- retention of initial *ff*, in the form *Ff* at the beginning of lines, and *ff* within words; retention of the ampersand;
- as in HF, abbreviations signalled by the use of italics: for example, 'S*ir*' for 'Sʳ', 'K*night*' for 'Kᵗ', '*that*' for 'yᵗ', '*the*' for 'yᵉ';
- initial capitalization of words, where present in the MS, but also following modern usage: thus, for the first word of each line; when commencing direct speech; and where a title or proper name is concerned (hence 'King Arthur');
- square brackets to indicate omission of letters/addition of characters where the original is obscured/missing, owing to blots, holes, or bleed-throughs, or where a scribal overbar is present (hence MS 'lem̄an' transcribed as 'lem[m]an'). Blemishes, holes, and defects that do not affect a reading are not routinely recorded. Square brackets are also employed where the MS is damaged but the text was seemingly visible to HF, or when their transcription of punctuation now lost aids interpretation;
- for the texts themselves, marginal glosses are provided for unfamiliar words, with use of an asterisk at the end of a line to signal an Explanatory Note.

J.W.

Appendix: Extract from letter by Percy to Thomas Warton, dated 28 May 1761

Spencer having made the old fabulous History of King Arthur and his Knights, if not the basis of his plan, yet the subject of many Allusions, which occur in his poem; It is natural to inquire where he first met with such history. You have very plainly proved that he had that Old Romance intitled *Mort. Arthur* in his eye: And seem to think that the Atchievements of Arthur, The Names of his Knights &c were invented by the Author of that piece: – But, Sir, I can prove to you, that the Author of *Mort. Arthur* (however he came by them in French) only drew upon a prose narrative of, and threw together into a regular story the Subject of a hundred Old Ballads, which had been the delight of our Ancestors for many ages before–; the contents of which had possibly found their way into other languages.

The settling of this point would be a matter of little consequence, if I had not a farther end in it, and that is to shew that many passages in our ancient English Poets may be illustrated from these Old Ballads, few of which were ever in print, and tho' generally forgotten are not wholy lost: For I have the good fortune to have in my possession an ancient *Folio MS.* which contains a great number of them which bear evident marks of very remote antiquity. They are many of them earlier than Chaucer, a plain proof of which is, their being expressly quoted, or particularly alluded to, by him.

Of this I am going to produce a striking instance; previous to which let me just observe that the Old Ballads about King Arthur and his Knights seem to have been as current among our plain but martial Ancestors, as the *Rhapsodies* of Homer were among his countrymen: and that the several Characters of *Agamemnon*, *Achilles*, *Ajax*, *Thersites* &c were not more familiarly known among the Greek's, or more distinctly marked by them; than those of *Arthur*, Dame *Guenever*, Sir *Gawaine*, Sir *Kay* &c were formerly in England.

Accordingly in those several unconnected Ballads, they almost always appear with the same attributes and manners: thus *Gawaine* is always drawn courteous and gentle: *Kay* rugged and brutal: *Guenever* light and inconstant: &c. ... [Percy then mentions Chaucer's reference to Gawaine in 'The Squire's Tale', a work that he was later to exhort Warton to complete] ... But that Chaucer did something more than meerly quote or allude to these Old Ballads, I think will appear from a fragment of one of them, which I here inclose. I am of opinion that he borrowed his *wife of Bath's Tale* from it ... I conclude this Old Song to have been Prior to Chaucer ... But that my Old Ballads were more ancient than the times of Chaucer, appears also from the *Rhyme of Sir Thopas*, which he wrote in express imitation of the manner, style, and Meter of these Old Ballads: many of those quoted in it being extant in my Collection: to mention only one, That of *Sir Libeaux*, which I have intire. &c. ...

Besides the Fragment above mentioned, I have inclosed an Old Song intitled *The Boy and the Mantle*, wherein you'll find the Trial of Chastity made by the Cup or Horn mentioned by Spenser ... and I think it also not impossible, but that Mantle &c described in this Ballad, may have furnished the Hint to *Spencer* of his *Florimel's Girdle*.

(*Letters*, III, 2–6)

The Texts

King Arthur and King Cornwall

Gillian Rogers and John Withrington

Both *The Turke & Gowin* (*TG*) and *King Arthur and King Cornwall* (*KAKC*) survive uniquely in the PF, but, unlike *TG*, *KAKC* lacks both the beginning and the end. In addition, as well as lines lost through damage, on seven occasions complete half-pages are missing, owing to the manuscript being used to light a fire at Mr Pitt's house. Overall, one may surmise that as well as the opening title we have lost two or three opening stanzas, a final six or seven, and perhaps some nine through the lost half-pages. This would imply an original length for the work of almost 600 lines.[1] Assigning a date is problematic. While *KAKC* and *GK* (late fifteenth century) share a character in the form of Bredbeddle, there is nothing to show that one borrowed the name from the other.[2] As for the language of this ballad, while the word 'trauckled', meaning 'plodded wearily', is Scottish (see Explanatory Note to line 34, below), and might hence imply that the ballad originated north of the Border or from northern England, as with so many other texts in the Percy Folio, such dialectal clues may simply reflect revisions as a result of recitation or performance.

Stylistically, *KAKC* may be called a 'romance ballad', comprising mainly 4-line stanzas rhyming *abcb*, mostly with 4-stress lines followed by those with 3 stresses. Occasionally, however, 6-line stanzas are present, rhyming *abcbdb*.[3] In addition, the versification contains frequent irregularities, e.g., hypermetrical lines, faulty rhymes, and cases where whole lines appear to have dropped out, while some passages are scrambled almost beyond sorting, notably the whole scene after Bredbeddle has subdued Burlow Beanie. Characteristic of ballad material is the use of familiar tags and phrases, a formulaic approach that provides rhythm and performs a mnemonic function.[4] Despite its fragmentary state, this idiosyncratic and inventive text displays an extraordinary range of references to Arthurian and non-Arthurian material. The fact that the author felt comfortable about including such a wide range says much about his intended audience, who seemingly would have appreciated not just performance and humour, but presumably would have been conversant with at least the basics of Arthurian romance and stereotypes.

The main influence upon *KAKC* was the *Le Pèlerinage de Charlemagne* (*Pèl*), most likely written in the latter half of the twelfth century, and which was found in BL MS Royal 16 E. VIII, dating from the thirteenth or possibly fourteenth century.[5] The story proved popular for some time to come: for example, in the thirteenth century it was translated into Old Norse (the Karlamagnus saga, Branch I); into Welsh (the *White Book of Rhydderch*, MS NLW Peniarth 5, *c*.1350); and several

French versions date from the late Middle Ages, including the cyclical *Garin de Monglane*, the *Charlemagne* of Girart d'Amiens, and *Galien le Restoré* (Burgess and Cobby, 2019, 13). The publication of the latter *c.*1500 by Antoine Vérard could well have resulted in translations into English appearing in succeeding years, subsequently mutating into forms appropriate for a ballad audience and thus drawn upon by the author of *KAKC*. However, no such translations are known.[6]

The first part of *KAKC* contains the same basic elements in the same basic sequence as *Pèl*, where Charlemagne boasts of his own magnificence, eliciting his wife's scornful reply that she knows of a far more magnificent king in Constantinople. Charlemagne instantly determines to visit this king, giving as the ostensible reason for his journey a pilgrimage to Jerusalem (Arthur and his companions dress as palmers), where they acquire certain holy relics (in *KAKC* they find a 'litle booke'), before continuing to Constantinople, Charlemagne's true destination. There, he and his peers are overwhelmed by the magnificence of their reception by King Hugo. After dinner, the travellers retire to a bedchamber, and each makes an impossible 'gab', or vow, although unknown to them, Hugo sets a man to spy on them from a recess in a stone wall (cf. *KAKC*, 193), with instructions to report back.[7]

However, while the ultimate debt to *Pèl* is clear, retaining the fulfilment of the vows as the motivating force of the action, the author of *KAKC* draws also upon Arthurian stereotypes and folkloric themes for what at times is a heady mix. In *Pèl*, Olivier's vow to lie with Hugo's daughter is echoed at *KAKC* 149–54 by Gawaine's crude boast: Gawaine's encounters elsewhere with the daughters of Imperious Hosts (see *CARLE*, pp. 331–34, below) make him an obvious choice for Olivier's role. Roland's vow to blow Hugo's horn so hard that the sound will bring down the walls of his palace is paralleled by Tristram undertaking the task of blowing King Cornwall's magic horn: although Tristram might seem a surprising choice of companion for Arthur on a journey of this nature, he was famed for his knowledge of hunting and his skill at blowing the horn.[8] The presence of Marramiles – who, we assume, vowed to ride Cornwall's magic steed – is a puzzle, given that this is his only appearance in Arthurian romance or ballad. Nor is there an obvious reason why Bredbeddle should have been one of Arthur's companions, or why he should have been called 'the Greene Knight', although of course he is the hero of *GK*, his only other appearance in Arthurian romance.[9] Cornwall, the powerful and boastful necromancer-king, is akin to the various Imperious Host figures encountered in *TG*, *CARLE*, and *GK*. The subject of his boasting – the magic steed, the gold wand, and the horn – mark him out for certain as a magician. He is not enchanted, as are the Carl and *GK*'s Bredbeddle, but he has much in common with the daughterless King of Man in *TG*: both have evil intentions towards their guests. In contrast to the more sombre folkloric elements, Burlow Beanie proves an unexpected and delightful creation, bursting out of his hiding place breathing fire and sparks. His jack-in-the-box appearance has obvious potential when it comes to performing the text, and while his manifestation as a seven-headed beast has distinctly apocalyptic connotations,[10] his later calmer aspect is as a friendly helpful household spirit, akin to Belly Blind, or Billie Blin, who appears in several ballads in Child's collection.[11]

Pèl resists simple classification; although it contains elements of the epic, the pious, and the richly comic, it is 'neither a true *chanson de geste* nor an authentically pious tale' (Burgess and Cobby, 2019, 6).[12] But, whatever the source inherited by the *KAKC* poet, his is a version that fizzes with similar invention and delight. As with *Pèl*, the catalyst for this Arthurian tale is not the arrival of an outside figure prompting a quest or challenge, but a fit of domestic pique, as Arthur is determined to find out who has a better Round Table than he. As in *Pèl*, Arthur decides that he and his company should adopt the disguise of pilgrims in order not to arouse suspicion or attention, but they seek shelter in Cornwall's impressive castle, Cornwall promptly identifies these 'pilgrims' as from Brittany, and immediately boasts of his affair with Arthur's wife, presumably to Arthur's surprise and discomfort.[13] Notwithstanding the heroes' extravagant gabs in *KAKC*, success is due not to their efforts but to the work of the effervescent Burlow Beanie, who, controlled and conjured by Bredbeddle, thanks to the happy discovery of the 'litle booke',[14] enables Marramile to ride the horse, Tristeram to blow the horn, and Arthur to obtain Cornwall's sword.[15]

Of *Pèl*'s author, it has been observed that 'skilful weaving of his varying threads is crucial to his artistic aim (Burgess and Cobby, 2019, 20), but the same could be said of the author of *KAKC*. While the framework of this tale may be derived from a version of an old *chanson de geste*, the boastful gabs, the bickering between Arthur and Gawaine (135–44), the tension as Bredbeddle's three weapons fail in turn, only to be saved by a little book, and the slapstick Burlow Beanie would have made for a particularly entertaining performance as part of a fusion of folklore, romance, and burlesque in which realism can safely be left behind.[16] Alternating the slower-paced, more-descriptive, 'romance' sections with faster-paced, heavily formulaic 'ballad' passages would have helped to create and maintain the suspense, as would the use of repetition and refrains, which could have created an almost hypnotic effect. It is likely that *KAKC* would have made for very effective theatre.

Notes

[1] Bearing in mind that titles in the PF usually occupy three to four lines, it seems likely that only two to three stanzas are missing from the beginning. The previous item, *Robin Hood his Death*, possibly lacks five to seven stanzas, and the one following, *Sir Lionell*, starts at the top of a verso, hence the assumption that *KAKC* lacks some six or seven stanzas at its conclusion.

[2] The implication at line 15 that Arthur is king of 'Litle Britaine' could indicate a revision by a later hand, influenced by the *c.*1555 publication of Lord Berners's *Arthur of Little Britain*, a translation undertaken before 1521 of the French romance *Artus de la Petite Bretagne* (see Kenneth J. Oberempt, 'Lord Berners' "Arthur of Lytell Brytayne": Its Date of Composition and French Source', *Neuphilologische Mitteilungen* 77(2) (1976), pp. 241–52). Berners's work was later printed by East *c.*1582, some four years after he published Malory's *LMD*: it is possible that this reinforced a confusion between the two Arthurs. See also Explanatory Note to line 198, below.

[3] In this edition, and that of Hahn, there are nine 6-liners, while HF has 10, plus one 7-liner (13–19). The predominant rhyme *–ee* also makes it difficult to be certain about the length of some stanzas. P seems to have tried to impose a 4-line stanza pattern on the poem in places.

4   For example, variations of the phrase, 'These were the words said he/she' occur 22 times in *KAKC*.
5   Glynn S. Burgess and Anne Elizabeth Cobby (eds), '*The Pilgrimage of Charlemagne*' and '*Aucassin and Nicolette*' (Abingdon and New York: Routledge, 2019), pp. 1–2. BL MS Royal 16 E. VIII went missing in 1879. See Carla Rossi, 'A Clue to the Fate of the Lost MS. Royal 16 E VIII, a Copy of the *Voyage de Charlemagne*', *Romania* 126(501–2) (2008), pp. 245–52.
6   'The English ballad retains too little of the French story to enable us to say what form of it this little was derived from. The poem of Galien would cover all that is borrowed as well the Journey of Charlemagne' (Child, I, 280). J. W. Davis has suggested that an English translation of the *White Book of Rhydderch* was the most likely original source for *KAKC*, given particular affinities between the two tales (J. W. Davis, '*Le Pèlerinage de Charlemagne* and *King Arthur and King Cornwall*: A Study in the Evolution of a Tale', PhD thesis, Indiana University, 1973, pp. 379–80).
7   In *KAKC*, the 'gabs' are linked to the magic objects that the boastful Cornwall displays to his guests. In *Pèl*, the gabs occur independently as part of a post-feast bragging session.
8   In the thirteenth-century Middle English *Sir Tristrem*, Tristrem shows King Mark's huntsmen the right way to blow the various notes associated with the hunt (Alan Lupack (ed.), *Lancelot of the Laik* and *Sir Tristrem* (Kalamazoo: Medieval Institute Publications, 1994), lines 507–28, https://d.lib.rochester.edu/teams/publication/lupack-lancelot-of-the-laik-and-sir-tristrem (accessed July 2023)); and in Malory's *LMD*, Tristram is called the 'best chacer of the world and the noblest blower of an horne of all manere of mesures' (Book X, Chapter 52). Because of the gap in the MS at this point, we do not know what Cornwall's magic horn was intended to do.
9   The fact that Bredbeddle's mother-in-law is a witch with the power to shape-shift him into the Green Knight may have suggested his appropriateness for dealing with a shape-shifting fiend in *KAKC*.
10 The seven-headed Burlow Beanie brings to mind the beast with seven heads and ten horns which John sees rising from the sea (Revelation 13:1). See also Explanatory Note to line 191.
11 In *Gil Brenton*, he is known as Billie Blin (Child #5C); in *Willie's Lady* as Belly Blind (Child #6A); in *Young Beichan* as Belly Blin (Child #53C); and in three versions of *The Knight and Shepherd's Daughter* we have Belly-Blind, Billy-Blin, and Billie Blin (Child #110, D, F, G). It is possible that 'Beanie' might be a corruption of 'Brownie': 'Almost all authorities are at one in regarding [the Brownie] as a species of *lar familiaris*, the humble retainer of old farming families' (Lewis Spence, *The Fairy Tradition in Britain* (London: Rider & Co., 1948), p. 35). What is not clear in *KAKC* is whether Burlow Beanie's true form is the fire-breathing fiend or the friendly household spirit.
12 Of *Pèl*, it has been remarked that 'Such divergence of opinion is fostered by the tendency of scholars to study the *Pèlerinage* primarily as an example of one medieval genre or another' (Burgess and Cobby, 2019, 3, who go so far as to argue that *Pèl* is, strictly, speaking, a parody of the various genres it draws upon). *Pèl's* refusal to be pigeonholed neatly into one category or another is a characteristic it shares with other Arthurian texts in PF: see note 38, p. 28, above.
13 While Guenevere's lustful disloyalty is a common theme in ballad material – see, for example, *LAMBE* and *BM* below – *KAKC*'s reference to her having another man's child is seemingly unique.
14 In Revelation 10:2, St John sees a mighty angel holding a 'little book' in his hand, who 'set his foot upon the sea'.
15 It should be noted that Arthur decapitates Cornwall while he is asleep. This action – unlike the ritual disenchanting of *CARLE*, *TG*, and *Sir Gawain and the Green Knight* – is more farcical than heroic.
16 For example, how could Cornwall have spent seven years in Guenevere's company without Arthur knowing, let alone have fathered a child on her? All the more so since, given that Cornwall calls Arthur a cuckold, Arthur and Guinevere must have been married at the time.

Editions and Related Texts
Child, Francis James (ed.), *The English and Scottish Popular Ballads*, 5 vols (Boston: Houghton, Mifflin, 1882–98; repr. Cambridge: Cambridge University Press, 2014, online 2015), I, 274–88 (#30).

Hahn, Thomas (ed.), *Sir Gawain: Eleven Romances and Tales* (Kalamazoo: Medieval Institute Publications, 1995), pp. 419–36.

Hales, John W., and Furnivall, Frederick J. (eds), *Bishop Percy's Folio Manuscript: Ballads and Romances*, 3 vols (London: Trübner, 1867–68), I, 59–73.

Madden, Sir Frederic (ed.), *Syr Gawayne: A Collection of Ancient Romance-Poems, by Scotish and English Authors, Relating to that Celebrated Knight of the Round Table, with an Introduction, Notes, and a Glossary* (London: Richard and John Taylor, 1839), pp. 275–87, https://archive.org/details/syrgawaynecoll6100madduoft/page/n5/mode/2up (accessed July 2023)

Further Reading
Burgess, Glynn S., and Cobby, Anne Elizabeth (eds), '*The Pilgrimage of Charlemagne*' and '*Aucassin and Nicolette*' (Abingdon and New York: Routledge, 2019).

Niles, John D., 'On the Logic of *Le Pèlerinage de Charlemagne*', *Neuphilologische Mitteilungen* 81(2) (1980), pp. 208–16.

Rogers, Gillian, '*King Arthur and King Cornwall*', *AE*, 215–19.

King Arthur and King Cornwall

    [Saies, 'Come hither, S*i*r Gawaine the] gay,*   p. 24/f. 10v
        My sister's sonne be yee,
    Ffor you shall see one of the fairest round tables*
        That ever you see with your eye.'

5   Then bespake Lady Qu*een* Guenever,*
        & these were the words said shee:
    'I know where a round table is, thou noble K*ing*,*
        Is worth thy Round Table & other such 3:

    'The trestle that stands under this round table,' she said,
10   'Lowe downe to the mould,   *ground*
    It is worth thy Round Table, thou worthy K*ing*,
        Thy halls & all thy gold.

    'The place where this round table stands in,*
        It is worth thy castle, thy gold, thy fee,   *lands*
15 And all good Litle Britaine.'*   *Brittany*

    'Where may that table be, Lady?' q*uo*th hee,
        'Or where may all that goodly building be?'
    'You shall it seeke,' shee says, 'till you it find,
        For you shall never gett more of me.'

20 Then bespake him Noble K*ing* Arthur,
        These were the words said hee,
    'Ile make mine avow to God,*
        & alsoe to the Trinity,

    'Ile never sleepe one night there as I doe another,*
25   Till t*ha*t Round Table I see.
    S*i*r Marramiles & S*i*r Tristeram,*
        Fellowes *tha*t ye shall bee,

    'Weele be clad in palmer's weede,*   *pilgrims' clothes*
        5 palmers we will bee.

30 There is noe outlandish man will us abide,*
        Nor will us come nye.'
    Then they rived east & the[y] rived west   *travelled*
        In ma[n]y a strange country.

    Then they trauckled a litle further,*
35   They saw a battle new sett.*

'Now, by my faith,' saies Noble K*ing* Arthur,*
    .... [well mett]

[*Half a page missing. The five companions travel on, and find a 'litle booke' washed up on the seashore.*]

[But when he came that castle to],
    & to the palace gate,   p. 25/f. 11r
40 Soe ready was ther a proud porter,
    & met him soone therat.

Shooes of gold the porter had on,*
    & all his other rayment was unto the same.
'Now, by my faith,' saies noble K*ing* Arthur,
45 'Yonder is a minion swaine.'*   *dainty fellow*

Then bespake noble K*ing* Arthur,
    These were the words says hee,
'Come hither, thou proud porter,
    I pray thee come hither to me.

50 'I have 2 poore rings of my finger,
    The better of them Ile give to thee.
Tell who may be Lord of this castle,' he sa[y]es,
    'Or who is lord in this cuntry?'

'Cornewall K*ing*,' the porter sayes,
55   'There is none soe rich as hee,
Neither in Christendome nor yet in heathennest,   *heathendom*
    None hath soe much gold as he.'

& then bespake him noble K*ing* Arthur,
    These were the words sayes hee,
60 'I have 2 poore rings [o]f my fingar,
    The better of them Ile give thee,
If thou wilt greete him well, Cornewall K*ing*,
    & greete him well from me.

'Pray him for one night's lodging & 2 meales meat[e],
65   For His love that dyed uppon a tree.*
A une ghesting & 2 meales meate,*   *one night's lodging*
    For His love that dyed uppon a tree.

'A une ghesting of 2 meales meate,
    For His love that was of virgin boirne,   *born*
70 & in the morning *tha*t we may scape away,*   *escape*
    Either w*i*thout scath or scorne.'   *harm or disgrace*

Then forth is gone this proud porter,*
    As fast as he cold hye,
& when he came befor Cornewall King,
75   He kneeled downe on his knee,

Sayes, 'I have beene porter-man at thy gate…'*

[*Half a page missing. The porter says he has never seen such a strange sight as these five palmers. King Cornwall consents to see them, and they are brought to him. Arthur recounts the tale of their travels, which leads King Cornwall to believe that they have come from Brittany.*]

    '… Our Lady was borne.'*   p. 26/f. 11v
Then thought Cornewall King these palmers had beene in Britt[aine].
Then bespake him Cornwall King,
80   These were the words he said there,*
'Did you ever know a comely King,
    His name was King Arthur?'

& then bespake him Noble King Arthur,
    These were the words said hee,
85   'I doe not know that comly King,
    But once my selfe I did him see.'
Then bespake Cornwall King againe,
    These were the words said he,

Sayes, '7 yeere I was clad & fed*
90   In Litle Brittaine, in a bower.
I had a daughter by King Arthur's wife,
    *Tha*t now is called my flower,
Ffor King Arthur, that kindly Cockward,   *cuckold*
    Hath none such in his bower.*

95   'For I durst sweare, & save my othe,   *keep my oath*
    *Tha*t same lady soe bright,   *[is] so fair*
That a man *that* were laid on his death bed
    Wold open his eyes on her to have sight.'
'Now, by my faith,' sayes noble King Arthur,
100   '& that's a full faire wight!'   *person*

& then bespake Cornewall againe,
    & these were the words said he,*
'Come hither, 5 or 3 of my knights,*
    & feitch me downe my steed.
105   King Arthur, that foule Cockeward,
    Hath none such, if he had need,

King Arthur and King Cornwall

  'For I can ryde him as far on a day
    As King Arthur can doe any of his on 3.
  & is it not a pleasure for a K*ing*,
110 When he shall ryde forth on his Journey?

  'For the eyes that beene in his head,
    The[y] glister as doth the gleed.'   *sparkle; live coal*
  'Now, by my faith', says Noble King Arthur,
    ['& that's a full faire steed.']

[*Half a page missing. King Cornwall boasts of his other treasures: his magic horn, his sword, and, possibly, his household spirit. The companions are entertained to dinner, at which Cornwall's daughter is present; afterwards, they retire to their bedchamber for the night.*]

115 'Nobody [say] …*   p. 27/f. 12r
  But one *that*'s learned to speake.'

 Then K*ing* Arthur to his bed was brought,
  A greeived man was hee,   *angry*
 & soe were all his fellowes with him,
120 From him the[y] thought never to flee.

 Then take they did that lodly boome   *loathsome creature*
  & under thrub chadler closed was hee;*   *barrel*
 & he was set by K*ing* Arthur's bed side,
  To heere theire talke & theire com[mu]nye, *conversation*

125 *Tha*t he might come forth & make p*r*oclamation,
  Long before it was day.
 It was more for K*ing* Cornwall's pleasure
  Then it was for K*ing* Arthur's pay.   *liking*

 & when K*ing* Arthur in his bed was laid,
130 These were the words said hee,
 'Ile make mine avow to God,
  & alsoe to the Trinity,
 That Ile be the bane of Cornwall Kinge,
  Litle Brittaine or ever I see.'

135 'It is an unadvised vow,' saies Gawaine the gay,*
  'As ever K*ing* hard make I,   *heard*
 But wee *that* beene 5 Christian men,
  Of the Christen faith are wee,
 & we shall fight against anoynted K*ing*
140 & all his armorie?'   *armed men*

    & then bespake him Noble Arthur,
        & these were the words said he,
    'Why, if thou be afraid, S*i*r Gawaine the gay,
        Goe home & drinke wine in thine owne country!'

The 3.^d part*

145   And then bespake S*i*r Gawaine the gay,
        And these were the words said hee,
    'Nay, seeing you have made such a hearty vow,
        Heere another vow make will I.

    'Ile make mine avow to God,
150   & alsoe to the Trinity,
    *Tha*t I will have yonder faire lady
        To Litle Brittaine with mee.

    'Ile hose her homly to my hurt*
        & with her Ile worke my will ...'

[*Half a page missing. The other knights also make vows, probably using the same formula as that of Arthur and Gawaine. They discover the hidden watcher (presumably before he has had time to report to King Cornwall), but three of Arthur's companions in turn refuse to fight with the fiend.*]

155   These were the words sayd hee,*   p. 28/f. 12v
    'Befor I wold wrestle with yonder feend,
        It is better be drowned in the sea.'

    And then bespake S*i*r Bredbeddle,
        & these were the words said he,
160   'Why, I will wrestle w*i*th yon lodly feend,
        God, my governor Thou wilt bee.'

    Then bespake him Noble Arthur,
        & these were the words said he,
    'What weapons wilt thou have, thou gentle knight?
165   I pray thee tell to me.'

    He sayes, 'Collen brand Ile have in my hand,*   *Cologne sword*
        & a Millaine knife fast by me knee,   *Milanese*
    & a Danish axe fast in my hands,
        *Tha*t a sure weapon I thinke wil be.'

170   Then, with his Collen brand *tha*t he had in his hand,
        The bunge of the trubchandler he burst in 3.

King Arthur and King Cornwall

With that start out a lodly feend,
    With 7 heads & one body.

The fyer toward the element flew*
175   Out of his mouth, where was great plentie.
The knight stoode in the middle & fought,
    That it was great joy to see,

Till his Collaine brand brake in his hand,
    & his Millaine knife burst on his knee,
180 & then the Danish axe burst in his hand first,
    That a sur weapon he thought shold be.

But now is the knight left without any weapons,
    & alacke, it was the more pitty!
But a surer weapon then had he one,*
185   Had never Lord in Christentye,
& all was but one litle booke,
    He found it by the side of the sea.

He found it at the sea side,
    Wrucked upp in a floode.   *Thrown up in a heap by the tide*
190 Our Lord had written it with His hands
    [& sealed it with His bloode.]*

[*Half a page missing. Bredbeddle subdues the fiend by means of the charm or conjuration written on the back of the title-page of the holy book, and bends him to his will.*]

'That thou doe not s…*   p. 29/f. 13r
    But ly still in that wall of stone,
Till I have beene with Noble King Arthur,
195   & told him what I have done.'

And when he came to the King's chamber,
    He cold of his curtesie,   *bowed*
Says, 'Sleepe you, wake you, noble King Arthur?*
    & ever Jesus waken yee!'

200 'Nay, I am not sleeping, I am waking,'
    These were the words said hee,
'Ffor thee I have card, how hast thou fared?
    O gentle knight, let me see.'

The knight wrought the King his booke,   *held out to*
205   Bad him behold, reede, & see,
& ever he found it on the backside of the leafe,*   *verso*
    As Noble Arthur wold wish it to be.

  & then bespake him K*ing* Arthur,
   'Alas, thow gentle knight, how may this be,*
210 That I might see him in the same licknesse   *likeness*
   Tha*t* he stood unto thee?'

  & then bespake him the Greene Knight,*
   These were the words said hee,
  'If you'le stand stifly in the battell stronge,   *stand firm*
215 For I have won all the victory.'

  Then bespake him the K*ing* againe,
   & these were the words said hee,
  'If wee stand not stifly in this battell strong,
   Wee are worthy to be hanged all on a tree.'

220 Then bespake him the Greene Knight,
   These were the words said he,
  Saies, 'I doe conjure thee, thou fowle feend,*   *call upon you*
   In the same licknesse thou stood unto me.'

  With that start out a lodly feend,*
225 With 7 heads & one body.
  The fier towards the element flaugh,   *flew*
   Out of his mouth, where was great plenty.

  The knight stood in the Middle …

[*Half a page missing. Bredbeddle, the Green Knight, subdues the fiend again with his 'litle booke'. Possibly, Gawaine's encounter with King Cornwall's daughter follows.*]

  … they stood the space of an houre,*   p. 30/f. 13v
230 I know not what they did.

  And then bespake him the Greene Knight*
   & these were the words said he,
  Saith, 'I conjure thee, thou fowle feend,
   Tha*t* thou feitch downe the steed that we see.'

235 & then forth is gone Burlow Beanie,*
   As fast as he cold hie,   *go*
  & feitch he did *that* faire steed,
   & came againe by & by.

  Then bespake him S*ir* Marramiles,*
240 & these were the words said hee,
  'Riding of this steed, brother Bredbeddle,
   The mastery belongs to me.'

Marramiles tooke the steed to his hand,
    To ryd him he was full bold.
245 He cold noe more make him goe,
    Then a child of 3 yeere old.

He laid uppon him with heele & hand,
    With yard that was soe fell;   *stick; cruel, brutal*
'Helpe, brother Bredbeddle,' says Marramile,
250   'For I thinke he be the devill of Hell.'*

'Helpe, brother Bredbeddle,' says Marramile,
    'Helpe, for Christ's pittye!
Ffor without thy help, brother Bredbeddle,
    He will never be rydden p*er* me.'   *by*

255 Then bespake him S*ir* Bredbeddle,
    These were the words said he,
'I conjure thee, thou Burlow [B]eane,
    Thou tell me how this steed was riddin in [t]his country.'
He saith, 'There is a gold wand
260   Stands in K*ing* Cornwall's study windowe.

'Let him take that wand in *tha*t window
    & strike 3 strokes on that steed,
& then he will spring forth of his hand
    As sparke doth out of Gleede.'

265 [& then bespake him the Greene Knight,] …*

[*Half a page missing. Bredbeddle commands Burlow Beanie to fetch the wand. He does so, his instructions are carried out, and Marramiles is able to ride the horse. Next, Tristram wants to fulfil his vow of blowing King Cornwall's horn. He is unable to do so. Bredbeddle commands Burlow Beanie to tell him how it may be blown.*]

'A lowd blast [he may blow then].'   p. 31/f. 14r

& then bespake S*ir* Bredebeddle,
    To the feend these words said hee,
Says, 'I conjure thee, thou Burlow Beanie,
270   The powder-box thou feitch me.'

Then forth is gone Burlow Beanie,
    As fast as he cold hie,
& feich he did the powder-box,
    & came againe by & by.

275 Then S*i*r Tristeram tooke powder forth of *tha*t box,
  & blent it with warme sweet milke;   *mixed*
& there put it unto that horne
  & swilled it about in that ilke.   *the same* (*horn*)

Then he tooke the horne in his hand
280 & a lowd blast he blew.
He rent the horne up to the midst,   *split*
  All his fellowes this the[y] knew.

Then bespake him the Greene Knight,
  These were the words said he,
285 Saies, 'I conjure thee, thou Burlow Beanie,*
  *Tha*t thou feitch me the sword *tha*t I see.'

Then forth is gone Burlow Beanie,
  As fast as he cold hie,
& feitch he did that faire sword,
290 & came againe by & by.

Then bespake him S*i*r Bredbeddle,
  To the K*i*ng these words said he,
'Take this sword in thy hand, thou noble K*i*ng A[rthur],
  For the vowe's sake *tha*t thou made, Ile give it t[hee],*

295 And goe strike off K*i*ng Cornewall's head,*
  In bed were he doth lye.'
Then forth is gone Noble K*i*ng Arthur,
  As fast as he cold hye,
& strucken he hath off K*i*ng Cornwall's hea[d],
300 & came againe by & by.

He put the head [upon] a sword['s point] …*

[*The end is missing.*]

Explanatory Notes

It is possible that the first two lines of the first extant stanza began, 'And then bespake him noble King Arthur/(And) these were the words sayd hee', which would make this a 6-line stanza.

1   'Sir Gawaine the gay' is a common alliterative epithet for the hero: cf. lines 135, 143, 145. Arthur's eagerness to show off the Round Table suggests that Gawaine has only lately come to court. See also note to lines 135–50, below.

3   The idea that there is more than one round table is unique to *KAKC*. The effect is to make a mere piece of furniture of this celebrated feature of Arthur's court: after the opening sequence, we hear no more of it.

KING ARTHUR AND KING CORNWALL 65

5–6	*Then bespake*: a mnemonic device to aid recall and rhythm during performance, this is the first of five refrains running throughout the poem, occurring 23 times.
7–19	Guenevere's response to Arthur's boast, and her sharp retort when Arthur asks where this other round table may be found, implies that, as is the case with Charlemagne and his queen, all is not well between husband and wife.
13–19	HF construed 13–19 as a single block of seven lines. P puts a division after 15, but crosses it out and places one after 16, possibly following the rhyme rather than the sense. Nonetheless, lines 16–19 constitute an acceptable unit as they stand.
15	*Litle Britaine*: see note 2, p. 53, above.
22–23	*Ile make mine avow*: the second of the refrains. See also 131 and 149.
24	'I'll never sleep two nights in the same place': a common practice of knights errant. In effect this is Arthur's first vow, unrelated to the main sequence at Cornwall's castle, but one that sets the whole action of the poem in motion. Unlike those of knights on a serious quest, Arthur's vow is a trivial undertaking, motivated by pique.
26	*Marramiles*: although 'miles' (Latin, *knight*) could be a suffix to the proper name 'Marra' (the romance *Sir Launfal*, found in BL MS Cotton Caligula A. ii is headed 'Launfal Miles'), no Arthurian character of this name is known. It may be a corruption of 'Marrocke', who appears in *CARLE* as one of Arthur's companions.
28	*palmer's weede*: a palm leaf or branch brought back from the Holy Land was seen as a mark of a successful pilgrim. By association, a 'palmer' was another word for a pilgrim.
28–33	P makes divisions after 31 and 33, thus making 32–33 a couplet. Hahn prints 28–31 as a unit of four lines, with 32–33 as the couplet. HF print 28–33 as a 6-liner.
30–31	'No foreigner will delay us, or (slow us down) by coming near us'. Whereas in *Pèl* Charles uses a pilgrimage as cover for his travels, in *KAKC* this forms 'no part of Arthur's programme. The five assume a palmer's weed simply for disguise' (Child, I, 279).
34	'plodded wearily': *OED trachle	trauchle*, to tire out or fatigue greatly by long walking; to exhaust by over-exertion, v,2(a): the first two examples quoted are Scottish, from the sixteenth and seventeenth centuries. 'Then' suggests that some preceding text has been lost.
35	'They saw an army, newly drawn up'. The appearance of an army does not make much sense in context, but in *Galien le Restoré* Charlemagne and his peers are threatened by an army of Turks.
36	*Now, by my faith*: the third of the refrains. See also 44, 99, and 113.
42–43	*Shooes of gold*: in *Galien le Restoré* the travellers are overwhelmed to see that even King Hugo's swineherds are all dressed in gold.
45–71	This entire passage makes use of incremental repetition.
65–66	P placed stanza divisions after 61, 65, and 67, implying that he thought the stanzas should be divided up as 58–61 and 62–65, with 66–67 as a couplet. From its rhymes, this floating couplet clearly belongs to the stanza beginning at 64, forming another example of incremental repetition which is carried on into the next stanza. That this last is a stand-alone quatrain, however, is shown by the fact that 69 rhymes with 71.
66	*A une*: it is unclear why the French 'to have one' is employed here and at 68.
70–71	Cf. *CARLE*, 145–46.
72–73	*Then forth is gone*: the fourth refrain: see 235, 271, 287, 297.
76	After 76, HF records 'this 30 winter and three … [? MS.]' as line 77. There is no trace of any line remaining in the MS, which has been cropped at this point; Madden did not record a reading, nor is there any comment by P. The assumption must be that HF's line was simple conjecture. On that basis this line has not been included in this edition.
77	Why Arthur's reference to 'Our Lady' should lead Cornwall to infer that the heroes have come from, or hail from, Brittany is unclear. However, Arthur's plan to avoid attention by dressing as pilgrims has gone sadly awry.
80	In order to provide an (approximate) rhyme for 'Arthur' in 82, the formulaic 'These were the words said hee' was changed to the weaker 'he said there'.
89–94	Cornwall's sarcasm (Arthur kindly allowed Cornwall to cuckold him; compare 105) and double insult (not only has he cuckolded Arthur, he has fathered a child on his wife), together with the shock of Cornwall's revelation, provides a more effective motivation for

	the vows than is provided by the 'gabs' in *Pèl*. Cornwall's reference to Arthur as a cuckold and his scorn about Arthur's apparent lack of children (94) form another double insult; i.e., implied criticism of Arthur's virility, as well as his failing as a king to supply an heir. It is a remarkably restrained response from Arthur in the circumstances, although his subsequent anger and vow to kill Cornwall reflect his true feelings.
94–105	P has stanza divisions after 94, 98, and 102, suggesting that he was trying to make three 4-line stanzas out of these 12 lines. The rhymes go against this.
102	*said he*: while the formulaic 'said he' is common enough in this text, HF's alternative 'he said' does at least have the virtue of attempting a close rhyme with 104.
103	Owing to defects in the manuscript, the magic steed is the only one of Cornwall's possessions that we know was the subject of boasts by King Cornwall. The steed recalls the 'steede of bras' in Chaucer's *Squire's Tale*, which can, in 'foure and twenty houres', bear a man wheresoever he wishes to go, and can only be activated by twirling a pin in his ear. Subsequent events show that Cornwall must also have boasted of his horn (which none but he could blow), and his sword (the only weapon that could kill him), quite possibly saying on both occasions that Arthur had nothing to compare. Cornwall must also have spoken of his seven-headed, fire-breathing household spirit, since 155–57 implies that Gawaine, Marramiles, and Tristram all refuse to fight Burlow Beanie until Bredbeddle breaks open the bung of his hiding place.
115–16	The meaning of these lines is obscure.
122	*thrub chadler* (cf. line 171, where it is called a 'trubchandler'). No satisfactory explanation has ever been given for this mysterious object. *OED chandler*, a stand or support for a candle, a candlestick … Chiefly *northern*, now *Obsolete*, n,1, implies a stand by the bed upon which a candle has been placed. Given that Bredbeddle smashes the bung confining Burnow Beanie, it presumably means a barrel of some sort.
135–44	Gawaine's rebuke of Arthur has a long history behind it, stretching back to Chrétien de Troyes's *Erec et Enide*. However, Arthur's angry reaction and his accusation of cowardice (143) are unusual, as is the suggestion that Gawaine should go home to his own country, which perhaps reinforces the impression that Gawaine is newly come to court. Note that Gawaine's objection is couched in strictly Christian terms (cf. his attempt to convert the King of Man to Christianity in *TG*, 259–61). There is also a note of caution in his objection: they are five knights against all of Cornwall's 'armorie'.
144	After this line the scribe records in the LH margin the beginning of the third part of the tale, the only such structural notice to have survived. A more logical place for a division would have been after 116, at the change of scene to the bedchamber.
153	'I'll clasp her closely to my heart'. Note the alliteration on 'h' and 'w' in the following line. Gawaine's vow is in contrast to his chaste reply to Bredbeddle's wife in *GK*, 382–89.
155	The preceding line is missing but is likely to have commenced with the familiar form 'And then bespake him Sir …' Because of the lacuna in the text at this point we do not know how the companions discover the presence of Burlow Beanie in his 'trubchandler'.
166	*Collen brand*: Cologne was particularly associated with the production of weapons. *OED Cologne*, n,(a) cites the ballad 'Otterburn' of *c*.1550: 'They swapped together … Wyth swords of fine collayne'.
174	'The fire flew heavenwards', i.e., up into the air.
184	Bredbeddle's weapons have all failed: the only sure weapon is the Word of God, enshrined in the 'litle booke' written in Christ's own hand.
191	Assuming we have the correct reading, 'sealed' recalls the seven seals on the book which Christ holds in His right hand in the Bible's Book of Revelation (6:1). A number of books claimed to have been written by Christ with His blood, among them, a fourteenth-century forgery called the *Carta humani generis*, which was 'said to have been delivered by Christ at Calvary, using his blood as ink, the nails that pierced his body as a quill and his skin as parchment' (Nicholas Vincent, *The Holy Blood: King Henry III and the Westminster Blood Relic* (Cambridge: Cambridge University Press, 2001), p. 34).
192	This whole passage seems confused but may perhaps be explained by supposing that the fight between Bredbeddle and Burlow Beanie has moved out of the bedchamber, away

198	from Arthur and the others, so that they do not see the outcome, and Bredbeddle has to return to the bedchamber to report his success.
198	Madden, in his edition of *KAKC* (p. 357), noted that this phrase 'seems to have been popular at the end of the sixteenth century, and may, perhaps, mark the age of the ballad'. One of the analogues he cites is 'Old Robin of Portingale' (*Reliques*, III, 49: 'Sleepe you, wake you, faire Syr Gyles?'), while noting that the phrase also appears in Act III, scene v of *King Lear*. Again, the very popularity of the phrase may account for its presence as a later insertion.
206	Arthur wishes to see the words written on the verso, which presumably contains the secret of how to subdue Burlow Beanie. Hahn suggests that the words may include Burlow Beanie's real name, or an image of what Burlow Beanie really looked like before changing its shape.
209	It is unclear why Arthur should use the word 'Alas' at this point, and why he should ask to see Burlow Beanie as he had appeared to Bredbeddle: Arthur must already have seen him in his fiendish shape when the bung was burst open.
212	This line invites an association with *GK*, which has Bredbeddle as its hero.
222	'I doe conjure thee': the fifth and final refrain: see 233, 257, 269, and 285.
224–27	A repetition of 172–75. This time Bredbeddle's weapon is now the 'little booke'.
229–30	It is difficult to know where the fulfilling of Gawaine's vow would have fitted into the narrative. These lines might refer back to Gawaine meeting Cornwall's daughter and what happened next – this could explain the likely faux coy 230 – but why the parties concerned should have been standing for 'the space of an houre' is not clear. The sequence may have ended with a repetition of Gawaine's vow of 153–54.
231	The fulfilling of the vows made by Marramiles and Tristram now begins. Bredbeddle is in control of events as master of ceremonies, with complete power over Burlow Beanie. The poem becomes distinctly more ballad-like from this point on.
235	From here, Burlow Beanie becomes a Helpful Attendant figure, although, unlike the Turke in *TG*, he is constrained by conjuration to obey Bredbeddle.
239	Possibly originally '& then …'; cf. line 231.
250	*the devill of Hell*: a reminder that this recalcitrant steed has eyes that 'glister as doth the gleed' (112), and also a hint of the apocalyptic nature of Cornwall's 'familiars'.
265	It is quite possible that the succeeding line would have been 'And these were the words said he'. See Textual Note.
285	There are here none of the preliminaries that attend the fulfilling of the two previous vows, no failure before success. The culmination of the tale, this is the fulfilling of Arthur's vow to 'be the bane of Cornwall Kinge'.
294	The sword evidently relates to Bredbeddle's vow, whatever that may have been, but he appears to consider that Arthur's vow is more important, since he renounces his own right to it.
295	The motif that a man may only be killed with his own sword is found in the early Irish tale, *The Tragic Death of Cu Roi Mac Dairi*, and the twelfth/thirteenth century *De Ortu Waluuanii Nepotis Arturi* ('On the Rise of Gawaine, Arthur's Nephew'), where the motif is attached to Gawaine.
301	Presumably, Arthur took Cornwall's head back with him, to confront Guenevere. It is possible that this beheading may have broken the 'evil custom of the castle', as does the Turke's upending of the King of Man into the vat of boiling lead in *TG*, and Gawaine's obedience in *CARLE*.

Textual Notes

The presence of so many comments by Percy suggests that he may have considered including this ballad in his *Reliques*, possibly adapting it in the same way as he revised both *BM* and *MSG*. In the LH margin, at the start of the surviving text, P wrote: 'Fragment of *the* Ballad of K*ing* Arthur & *the* King of Cornwall'.

1	Top half of line cropped. 'Come heere my Cu*z*en Gawain so gay. [To] the best of my remembrance this was the first Line before the Binder cut it' [P]. While both Madden and

	HF follow P's recollection, there is the descender of a secretary *h* in the line, suggesting that this should be 'hither' rather than 'here': the word 'come' appears five times elsewhere in *KAKC*, on three occasions being succeeded by 'hither', and never by 'here'. Following this word there appears to be a capital *S*, hence interpreted as S*ir*, and the descender of the *g* for 'Gawaine' is clearly visible. For 'the' as opposed to 'so', compare the bottoms of the letters in this word to 'S*ir* Gawaine the gay' at 143.
13	*where*: emended from 'weere' or 'waere' by scribe.
22	*Ile*: written over another word containing a long-tailed *s*.
23	*alsoe*: *l* inserted between *a* and *s*.
31	A stanza break by Percy in thick red pencil after this line.
32	*the*[*y*]: the [MS], also at 112, 120, 282; *rived*: 'rived: i.e. arrived.' [P].
33	*ma*[*n*]*y*: one minim too few on *n*; letter *a* written above the line by scribe, with caret.
34	*trauckled*: 'travelled qu.' [P]. While HF and others have 'tranckled', the scribe's *u* is frequently indistinguishable from his *n*. Explanatory Note to line 34 above favours the spelling adopted in this edition.
37	[*well mett*]: line missing, reading supplied by HF. The 'mett' is presumably conjectural, but plausible given context and rhyme with 35.
38	MS torn and line missing, reading supplied by P in marginal comment. HF has 'But when he cam to this … C …', but considered that the last three words by P did not match the parts of the letters left, which suggests that they could read more of the line than is now the case. It is now impossible to come to a firm conclusion on the matter.
41	*him*: written above the line, with caret, by scribe.
51	*The*: they [MS].
52	*sa*[*y*]*es*: lacks minim on *y* [MS].
60	[*o*]*f*: *f* [MS], what appears to be an *o* is actually the faint off-set from the first *e* of 'were' (97) on the following recto.
61	A stanza break by P after this line.
64	*meat*[*e*]: final *e* masked by mount.
66	*A une*: 'Atone' [P].
68	*A une*: 'A tone' [P].
72	*is*: his [MS].
77	First half of line now missing. *Our Lady was borne*: the two preceding words may have been 'night' (on the grounds that descenders of 'gh' may be discerned) and 'that' (based on the shape of the descender just before the following word, i.e., suggesting the form 'y*t*').
78	*Britt*[*aine*]: Britt [MS]. This overlong line stretches across the page. Hahn splits the line in two, but such a division sits uneasily with the rhyme and structure of the text.
82	A stanza break by P after this line.
93	*Cockward*: 'cuckwold' [P].
94	A stanza break by P after this line and after 98.
102	*said he*: 'he hight' [P].
106	*if*: beginnings of a loop over the *i*, possibly for a 'he', 'he' being the next word.
108	*on* written above the line, with caret, by scribe.
112	*gleed*: 'In Shropshire Gleed or Gleeds signifies glowing Embers: Vid. pag. 30' [P]. P's reference here is to line 264.
114	[*& that's a full faire steed.*]. Only the very tops of a few letters are discernible in this line, with interpretation complicated by the heavily blotted state of 111 to the end of the page. However, while P records 'That is a noble steed qu' at this point, the formulaic nature of 100, together with alliteration, makes a strong case for the reading adopted in this edition. HF has the tentative '*that* is a well faire steed' [? MS.]'.
115	*Nobody* [*say*]: 'No body' [P]. While the bottom half of 'no body' is relatively clear, HF's succeeding 'say' is supported by a descender, although the form of the *y* is more usually found mid-word rather than at the end of one.
124	*com*[*mu*]*nye*: HF interpreted the word as 'com*u*nye', while Madden has 'com'nye' and Hahn 'cumunye'. The precise spelling is uncertain, a scribal overbar indicating a missing letter *m*, but is likely to be associated with *OED communy*, derived from Middle French *communier*, 'to share, to transmit, to spread'. However, the *OED* records only a single

	instance of the word as a noun, and that is by citing this line from Hahn's edition; as a verb the only example quoted dates from 1530. The sense here is surely that Burlow Beanie listens not just to what Arthur and his companions say, but also to the flow and import of their discussions.
127	*Cornwall's*: 'Arthurs' struck through and 'Cornwalls' substituted below the line by scribe.
128	*pay*: 'i.e. pleasure' [P].
131–32	Written as one line in MS.
135	*an*: a capital *V* or *U* crossed out before this word, the scribe anticipating the following word 'unadvised'.
138	A stanza break by P after this line and after 140.
139	*against*: inserted above the line, with caret, by the scribe.
144	Scribal 'The 3ᵈ part' in LH margin.
145	Line begins with a large 'And', preceded by stanza break.
151–54	Bracketed in LH margin, and seemingly an afterthought to his comment at 112, 'N.B. 3led A. Sax. est pruna a live coal' [P].
163	*the*: they [MS].
166	*Collen brand*: most of this word slightly obscured by bleed-through from the crossed-out word 'Arthurs' (127) on preceding recto.
178	*brand brake*: a second 'brand' (partially obscured by hole) crossed out, and 'brake' substituted.
181	*sur*: 'sure' [P].
185	A stanza break by P after this line and after 187.
189	*Wrucked*: 'rucked, i.e. crowded all of a heap or ruck' [P].
190	*it*: inserted above line, with caret, by scribe.
191	[*& sealed it with His bloode*]. While this line is now missing from the MS, Madden, HF, and Child all included it. P does not comment. The tops of the letters of the first part of the line could well be '& sealed it with'.
192	Latter part of this line lost. It is possible that 'not' is succeeded by 'stirre': the sense is appropriate, and the remains of the descender of a long-tailed *s* open the following word, although the bottom of the remaining letters are not apparent.
203	*knight*: the scribe seemingly started to write 'Bredbeddle', and got as far as the opening capital letter, before realizing his mistake, overwriting with a lower case *k*, and then finishing the word.
205	*reede*: 'reede' [P]. The end of the word is partly obscured, necessitating P's gloss.
213	'See the Romance of the Green Knight. pag. 203.' [P]
218	*strong*: the edge of the page is cropped, and the downstroke of the *g* is also missing.
226	*flaugh*: 'flew' [P].
228	*The knight stood in the Middle* …; HF has 'The knight stood in the Middle p…' at this point, but this last letter is no longer visible, and was not recorded by Madden.
229	*they stood*: only the lower parts of these words can be made out, but given the narrative at this point the preceding words might have been 'And then'.
244	*full*: *f* written over a *b*. The scribe began to write 'bold'.
246	*Then*: the scribe originally wrote 'th' with a secretary *h*, followed by an italic one, then changed this to *e*.
249	*Bredbeddle*: first *b* overwritten with a *d*.
256	*words*: a long-tailed *s* crossed out before the *w*. The scribe began to write 'said', but realized he had missed out 'words'.
257	*Burlow [B]eane*: leane [MS].
258	[t]*his*: his [MS].
264	*Gleede*: 'Vid. note Pag. 26.' [P].
265	From the final word of 262 to the end of the page the lines are blotted. Line 265 is missing, with only the tops of a few letters visible: reading supplied by HF, and recorded by Madden.
266	[*he may blow then*]. Only the very bottom of the last two words remain. Madden only recorded 'A lowd blast'. HF has 'A lowd blast he may blow then', but qualified with a question mark: 'blow' is certainly plausible.

278	*swilled*: 'i.e. rinsed it washt it. Verb. Salop.' [P].
285	*thee*: second *e* inserted by scribe above the line, without caret.
286–301	Running the length of these lines in the LH margin: 'The Decapitation occurs in the Romance of the Green Knight. See that Romance beginning at pag. 203.' [P]
293	*A[rthur]*: MS crumbled at this point, leaving only a lower case ?*a*.
294	*t[hee]*: MS crumbled at this point. Stanza break by P after this line.
299	*off*: written above the line by scribe, with caret; *hea[d]*: page torn at this point.
301	*He put the head [upon] a sword['s point]*: the first three and the seventh words can be construed. Complete line supplied by HF.

Sir Lancelott of Dulake

Raluca Radulescu

This ballad is among those that have suffered most from the attention of Pitt's housemaid, with a large number of stanzas missing after lines 30 and 60, and one missing in the middle (as noted by Percy in the margin of the manuscript by lines 42–43). The text, as it survives in PF, consists of sixteen 4-line stanzas: the scribe has numbered the stanzas in large bold numerals on the left-hand side of the text (1–7, 16–22).[1] The half-leaf on which the poem starts has been mounted at the top of f. 16v (p. 36), and the second half-leaf has been mounted at the bottom of f. 17r (p. 37).[2] The story is based on an episode in *LMD*, where Launcelot defeats Sir Tarquin in single combat, liberating as a result three score and four of King Arthur's knights who had been imprisoned by him. Launcelot thus emerges from this encounter as the quintessential Arthurian knight, and Tarquin as its very antithesis, using his superior strength and cunning to exploits the trust of Arthur's knights in his (presumed) chivalric conduct.

SLDL is the most popular Arthurian piece to have found its way into the PF. The ballad was written by Thomas Deloney between 1595 and 1596, versifying the story he found in East's ?1585 edition of *LMD*, before including it in his *The Garland of Good Will*.[3] The *Garland* proved to be phenomenally successful; earlier editions have not survived, but a copy published by Robert Bird in London in 1628 is currently housed in Yale University Library (*Y*), while Mann's *The Works of Thomas Deloney* reproduces an edition from 1631 (*M*): approximately a dozen editions of this collection of ballads were to appear in the course of the seventeenth century, with further editions continuing to be augmented and printed very many years after Percy's death.[4] Independent of its existence in the *Garland*, the ballad enjoyed a flourishing life as a broadside: it was licensed to Edward Allde in 1603, and while the earliest extant version seemingly dates to *c.*1615 (Nastali and Boardman, 2004, I, 25), a broadside from *c.*1620 has survived, and is housed in Harvard University Library (*B*).[5] Such was the ballad's popularity that Falstaff quotes from it in Shakespeare's *The Second Part of King Henry IV*, Act II, scene iv (*c.*1598), and it features in both Marston's *The Malcontent* (*c.*1603) and Fletcher and Massinger's *The Little French Lawyer* (1619–23). Under the title 'The Noble Acts of King Arthur and the Knights of the Round Table; with the Valiant Atchievements of *Sir Lancelot du Lake*' this widely known ballad was included in the popular *A Collection of Old Ballads* (1723–25), a work that played a key role in Percy's development of the *Reliques* (see Introduction). Paradoxically, the popularity of the ballad seems to have had a limited effect on the scribe of the PF: writing *c*.1650, he uniquely calls the Arthurian hero Sir Lancelot 'of Dulake', and was seemingly oblivious to the fact that he had left out a stanza, notwithstanding the fact that he assigned a sequential number to each.[6]

One of the more remarkable features of this text is its fidelity to Malory's original story, which Deloney would have found in Book VI, Chapter i of the Caxton edition of *LMD*. An assessment of the relationship between *SLDL* as it appears in the PF and the many versions found after 1650 is beyond the scope of this chapter, but it is striking how the PF ballad differs on occasion in its readings from *B*, *M*, and *Y*. For example, at line 10, *B* and *Y* follow variations of *M*'s 'before them there were drest',[7] and similarly at line 12 *B*, *M*, and *Y* have 'and far' instead of '& eke' in the PF (the PF seems to favour ampersands in this text); at line 15 the three antecedents have 'He in his fights and deeds of arms'; 'good' for 'great' (24), 'right' for 'good' (37), the preferable 'void' for 'avoyd' (41), 'and like' for 'like to' (51), and 'quoth Lancelot' for 'said Lancelott' (55). At line 59, all three texts have a different word order that would have affected the rhyme scheme, i.e., 'His name is Sir Lancelot du Lake' instead of the PF's awkward 'His name Sir Lancelott Dulake is'.[8] Given the number of times *SLDL* appeared in print, was read and enjoyed between its original composition towards the close of the sixteenth century, and its appearance in the PF some 150 years later, it is not too surprising that different readings emerged.

However, a contributory factor would have been the tune to which the ballad was sung, i.e., 'Flying fame'. 'Flying fame' was popular enough that it lent itself to a wide range of songs within the seventeenth century, for example 'Chevy Chase', 'St George', 'The Dead Man's song', 'The Shooe-makers travel', 'The battel of Agen-Court', 'Of the faithful friendship that lasted between two faithful friends', 'The Shepherd and the King', 'St. Bernard's vision', 'A Caroll for Saint Iohns day', and 'The Wanton wife of Bath'.[9] The tune also accompanied 'The faire Lady Rosamond', which opens the Yale 1628 edition of the *Garland* and which includes our Arthurian ballad as item 8 in that publication. The ingredients of an action-packed ballad, an Arthurian theme, a readily recognizable tune that would have encouraged circulation, all in a medium which lent itself readily to vigorous performance that exploits to the full the potential offered by different voices and physical gestures,[10] was surely enough to keep audiences rapt in Elizabethan times and for centuries beyond.

Notes

[1] The text as published in previous editions of *The Garland of Good Will* and as a broadsheet would have been continuous, with alternate lines indented. This was the case for the broadsides in the Roxburghe collection: BL C.20.f. 9.25 (ESTC R216001), ?1669; Bodl. Wood 401(61) (ESTC R179003), 1674–79; and Pepys Library, Magdalene College, Cambridge (ESTC R234299), 1693. The Roxburghe text formed the basis for the reprint of the ballad by the Percy Society in 1886, although its editor, J. Woodfall Ebsworth, chose to set out the text in extended quatrains, e.g., lines 1–8 in the PF forming the first stanza.

[2] For a brief discussion of the mounting of the leaves, and the likelihood that they are both bottom half-leaves, see Gillian Rogers, 'The Percy Folio Manuscript Revisited', in Maldwyn Mills, Jennifer

Fellows, and Carol M. Meale (eds), *Romance in Medieval England* (Cambridge: D. S. Brewer, 1991), pp. 42–43.

[3] For the likely date of composition, see Merritt E. Lawlis, 'Shakespeare, Deloney, and the Earliest Text of the Arthur Ballad', *Harvard Library Bulletin* 10 (1956), pp. 130–35. Mann (*The Works of Thomas Deloney. Edited from the Earliest Extant Editions & Broadsides with an Introduction and Notes by Francis Oscar Mann* (Oxford: Clarendon Press, 1912), xii) noted that Thomas Nash mentioned Deloney's authorship of the *Garland* in 1596, but argued that an entry in the Stationers' Registers of 1592–93 implied an earlier date.

[4] Nastali and Boardman state that there was an edition in 1604 (Daniel P. Nastali and Phillip C. Boardman, *The Arthurian Annals: The Tradition in English from 1250 to 2000*, 2 vols (Oxford: Oxford University Press, 2004)). Mann (Deloney, 1912, 563) noted that one critic had spoken of fragments of a 1604 edition, and another had professed to have seen a complete copy, but 'neither, however, gives any references'.

[5] ESTC S2568, printed by 'W. I.', in London. The ballad remained popular beyond the likely date of the composition of the PF and was frequently paired with the 'The Jolly Pindar of Wakefield' (see n1, above). The PF includes the fragmentary 'Robin Hood and the Pindar of Wakefield' (HF, I, 32–36).

[6] At *GK*, 218, the scribe also refers to 'Sir Lancelott Dulake', and the same spelling is used elsewhere in the PF, i.e., line 76 of 'The Fall of Princes' (HF, III, 172).

[7] *B* seems to read 'brest' as the final word.

[8] The reading from *B* at this point is the most colloquial: 'His name's Sir Lancelot du Lake'. The line that would have rhymed in PF has been lost, along with the remainder of the ballad. Interestingly, at line 56, the three texts diverge: *M* and *Y* agree with the PF ('But sith it must be so'), but *B* echoes the PF ('but sith it so must be').

[9] Numerous examples of ballads sung to 'Flying Fame' may be found by consulting the ESTC. Some of these songs, albeit with different words, were included by Percy in the 1765 *Reliques*, e.g., 'The Ancient Ballad of Chevy Chase' (I, 1–17), 'Fair Rosamond' (II, 133–45), and 'St. George and the Dragon' (III, 225–35). 'The Wanton Wife of Bath' (III, 146–51) was copied by Percy from a broadsheet in the Pepys Collection, and undoubtedly sung to 'Flying Fame'.

[10] Deloney 'altered the emphasis and structure of Malory's tale radically, turning the moral drama of his source into a tale of pure action with little, if any, moral import' (Robert A. Schwegler, 'The Arthur Ballad: From Malory to Deloney to Shakespeare', *Essays in Literature* 5(1) (1978), p. 5).

Editions, Related Texts, and Sigla

HF, I, 84–87.

Anon., *A Collection of Old Ballads. Corrected from the best and most Ancient Copies Extant. With Introductions Historical, Critical, or Humorous. Illustrated with Copper Plates*, 3 vols (London: J. Roberts and D. Leach, 1723–25), II, 18–24.

Anon., 'The noble acts newly found, of Arthur of the table round to the tune of Flying Fame'. Broadsheet published in London *c.*1620, by W. I. (ESTC S2568) (*B*).

Deloney, Thomas, *The Garland of Good Will* (London: Edward Brewster and Robert Bird), 1628 (*Y*).

—— *The Works of Thomas Deloney. Edited from the Earliest Extant Editions & Broadsides with an Introduction and Notes by Francis Oscar Mann* (Oxford: Clarendon Press, 1912), pp. 323–26. Based on *The Garland of Good Will* (London: Robert Bird, 1631), pp. 323–26, 570–72 (*M*).

Further Reading

Lawlis, Merritt E., 'Shakespeare, Deloney, and the Earliest Text of the Arthur Ballad', *Harvard Library Bulletin* 10 (1956), pp. 130–35.

Rogers, Gillian, 'Themes and Variations: Studies in Some English Gawain-Poems', PhD thesis, University of Wales, 1978, pp. 433–37.
—— 'The Percy Folio Manuscript Revisited', in Maldwyn Mills, Jennifer Fellows, and Carol M. Meale (eds), *Romance in Medieval England* (Cambridge: D. S. Brewer, 1991), pp. 39–64.
Schwegler, Robert A., 'The Arthur Ballad: From Malory to Deloney to Shakespeare', *Essays in Literature* 5(1) (1978), pp. 3–13.

Sir Lancelott of Dulake

    When Arthur first in Court began*   p. 36/f. 16v
       & was approved king,
    By force of armes great victorys wonne
       And conquest home did bring.

5   Then into England straight he came*
       With 50^{ty} good and able
    Knights that resorted unto him,
       & were of the Round Table.

    And many Justs and turnaments   *jousts*
10   Wherto were many prest,   *ready*
    Weherin some knights did farr exell
       & eke surmount the rest.

    But one, S*ir* Lancelot of Dulake,
       He was approved well,
15   He for his deeds & feats of armes
       All others did exell.

    When he had rested him awhile
       In play & game to sportt,
    He said he wold goe prove himselfe
20   In some adventurous sort.

    He armed rode in a forrest wide,
       & met a damsell faire,
    who told him of adventures great,
       wherto he gave great eare.   *listened carefully*

25   'Why shold I not?' qu*o*th Lancelott tho,*
       'for that cause came I hither.'
    'Thou seemst,' qu*o*th shee, 'a K*nig*ht full good,
       & I will bring thee thither

    'Weras the worthiest k*nig*ht doth dwell'
30   [th] .....

[*Half a page lost. The damsel asks his name, then tells him that a knight nearby holds prisoners a large number of Arthur's knights, and he has never been beaten in combat. Lancelot challenges Tarquin to a fight. Tarquin tells Lancelot that if he is indeed of the Round Table, then he defies him and his fellowship.*]

    'Thatt's over much,' qu*o*th Lancelott tho,   p. 37/f. 17r
       Defend thee by & by.'

They sett their [spurs] unto their steeds,*
    And eache att other flie.

35 They coucht theire speares, their horses run
        As though there had beene thunder,
    & every stroke in midst their sheelds,
        Werewith they broke in sunder.

    The[ir] horsses bakes brake under them,*
40   The knights were both astond;   *stunned*
    To avoyd their horsse they made great hast,*
        & light upon the ground.

    They wounded were, & bled full sore,
        They both for breath did stand,
45 & leaning on their swords awhile,
        Quoth Tarqine, 'Hold thy hand,

    'And tell to me what I shall Aske.'
        'Say on,' quoth Lancelott tho:
    'Thou art,' quoth Tarqine, 'the best knight
50   That ever I did know,

    'Like to a knight that I doe hate,
        Soe that thou be not hee,
    I will deliuer all the rest,
        & eke accord with thee.'

55 'That is well said,' said Lancelott tho,
        'But seeth it must soe bee,   *since*
    What knight is that, that thou dost hate?
        I pray thee show to mee.'

    'His name Sir Lancelott Dulake is,
60   He slew my brother deere …

[*The rest is lost. Tarquin reveals that of all men, he wishes to meet Lancelot. Lancelot reveals his identity, and they fight to the death. Lancelot defeats and beheads Tarquin, and frees the prisoners.*]

Explanatory Notes

1–4   The first stanza provides a rather abrupt introduction to the story, the result of which is awkward ('first began'); in *LMD*, a smoother transition is visible at this point between the conclusion of Arthur's war against the Emperor Lucius (Book 5, Chapter vi) and the beginning of Lancelot's adventures (Book VI, Chapter i).

5   The textual variations in the editions (Britain for England) reflect the post-medieval preference for 'Britain', whereas in *LMD* 'England' is the preferred term throughout. PF's 'England' is true to *LMD*, as it is clearly in opposition with the 1726 edition Percy mentions in a side note (and all the other ones).

25	Lancelot's abrupt question marks a break in the narrative. As in Malory's original story, the damsel provokes him by implying that he might be wary of adventures; there Lancelot's reply comes as a natural progression of his argument in favour of pursuing 'strange adventures'.
33	*spurs*: rather than the MS *speares*, 'spurs' is the usual reading elsewhere at this point: it is quite likely the scribe had unconsciously in mind the references to spears two lines later.
39–40	The two knights' actions are typical of a violent encounter as they place their spears in position; the force of the clash shatters the spears, and the knights are stunned by the impact. As their horses fall, the audience can almost feel the force of the encounter, which may justify the appeal of the story and the initial decision to select it from among so many of Malory's descriptions of combat.
41	They dismount their horses in order to avoid being caught under them in their fall.
42?ff.	A stanza missing here, recounting the fight after they dismounted.

Textual Notes

In the LH margin, P has noted: 'In the printed collection 1726 – [v]ol. 2d: p. 18. N. III'. The reference is to the second edition of *A Collection of Old Ballads*, the first edition having been published in 1723.

30	[*th*]: text lost through cropping. HF recorded these letters as *ch* although, as they note, the line is likely to have read 'That now is of great fame'.
33	*They*: the *e* superscript; *spurs*: speares [MS].
39	*The*[*ir*]: They [MS].
40	*The*: they [MS].
42	In the space between lines 42 and 43, stanzas 18 and 19, P has written 'A stanza is here wanting w*hic*h is to be found in *th*e printed Copy'.
47	*I*: interlined, with caret; *Aske*: prior to the initial capital letter in the MS there appear to be two characters that have been blotted out. The opening character may be an *s*. It is possible that the scribe, when writing, had either the preceding or succeeding word in mind, both of which start with this letter, then realized his mistake.

The Turke & Gowin

Gillian Rogers and John Withrington

The unique copy of this rich, evocative, and eclectic tale, generally dated to about 1500 and written possibly in Cheshire, is contained in the damaged portion of the PF on ff. 17v–21v, comprising 336 lines, or parts of lines, out of an estimated 646.[1] The beginning and ending are both intact. It is in tail-rhyme, with 58 stanzas or parts of stanzas surviving. Six-line stanzas predominate, with a basic rhyme scheme of $aa_4b_3cc_4b_3$, but there are also five 9-liners, three marked off as such by Percy, and 20 stanzas where the rhyme scheme suggests that the original poem may have been written in units of 12 lines.[2] On occasion, it seems that both the scribe and Percy were confused as to where the stanza divisions came, possibly because neither was familiar with the verse form.[3] There are frequent lapses in the rhyme scheme: in some cases no attempt has been made to rhyme, others are caused by modernization of spelling.[4] Alliteration is confined mainly to set phrases and 'tags', of which there are many, but some lines alliterate on two letters, and there are instances where the alliteration stretches over two lines, or crosses stanza divisions.

The choice of the word 'turk' to describe *TG*'s protagonist is particularly interesting. On the one hand, the word simply means a dwarf, the arrival of which at Arthur's court to herald a new adventure is conventional enough (see, for example, Teddelyne in *LD*). Sir John Paston, writing to his brother in about February 1470, noted the arrival at court of 'a newe littell Torke, whyche is a wele vysagyd felawe off the age off xl yere, and he is lowere than Manuell by an hanffull and lower then my lytell Tom by the scholderys ... And he is leggyd ryght j-now'.[5] However, the use of the word in the sense of 'Turkish' adds a layer of exoticism to *TG*: 'like "Saracen," "Turk" defines otherness through geography, politics, religion and class'.[6] Derek Pearsall has suggested that *TG*'s verse form may reflect performance by a popular entertainer,[7] and the appearance of a Turk in such entertainment is well documented: Hahn (1995, 352n) notes that in Gloucester in 1595 payment was made, presumably for a lavish costume, 'for a wagon in the pageant and for the turke', observing that the adversary in mummings and St George's plays is known variously as, e.g., 'The Turk', 'The Turkish Knight', and 'Turkey Snipe'. David Lawton has also written on the figure of what he calls the 'festive Turk' in the world of folk drama. Of the Turk in *TG*, he writes:

> Reborn, his full name is Sir Gromer Somer Joure, which places him in a context of folkloric and festive representation, Midsummer, equivalent to the Christmas games of the

Mummers' combat play and of *Sir Gawain and the Green Knight*. He belongs there with … [the Grene Knyght] … Sir Bredbeddle. These romances are best seen as scripts for festive performance, where the worlds of drama and romance converge.[8]

This duality of romance and folk-tale, in which the romance elements form the framework of the whole tale and the folk-tale elements constitute its main action, sets *TG* apart from many other Arthurian texts. The unknown author shows an impressive knowledge both of the Arthurian milieu itself and of Gawaine's traditional characteristics within that milieu. There is, however, a sharp dichotomy between the Arthurian world and that of folk-tale. In romances such as *SGGK*, *GK*, and the two *Carle* tales, Gawaine takes his 'Arthurian' characteristics with him on his adventure – his courtesy, his modesty, his eye for beauty, his championing of the underdog, and his adherence to his sworn word – and these come into play in the course of the narrative; but, with the exception of the last, once he steps out of the Arthurian framework in *TG*, Gawaine largely sheds these characteristics and, apart from one brief moment (168–71), becomes the kind of folk-hero whose chief and most necessary attribute is passive obedience. The hero, however, is at times portrayed in a distinctly anti-heroic fashion, thereby aligning himself with a time-honoured tradition stretching back to Chrétien de Troyes and his successors, for in the folk-tale section, Gawaine does not perform well, displaying hunger and becoming querulous when denied food, being frightened by the hill opening before him, and even complaining about the weather.[9] Furthermore, he performs none of the three tasks set by the King of Man, leaving them to his 'boy', the omniscient and omnicompetent Turk.[10] Once back at court, however, he resumes his normal character and behaviour.

As in many folk-tales, a triadic structure runs through *TG*. The Turk promises to make Gawaine '3*ise* as feard/As ever was man on middlearth' (39–40), the King of Man imposes three tests on his 'guest' (195–97), and the Turk whirls the 'chimney' '3*is* about his head' (222). These three tests are so unlikely as tests for a hero that an unmistakable element of burlesque emerges: the comic potential offered for performance is obvious. In structural terms, *TG*'s chief affinities lie with *SGGK* and, to a lesser extent, its alter ego, *GK*, particularly in its opening sequence: the appearance of an antagonistic and enchanted stranger at Arthur's court during a feast, the challenge to an exchange of blows,[11] Gawaine's acceptance of the challenge and his subsequent obligation to leave the court in order to fulfil his part of the bargain at a different time and place (although in this case, the challenger accompanies him), and the hospitality offered to him on the way by this challenger. Also common to the two tales is the challenger's contemptuous treatment of Arthur and Gawaine, the three tests imposed on the latter, the weather encountered by him on his journey, and the presence of two Otherworlds. In *TG*, however, an additional motif has been added: Disenchantment by Decapitation.[12]

No direct source is known for *TG*, although a number of analogues have been identified. Snorri Sturluson's thirteenth-century *Gylfaginning* has Thór journey to the giant Útgarđa-Loki and visit the Otherworld king, and undergo imposed tests.[13] Webster saw a general resemblance between the scene in the King of Man's castle and Charlemagne's visit to King Hugo of Constantinople in *Le Pèlerinage de Charlemagne*, particularly between William of Orange's *pelote* and *TG*'s 'tennisse ball', Aimer's *capel* and the Turk's grey cloak of invisibility, and the bath of molten lead that Ernalt vows to sit in (a similar bath being used to kill one of the Turk's giants).[14] The fourteenth-century *Thomas of Erceldoune* supplies parallels to Gawaine's journey to the first Otherworld, particularly in the description of the travellers' entrance through the hill, with its attendant climatic conditions, and the prohibitions on eating and speaking while there. Its ballad counterpart, *Thomas the Rymer* (*TR*), also contains these prohibitions, the first of which is misunderstood in exactly the same way as in *TG*, since the guide supplies other food for the famished hero to eat.[15] The hill or mound as entrance to the Otherworld is also found in *Sir Orfeo* (late fourteenth-/early fifteenth-century), where the classical Hades of Pluto, the King of the Underworld, has been transformed into a Celtic realm whence no mortal returns, inhabited by the beautiful but sinister elves.

TG follows a common pattern of double Otherworlds, the second being either separate from the first and visited after it, or situated within the first, as happens, for instance, in Chrétien's *Lancelot*.[16] In *TG*, the apparently deserted, but well-provisioned castle beneath the mound, the first Otherworld visited by Gawaine and his companion, possibly belongs to the Turk himself. Food is laid out and a fire is burning in the hearth. These are common features of Otherworld castles, and Gawaine comes across many such in various romances.[17] The gap in the MS at this point makes it unclear whether they emerged from an underground realm and then travelled on to the sea and thence to the second Otherworld, the Isle of Man, or simply continued until they reached the sea and embarked on the self-steering boat.[18] Waldron cites a belief that the Isle of Man was populated by a race of giants who had overcome the original (fairy) inhabitants and who had themselves been overcome and spell-bound by Merlin, and Moore cites traditions of Manannan, variously a 'paynim' necromancer and terrible giant.[19] The Kingship of Man was granted to Sir John Stanley in 1405, and Byrne and Flood put forward the interesting suggestion that 'What we appear to have in *The Turke and Sir Gawain* is an origin myth for the Isle of Man, firmly located in the Arthurian past, but which deploys a range of motif and plot elements that foreshadow the coming of the Stanley kings'.[20] However, Gawaine's refusal of the Kingship of Man owes more to his literary reputation for refusing such honours than to any identification with Sir John.

The text of *TG*, as we have it, contains many puzzling, sometimes contradictory, features, quite apart from the problems of interpretation arising from the gaps. For example, if the Turk is simply an enchanted knight, what is he doing with an underground 'Otherworld' castle, playing the host and bringing alternative food and drink for the famished Gawaine? Why is he so hostile to the knight he hopes will deliver him from his enchantment? How does he come to possess a cloak of invisibility? Does his exceptional strength arise only from his enchanted state? Was there ever a return blow, and where would it have been given? Over and above all these enigmas is the paradox that *TG* is a folk-tale about an enchanted knight requiring the help of another to regain his normal shape, and hence arguably more the Turk's story than Gawaine's; while at the same time the narrative – being located in an Arthurian milieu, with echoes of *SGGK* and containing a considerable number of motifs traditionally, indeed persistently, associated with Gawaine – contextually make it more Gawaine's story than the Turk's. As with *BM*, *TG* defies simple classification.

Notes

[1] See Griffith, *AE*, 201. Rhiannon Purdie dates *TG* to the second half of the fifteenth century or the sixteenth century, adding that 'there is a clear Northern colouring to the language despite the brevity and lateness of the extant text' (Rhiannon Purdie, *Anglicising Romance: Tail-Rhyme and Genre in Medieval English Literature* (Cambridge: D. S. Brewer, 2008), pp. 236–37). It is difficult to be precise about the length of the text since the number of lines to a half-page varies between 34 and 44, with 38 on five of the 9 half-leaves, and 27 on the last (which it shares with the opening of *MSG*).

[2] The tail-rhyme romance *Sir Triamore*, which appears in the PF, is also to be found in Cambridge University Library MS Ff.2.38. While the PF version was most probably copied from Copland's print of 1561, the Cambridge version was also likely to have been framed in 12-line stanzas and shares structural similarities to *TG*: 'a good number of stanzas are split into two six-line stanzas. There are also several nine-line stanzas, and even the occasional fifteen-line stanza … However, many of these six-line stanzas are shown by their tail-rhymes to be divided twelve-line stanzas' (Demelza Jayne Curnow, 'Five Case Studies on the Transmission of Popular Middle English Verse Romances', PhD thesis, University of Bristol, 2002, p. 185). I am grateful to Prof. Ad Putter for bringing this work to my attention [J. W.].

[3] The scribe marks off stanzas with a space, albeit not always consistently; P marks off with a short thick black line. The confusion over stanza divisions is particularly noticeable on f. 20r, where the scribe has left prominent spaces between lines 197–98, 203–4, 209–10, and less prominent ones between 215–16 and 218–19. Percy followed the scribe at 203–4, 209–10, and 218–19, but inserted divisions between 194–95 and 212–13 and erased those he had made at 191–92, 197–98, and 215–16. Reconstruction of stanzas, particularly units of nine lines, must remain largely a matter of interpretation for this text, as P's erasures indicate.

[4] Occasionally, the first tail-line of a stanza is made to rhyme with the next line (221–22, 279–80); 56–59 and 118–21 even show series of line-by-line rhyming. There are many examples of modernization of spelling, e.g., 60–61 (*sore* (*sare*)/*care*) and the tail-rhymes at 68 and 71 (*adread* (*adradd*)/*had*) and 92–93 (*fay*/*maid* (*may*)).

[5] Norman Davis (ed.), *Paston Letters and Papers of the Fifteenth Century*, 2 vols, EETS SS 20, 21 (Oxford: Oxford University Press, 2004), I, 415. Paston's comment suggests that, notwithstanding his height, the 'Torke' was well proportioned.

[6] Hahn, 1995, 338. In a deft reversal of roles, Gawaine himself of course becomes the outsider in the King of Man's realm.

[7] Derek Pearsall, *Old English and Middle English Poetry* (London: Routledge & Kegan Paul, 1977), p. 260.

[8] David Lawton, 'History and Legend: The Exile of the Turk', in Patricia Clare Ingham and Michelle R. Warren (eds), *Postcolonial Moves: Medieval through Modern* (Basingstoke: Palgrave Macmillan, 2003), p. 189. As with other Arthurian texts within the PF, *TG*'s potential for performance and entertainment is clear.

[9] Compare his stoical endurance of the icy conditions he experiences on his way to Bertilak's castle in *SGGK*.

[10] While the first two tests have been lost due to damage to the PF, the Turk certainly performed the third (219). That the Turk performed all three is made clear by his heartfelt thanks to Gawaine

after he has reluctantly beheaded him (296–97). Furthermore, Gawaine, on refusing the kingship of Man, declares, 'Give it him, for he it wan' (324).

[11] That this, unlike the challenge in *SGGK*, was never intended to be an invitation to a Beheading becomes clear when Gawaine later asks for his return blow at the castle beneath the mound. Beheading as a means of 'unspelling' occurs only here and in *CARLE*. As a motif, it is quite separate from the Beheading Game seen in *SGGK*, although it is possible that it was drawn into Gawaine's orbit as a result of the association of ideas.

[12] Compare the very similar sequence in *CARLE*, 380–404. For a detailed discussion of the many motifs that make up *TG*, together with that of Disenchantment by Decapitation, see Gillian Rogers, 'Themes and Variations: Studies in Some English Gawain-Poems', PhD thesis, University of Wales, 1978, 252ff.

[13] A strong element of burlesque is present in the tests imposed on Thor, whose small stature is commented upon by the giants (Snorri Sturlson, *Edda*, trans. and ed. Anthony Faulkes (London: Dent, 1987), p. 46).

[14] K. G. T. Webster, 'Arthur and Charlemagne', *Englische Studien* 36 (1906), pp. 357–60. *KAKC* is particularly reminiscent in places of *Le Pèlerinage*: it is interesting to note the presence of two unique Arthurian romances in the PF, both seemingly indebted to the same text, the one following the other.

[15] For the prohibition on eating and drinking, and the proffering of alternative food in *TR* and *TG*, see Child, I, 37A, Introduction, and stanzas 9–10 and 15, and E. B. Lyle, '*The Turk and Gawain* as a Source of *Thomas of Erceldoune*', *Forum for Modern Language Studies* 6(1) (1970), pp. 100–01. Two versions of *TR* can be traced back in Scotland 'to the first half of the 18th century', with a further version 'possibly into the late 17th century' (Ingeborg Nixon (ed.), *Thomas of Erceldoune, Parts 1–2* (Copenhagen: Publications of the Department of English, University of Copenhagen, 1980–83), II, 82).

[16] Lancelot lodges overnight in a place evidently already within the Otherworld of Gorre, since his hosts are prisoners there, before crossing the Sword-Bridge to rescue the imprisoned Guenevere.

[17] For example, the castle in *La Mule sanz Frein* (perhaps the closest analogue to the situation in *TG*), Chrétien de Troyes's *Perceval* (the 'Roche de Canguin' episode), episodes 4 and 6 of the *First Continuation* of that poem (the 'Chastel Orguellous' and the 'Guiromelant' sections), *La Vengeance Raguidel*, and Perre Bercheur's *Reductorium Morale*. See Rogers, 1978, 281–83.

[18] See Tom Peete Cross, *Motif-Index of Early Irish Literature* (Bloomington: Indiana University Press, 1952), F134.1, p. 232: 'Hebrides, Isle of Man (Falga) as otherworld'. Traces of this double Otherworld pattern are to be found also in *SGGK*. Since the visits to the second Otherworld represented by the Green Chapel in *SGGK* and the Isle of Man in *TG* are both connected to the giving of the return blow, it is possible that *TG* is again following the same structural pattern as *SGGK*. See Rogers, 1978, 271–87 for a discussion of the double Otherworld motif.

[19] George Waldron, *A Description of the Isle of Man*, ed. William Harrison (Douglas: The Manx Society, 1865): a reprint of Waldron's 1731 edition, www.isle-of-man.com/manxnotebook/manxsoc/msvol11/p01.htm (accessed July 2023); A. W. Moore, *The Folk Lore of the Isle of Man* (London: David Nutt, 1891), pp. 5–6.

[20] Aisling Byrne and Victoria Flood, 'The Romance of the Stanleys: Regional and National Imaginings in the Percy Folio', *Viator* 46(1) (2015), p. 348. See Introduction, p. 5, above, for the PF scribe's apparent interest in the Stanley family.

Editions and Related Texts

Hahn, 337–58.

HF, I, 88–102.

Madden, 243–55.

Williams, Jeanne Myrle Wilson, 'A Critical Edition of "The Turke and Gowin"', PhD thesis, University of Southern Mississippi, 1987.

Further Reading

Griffith, David, '*The Turke and Gowin*', *AE*, 1201–3.

Jost, Jean E. 'The Role of Violence in "Adventure": "The Ballad of King Arthur and the King of Cornwall" and "The Turke and Gowin"', *Arthurian Interpretations* 2(2) (1988), pp. 47–57.

Lyle, E. B. '"*The Turk and* Gawain" as a Source of *Thomas of Erceldoune*', *Forum for Modern Language Studies* 6(1) (1970), pp. 98–102.

Sturlson, Snorri, *Edda*, trans. and ed. Anthony Faulkes (London: Dent, 1987).

Thompson, Raymond H., '"Muse on Þi Mirrour …": The Challenge of the Outlandish Stranger in the English Arthurian Verse Romances', *Folklore* 87(2) (1976), pp. 201–8.

The Turke & Gowin

	LISTEN lords, great & small,	p. 38/f. 17v
	What adventures did befall	
	In England, where hath beene	
	Of knights that held the Round Table,	
5	Which were doughty & profittable,	*valiant; worthy*
	Of kempys cruell & keene.	*warriors; fierce; brave*
	All England, both East & west,	
	Lords & ladyes of the best,	
	They busked & made them bowne,	*got ready*
10	& when the king sate in seate,	
	Lords served him att his meate,	
	Into the hall a burne there ca[m]e;	*man*
	He was not hye, but he was broad,	
	& like a turke he was made,*	*dwarf*
15	Both legg & thye,	
	& said, 'Is there any will, as a brother,*	
	To give a buffett & take another,	
	Giff any soe hardy bee?'	*If*
	Then spake Sir Kay, that crabbed knight,*	*churlish*
20	& said, 'Man, thou seemest not soe wight*	*clever*
	If thou be not adread,	
	For there beene knights within this hall	
	With a buffett will garr thee fall,	*make*
	& grope thee to the ground.	*throw*
25	'Give thou be never soe stalworth of hand,	*If; strong*
	I shall bring thee to the ground,	
	That dare I safely sweare.'	
	Then spake Sir Gawaine, that worthy knight,	
	Saith, 'Cozen Kay, thou speakest not right,	
30	Lewd is thy answere.	*ignorant*
	'What & that man want of his witt,*	*if*
	Then litle worshipp were to thee pitt*	
	If thou shold him forefore.'	
	Then spake the Turke with words thraw,*	*angry*
35	Saith, 'Come the better of yo[u] tow,	*two*
	[Though y]e be bre[m]e as bore ...'	*fierce as a boar*

[*Half a page missing. The Turk promises them a better blow than they can give him. Gawaine claims the right to give the blow and strikes the Turk. Instead of returning the blow immediately, the Turk proposes an adventure to Gawaine, in the course of which he will repay his blow with interest.*]

	'This buffett thou hast ...*	p. 39/f. 18r
	Well quitt that it shall be,	*repaid*
	And yett I shall make thee 3^{ise}as feard	
40	As ever was man on middlearth,	*earth*
	his court againe ere thou see.'	
	Then said Gawaine, 'My truth I plight.*	*I pledge my word*
	I dare goe with thee full right,	
	& never from thee flye.	
45	I will never flee from noe adventure,	
	Justing nor noe other turnament,	*jousting*
	Whilest I may live on lee.'	*While I live*
	The Turke tooke leave of king with crowne,	
	Sir Gawaine made him ready bowne,	*prepared to leave*
50	His armor & his steed.	
	They rode northward 2 dayes and more;	
	By then, Sir Gawaine hungred sore,*	
	Of meate & drinke he had great need.*	
	The Turke wist Gawaine had need of meate,	*knew*
55	& spake to him with words great,	
	Hawtinge uppon hee;*	
	Says, 'Gawaine, where is all thy plenty?*	
	Yesterday thou wast served with dainty,*	
	& noe part thou wold give me,	
60	'But with buffett thou did me sore.	
	Therfore thou shalt have mickle care,	*much*
	& adventures shalt thou see.	
	I wold I had King Arthur heere,	
	& many of thy fellowes in fere,	*together*
65	That beh[o]ves to try mastery.'*	
	He led Sir Gawaine to a hill soe plaine;*	
	The earth opened & closed againe,	
	Then Gawaine was adread.	
	The Merke was comen & the light is gone,	*darkness*
70	Thundering, lightning, snow, & raine,*	
	Therof enough they had.	
	Then spake Sir Gawaine, & sighed sore,	
	'Such wether saw I never afore,	
	In noe stead where I have beene stood ...'	*place, i.e., nowhere*

[*Half a page missing. They journey on beneath the hill, to a point where they see a castle. Here they pause while the Turk warns Gawaine not to eat or drink anything in that place, nor to speak to anyone but himself.*]

75 '... make them noe answere,* p. 40/f. 18v
    But only unto mee.'

    To the Castle they then yode.   *went*
    Sir Gawaine light beside his steed,   *dismounted*
        For horsse the Turke had none.*
80 There they found chamber, bower & hall,
    Richly rayled about with pale,   *richly adorned with fine cloth*
        Seemly to looke uppon.   *Pleasing*

    A Bord was spred within that place,
    All manner of meates & drinkes there was
85   For groomes that might it againe.*
    Sir Gawaine wold have fallen to that fare,
    The Turke bad him leave for care,   *warned him to stop*
        Then waxt he unfaine.*   *became displeased*

    Gawaine said, 'Man, I marvell have
90 That thou ma[y] none of these v[i]ttells spare,   *this food*
        & here is soe great plentye.
    Yett have I more mervaile, by my fay,   *faith*
    That I see neither man nor maid,
        Woma[n] nor child soe free.

95 I had lever now, att mine owne will,   *rather*
    Of this fayre meate to eate my fill
        Then all the gold in Christenty.'   *Christendom*
    The Turke went forth & tarryed nought,
    Meate & drinke he forth brought
100   Was seemly for to see.

    He said, 'Eate, Gawaine, & make thee yare.   *ready*
    In faith, or thou gett victalls more,
        Thou shalt both swinke & sweat   *labour*
    Eate, Gawaine, & spare thee nought.'
105 Sir Gawaine eate as him good thought,
        & well he liked his meate.

    He dranke ale, & after, wine.
    He saith, 'I will be att thy bidding baine*   *obey you willingly*
        Without bost or threat.
110 But one thing I wold thee pray,*

Give me my buffett & let me goe my way,
    I wold not longer be hereatt.'

[*Half a page missing. The Turk refuses to give the return blow, but holds Gawaine to his promise, thereby forcing him to go with him still further until the bargain is kept. They set off once more and arrive at the seashore.*]

	There stood a bote, and ...*	p. 41/f. 19r
	Sir Gawaine left behind his steed,*	
115	He might noe other doe.	
	The Turke said to Sir Gawaine,	
	'He shal be here when thou comes againe,	
	I plight my troth to thee.'	
	Within an hower, as men tell me,	
120	They were sailed over the sea.	
	The Turke said, 'Gawaine, hee!	
	'Heere are we withouten scath,	*harm*
	But now beginneth the great othe,*	
	When [w]e shall adventures doe.'	
125	He lett him see a castle faire,*	
	Such a one he never saw yare,*	*before*
	Noe where in noe country.	
	The Turke said to Sir Gawaine,	
	'Yonder dwells the King of Man,	
130	A heathen soldan is hee.	*sultan*
	'With him he hath a hideous rout	*gang*
	Of giants strong & stout,	
	& uglie to looke uppon.	
	Whosoever had sought farr & neere,	
135	As wide as the world were,	
	Such a companye he cold find none.	
	'Many aventures thou shalt see there,	
	Such as thou never saw yare	
	In all the world about.	
140	Thou shalt see a tenisse ball	
	That never knight in Arthur's hall	
	Is able to give it a lout,	*blow, clout*
	& other adventures there are moe.	*more*
	Wee shall be assayled ere we goe,*	*tested*
145	herof have thou noe doute.	
	'But & yee will take to me good heed,*	*if*

I shall helpe you in time of need.
    For ought I can see,
There shall be none soe strong in stower,   *combat*
150   But [I shall bring thee againe to hi …]'*

[*Half a page missing. The Turk promises that he will deal with any trouble. The two of them make their way to the castle, and possibly encounter a porter, with whom they exchange words, and who takes news of their arrival to the King of Man. They enter the hall to find him feasting, with all his giants about him. The King greets Gawaine.*]

'[… S*ir* Gawaine], stiffe & stowre,   p. 42/f. 19v   *strong in battle*
How fareth thy unckle K*ing* Arthur,*
    & all his company,
& that Bishopp S*ir* Bodwine,*
155   'That will not let my gods alone,
    But spiteth them every day?   *But treats them with contempt*

'He preached much of a crowne of thorne;
He shall ban the time *tha*t he was borne   *curse*
    & ever I catch him may!   *If*
160   I anger more att the spiritual[t]y*   *clergy*
In England nor att the temporaltie,   *than at; laity*
    They goe soe in theire array.   *fine attire*

'And I purpose in full great ire
To brenn their clergy in a fire,*   *burn*
165   & punish them to my pay.'   *satisfaction*
Sitt downe, S*ir* Gawaine, at the bord.'
S*ir* Gawaine answered at that word,
    Saith, 'Nay, that may not be.

'I trow not a venturous k*nigh*t shall   *think*
170   Sitt downe in a king's hall
    Adventures or [he] see.'   *before*
The K*ing* said, 'Gawaine, faire mot then fall!*
Goe feitch me forth my tennisse ball,
    For play will I and see.'*

175   They brought it out w*i*thout doubt.
W*i*th it came a hideous rout
    Of Gyants great & plenty.
All the giants were there then
Heire by the halfe then S*ir* Gawaine,   *Taller*
180   I tell you withouten [n]ay.

There were 17 giants bold of blood,

The Turke & Gowin

      & all thought Gawaine but litle good
          When they thought w*i*th him to play.
      All the giants thoughten then*
185   To have strucke out S*ir* Gawaine's braine.
          Help him God, that best may!

      The ball of brasse was made for the giant's hand,
      There was noe man in all England
          [Were able to carry it ...]

[*Half a page missing. The test with the tennis ball is duly carried out, not by Gawaine but by the Turk, now invisible and who presumably accounts for some of the giants in this way. The test with the axletree, also performed by the Turk, follows*].

190	And sticked a giant in the hall,	p. 43/f. 20r *ran through*
	That grysly can hee grone.	*dreadfully; did*
	The K*i*ng sayd, 'Bray away this axeltree,	*destroy*
	For such a boy I never see.*	
	Yett he shal be assayd better ere he goe,	*tested*
195	'I tell you, soe Mote I tho,*	*so may I thrive*
	W*i*th the 3 adventure & then no more*	
	Befor me at this tide.'	*time*
	Then there stood amongst them all	
	A chimney in the K*i*ng's hall,	*brazier*
200	With barres mickle of pride.	*magnificent*
	There was laid on in that stond	*at that time*
	Coales & wood that cost a pound,	
	That upon it did abide.	
	A giant bad Gawaine assay,	*try*
205	& said, 'Gawaine, begin the play!'*	
	'Thou knowest best how it shold be;	
	& afterwards, when thou hast done,	
	I trow you shal be answered soone,	*I think*
	Either w*i*th boy or me.'	
210	A great giant, I understand,	
	Lift up the chimney with his hand,	
	& sett it downe againe fairly.	
	S*ir* Gawaine was never soe adread	
	Sith he was man on midle earth,	*Since*
215	& cryd on God in his thought.	
	Gawaine unto his boy can say,	
	'Lift this chimney, if you may,	
	*Tha*t is soe worthily wrought.'	*richly made*

	Gawaine's boy to it did leape,	
220	& gatt itt by the bowles great,	*handles*
	& about his head he it flang.	
	3ⁱˢ about his head he it swang,	*thrice*
	That the coales & the red brands …	

[*Half a page missing. Possibly, the Turk accounts for all but one of the rest of the giants. If he is indeed invisible at this point the King of Man may assume that Gawaine is now alone and defenceless. He boasts of how he has slain those of Arthur's knights who have journeyed to his court to challenge him in the past, despite their strength and prowess in battle.*]

	… [he saw] of mickle might, p. 44/f. 20v	*great*
225	& strong were in battell.	

	'I have slaine them thorrow my mastery,	
	& now, Gawaine, I will slay thee,	
	& then I have slaine all the flower.*	
	There went never none againe no tale to tell,	
230	No[e] more shalt thou, thoe thou be fell,	*fierce in combat*
	Nor none that longeth to King Arthur.'	*belongs*

	The Turke was clad invissible gay,*	
	No man cold see him, withouten nay,	
	He was cladd in such a weede.	*garment*
235	He heard their talking lesse & more,	
	& yet he thought they shold find him there*	
	When they shold do that deed.	

	Then he led him into a steddie	*place*
	Werhas was a boyling leade,	*where*
240	& welling uppon hie,	*bubbling up*
	& before it a giant did stand	
	With an Iron forke in his hand	
	That hideous was to see.	

	The giant that looked soe keene,	*fierce*
245	That before Sir Gawaine had never seene,	
	Noe where in noe country.	
	The King said to the giant thoe,	*then*
	'Here is none but wee tow,	
	Let see how best may bee.'	

250	When the giant saw Gawaine's boy there was,*	
	He leapt & threw, & cryed alas	*writhed*
	That he came in that stead.	*place*
	Sir Gawaine's boy to him lept,	

255	& with strenght up him gett, & cast him in the lead.	
	With an Iron forke made of steele He held him downe wondorous weele, Till he was scalded to the dead. Then Sir Gawaine unto the King can say,	*to death*
260	'Without thou wilt agree unto our law,* Eatein is all thy bread.'	*Unless*
	The King spitt on Gawaine the knight. With that, the Turke hent him upright* & into the fire him flang.	
265	& said to Sir Gawaine at the last, 'Noe force, Master, all the perill is past, [Thinke not we tarried too longe] … '	*No matter*

[*Half a page missing. Gawaine thanks the Turk for his aid, and again asks for his return buffet, and is again put off. The Turk wishes him to do one more thing for him instead. Gawaine agrees to do so; whereupon, the Turk leads him to another room, where* …]

	He tooke forth a bason of gold* As an Emperour washe shold,*	p. 45/f. 21r
270	As fell for his degree.	*As befitted his rank*
	He tooke a sword of Mettle free,	*precious metal*
	Saies, 'If ever I did any thing for thee, Doe for me in this stead.	*here*
	Take here this sword of steele	
275	That in battell will bite weele, Therwith strike of my head.'	
	'That I forefend!', said Sir Ga[w]aine,*	*God forbid!*
	'For I wold not have thee slaine For all the gold soe red.'	
280	'Have done, Sir Gawaine, I have no dread,* But in this bason let me bleed,	
	That standeth here in this steed,	*place*
	'And thou shalt see a new play,	*sight*
	With helpe of Mary, that mild mayd,	
285	That saved us from all dread.'	
	He drew forth the brand of steele	*sword*
	That in battell bite wold weele, & there stroke of his head.	
	And when the blood in the bason light,	*fell into*

290 He stood up a stalwortht K*nigh*t,
    *Tha*t day, I undertake,
    & song, 'Te deum laudam[u]s,*   *'We praise thee, O Lord'*
Worshipp be to our lord Jesus,
    That saved us from all wracke!   *ruin*

295 'A, S*ir* Gawaine, blesed thou be!
For all the service I have don thee,
    Thou hast well quitt it me.'   *repaid me*
Then he tooke him by the hand,
    & many a worthy man they fand*   *found*
300 *Tha*t before they neve[r] see.

He said, 'S*ir* Gawaine, w*i*thouten threat,*
Sitt downe boldly at thy meate,
    & I will eate w*i*th thee.
Ladyes all, be of good cheere,
305 Eche ane shall wend to his owne dee[r]
    In all hast that may be.

'First, we will to K*ing* Arthur's hall,
& soone, after yo*ur* husbands send we shall,
    In country where th[ey beene] …'

[*Half a page missing. They travel, with the ladies, to Arthur's court, where Gawaine recounts their adventures to the King.*]

310 'Thus we have brought 17 ladys cleere,   p. 46/f. 21v *beautiful*
*Tha*t there were left in great danger,
    & we have brought them out.'
Then sent they for theire husbands swithe,   *without delay*
& every one tooke his oune wife,
315   & lowlye can they lowte,   *humbly; bow*
And thanked the 2 k*nigh*ts & the K*ing*,
& said the[y] wold be at theire bidding   *service*
    In all England about.

S*ir* Gromer kneeld upon his knee,*
320 Saith, 'Sir K*ing*, & yo*ur* wil be,   *if it be your will*
    Crowne Gawaine K*ing* of Man.'
S*ir* Gawaine kneeled downe by,
& said, 'Lord, nay, not I.
    Give it him, for he it wan,   *won*

325 'For I never purposed to be noe K*ing*,
Never in all my livinge,
    Whilest I am a living man.'

	He said, 'Sir Gromer, take it thee,	
	For Gawaine will never King bee	
330	For no craft that I can.'*	
	Thus endeth the tale that I of meane,	*am telling*
	Of Arthur & his knightes keene,	
	That hardy were & free.	*noble*
	God give them good life, far & neere,	
335	That such talking loves to heere.	
	Amen, for Charity!	ffins

Explanatory Notes

14	*& like a turke he was made*: see Headnote for a discussion about the various meanings of the word 'turke'. At his entrance, the Turk is described merely as 'not hye, but he was broad' (13). Kay's scornful reaction to him certainly suggests that we should see him as an ugly dwarf, but not necessarily deformed.
16–17	The Turk comes in peace, 'as a brother', asking for a 'buffett', i.e., a blow or stroke, usually given with the hand. Gawaine, when asking for his return blow at the Turk's castle, also calls it a 'buffett': decapitation is not in question here.
19	*crabbed*: an epithet used more than once for Kay in the English Arthurian tradition. Note that, as well as neatly describing his character, it also alliterates on his name. Kay's boast at 25–27 is typical of his characterization in this tradition, as is Gawaine's rebuke at 29–30. Cf. the similar scene in *GK* and *CARLE*.
20	*wight*: MED and OED definitions both carry connotations of courage or strength, but the tenor of Kay's speech seems to require 'clever', meaning 'You seem not so bright, if you are not afraid'.
31	It is unusual for Gawaine to be so blunt as to suggest that their visitor might be mad. The Turk takes umbrage at the implication and thus challenges both, as he thinks, hostile knights.
32–33	'You would gain little honour, if you were to kill him'. HF were surely right to interpret 'kill' as the most likely meaning of 'forefore', i.e., derived from the Old English 'forfaran'. *MED forfaren*, of persons: to perish, be destroyed, v,1(a).
34	*thraw*: OED thro | thra, angry, wroth, furious, violent, adj., A3.
37	Note that the Turk addresses Gawaine as 'thou' here, as to an inferior, and indeed does so throughout the poem, except at 146–47, where he is offering him his help.
42–47	A speech so characteristic of Gawaine that it has become almost a commonplace, an epitome of his creed on such matters; see, e.g., *SGGK*, 2132–35, 2156–59; *GK*, 226–31; and *WSG*, 342–53.
52	From this point, Gawaine sheds his knightly, 'Arthurian' characteristics, and becomes the (passive) 'folk' hero rather than the (proactive) 'Arthurian' hero.
53	*& drinke*: the scribal addition of this phrase in 53, above the line, turns this tail-line into a 4-stress line. Line 54 omits '& drinke' (which would have made the line hypermetrical). An example of stanza-linking, where 54 echoes, but does not repeat, 53.
56	'In a loud, haughty voice'. The scribe's 'hawtinge' suggests that he may have mistaken the ending of the word 'hautein' or 'hautin' for '–ing', i.e., a present participle. *MED haut*, proud, haughty, adj.,1(a); of words, speech: loud, adj.1(c).
57–65	This speech seems more appropriate for the King of Man than to the Turk. The Turk's aggressive stance is a high-risk strategy since, as it transpires, he desperately needs Gawaine's help to disenchant him.
58	*Yesterday*: the word can mean not just the previous day, but also recently, lately, some time ago. *MED yesterday*, adv.,1(b).
65	'That mastery can be tested'.

66	*a hill soe plaine*: *MED*'s definition of the adjective 'plaine' – i.e., low in elevation, 1,a(a) – surely indicates that what the poet had in mind was a rounded, smooth, and treeless burial mound. Such mounds feature frequently in folk-tale and myth as entrances to the Otherworld, or to the fairy realms.
70	Possibly the Turk himself conjures up these extreme weather conditions for the occasion.
75	*make them noe answere*: this is the tail-end of the Turk's instruction not to speak to anyone but himself while they are in this Otherworld.
79	The Turk appears to have lost his horse somewhere along the way, since at 51 it is said that 'They rode northward'.
85	'For men who might benefit from it'.
88–97	Gawaine's anger at the Turk's prohibition carries more than a hint of petulance – why should he starve in the midst of plenty?
108–9	Cf. the same sentiment in, e.g., *SGGK*, *GK*, *CARLE*, and the related *Syre Gawene and the Carle of Carelyle*.
110–12	Comically, immediately after his declaration of obedience, Gawaine asks for his return blow there and then, so that he can return to court immediately.
113	The conveniently awaiting boat may be one of those 'Otherworld' self-steering boats common in romance and folk-tale.
114–15	Gawaine has to leave behind his horse – a further abandonment of his knightly status. He is now truly on a par with the Turk, who senses his anxiety about his mount, and comforts him.
123–24	*The great othe*: Gawaine had sworn to go with the Turk whatever happened (42–47), and must now keep his word.
125	The use of the word *lett* seems to imply that Gawaine could not see the castle until the Turk allowed him to.
126	*yare*: possibly an error for 'ere' or 'are', meaning 'before'; the normal meaning of the word is 'ready', as in 101. The same error occurs at 138.
144	*assayled*: 'assailen' means to attack or assault, *MED* v,1(a), but this is more likely to be an error for 'assayed', meaning 'tried', 'tested', as at 194, 204.
146–47	The Turk is plainly telling Gawaine to do what he tells him, and to leave the rest to him.
150	This incomplete line appears to be part of the Turk's promise to Gawaine to overcome the opposition, no matter how strong it is.
152–53	An ironic question on the King of Man's part, Arthur being his mortal enemy.
154 ff.	Cf. the Carle's attack on the clergy, also aimed at Baldwin, in *CARLE*, 269–72. As in that romance, Baldwin is both bishop and knight.
160–62	Hahn considers that this might be a post-Reformation insertion; however, Purdie (2008, 237) suggests that 'it is not impossible that the *Turke* is itself post-Reformation'.
164–71	Comically, the king declares his intention of burning all the clergy in a fire (the fate that eventually overtakes *him*), and in the same breath invites Gawaine to sit and eat. Gawaine's declaration may be an echo of Arthur's habit of not eating on feast days before some 'adventure' has occurred, but equally it may be that in this Otherworld the prohibition on eating and drinking holds, as in the first Otherworld. His appearance at the King of Man's court perhaps mirrors that of the Turk's at Arthur's, also at a mealtime. Here, Gawaine himself is the 'other', the mysterious stranger.
172	'Let things turn out as they may'.
174	*play*: the three tests are all forms of 'Duelling by Alternation', although the 'brazier' test is the only one where this is clear, because of the mutilation of the manuscript. They are evidently seen by the king as an opportunity for sport or entertainment at Gawaine's expense. The rustic connotations of throwing the axletree, and casting the tennisse ball, signal the burlesque nature of this testing of Arthur's chief knight, activities well suited to performance of the text itself.
184–85	In the *Skaldskaparmal*, Thor visits the giant Geirröd, who flings a ball of molten iron at him. Thor catches it and throws it back at Geirröd, who has ducked behind a pillar for protection, only for the ball to pierce both pillar and giant (Faulkes, 1987, 82–83).
193	'Boy' presumably refers to Gawaine himself, the only visitor visible to the giant King of Man, and perceived by him as being very small, rather than to the Turk (cf. Thor

	in the hall of Útgarda-Loki, who refers to him as 'this little fellow' (Faulkes, 1987, 46)). References to 'boy' at 216, 219, 250, and 253 imply that the Turk was invisible throughout the tests, although 232 is the first intimation that the Turk is wearing a 'weede' that renders him invisible.
195	*tho*: a variant of 'thee', i.e., to thrive. Originally, it would have rhymed with 'moe' in the line below, here modernized by the scribe.
196	*the 3 adventure*: Williams (1987, 137) suggests that '3rd' was intended here, which would explain the use of the singular 'adventure' and the comment '& then no more'. There is, however, no evident gap in the MS between '3' and 'adventure'.
205–12	Previous editors have assumed that lines 205–12 are all spoken by the giant, but 206–9 make it clear that it is Gawaine speaking. Lines 208–9 seem to be a retort by Gawaine and an open reference to his 'boy', the Turk, i.e., a slip on the part of an author or scribe. If Gawaine is the speaker, 208–9 could be glossed, 'You'll be answered quick enough by me, whether I'm a "boy" or a knight!', i.e., in response to the king's insult at 193. Fearing the outcome of the test, Gawaine cannily asks the giant to perform it first so that he can see how it is meant to be done. The giant obligingly does so.
228	'And then I shall have slain all the best' (of Arthur's knights).
232–33	'The Turk had on a brightly coloured cloak of invisibility, so that no one could see him'. *OED gay*, bright or lively-looking, esp. in colour; brilliant, showy, adj., A1(a).
236–37	'And yet he was determined to be there when they tried to do that deed'.
250	The Turk becomes visible at this point, throwing the giant into dismay, and thus taken by surprise as the Turk picks him up and casts him into the lead.
260	*law*: HF suggested that this word may have been 'laye' in the original, to rhyme with 'say' in the preceding line. *MED laue*, a rule or set of rules prescribing or restraining conduct, n,1(a).
263	'With that, the Turk seized him and lifted him up'.
268	*a bason of gold*; cf. the ballad *Lamkin* (Child, II, 320–41) in which a gold basin is used for similar purposes. The basic assumption underlying both texts is that the blood of someone of noble birth must be caught in a bowl of precious metal; but whereas nothing comes of it in *Lamkin*, where the Lady and her child are simply killed by Lamkin as an act of revenge, in *TG* the poet links the blood in the basin with the Turk's transformation (282, 289–90). The scene is very much more ritualistic than the beheading in *CARLE* (380–400).
269	'Fit for an emperor to wash in'.
277ff.	Compare Gawaine's horrified reaction to the Carle's similar request for decapitation in *CARLE* (386–88).
280	Unlike the Carle, the Turk does not threaten Gawaine with death if he refuses to comply with his request but comforts and reassures him. This reaction fits its context much better than that of the Carle, who reassures with one breath and threatens with the next.
292	The *Te Deum* is part of the liturgy, but was also sung at times of rejoicing, or for deliverance from evil.
299	The sense demands 'woman' as opposed to 'man' here, since at 304 the Turk addresses the rescued people as 'Ladyes' and promises to send for their husbands as soon as they reach Arthur's court (307–8), although at 305 he slips back into 'his'. At 310–12, the adventurers tell Arthur that they have rescued 17 ladies from 'great danger'. It is possible that lines 299–300 refer to the King of Man's giant companions who were also disenchanted when Gawaine beheaded the Turk; since there are 17 giants as well as 17 ladies, it may be that they were originally the husbands. This would not explain, however, why husbands are produced once the company has returned to court.
301–3	Significantly, the Turk now tells Gawaine to sit and eat, and he himself will eat with him, which suggests that he too was prohibited from eating in this Otherworld until he too had been disenchanted. Now the enchantments are over, the prohibitions on eating and drinking apparently no longer apply. Note that the Turk is still organizing Gawaine even now, and retains the initiative right up to the moment when Gawaine refuses the Kingship of Man.

319   *Sir Gromer*: it is not clear where this name comes from, or if it is in any way related to the antagonist of *WSG*, Sir Gromer Somer Joure (see note to line 183, p. 111, below), or to his counterpart of the same name in *LMD*, also called Grummor Grummorson. See John Withrington, '"He Telleth the Number of the Stars; He Calleth Them All By Their Names": The Lesser Knights of Sir Thomas Malory's *Morte Darthur*', *Quondam et Futurus* 3(4) (1993), p. 19 and Sir Thomas Malory, *Le Morte Darthur*, ed. P. J. C. Field, Arthurian Studies LXXX, 2 vols (Cambridge: D. S. Brewer, 2013), II, 875.

330   'No skill that I have would persuade him'. Gawaine's reluctance to take rewards for himself is a persistent theme running through Arthurian romance, particularly in the French tradition.

Textual Notes

Possibly because he was not intending to make use of *TG* in his collection, or perhaps because he could find no source for it, Percy made no general comments concerning provenance or similarities with other texts. This is in contrast to *MSG*, which immediately follows *TG* in the PF.

6   *kempys*: 'kempys i.e. Warriors.' [P].
12   *burne*: 'barne. i.e. homo.' [P]; *ca[m]e*: cane [MS]. Hahn makes the plausible suggestion that P may have overwritten this word himself, on the grounds that P assumed the word read 'taite' (which is also what Madden transcribed).
14   *a turke*: throughout *TG* this word is written with an initial lower case *t*. Where reference is made in the text and critical apparatus to this individual as Gawaine's protagonist, an initial capital has been adopted ('the Turke').
25   *stalworth*: 'i.e. stout.' [P].
29   *Kay*: scribe first wrote 'hay' and emended clumsily.
34   *Turke*: turkes [MS].
35   *yo[u]*: your [MS].
36   [*Though y*]*e*: illegible because of dampstain, reading taken from HF; *bre[m]e*: brenne [MS]; 'breme. i.e. fierce' [P].
37   Only the lower parts of this line are now visible: reading supported by HF. Sense and rhyme support that the line should conclude 'given me', but there is no sign of a descender for a *g*. While there is the trace of another letter towards the end of the line – the descender of a long-tailed *s* or an *?f* – neither of these letters would fit this interpretation, and it may not be part of the line at all.
40   *middlearth*: 'middle-eard i.e. middle earth' [P].
51   *northward*: 'northard': [MS], *w* interlined, with caret; 'and' interlined, with caret [MS].
53   *& drinke*: interlined, with caret [MS].
58   *wast*: loop above *w* suggests that the scribe began to write 'hast'.
62   *shalt*: 'shat', with *l* inserted [MS].
63   *heere*: 'heer', with *e* added afterwards [MS].
65   *beh[o]ves*: 'behaves' [MS], 'behoves qu' [P].
66   *hill*: 'his' emended to 'hill' [MS].
75   '... *make them noe answere*'. The top half of this line has been cropped, and only the last three words can be discerned relatively clearly. Given line 76, it seems reasonable to assume that the couplet represents an instruction by the Turk, in which case 'make' makes more sense than HF's 'made'. The opening words to 75 could well have been 'Look thou'.
80   *& hall*: *h* squeezed in between *&* and *a* [MS].
81   *rayled*: 'rayled' [P].
83   *spred*: 'sped', with *r* inserted above, without caret.
85   *againe*: first *a* blotted, possibly erased, to read 'gaine' [MS].
88   'he' interlined, with caret [MS].
90   *ma[y]*: *y* blotted, most likely by scribe overwriting an *n*, i.e., mistakenly repeating the word 'man' from the line above [MS]; *v[i]ttells*: 'vttells' [MS], 'vittells' [P].
94   *woma[n]*: hole in MS.

100	*see*: 'eate' crossed out, replaced by 'see' [MS], possibly in unconscious anticipation of the following line.
103	*swinke*: 'swinke. i.e. labour.' [P].
112	*hereatt*: 'hereat' [P].
113	Tops of last three words missing because of upward slant of line at top of page. The first letter of the last word, however, could well be a *y*, as in 'in he yode/in they yode': 'yode' would fit both the sense and rhyme, and the fragment remaining is strikingly similar to the conclusion of 77.
117	*againe*: first *a*: scribe wrote *g*, then crossed out the tail to make an *a* [MS].
124	[*w*]*e*: 'he' [MS]; *doe*: the tail-rhymes in this stanza suggest that 'see' might have been the original rhyme (cf. 'country', 127 and 'hee', 130).
127	*wher in*: 'wherin' [MS], 'where in' [P].
142	*lout*: 'Lout. i.e. blow' [P].
150	But [*I shall bring thee againe to hi* ...]: reading supplied by HF. Only the tops of some letters now visible after *I*, but the remains of 'shall' are very similar to the identical word just above it, and the 'agai' of 'againe' is still just visible.
151	[... *Sir Gawaine*]. No trace remains: reading supplied by HF. The lower parts of 'stiffe & stowre' are just legible.
155	*gods*: 'goods', with second *o* blotted [MS].
160	*spiritual*[*t*]*y*: 'spiritually' [MS], 'spiritualty' [P].
161	*nor* inserted above line, with caret [MS].
171	[*he*]: 'you' [MS], 'hee see' [P].
179	*Heire*: 'heires' [MS], 'higher' [P].
180	[*n*]*ay*: 'may' [MS].
182	*all*: 'all' repeated and crossed out [MS]; *litle*: 'lille', second *l* corrected to large *t* [MS].
185	*braine*: the *b* possibly emended from a *t* [MS].
187	*hand*: possibly 'hands' [MS]: misshapen tag on *d*.
189	Reading supplied by HF. The line is now completely missing, although Madden records the first three words.
194	*shal be*: 'shalbe' [MS], *b* corrected from an indecipherable letter.
197–98	The scribe left a space between these lines. P added a stanza-division, but then erased it, leaving it as part of a 9-liner.
198	*amongst*: 'amonght' [MS], emended to 'amongst' by adding a downward loop to the secretary *h*.
199	*the*: 'they' [MS].
209–10	The scribe left a space after 209; P added a stanza-division, but the rhymes match, indicating a 9-line stanza.
210	*understand*: *r* interlined, without caret. The scribe wrote an *r* but masked it with the following *s*, thereby necessitating the interpolation.
215	*cryd*: 'chyd', corrected clumsily [MS]. Between 215 and 216 there is another scribal gap, with an erased stanza-division.
216	*his*: 'bis'. The scribe began to write 'boy' and emended [MS].
224	Reading supplied by HF. The top of the page is cropped at this point. While the last three words of the line are relatively clear, 'he saw' can be inferred from the scribal strokes remaining.
230	*No*[*e*]: 'nor' [MS].
231	*longeth*: 'longhth', emended to 'longeth' [MS].
232	*invissible*: 'invissible' [P].
235	*talking*: 'talkings' [MS].
238	*steddie*: 'stede, place' [P].
239	*Werhas*: 'whereas' [P].
240	*welling*: 'walling up, on high boiling up &c.' [P].
243	*see*: 'hee' emended to 'see' [MS].
267	Entire line cropped. HF has 'thinke not we tarrie too long', but P's 'tarried too longe' fits better the sense. Madden has 'Thinke not we tarried too long'.
271	*a* interlined, with caret [MS].

276	*strike*: 'stricke' [MS].
277	*Ga[w]aine*: 'Gavaine' [MS].
292	*laudam[u]s*: 'laudams' [MS].
293	*our*: 'uur', with first *u* emended to *o* [MS].
300	*neve[r]*: *r* incomplete [MS]; 'neuer' [P].
308	*your*: superscript *r* obscured by downstroke of *K* in line above [MS].
309	*In country where th[ey beene]* ... : reading supplied by HF; scribe began to write 'coutry' and emended in mid-word. Only 'where th[ey]' (or possibly 'wherat') now discernible.
310	HF's edition for 310 reads 'There they wold ... abide'. However, the MS has deteriorated at 309 to the extent that there is no trace of a succeeding line on this page. Madden's edition, published 28 years before HF, also concludes at 309, and P offers no comment at this point. It seems odd that HF were able to read a line that was not visible to Madden almost 30 years beforehand. On that basis, HF's reading has not been followed.
314	*one*: interlined, with caret [MS].
317	*the[y]*: 'the' [MS].
320	*your*: superscript *u* clumsily emended to *r* [MS].
336	*ffins*: following the last word of this line, the scribe has written 'ffins' to signify the end of the piece. The title of *MSG* follows almost immediately afterwards.

The Marriage of Sir Gawaine

John Withrington

The Marriage of Sir Gawaine (*MSG*) has suffered particularly at the hands of Humphrey Pitt's household, the tearing in half of the PF resulting in the loss of approximately 54 stanzas out of a probable total of 111.[1] The ballad is written as a series of 4-line stanzas rhyming *abcb*, the first and third lines containing four stresses with the second and fourth containing three. As elsewhere in the PF, incremental repetition contributes significantly to the ballad's dramatic effect, creating a sense of rhythm and tension as the narrative progresses.[2]

Alongside 'Boy and Mantle' (*BM*), *MSG* played a pivotal role in the development of the *Reliques*. From the outset, *MSG* represented for Percy a bridge between the ancient and the modern, firm evidence of a tradition of minstrelsy reaching back to the Middle Ages and beyond, so much so that he argued that the ballad was the direct inspiration for Chaucer's 'The Wife of Bath's Tale'.[3] The first sheet to be pulled from publication in the *Reliques* of 1765, the so-called sheet B, contained *BM* and part of *MSG*, and it was at this point that Percy, having sent Sheet B to Warton on 28 February 1762 (*Letters*, III, 33), abandoned the idea of publishing the 'Fragment' as it stood, deciding instead to rewrite *MSG* in its entirety.[4] This decision altered the course of the whole enterprise, steering it away from being an antiquarian collection of rough-hewn curiosities towards an anthology of burnished material suited to the popular taste of the period. The revision of this single text thus changed the ethos of the entire collection and proved fundamental to the success of the project (Groom, 1999, 225–27). The version of *MSG* published in 1765 represented therefore a text far removed from the original: of the 217 lines found in PF only 36 made it either unchanged or with occasionally modernized spelling into what now became a 316-line rewrite, representing not so much the ballad as it was as the ballad as it should have been.[5] But while Percy indicated that revisions had taken place,[6] the extent of these changes only became apparent some 30 years later when a transcription of *MSG* as it appears in the Folio MS was published at the end of the fourth edition of the *Reliques*.[7]

The mutilation of the text in PF is particularly unfortunate since *MSG* occupies a significant place in our literary heritage, not just in the history of Arthurian romance and popular ballads, but because it is one of only three known analogues to Chaucer's 'The Wife of Bath's Tale' (*WBT*), the others being 'The Tale of Florent' in *Confessio Amantis* (*FLOR*), the work of the fourteenth-century poet John Gower, and the anonymous fifteenth-century poem *The Wedding of Sir Gawain and Dame*

Ragnell (*WSG*).[8] All four texts make use of two motifs, i.e., an individual must answer the riddle 'What is it that women most desire?', and a 'Loathly Lady' is transformed into a beautiful woman. P. J. C. Field categorizes *FLOR*, *WSG*, and *MSG* as 'first-order analogues' to *WBT*, observing that Maynadier wanted to add two texts to this grouping, i.e., the popular seventeenth-century ballad, 'The Knight and the Shepherd's Daughter', and 'King Henry', first recorded *c.*1800 by Sir Walter Scott.[9] But the deeper origins of the English 'Loathly Lady' stories lie in what Field calls the 'second-order analogues', i.e., 'Irish stories recorded from the eleventh century onwards which contain material from Irish mythology, legend and early history' and which, as Maynadier noted, allegorize the granting of sovereignty over Erin (Field, 2010, 61).[10] Sigmund Eisner, while following Maynadier, disagreed that an Arthurian setting for the Loathly Lady stories was a relatively late development, and concluded that in place of the lady granting the man sovereignty over territory, the man granting her sovereignty over himself reflected the influence of what has become known as 'courtly love'.[11] As a result Field argues convincingly that this means that the archetype of the English Loathly Lady stories most likely emerged from the court of Marie de Champagne in the twelfth century, a court that, of course, supported the Arthurian poet Chrétien de Troyes.[12]

But while the Arthurian content in Chaucer is minimal and in Gower non-existent, there is clearly a close relationship between the narratives found in *MSG* and *WSG*, although it is impossible to be more precise than this. Nonetheless these two texts differ quite widely in tone: to take but one example, in *WSG* the hag specifically asks for Gawain's hand in marriage as the price Arthur must pay to solve the riddle 'What is it that women love best?', while in *MSG* Arthur freely offers her Gawaine without even being asked. Whether both texts derive independently from a descendant of the original archetype, or *MSG* from *WSG*, is impossible to say, but it is not inconceivable that the ballad should have appeared as part of a collection in the PF some 150 years after the date of *WSG* by means of a circuitous route, having been shaped in the intervening years by various performances.[13] However, unlike *MSG*'s cheerful simplicity, *WSG* is a more complicated work. Stephen Shepherd was the first to draw attention to the text's burlesque dimension and comic features, for example the less than flattering portrayal of Arthur and the poet's seemingly deliberate series of false endings,[14] and yet *WSG* is not wholly light entertainment in nature: references to the death of Ragnell and Gawain's lasting sorrow are in direct contrast to the poem's more humorous touches, while the anonymous author's references to his imprisoned state are surely sincere.[15] Complicating the extent of a possible relationship between the two texts is that both texts as we have them are damaged: *MSG* has suffered omissions through the host manuscript being torn in half in places, while the Rawlinson MS has a leaf missing between folios 136 and 137, its stanzaic structure is corrupt, and the text appears as a single narrative block.[16]

Assumptions that *WSG* and *MSG* have both come down to us unchanged and in a state that reflects the original author's intentions is to deny the possibility of either tale 'growing in the telling', and to impose modern values that probably would have been alien to a contemporary audience. For example, of Ragnell's death in *WSG*, Mary Leech pronounces that 'Masculine authority is reaffirmed and the troublesome female grotesque is transmuted into an iconic ideal of patriarchal womanhood', and this is why Ragnell's demise is inevitable.[17] However, a far more likely explanation is simply that for a late fifteenth-century audience Gawaine's reputation as a ladies' man precluded the possibility that the hero would settle down with Ragnell and enjoy a long life of connubial bliss.[18] Similarly Leech's argument that Ragnell's teeth and tusks relate to a type of 'threatening sexual imagery, yet a disruptive sexual nature is associated with all women as fallen daughters of Eve' ignores the possibility that such a description exploits the grotesque for simple humorous effect, deliberately subverting ideals of feminine beauty, and thus offering comic possibilities as part of a dramatic performance.[19] The appearance of *MSG* in the mid-seventeenth-century PF was surely attributable to its entertainment value as a text that was read and performed, and which, like *WSG*, would have been shaped by authors, performers, and audience alike. Ignoring the possibility of organic growth and the richness that comes with refining and performing pieces that were undoubtedly meant to be seen, heard, and read is to invite the imposition of a patina of latter-day values. In the case of *WSG*, while there is evidence of a serious undercurrent to the poem, its humour and dramatic potential are obvious. These are attributes which also apply and are most certainly to the fore in its later, balladic counterpart *The Marriage of Sir Gawaine*.

Notes

[1] Percy estimated that the loss of half a page was equivalent to nine stanzas (1794 *Reliques*, III, 350).

[2] For example, lines 3–4 and 5–6; 22–23 and 24–25; 32–33 and 84–85; 130–31 and 134–35. While the dialect of *WSG* is probably Midlands, identifying the provenance of *MSG* through its use of language is next to impossible, given the likely number of iterations it will have undergone, through recital and performance, in the course of its history (Rhiannon Purdie, *Anglicising Romance: Tail-Rhyme and Genre in Medieval English Literature* (Cambridge: D. S. Brewer, 2008), p. 239).

[3] Percy's belief that Chaucer was indebted to *MSG* is reflected in his marginal comment next to the title on f. 21v (see Textual Notes). He stated this belief boldly in a letter to Thomas Warton of 28 May 1761, enclosing transcripts of both *MSG* and *BM*, writing of the former that 'I am of opinion that he borrowed his *wife* [sic] *of Bath's Tale* from it' (*Letters*, III, 4), repeating this view as fact six months later in a letter to Evan Evans: 'The *fragment* is certainly more ancient than the time of Chaucer, who took his *Wife of Bath's Tale* from *it*, as any one upon perusal will be convinced, and not that *the song* was taken from Chaucer' (*Letters*, V, 22).

[4] The Percy–Darby papers, Percy's own working copy of the *Reliques*, show that Percy continued *MSG* after the point at which the printed extract had finished, drawing upon PF itself. As for the argument that the language of *MSG* was 'not so ancient' as the time of Chaucer, Percy wrote 'let it be remembered, that an old ballad cannot be expected to have been preserved so faithfully, as compositions of a less popular kind. This perhaps was only handed down from mouth to mouth, and at length communicated to writing from the fallacious memory of some illiterate harper' (quoted by Groom, 1996, III, 392; Groom provides a complete transcript on pp. 391–401).

[5] While Percy not unreasonably attempted to fill some gaps in the original, its content and order were not sacrosanct: for example, the 'happy ending' postscript to the story, whereby the lady is welcomed into Round Table society, is completely missing in his version.

6 Percy's annotation on f. 21v – 'To supply *the* Defects' – may be a personal aide-memoire about the perceived need to revise the text as he found it. In the 1765 foreword to *MSG* (*Reliques*, III, 11), he wrote that 'The original was so extremely mutilated, half of every leaf being torn away, that without large supplements, etc. it would have been improper for this collection: these it has therefore received, such as they are. They are not here particularly pointed out, because the FRAGMENT itself will some time or other be given to the public'.

7 Provoked by Ritson into publishing the original, Percy continued vigorously to defend his earlier revisions: by printing the text as found in the manuscript critics would hence see 'how unfit for publication many of the pieces would have been, if all the blunders, corruptions, and nonsense of illiterate Reciters and Transcribers had been superstitiously retained, without some attempt to correct and emend them' (1794 *Reliques*, III, 350).

8 The *Confessio Amantis* was written by 1389 and underwent several revisions in the period up to about 1399, while *WBT* is thought to have been written in the early to mid-1390s. Whereas the *Confessio Amantis* exists in three different recensions and has survived in 49 manuscripts, *WSG* is found uniquely in Bodl. MS Rawlinson C.86 (*c*.1500). See John Withrington and P. J. C. Field, 'The Wife of Bath's Tale', in Robert M. Correale and Mary Hamel (eds), *Sources and Analogues of the Canterbury Tales*, 2 vols (Cambridge: D. S. Brewer, 2005), II, 405–9.

9 P. J. C. Field, 'What Women Really Want: The Genesis of Chaucer's Wife of Bath's Tale', in Elizabeth Archibald and David F. Johnson (eds), *Arthurian Literature* 27 (Cambridge: D. S. Brewer, 2010), pp. 59–61. Field also considers the early seventeenth-century ballad, 'Of a Knight and a Fair Virgin', which appears to be based on *WBT*. In October 1762, Warton drew Percy's attention to the fact that 'A New Sonnet of a knight & a faire Virgin', set in King Arthur's time, and featuring 'the old story of Q. Guenever desiring to know *What* women love most', was to be found in Richard Johnson's 1612 *A crowne garland of goulden roses* (*Letters*, III, 52). See Explanatory Note to line 183, below.

10 See G. H. Maynadier, *The Wife of Bath's Tale: Its Sources and Analogues* (London: David Nutt, 1901).

11 See Sigmund Eisner, *A Tale of Wonder: A Source Study of the Wife of Bath's Tale* (Wexford: John English, 1957).

12 Field (2010, 59–64) provides an excellent summary of Maynadier and Eisner's positions, the implications for the origin of the English Loathly Lady tales, and how such themes came to be placed in an Arthurian context.

13 See above, pp. 21–24. 'Syr Gawen' featured as part of Captain Cox's repertoire in 1575 (above, p. 34). The Rawlinson MS also contains the unique copy of *Sir Landevale* (see pp. 114–19, below).

14 Stephen H. A. Shepherd, 'No Poet Has His Travesty Alone: *The Weddynge of Sir Gawen and Dame Ragnell*', in Jennifer Fellows et al. (eds), *Romance Reading on the Book: Essays on Medieval Literature Presented to Maldwyn Mills* (Cardiff: University of Wales Press, 1996), pp. 112–28.

15 Field was the first to raise the possibility that references to imprisonment indicated that Malory could have been the author of *WSG*: see his 'Malory and *The Wedding of Sir Gawen and Dame Ragnell*', *Archiv für das Studium der neueren Sprachen und Literaturen* 219 (1982), pp. 374–81. Field (2010, 80) describes as 'persuasive' the agreement of Ralph Norris with this view. See Ralph Norris, 'Sir Thomas Malory and *The Wedding of Sir Gawain and Dame Ragnell* Reconsidered', *Arthuriana* 19 (2009), pp. 82–102. Were Malory the author of *WSG*, then this would mean the text was composed before Malory's death in March 1471.

16 Some tail lines in *WSG* have an extra stress (e.g. 227), some couplets are overlong (167–68), and on several occasions the stanzaic structure breaks down completely. Norris thinks it likely that 'the author of the *Wedding* constructed his poem by combining elements from "The Tale of Florent" and "The Wife of Bath's Tale" and added details from minor sources' (2009, 85). However, 'The poem suffers from corruptions which make it impossible to say with certainty how accurate a reflection the existing version is of the poet's original work' (John Withrington, *The Wedding of Sir Gawain and Dame Ragnell*, Lancaster Modern Spelling Texts (Lancaster: Lancaster University, 1991), p. 19). The clumsy nature of plagiarism, down to *WBT*'s use of the first person plural,

surely points to the prospect of at least one later hand seeking to 'improve' upon an original (see also Shepherd, 1996, 117–18).

[17] Mary Leech, 'Why Dame Ragnell Had to Die: Feminine Usurpation of Masculine Authority in "The Wedding of Sir Gawain and Dame Ragnell"', in S. Elizabeth Passmore and Susan B. Carter (eds), *The English 'Loathly Lady' Tales* (Kalamazoo, MI: Medieval Institute Publications, 2007), p. 228. 'To feel sad or perturbed ... at the death of Ragnell risks missing the joke' (Shepherd, 1996, 121).

[18] Withrington, 1991, lines 817–22n; Field, 2010, 70.

[19] Leech, 2007, 217. Indications that the physical descriptions of Ragnell may have been subject to subsequent embellishment include the statement at line 238, which says that her neck was 'long and therto greatt', an image contradicted by line 555, which states that 'Nek forsoth on her was none i-seen'.

Editions

Child, I, ii, 288–96.

Hahn, 359–71.

HF, I, 103–18.

Madden, 288–97.

Shepherd, Stephen H. A., *Middle English Romances: Authoritative Texts, Sources and Backgrounds, Criticism* (New York: W. W. Norton & Co., 1995), pp. 380–87.

Withrington, John, *The Wedding of Sir Gawain and Dame Ragnell*, Lancaster Modern Spelling Texts (Lancaster University: Lancaster, 1991).

Further Reading

Field, P. J. C., 'What Women Really Want: The Genesis of Chaucer's Wife of Bath's Tale', in Elizabeth Archibald and David F. Johnson (eds), *Arthurian Literature* 27 (Cambridge: D. S. Brewer, 2010), pp. 59–85.

Rogers, Gillian, 'The Percy Folio Manuscript Revisited', in Maldwyn Mills, Jennifer Fellows, and Carol M. Meale (eds), *Romance in Medieval England* (Cambridge: D. S. Brewer, 1991), pp. 55–56.

Withrington, John, '*The Weddynge of Sir Gawen and Dame Ragnell* and *The Marriage of Sir Gawaine*', *AE*, 207–10.

Withrington, John, and Field, P. J. C., 'The Wife of Bath's Tale', in Robert M. Correale and Mary Hamel (eds), *Sources and Analogues of the Canterbury Tales*, 2 vols (Cambridge: D. S. Brewer, 2005), II, 405–48.

The Marriage of Sir Gawaine

  Kinge Arthur lives in merry Carleile,   *p. 46/f. 21v*
    & seemely is to see,   *comely*
  & there he hath with him Queene Genev*er*,
    *Tha*t bride soe bright of blee.   *lady; fair of face*

5 And there he hath with him Queene Geneve[r],
    *Tha*t bride soe bright in bower,
  & all his barons about him stoode
    *Tha*t were both stiffe & stowre.   *bold and strong*

  The K*ing* kept a royall Christmasse
10   Of mirth & great honor,
  [& when] …

[*Half a page is missing. Arthur travels to Tarn Wadling, and there meets with a bold baron. The baron gives Arthur an ultimatum: either to fight or pay a ransom. Arthur agrees to the latter, and to return on New Year's Day.*]

  'And bring me word what thing [it] is   *p. 47/f. 22r*
    *Tha*t a woman most desire.
  This shal be thy ransome, Arthur,' he sayes,
15   'for I'le have noe other hier.'   *reward*

  K*ing* Arthur then held up his hand,
    According thene as was the law;
  He tooke his leave of the baron there,
    & homward can he draw.   *did he go*

20 And when he came to Merry Carlile,
    To his chamber he is gone,
  & ther came to him his Cozen S*ir* Gawaine   *kinsman*
    As he did make his mone.   *complaint*

  And there came to him his cozen S*ir* [G]awaine
25   *Tha*t was a curteous knight,
  'Why sigh you soe sore, unckle Arthur?' he said,   *sorely, heavily*
    'Or who hath done thee unright?'   *wrong*

  'O peace, O peace, thou gentle Gawaine,
    *Tha*t faire may thee beffall,*
30 For if thou knew my sighing soe deepe,
    Thou wold not mervaile att all;

  'Ffor when I came to Tearne Wadling,
    A bold barron there I fand,*   *found*

The Marriage of Sir Gawaine

With a great club upon his backe,
35   Standing stiffe & strong;*

'And he asked me wether I wold fight,
   Or from him I shold begone,
O[r] else I must him a ransome pay
   & soe depart him from.

'To fight with him I saw noe cause,
40   Methought it was not meet, — *appropriate*
For he was stiffe & strong withall,
   His strokes were nothing sweete; — *would have been*

'Therfor this is my ransome, Gawaine,
45   I ought to him to pay:
I must come againe, as I am sworne, — *return*
   Upon the New Yeer's day.

'And I must brin[g] him [word] [w]hat thing it [is] ...'

[*Half a page missing. Gawaine probably suggests to Arthur that they collect answers to the riddle posed in 12–13. Arthur then makes himself ready to meet with the baron on the appointed day and to present him with his findings, i.e., the 'letters' referred to at 88.*]

Then King Arthur drest him for to ryde,   p. 48/f. 22v   *got ready*
50   In one soe rich array,*
Toward the fore-said Tearne Wadling,
   That he might keepe his day. — *In order (that)*

And as he rode over a more, — *moor*
   Hee see a lady where shee sate
55 Betwixt an oke & a greene hollen: — *holly tree*
   She was cladd in red scarlett.

Then there as shold have stood her mouth*
   Then there was sett her eye,
The other was in her forehead fast
60   The way that she might see.

Her nose was crooked & turnd [out]ward,
   Her mouth stood foule a-wry;
A worse formed lady then shee was
   Never man saw with his eye!

65 To halch upon him, King Arthur, — *greet*
   This lady was full faine, — *willing*

But *K*i*ng* Arthur had forgott his lesson,*
    What he shold say againe.   *in return*

70 'What knight art thou,' the lady sayd,
    'That will not speak to me?'
Of me be thou nothing dismayd
    Tho I be ugly to see;

'For I have halched you curteouslye,
    & you will not me againe;
75 Yett I may happen, *S*i*r* Knight,' shee said,
    'To ease thee of thy paine.'   *unhappiness*

'Give thou ease me, lady' he said,   *If, assist*
    'Or helpe me any thing,   *in any way*
Thou shalt have gentle Gawaine, my cozen,
80   & marry him with a ring.'

'Why, if I help thee not, thou noble *K*i*ng* Arthur,
    Of thy owne heart's desiringe,
[Of gentle Gawaine …']

[*Half a page missing. Arthur and the hag presumably agree to the terms by which she will save the King's life, and Arthur keeps to his appointed rendezvous.*]

And when he came to the Tearne Wadling,   p. 49/f. 23r
85   The baron there cold he [finde],*   *did*
With a great weapon on his backe,
    Standing stiffe & stronge.

And then he tooke *K*i*ng* Arthur's letters in his hand
    & away he cold them fling,
90 & then he puld out a good browne sword,   *bright*
    & cryd himselfe a *k*i*ng.*   *proclaimed*

And he sayd, 'I have thee & thy land, A[r]thur,
    To doe as it pleaseth me,
For this is not thy ransome sure:*
95   Therfore yeeld thee to me.'

And then bespoke him noble Arthur,
    & bad him hold his hand,   *commanded*
'& give me leave to speake my mind
    In defence of all my land.'

100 He said 'As I came over a more,
    I see a lady where shee sate

Betweene an oke & a green hollen;
    Shee was clad in red scarlett;

'And she says "A woman will have her will,
105   & this is all her cheef desire":
Doe me right, as thou art a baron of sck[i]ll,*
    This is thy ransome & all thy hyer.'

He sayes, 'An early vengeance light on her!   *befall*
    She walkes on yonder more;
110 It was my sister that told thee this;
    & she is a misshappen hore!

'But heer I'le make mine avow to God
    To doe her an evill turne,
For an ever I may thate fowle theefe ge[tt],   *if*
115   In a fyer I will her burne!'

[*Half a page missing. Having disposed of the threat posed by the baron, Arthur visits the hag to keep his part of the bargain.*]

[T]he 2ᵈ part:

Sir Lancelott & Sir Steven bold*   p. 50/f. 23v
    They rode with them that day,
And the formost of the company
    There rode the steward Kay.

120 Soe did Sir Banier & Sir Bore,
    Sir Garrett with them soe gay,
Soe did Sir Tristeram that gentle knight,*
    To the forrest f[r]esh & gay.

And when he came to the greene forrest,
125   Underneath a greene holly tree
Their sate that lady in red scarlet
    That unseemly was to see.

Sir Kay beheld this Lady's face
    & looked upon her s[w]ire,*   *neck*
130 'Whosoever kisses this lady,' he sayes,
    'Of his kisse he stands in feare!'

Sir Kay beheld the lady againe,
    & looked upon her snout,
'Whosoever kisses this lady,' he saies,
135   'Of his kisse he stands in doubt!'   *fear*

'Peace, cozen Kay,' then said Sir Gawaine,*
    'Amend thee of thy life;   *change your ways*
For there is a knight amongst us all
    That must marry her to his wife.'

140 'What! Wedd her to wiffe?' then said Sir Kay,
    'In the Divell's name anon!
Gett me a wiffe where e're I may,
    For I had rather be s[l]aine!'

Then some tooke up their hawkes in hast,   *haste*
145   & some tooke up their hounds,
& some sware they wold not marry her
    For Citty nor for towne.*

And then be-spake him noble King Arthur,
    & sware there 'By this day,
150 'For a litle foule sight & misliking ...'*

[*Half a page missing. Gawaine agrees to marry the hag, the wedding takes place, and the couple retire for the night. The hag magically turns into a beautiful woman.*]

Then shee said 'Choose thee, Gentle Gawaine,   p. 51/f. 24r
    Truth as I doe say,
Wether thou wilt have me in this liknesse
    In the night or else in the day.'

155 And then bespake him gentle Gawaine,
    With one soe mild of moode,*   *to*
'Sayes, "Well I know what I wold say –*
    God grant it may be good!"   *the right thing to say*

To have thee fowle in the night
160   When I with thee shold play;
Yet I had rather, if I might,
    Have thee fowle in the day.'

'What! When lords goe with ther [f]eires,' shee said,   *companions*
    'Both to the ale & wine?
165 Alas! Then I must hyde myselfe,
    I must not goe withinne.'*

And then bespake him gentle Gawaine,
    Said 'Lady, that's but a skill;*
And because thou art my owne lady,
170   Thou shalt have all thy will.'

The Marriage of Sir Gawaine

Then she said, 'Blesed be thou gentle Gawain[e],
    This day *tha*t I thee see;
For as thou see me att this time,
    From henc[e]forth I wil be:

175 'My father was an old knight,
    & yett it chanced soe   *happened*
That he marryed a younge lady
    *Tha*t brought me to this woe.

'Shee witched me, being a faire young Lad[y],   *bewitched*
180   To the greene forrest to dwell;
& there I must walke in woman's liknesse,
    Most like a feend of hell.

'She witched my brother to a Carlis[h] [b] ...'*

[*Half a page missing. Gawaine's wife explains that by granting her the sovereignty of choice the transformation to beauty is permanent, and Gawaine rejoices in his good fortune. Arthur's court is informed of the circumstances behind the transformation, and she is presented to the court.*]

'That looked soe foule, & that was wont   p. 52/f. 24v
185   On the wild more to goe.'

'Come kisse her, Brother Kay,' then said S*i*r Gawaine,
    '& amend the of thy liffe;   *thee*
I sweare this is the same lady
    *Tha*t I marryed to my wiffe!'

190 S*i*r Kay kissed that lady bright,   *fair*
    Standing upon his feete;
He swore, as he was trew knight,
    The spice was never soe sweete.

'Well, Co*zen* Gawaine,' sayes S*i*r Kay,
195   'Thy chance is fallen arright;
For thou hast gotten one of the fairest maids
    I ever saw w*i*th my sight.'

'It is my fortune,' said S*i*r Gawaine;
    'For my unckle Arthur's sake
200 I am glad as grasse wold be of raine,*
    Great Joy that I may take.'

S*i*r Gawaine tooke the lady by the one arme,
    S*i*r Kay tooke her by the tother,

They led her straight to King Arthur
205   As they were brother & brother.*   *As if*

   King Arthur welcomed them there all,
      & soe did Lady Genever, his queene,
   With all the knights of the Round Table
      Most seemly to be seene.

210   King Arthur beheld that lady faire
      That was soe faire & bright;
   He thanked Christ in Trinity
      For Sir Gawaine, that gentle knight.

   Soe did the knights, both more & lesse,
215   Rejoyced all that day
   For the good chance that hapened was
      [To] Sir Gawaine [&] his l[ady gay].

Explanatory Notes

29 'That good fortune will come your way'.
33 *fand*: the failure to rhyme with the last word of line 35 makes it likely that the original readings for these lines was '… me fang' (i.e., 'took me prisoner'; *OED fang*, to catch, apprehend, get into one's power, v,1(c)) and 'strang', i.e., 'strong'. Alternatives could be 'feng/streng' or 'fong/strong' (*MED fongen*, to capture (someone), take (prisoner), v,3 cites several examples of both 'fange' and 'fonge'). See also note to line 85, below, and Textual Notes 33 and 85.
35 'Standing resolute and strong' (*MED stif*, resolutely, determinedly, staunchly, adv.,1(b)).
50 'Suitably dressed in the finest manner'.
57–60 'Where her mouth should have been, she had one eye. The other eye was set in her forehead, so that she could see her way'. Presumably the hag has a Cyclopean appearance, with her mouth set off to one side of her face (62).
67–68 Perhaps from shock, Arthur forgets to behave in the courteous fashion to be expected from one of his rank.
85 See line 33 and note above.
94 'This is not the ransom we agreed'.
106–7 'Do right by me, as you are a reasonable man. This is your ransom and reward' (*MED skil*, n,2(a), reasonableness, discretion; moderate behaviour, moderation, self-control; 2(b) sound judgment, good sense). See also note to line 168, below.
116 An interesting roll call of knights of the Round Table: Lancelot, Kay, Banier (either Bedivere or possibly Ban), Bors, and Tristram are all present, as is Gareth. As Madden noted, 'Sir Steven' is not a familiar figure in romances of the Round Table.
122 *Sir Tristeram*: the same spelling as in *KAKC*.
129–31 *s[w]ire*: literally the neck. *OED swire*, the neck, *obsolete*, cites P's version of *MSG* in the *Reliques* as an example of the word. In medieval times used to denote feminine beauty (*MED swire*, n,1(b)). Kay sees the hag and observes sardonically that, since she is so ugly, anyone kissing her would naturally be frightened (to death). (*MED dout(e*, anxiety; fear, fright; 'for doute of', for fear of (death), n,3(a)).
136–37 As so often in the English Arthurian tradition, Gawaine rebukes Kay for his spiteful behaviour.
147 *For Citty nor for towne*. P understandably revised the corresponding line in his version in the *Reliques* to a plural form in order to preserve the rhyme scheme of 145, i.e., the comparable line reads 'For cities, nor for townes' (76).

150	Having seen some of his knights beat a hasty retreat on learning that someone has to marry the hag, Arthur plays down both the ugliness of the lady and the natural revulsion of those upon seeing her. Whether he is genuinely dismayed that none of his men is prepared to make such a sacrifice for him, or whether, knowing that it is Gawaine who is to marry her, he can afford to express publicly his disappointment, the end result is richly comic.
156	Gawaine is speaking to a mild-mannered person, but P's gloss 'which was soe' implies that it is Gawaine who is speaking mildly to the transformed hag.
157–58	Gawaine's hesitancy indicates a degree of uncertainty as to how the lady will react to his preference: her response (163–66) is immediate.
166	'I will not be able to accompany you into the hall to dine'.
168	*skill*: HF suggested 'reason, feint, pretence'. Although the word might be interpreted as at 106, the context seems to imply that Gawaine responds instinctively and selfishly when given the choice, only to backtrack immediately once he witnesses his wife's evident distress, relinquishing to her the ultimate decision.
183	*Carlis[h]* [*b*]. See also Textual Note. Assuming this reading of the MS, and that P's 'carlish boore' of the *Reliques* is a reasonable extrapolation on his part, the missing stanzas at this point may have explained that the wicked stepmother's evil spells were designed to humiliate and disadvantage the offspring of her aged husband; in the case of the daughter by perverting the idea of feminine beauty to the extent of making her a hideous hag, and in the case of the girl's brother by destroying the social standing of the son and heir of a knight by reducing him to the level of a commoner (*MED carl*, a man (usually of low estate); often patronizingly or contemptuously: fellow, n,1(a); a serf, servant, slave …; a peasant, a rustic, n,2(a)–(b). Hence adjectival *carlish*). The earliest example cited by the *OED* of *boore* (a peasant, countryman (*boor*, n,1) dates from 1548, although the word also appears in *The Nine Worthies of London* (1592) by Richard Johnson, who also published *A crowne garland of goulden roses*. Whereas in *WSG* Arthur's adversary, Sir Gromer Somer, is described as a knight who is aggrieved that his lands have been given to Gawaine, in *MSG* the adversary is clearly not of a knightly class. As Field notes (2010, 68), in the latter text the weapon of choice is a club, an instrument traditionally associated with a giant.
200	Gawaine's metaphor is both homely and vivid, expressing his relief that his uncle's life is no longer in danger, and his joy at the pleasure to come.
205	A rare and touching example in Arthurian romance of a rapport between Gawaine and Kay.

Textual Notes

In the LH margin, opposite the title, P has written: '[N.]B. To supply *the* Defects. P:' In the RH margin, against the title: 'This is upon th[e] same Subject as the Wife of Bath's Tale in Chaucer. from which Chaucer very probably took the Story.'

1	'in' before 'lives' struck through [MS].
3	*Queene*: Qqueene [MS]. The second *q* is thickly drawn, and could indicate an intended deletion.
5	*Geneve[r]*: Geneve [MS].
11	[*& when*]: MS cropped, reading supplied by HF.
12	[*it*]: this word no longer visible as the top of the page is missing; there is, however, a caret between 'thing' and 'is', suggesting the presence of an interlined word.

12–48	Running the length of the leaf, in the LH margin, P has written: 'In the Collection of Scots Poems written before 1600, intitled *the* Evergreen by Allan Ramsay, 2 vol. Edinburgh 1724. In Dunbar's Lament for the Loss of the Poets; Stanza 16th. are these Words, speaking of Death.'
	    "Clerk of Tranent eik he has tane,
	    "That made the Aventures of Sir Gawane, &c."
	    "Sir Gilbert Gray endit has he' &c. Vol. 1st pag. 133
	    NB. These are printed from a Collection made 1568.
	    NB. Dunbar liv'd in *the* Time of ou[r] Henry 7.th

Running the length of the leaf, in the RH margin, P has written:
'Dunbar mentions Chaucer 4 stanzas before He comes to *th*e Author of Gawane, but this may not be on Acc*oun*t of his being the more ancient Bard: but from his being the more eminent in his Art & by far more celebrated: On w*hi*ch Acc*oun*t he begins with him in *th*ese Words

   He (Death) has done petously devore
   The nobil Chawser of Makkars flowir
   The Monk of Berry & Gowre all thre &c.
    St. 12. p. 137.'

24	[*G*]*awaine*: Cawaine [MS].
26	*soe*: 'sore' changed to 'soe', the scribe anticipating the following word.
33	*fand*: 'fonde' [P].
37	*Or*: 'i.e. e'er' [P].
38	*O*[*r*] *else*: O else [MS]; 'or else' [P].
48	While much of the line remains legible, the complete line is recorded by HF.
49	*drest*: 'i.e. addrest' [P].
52–79	In the LH margin, P has written (opening two words discernible, but supplied by HF): '[It appears] also from <u>The Squire's Tale in Chaucer</u> that these were old ballads in his Time. See lin. 109 &c

   "A strange kn*igh*t …
   "Salued the King & Queen & Lordis all &c …
   "With so hie reverence and obeisance &c …
   "That Sir Gawin with his old Curtesy
   "(Altho he come again out of faierye)
   "He could him nought amend in with no word," &c …'

53	*a* interlined by scribe with caret.
55	*hollen*: 'holly' [P].
57	*there*: 'where' [P].
61	[*out*]*ward*: toward [MS]. P corrected to 'outward', striking out the opening two letters and adding 'out' above the line.
79	The MS is cropped at this point, the entire line being supplied by HF. The equivalent line (92) in the Percy–Darby *Reliques* reads 'Let gentle Gawaine' (Groom, 1996, III, 396).
85	*cold he* [*finde*]: frinde [MS]; 'he fonde' [P]. Opposite this line, in the LH margin, P has the following faint comment: 'he found e'er long', and below this, 'Qu.'.
88	*hand*: HF recorded 'hands' here and observed of the same word at 97 that 'there is a tag to the *d*, as if for *s*'. However, in the MS, there is no difference between the way the two words are written, and in context the singular use of the noun in lines 88 and 97 is to be preferred. The rhyme 'land' (99) for line 97 in the MS is very clearly in the singular form.
89	*cold*: 'did' [P].
92	*sayd*: HF observed that 'the *d* and final curl could have been meant for *es*, "sayes"'. However, the 'final curl' is vestigial to the point of invisibility, the short ascender of *d* making it look possibly like an *e*; *A*[*r*]*thur*: Aithur [MS].
100	*He*: the [MS], clumsily overwritten to read 'He'; *I* interlined by scribe with caret.
102	*hollen*: 'holly' [P].
106	*sck*[*i*]*ll*: sckll [MS], the *c* dotted as for an *i*.
112	*mine avow*: 'my Vo[w]' [P]; margin torn.
114	*ge*[*tt*]: supplied by HF, corner of leaf missing.
116	In LH margin [*T*]*he 2*^d *part*:
117	*them*: 'him Qu' [P].
123	*f*[*r*]*esh*: flesh [MS]. The thickness of the *l* – which has a superscript *r* added above, and a half-caret below – indicates a clumsy attempt by the scribe at deletion.
129	*s*[*w*]*ire*: smire [MS]. HF acknowledged the possibility of 'swire', but the text is reasonably distinct. It is possible that the archaic 'swire' was unfamiliar to the scribe, who hence wrote 'smire' instead. See Explanatory Note.
139	*marry*: interlined by scribe with caret.
140	*to*: A *t* superimposed over *d*.

The Marriage of Sir Gawaine

143   *s[l]aine*: shaine [MS]; 'I'm sure she shall be none, qu.' [P] – very faint, reading supplied by HF.

156   *with one soe*: 'wh*i*ch was soe Qu.' [P].

161   *rather*: A *t* crudely superimposed over another letter.

163   [*f*]*eires*: seires [MS]. Most editors choose to follow 'feires' (*OED fere*, a companion, comrade, mate, partner, n,1(a)): the speaker laments her anticipated social exclusion. A thick downward stroke obscures the *i*.

171   *Gawain[e]*: MS cropped. Reading supplied by HF, although beginning of final letter faintly discernible.

174   *henc[e]forth*: hencforth [MS].

179   *Lad[y]*: corner of MS torn away.

183   *Carlis[h]* [*b*]: The incomplete state of the MS makes it impossible to know what was written originally at this point. In his continuation of the ballad in sheet B, Percy recorded the fragmentary line as 'She witched my brother to a carlish B…' (Groom, 1996, III, 400). For all four editions of the *Reliques*, the text at this point reads 'carlish boore', the adjectival 'carlish' being applied to Arthur's adversary six times. However, having reluctantly agreed to publish the text from the MS itself at the conclusion of the fourth edition, P provided the nonsensical transcription – possibly a simple slip on his part – 'Carlist B…', a reading subsequently followed by Ritson in his *Ancient Engleish Metrical Romanceës* of 1802, Madden in 1839 (albeit that all transcripts from PF were undertaken for him by a third party), HF, and others since. The final letter of the first word seems to have a loop, which would imply an *h* instead of a *t*. The letter that would have opened the following word is indistinct, but *b* – or less likely *B* – is plausible. See Explanatory Note.

216   'I suppose ffinis' [P]. Any scribal annotation confirming an actual conclusion has been lost owing to damage to the end of the leaf: P's disappointment is palpable. However, his transcription of *MSG* for the fourth edition of the *Reliques*, entitled 'The Ancient Fragment of The Marriage of Sir Gawaine', concludes with 'Ffinis', presumably on the grounds that Percy felt inclusion of the word was by now warranted. Madden, HF, and Hahn followed suit, recording 'FINIS', 'ffins', and 'Fins' respectively.

217   [*To*] *Sir Gawaine* [*&*] *his l[ady gay]*. Lower half of line missing, full reading supplied by HF, presumably following the reading in the fourth edition of the *Reliques*.

Sir Lambewell

Elizabeth Williams and John Withrington

The Breton lai *Lanval* by Marie de France, composed before 1170, was probably first translated into English in the early fourteenth century, drawing upon Celtic tales.[1] This translation is no longer extant, but it gave rise to two offshoots, of which the first is Thomas Chestre's 12-line tail rhyme *Sir Launfal*, composed in the late fourteenth century and found uniquely in BL MS Cotton Caligua A.II.[2] The second, and more popular, offshoot comprises the anonymous *Sir Landevale*, a complete text of 538 lines in octosyllabic couplets dating most likely from the first half of the fourteenth century, and found in Bodl. MS Rawlinson C.86 (*c.*1500); *Sir Lamwell*, existing in two fragmentary prints from the sixteenth century (Bodl. Malone 941 and Bodl. Douce Fragm. e.40),[3] and the incomplete Cambridge University Library MS Kk.5.30 (late fifteenth/early sixteenth century);[4] and PF's *Sir Lambewell* (*LAMBE*), the only other complete text, running in this edition to 631 lines. The *Sir Lamwell* pieces represent a text that is closer to *LAMBE* than to *Sir Landevale* but are not sufficiently close to be regarded as the source for the PF scribe: despite their different poetic forms, *Sir Landevale* and *Sir Launfal* would seem to represent an older version of the poem than *Sir Lamwell* and *LAMBE*.

The relationship between these offshoots is uncertain,[5] but it is clear that Marie's decision to place her lai within an Arthurian setting undoubtedly contributed to the tale's lasting popularity, spanning as it does some four and a half centuries in the period up to the transcription of PF. The presence of *Sir Landevale* in the Rawlinson MS, a manuscript that contains the contiguous and unique *The Wedding of Sir Gawain and Dame Ragnell* (*WSG*), itself closely related to PF's *The Marriage of Sir Gawain*, is witness to an interest in Arthurian material by a mercantile middle class audience in London *c.*1500: of 25 surviving medieval manuscripts containing Arthurian works, 'eleven are known either to have been copied or to have been in circulation, in the city'.[6] As Boffey and Meale point out, however, several of the pieces in the Rawlinson MS were already available in print; i.e., whether the MS copied printed texts, or printers foraged copy from manuscript collections is unclear, but 'some cross-over certainly exists' (Boffey and Meale, 1991, 167–68).

The Lanval story, as with the PF ballad *Sir Launcelott of Dulake*, seems to have been popular in printed form in the sixteenth century, paving the way for a version to be included in the Percy Folio in the following century. As well as the examples of the Malone and Douce fragments, a romance of 'Sir Lamwell, knight' may have been printed by Wynkyn de Worde, who died *c.*1535 (Boffey and Meale, 1991,

167), while Sir Lamwell features as a knight of the Round Table not only in the early sixteenth-century Thomas Feylde's *Controversy between a Lover and a Jay*, but also in the collection of Captain Cox as narrated by Robert Laneham in 1575.[7] Such interest was not confined to south of the border. Bawcutt has demonstrated that *Sir Landevale* in Cambridge University Library MS Kk.5.30 'derives from an English work, first printed in the early sixteenth century, which has been lightly Scotticized in style and language' (Bawcutt, 2005, 83). While the MS contains for the most part a Scottish copy of Lydgate's *Troy Book*, the owner James Murray added a supplement in 1612, which contains the first 90 lines of *Sir Landevale*.[8] Reference to an item of music called 'Sir Lamuel' in National Library of Scotland MS 9450, a compilation by the Scottish minister Robert Edward (b. 1617), would indicate that by the time the Percy Folio was being transcribed, the literary offspring of Marie de France was being celebrated in Scotland on the dance floor as well as in verse.[9]

While the story told in the twelfth century *Lanval* has retained its general shape in the English versions, changes in tone and emphasis inevitably reflect developments in audience and literary taste over the years that followed. Marie's *Lanval*, written for a courtly audience, depicts accordingly an affluent and confident society. By way of contrast, the later English versions of the tale display a particular interest in the social implications of an unexpected fall from a state of wealth to poverty. Thus, of *Sir Launfal*, Bliss notes that 'The most important possession of a knight is his wealth, and his most important virtue his generosity … once he loses his wealth he is no longer respected' (Chestre, 1960, 42). The depiction of unexpected good fortune and its material benefits, a sort of medieval lottery win, would surely have been of interest to those of a mercantile, middle-class background. However, Colette Stévanovitch has argued convincingly for a more subtle portrait of the hero as he appears in the later PF, in which the stress is more on interpersonal relationships than simple wealth, and the hero is far more conscious of the social difference between him and his lady, to the point of being both humble and hesitant: 'In all of these instances Lambewell behaves not so much like medieval hero as like a seventeenth-century gentleman transported into a romance setting to which he tries to apply the social norms of his time'.[10]

Changes in audience and attitude are reflected also in the language and characterization employed. Part of that process over a time has been a loss of succinctness. *Sir Landevale* is far more pithy than *LAMBE*, whose greater length is partly to be explained by successive attempts to replace words that had become archaic or obsolete, while attempting, often in vain, to retain the rhyme scheme. Speeches in particular also tend to be expanded and the result, while formulaic and aiding recitation, is often inflated and repetitious, an effect compounded by the redactor's tendency to repeat, almost verbatim, passages in scenes that describe closely similar events.[11] Inevitably, the language of *LAMBE* reflects also a more modern audience, in which

> the grammar of *Sir Lambewell* is not Middle English, nor is its vocabulary medieval. A process of modernization, no doubt spread over the whole period of transmission, has

been at work … Modernization has been systematic except at the end of lines, where the reviser was faced with the dilemma of letting an archaic word stand or losing the rhyme.[12]

While Sir Lambewell may be a more sensitive figure than his predecessors, and while his lady is both rich and powerful but not necessarily of fairy-kind (in *Sir Landevale*, she is 'The kyngys doughter of Amylion;/That ys an ile of the fayré'), the character of Guinevere remains that of the faithless, promiscuous, and vengeful queen, a depiction found elsewhere in the PF.[13]

Few of the apparently unique additions to *LAMBE* are substantive. The main exception is Lambewell's farewell soliloquy to his fellow knights as he leaves Carlisle (lines 35–50), which have no precise equivalent in other texts and are presumably intended to add to the Arthurian flavour of the narrative. This scene occurs at the beginning of *Sir Launfal*, with a similar list, but the only names in common are Kay, Percival, Agravaine, and probably Gawaine, who appears at this point in *LAMBE* in the garbled form 'Gaion', the rhyme on 'faine' explaining Percy's suggestion of a change to 'Gawaine', whose name appears correctly later in the text.[14] Also rhyming (falsely) on 'faine' is the therefore suspect and otherwise unrecorded Sir Griffine. The name of Sir Huon could have been influenced at some point in *LAMBE*'s genesis by Lord Berners's translation of the romance *Huon of Bordeaux*, in print in England since 1534, but the name recurs at line 463, and is presumably the same person referred to as Haion or Hayon at 222, 354, and 503, often in association with Gawaine.[15] Also mentioned are Sir Garrett (i.e., Gareth) and Sir Ironside, who appears in both *Syre Gawene and the Carle of Carelyle* and PF's *CARLE*.[16] One other passage that is somewhat longer in *LAMBE* than in the other versions comes at the end when Lambewell pleads for forgiveness before riding away to 'Amilion' with his lady. This scene of reconciliation is absent from *Sir Launfal*, but is present, more briefly, in *Sir Landevale*. In PF, it is considerably expanded, with Lambewell not only pleading himself, but begging Arthur and his knights to plead also on his behalf. He wins forgiveness in *Sir Landevale* but in *LAMBE* the lady says nothing, and when he leaps uninvited on to her horse to go with her she simply rides away with him, apparently accepting the fait accompli.

LAMBE appears on ff. 28v–33v of PF at the point where the pages, though torn in half, are all present, so no major areas of text have been lost.[17] Frequent small losses occur, however, at the centre of the pages where the two halves have been rejoined, and where the tops and bottoms have been trimmed by the binder.

Notes

[1] 'There can be no doubt that the story told in *Lanval* and immediate analogues is of genuinely Celtic origin' (Thomas Chestre, *Sir Launfal*, ed. A. J. Bliss (London: Thomas Nelson, 1960), p. 19).

[2] Percy's access to the Cotton manuscripts meant that he knew *Sir Launfal*, which he not unreasonably supposed to be the source of *LAMBE*. His assumption that it dated to 'before the Reformation' (see introduction to the Textual Notes, below) is predicated upon line 525 of the present edition, which contains a reference to the 'sacring' of the Host at Mass.

3 Bodl. Malone 941 comprises two complete leaves and six fragmentary leaves from the edition published by John Mychell in 1548 (ESTC S100264). Bodl. Douce Fragm. e.40 comprises a single leaf from the edition printed by John King in 1560 (ESTC S125060). I am grateful to Ms Sarah Weale, Head of Rare Books at the Weston Library, University of Oxford, for clarification of details in respect of this note (J.W.).

4 Priscilla Bawcutt, '*Sir Lamwell* in Scotland', in Rhiannon Purdie and Nicola Royan (eds), *The Scots and Medieval Arthurian Legend*, Arthurian Studies LXI (Cambridge: D. S. Brewer, 2005), pp. 83–93.

5 For example, Laskaya and Salisbury state that Chestre borrowed 'whole lines' from *Landevale* (Anne Laskaya and Eve Salisbury (eds), *The Middle English Breton Lays* (Kalamazoo, MI: Medieval Institute Publications, 1995, 201), while Bliss (Chestre, 1960, 99–100) thought it likely that for line 886 of *Sir Launfal* 'Chestre worked from a MS closely related to MS Rawlinson C.86'.

6 Julia Boffey and Carol M. Meale, 'Selecting the Text: Rawlinson C. 86 and Some Other Books for London Readers', in Felicity Riddy (ed.), *Regionalism in Late Medieval Manuscripts and Texts: Essays Celebrating the Publication of* A Linguistic Atlas of Late Mediaeval English' (Cambridge: D. S. Brewer, 1991), p. 161. Boffey and Meale note that one leaf and the conclusion to *Landevale* and all of *WSG* are the work of a single scribe, adding of the booklet of which these texts is part that it was 'evidently planned as a whole from the outset, as the various texts lead on one from another with no significant breaks' (169).

7 Bawcutt, 2005, 84–85, citing Boffey and Meale. Feylde's work is particularly interesting. Framed as a traditional dream poem, drawing upon Chaucer and Lydgate, a 'jangling' jay advises a mournful lover on the inconstancy of women. 'Lamwell' is bracketed among some of the most notable names of the Round Table, i.e., Trystram, Lamaroke, Gawayne, Launcelorte, Garathe, and Craddock. (A scan of the ?1527 edition by Wyknyn de Worde is available at www.proquest.com (accessed July 2023).) See Explanatory Note to lines 510–12, below, and for Captain Cox, p. 34, above.

8 Bawcutt's transcription may be found at 2005, 91–93. Alongside BL MS Cotton Caligua A.II and the Rawlinson MS, the Cambridge MS is another example of Arthurian material being found with works by the extraordinarily popular poet John Lydgate.

9 Bawcutt (2005, 88), after Helena Shire, notes that while the words have not survived, the music is in the style of a sixteenth-century dance that would have suited an octosyllabic couplet were an alternating refrain added.

10 Colette Stévanovitch, 'Enquiries into the Textual History of the Seventeenth-Century *Sir Lambewell* (London, British Library Additional 27897)', in Leo Carruthers et al. (eds), *Palimpsests and the Literary Imagination of Medieval England: Collected Essays* (New York: Palgrave Macmillan, 2011), pp. 201–2. Stévanovitch's reference at this point to Twain's *A Connecticut Yankee*, while apposite, perhaps fails to take into account the potential for humour and performance that exists in the PF ballad. Stévanovitch concludes that *LAMBE*'s emphasis upon the hero's sensitivity and the ballad's lack of emphasis upon Lambewell's lavish spending suggests an audience that is more refined and less interested in texts portraying a 'materialistic outlook on life'.

11 Changes in pronunciation over time have affected both language and metre: 'The original fourteenth-century translation was written in the equivalent of the French octosyllable, but the loss of the final –*e* means that many lines are too short to scan properly. To remedy this, the *Lambewell* reviser added line fillers, and sometimes overdid it' (Stévanovitch, 2011, 198).

12 Stévanovitch, 2011, 196. Curnow argues convincingly that *LAMBE* was memorially transmitted, which would support Stévanovitch's view (Demelza Jayne Curnow, 'Five Case Studies on the Transmission of Popular Middle English Verse Romances', PhD thesis, University of Bristol, 2002, 222–36).

13 Uniquely, in *Sir Launfal*, the Queen rashly vows to be blinded if the hero's lady is fairer than she, and suffers this fate accordingly.

14 Curnow (2002, 232) points out that while *Launfal* lists the names of several knights, *LAMBE*'s list underlines how much the hero will miss the companionship of friends and their society.

15 At lines 35, 222, and 354, Percy corrects these variants to 'Hayne', presumably in order to rhyme with 'Gawaine'. For 'Huon', HF suggested Sir Uwayne as a possibility. 'Syr Ewayn' is mentioned at the beginning of *Sir Launfal*.

[16] See Explanatory Notes to lines 37ff. of *CARLE* on p. 346, below, where Sir Ironside is provided with a lengthy and entirely irrelevant biography. Intriguingly, Sir Gareth faces the formidable Sir Ironside in Malory's *LMD*. No source has been identified for this particular tale by Malory, although it was likely to have been an English poem of the type known as a 'Fair Unknown' romance.

[17] The page on which the poem begins, f. 28v, is the first of which both halves survive, but at some stage after Furnivall examined the manuscript the two halves were mounted separately and in the wrong order. As a result, 'fol. 28r ought be the upper half of fol. 29r and fol. 28v should be the upper half of fol. 29v, so forming fol. 29 containing the end of … *[King] James & Browne*' (St Clair-Kendall, 2007, 5).

Manuscripts and Editions

Sir Launfal

BL MS Cotton Caligula A.II [printed in Thomas Chestre, *Sir Launfal*, ed. A. J. Bliss (London: Thomas Nelson, 1960)].

Johnson, Lesley, and Williams, Elizabeth (eds), *Sir Orfeo and Sir Launfal* (Leeds: University of Leeds, School of English, 1984).

Laskaya, Anne, and Salisbury, Eve (eds), *The Middle English Breton Lays* (Kalamazoo, MI: Medieval Institute Publications, 1995), pp. 201–62, https://d.lib.rochester.edu/teams/text/laskaya-and-salisbury-middle-english-breton-lays-sir-launfal-introduction (accessed July 2023)

Sir Landevale

Bodl. MS Rawlinson C.86 [printed as an appendix in Thomas Chestre, *Sir Launfal*, ed. A. J. Bliss (London: Thomas Nelson, 1960), with the text of Marie de France's *Lanval* in parallel].

Sir Lamwell

Bodl. Malone 941 and Bodl. Douce Fragm. e.40 [fragmentary prints transcribed at HF, I, 522–33 and 533–35 respectively. N.B., of the Malone fragment, Furnivall wrote on p. 521 that 'some of the lost part filled up in italics, by guess and by comparison with the text of the Folio and the Douce leaf']. Bawcutt corrects some of HF's readings by comparing them with the Cambridge MS (Priscilla Bawcutt, '*Sir Lamwell* in Scotland', in Rhiannon Purdie and Nicola Royan (eds), *The Scots and Medieval Arthurian Legend*, Arthurian Studies LXI (Cambridge: D. S. Brewer, 2005), pp. 87–88).

Cambridge University Library MS Kk.5.30 (incomplete, but printed in Bawcutt, 2005, 91–93).

Sir Lambewell

HF, II, 142–64.

Further Reading

Bawcutt, Priscilla, '*Sir Lamwell* in Scotland', in Rhiannon Purdie and Nicola Royan (eds), *The Scots and Medieval Arthurian Legend*, Arthurian Studies LXI (Cambridge: D. S. Brewer, 2005), pp. 83–93.

Curnow, Demelza Jayne, 'Five Case Studies on the Transmission of Popular Middle English Verse Romances', PhD thesis, University of Bristol, 2002.

Lyle, E. B., '*Sir Landevale* and the Fairy-Mistress Theme in *Thomas of Ercedoune*', *Medium Aevum* 42 (1973), pp. 244–50.

Stévanovitch, Colette, 'Enquiries into the Textual History of the Seventeenth-Century *Sir Lambewell* (London, British Library Additional 27897)', in Leo Carruthers et al. (eds), *Palimpsests and the Literary Imagination of Medieval England: Collected Essays* (New York: Palgrave Macmillan, 2011), pp. 193–204.

Stokes, Myra, '*Lanval* to *Sir Launfal*: A Story Becomes Popular', in Ad Putter and Jane Gilbert (eds), *The Spirit of Medieval English Popular Romance* (Harlow: Longman, 2000), pp. 56–77.

Williams, Elizabeth, '*Sir Landevale, Sir Launfal, Sir Lambwell*', *AE*, 130–35.

Sir Lambewell

	Doughty in King Arthure's dayes,	p. 60/f. 28v
	When Brittaine was holden in noblenesse,	
	And in his time a long while	
	He sojourned in merry Carlile.	
5	With him he had many an heire,*	
	As he had else ma[n]y a wide where.	*far and wide*
	Of his Round Table they were Knights all,	
	& the[y] had much Mirth in bower & hall.	
	In every Land of the world wide	
10	The[y] came to the court on every side,	
	Both yonge knights & Squiers eke,	
	All the[y] came [to] the courte to seeke.	
	& with him there longed a bold bachelor,	*lived; young knight*
	And soe he did many a yeere:	
15	A yonge Knight of much might,	
	Sir Lambewell forsooth he hight;	*was named*
	And ever he spent worthilye	
	& he gave gifts that were larglie.	*generous(ly)*
	[Soe largely] his good he spent,	p. 60/f. 29v *property*
20	Much more than ever he had rent,	
	& soe outragiouslie he it sett	
	That he became far in debt.	
	And when he saw that all was gone	
	Then he begunn to make great moane.	
25	'Alacke,' he said, 'noe goods I have.*	
	I know not how to doe, soe [Go]d me save,	
	& I can neither begg nor [b]orrowe!	
	[Thus] I am brought far in sorrow,	
	& I am far in a strange land	*foreign*
30	& have noe goods, as I understand.	
	Of all these Knights that are soe feirce	
	Of the Round Table, which are my peeres,	
	Eche one to have me they were glad	
	& now for me the[y] wil be sad.	
35	Both Sir Huon & Sir Gaion,	
	Some time of me that you were faine.	*glad*
	Ffarwell, Sir Kay, that crabbed Knight,	*short-tempered*
	Farwell, Sir Percivall the wight;	*valiant*
	Of my companie that thou was faine;	
40	The good Knight, Sir Agravaine,	
	Farwell S[ir G]arrett & Sir Griffine:	
	Of my company that thou was faine;	
	Ffarwell the Knight, Sir Ironside:	
	Of my company thou had much pride	
45	Ffor my expence [&] noble wray	*expenditure; array*

	& the rich gifts that I gave aye;	*always*
	Certes you shall me neve[r] see.	
	Ffarwell, I take my leave of you	
	As a simple batchlour without blame,	
50	Where before I bare a good name.'	
	Then he leaped uppon a fresh courser,	*charger, steed*
	Without page or any squier,	
	& tooke his way towards the west	
	Betweene the water & a faire forrest.	
55	The sun was [at the even-tide],	p. 61/f. 30r
	The Knight light downe & thought to a[bide]	
	& layd him downe, the Knight free,	
	Under the shadow of a tree.	
	And what for Weeping much & warle*	
60	Asleepe, Iwis, this Knight fell,	*assuredly*
	& what for sobbing & greet,	*lamentation*
	When he wakned, up he him sett,	
	And then he looked afore him tho:	*then*
	Out of a forrest came Maydens tow.	*two*
65	Towards Sir Lambewell they did [draw];	
	Ffairer befor he never sawe.	
	Mantles they had of Red velvett,	
	Fringed with gold, full well sett,	
	& kirtles of purple sandall:	*fine linen*
70	They were small lace[d] & fitted well.	*tightly*
	They were tyred above over all	*wore head-dresses*
	& either of them had a fresh color.*	
	They had faces as white as snowdowne;	
	They had lovesome color & eyen Browne;	
75	& one of them had a go[ld] Bason	
	& the other a towell of silke fine.	
	Towards Lamewell drew these maids twaine;	
	The Knight was curteous & rose them againe.	*to meet them*
	The[y] said, 'God speede thee, thou Knight free,	
80	There as thou lyest, full of povirty!'	
	'Damsell,' saies Lamwell, 'welcome to mee.'	
	'Sir,' quoth the one, 'well may thou bee.	
	My Lady, that's bright as blossome or flower,	
	Thee greets, Sir Lamwell, as her paramoure	
85	& prays you for to speake with her,	
	& if it be your will, faire Sir.'	
	Lamwell answered them both there,	
	'& I am faine with you to fare:	*happy*
	for which way soever your gate lies	*way*
90	I deeme certaine be paradice;*	
	For fairer maids then you tow bee	*two*
	I never saw [none] with mine [eye].'	

The[y] thanked Lambwell, *that* K*nigh*t Curteous,
For giving them soo great a praise:
95 'But shee as much fairer then wee are seene,*
& over us might be a queene.
Her bewtie passeth us as far
As betweene the flower & the steale.'   *stem*
They washed their hands & face alsoe
100 & forth w*i*th those maids the K*nigh*t did goe.
Within that forrest the[y] did see
A rich pavillion pight full hee,   *pitched*
& every pomell of the pavillion
Was well worth a 100 pound.*
105 Upon the topp a gripe stood   *griffin*
Of shining gold, fine & good.
In his mouth he bare a carbunckle bright;
Like the moone it shines every night.
K*ing* Alexander the conquerour,
110 Nor Salamon in his most honour,
Nor Charlemount the rich K*ing* –   *Charlemagne*
They never welded such a thing.   *possessed*
For sooth there was in that pavillion
The K*ing*'s daugter of Million.*
115 In that pavillion was a bed of price
*Tha*t was covered ore w*i*th goodlie vice,*
& therein sate a lady bright;
From the Middle shee was naked upright*
And all her cloathing by her lay.
120 Ffull seemlie shee sate, I say,
All in a mantle of white Ermines;
Was fringed about w*i*th gold fine.
Her mantle downe for heat shee did
Full right unto her girdle steed.   *waist*
125 Shee was as white as lilly in May,
Or snow that falls on winter's day.
The blossome, nor the bryar, nor [noe K*i*nd of flower]*
[It hath noe hue unto her color.]
[And the red Rose] when it is new   p. 62/f. 30v
130 To her rednesse hath noe hue,
For it shone Like the gold wyer,
Yett noe man can tell of her attyre.
When of her he had had a sight
Downe of his knees then fell the K*nigh*t
135 & saluted her w*i*th mild steven   *voice*
As though that shee had come from heaven,
& spake to her when he had space:
'I put [me], lady, into your grace.'
'S*ir* Lambewell,' shee said, 'my hart's sweete,

140	For thy love my hart I leete,	*lose, surrender*
	& there's noe K*ing* nor emperour	
	But & if I loved him paramour	*as a true lover*
	As much, S*ir* L[amb]ewell, as I doe thee,	
	He wold be right glad of me.'	
145	He sett him downe the lady beside.	
	'Lady,' he saies, 'what ere betide,	*whatever*
	Both earl[y] & late, loud & still,	
	Com[m]and [me] ready [at] your will.	
	But as helpe me God, my lady deere,	
150	I am a k*nigh*t without hawere.*	
	I have noe goods noe more, nor men	
	To maintaine this estate I find yo[u] in.'	
	Then said that Lady, 'I doe you soe kind,*	
	I know thy estate, first & end:	*from beginning to end*
155	& thou wilt trustilie to mee take,	*if*
	& for my love all other forsake,	
	Then I will maintain thine honour	
	W*i*th gold, w*i*th silver, & w*i*th rich treasure;	
	& w*i*th every man thou shalt spend larglie,*	*generously*
160	& I will give thee great plentie.'	
	Then of *that* pr*o*fer he was full blithe	
	& thanked this lady often sithe.	*many times*
	He obaid him unto her ther,	*made obeisance*
	He list this lady that was soe faire,	*desired*
165	& by that Lady downe him sett,	
	& bad her maides downe meat fet,	*fetch*
	& to there hands watter cleer;	
	for then shee wold unto supp*er*.	*wished to go*
	There was meate & dri[n]ke great plentie	
170	Of every thing *that* was daintye.	
	When they had eaten & dru[n]ken both	
	Then to her bed this lady wold goe.	
	S*ir* Lambwell, like a hailow K*nigh*t,*	
	By her bedside stood up full right,	
175	Said, 'You displease that wold I nought,	
	But Jesus leeve, [you] knew my thought.'	
	Then spake *that* Lady [f]ree,	*noble*
	Saies, 'Undight thee, Lambewell, & come to me.'	*undress*
	Then was Lambwell soone undight	
180	& in bed with this Lady bright,	
	& did all that night lye there	
	& did whatsoever their wills were.	
	For play the[y] slept but litle *that* [n]ight	
	Till it began to be daylight.	
185	& when the daylight was comen tho	*then*
	Shee said, 'Rise, Lambewell, & now goe.	

	Gold & silver take inoughe with thee	
	& with every man thoust spend larglie;	*you may*
	& more thou spendest, meryer thoust sitt,	
190	& I will send thee innoughe of it.	
	But one thing, Knight, I thee forefendant,	*forbid*
	That of mee thou never avant.	*boast*
	For & thou doe, I tell thee before,	*if*
	For ever thou hast my love forlore.	*lost*
195	& when thou wilst, thou gentle Knight,	
	Speake with me by day or night,	
	Into some secrett place looke you goe	
	& thinke uppon me soe & soe	
	& shortly I will with you bee:	
200	Not a man save you that shall me see.'	
	A maid brought him his horsse anon;	
	Hee tooke his leave & leapeth uppon:	
	'Ffarewell [my hony, farwell my sweete]!'	*p. 63/f. 31v*
	'Farewell, Sir Lambwell, till oft wee meete.'*	
205	Of treasure then he had great plentie	
	& thus he ryds thorrowout the cittye	
	While he came there he shold have beene:	*until*
	A merryer man they neere had seene.	
	Now Lambwell he makes rich feasts;	
210	Lambewell feeds minstrelsie their Jests;	
	Lambwell rewards religious;	*members of religious orders*
	Lambewell helpes every poore howse;	
	Were it Knight, squire, or swaine	
	With his goods he helpeth them.	
215	Of his largnesse every man wotts	
	But noe man witts how he itt gotts.	
	Always when he lyed privy & still	
	His lady was ready at his will:	
	But well happy were the man	
220	That in these dayes had such a one!	

The 2ᵈ parte

	Soe uppon a day Sir Gawaine	
	The gentle knight, & Sir Haion,	
	Sir Lambewell with them alsoe	
	& other knights 20 & moe,	
225	Went for to play them on a greene	
	Underneth the tower where lay the queene.	
	These knights on there game plaid thoe*	*then*
	But sithe to dancinge they wold goe.	*afterwards*
	Sir Lambell he was before sett:*	
230	For his large spending they loved him best.	

Sir Lambewell

The queene in a bower beheld them all
& saies, 'Yonder is Large Lambwell! — *generous*
Of all the knights *tha*t be there
There is none soe faire a bachlour,
235 & he hath neither lem[m]an nor wiffe – — *sweetheart*
I wold he loved me as his life!
Betide me well, betide me ill,
I shall,' shee said, 'goe witt his will.'
Shee took w*i*th [h]er a companie
240 Of damsel[ls th]at were right pretty,
& down[e she go]es anon wright
For to [goe dance w*i*th a knight],
& shee went to the first end
Between Gawaine & Lambwell the hend, — *courteous*
245 & all the maids soe forth right
One & one, betweene 2 knig[hts].
& when this dancing did aslake — *came to an end*
The queene S*i*r Lambwell to councell did take.
'Lambwell,' shee saies, 'thou gentle K*nigh*t,
250 I have loved thee & doe w*i*th all my might,
And as much desire I thee
As Arthur, that K*nigh*t soe free.
Good hap is now to thee tane*
*Tha*t thou wilt love me & noe other woman.'
255 He saies, 'Madam, noe, certez; — *indeed*
I wil be noe traitor never in all my daies.
For I owe my king fealtie & homage
& I will never doe him that damage.'
She said, 'Fie upon thee, faint Coward!
260 Dastard harllott as thou art! — *rogue, knave*
That thou livest it is great pitye –
Thou lovest noe woman nor noe woman loves thee!'*
He said, 'Ma[da]m, say yee your will,
But I can love both lowde & still,
265 & I am loved w*i*th my lem[m]an
*Tha*t fairer hath noe gentleman,
Nor none soe faire, yett say I,
Neither mayd nor yett Lady.
The simplest maiden w*i*th her, I weene,
270 Over you, Madame, may be queene!'
Then she was ashamed & full wroth.
Shee clippeth her mayds & forth goeth. — *calls*
To Chamber shee wold, all heavye; — *vexed*
For teene & anger shee wold die. — *rage*
275 Then K*ing* Arthur came from hunting,
Glad & merry for all thing:
To the Queene's chamber gone is hee,

        & then she fell downe upon her knee,
        & fast 'Lord!' *tha*t shee did crye,
280 'Helpe me, Lord, or ever I dye!
        [Without .... might]   p. 64/f. 31v
        I shall die this yenders night!   *this very night*
        I spake to *Si*r Lambwell in my game   *in jest*
        & he desired my body of shame.
285 As a false villane traitor
        He wol[d] have done my body dishonor,
        And when I wold not to him aply   *attend*
        He shamefully rebuked me,
        & of [his] Lem[m]an praisment he made
290 That the lowest maiden that shee had
        Might be a queene over mee –
        & all, Lord, was in despight of thee!'*
        The K*ing* t*herwith* he waxed wroth,
        & for anger he sware an oathe
295 that Lambwell shold abide the law,
        P*er*adventure both to hang & draw.
        & he com[m]anded 4 knights
        To feitch the traitor to his sight.
        Theese 4 knights seeken him anon;
300 & to his chamber he is gone:
        'Alacke,' he say[d], 'now my life is lorne!*   *lost*
        Hereof shee warned me beforne:
        Of all things *tha*t I did use
        Of her I shold never make my rowze!'   *boast, brag*
305 He clipped, hee called, he her besought,   *cried out*
        But al availed him of nought.
        He sorrowed & he did cry
        & on his knees besought her mercy:
        'O my Lady, my gentle creature,
310 How shall my wreched liffe endure?
        My worldlie blisse I have forlorne   *utterly lost*
        & falslie to my lady forsworne.'   *perjured myself*
        For sorrow & care he made that stond,   *outcry*
        He fell in soonde to the ground.   *swoon*
315 Soe long he lay *tha*t the Knights came
        & in his chamber too[ke hi]m then,
        & like a theefe they led him [tho]
        Thus was his sorrow, weale & woe.*
        The[y] brought [the] K*nigh*t before the Kinge,
320 & this he said at his com[m]inge:
        'Thou false & untrue traitor,
        Thou besought my wife of dishonor:
        *Tha*t shee was lothlier, thow her upbraid,   *reproached*
        Then was thy Lem[m]an's lodlyest maid.'

325 Sir Lambewell answerd with Mild moode,
& tooke himselfe sworne by the roode   *the Cross*
Tha*t* it was noe otherwise but soe,
'& that my selfe will make good thoe,
& therto over your court Looke.'
330 12 knights were d[r]iven to a booke*
The sooth to say in that case
Altogether as it was.
These 12 knights, as I weene,
The[y] knew the rule of the queene: *custom, habit*
335 Although the K*ing* were bold & stout   *valiant*
That shee was wicked, out & out;
But shee had such a comfort
To have Lem[m]ans under her Lord.
Therfore the[y] accquitt the trew man;
340 But sithe the[y] spake forth then,   *afterwards*
For why *that* he is lem[m]an bring*
Wherby he made his advantin*g*,   *boast*
And alsoe *tha*t he prove in place
That her maids fairer was,
345 & alsoe more bright & sheene
& of more beutye then the queene,
& alsoe countenance & hue,
They wold quitt him as good & trew.   *acquit*
& if he might not stand ther till   *hold to that*
350 He shold abide the K*inge*'s will.
This verditt was given before the King.
The day was sett …   *p. 65/f. 32r*
Sureties he found to come againe,*
Both S*ir* Gawaine & S*ir* Hayon.
355 'Alacke,' he said, 'now my life is lorne!
Herof shee warned [mee] beforne:
Of all things *tha*t I did use
Of her *tha*t I shold never make rowze.'
He cleped, hee called, he her besought,
360 But all avayled him of nought.
He bet his body & his head eke,*
He curst his mowth *tha*t of her did speake,
And thus he was w*i*th sorrow Mun,*
He wold his endinge day were come
365 *Tha*t he might from his life goe.
Eche man for him was full woe,
For a large[r] spender then hee
Never came in that countrye,
& therto he was feirce & bold –
370 None better in the King's houshold.
The day was come of his appearing:

The[y] brought the Knight afore the King.
His barons *tha*t his surties was   *guarantors*
They brought him forth, alas!
375   The King let it be rehersed there   *repeated*
Both the plaintiffe & the answere.*
The King bad him bring his lem[m]an in sight.
He answered that he ne might:
'But this I say to you alone:
380   A fairer then shee was never none,
Both of bewtye & of shape.
I am to simple to tuch her lappe,   *clothing*
Or yett to come unto her bower
Eccept it were for her pleasure,
385   Not displeasing her sickerlie.   *truly*
Yet wold I you saw her ere I dye.'
'Bring her forth!' the King sayes,
'That thou dost now soe fast praise,
To proove the sooth *tha*t thou sayst of.'*
390   'Forsooth, my Lord, *tha*t can I nought.'
Then sayd the King anon thoe:
'Fforsooth thy disworshipp is the more.   *dishonour*
What may wee all know therby
But that thou lyest loud & hye?'
395   He bade the barons give Judgment.*
The Barons answered, 'Verament,   *assuredly*
To it, Lord, wee will gone.
Wee will to it soone & anon.'
& then bespake the Erle of Cornwayle,
400   Who was one of the councell,
& say[d]: 'Wee know thee King, our Lord:*
Hees owne mouth beares record,
The wich, by his owne assent,
Hath the g[i]ven the Knight Judgment.
405   Therefore, & we shold by the law*
Lambewell shold both hang & draw.
But villany it were to eche of us one
To let us fordoe soe a noble man,   *destroy*
Or yett soe doughtie a bachlour –
410   Amongst us all had never peere.
& therfore say by our reede   *counsel*
Wee will the King such way leade
That he shal be com[m]anded to goe
& void the court for evermore.'
415   & while they stood thus speaking
They saw 2 Ladyes come ryding
Upon 2 ambling palfrayes,
Much fairer then the sum[m]er's days,

Sir Lambewell

   & they were clothed in rich attire*
420 That every man had great desire.
   Them espied Gawaine, the gentle K*night*.
   'Lam[bwell,' he said, 'dread] for noe wight!   p. 66/f. 32v
   Yonder comes thy life, yond maist thou see:
   The love of thee, I wott, is shee.'
425 Lambewell beholds them w*i*th much thought
   & said, 'Alacke, I know them nought!
   My lady is much fairer, certainlie.'
   When they came S*ir* Lambwell by,*
   Not tarrying w*i*th him the[y] yode,   *went*
430 But to the King both the[y] rode
   & said, 'Thou Lord of worshipp, Arthur,
   Lett dresse thy halls & thy bowers,
   Both by ground, roofe & wall,
   W*i*th clothes of gold rich over all.
435 It must be done att device:*   *to perfection*
   Heere comes our Lady of much price.
   Shee comes to you, as I weene,
   Before yee, my lord, shee shal be seene.'
   The [king] com[m]anded for her sake
440 The fairest chamber to them to take.
   The Ladyes are gone to bower on hye.   *at once*
   The K*ing* bade his barronrye
   Have done & give their judgment.
   The Barons were att 'Verament:*   *assuredly*
445 Wee have beholden this maiden bright
   & yee have letted us, by this light!   *delayed us*
   But to it, Lord, we will gone:
   Wee will have done soone & anon.'
   A new speech they began thoe.   *then*
450 Some said 'well' & some said 'not soe.'
   Some to death wold him deeme,   *condemn*
   For to please the K*ing* & queene,
   & other some wold make him cleere.
   Whilest they stood pleading in feare,*   *together*
455 The whilest the[y] stood thus speaking,
   Other tow Ladies came ryding,
   Uppon tow goodly mules of Spaine.
   They had s[ad]les, & [bridles] were champaind.*
   They were clothed in rich attire,
460 That every man had great desire
   Ffor to behold their gentryes: *nobility*
   They came in oft soe rich a wise.   *manner*
   Them espyed Huon the hind.   *courteous*
   'Lambewell,' he said, 'my brother & freind,
465 Yond comes thy life, yond may thou see

      The tone of these I wott is shee,   *that one*
      Ffor fairer then shee there may be none!
      If it be not shee, choose thee none.'
      Lambwell beholds them both, iwis,
470   & said, 'Of them 2 none it is.
      My Lady is much fairer certainly,
      But of her servantes they may be.'
      These ladies that thus came ryding
      Rode to the Castle, to the K*ing*,
475   & when the[y] came [Sir] Lamw[ell] by
      Baysance the[y] made certainly.
      Not tarrying w*i*th him the[y] made
      But to the K*ing* both the[y] rode
      And the[y] said, 'You, Lord of worship, Arthur,
480   Let dresse thy halls & bowers,
      By ground, by roofe, & by wall,
      W*i*th clothes of gold hang it all,
      & cleath thy carpetts under her feete.*
      It must be done at device,   *to perfection*
485   For heere comes our lady of much price.'
      Much sorrow had Dame Genever*
      When shee saw the ladies' color.   *i.e., beauty*
      Then shee trowed of some guile   *suspected some trick*
      Tha*t* Lamwell shold be holpen w*i*thin a while
490   By his ladye that was coming.
      Fast shee cryed upon the K*ing*
      And said, 'Lord, if thou love thine hono*u*r
      Avenge me on this traitor!'
      To hang Lambwell shee wold no[t spare]:   *p. 67/f. 33r*
495   'Yo*u*r barons make you not to care.
      W*i*thout you him sloe without more*
      I shall die my self before.'
      He bad his barons give judgment,
      'Or I will my selfe, by Mary gent!'
500   'We will him doome, S*ir*, soone anon!'
      To tell the[ir] tale they once began.

[T]he 3ᵈ parte

      'My lord, thus for sooth agreed are wee ... '
      'Peace!' said S*ir* Haion, 'noe more say yee,
      Ffor yonder I see her come rydinge
505   On whome S*ir* Lambwell made his ava[n]ting!
      A damsell by her selfe alone –
      On earth was fairer never none –
      Upon a fresh ambling palfray,
      Much fairer then the sum[m]er's day;

Sir Lambewell

510 Her eyes beene blossome[s] cleere & faire,*
     Jolly & jocund as the faulconer
     Or the Jay that sitts on a bough;
     Of all things shee is faire enoughe.
     Lord, shee's a lovely creature,
515 & rides thus att her pleasure!'
     A sparhawke shee had on her hand;
     A softly pace her palfray fand;*   *went*
     3 white greyhounds running her by,
     As well beseemed for such a lady.
520 She had a crowne uppon her head
     Of precious stones & gold soe red.
     Wife & child, yonge & old,
     All came this lady to beholde;
     & all still uppon her gazing*
525 As people that behold the sacring;   *close attention*
     & all they stood still in their study,
     & yet they thought them never weary;
     for there was [n]ever man nor woman *tha*t might
     Be weary of this ladie's sight.
530 As soone as S*ir* Lambwell did her see
     On all the people cryed hee,
     'Yond comes my life & my likinge!
     Shee comes *tha*t me out of baile shall bring.   *torment*
     Yond comes my lem[m]an, I make you sure:
535 Treulie shee is the fairest creature
     *Tha*t ever man see before indeed.
     Looke where shee rydes uppon her steed!'
     This Lady, when shee came thus ryding,
     Rode to the castle to the K*ing*.
540 The K*nigh*t there his owne worshipp did:
     He rose up & he gave her the steed,*   *deferred to her*
     & lovely he can her greete*
     & shee againe with words sweete.
     The queene & other Ladyes stout   *stately*
545 Behold her comlye round about;   *from all sides*
     And there the[y] sate as dum[m]be*
     As the moone is light from the sunn.
     Then shee said to the K*ing*,
     'Hither am I come for such a thing:
550 My trew lem[m]an, S*ir* Lambewell,
     Is Challenged, as I heere tell,   *accused*
     How that he shold w*i*th villanie
     Beseech the queene of adoutry.   *adultery*
     That is false to bleeve, S*ir* K*ing*:
555 He bade not her, for shee bade him!
     If he h[a]d de[sir]ed her, w*i*th[o]ut let,*   *without fail*

Not a fo[ot] hi[ther] I wo[l]d have sett.
You may beleeve me every word.
That this is right I will make good.
560 & for the other praisment that he made
That mine owne Lowtest mayd*
Was mor of beawtye then thy queene –
Let the proofe, Sir, soone be seene.'
The King said, 'Verament,
565 Barrons, heere shall be noe judgment   *judge*
But I my selfe the same will deeme
Both of the queene & of the Mayden.
If I doe not right then you may say
But Sir Lambwell …'
570 … [quoth the] Knight,   p. 68/f. 33v
'I will love [her] with all my might,
Both in place & in stead
Much better then ever I did.'
& when shee heard him soe say
575 She leaped on her palfray
& obayd her to the King soe hind*   *made obeisance*
& tooke leave away to wend.
Then of all that while to Sir Lambwell
Shee wold not speake nor looke never soe deale.   *in the least*
580 But wott you well sorry was hee:
Befor her he fell on his knee
& said, 'Madam, trespassed I have,*
& I am come of your mercy to crave.
I k[n]ouledge me of that wicked deed   *confess*
585 That was forbidden me when you yode.   *departed*
I am well worthy therfor to hange
Or leade my life in pai[n]es strange.   *strong*
What pennance, Lady, you will to me say
Or you depart from me away   *before*
590 Lady, I desire noe more of thee
But once aside to looke on me.
My lord the King, of soe high a prow,   *valour*
For all the service I have done you,
One good word for me to speake!
595 & all my fellowes, I you beseeke,   *I pray you*
With the King pray you alsoe
Of her good word; I aske no moe.'
Ffor that they saw he mad such mone
The King & the[y] prayd, every one,
600 But for all that ever he cold doe
Not a word shee wold speake him too,
But obayd her to the King soe hind
& tooke her leave away to wend.

	Then Lambewell saw *tha*t shee wold fare,	
605	His owne hart he tooke to him there.	
	When shee turned her horse to have gone	
	He leaped upon soone anon	
	Upon her palfray, whatsoever betide –	
	Behind her he wold not abide –	
610	& he said, 'Madam, w*i*th reason & skill,	
	Now goe w*hi*ch way soe ere you will,	
	For when you light downe, I shall stand,	
	& when you ryd, all at yo*u*r hande,	
	& whether it be for waile or woe	
615	I will never dep*ar*t you froe.'	
	This Lady now the right way num[m]	*took*
	With her maids, all and some,	
	& shee brought S*ir* Lambwell from Carlile	
	Farr into a Jolly Iland	
620	*Tha*t clipped was Amilion,*	*called*
	W*hi*ch knoweth well every Briton.	
	& shee came there, that Lady faire;	
	shee gave him all that he found there,	
	*Tha*t was to say, all manner of thing	
625	*Tha*t ever might be to his likinge,	
	& further of him hard noe man,	
	Nor more of him tell can;	
	But in that Iland his life he spend;*	
	Soe did shee alsoe tooke her end.	
630	Butt God that is the K*i*ng of blisse	
	Bring us thither as his woning is! ffins	*dwelling*

Explanatory Notes

5	Although Malone reads '… m many an heyre' at this point (5), the meaning is not that Arthur was accompanied by many of his approved successors. Rawlinson (5) provides an explanation with, 'He had with hym a meyné there' (*OED meinie*, a body of people attending a lord or other powerful person, n,2). It seems likely that the term, already increasingly archaic by the time of Malone and PF, was either misunderstood, or an error picked up as a result of aural transmission.
25–50	Of the Lanval tales, only PF develops the occasion into an expansive list of names as part of a single, formal soliloquy (see Headnote). The passage is one of the longest that is unique to the MS and looks like padding, with names selected perhaps partly at random: note, for example, the banal repetition with redundant relative pronouns at 36, 39, and 42. Kay's epithet of 'crabbed' (37) plays to the stereotypical characterization found in ballad material, but the description of Agravaine as 'the good knight' would come as a surprise to those versed in the romance tradition, where Agravaine and his brother Mordred are the architects of Arthur's downfall.
59	'Warle' is nonsensical, although it is possibly related to the northern dialect *wrawl*, to utter an inarticulate noise or sound; to bawl, squall (*OED*, v,1). While P's tentative suggestion ('waile') fits the context, it does not help the rhyme.

72	Stévanovitch observes of this singleton that in *Sir Landevale* the companion line reads, 'With facys white as lely floure'. She adds, 'Since *flower* and *color* no longer rhymed in seventeenth-century English, the link between the two lines was weakened, paving the way for the loss of the first one' (Stévanovitch, 2010, 199).
90	The reference to paradise is unique to PF. However, other versions compare the maidens to angels from heaven – Malone (74), Cambridge University Library MS Kk.5.30 (72), Rawlinson (64) – cf. line 136.
95–98	These lines are unique to PF but in part anticipate Lambewell's outburst at 269–70 and the Queen's outraged repetition of his supposed slur at 289–91.
104	*Sir Landevale*'s 'Was worth a citie, or a towne' (82) would provide a better rhyme than PF's 'pavillion', but both texts underline an emphasis upon prodigious wealth.
114	*Million*: 'Mylon' in Malone (104) and 'Amylion' in Rawlinson (92). Although *LAMBE* later identifies the place as an island called 'Amilion' (619–20), unlike Malone and Rawlinson there is no reference to it being located in fairy. Line 621 states of Amilion, 'Which knoweth well every Briton'. It is quite likely that *LAMBE*'s audience would have been more familiar with the traditional name of Avalon, as Marie de France recorded in *Lanval* ('Avalun', 641). See also note to line 620 below.
116	*goodlie vice*: the lady has a rich, purple covering on her bed. At this point *Sir Landevale* calls it 'byse (96) and *Sir Launfal* 'bys' (284): *OED byse*, some kind of (?brown) fur, much used in the 15th cent. for trimming gowns, etc. *OED*'s last citation dates from 1513, which would explain why the archaic 'byse' transformed into *LAMBE*'s 'vice'; 'probably to be understood as *device*, that is to say *pattern*' (Stévanovitch, 2011, 198). See also Textual note to this line.
118	'She was sitting upright, naked to the waist'.
127	The length of this line and the internal rhyme perhaps suggest two lines written as one.
150	'I am a knight without wealth': 'hawere' is likely derived from *MED aver*, things owned; possessions, property, wealth, n,2(1).
153	*kind*: P's suggestion – 'to ken' – is plausible (*MED kennen*, ppl. *kend*, to make known, v(1),1a). The lady makes it clear that she understands Lambewell's impoverished state.
159	Repeated almost verbatim at 188.
173–78	*hailow*: the word is unique to PF. P made no suggestions as to a possible meaning, while HF ventured that it might be a form of the Old English 'halig', i.e., 'holy'. If so, it may be an ironic reference to line 90, i.e., the hero displaying a deference for the lady which borders on the sacred (cf. note to lines 524–27, below). Whatever the meaning, Lambewell's wishful thinking at this point is in sharp contrast to the lady's remarkably frank proposition at 178. While the comedic potential offered by this scene is obvious, and such openness typical of fairy mistresses, there is no indication in this text that she is unquestionably of fairy kind. Nonetheless, 195–200 and 217–18 hint at a supernatural origin.
204	*oft*: most likely an error for 'eft': *MED eft*, a second time, another time, once more, again, adv.,1.
227	*game*: Rawlinson (191) indicates a board game, perhaps chess.
229	*before sett*: i.e., set to lead the dance. The form of dance is unknown, but likely to have been of a processional type. Guinevere invites herself to the dance, placing herself between Lambewell and Gawaine, presumably at the head of the line (243–44).
253–54	'Good fortune has now befallen you, provided that you love me and no other woman'.
262	Lambewell's blunt rejection and protestation of loyalty to his king, her husband, provokes the Queen's spiteful response. Her accusation that the knight loves no woman, and no woman loves him, is echoed in *Sir Launfal*, *Sir Landevale*, and Malone, but may carry with it an underlying insinuation: in Marie de France's *Lanval*, the queen accuses the knight of being gay.
292	The Queen spins the alleged incident as not only a personal affront, but as an insult to her husband (and king).
301–6	These lines repeated almost verbatim at 355–60.

318	The alliterative doublet 'weale and woe', i.e., 'good and ill', was common enough a phrase, but does not make sense given the context; cf. line 614, where the usage would be correct, but 'weale' has been corrupted to 'waile'.
330	'Were ordered to swear on the Bible.'
341	'That if he could produce his beloved ...'
353	Lambewell secures guarantors to stand bail for him in order to ensure his return to court.
361	'He beat his body and also his head': Lambewell strikes and berates himself for his stupidity. The MS 'bent' is nonsensical.
363	*Mun*: P glossed as 'taken', from 'nome'. HF recorded the word as 'Num', but wondered if it might be 'Mun'. However, *OED mun*, the mouth, n,1, provides a possible explanation, carrying over the sentiment of the previous line. In which case 362–63 might be glossed: 'He cursed his mouth that spoke of her in that way, And thus he was, with a sorrow[ful] mouth, [that] ...' See also Textual Notes for 363 and 616.
376	*plaintiffe*: Malone's 'playnte' (374) makes more sense (*OED plaint*, a statement or representation of wrong, injury, or injustice suffered, n,2(a)). Arthur ensures that both the grievance and the accused's response are heard.
389	This singleton line implies that a rhyming line was omitted at some point.
395–98	Repeated almost verbatim at 442–44.
401–14	Arthur has already sworn that Lambewell shall die (295–96). The Earl concedes that Lambewell seems to have incriminated himself but argues that Lambewell's record and character means that banishment from the court should be the outcome, as opposed to execution. The Earl's viewpoint testifies to the strength of feeling in support of Lambewell, as well as to the Queen's malice and the king's weakness.
405	'If we were to abide by the [strict letter of the] law'.
419–20	These lines are repeated at 459–60 when the second pair of maidens arrive.
428–36	cf. lines 475–85.
435–36	cf. lines 484–85: again, part of a deliberate repetition.
444	*were att*: the sense is surely that they responded. The corresponding line in Rawlinson is the straightforward 'The barones saide, "Verament" (376).
454–55	The repeated 'whilest' indicates a garbled couplet.
458	Champagne was a kind of cloth as well as a place name: *MED champain(e*, n.(2) cites three examples, the latest of which dates from 1500, but there is no evidence to suggest that the word was used as a verb, and cloth is hardly suitable as a material for saddles and bridles. In Rawlinson, the saddles and bridles are 'of Almayn' (388).
483	*cleath*: contextually the meaning implies 'spread', but neither *OED* nor *MED* supplies comparable usages. N.B. *OED clead	cleed*, to clothe (northern dialect).
486–97	These lines, unique to *LAMBE*, underline the Queen's vindictive behaviour.
496	'Unless you kill him, without any more delay'.
510–12	The confused use of conventional phrases denoting beauty implies a history of corrupt transmission. At this point, while Rawlinson has 'Jentyll and joylyff as birde on bowghe' (433), it is not obvious why a falconer, or even a falcon, should be 'jolly and jocund', especially given that jays were known for their plumage and chattering. (From the early sixteenth century onwards, the word was being applied in a less than complimentary sense: *OED jay*, a stupid or silly person; a simpleton, n,3(d). See also Headnote for a reference to Lamwell in the early sixteenth century *Controversy between a Lover and a Jay*.)
517	*fand*: While the MS clearly reads 'fand', HF's puzzling reading of 'sand' is nonsensical, Furnivall suggesting instead 'fand', i.e., 'to try', as an alternative reading. While *OED* cites *LAMBE* as evidence of *fand*, to go, proceed, v,8, only three other such examples are cited, all from the early fifteenth century.
524–27	'Sacring' refers to the consecration of the Host at Mass. These lines, unique to *LAMBE*, convey an atmosphere of religious awe.
541	'He rose, and deferred to her the place': Lambewell rises to greet her, and acknowledges her precedence (*OED stead*, the place designated by the context, n,II.2(d)).
542	P's marginal comment of 'lowly' for 'lovely' was rejected by HF ('no: lovely'). While P's reading reflects the respect the hero publicly shows his beloved, his loving attitude is in keeping with the tenderness Lambewell and his lady feel for each other.

546	*dum[m]be*: *OED dun*, dark in colour; *spec.* characterized by or causing a lack of light; murky, gloomy; (of light) dim, obscure, adj., 2.
556–59	This emphatic assertion by the lady is unique to PF.
561	*Lowtest*: while P's 'lowliest' is adequate, 265–70 and the context of 562 surely imply that Guinevere means 'loathliest' at this point (cf. Rawlinson 486, 'my lothliest maide').
576–77	cf. lines 602–3.
582–97	Lambewell's impassioned plea to the lady, extended to his peers to plead for him, is one of PF's longest, and most effective, apparent additions.
620	Chestre's 'Olyroun' (Oléron), noted by P in a marginal comment, is a real island off the coast of Brittany. See also note to line 114, above.
628–31	While 630–31 constitute a conventionally pious conclusion, this version of the Lanval tale is the only one to speak of the deaths of the hero and his lady, again reinforcing the down to earth nature of this story, as opposed to the openly fairy context of other versions, or the legend of King Arthur's supposed survival in an otherworldly Avalon.

Textual Notes

Underneath the title Percy has written 'In 3 Parts'. (The division of the text into parts, unique to this version of the story, is indicated by the scribe, who inserted headings after 220 and 501. See also notes, below, for line 441 and after 501.) In the LH margin, opposite the title: 'A curious old romantic ballad written before the Reformation. See part 3.^{d} v. 24. This is upon the same Subject as the old Romance of S*ir*. Launfal but differs in Some Parts of the Story: probably altered. by some Minstrel.' [P].

4	*Carlile*: 'In other Ballads it is Carleile, v*id* p. 284' [P]. The page reference is to *BM*, line 2. Underneath, P wrote and then struck through, 'It means Caer-leon': see note 38, p. 43 above, for P's debt to Evans on this point.
6	*ma[n]y*: one minim too few; *wide*: the scribe started to write 'wh–', presumably with the following word in mind, but then struck through part of the letter.
8	*the[y]*: the [MS]. See also 10, 12, 34, 79, 93, 101, 183, 319, 334, 339, 340, 372, 429, 430, 455, 475, 476, 477, 478, 479, 546, 599.
9	*In every*: 'From every' [P]; *world*: half-loop over *r*, as if scribe began to write letter *l*.
12	[*to*]: hole in MS, although there is the beginning of a letter.
19	[*Soe largely*]: 'Soe largelye' [P]. Reading supplied by HF, folio torn in half at this point; – *gely* still partly visible.
24	*moane*: the *n* is relatively clear but is preceded by what appears to be an extra minim, possibly crossed through with a blot above.
26	[*Go*]*d*: hole in MS, also [*b*]*orrowe* in next line.
28	[*Thus*]: hole in MS. Reading supplied by HF.
35	*Sir Huon & Sir Gaion*: 'Sir Hayne & S*ir* Gawa[ine]' [P]. Margin cropped. Reading supplied by HF.
41	*Farwell*: *r* interlined by scribe, no caret; *Si[r G]arrett*: hole in MS. Reading supplied by HF.
44	*company*: preceded by beginnings of an *h* overlaid by a Greek *e*.
45	[*&*]: smudged; *wray*: 'Qu array' [P].
47	*neve[r]*: neve [MS].
48	*of you*: *of* interlined by scribe, with caret [MS]; 'of yee' [P]. P's correction for rhyme creates a grammatical error ('ye' for 'you'), also found at 438.
49	*simple*: HF has the tautological 'single', but the word is clear.
55	*The sun was* [*at the even-tide*]: line cropped by binder. The bottom of the opening three words is just discernible. Reading supplied by HF, supported by Malone's 'The sonne was at the euyn[tide] …' (line 41, HF, I, 523); 'The Sun was low at the Even-tide qu' [P].
56	*a[bide]*: most of word lost. Reading supplied by HF.
59	*warle*: 'perhaps (waile' [P]. Final parenthesis lost through cropping.
64	*a*: interlined by scribe, with caret.

Sir Lambewell

65	[*draw*]: grow [MS]. 'draw qu' [P]. P's comment is supported by 'Come out off the forrest & to him drau' of Cambridge University Library MS Kk.5.30 (line 61), but all texts show evidence of corruption at this point.
70	*lace*[*d*]: hole in MS. Reading supplied by HF.
71	*above over all*: 'above all over' [P].
75	*a go*[*ld*]: two holes in MS. Reading supplied by HF.
76	*a*: interlined by scribe, with caret.
88	*faine*: 'i.e. glad' [P].
90	*certaine*: 'to be' [P].
92	[*none*]: 'I never saw none with mine eye' [P]. The torn folio is repaired across the scribal line. The opening three words may be discerned, but in recording P's annotation HF declared that 'the first letter of *none* is clearly *m*', thus resulting in the awkward line 'I never saw moue with mine eye'. While an opening letter *m* is faintly possible, P's 'none' fits the context much better.
93	*Curteous*: 'forte cer[tes]' [P]. Reading supplied by HF.
98	*steale*: 'i.e. stalk' [P].
99	*their*: 'perhaps his' [P].
102	*hee*: '<u>hie</u> or high <u>olim</u> pronounced <u>hee</u>.' [P].
105	*gripe*: 'Grype i.e. Griffin' [P].
111	*Charlemount*: 'Charlemagne' [P].
114	*Million*: 'Olyron (Oleron) in the original by T. Chester' [P]. See note to line 620, below.
116	*vice*: 'perhaps devic[e]' [P]. Page cropped, reading provided by HF.
121	*Ermines*: 'Ermine' [P].
124	*steed*: i.e., 'pla[ce]' [P]. Page torn, reading provided by HF.
127	*blossome*: *l* corrected by scribe from *r*, having anticipated 'bryar'; *noe* [*Kind of flower*]: 'noe' interlined with carat by scribe, but the remainder of the line is torn away. HF supplied the reading 'noe Kind of f[lower]', implying that at least some of the text was still legible at that point.
128	[*It hath noe hue unto her color*]: paper torn away at foot of page. Reading supplied by HF.
129	[*And the red Rose*]: paper torn at top of page. Reading supplied by HF.
133	*he*: added by scribe.
134	*of his*: 'on his' [P].
138	[*me*]: my [MS]; 'me qu' [P].
143	*L*[*amb*]*ewell*: hole in MS; *as*: interlined by scribe, with caret.
147	*earl*[*y*]: hole in MS.
148	*Com*[*m*]*and* [*me*]: [*me*] supplied by P with caret; [*at*]: hole in MS.
150	*hawere*: 'harbere i.e. home' [P].
152	*To maintaine*: 'find' struck through before 'maintaine'; *yo*[*u*]: you*r* [MS].
153	*soe kind*: 'to ken' [P].
167	*hands*: 'qu [h]ands' [P]. The writing is faint and the MS damaged at this point; *hands*: scribe began with a letter *w*, obviously anticipating the following word, then changed it to *h*. He then added 'for then she wold' at the end of the line, anticipating the opening to 168, only to strike it through on realizing his mistake.
168	*supper*: supp [MS]; '[suppe]re' [P].
169	*dri*[*n*]*ke*: drimke [MS].
171	*dru*[*n*]*ken*: druken [MS]; 'drünken' [P].
172	*wold goe*: 'goeth or gothe' [P].
173	*hailow*: opening *s* changed to an *h*, *r* to an *i*. Large cross in LH margin, opposite this line: similar large X at 368–69.
176–77	[*you*]; *f*[*ree*]: hole in MS affecting both lines. Reading supplied by HF.
183	[*n*]*ight*: Knigh*t* [MS]; 'night' [P].
185	*tho*: 'i.e. then' [P].
187	*take inoughe*: 'take enoughe' [P].
192	*avant*: 'avaunt, i.e. boa[st]' [P]. Margin cropped, reading provided by HF.
202	The bottom half of this line is mostly lost. Reading supplied by HF.

203	[*my hony, farwell my sweete*]. The top line of the page is now largely lost, with only the descenders of some letters visible. Reading supplied by HF, who seem to have been able to read the whole line with the exception of 's[weete]'. '*Ffarewell*' is still discernible, the reading confirmed by the catchword on the previous page; 'Farewell my honey farewell my sweete:' [P].
204	*oft*: 'next' [P].
206	*thorrowout*: 'perhaps towards' [P].
207	*while*: 'when q' [P].
210	*Jests*: 'Gests q' [P].
213	*were*: where [MS]; 'were' [P]. After the line P has written and then struck through 'where (ie whether) it were'. This phrase preceded by several characters, including the Greek letter phi, variously blotted and unclear.
215	*wotts*: 'wot' [P].
216	*gotts*: 'got' [P].
220	After this line the scribe has written in the LH margin 'The 2$^{\underline{d}}$ parte'. P starts renumbering from this line onward.
222	*Haion*: 'qu Hayne' [P].
226	*the tower*: 'the' added above line by scribe, with caret.
234	*bachlour*: 'batchelere' [P].
240–42	Extensive hole in MS and damage at half-page repair; readings supplied by HF.
240–45	Illegible comment by P struck through in LH margin, next to these lines, with two large figure 3s with mark below, ranged one above another, in P's writing.
246	*knig*[*hts*]: hole in MS.
256	*I wil be*: 'I will be' [P].
262	*Thou*: the *u* squeezed in above the line.
263	*Ma*[*da*]*m*: Madadam [MS].
272	*clippeth*: 'clepeth' [P].
274	*teene*: 'greif [*sic*], indignation' [P].
281	[*Without ... might*]: reading supplied by HF, although the opening four letters can be deduced from preceding catchword. All that remains of this line are the possible letters '–ght' at the end, which would rhyme with 'night' at 282. At this point line 277 of Malone reads, 'And without ye Juge ryght' (HF, I, 528).
286	*He wol*[*d*]: *d* obscured; 'he wold' [P].
287	*aply*: 'perhaps comply' [P].
289	*of* [*his*]: 'of [MS]; 'of his' [P].
301	*say*[*d*]: the *d* partially obscured by hole.
305	*clipped*: 'cleped' [P].
306	*al*: interlined by scribe, with caret.
313	*sorrow*: letters 'rr' smudged and corrected by scribe above line.
315	*the*: they [MS]; 'the' [P].
316	*too*[*ke hi*]*m*: hole in MS, extending to following line. Reading supplied by HF.
317	*him* interlined by scribe; [*tho*]: letters lost through hole and by half-page repair. Malone at this point (line 313; HF, I, 529) reads, 'And as a thefe they ledde hym th ...'; however, the bottom half and end of the last word of this printed line, as well as several lines thereafter, is missing. HF assumed, both for the transcription of Malone and of *LAMBE*, that the incomplete word must have been 'th[en]', although the result for 315–17 is to produce consecutive rhymes of 'came', 'then', and 'then'. Lines 757–58 of *Sir Launfal* – 'And bond hym, & ladde hym þo/Þo was þe kny3te yn doble wo' – provide an alternative reading: replacing HF's 'then' at 317 for its older form 'tho' follows a reading in an older text and provides a clear rhyme with 318.
318	*weale*: 'wail' [P], the *a* blotted.
319	[*the*] *Knigh*t: 'the Knight' [P].
323	*lothlier*: lothher [MS]; 'lothlier, i.e. more loathsome' [P].
324	'i.e. ugliest' [P].
330	*d*[*r*]*iven*: diven [MS]; 'i.e. a Jury of 12 of his Peers' [P].

331–32	*altogether* struck through at end of 331 by scribe, and *as it w* similarly struck through at beginning of 332.
341	*is*: 'his' [P].
342	*advanting*: 'avaunting' [P].
347	*alsoe*: 'of' [P], with caret before 'countenance'.
349	*ther till*: 'i.e. thereto' [P].
352	*The day was sett* ... top half of line pared by binders. P commented 'The day was sett' at this point, indicating that at least the opening of this line was visible. Line 9 of Douce reads 'The day was set her in to bring' (HF, I, 533).
354	*Hayon*: 'Hayne Qu' [P].
356	[*mee*]: omitted in MS, but *mee* added, in RH margin by P, with caret before 'beforne' in the line.
361	*bet*: bent [MS].
363	*Mun*: 'nome i.e. taken' [P]. See Explanatory Note and note 616, below.
367	*large[r]*: large [MS]; 'larger' [P].
373	*surties*: 'sureties' [P].
378	*he ne*: 'ne' [P].
387	*sayes*: word damaged at half-page repair; 'sayes' [P].
392	*more*: 'moe' [P].
401	*sayd*: say [MS]; 'sayd' [P].
402	*hees*: 'his' [P].
404	*g[i]ven*: one minim too few in MS.
405	*by*: 'bide or byde but bye means th[e] same' [P].
409	*bachlour*: 'batchelere' [P].
411	*reede*: 'reade, i.e. counsel' [P].
414	*evermore*: 'evermoe' [P].
422	Top of leaf cropped by binder. *Lam[bwell*: HF prints 'Lamwell' on the basis that the word is 'supplied from foot of p. 65'; however, only the opening three letters of this catchword now survive, and it is an uncommon spelling of the hero's name in this text. In the LH margin by 422, P has written: '[La]mbwell', one of a number of comments by P not recorded by HF in this text. Remainder of line supplied by HF: only last three words clearly discernible.
432	*halls, bowers*: 'hall – bower' [P].
438	*shee*: interlined by scribe, with caret; *it* struck through.
439	*The [king] com[m]anded*: the com[m]anded [MS].
441	'Here I w*ould* begin *the* 3ᵈ Parte if not at verse 200.' [P] (i.e., 415, which would be a better place to break than at 503, which cuts across a scene).
448	*&*: interlined by scribe, with caret.
454	*in feare*: 'in-fere, i.e. together' [P].
458	*s[ad]les & [bridles]*, obscured by half-page damage and repair. Reading supplied by HF.
461	*gentryes*: 'gentrise, vid. pag[e] 358. st.11' [P], page cropped. The reference is to the text of *John de Reeve* (HF, II, 559, line 65), where P notes: 'Genterice is still in use in Scotland, for Gentility honourable birth See Gloss. to Ramsey's Evergreen'.
462	*oft*: 'delend' [P].
463	*hind*: 'hend' [P].
466	*The tone*: '[t]he tone of' [P].
475	[*Sir*]: it [MS]; *Lamw[ell]*: '*Sir* Lambwell' [P].
476	*baysance*: '[i.e.] obeysance' [P] – MS cropped. Reading supplied by HF.
480	*halls & bowers*: 'hall & bower' [P].
483	Of this singleton, P commented opposite lines 483–84 that '[a] verse is here wanting'. HF recorded P's comment but signalled the want of a line to rhyme with 483 by inserting a series of dots and calling it 484, numbering sequentially thereafter as a result. The presence of this 'phantom' line is not included in the present edition, and hence the total number of lines (631) does not accord with HF's count of 632.
494	*no[t spare]*: 'not spare' [P]; MS cropped. Reading supplied by HF.
496	*sloe*: 'i.e., slay' [P].

501	*the[ir]*: they [MS]; 'the or their' [P]. After this line the scribe has written, in the LH margin: '[T]he 3ᵈ parte' (opening letter mostly lost). Immediately thereafter P adds, 'I would rather chuse to begin *the* 3ᵈ. Part at the 226th verse of the preceding as well in regard to *the* sense, as to *the* equality of *the* division.' P starts renumbering from this line onward.
505	*ava[n]ting*: one minim too few; 'avaunting' [P].
510	*blossome[s]*: blossomed [MS].
527	*yet*: beginning of a superscript *t* on *yt* [MS]. The scribe may have begun to write *yᵗ*, then realized that it should be 'yet', not 'that'.
528	*[n]ever*: one minim too many on the *n*.
534	*sure*: 'sure' [P]. The second letter resembles an *a*, which may explain P's need to gloss.
541	*steed*: 'i.e. place' [P].
542	*lovely*: 'lowly' [P].
545	*behold*: first letter scribal correction from *s*.
551	*Challenged*: the word written with a blurred capital C, which P may have felt needed elucidation, hence 'challenged' [P].
553	*beseech*: 'Beseek, i.e. seek, solicit' [P]; *adoutry*: 'avoutry, i.e. adultry.' [P].
554	*bleeve*: 'i.e. believe' [P].
556–57	Holes in page. Readings taken from HF.
561	*Lowtest*: 'lowliest q.' [P].
567	'Perhaps Both of the mayden and the Queene' [P].
569–70	Damage to lower half and top of lines respectively. Reading based on HF, although the bottom half of the opening letter of 'knight', with its required rhyme for the following line, can be discerned.
571	*[her]*: him [MS].
576	*obayd*: 'i.e., made obeysance.' [P]; *hind*: 'hend' [P].
579	*soe*: 'a qu' [P].
584	*k[n]ouledge*: kouledge [MS]; 'i.e., acknowledge.' [P].
585	*you yode*: 'yede, or I yede i.e., went' [P].
587	*pai[n]es*: one minim too few on the *n*.
589	*me away*: blurred word before 'away', possibly 'and'.
599	*The King & the[y]*: They King & the [MS].
602	*hind*: 'hend' [P].
608	Words damaged by mid-page break and repair. Reading taken from HF.
614	*waile*: 'weale' [P].
616	*num[m]*: 'nome i.e. took' [P]. As at 363, this word causes problems. At 363, HF transcribed as 'Num', but wondered if it might be 'Mun'; here (617 in HF's edition) they transcribe as 'numm'. The scribal overbar certainly indicates an additional *m* is required, but at this point HF wondered if the word could be 'run'. (The opening letters in both cases appear to be virtually identical: *r* is not plausible.) P's suggested meaning for 'numm' is as good an explanation as any.
618	*Carlile*: added later by scribe in ?different ink. P wrote and struck through 'Line wanting', in LH margin, perhaps momentarily confused by the apparent lack of rhyme at 619.
619	*Iland*: 'Isle' [P]. P's annotation was likely prompted by the need for this line to rhyme with 618. Rawlinson, which P would not have known, rhymes 'from Cardoyll/joly yle' at this point (531–32).
620	*clipped*: 'cleped' [P]; *Amilion*: 'Olyron (Oleron) in Chester's original Poem' [P]. Large asterisk by P after 'Amilion' and before his gloss; cf. note to line 114, above.
631	*woning*: 'i.e. dwelling' [P]; *ffins*: following the last word of this line, the scribe has written 'ffins' in a larger and thinner hand to signify the end of the piece.

Merline

Elizabeth Darovic, Gillian Rogers, and John Withrington

The roots of the Merlin story lie deep in both North British and Welsh legend.[1] It began to take its present shape with Geoffrey of Monmouth's *Historia Regum Britanniae* (*HRB*) (*c*.1138), in which he borrows the episode of Vortiger's tower and the warring dragons from the anonymous ninth-century *Historia Brittonum*, formerly attributed to Nennius, calling its hero Merlinus rather than the Ambrosius Merlinus of the earlier chronicle.[2] A later work by Geoffrey, the *Vita Merlini* (*c*.1150), makes Merlin the king of the Demetae, the southern Welsh, who is driven mad by the death of three brothers, who were his close companions, at the battle of Arthuret, and flees into the forest. In this version, we perhaps see the origin of the prophetic laughter to which the child Merlin gives vent on his journey to Vortiger, accompanied by the king's messengers. To Geoffrey is due the failed demonic plot to create Merlin as Antichrist.

Around the beginning of the thirteenth century, a *Merlin* formed part of a prose trilogy attributed to Robert de Boron, recounting the whole story of Merlin's life up to the time of Arthur's coronation. This formed the basis of the Merlin section of the Old French Prose Vulgate-cycle, the *Estoire de Merlin*, which was itself translated reasonably closely into the English prose *Merlin* in the mid-fifteenth century, and into somewhat long-winded verse by Henry Lovelich, a London skinner, *c*.1430.[3] However, in terms of a retelling of the story in English verse, as opposed to in translation, two distinct groups may be discerned. The first is an adaptation of the Vulgate *Merlin*, written in couplets and running to 9,938 lines and found uniquely in NLS Advocates Library MS 19.2.1: 'the Auchinlek manuscript' (*A*).[4] Known by the name *Of Arthour and of Merlin*, or simply *Arthour and Merlin* (*AM*),[5] it takes the narrative from the death of King Costaunce and the seizure of his throne by Fortiger up to Arthur's battle against Rion, displacing the tale of the birth of Merlin from its original place at the beginning of the tale to the point where Vortiger's messengers are sent in search of a child without a father. It also incorporates an episode that does not appear in the French versions, the story of the female chamberlain (*MER*, 1340–1420).

The second group is a much shorter version, typically running to some 2,000 lines, focusing on Merlin's birth and events up to the death of Uter's brother, and hence by implication Uter's succession. These texts are so obviously related to *AM* that 'independent descent from the French source is out of the question', Macrae-Gibson thus assigning to this group the collective name *AM2* (Macrae-Gibson,

II, 1). Texts in this group comprise the early fifteenth-century London, Lincoln's Inn MS 150 (*L*); the fifteenth-century Bodl. MS Douce 236 (*D*), the beginning and ending of which are missing; the PF version; a late sixteenth-century transcript of the first 62 lines by John Stow (BL Harley MS 6223) (*H*); and a print by Wynkyn de Worde, *Marlyn*, of 1510 (*W*), the only surviving complete copy of which is in the Pierpont Morgan Library in New York.[6] All versions are in octosyllabic couplets, apart from the first 12 lines of *W*, which are in tail-rhyme. *L* and PF resemble each other closely, so closely in fact that Macrae-Gibson felt able to use the latter in those places where *L* is defective. *L* is not, however, the immediate source of PF.[7] It ends with the death of Fortager (Vortiger), followed by a short prayer and an explicit. This prayer, without the explicit, is incorporated into PF, which then continues up to the death of Pendragon. That the death of Pendragon was the usual ending for *AM2* is shown by the fact that *W* also ends at this point, albeit without the prayer that ends the Vortiger section of the story in *L* and PF. A line in *L* (1812), also found in *W* (1914) and PF (1713), contains a promise to describe the death of Aungys, a promise fulfilled in the two latter versions, but not in *L*, which cuts off after that point. The implication is that there must have been two versions of *AM2* in circulation: one, the truncated version, ending with Vortiger's death, followed by the prayer, represented by *L* and the first part of PF; the other, the fuller version, taking the story up to the death of Pendragon, represented by *W* (first printed 1510) and the second part of PF. After he had transcribed his truncated version, the PF scribe must then quite quickly have come across a source that carried the story on to the death of Pendragon, and simply added that, omitting to cross out the intermediate prayer.[8] Allowing for omissions, additions, dropped couplets, misunderstandings, and eye-slip, both parts of PF resemble *W* very closely, despite the 240 or so years between them. They both end with a very similar prayer.[9] PF is the only version of *AM2* to divide the text into parts, nine in all. Unlike some of the other texts the scribe treats in this way, the breaks are mostly at key stages in the narrative, where the action switches from one set of characters or one situation to another, the only exceptions being the divisions between Parts 3 and 4, and 5 and 6.[10]

Although Percy did not include *MER* in his *Reliques*, his opening note to the text observes that this 'very curious old Poem … may be considered, as one of the first Attempts in Epic Poetry by the English', and his reference to the text being in 'cantos' undoubtedly reflects his interpretation of the work as part of an epic tradition.[11] In this respect, *MER* and *LD* both occupy a valued place in what he considered to be the bardic canon. Subsequent criticism of the text as found in PF has not always been kind, but recent research on *L* – which, like the PF, also includes *Libius Disconius* – offers some possibilities as to why this tale should have ended up in the mid-seventeenth-century PF. Horobin and Wiggins have noted that while the dialect of the scribe is from Shropshire, the contents of *L* most likely came from London exemplars. This would sit easily with other collections of Middle English verse, whereby in the fifteenth century, compilations would be read out in a household environment.[12] Changes made by the *L* scribe, who was responsible for copying out the entire manuscript, focus particularly on scenes showing comic and physical actions: for example, 'revisions and additions in the episodes that involve Merlin's mother suggests these scenes were the most attractive to the reviser and regarded as offering the most potential for dramatic enhancement' (Horobin and Wiggins, 2008, 38). Moreover, marginal annotations show that the scribe 'was not just a hired copyist who disappeared from the scene once the task of copying was complete. They show that the scribe of *L* was in some way involved in the reception of the texts he copied' (Horobin and Wiggins, 2008, 40). Marginal annotations may even indicate performance cues: 'it is difficult to resist the impression of a single scribe who set out to overhaul this collection of texts and whose agenda was to dramatize and make them more suitable for a listening audience'.[13] As with other Arthurian pieces in PF, *MER* may owe its inclusion at least in part to a tradition of performance. This is supported by the history of the Lincoln's Inn manuscript, which, while dating from the early fifteenth century, was still being annotated by one Anthony Foster, who died in 1643, i.e., contemporaneous with the writing of the PF itself.[14] While *L* is in the dialect of Shropshire but its story is the child of London audiences, the language and ancestry of *MER* itself is hard to evaluate. The lively narrative and performance potential of the versions of the Merlin story as found in the *AM2* texts undoubtedly contributed to their longevity, but performance, the passage of time, and audience response will have impacted upon vocabulary and dialect. As with *LAMBE*, it is likely that 'the modernized language of the Percy Folio demonstrates that *Arthour and Merlin* was a living, popular text, worth the trouble of updating for the sake of its exciting story' (Clifton, 2014, 86).

Notes

[1] A. O. H. Jarman, 'The Merlin Legend and the Welsh Tradition of Prophecy', in Rachel Bromwich, A. O. H. Jarman, and Brynley F. Roberts (eds), *The Arthur of the Welsh: The Arthurian Legend in Medieval Welsh Literature* (Cardiff: University of Wales Press, 1991), pp. 117–45.

[2] Evan Evans wrote to Percy on 23 October 1762 informing him that the story of the conception of Merlinus Ambrosius was to be found in Geoffrey of Monmouth's *HRB*, 'but it is set in another light by Nennius a British historian who lived three hundred years before him' (*Letters*, V, 42).

[3] Lovelich also translated the French *Estoire del Saint Graal* as *The High History of the Holy Grail*. For a discussion of both works and the English prose *Merlin*, see Karen Hodder, 'Henry Lovelich's History of the Holy Grail', *AE*, 78–83.

[4] Bodl. MS Douce 124 is an early nineteenth-century copy in the hand of Sir Walter Scott.

[5] *Of Arthour and of Merlin*, ed. O. D. Macrae-Gibson, 2 vols, EETS OS 268, 279 (Oxford: Oxford University Press, 1973, 1979). See also David Burnely, 'Of Arthour and Merlin', *AE*, 83–90. The Auchinlek MS also contains the romance *The Seven Sages of Rome*, which features a brief appearance by Merlin as 'the child with no father', an appearance which, as Hodder says, is 'further testimony to the popularity of Merlin in English romance' (*AE*, 81).

[6] See Macrae-Gibson (II, 35–44) for details of the MSS. There were two other prints of Wynkyn's version, one of 1500 and another of 1529, both of which survive only in fragments. The text of *W* can be found at Early English Books Online, available at www.proquest.com (accessed July 2023).

[7] That *PF* is not a copy of *L* is shown chiefly by the names of the principal characters: Constaunce, the father of the three princes in *L*, appears as Constantine in *PF*, Uter appears as Uther, Fortager becomes Vortiger, and Aungys (Hengist) becomes Anguis. PF also contains many variant lines and some omission of couplets where scribal errors such as eye-slip are not in question. Macrae-Gibson (II, 50) was of the opinion that PF and *H* 'probably had a distinct common source, which

derived from a close ancestor of L'. The names of the royal family in *D* are identical to those of PF, allowing for spelling; those of *W* are identical to those of both *L* and PF.

[8] Holland argues, however, that the continuation as found in Parts 8 and 9 in PF was a relatively late development by someone 'not fully familiar with romance convention', and that as a result 'P[F] appears to have descended by written transmission from a version closely related to L, with further incidents grafted on at a late date' (William E. Holland, 'Formulaic Diction and the Descent of a Middle English Romance', *Speculum* 48 (1973), pp. 99, 105).

[9] *W*, however, adds two lines after 'Amen for his moders loue' (the line that ends PF's version), closely resembling 3–4 in both *L* and *PF*. Immediately before this prayer, the scribe rounds off his version with two lines describing Uther's coronation, a passage that occurs in neither *L* nor PF.

[10] As with other long pieces in PF, each part is ruled off from the next, which begins with the part number in large italics straddling the margin, with the first eight lines bracketed and indented. This seems to be a quirk of the scribe rather than something he simply copied from his exemplars. There is no apparent change in either the ink or the handwriting between parts seven and eight, where PF carries on past the prayer that ends *L*.

[11] Percy's comment 'in 9 Parts or Cantos' immediately following the title of the work is in bold, upright script with separated letters, testifying to his belief that the poem is an early attempt at an English epic. While he numbered lines afresh at the start of each Part, his counting was occasionally erratic: for example, line 95 was numbered by him as 100; 331 as 100 instead of 95; 1697 as 265 instead of 245. In their edition, HF incorrectly label line 2289 as 2288.

[12] Simon Horobin and Alison Wiggins, 'Reconsidering Lincoln's Inn MS 150', *Medium Aevum* 77(1) (2008), pp. 31–32.

[13] Horobin and Wiggins, 2008, 48–49. The different voices and settings in the PF version and its analogues would, of course, lend themselves to performance by more than one individual.

[14] For Foster and his annotations, see Nicole Clifton, 'Modern Readers of the Romance "Of Arthour and Merlin"', *Arthuriana* 24(2) (2014), pp. 71–91.

Editions and Sigla

Geoffrey of Monmouth, *Life of Merlin: Geoffrey of Monmouth* Vita Merlini. *Edited with Introduction, Facing Translation, Textual Commentary, Name Notes Index and Translations of the* Lailoken *Tales, by Basil Clarke* (Cardiff: University of Wales Press, 1973).

HF, II, 417–96.

Macrae-Gibson, O. D. (ed.), *Of Arthour and of Merlin*, 2 vols, EETS OS 268, 279 (Oxford: Oxford University Press, 1973, 1979). This edition has *L* and *A* in parallel-text, with *P* filling in the gaps in the former.

Further Reading

Calkin, Siobhain Bly, 'Violence, Saracens, and English Identity in *Of Arthour and Merlin*', *Arthuriana* 14 (2004), pp. 17–36.

Clifton, Nicole, 'Modern Readers of the Romance "Of Arthour and Merlin"', *Arthuriana* 24(2) (2014), pp. 71–91.

Goodrich, Peter H., *Merlin: A Casebook* (New York: Routledge, 2003).

Holland, William E., 'Formulaic Diction and the Descent of a Middle English Romance', *Speculum* 48 (1973), pp. 89–109.

Horobin, Simon, and Wiggins, Alison, 'Reconsidering Lincoln's Inn MS 150', *Medium Aevum* 77(1) (2008), pp. 30–53.

Jarman, A. O. H., 'The Merlin Legend and the Welsh Tradition of Prophecy', in Rachel

Bromwich, A. O. H. Jarman, and Brynley F. Roberts (eds), *The Arthur of the Welsh: The Arthurian Legend in Medieval Welsh Literature* (Cardiff: University of Wales Press, 1991), pp. 117–45.

Sklar, Elizabeth, 'Arthour and Merlin: The Englishing of Arthur', *Michigan Academician* 8 (1975), pp. 49–57.

MERLINE

    Hee that made with his hand,   p. 145/f. 72v
    Both winde, water and lande,
    Give them all good ending
    That will Listen to my talking,
5   & I shall you informe
    How Merlyn was gotten & borne,
    & of his wisdome alsoe,
    & other happs many mooe   *events; more*
    Which then befell in England.
10 He that will this understand:
    In England there was a King,
    A No[b]le man in all thin[ge].
    In warr he was ware & wight,   p.146/f. 73r   *swift and valiant*
    Constantine forsooth he hight;
15 A doughtye man he was of deed,
    & right wise he was of reede.   *counsel*
    King he was of great honor,
    & holden prince & Emperour,
    For King Anguish of Denmarke
20 & many a Sarazen stoute & starke*   *fierce*
    Warred on him withouten fayle,
    & he overcame them in battaile
    That they durst him not abyde,*
    & drove them out of feild that tyde.   *that time*
25 Then had The Kinge sonnes 3,
    The fairest children that might bee.
    The eledest so[nn]e that shol[d] be King
    Was called Moyne, with[out] Leasing;   *without a lie*
    The othe[r] were of great renowne,
30 Both Uther & Pendragon.
    In that time, wee find in booke,*
    A great sicknesse the King tooke,
    That out of this world he must wende,   *go*
    & after his Barrons he did send.
35 & wen they were comen everecheone,
    The King said to them anon,
    'Lords,' he said to the[m] anon,*
    'Out of this world must I gon.
    For God's love & Charitye,
40 & for the love you owe to me,
    When I am dead & locked in clay,
    Helpe my Children in what you may,
    & take Moyne my Eldest so[nn]e
    & make him King & give him crowne.
45 Hold him for your Lord,' said hee.

All they granted itt shold soe bee.
Then had the King a steward fayre,   *excellent*
That was cal[l]ed Sir Vortiger.
His truth to the King he plight,   *he promised*
50 To helpe his children with all his might;
But soone the traytor was forsworne   *treacherous*
& brake troth he had made beforne.
For the King out of this world went
& faire was buryed verament.   *truly*
55 Att Winchester, without Leasinge,
There was made his buryinge.
Erles & Barons soone anon,   *straightway*
Tooke them together everechone.
Without any more dwellinge   *delay*
60 They made Moyne Lord & King,
But the Steward, Sir Vortiger,
Was full wrath, as you may heere,
& stoode there againe with all his might   *against it*
Both by day & eke by night,   *also*
65 For he thought himselfe with treason
To be Lord & King with Crowne.
As soone as Moyne was chosen King
Into Denmarke the word can springe.
King Anguis hard it the[n],   *heard*
70 & therof was both glad and faine.   *happy*
Soone M[e]ssengers in that ilke tyde   *same*
He sent over all the land wyde
After many sarazens stout & starke,
& of Saxons & of Denmarke
75 A 100 thousand & yett moe,
On horss backe & on foote alsoe.
Then wold they noe longer abyde,
But dight them to shipp that tyde*
& brought into England, I saine,
80 Many a doughtye Sarazen.   *fierce*
But England was called the[n]*
Mikle Brittaine of every man.   *Great*
Then the word wyde sprange   p. 147/f. 73v
How the Danish King with wronge
85 Wrought in England Mickle woe.   *caused*
King Moyne heard that it was soe;
He went unto Sir Vortiger
& prayed him with lowlye cheere,   *humbly*
& besought him of his honour   *begged*
90 For to be his governor
Against his foemen to fight.
He answered him anon right,

    && fained himself sicke, as traytor strong,   *pretended to be*
    & said w*i*th wright & not w*i*th wrong,
95 He wold nev*er* come i[n] battaile
    When his strenght began to faile.
    For all this he said aforehand,
    For he thought to be K*ing* of *tha*t Land.
    The K*ing* he wold him noe more pray,
100 But tooke his leave & went his way.
    Messengers he sent *tha*t tyde
    To all the Lands on every side,
    For Erles, Barons & K*nigh*ts
    To come & helpe him in his fights.
105 & when they were all come,
    & their armes done upon,
    the[y] pricked forth w*i*thout fayle   *set forth*
    to give the Danes' K*ing* battaille.
    There was cloven many a sheeld
110 & many k*nigh*t fallen in feild.
    All *tha*t they mett in strond,*   *there*
    Horsse & man fell to the ground.
    Soone the English men, the sooth to say,
    Were discomffitt & fled awaye;   *defeated*
115 To Winchester the[y] fledden thoe,
    W*i*th much sorrow, care & woe.
    But the Danish K*ing* before,
    Much of his folke he had forlore,   *lost*
    & then forthe he sent his sond   *summons*
120 So[n]e into his owne Land,
    To all *tha*t might weapons beare
    Shold come & helpe him in this warre;
    Of warre wold he nev*er* blinne,   *cease*
    Cytyes & castles for to winne.
125 In England he warrd full sore   *waged bitter war*
    Halfe a yeare & some deale more.
    All the Barons in England
    Tooke them together in *tha*t stond   *in that place*
    What was best for them to done
130 For to avenge them of their fone.
    When they were comen all arright
    Erles & Barrons, Lords & Knights,
    The[y] said Moyne their young K*ing*
    Was but a Brotherlinge,   *worthless creature*
135 & said if Vortiger K*ing* were
    He wold bring them out of care.
    They said anon, both old & younge,
    *Tha*t Vortiger shold be their K*ing*;
    & when they had spoken all this,

140	12 barrons they send, Iwis,	
	To S*i*r Vortiger the bold,	
	To witt whether he nay wold*	
	Against their foemen to stand,	
	To drive them out of England.	
145	& when the Barrons all in fere	*all together*
	Were come to S*i*r Vortiger,	
	Well & hendlye they him greete,	*courteously*
	& on the d[e]ske by him they seete,	*dais*
	& [he] bade them w*i*th words still	*quietly*
150	For to say what was their will.	
	& the[y] answered fayre againe,	
	& bade *tha*t he shold them saine	
	Why he wold not w*i*th them gone	
	For to avenge them of their foone,	p.148/f. 74r *foes*
155	& sayden 'Sith Constantine was dead	
	Wee have had a sorry read,'	*counsel*
	& bade *tha*t he shold take in hand	
	To warre them out of England.	
	Then answered S*i*r Vortiger	
160	As a man of great power,	
	'I was yett nev*er* yo*u*r K*ing*,	
	Why pray you me of such a thinge?	
	Nor yett nev*er* here beforne,	
	Nor to you was nev*er* sworne	
165	For to helpe you att yo*u*r neede,	
	& therfore, soe God me speede,	*so help me God*
	Wend home unto [yo*u*r] K*ing*,	
	& pray him in [all thing]	
	To helpe you against yo*u*r fone,	
170	For helpe of me gett you none.'	
	Then answered a bold Barron,	
	'Our K*ing* is but a younge one,*	*fool*
	For when he seeth a sword drawne	
	He weeneth to bee slowen.*	
175	Hee doth us noe other good,	
	But flyeth away as he were wood.	*mad*
	Had thou beene amongst us all,	
	*Tha*t chance had nev*er* beffalle;	
	Thus saine all our Peeres.'	
180	'I trow well,' said Vortiger,	*I believe so*
	'Certaine it was great dole	*pity*
	To make a kinge of such a foole.	
	Had you made a Man yo*u*r K*ing*,	
	He had saved you in all thinge.	
185	But sithen siker you bee,	*But since you are safe*
	Helpe gett you none of mee.	

	But if your King were dead, aplight,	*I assure you*
	I wold helpe you with all my Might.'	
	Then said the Barrons eche one,	
190	'Will yee that wee our King slowen?'	
	'Nay,' he sayd withouten strife,	*calmly*
	'While your younge King is alive,	
	Helpe gett you None, Iwis.'	
	The Barrons tooke leave with this.	
195	To Winchester they went all	
	There the King was in halle.	
	& as he sate att Meate,	*at his meal*
	They run to him in great heate;	
	& as he sate att the bord,	*table*
200	Or ever he spake any w[or]d,	
	The[y] run all to him anon	
	& smitten of his head full soone.	*struck*
	& when the King was thus slowe,	
	Ereles, Barrons, hye & lowe,	
205	Tooken them all to reede	
	That a King they must have need,	*must needs have*
	All England for to warre*	
	Against them that will or darre.	
	Then had Moyne brethren tow,	
210	Younge Children they were alsoe;	
	The one hight Uther, the other Pendragon.	*was called*
	Then saiden the Barrons everye one	
	That they shold never speede	
	But if a doughtye man of deede	*powerful*
215	Were chosen to be their King in fere,*	
	& sweren that Sir Vortiger	
	Was a doughtye man of deede,	
	Stout & staleworth of a steede.*	
	The[y] swearen then together eche one	
220	That other King they wold have none.	
	Then was there neither Knight nor swaine	
	That durst speake them againe,	*against*
	But granted it, both old & younge,	
	To make Sir Vortiger their King.	
225	Soe in the time of Aprill, as yee may heere,	
	[The 12 Barrons] came to Vortiger	
	And said that England's right	p. 149/f. 74v
	Was lorne thorrow their King, aplight,	*lost; certainly*
	& he was dead without Leasing,	
230	& his 2 brothers were to young	
	To hold the Kingdome in hand.	
	'Therfore, the com[m]ons of the Land	
	Have you chosen with Honour	

	For to be their Emperour.'	
235	Blithe & glad was Vortyger	
	& anon was K*ing* w*i*thout danger.	*without any resistance*

2ᵈ parte:

	Att the feast of the turnament	
	The barrons *tha*t were gent,	*noble*
	*Tha*t all the tre[a]son unde[r]stoode,	*understood*
240	They had ruth of the right blood,*	
	*Tha*t the children shold be done to dead.	
	Therfore, they tooke another reade	*advice*
	& tooken Uther & Pendragon	
	& passed ov*er* the seas anon.	
245	Of theire passage wist noe moe*	
	But the hend barrons 2.	
	& when the feast was all hold,	
	Vortiger the traitor bold	
	Lett make accompackement	*a compact*
250	Of erles & barrons *tha*t were gent,	
	Att w*h*ich Parlament they had hight	*summoned*
	For to have slaine the children right.	
	Vortiger com[m]anded anon	
	For to feitch Uther & Pendragon.	
255	Fast about all they sought	
	But they cold find them nought.	
	When Vortiger this understoode	
	Then hee waxed almost woode.	*mad*
	But nev*er*thelesse, S*i*r Vortiger	
260	Did give com[m]andment far & neere	
	To Duke, Erle, Barron & K*nigh*t,	
	To make them ryedey for to fight.	*ready*
	& soone the[y] dight them, Iwis,	*prepared themselves*
	W*i*th armes & w*i*th horsses of price.	
265	& when they were ready dight,	
	Forsooth it is a seemlye sight.	
	W*i*th helme one head & bright banner,	
	All went forth w*i*th Vortiger.	
	The K*ing* of Denmark w*i*th pryde	
270	Brought his host by his syde.	
	Either host can other assayle;	
	There might you see a strong battele.	
	The English folkes, sooth to say,*	
	They foughten so well *tha*t day	
275	*Tha*t K*ing* Anguish in *tha*t tyde	
	Was upon the worsse side,	
	& fledd away as he were woode	

  Into a Castle faire & goode,
  & manye of his host alsoe.
280 Fast away can they goe,
  & Vortiger with his rowte   *company*
  Besett the castle all aboute.
  & when t[h]ey had Longe Laine,
  Vortiger send to them for to [s]aine,*
285 If he [in] peace passe must,*
  Hee wolde take all his host
  & wende into his countrye,
  & never after that day
  Wold he passe the sea stronde*
290 Ne come to warr in Englande.
  & when this covenant was all done,
  That they wold not into England come,
  Vortiger tooke his councell
  & lett them passe certaine.
295 & soe they went to the sea
  & passed to their owne countrye.
  Vortiger then tooke his ost   *army*
  & went thence with a great boaste;
  He held feast many a day
300 With much s[o]lace & with play.
  And when the feast was all helde   p. 150/f. 75r
  The 12 barrons that I erst of told,
  That had slaine Moyne the King,
  They bethought them of a wonderous thing,
305 That they wold wend to Vortiger
  & aske him meede & liverr,*
  & said, 'Vortiger, now you bee above,
  Now yeelde us meede. For thy Love
  Wee slew our right King by kind.   *by right of birth*
310 Now will wee see if thou bee hynde,   *generous*
  For wee brought thee to thine above;   *to your victory*
  Thinke what wee did for your love.'
  King Vortiger answered againe;
  With Egar Moode he can saine,   *angrily*
315 'By the law that God made,
  You shall have as yee bade!
  For yee are traitors starke & stronge,
  & have slaine your King with wronge,
  & yee have wrought against the law,
320 & therfore yee shall both hang & draw'.
  He did take horsses fleete
  & tyed them to their feete,
  & then drew them on a pavement
  & sithen hanged them verament.

325	Then Many an Erle & Barro[n] hynde,	
	That were of the barrons' Kinde,	*kin*
	To Vortiger they ran anon	
	As his most deadlye fone.	
	Hard on him can they fight,	
330	For to slay him the[y] thought right.	
	Vortiger with Might & Maine	*with great force*
	He with his host went them againe.	*against*
	A strong battell there was dight,	
	& many a head therof smitt,	
335	Soe that Vortiger that day	
	Was glad for to scape away.	
	Anon the Barrons send their sonde	*summons*
	Wyde over all England,	
	To all their freinds, sibb & couthe	*kinsmen and acquaintances*
340	East, west, North & southe,	
	& told them that sooth tyde	*the truth*
	How Vortiger with great despighte,	
	With great treason & with wrong,	
	Their kinred had drawen & honge.	
345	Wrath then was many a man,	
	& al together swarren then	
	That they wold not assunder breake	
	Till they were on him wreake.	*avenged*
	Everye man on other besought,	
350	A great host on him they brought,	
	& foughten with Sir Vortiger	
	9 monthes of this yeere,	
	That many a Lady fayre & free	
	Lost her Lord & her meanye.	*household*
355	Then the warr endured long,	
	& the Barrons waxed strong,	
	That Vortiger had not power	
	Against them longer to endure.	
	Messengers anon hee tooke	
360	& made them sworne upon a booke	
	That they shold his arrand gone.	*errand*
	& letters he tooke to them anon	
	& sent them over the seas, Iwis,	
	To Denmarke unto King Anguis,	
365	& that hee shold come att neede	
	With all the power that he might lead,	
	Against his foemen for to fight	
	That wold deprive him of his right.	
	Then was King Anguis blythe,	
370	& Messengers hee sent swithe	*straightaway*
	To Duke, Erle, Barron & Knight,	

	& to all *that* weapon beare might.	
	Th[en to shipp they went] blith[e],	*quickly*
	And ov*er* the sea can they drive.	p. 151/f. 75v
375	& when they came to Vortiger,	
	He welcomed them w*i*th merry cheere,	
	& seazed there into his hands*	
	Halfe the realme of England	
	*Tha*t he had, or have might,	
380	For to helpe him in his right.	
	When this covenant was made fast,	
	All they dighten them in hast,	*armed*
	Into Battelle for to wend	
	W*i*th the Barrons *tha*t were hende.	
385	Besids Salsbury a Lyte	*near*
	There the battell can the[y] smite.*	*strike*
	Many a bold Champion,	
	& many a 1000 in *tha*t stonde	*place*
	Were slaine & brought to ground.	
390	Many a Ladye & damsell	
	Can weepe *tha*t day w*i*th teares fell.	*bitter*
	Then had Vortiger 10	
	Against one of the Barrons' men.	
	Discomffitted they were *tha*t day;	
395	W*i*th great sorrow the[y] fled away.	
	& Vortiger, *tha*t wold not spare,	
	But hunted them as hound doth hare.*	
	Them *tha*t he did ov*er*take	
	Noe other peace did he make,	
400	But did them all to-draw & hange.	
	But sithen all *tha*t was wrong,	*since*
	Many a Barron hynde & free	
	Fled out of his owne countrye,	
	& dwelled out many a yeere	
405	For love of *Si*r Vortiger*	
	Then Vortiger ceazed into his hands	
	The Lands & rents of all the Barrons,	
	& both wiffe, Chylde & swaine	
	He drove out of the Lannd certaine.	
410	K*ing* Anguis had verament	
	A daughter *tha*t was faire & gent,	
	*Tha*t was heathen Sarazen,	
	& Vortiger for love fine	
	Undertooke her for his wiffe	
415	& lived in cursing all his liffe.	*damnation*
	For he did make the Christen Men	
	To Marry the heathen women,	
	Soe *tha*t nighe all England	

	Was fallen into the Devill's hand;	
420	& thus they lived many a yeere.	
	Soe on a day, *Sir* Vortiger	
	Bethought him on the children tow	
	*Tha*t out of the Land were fledden thoe,	
	& alsoe he bethought him then	
425	Of many another doughtye Man	
	*Tha*t hee had fleemed out of the Land,	*banished*
	& in his hart gan understand	
	*Tha*t it was a sorry happe,	*chance*
	& doubted him of an afterclappe.	*reprisal*
430	Anon, he sent Messengers	
	Ov*er* all the Land for Carpenters,	
	& for good Massons alsoe,	
	The best *that* were in Land thoe.	
	Many a 1000 there came anon,	
435	*Tha*t colde worke Lime & stone.	
	& when they were comen all,	
	The K*ing* anon to them gan call,	
	& said, 'Lordings, I have thought	
	A strong castle to be wrought	
440	Of bigge timber, lime & stone,	
	*Tha*t such another be noe were none,	*nowhere*
	If ev*er* I have any need,	
	My liffe therin *th*at I may Lead.	
	The Castle yee shall make surlye	*surely*
445	Upon the plaine of Salsburye.	
	Goe & doe as I you bade	
	*Tha*t itt be [surlye &] well made,	
	And you shall have to yo*ur* hye	152/f. 76r *reward*
	As much as you shall desire.'	
450	The workemen went forthe thoe,	
	15,000 & yett moe,	
	Hewen timber, carving stone,	
	& Laid a foundation there anon.	
	Some laid, & some bore,	
455	& some can the worke arreare.	*erect*
	*Tha*t ilke day, round about,	
	Itt was brest high w*i*thout doubt.	
	When itt came to the night,	
	To their bedd they went wright,	
460	& came again upon the Morrow	
	& found a thing of much sorrow.	
	For all the fondation the[y] found,	
	Lying abroad upon the ground,	
	& all to torne, both Lime & stone.	
465	The[y] had great wonder ev*er*ye one;	

Better read then cold they None,*
But began it new againe,
& sped as well, the sooth to say,
As the[y] did the first daye.
470 & when the evening was comen,
The[y] went to bedd all soone.
On morrow they came anon,
& found it cast downe, lime & stone,
& was spredd both heere & the[r]e,
475 & thus they faren halfe a yeere.
When the King heard of this,
Great wonder he had, Iwis,
& oft asked both young & old,
& of the wonder wold be told,
480 & why the worke might not stand.
There was none within the la[n]d,
Highe nor lowe, Learned nor Clarke,*
That cold tell him of the worke.
King Vortiger sate in his hall
485 Amongst his Barrons & Knights all,
& sware he wold never spare   *spare no effort*
Untill he wist why it were.
& anon he sent his sonde
Over all England,
490 After Clerkes old & younges,
That cold tell him wonderous things.
The Messengers forth went
& did the King's Com[m]andment.
Many a wise Clarke they sought;
495 Before the King they all we[re] brought.
King Vortiger opposed them all   *questioned*
Why his worke did downe fall,
But there was none that cold him tell.
Then he sware he wold them quell   *kill*
500 But if they wold say in hast   *Unless*
Why this worke was downe cast.
10 Masters he tooke anon,
The wisest of them every one.
Into a chamber they were doe
505 That no[e] man might come them to.
Soe one day, verament,
The[y] looked into the firmament,
& under the welkin their shewd a skye,   *there appeared a sign*
That shewedd them witterlye,   *certainly*
510 That in 5 winters there beforne,
A knave child there was borne,
Begotten without any man.

  & if they had *tha*t child then,
  & sley him hastilye then
515 Or he spoke to any man,   *Before*
  & smeere the worke w*i*th his blood,
  Then shold *tha*t worke be sure & goode.
  [Thus the sky] shewed them there
  And passed away w*i*thout more.   p. 153/f. 76v
520 Then were the clarkes gladd & blythe,
  & came to Vortiger sithe,*   *quickly*
  & told him w*i*thout lesse   *without a lie*
  Of a knave child *tha*t was gotten, Iwis,
  W*i*thout seede of any man.
525 Thus they saydden ev*er*ye one,
  'Doe send & feitch *tha*t child,
  Whether hee bee in towne or field,
  & doe him slay hastilye,
  & take the blood of his bodye
530 & smere the worke rond about,
  & it shall stand, w*i*thout doubt.'
  Glad & blithe was Vortiger,
  & called to him 12 Messengers,
  & p*ar*ted them in veritye,
535 *Tha*t nev*er* a one might other see.
  He sent them forth upon his sond
  Unto 4 p*ar*ts of England,
  & com[m]anded *tha*t they stint nought   *did not give up*
  Till he were befor him brought.
540 Anon the Messengers forth went,
  And did the K*ing*'s com[m]andement.
  & S*i*r Vortiger the bold
  Caused the clarkes to be hold   *kept confined*
  Till the Messengers came againe,
545 To witt what the[y] wold saine,   *know; say*
  & sware by Jesu, Heaven K*ing*,
  If they made any Leasinge
  Noe ransome shold for them gone,
  But they shold dye ev*er*ye one.
550 Now let us tell of these Messengers
  *Tha*t went from S*i*r Vortiger's
  For to seeke the child soe younge,
  & yee shall heare a wonderous thing.
  & if yee will a stond dwell,   *wait a while*
555 Of *tha*t Chyld I shall you tell,
  On what Manner the Messenger
  Brought him to S*i*r Vortiger,
  & what hee hight w*i*thouten lesse,
  & of what kind he is,

560 *Tha*t yee may understand & witt — *purpose*; *begotten*
Thorrow what skill he was gett.

3ᵈ parte:

David the prophet, & Moyses,
Wittenesse & saith how itt was
*Tha*t God had made, thorrow His Might,
565 Heaven full of angells bright.
The joy *tha*t the[y] hadden then,
Forsooth no tounge tell can,
Til[l] Lwcifer w*i*th guilt of pryde,
& all *tha*t held w*i*th him *tha*t tyde,
570 Such vengeance God on them can take
*Tha*t they are now feinds blake. — *black*
& I find in Holy Ritt, — *Holy Writ*
The[y] fell from Heaven to Hell pitt
6 dayes & 7 nights,
575 As thicke as hayle in thunder lights.
& when it was Our Ladye's will,*
Heaven closed againe full still.
The feendes *tha*t I told of ere,
Fellen out of heaven w*i*th Lucifer.
580 Those *tha*t bidden on the ayre on haight, — *remain*
Fell the[y] beene, stronge & sleight. — *Evil; cunning*
Of the ayre the[y] take their light
& have great strenght & might*
After man to make a bodye
585 Fayre of coulour & rudye,
Discending downe among mankind
To tise men to deadlye sinne. — *tempt, lure*
All they wist well beforne
*Tha*t Jesu wold on Mary be borne.
590 Therto the feendes hadden envye,
& said to the earth the[y] wolden hye — *go*
To neigh on earth a maiden mild, — *approach*
& begett on her a child.
Thus the[y] w[end] the world to have [filed],* — p. 154/f. 77r
595 But att the Last they were beguiled. — *outwitted*
I shall you tell how itt was,
Now yee may heere a wonderous case.
In *tha*t time, I unde[r]stand,
A rich man was in England
600 & had a go[o]d [wo]man to his wiffe,
& lived together a cleane liffe.
A sonne they had, & daughters 3,
The fairest children *tha*t might bee.

Anon, a feende *that* I of told,
605 *That* woonen in the ayre soe bold,   *lived*
& for to tempt *tha*t good woman,
He light on the earth then,
& in her body had great might
& brought her into striffe & fight,
610 & made her after w*i*th Egar Moode,
To cursse her child as shee was woode.
Upon a day att Even Late
Thorrow the feend, w*i*th great hate
W*i*th her sonne shee gan to grame   *became angry*
615 & curst him fast by his name,
& to the Devill shee him behight*
With all her power & her might.
Then was the feende glad & blythe,
& thought to doe him shame swithe.
620 & when it was come to night,
The feende went to her house right
& strangled her sonne where he lay.
The wiffe rose up when it was day,
& found her ssonne dead att morrow,
625 & went & strangled herselfe for sorrowe.*
& when her Lo*rd* heard this,
Anon swithe for sorrow, Iwis,
Sodainlye he dyed thoe
W*i*thout shrift or houzell alsoe.*
630 The folke of the cuntrye *tha*t tyde,
*Tha*t wooned there neere beside,   *lived*
Came together then to see,
& had ruth & great pittye.
& many a man *tha*t day
635 Weeped & sayd 'Wellawaye'   Alas!
For *tha*t good man & his wiffe,
*Tha*t had lived soe good a liffe.
An Hermitt *tha*t wooned there beside
Came to see them there *tha*t tyde.
640 Blasye, forsooth, his name was,*
& oft for them he sayd alas
*Tha*t it was beffallen soe.
In his heart he was full woe,
& said it was verament
645 Thorrow the feende's incomberment.*
The daughters he found there alive;
The Hermitt hee can them shrive,
& when he had done & sayd,
Fayre penance on them he Layd.
650 & when hee had done soe,

	Home againe can he goe.	
	Then the Maydens all in fere	*together*
	Served God *with* blythe cheere.	
	In all England then was the usage	*custom*
655	If any woman did outrage,	*behaved wantonly*
	But if itt were in her spousage,	
	If any man, old or younge	
	Might it witt of *tha*t countrye,	
	All qu[i]cke shee shold dolven bee,	*buried alive*
660	But if it were a light woman called*	
	To all men *tha*t aske her wold.	
	Soe the feend *tha*t had might,	
	*Tha*t wooned in the ayre light,	
	Into the earth he light downe then,	
665	& went unto an old woman,	
	& hight her both gold & fee	*promised*
	To wende to the sisters 3	
	The eldest mayden to enchant,*	
	[Some younge man's body] to enfante.*	
670	And shee might bring her t[hert]o,*	p. 155/f. 77v
	He hett her gold for ev*er* more.	*promised*
	*Tha*t old Queane was full glad	
	& did as the Devill her badde,	
	& went to the sisters 3.	
675	As soone as shee might them see,	
	To the eldest sister soone s[hee] saiyd,	
	'Alas, my deere sweete Mayd,	
	Thou hast fayre feete & hande,	
	A gentle body for to sounde,*	
680	White hayre & long arme.	
	Iwise it is much harme	
	*Tha*t thy bodye might not assay	*try*
	W*i*th some younge man for to play,	
	*Tha*t yee might find in ev*er*ye place	
685	Game, mirth, & great solace.'	*comfort*
	'Certaine,' said the maiden then,	
	'If *tha*t I take any man	
	But if it were in spousing,	*marriage*
	Any man either old or younge,	
690	& itt were knowen in this countrye,	*if*
	All quicke I shold be dolven be.'	
	'Nay, certaine,' said the old queane,	
	'Yee may it doe w*i*thout deane,	*noise*
	Both in bower & in bedd,	
695	Although noe man doe you wedd.	
	& therfore dread thee nought,	
	For it needs nev*er* be forth brought,	

	& if thou wilt doe by my read,	
	Thou diddest never a better deede.'	
700	Soe thorrow the queane's inchantment	
	& the feend's incumberment,	*temptation*
	The eldest sister, the sooth to say,	
	Lett a young man with her play;	
	& when shee liked best the game,	
705	It turned her to much shame,	
	For shee was taken & forth drawen,	*taken away*
	& of her game shee was knowen	
	& for that worke dolven was.	
	Many a man sayd for her 'alas.'	
710	The feende yett another while	
	The other sister h[e] can beguile,	
	& made her to love a faire young man,	
	& after was his lem[m]an then	*lover*
	Shee was taken forthwise,*	*forthwith*
715	& brought before the hye Justice	
	Her judgment to understand,	
	As itt was the law of the land.	
	The Justice opposed her thoe	*questioned*
	Wherfore shee had done soe.	
720	Shee answered as shee was taught,	
	& said shee forsooke itt nought,	
	& said shee was a light woman	
	To all that wold come to her com[m]on.	*come*
	& soe shee scaped them away,	
725	Soe that her followed all that day*	
	Of Harlotts a great race	
	To fyle her body for that case.	*defile*
	Yett the feende in that while	
	The 3.ᵈ sister can beguile.	
730	Then was the youngest sister soe woe	
	That nye her hart burst in tow,	
	For her mother had hangd her selfe	
	& her one sister quicke was delfe,	*was buried alive*
	& for that her father dyed amisse	
735	& her brother was strangled, Iwis,	
	Her other sister a whore stronge,	
	That harlotts was ever among.	
	Almost for sorrow & for thought,	
	In wan hope shee was brought.	*despair*
740	To the Hermitt shee went then,	
	To that hight Blassye, that good man,	*called*
	& told him all the sooth be[forne],	
	How all her kindred were forlorne.	p. 156/f. 78r
	The Hermitt had wonder great;	

745	On God's halfe he her besett,*	
	'I bid thee have God in thy minde,	
	& lett be the lore of the feende,'	
	& bade her forsake in any wise	
	Pryde, hate & covetise,	
750	Alsoe s[l]oth & envye,	
	& man's flesh in lecherye,	
	All such workes for to flee;	
	& bade her God's servant bee,	
	& bade her to take good keepe	*good care*
755	*Tha*t shee layd her not downe to sleepe,	
	& namelye not in the night,	*especially*
	Unlesse shee had a Candle light,	
	& windowes & dores in *tha*t stond	
	To be spurred to roafe and ground,	*barred; roof*
760	& make there againe wi*t*h good noyce	
	The signe of the Holy Crosse.	
	& when he had taught her soe,	
	Home againe can shee goe	
	& served God wi*t*h hart glad,	
765	& did as the hermitt her bade.	
	& yett the feende thorrow envye	
	Beguiled her wi*t*h treacherye	
	& brought her into a dreerye cheere:	
	I shall you tell in what manner.	
770	Upon a day, verament,	
	Wi*t*h neighbors to Ale shee went.	
	Long shee sate & did amisse,	
	*Tha*t drunken shee was, Iwis.	
	Her other sister *tha*t I of told,*	
775	*Tha*t was a whore stout & bold,	
	Came thither *tha*t same day	
	Wi*t*h many harlotts for to play,	
	& missaide her sister as shee was wood,	*mad*
	& called her other then good.	
780	Soe long shee Chi[d]d in a resse,	*chided; rage*
	The whore start up, wi*t*hout lesse,	
	& went to her sister in a rage	
	& smote her on the visage.	
	Then home to her chamber can shee can goe	
785	& made to the dores betweene them tow	
	& cryed out, & Neighbors came,	
	& the whore soone the[y] name	*took*
	& droven her away anon,	
	& the harlotts eve*r*ye one.	
790	When they were driven away,	
	The maid *tha*t in the chamber Lay	

Merline 163

	All made as shee were woode,*	*mad*
	Weeped & fared as shee were w*i*th ill moode.	
	& when it was come to night,	
795	Upon the bed shee fell downe right,	
	All both shodd & cladde.	
	Shee fell on sleepe & all was madd,	
	& forgott her howse unblessed,	
	As the hermitt had her vised.	*advised*
800	Then was the feende glad & blythe	
	& thought to doe her shame swithe.	
	Over all well hee might,	
	For there was noe crosse made *tha*t night.	
	& to the Mayd anon he went,	
805	& thought all Christendome to have shent.	*destroyed*
	A [t]raine of a childe he put in her, thoe,*	
	& passed away where hee cam froe.	
	& when *tha*t woman was awaked	
	& found her body lying naked,	
810	& shee grope w*i*th her hands	
	& some seed there shee found,	
	Wherby shee wende witterlye	*understood clearly*
	*Tha*t some man had Lyen her by.	
	Then shee rose up in hast	p. 157/f. 78v
815	& found her dore sparred fast.	*fastened*
	When shee found *tha*t it was soe,	
	In her hart shee was full woe,	
	& thought itt was some wicked thinge	
	*Tha*t wold her to shame [bringe].	
820	All the night shee made great sorrowe	
	& to the Hermitt shee went att morrowe,	
	& told him all the case.	
	The hermitt sayd, alas, alas,	
	*Tha*t shee had broken her pennance,	
825	& said it was the feend's combrance.	*temptation*
	'A, good father,' said shee thoe,	
	'What if itt be fallen soe	
	*Tha*t a child be on me gotten	
	& any man may it witten?	
830	Then shall I be delven anon,	
	All quicke both bodye & bo[n]e.'	
	'Certaine,' said the goodman,	
	'My deere daughter, after then	
	I shall you helpe w*i*th all my might,	
835	Till of itt I have sight.	
	Goe home daughter now mine.	
	& have God's blessing & mine,	
	For He may, & His will bee,	*if*

Out of thy sorrow bringe thee.'
840 Home shee went with dreerye moode
& served God with hart good.
& everye day after then
Her wombe will greater began*
Soe that shee might it not hyde,
845 But itt was perceived in that tyde.
Then was shee taken forsoothe, Iwisse,
& brought afore the hye Justice.
The Justice opposed her thoe,
Why shee had done soe.
850 & for shee wrought against the law,*
He Judged her for to be slowe.   *killed*
& shee answered & said, 'Nay,
I wrought never against the law,*
& sware by Him that dyed on tree,   *the Cross*
855 'Was never man that neighed mee   *came near*
With fleshly lust or Lecherye,
Nor kissed my body with villa[n]ye.'
The Justice answered anon,
'Dame, thou lyest, by St John!
860 Thy words beene false & wylde
When men may see thou art with childe.
In this world was never childe borne
But man's seede there was beforne,
Save Jesu Christ thorrow His might
865 Was borne of a mayden bright.
How may thou for shame then,
Say thou had never part of any man,
When I myselfe the soothe may see
That a child is gotten of thee?'
870 'Certaine, Sir,' shee said then,
'I goe with child without any man.
By Him,' shee sayd, 'that made this day,
There was never [man] that by me Lay,
But as I sleeped one night,
875 By mee lay a Selcoth wight,   *strange being*
But I wist never what it was.
Therfore, I doe me in thy grace.'
The Justice said withouten fayle,
'I never hard of such a marveile!
880 Today nay shall the woman be delfe   *buried*
Till I have asked wiffes 12
If any child may be made
Without getting of manhood;
& if the[y] say itt may soe bee,
885 All quitt shalt th[ou goe], & free.

```
        And if the[y] say that it may nay,                  p. 158/f. 79r
        All quicke, men shall delfe thee today.'
        On 12 wives [hee] did [him] anon,
        & they answered every one
890     That never child was borne of maiden
        But Jesu Christ, they all saydden.
        Blasye the Hermitt upstartt then.
        To answer the Justice he began:
        'Sir Justice,' he sayd thoe,
895     'Hear me in a word or tow.
        That this woman hath told eche deale,              everything
        Certez I beleeve itt weele,
        & yee beleeven her right nought.
        By God & all this world wrought,
900     I have her shriven & taught the law.
        To mee wold shee never a-know                       confess
        That any man for any meede                          reward
        Neighed her body with fleshlye deede.
        Therfore, it is against the law
905     That shee dolven shold be this day.
        Giff shee have served for to spilt*
        The chylde in her wom[be] hath not gilt.
        Therfore, Sir, doe by my reade                       advice
        & put her not this time to dead,
910     But doe her in warde before*
        Till the childe be bore.
        & then', he sayd, 'God itt wott,
        2 yeere keepe it shee motte,
        '& peradventure,' he sayd, 'then,
915     The child may proue a good man.'
        Then said the Justice,
        'Hermitt, thy words are full wise.
        Therfore, by thy doome I will,                    judgement
        Noe man today shall her spill.'
920     The Justice com[m]anded anon
        To lead her to a tower of stone,
        & that noe wight shold with her goe                  nobody
        But a midswiffe & noe moe.
        The tower was strong & hye
925     That noe man might come her nye.
        A window there was made thoe,
        & a cord tyed therto,
        To draw therein all thin[g]e,                        things
        Fire & water, Meate & drinke.
930     & when the time was comen,
        Shee bare a selcoth sonne.
```

4ᵈ parte

     Right faire shape he had then,
     All the forme *tha*t fell for a man.
     Blacke he was, w*i*thout lase,   *without a lie*
935 & rough as a swine he was.
     Then the midwiffe anon-right
     Was afeard of that sight,
     & for he was soe rough of hyde,
     Full well shee wist *tha*t tyde
940 That he was nev*er* gotten by [any] man.
     & full faine shee wold then   *wished*
     In hell *tha*t he had beene her froe,
     *Tha*t nev*er* man had seene him moe.
     The Hermitt *tha*t hight Blassye
945 Wist full well, sikerlye,
     The time the Child shold be borne,
     & to the tower he came att Morne,
     & called upward to them yare   *quickly*
     & asked them how they did fare.
950 The midwiffe said w*i*thout lesse   *lying*
     A knave child there borne was.
     'Take him me,' he sayd then,
     '& I shall make him a Christen man.
     Whether he dye or live abyde,   *remain alive*
955 The fairer grace he may betyde.'   *may befall him*
     Full glad was the midwiffe,
     & caught the chylde belive,   *immediately*
     & by a cord shee lett him downe
     & Blassy gave him his benison,   *blessing*
960 & bare him home w*i*th merry moode,
     & batptized him in the holy floode,
     And called him to his Christendome*   p. 159/f. 79v
     & named him Merlyin in God's name.
     Thorrow *tha*t name, I you tell,
965 All the feends *tha*t were in hell
     Were agreeved, & that full sore;
     Therfore was their power [l]ore.   *lost*
     & when he had christened him soe,
     Home againe he bare him thoe,
970 & in the cord he can him laine.
     The Midwiffe drew him up againe
     & he bade her w*i*thout blame
     Call him Merlyne by his name.
     The midwiffe bare him anon right
975 To the fyer *tha*t was bright,
     & as shee warmed him by the fyer*

Merline

  Shee beheld his lodlye cheere.   *his hideous appearance*
  'Alas,' said shee, 'Art thou Merlyn?
  Whence art thou? Of what kinne?
980 Who whas thy father by night or day,
  That noe man Iwitt itt may?   *know*
  It is great ruth, by Heaven's K*ing*,   *pity*
  Tha*t* for thy love, thou foule thinge,
  Thy mother shal be slaine w*i*th woe.
985 Alas the time it shal be soe!
  I wold thow were farr in the sea
  Tha*t* thy mother might scape free.'
  When Merlyn hard her speake soe,
  He bradde open his eyen towe.*
990 & lodlye on her can hee looke   *angrily*
  & his head on her hee shooke,
  & gan to cry w*i*th lowd dinne,
  'Thou lyest,' he sayd, 'thou foule queane!
  My mother,' he sayd, 'shall no man quell
995 For nothing *that* men can tell!
  Whilest I may speake or gone,
  Mauger them *that* wold her slone,   *in spite of; kill*
  I shall save her liffe for this.
  Tha*t* you shall see & heare, Iwis.'
1000 When the Midwiffe shee heard *that*,
  Shee fell downe almost flatt.
  Shee gan to quake as shee were wood,
  & had rather then any good
  Tha*t* shee had beene farr away;
1005 Soe had his mother where she Lay.
  Soe sore they were of him agast,
  The[y] blessed them & that full fast,
  & cryed on him, in God's name,
  Tha*t* he shold doe them noe shame.
1010 & fast on him they can crye,
  In God's name & St Marye,
  He shold them tell what hee were
  & what misadventure brought him there.
  He did lye & held him still
1015 & lett them crye all their fill.
  & if they shold have slaine him tho,
  He wold not speake a word moe.
  & the 3 lived there
  W*i*th much sorrow & w*i*th care.
1020 & for after halfe a yeere,
  As shee held him by the fyer,
  Rufullye shee gan to greete   *weep*
  & said to him, 'My sonne sweete,

	For thy love, withouten weene,	*without doubt*
1025	All quicke dolve shall I beene.'	
	He answered & said, 'Nay,	
	Dame, thou gables, by this day.	*talk nonsense*
	There is neithe[r] man nor Justice	
	That shall yee deeme in noe wise	*judge you*
1030	Then whilest I may either goe or speake,	
	In earth thy body for to wreake.'*	
	Then was his mother a blythe woman,	p. 160/f. 80r
	& everye day after then	
	He made her gladd & bold,	*courageous*
1035	& Marvelous tales to her he told.	
	When he cold speake & gone,	*walk*
	The Justice was ready anon,	
	& bade bring forth anon then	
	Befor him that ilke woman	*same*
1040	For to receive her judgment.	
	& when shee came in present,	
	The Justice forgatt itt nought,	
	But Egerlye he said his thought,	
	& sware anon by Heaven's Queene	
1045	All quicke shee shold dolven beene.	
	Then the childe answered with words Bold	
	(& he was but 2 yeeres old),	
	He sayd to the Justice with Egar Moode,	
	'Sir Justice, thou can but litle goode*	
1050	To doe my mother to the dead,	
	& wotts not by what reade,	
	Save a chance that to her fell.	
	Therfore, thou dost not to her well,	
	For everye man will wott well then	
1055	That against chance may be noe man,	
	& thorrow chance I was begott.	
	Therfore everye man may well wott	
	That my mother ought nought	
	For my love to death be brought.'	
1060	Great wonder had both old & younge	
	Of the child's answering.	
	Then the Justice was full wrath	
	& on Loud sware an oathe,	
	All quicke shee shold dolven bee.	
1065	'Nay,' said Merlyn, 'soe Mote I thee,	*as I hope to thrive*
	Thou shalt her never br[in]g therto	
	For ought that ever thou canst doe!	
	'It shall not goe as thou wilt	
	For shee hath done no guiltt,	
1070	& I shall prove itt through skill,	

Mauger of them *tha*t wold her spill.   *In spite of; kill*
My father *tha*t begatt mee
Is a feende of great potencye,
& is in the ayre above the light,
1075 & tempts men both day & night.
& therfore to my mother he went,
& wend all Christendome to have shent*
& gott mee on her w*i*thout Leasinge,   *lying*
& shee therof wist no thing.
1080 & for shee wist not when it was,
I prove *that* shee is guiltlesse.
For all the feends wenden by mee
To have shent all Christentye
& had of me a wicked foode.   *an evil son*
1085 But God hath turned me to goode,
For now I am of God sende
For to helpe all Englande.
& forsoothe,' hee said then,
'P*a*rdie, tell you I can
1090 All *tha*t ever was & now is;
I can you tell well, Iwis,
Thou dost not wott, Justice then,
Who was thy father *tha*t thee wanne,
& therfore I prove *tha*t mother thine
1095 Rather to be dolven then mine.'
Hearknen now all the striffe,
How Merlyne saved his mother's liffe!
Then was the Justice in hart woe,
& to Merlyne he said thoe,
1100 'Thou Lyest!' he sayd, 'thou glutton!*
My father was a good Barron
& my mother a ladye free.
Yett on live thou may her see.'
'S*i*r,' said Merlyne then anon,
1105 'Say[n]d after her full soone   *send*
And I shall make her to be knowen,   p. 161/f. 80v
Or else hange me on to drawen.'*
The Justice after his mother sent,
& when shee was comen p*re*sent,
1110 The Justice before them all
To Merlyn can he call.
He said to him, 'Bela[m]ye,   *fair friend*
Be now soe bold & hardye
To prove thy tale, if thou can,
1115 *Tha*t thou saidest of this woman.'
Merlyn said to the Justice,
'S*i*r, thy words be not wise.

If I tell theese folke beforne
How thow was getten & borne,
1120 Then shold it spring wyde & broad
& thou shold lose thy manhood.
Then shall thy mother dolven bee,
& all were for the love of thee.'
The Justice then understoode
1125 *That* Merlyn cold mikle good.*
Then to a chamber can they goe,
He and Merlyne, & noe moe.
'Merlyn,' he said, 'I pray thee,
What was *that* man *that* begatte me?'
1130 '*Sir*,' he said, 'By St Simon,
It was the p*ar*son of the towne!
Hee thee gott, by St Ja[m]e,
Upon this woman *that* is thy dame.'
The Lady said, 'Thou fowle thinge!
1135 Thou hast made a stark Leasinge!
His father was a noble Baron,
& a man holden of great renowne,
& thou art a mis[e]begott wretch!
I pray thee, God, Devill thee feitch!
1140 In wyld fyer thou sha[l]t be brent
For w*i*th wronge thou hast m[e] shent.'
'Dame,' sayd Merlyn, 'hold thee still,
For itt were both right [&] skill.*
For I wott w*i*thouten weene
1145 Thou deserve dolven to beene,
Ffor sithe thou was to this world brought,
All the worke *that* thou hast wrought
I can tell itt ev*er*ye word
Better then thou, by Our Lord,
1150 How thy sonne was [be]gotten.
Dame, if thou have forgotten,
I can tell you all the case,
How, & where, & when itt was,
& thou shalt be ashamed sore;
1155 Thee were better speake noe more.'
The Lady was sore dismayd,
& Merlyn forth his tale sayd.
'Dame,' he said, 'Verament,
That time thy Lo*r*d to Carlile went,*
1160 (Itt was by night & not by day),
The p*ar*son in thy bed Lay;
Att thy chamber dore thy Lo*r*d can knocke,
& thou didest on thy smocke
& was sore afrayd *that* tyde,

1165	& undidst a windowe wyde.	
	& there the parson thou out Lett,	
	& he ran away full tyte.	*speedily*
	Dame,' he said, 'that ilke night	
	Was begotten thy sonne the Knight.	
1170	Dame,' he sayd, 'Lye I ought?'	*Do I lie?*
	Shee stood still & sayd nought.	
	Then was the Justice wrath & woe	
	& to his mother he sayd thoe,	
	'Dame,' hee sayd, 'How goeth this?'	
1175	'Sonne,' shee said, 'All sooth, Iwis!	*true*
	For if thou hang me with a corde,	
	Hee belyeth me never a word.'*	
	The Justice for shame waxes redd	p. 162/f. 81r
	& on his mother shooke his head,	
1180	& bade her in hast wend home	
	With much shame as shee come.	
	'Belyve,' sayd Merlyn, 'Send after a spye,	*immediately*
	For to the parson shee will her hye,	
	& all the sooth shee will him saine	
1185	How that I have them betraine.	*betrayed*
	& when the parson hath hard this,	
	Anon for shame & sorrowe, Iwis,	
	To a bridge he will flee,	
	& after noe man shall him see;	
1190	Into the watter start he will	
	Liffe & soule for to spill.	*destroy*
	& but itt sooth that I say,	
	Boldlye hang me today.'	
	The Justice withouten fayle	
1195	Did after Merlyn's counsayle.	
	He sent after a spye bold,	
	& found itt as Merline told.	
	& the Justice, for Merlin's sake,	
	Him & his mother he lett take,	
1200	& le[t]t them goe quitt & free	
	Before the folke of that countrye.	
	& when Merlin was 7 yeere old,	
	He was both stout & bold.	
	His mother he did a Nun make	
1205	& blacke habitt he let her take,	
	& from that time, verament,	
	Shee served God with good entent.	

5:d parte

      Now let us of his mother fayle*
      & turne us to another tale,
1210 & speake wee of the messenger
      That wenten from Sir Vortiger
      For to seeke Merlin the bold,
      To have his blood, as I you told.
      Soe 3 of them came, by chance,
1215 Into the place where Merlyn was,
      On playing as he can goe
      With other children many moe.
      & as the[y] played in that stead,
      One of his fellows him misdeed,*   *insulted*
1220 & gan to crye on Merlyn thoe,
      'Thou cursed srow, thou goe us fr[o]e!   *shrew*
      Thou art a fowle thing gotten amisse.
      Noe man wotts what thy father is!'
      The Messengers came fast bye
1225 & hearden well the child crye.
      Soone anon they were bethought
      That it was the childe they after sought,
      & eche one his sword out droughe.
      & Merlin shooke his head & laughe,
1230 'Heere comen the King's Messengers
      That have me sought both farr & neere
      For to have my hart's blood!
      Now the[y] thinke itt in their Moode
      For to slay me this day;
1235 But, by my truth, if that I may,
      Or that they part away from mee   *Before*
      Well good freinds shall wee bee.'
      Merlyn anon to them ran.
      Hee greetes them fayre as he well can,
1240 & welcomed the Messenger,
      & sayes, 'Yee come from Sir Vortiger;
      Me to slay is all your thought,
      Therof shall yee speed nought,   *not succeed*
      & for to beare your King my blood,
1245 That never shall doe him good.
      For they that told him that tydinge
      Lyed of me a strong leasing,   *told a wicked lie about me*
      & said my blood without wronge
      Shold make h[i]s castle stiffe & strong.'   p. 163/f. 81v
1250 The Messengers had wonder then,
      & sayd to Merlyn anon,
      'How can thou tell us this priv[i]tye?   *secret*

	Tell us the sooth, I pray thee,	
	That wee may have tokeinge	*a token*
1255	To avow our tale before our K*ing*.'	
	Merlin Led them a good pace	
	Till hee came where his mother was.	
	Shee told them all the sooth beforne,	
	How Merlyne was gatten & borne,	
1260	& of his wisdome & of his reede,	*advice*
	& how hee saved her from deade.	
	The Messengers, as I you tell,	
	All night there did dwell.	
	Att Morrow, soone when it was day,	
1265	The[y] tooke leave to wend awaye.	
	Alsoe, Merlyn *tha*t ilke tyde	
	Rode on a palfray them beside,	
	& wentt forth all in fere	*all together*
	Towards K*ing* Vortiger.	
1270	As they thorrow the countrye came,	
	In a towne their inne they tane,	
	Soe *that* Merlyne, as I you tell,	
	Came there as shoone were to sell.	*shoes*
	A great laughter up he tooke;	
1275	The Messengers fast on him can lookee	
	& full soone asked him thoe	
	Wherfore *tha*t he laughed soe.	
	Then sayd Merlyne, 'See yee nought	
	The young man *tha*t the shoone hath bought?	
1280	He wendes to live them to weare,	*thinks*
	But by my hood I dare well sweare	
	His wretched liffe hee shall forgoe	
	Or *tha*t he is one gate come to.'*	
	The Messengers att *tha*t tyde	
1285	After *tha*t man can they ryde,	
	& found him dead as any stone	
	Or *tha*t he had a furlong gone.	
	In *tha*t towne the[y] dwelled all night.	
	On morrow when it was daylight,	
1290	The[y] dight their horsses & made them yare	
	On theire journey for to fare.	
	& as they went on their Journey,	
	Thorrow a towne in *tha*t countrye,	
	He came by a churchyard.	
1295	He mett a course thith[er]ward,	*corpse*
	W*i*th preists & Clarkes singing befor[n]e.	
	The corpes were on a beere borne,	
	Many a man therwith can gone.	
	Merlyn beheld them ev*er*ye one;	

1300	A great laughter he uptooke.	
	The Messengers on him can looke,	
	& asked him with hart free	
	Why he laughed soe hartilye.	
	He said, 'Amongst these folkes then	
1305	I see an old sillye Man	*simple*
	That doth sore & fast weepe;	
	He ought better to skipp & leape!	
	& others here goe & singe,	
	That ought better their hands to wringe.	
1310	I shall you tell certainlye,	
	That you may know the cause whye.	
	That corse that dead is & cold,	
	Was a childe of 10 yeeres old.	
	That ilke preist,' he sayd thoe,	*same*
1315	'That goeth before & singeth soe,	
	He was the father that the child begott,	
	& if he were bethought of that,	
	He wold his hands wring sore	
	& for that child sorrow more.	
1320	Now he singeth with Joy & blisse,	p. 164/f. 82r
	As the chyld had never beene his.	
	& to see the seely husband	
	For sorrow & care wring his hands	
	Therfore, he is a Mickle foole	
1325	That for his fooman maketh dole.'	*grieves*
	The Messengers everiche one	
	To the chyld's mother went anon,	
	& Merlyn in a litle throw	*little while*
	Made the Mother to be know,	*to be known*
1330	Wherfore shee cold not say nay,	
	But ever prayd them naught to say.	
	Then were the Messengers blythe	
	& on their Journey ridden swithe.	
	As they ridden on their way,	
1335	It was upon the 3.d daye,	
	When it was about the prime,	
	Then laughe Merlyne the 3.d ti[m]e.	
	Then asked they all in fere	
	Why he Made such laughing cheere.	
1340	Then said Merlyne Iwisse,	
	'Thereof I laugh noe wonder is,	
	For sithe the time that yee were borne,	
	Such wonder heard yee never beforne.	
	I shall you tell withouten othe	
1345	That yee shall find trew & soothe:	
	This ilke day, by my truth,	

	In the King's house is mickle ruth	*pity*
	Of the King's Chamberlaine.	
	For the Queene, sooth to sayne,	
1350	Hath Lyed on him a leasing stronge.*	*lie*
	Therfore, shee shall be dead with wronge,	
	For his chamberlaine is a woman	*i.e., the king's*
	& goeth in the clothing as a man.	
	& for shee is fayre & bright of hew,	
1355	The false Queene that is untrew,	
	Besought her to her Lem[m]an dearne.	*to be her secret lover*
	& shee answered & can her warne,*	*refused her*
	& sayd shee must that game forsake,	
	For noe comfort shee wold her make.	
1360	Therfore, the Queene was a foole,	
	For had shee witt of her toole	
	& how short itt was wrought,	
	Shee wold of love asked her nought.	
	The Queene forthwith was affrayd	
1365	& wend well to have beene bewrayd*	
	& thought that shee shold be shent;	
	& before the King anon shee went,	
	& sayd that his chamberlaine	
	With strenght wold have her forlaine.	*raped*
1370	The King therof was wonderous wrath,	
	& swore many a great othe	
	That shee shold both hang & draw,*	
	& that were against the law!	
	Therfore, wend you whome belyve,	*hurry home*
1375	As fast as yee may drive,	
	& say to Vortiger the king	
	The Queene hath made a strong Leasing	
	Upon his chamberlaine for hate.	
	Therfor, bydd that shee be take,	
1380	& search the chamberlaine then,	
	& he shall find shee is a woman!'	
	A knight there was both stout & stearne,	*strong in fight*
	& pricked forth the truth to Learne,	
	& he made noe tarrying	
1385	Till he came before the King.	
	When hee came into the hall,	
	Downe on his knees can hee fall,	
	& said, 'Thorrow many a country [w]e went	
	On thy Message as thou us sent,	
1390	To seeke a child of selcoth Land,	
	& such a one have wee founde,	
	That is but 5 wynters old.	
	You heard never none soe bolde.	

	He is clypped child Merline.	*called*
1395	He can tell all Mannour of thing;	
	Of all *tha*t was & now is	
	He can tell you well, Iwis.	p. 165/f. 82v
	He can tell you full well	
	What thing troubles y*o*ur castell,	
1400	Why itt may not stand on plaine,	
	& alsoe of y*o*ur chamberlaine	
	*Tha*t yee have mentt to draw & hang.	
	He saith, forsoothe, itt is for wrong	
	For to slay a woman	
1405	*Tha*t goeth in clothing as a man.	
	& therfore, doe as I you [s]ayne,	
	& doe take the chamberlayne,	
	& of her bonds yee her unbinde	
	A woman fayre yee shall her finde.	
1410	& but itt be soe, w*i*th right Lawe	
	Doe mee to hang & drawe.'	
	Vortiger a-wondred was,	*astonished*
	& all *tha*t hearden of *tha*t case.	
	He com[m]anded his men all	
1415	His chamberlayne to bring in [h]all.	
	Anon the[y] serched her *tha*t stonde,	*then*
	& a woman shee was founde.	
	Wrath then was S*i*r Vortiger	
	& asked of *tha*t Messenger	
1420	Who told him he was a woman.	
	'Fforsooth, S*i*r,' hee sayd then,	
	'Merlyn it was *tha*t this can say	
	As wee rydden by the waye.	
	For he can tell, & lye nought,	
1425	All things *tha*t ev*er* were wrought,	
	& all *tha*t ev*er* you can him saine,*	
	He will tell you sooth, Certaine.'	
	Vortiger was glad & blythe,	
	& said to the Messenger swithe,	
1430	'I shall yee give both Land & ploughe	
	& make yee a man right good enoughe.	
	Therfore, I com[m]and anon-right	
	Duke, Erle, Barron & K*nigh*t,	
	To dight their horsses & make them yare,	
1435	Forth w*i*th Vortiger to fare!'	
	Then wold he noe longer abyde,	
	But leapt to horsse & forth gan ryde	
	To speake w*i*th Merlyn the younge,	
	For glad he was of his com[m]inge.	
1440	But when it was come to night,	

With Merlyne he Mett right.
As soone as he can him meete,
With fayre words hee can him greete.
Of many things he spoke then;
1445 Some of them tell I can.
With much Joy, & verament
To the King's court the[y] went,
& were att ease all that night.
& on the Morrow when it was light,
1450 To that steede they went, by-deene,   *place; immediately*
Where the castle shold have beene.

6ᵈ parte:

'Sonne,' he sayd to Merlin then,
'Tell me, chyld, if thou can,
Why my castle in this stonde   *place*
1455 Is everye night fallen to ground,
& why it may stand nought,
Of soe strong things as itt is rought?'
Then said Merlyn to the King,
'Yee shall heare a wonderous thing.
1460 Heere in this ground Deepe
Is [a] water strong & steepe.
Under the watter are stones towe,   *two*
Much & strong & broad alsoe.
Beneathe the stones, under the Mold,   *ground*
1465 Tow dragons Lyen there fould.   *coiled*
The one is white as Milke reeme,   *cream*
The other red as any gleame.
Grislye they are of sight both,
& fare together as the[y] wrothe;   *as if they were angry*
1470 & everye day when itt is night,
They begin a strong fight
That through the strenght of their blast.
The worke the[y] can downe cast.   p. 166/f. 83r
& if the dragons were away,
1475 Then might the workemen worke everye day,
& make thy worke both strong & still,
& to stand att thy owne will.
Doe now looke & thou shalt see
That it is soothe that I tell thee.'   *true*
1480 Vortiger Com[m]anded anon
All his workemen everye one,
15,000 & yett moe,
He bade them looke whether it were soe.
Anon they dolven in the ground,

1485	& a watter there they found.	
	Amonge them all, the soothe to tell,	
	The[y] Made a full deepe well,	
	& the watter the[y] brought out thoe.	
	& when the[y] hadden done soe,	
1490	Beneath the watter in the ground	
	2 great stones there they found.	
	Many men there they were	
	The 2 stones up to reare,	*to lift up*
	& when they were up hent,	*taken up*
1495	2 dragons there were bent.	
	Foule they were for to behold,	
	& found itt right as Merlyn tolde,	
	The one dragon as red as fyer,	
	With bright eyen as Bason cleare;	
1500	His tayle was great & nothing small,	
	His bodye was unryde withall,	*monstrous*
	His shape May noe man tell,	
	He looked like a feende of hell.	
	The white dragon lay him by,	
1505	Sterne of Looke & grislye.	
	His mouth & throate yawned wide,	
	The fyer brast out on every side.	
	His tayle was ragged like a feend,	
	& upon his tayle's end	
1510	There was shaped a grislye head	
	To fight with that dragon redd.	
	For Merlyn said, forsooth Iplight,	
	Soe grislye they were both in fight,	
	That when the[y] shold up rise	
1515	Many a man they shall agrise.	*terrify*
	Anon the[y] ryssden out of their den,	*rose up*
	Then was feard many a man.	
	Of all the folke there was that tyde	
	Durst not one of them abyde.	
1520	The redd dragon & the white	
	Hard together can the[y] smite	
	Both with mouth & with tayle.	
	Betweene them was a hard battele	
	That the earth quaked thoe,	
1525	& lodlye whether waxed alsoe.	*weather*
	Soe strong fyer they cast anon	
	That the plaines therof shone.	
	Soe they fought, forsoothe to say,	
	All the long sum[m]er's day.	
1530	They never stinted their fighting	
	Till men to Evensong did ri[n]ge.	

Soe in *that* time, as I you tell,
The red dragon, *that* was soe fell,
Drave the white from a downe
1535 Into the plaines a great verome* *a great distance*
Till they came into a valley;
& there they rested them both tway,
& there the white recov*er*ed his flight
& waxed Egar for to fight.
1540 & Egerlye, w*i*thout fayle,
The redd dragon he can assayle.
& there the wh[i]te w*i*th all his might
Hent the red anon-right,
& to the ground he him cast,
1545 & w*i*th the fyer of his blast
Altogether he brent the red,
That nev*er* after was found shread, p. 167/f. 83v *a shred*
But dust upon the ground lay.
& the white went away,
1550 & nev*er* sithe *tha*t time then
Heard noe man where he became.
Then sayd Merlyn the younge
Among them all before the K*ing*,
& said to him w*i*th words bold,
1555 'Now is itt sooth *that* I you tolde?
Itt is soothe, yee may itt see.
Therfore, S*ir* K*ing*, I pray thee,
Doe yee the clarkes afore mee bring
*Tha*t Laid on mee that Leasing.'
1560 & he asked them the K*ing* beforne
Why the[y] wold his blood were Lorne.*
& the[y] answered w*i*th words myld,
Dreadfullye before the chylde, *fearfully*
& sayden the[y] saw witterlye *clearly*
1565 Beneath the welkin a skye, *apparition*
& shewed him all his begott,*
How hee was on earth lote,
& thorrow his blood the K*ing*'s castle
Shold stande both strong & weele.
1570 Then sayd Merlyn thoe,
'Hee was a shrew *that* told you soe.
*Tha*t skye,' he sayd, '*that* showed you *tha*t, *apparition*
He was the father *that* mee begatt,
& for I serve him not att will,
1575 Therfore, he wold my blood spill,
& for *that* he hath beguiled you soe.
S*ir* Vortiger, I pray you thoe,
*Tha*t yee grant them their liffe;

	All my wrath I them forgive.'	
1580	The K*ing* his asking granted swithe.	
	Then were the clarkes glad & blythe.	
	Forth they went, both more & mynne,	*all together*
	& w*i*th them went Merlyne.	
	Merlyn was w*i*th Vortiger	
1585	To his counsell all *tha*t yeere.	
	Through his wisdome & consayle	
	The castle was built strong & well.	
	& when the castle was all wrought,	
	Erles & Barrons the K*ing* besought	
1590	*Tha*t he wold know att Merlyn thoe,	
	Why the dragons foughten soe.	
	'Itt was some tokening,' the[y] sayd all,	
	'*Tha*t some adventure shold befall.'	
	Merlyn was brought befor the K*ing*,	
1595	& he him asked w*i*thout Leasinge	
	What *tha*t tokening might meane,	
	The fighting of the dragons keene.	*fierce*
	Merlyn stoode & Made danger.	*resisted*
	Then bespake S*i*r Vortiger,	
1600	& sayd, 'Merlyn, but thou me tell,	
	Anon I shall cause thee to be quell.'	
	Then answered Merlyn aplight,	*in truth*
	W*i*th great wrath anon-wright,	*immediately*
	& sayd 'W*i*thouten weene,	*without doubt*
1605	*Tha*t day shall nev[er] be seene.	
	If thou take thy sword in hand	
	Me to slay or bring in band,	
	Yett may thou fayle of all thy fare,	*endeavours*
	As the hound doth of the hare.	
1610	I warne you well, S*i*r Vortiger,	
	I give nothing of thy danger!*	
	But if thou wilt find me a borrowe,	*pledge*
	*Tha*t thou shalt doe me noe sorrowe,	
	Then will I tell you all by-deene	
1615	The fightinge of the dragons keene.'	
	Then said Merlyn to the K*ing*,	
	'S*i*r, understand well my sayinge:	
	The red dragon, so foule of sight,	
	Betokeneth thy selfe & all thy Might,	
1620	For through thy false p*r*ocuringe	
	Moyne was slaine, the younge K*ing*.	
	Thou see the red dragon the white drove	
	Far downe into the grove:	p. 168/f. 84r
	*Tha*t betoekneth the heyres *tha*t thou di[d]st fleame	*banish*
1625	W*i*th wrong out of the realme.	

Soe all the folke *tha*t w*i*th them held,
Both in towne & in feilde,
The white dragon doth signiefie.
The right heyres have great envye
1630 *Tha*t thou holdeth all their Land
Against them w*i*th much wronge.
Alsoe, the wh[i]te, can you well say,
Recovered his flyght into the Valley
& drove the redd dragon againe
1635 Till he came to the plaine.
& to the ground he him cast,
& w*i*th the fyer of his blast
All to powder he burnt the redd,
*Tha*t neu*er* of him was found a shread.
1640 *Tha*t betokens the heyres soe younge   *grown up; help*
Are now waxen, & succour found,
& are readye w*i*th ma[n]y a Knight
Against thee to hold fight.
Into this castle they shall thee drive
1645 W*i*th thy child & thy wiffe,
& all beene w*i*th thee then,
Into the ground shall the[y] brenn.   *burn*
& the K*i*ng, S*i*r Anguis,
Shall be slaine, & hold noe price.   *be held of little worth*
1650 His kingdome, & thine alsoe,
Shall doe England Mickle woe.
The head upon the white dragon's tayle,
*Tha*t betokens, w*i*thouten fayle,
The heyres *tha*t be trew & good
1655 Shall destroy all thy blood.
S*i*r Vortiger, this is the tokeninge
Of the dragons fighting.
As I thee say, w*i*thouten othe,
Thou shalt it find siker & troth.'   *the sure truth*
1660 Still him stood S*i*r Vortiger
& bote his lip with dreery cheere,
& sayd to Merline w*i*thouten fayle,
'You must tell mee some counsell,
Without any more striffe,
1665 How I may best leade my liffe.'
Then Merlyne sayd w*i*thout weene,
'Thus must itt needs beene,
& therfore, soe have I rest,   *so help me*
I can noe read but doe thy best.'*   *unless you tell me*
1670 Vortiger sayd, 'But me tell,
Anon I shall doe thee quell!'
He start up & wold him have wrought   *seized*

	But where he was he wist nought.	*knew*
	Soe soone hee was away then	
1675	*Tha*t in the hall wist noe man,	
	Hye nor lowe, swaine nor groome,	
	*Tha*t whist where Merlyne was become.	
	Then went Merlyn hastilye	
	To the Hermitt *tha*t hight Blassey,	
1680	& told him w*i*thout leasing	
	How he had served the king,	
	& told him w*i*thout wronge	
	The fighting of the dragons stronge;	
	Of the red & of the white	
1685	A great Booke he did endite,	*he (Blassey) wrote*
	& told *tha*t the red dragon	
	Betokens much destruction	
	Through Vortiger's kinred Iwis,	
	& the heathen K*ing* Anguis;	
1690	In England shold be afterward	
	Strong battailes & happs hard.	*mischances*
	All *tha*t Merline tolde & sayd,	
	In good writting itt was layd,	
	Of all the ventures, I understand,	
1695	*Tha*t ever shold fall in England.	
	But for itt is soe darke a thing	p. 169/f. 84v
	*Tha*t Merlyn made in his sayinge,	
	*Tha*t few men w*i*thouten weene	*doubt*
	Can understand what itt meane.	
1700	But on yee will a stond dwell,*	
	Of other things I will you tell.	
	Of the hend children tow,	
	Uther & Pendragon alsoe.	
	I told, as I you understand,	
1705	How they were fleamed out of ther Land.	*banished*
	Now will I tell you in certaine	
	In what manner the[y] came againe	
	W*i*th great strenght & power,	
	& how [they] drave S*ir* Vortiger	*they*
1710	Forth into his castle strong	
	For his unright & for his wronge,	*injustice*
	& how the[y] brent him flesh & bone	
	& how they can K*ing* Anguis slaine,	
	I will yee in what Manno*ur*.	
1715	Listen now & you shall heere.	

7ᵈ ⸴ parte

   The merryest time itt is in May,
   Then springs the sum[m]er's day.
   Soe in *tha*t time, as yee may heere,
   The Barrons came to Vortiger
1720 & said, 'My Lord the Kinge,
   Wee have brought you heard tydinge   *bad (hard) news*
   Of Pendragon *tha*t is thye foe
   & of Uther his brother alsoe.
   They are comen into this Land
1725 With many a K*nigh*t doughtye of hand,
   & they will stint nought   *will not stop*
   Till thou be to ground brought.
   They are att Winchester almost,
   Therfore send about in hast
1730 To all thy freinds, I thee reed,   *I advise you*
   For thou had nev*er* soe much need.'
   Up him start Vortigers
   & called to him Messengers.
   To Winchester he them sent,
1735 & bade them thorrow his com[m]andement
   Against Uther & Pendragon
   The[y] shold shutt the gates anon.
   As they wold his love winne,
   They shold not let them come in,
1740 & he wold come anon-right
   To helpe them w*i*th all his might.
   Other Messengers he sent anon
   To K*ing* Anguis soone,
   & bade him come to helpe att neede,
1745 W*i*th all the folke *tha*t he might leade,
   For to fight against his fone
   *Tha*t were comen him to slone.
   When K*ing* Anguis he was come,
   The way to Winchester they nume,   *took*
1750 & or they were halfe way there,
   Uther & Pendragon comen weare
   To Winchester towne soe nye,
   & reard their Bannors on hye.   *raised*
   Armes the[y] shewed rich there
1755 *Tha*t had beene their father's before.
   Then the burgesse *tha*t the Banners knew,
   Att the first he can them rue
   The death of Constantine the K*ing*
   & of Moyne *tha*t was slaine soe younge,
1760 & said Vortiger was a traitor,

& all that wold him succor,
& said the[y] wold let into the towne
Both Uther & Pendragon,
& ceaze there into their hands,*   *deliver*
1765 For they were right heyres of the land.
They sett open the gates wyde
& lett Pendragon in ryde,
And Uther his brother alsoe,   p. 170/f. 85r
& all *tha*t came w*i*th them 2,
1770 & yeelden to them both towne & tower,
& didden them full great honor,
*Tha*t ever after Winchester then
Great thanke & freedome wan.
When *that* Vortiger the fell   *cruel*
1775 The sooth Tydings hard tell,
*Tha*t Uther & Pendragon
Were let into Winchester towne,
Then he comanded his men fast
To goe to Winchester in hast.
1780 & when Pendragon undernome   *perceived*
*Tha*t Vortiger did thither come,
He cast open the gates wyde
& all they can out ryde,
& dighten them w*i*thout fayle   *prepared themselves*
1785 To give S*ir* Vortiger battayle.
But the English Barrons all in fere
*Tha*t were comen w*i*th Vortiger,
When the[y] can the folke seene
*Tha*t were some time of their kine
1790 (W*i*th Vortiger was many a K*night*
*Tha*t knew the Banners anon right;
Well a 100 there were
*Tha*t had served their father deere,
& saiden Vortiger was false in feild
1795 & all *tha*t ever w*i*th him helde),
To Vortiger the[y] ran soone
& thought for to have slaine him anon.
They had ment to have slaine him there,
But all too litle was their power,
1800 For against one of them
Vortiger had 20 men
*Tha*t we[r]e comen altogether
W*i*th K*ing* Anguis thither.
K*ing* Vortiger & Anguis
1805 For wrath were neere wood, I wisse,
He com[m]anded all his route   *company*
To besett them all aboute,

& sware there shold scape none,
But they shold all be slaine.
1810 Lance they broke & shafts the[y] drew,
Many of the Barrons the[y] slew,
But they were strong & wight — *brave*
& fought againe w*i*th all their might,
For nothing wold the[y] yeeld then,
1815 But slew many a heathen man.
Fast on him they can hew, — *them*
But, alas, they were to few!
Yett one Baron was soe stronge
*Tha*t hee scaped out of the thronge.
1820 Hee pricked his steed w*i*th great randome — *speed*
Till he came to Pendragon.
He sayd, 'Thou art heyre of this land,
To my tale doe understand.
For the love of thy Brother & thee,
1825 Hither I come to helpe thee,
& therfor now are wee shent — *put to shame*
For our good will to thee meant.
K*ing* Vortiger & K*ing* Anguis
W*i*th many a Sarazen of great price,
1830 Shall hew us downe to the ground,
But yee us helpe in this stonde.'
Itt was noe reed to bid him ryde.*
The folke spurred out on ev*er*ye syde
& when they were together mett,
1835 There were strokes wel besett.
There fought Uther & Pendragon
As they were woode Lyons.
Many a sarazen's head anon
The[y] stroke of by the Necke bone.
1840 Many folke *tha*t ilke tyde — *same time*
Were slaine on both syds.
K*ing* Vortiger, w*i*thout fayle,
Was overcome in *tha*t battele; — p. 171/f. 85v
& Maugre him & all his — *in spite of*
1845 *Tha*t were with K*ing* Anguis,
The[y] were driven soe nye*
*Tha*t into a castle they can flee,*
& *tha*t was both strong & merrye,
Upon the plaine of Salsburye.
1850 Pendragon & his brother Uther
Pricked after S*ir* Vortiger,
& when they to the castle came,
Wylde fyer soone them nume*
& cast itt in w*i*th a gynne. — *siege engine*

	& as soone as itt was wi*th*in,	
1855	Itt gann to bren out of witt	*out of control*
	*Tha*t noe man might stanch itt.	
	& Vortiger, wi*t*h child & wiffe	
	*Tha*t were theere in their liffe,	
1860	Beast & man, wi*t*h lymes & lythe,*	
	Were brenned all forthwi*t*h.	
	Vortiger raigned heere	
	Fullye the space of 7 yeere.	
	Now pray wee all the Heaven's K*ing*,	
1865	& His mother, *tha*t sweet thinge,	
	He blesse us all wi*t*h His hand,	
	& send us peace in England!*	

8ᵈ⁺ parte

	Now, when Vortiger was brent,	
	Uther & Pendragon went	
1870	For to beseege K*ing* Anguis	
	In his castle soe strong of price,	
	Wither he was fled for dread & doubt.	
	& Pendragon wi*t*h all his rout	
	Besett him soe on every side	
1875	*Tha*t noe man might scape *tha*t tyde.	
	But K*ing* Anguis wi*t*hin *tha*t castle	
	Was bestowed soe wonderous well,	
	& soe stronglye itt was wrought	
	*Tha*t noe man might deere itt [n]ought.	*hurt, damage it*
1880	& when they had beseeged him longe	
	About the castle *tha*t was soe stronge,	
	& when noe man might him deere,	
	5 Barrons comen there	
	*Tha*t had beene wi*t*h Vortiger,	
1885	& told Pendragon & Uther	
	How Merlyne was begotten & borne,	
	& how he came the K*ing* beforne,	
	& what words he him tolde	
	Of the dragons under the Mould,	
1890	& how the K*ing* wold have him slaine	
	& noe man wott where he become.	
	& said, 'S*i*r, verament,	*in truth*
	& Merline were here p*re*sent,	*If*
	Throughe his councell you shall anon	
1895	Kinge Anguis ov*er*come.'	
	Pendragon was wound[r]ed thoe,	*full of wonder*
	& soe was his brother Uther alsoe,	
	& sent anon the K*nigh*ts 5	

	For to seeke Merlyn belive.	*as quickly as possible*
1900	& bade them, if they found the child,	
	To pray him w*i*th words milde	
	To come & speake w*i*th Pendragon	
	& Uther in his pavillyon,	
	Him to wishe, & them to reade.	*teach; advise them*
1905	& if hee might, helpe them att neede	
	For to winne *tha*t stronghold,	
	& he shold have what he wold.	
	The Messengers forth went	
	To seeke Merlyn w*i*th good entent,	
1910	& fare & wyde they him sought,	
	But of him they heard right nought.	
	Soe on a day the Messengers	
	As they were sett att their dinners	
	In a taverne in the west countrye,	
1915	W*i*th meate & drinke great plentye,	
	An old churle hee came in	*countryman*
	W*i*th a white beard upon his chine,	
	& a staffe in his hand he had,	
	& shoone on feete full well made,	
1920	And begunn to crave more,	p. 172/f. 86r
	& said he was an hungred sore,	
	& praid them on the bench above	
	To give him something for God's love.	
	& the[y] then sayd, w*i*thout Leasinge	
1925	*Tha*t he shold have of them nothinge,	
	& sayd if that the churle be old,	
	He is a stronge man & a bolde	
	& might goe worke for his meate	
	If he itt wold w*i*th truth get;	
1930	& called to him ev*er*eche one	
	& bade him trusse & away gone,	*take himself off*
	& sware by the ruth *tha*t God them gave,*	
	He shold drinke w*i*th his owne staffe.*	
	Then Merlyn answered yorne:*	*vehemently*
1935	'Fellow,' hee sayd, 'I am noe churle.	
	I am an old man of this worlde,	
	& many wonders seene & hearde,	
	& yee be wretches & younge of blood,	
	& forsooth can litle good.	
1940	& if yee knew as yee nay can,	
	Yee shold scorne noe old man,	
	Yee shold be in the K*i*ng's neede,	
	For old men can thee wishe & reede	*advise and guide you*
	Where yee shold find Merlyn the chylde.	
1945	Therfore, the K*i*ng was full wilde	

To send madmen out off rage
For to goe on such a message,
For Merlyn is of such Manner,
If he stood before you here
1950 & spake to you right att this dore,
You shold know him never the more.
For 3^se this day you have him mett*
& yett yee know him never the bett;
& therfore, wend home by my reed   *advice*
1955 For him to find you shall not speed.   *succeed*
  & bydd *tha*t prince take Barrons 5
  & bydde come & speake to Merlyn belyve,
  & say *tha*t he shall them abyde
  Right here by this forrest's side.'
1960 & when he had said to them this,
Anon he was away Iwisse,
& there wist none of them
Where this old man was become.
The Messengers wondred all
1965 Where the churle was befall
& all about they him sought,
But of him they heard nought.
For in story it is told
The Churle *tha*t was soe stout & bold,
1970 *Tha*t spake soe to the Messengers
As the[y] sate att their dinners,
Forsooth itt was Merline the younge
*Tha*t made to them this scorninge.
The Messenger went soone anon,
1975 & told Uther & Pendragon
& how the churle to them had tolde
& sware to them *wi*th words bold,
& told them how Merlyne the chylde
Was byding in the forrest wylde,
1980 & bade them take Barrons 5
To come & speake *wi*th him belyve,
& sayd Merlyn wold them abyde
Att such a place by the forrest syde.
Pendragon had wonder thoe,
1985 & Uther his brother alsoe.   *noble*
Pendragon bade his brother gent
To the seege to take good tent   *make sure*
*Tha*t King Anguis scaped not away,
Neither by night nor yett by day,
1990 Till they were of him wreake,   *avenged*
For he wold goe *wi*th Merlyn speake.
Then Pendragon *wi*th Barrons 5,

	Went forth alsoe belyve,	*immediately*
	[And when] Pendragon was forth went,	p. 173/f. 86v
1995	Merlin anon, verament,	
	Wist full well *tha*t he was gone,	
	& to Uther he came anon	
	As itt were a stout garrison.*	
	He came to Uther's Pavillyon	
2000	& said, 'Uther, listen to mee,	
	For of thy harme I will warne thee.	
	Ffor I know well w*i*thouten fayle	
	All K*ing* Angrius' counsaile.	
	For he will come this ilke night,	
2005	W*i*th ma[n]y a man full well dight,	
	& into the forrest slippe anon	
	For to waite thee for to sloen.	
	But herof have thou noe dowbt,	
	But warne thy host all about	
2010	*Tha*t they be armed swithe & weele,	*quickly; well*
	Both in Iron & eke in steele.	
	& gather together all thy host,	
	& hold yee still w*i*thouten bost,	
	Till *tha*t hee bee amonge ye co[m]en.	
2015	For he shal be the first groome	
	*Tha*t shall upon thy pavillion ren.	
	& looke *tha*t thou be ready then,	
	& heard on him looke thow hewe,	*hard*
	& spare not that old shrewe,	
2020	For thou shalt slay him w*i*th thy hand	
	& win[n]e the price from all this land.'	*victory over*
	& when he had told him all this case,	
	He vanished away from *tha*t place.	
	Great wonder had Uther thoe,	
2025	*Tha*t he was escaped soe,	
	& thought itt was God's sonde	*a messenger from God*
	*Tha*t warned him *tha*t stonde,	*then*
	*Tha*t had soe warned him of his fone	*foes*
	& was soe lightlye from him gone.	
2030	& when itt drew unto the night,	
	K*ing* Anguis anon-right	
	Did arme his men wrath & prest,	*immediately*
	3,000 men of the best,	
	& said how a spye had tolde	
2035	*Tha*t Pendragon, the prince bold,	
	Forth into the country is gone	
	& left his brother Uther att home.	
	Therfore, he sayd, he will out breake	
	& on [U]ther he wold him wreake.	

2040 & sware an othe by Mahound
He wold kill him in his Pavillyon,
& soone they were ready dight.
Then K*ing* Anguis anon-right
Forthe of the castle he can ryde
2045 W*i*th 3,000 by his syde,
& forthe he went w*i*thout bost
Untill he came to Uther's host.
& when he was comen right
Where Uther's Pavillyon was pight,
2050 K*ing* Anguis, a fell felon,
He hyed him to the Pavillyon
& thought to slay Uther therin,
But he was beguiled thorrow Merlyine,
For Merlyne had *tha*t ilke Morrow
2055 Warned Uther of all the sorrow,
How K*ing* Anguis was bethought.*
Therfore in his Pavillyon was he nought,
But had taken the feild w*i*thout,   *outside*
W*i*th many a hardye man & stout.
2060 & Uther was a hardy man;
Upon King Anguis hee ran
& smote him att the first blow
*Tha*t he cane him ov*er*throwe,
& Uther w*i*th his sword soe smart,
2065 He smote him thorrow the hart,
& hent him by the head anon
& stroke itt from the necke bone.
And when the Sarazens this can see,   p. 174/f. 87r
Fast away can they flee
2070 To the castle ev*er*eche one,
& left their Lord all alone.
But or the[y] Might scape againe,
500 were all slayne
Of the stoutest *tha*t were there
2075 *Tha*t came w*i*th their King Ifere.   *together*

9<u>d</u> parte

Now let us be for a season,
& let us turne to Pendragon
*Tha*t was gone to the forrest wilde
To speake w*i*th Merlyn the chylde.
2080 The first time he asked for Merlyn
He see a heardsman keeping swine,
W*i*th an old hatt upon his head,
& in gray russett was he cladd,

	And a good staffe in his hand,	
2085	& a white whelpe him followande.	
	Stalworth he seemed, & well made.	
	The prince anon to him roade,*	*rode*
	& well fayre he can him fraine	*ask*
	Giff he heard ought of Merlyn,	*If*
2090	& whether hee cold tell him any tythands	*tidings*
	Where was his most wininge.	*dwelling*
	'Yea, S*i*r,' he sayd, 'By St Marye,	
	Right now was Merlyn here w*i*th mee.	
	& thou had comen eare, indeed,	*before*
2095	Thou might have found him in *tha*t stead.	*place*
	& if thou can Merlyn ken	*recognize*
	He is not yett far gone.	
	& therfore ryde forth in this way,	
	As fast as ev*er* thou may,	
2100	& on thy right hand rathe,	*soon*
	Thou shalt find a verry faire path	
	*Tha*t thorrow the faire forrest Lyeth.	
	& in *tha*t way then ryde swithe	*swiftly*
	& seekerlye, w*i*thouten weene	*surely; without doubt*
2105	Soone thou may Merlyn seene.'	
	Then was the prince glad & blythe,	
	& sped him forth swithe,	
	& as he hard, soe he itt found,	*heard*
	A well faire path on his right hand.	
2110	The[y] turned their horsses ev*er*eche one	
	& in *tha*t path the[y] rydden anon.	
	& w*i*th Merlyn they Metten then,	
	& as itt were a stout Champyon,	*chapman, pedlar*
	& bare a great packe on his backe.	
2115	& to him the prince full faire spake	
	& asked him if hee see Merlyn.	
	'Yea,' said he, 'By St Martin,	
	A litle heere before yo*u*r sight,	
	He is not farr, I you plyght.	
2120	To you I say, by St John,	
	He is not yett far gone,	
	& therfore ryde forth belive,	*quickly*
	As fast as yo*u*r horsses may drive,	
	& yee shall find him in a wyle.	
2125	By then yee have rydden a myle,	
	W*i*th Merlyn yee shall meete then,	
	Or yee shall speake w*i*th some other man	
	*Tha*t shall you tell full right	
	Where you shall have of Merlyn a sight.'	
2130	& when he had thus sayd,	

The[y] pricked forth in a brayd*
& by they had rydden a stonde,
As he him said without wronge,
He mett with Merlyn on the playne
2135 As he were a doughtye swaine
All cloathed in robes soe gay,
As it had beene a monke's gray,
& bare a gavelocke in his hand; *staff*
His speeche was of another Land.
2140 He, when the prince had him mett,
Faire & hendlye he did him greete.
Then the prince was all heavye,
& asked him, of his curtesie,
If he mett by the way p. 175/f. 87v
2145 With chyld Merlyn *that* day.
'Yea, S*ir*,' hee said, 'By St Michaell,
Merlyn I know verry well,
For right now, sikerlye,
Merlyin was here fast by,
2150 & had yee rydden a litle bett, *a little faster*
With Merlyn yee might have mett.
But, S*ir*, I say without othee, *oath*
He is a quante boy forsoothe. *strange*
Soe well I know Merlyn's thought,
2155 Without my helpe you find him nought.
& if of him yee will have speech,
Then must you doe as I to you teache.
Att the next towne here beside,
There you must Merlyn abyde,
2160 & in the towne take yo*u*r ine. *inn*
& certainly then child Merlyn
Shall come to you this ilke night,
& there yee shall have of him have sight.
& then yee may both Lowed & still
2165 Speake with Merlyn all *that* you will.'
Then was the prince blythe & glad
& pricked forth as he were madd,
& tooke his inne in the towne
As shold a lord of great renowne.
2170 Now May you heare in this time
How Merlyn came the 5^(th) time,
& how he the prince Mett,
& on what manner he him grett,
& became to him as councellour.
2175 Hearken to me & you shall heare.
When itt was within the night,
Merlyn came to the K*ing* full right,

	Right in the guise of a swayne	
	As he was in the forrest seene,	
2180	& sayd, as I find in the booke,	
	'Sir Prince, God send you good lucke!	
	Loe, I am heere *that* thou hast sought!	
	Tell me what is thy thought,	
	& what thou wilt to me saine?	
2185	For I wold heare thee wonderous faine.'	*gladly*
	Then up start Pendragon,	
	& into his armes he him nume.	*took*
	To bide *wi*th him he did him crave,	
	& what hee wold aske, he shold have.	
2190	& Merlyn sayd, verament,	
	He wold be att his com[m]andment.	
	O*ve*r all, where-soe he were,	
	He wold be att his bydding yare.	*ready*
	Then was the prince gladd & blyth,	
2195	& thanked Merlyn many a sythe.	
	Then sayd Merlyn, 'S*i*r, will you heare?	
	I come from thy brother deere,	
	For through my councell hee hath this night	
	Slaine K*ing* Anguis, I you plight.'	
2200	Then was the prince blythe & gladd	
	& great solace & myrth made,	
	& all *tha*t were there were full faine.	
	& on the Morrow rod home againe	
	& found K*ing* Anguis slaine,	
2205	His head sett up, his body drawne.	
	Pendragon asked Uther, Iwis,	
	Who had slaine K*ing* Anguis,	
	& he answered & can saine	
	*Tha*t he [was] warned by a swayne.	
2210	When he had told all how he did	
	He thanked God in *tha*t steade.	
	Then bespake Pendragon	
	& sayd to Uther anon,	
	'Hee *tha*t thee holpe att need thine,	
2215	Forsooth itt was child Merlyn	
	That standeth now here by thee.'	p. 176/f. 88r
	Uther him thanked w*i*th hart free	
	& prayd him then in all thing	
	*Tha*t he wold be att his bidding.	
2220	Then the[y] wenten to the castle, w*i*thout lesse,	
	Wherein many a Sarazen was,	
	*Tha*t noe man might to them winne	
	By noe manner of gynne.	*ingenuity*
	& therfore the oste still lay,	*army*

2225 Till after, upon the 3ᵈ day,
　　　Word came from the Sarazen,
　　　Where the[y] lay in castle fine,
　　　That they wold yeeld up the castle
　　　If they might passe well
2230 To their Land withouten dere.　　　　　　　　　　　　　　　　*harm*
　　　Upon a booke the[y] wold sweare
　　　That they shold never againe come.
　　　But Merlyn sent them word soone
　　　That they shold passe eache one
2235 By leave of his Pendragon.
　　　& when they had all sworne & some
　　　That they wold never in this land come,
　　　They passed anon to the sea strond
　　　& went into their owne Land.
2240 Then to Pendragon the crowne they name,　　　　　　　　　　*took*
　　　& King of Englande he became,
　　　& in England he raigned King
　　　But 3 yeere, without Leasing,
　　　& after, he was slaine rathe*
2245 With Sarazens, & that was scathe.　　　　　　　　*a matter for regret*
　　　I shall you tell in whatt manner,
　　　Listen a while & you shall heare.
　　　That time in the Land of Denmarke
　　　2 Sarazens where stout & starke　　　　　　　　　　　　　　*were*
2250 & were of King Anguis' kinde,
　　　Of his next blood that was soe hynde.　　　　　　*near kin; courteous*
　　　The one was come of the Brother,
　　　& of the sister came the other.
　　　Strong men the[y] were & fell,
2255 & theire names I can you tell:
　　　The one was called Sir Gamor,
　　　& the other Sir Malador.
　　　Gamor came of the brother beforne,
　　　The other was of the sister borne.
2260 Great Lords were they of Land.
　　　Sir Malador held in his hand
　　　2 duchyes, & Gamor 3;
　　　Stowter men might none bee.
　　　When they heard how King Anguis
2265 In England was slaine, Iwis,
　　　Altogether can they speake,
　　　Theire unckle's death they wold wreake.　　　　　　　　　　*avenge*
　　　& soe great an oste together they brought
　　　That the number they can tell nought.
2270 But unto shipp they gone anon
　　　& the seas to flowe began.

The winde soe well [be]gan to blow
*Tha*t they landed att Bristowe.
Then Merlyn knew itt well anon,
2275 & told itt Uther & Pendragon,
How there was comen from Denmarke
A stronge oste stout & starke,
W*i*th many Sarazens of Price
For to Avenge K*ing* Anguis.
2280 'In England,' sayd Merlyn then,
'Such an oste was nev*er* seene.
I say to you w*i*thouten Layne, *a lie*
The one of you shal be slayne,
& whether of you soe ere it is,
2285 Shall have to meede Heaven's blisse.' *reward*
But for noe meede he wold not saine
Whether of them shold be slaine,
But neve*r*thelesse yee shall heare.
Merlyn Loved well Uther,
2290 The least heere *tha*t was on his crowne, *hair, head*
Then all the body of Pendragon.
Hee bade them dight them anon p. 177/f. 88v
Against their foemen for to gone,
& sayd Pendragon w*i*thout fayle
2295 Uppon the Land shold them assayle.
'& Uther, alsoe I bidd thee,
Thou shalt wend by the sea
& looke *tha*t theere scapen none
Till they be slaine ev*er*ye-eche one.'
2300 Pendragon was a doughtye Knight
& fell & Egar for to fight.
He nev*er* for stroakes wold forbeare
Against noe man w*i*th sheeld or speare,
Nor better did w*i*thouten fayle,
2305 & *tha*t was seene in *tha*t Battaile.
He tooke his oaste w*i*th might & mayne, *army*
& went the Sarazens fast againe. *against*
& when they were together mett,
There were strokes sadlye sett.
2310 Many a heathen Sarazen
He clove downe to the chin,
Many a man was sticked tho,
& many a good steed was slayne alsoe.
The Booke saith, w*i*thouten Lye,
2315 There was done such chivalrye, *deeds of chivalry*
Of the folke *tha*t Pendragon fell,
Noe man can the number tell.
& Uther to the sea went,

  & Merlyn told him verament
2320 That he shold not that day be slaine.
  Then was Uther wonderous fayne,
  & in his hart soe wonderous Lyght
  That hee was feirce & fell in fight,
  & Egerlye without fayle
2325 The Sarazens he can assayle,   *strive*
  & fast against them can stryde
  That many a Sarazen lost their liffe.
  Pendragon & his folke in hast
  The Sarazens fast to ground the[y] cast,
2330 That there were none against them stoode,
  But fledd away as they were wood.
  But Uther in that ilke tyde
  Kept them in on the other syde;
  With strong Battayle & strokes hard
2335 He drove them all againe backward.
  & when that they noe further might,
  On Pendragon can the[y] light.
  A 100 Sarazens on a rowte   *company*
  Att once Layd him all about.
2340 Who-soe had seene Pendragon then,
  He might have seene a Doughtye man,
  For all that he might ever reach,
  Trulye the[y] need noe other Leech.   *physician*
  The Sarazens, stout & grim,
2345 Slew his steed under him,
  & when hee had Lost his steed,
  Great ruthe itt is in bookes to reede
  How that he on foote stood
  Till that he lost his hart's bloode.
2350 A 100 Sarazens att a brayd
  All att once att him Layd,
  & broken him body & arme,
  & slew him there, & that was harme.   *sad*
  & when that Uither understoode
2355 His brother was slaine, he waxt neere woode
  & bade his men fast fight,
  & he bestirrde him like a Knight.
  Of all the Sarazens that were left alive
  There scaped noe more but 5.
2360 Of the Christian men were but slane
  3,031, certane.
  & in that ilke country thoe,
  A mile might noe man goe,
  Neither by dale nor by downe,
2365 But he shold tread on a dead man.

MERLINE   197

        And when itt was against the night,   p. 178/f. 89r
        Uther had discomfited them in fight.
        He went home into his inne,
        & asket councell of Merlyne.
2370 Pendragon was out sought   *searched for*
        & to the church full fayre brought.
        He was graven & layd full Merrye
        In the towne of Glasenburye.*   *Glastonbury*
        & thus ended *tha*t doughtye K*night*;
2375 God grant his soule to blisse soe bright.
        & all *tha*t done soe for the right,*
        I pray Jesu, for His might,
        He grant them Heaven's blisse above.
        Amen, Amen, for His mother's love!
                          ffins

Explanatory Notes

20	*Sarazen*: Saxons. For a discussion of this linguistic confusion, see Siobhain Bly Calkin, *Saracens and the Making of English Identity: The Auchinleck Manuscript* (New York, Routledge: 2005).
23	'So that they dared not stand against him'.
31	*L* (31–32) names the 'booke' as the 'bruyt', i.e., *Brut*.
37	*to the*[*m*] *anon*: eye-slip from the line above.
78	'Went to their ships at once'.
81–82	*But England was called the*[*n*]: a statement also found in *L* (85), *W* (68), and *A*, which follows it with an explanatory line: 'þe Bretouns þat beþ Inglisse nov' (119).
111	*in strond*: an error for 'stond', i.e., in that place.
142–43	*To witt whether he nay wold*: both *L* (146) and *A* (175) have 'why' here; that is, the barons want to know why Vortiger would not fight, not whether he would.
172	*younge one*: both *L* (178) and *A* (206) at this point have variations of the word 'conioun' (*MED conjoin*, a fool, nincompoop, a worthless person, a rascal, n,1). The word was unfamiliar for *W*, who substituted 'cowarde' (167), and presumably for the PF scribe too. See also note to line 1100.
174	'He thinks he will be killed'.
207–8	'To make war for England against those who wish to, or dare to, oppose them'.
215	*in fere*: this phrase usually means 'together'. *L* has 'chose to beon empere' (225).
218	'Bold and strong on a horse'
240	'They took pity on the rightful heirs'.
245–46	'None but the two noble barons knew where they had gone'.
273–74	*The English folkes*: a patriotic note, shared by *L* (289) and *W* (296). *A* merely has 'our men' (323).
284	*Vortiger*: a scribal error for 'Anguis'.
285	'If he [Anguis] wished to go in peace'.
289	'Would he come ashore' [i.e., land in England again].
306	'Meede' means something given in return for service, e.g., money or a reward (*OED meed*, n): Vortimer's response at 316 implies the latter sense here. 'Liverr' similarly means support in the form of an allowance, e.g., food and drink (*MED livere*, n,3(2)).
377	'And there took into his own hands'.
386	A line is missing after this line, i.e., to rhyme with 'Champion' in 387.
397	*But hunted them as hound doth hare*: a rare example of a simile in this work, repeated at 1609.

405	*For love of Sir Vortiger*: HF suggest '*?feare*' here; cf. *W* 'And many for drede and doute' (446), and *A* 'Sum for gret ay3e and dout' (465). For P's suggestion, see Textual Note.
466	'They had no other choice'.
482	*Learned*: both *L* (505) and *A* (561) have 'lewed' here, which preserves the distinction between the unlearned (lewed) people and the learned (clarkes).
521	*sithe*: HF identified that the word should be 'swithe' (i.e., quickly), a word found in both *L* (546) and *W* (601). Possibly a misreading by the PF scribe.
576	*Our Ladye's will*: cf. line 2379. These references to the Virgin Mary may reflect the pre-Reformation origins of the tale. *L* (604), *A* (645), and *W* (659) all refer to God here, not 'Our Lady'.
583–84	'They had the great power to take on the form of a man'.
594	'Thus they thought to have defiled the world'.
616	'She wished him to the Devil'.
625	*strangled herselfe*: a difficult feat, the scribe getting it right at 732.
629	'Without making confession or receiving communion'.
640	*Blasye*: a variant of the more usual form, 'Blaise', appearing also in *A*.
645	'It was through the fiend's devilish temptation': cf. line 701.
660	'Unless she were known to be a prostitute'. If the woman could prove that she was a prostitute, she would not be buried alive.
668	'The eldest daughter to bewitch'.
669	[*Some younge man's body*] *to enfante. OED enfaunte*, to bear a child, v, is clearly wrong here. *L* (704), *A* (726), and *W* (794) all have 'haunt(e)', meaning 'to resort to', which is obviously right. Lines 668–69 may be translated accordingly as 'To bewitch the eldest daughter into keeping company with some young man'.
670	'If she could persuade her'.
679	*for to sounde*: possibly a misreading for 'fonde', arising from a confusion between *s* and *f*, and supported by *L* (714): *MED fonden*, to subject (a person) to trial by tempting him with sin; to tempt to evil, v,2(a). The hag is telling the daughter that she has a body to tempt any young man to sin.
714	*Shee was taken forthwise*: L's 'Heo was taken forþ ywis (751), i.e., 'She was taken forth, certainly' makes more sense here.
725–27	By declaring herself to be a prostitute, the sister attracts a large number of lechers (*OED harlot*, n,2a). The meaning of 'a female prostitute ... or sexually promiscuous woman' (n,2b) is a later meaning, recorded from ?c.1475 onwards. See P's note line 726.
745	'In God's name he besought her'.
774 ff.	As it stands, the prostitute sister scolds her sibling, and then leaps up in a rage, strikes her sister, and then retires to that sister's chamber. *L* (817–27) gives the correct sequence: the virtuous sister, drunk as she is, answers the 'missayer' back. It is she who scolds, causing her harlot sister to leap up and strike her, beating her so hard that she flees to her chamber.
792–93	A scrambled couplet, leading to the extra-metrical line 793. *L* (835–36) again supplies a more comprehensible reading: 'Al mad and couþe no good/Wepte al day as heo weore wood', a reading confirmed by *W* (923–94).
806	*A* [*t*]*raine of a childe*: *L* (849) has 'a streone', that is, 'strain' (*OED strain*, offspring, progeny, n,1,4); hence, figuratively speaking, a sperm. See also Textual Note.
843	'Her womb began to increase'.
850	'And because she had broken the law'.
853	'I did not act against the law'.
906	'If she has deserved to be killed'.
910–11	'But keep her confined for now, until the child is born'.
962–63	'He christened him Merlin, in God's name'.
976–77	*fyer/cheere*: in 977, 'syer' is crossed out before 'cheere'. The scribe, not thinking, instinctively provided a rhyme, and then realized that his copytext had 'fyer/cheere'. That this rhyme probably did stand in the original is shown by the fact that both *L* (1023–24) and *W* (1142–43) contain it.
989	'He opened both his eyes'.

1031	'Condemn your body to the earth'.
1049–52	'You do ill to condemn my mother to death without knowing the cause of her misfortune'.
1077	'And thought to have destroyed all Christendom'.
1100	*glutton*: an inappropriate insult, given the circumstances. The PF scribe presumably could not follow the relevant word in his copytext and used an approximation. *L* (1151) and *A* (1071) both have 'conioun', and *W* (1289) 'congon'. See note to line 172, above.
1107	'Or else hang, draw (and disembowel) me'.
1125	'That Merlin knew a great deal about him'.
1143	'For it would be both right and proper'.
1159	*Carlile*: both *A* (1123) and *L* (1212) have variations of 'Cardoil' (i.e., Caerleon). The confusion between the two is common, as Evan Evans noted in a letter to Percy in March 1764 (*Letters*, V, 68). The scribe of *W*, or his source, evidently did not know this name, and produced the gloriously inappropriate 'was to the cardynall sent' (1358).
1177	'He says no word of a lie about me'.
1208	'Now let us stop talking of his mother'.
1219	*misdeed*: probably a scribal error for 'missaide' (see 778), which would rhyme with 'stead' in the line above. *L* (1274) has 'mysa[i]de' and *W* 'mysdede' (1432).
1283	'Before he comes to his own gate'.
1350	The use of pronouns in this passage causes some confusion. The 'him' of 1350 is the King, and the 'shee' of 1351 the Queen; i.e., the Queen has greatly deceived her husband and merits death as a punishment for adultery. P himself was understandably confused at this point, taking 'she' to mean the Chamberlain (see Textual Note 1351). However, the 'shee' of 1354 is the Chamberlain, whom Merlyn reveals to be female. See note to line 1372 below.
1357	*warne*: a misunderstanding of 'werne', to refuse.
1365	'And was certain she would be exposed'.
1372	*That shee shold both hang & draw*: since the King is speaking of someone he believes to be male, this ought to be 'hee'. Both *L* (1447) and *W* (1637) also have the feminine at this point, but *A* (1364) correctly has the masculine pronoun. The punishment for such treason by a man would have been hanging and drawing, by a woman it would have been burning (J. G. Bellamy, *The Law of Treason in England in the Later Middle Ages* (Cambridge: Cambridge University Press, 1970), p. 227).
1426	*saine*: while the sense is 'anything you say [to him]', the reading in *L* – 'Al þat euer þow konst him frayne' (1505), i.e., 'anything he is asked about' (obsolete *OED frayne*, to make inquiry of (a person) about (something), v,1) is much clearer. Possibly arising from a confusion between an *f* and a long-tailed *s*.
1535	*Into the plaines a great verome*: *L* (1618) has 'vyroun' and *W* (1814) 'feron' (*MED viroun*, n,1(b), defines 'a gret viroun' as meaning 'for quite a distance', citing *L* as its example).
1561	'Why they wished to shed his blood'.
1566–67	'That showed them how he was begotten and came to earth'.
1611	'I care nothing for your power!'
1669	'I can give you no other advice but to do your best'.
1700	'But if you will wait a while'. As HF points out, 'on' is a scribal error for 'an', meaning 'if'.
1764	'And deliver [the town] into their hands'.
1832	'There was no need to bid them ride'. PF mistakenly has 'reed' (counsel) for 'need': latter reading confirmed by *L* (1944), *A* (1847), and *W* (2210).
1846	'They were so hard-pressed'.
1847	*into a castle*: *W* (2104) is the only version to give this castle a name, i.e., 'Tyntagell'. Malory's *LMD*, printed by Wynkyn de Worde 12 years before *W*, records Tintagel as the birthplace of King Arthur. This may reflect a desire to associate the text of *W* more closely with the Arthurian legend.
1853–54	'They immediately took wild-fire and cast it over the walls with a siege-engine'. Wild-fire was a combination of highly inflammable substances, difficult to extinguish.
1860–61	'Beast and man, all were immediately completely consumed by fire'.

1867	*& send us peace in England!*: partisanship, or possibly a contemporary plea for peace in war-torn England. A powerful conclusion and a natural performance break at the end of Part 7.
1932	*& sware by the ruth*: 'ruth' (i.e., pity) does not make sense here. *W*'s 'trouthe' (2316) is preferable. Probably a transcription error by the scribe, who omitted the first letter.
1933	*He shold drinke with his owne staffe*: the intention is clearly 'to expect nothing', but the derivation is obscure: given that the old man is only accompanied by his staff (1918), it may simply be that the men jeer at Merlin to keep his own company. At this point, *W* (2317–18) simply says that the old man will be beaten with his staff.
1934	The revelation of Merlin's name at this point is premature, as P points out.
1952	This is the first encounter between Merlin and the messengers on this particular occasion, and not the third. Given that *W* (2338) also has this, it is likely to have stood in the original of both versions.
1998	*As it were a stout garrison*: a nonsensical reading, but *W*'s 'As it were a stoute garson' – i.e., garçon, lad, young man (line 2388) – provides the explanation: Merlin comes to Uther's pavilion in the guise of a young man.
2056	'What King Anguis had in mind'.
2087	*roade*: presumably, the original spelling was 'rade', to rhyme with 'made' in the line above.
2131–32	'They rode out hastily, and after they had ridden a short while'.
2248–49	'But afterwards he was quickly slain by Saracens, and that was a matter for regret'.
2377	*Glasenburye*: Glastonbury, the traditional site of Arthur's burial.
2380	'And all who fight for the Right'.

Textual Notes

In the LH margin, opposite the title: 'A very curious old Poem and may be considered, as one of the first Attempts in Epic Poetry by the English.' [P]. To the right of the title P added:

> in 9 Parts or Cantos Containing 2391. verses. ~~Containing~~ Giving an account of the Birth, Parentage & Juvenile Adventures of that Famous old British Prophet. N.B. This Poem is more correct & perfect than most in this book.

1	*Hee*: in heavy bold large script in LH margin.
8	*happs many mooe*: 'haps many moe' [P].
12	*No[b]le*: Nolle [MS]; *thin[ge]*: scribe wrote 'thinke' and crossed out the *k* before the now obscured 'ge'. Reading supplied by HF: cf. lines 184 and 928, where the same error occurs, corrected in the former, but not the latter, where the rhyme word is 'drinke'.
13	*wight*: 'stout, active' [P].
16	*reede*: 'counsel.' [P].
19	*King Anguish*: 'Corruptè pro Hengist' [P].
20	*Sarazen*: 'here it means only Pagan.' [P].
24	*feild*: 'field' [P].
25	*the*: scribe began to write a long-tailed *s*, and changed it to a crossed *t*.
27	*so[nn]e*: some [MS]; *shol[d]*: shole [MS].
28	*Moyne*: 'In the Old Chronicles his name is said to have been Constaunce, but for as much as he is also said to have been a Monk, that may Account for his being here called Moyne or perhaps it should be Le Moyne i.e. the monk.' [P]; *with[out] Leasing*: with Leasing [MS]; 'without leasing i.e. without Lying' [P].
29	*othe[r]*: othe [MS].
35	*wen*: 'when' [P].
37	*the[m]*: then [MS].
38	*gon*: 'gone, i.e. go.' [P].
43	*so[nn]e*: some [MS].
48	*cal[l]ed*: calbed [MS].
59	*dwellinge*: 'i.e. delaying. Vid. Page. 356 St. 21.' [P]. [The last three letters of 'Page' are indistinct, but HF was correct in their assumption: P's reference is to line 560 of *Guy & Colbrande*, found on p. 356 of the PF. See HF, II, 546.]

63	*there againe*: 'i.e., against that. so <u>thereto</u> is <u>to that</u>. &c' [P].
69	*Anguis*: Angius [MS]; *the[n]*: them [MS].
70	*faine*: 'faine, joiful.' [P].
71	*M[e]ssengers*: Missingers [MS]; the dot of the *i* is over the capital *M*, the downstroke looking as if the scribe subsequently attempted to turn it into an *e*; *ilke tyde*: 'i.e., that same time' [P].
72	*land*: 'world' crossed out and 'land' substituted above [MS].
73	*sarazens*: 'ver. 73 & 74. It plainly appears here that Saracens is not a misnomer for Saxons.' [P].
78	*dight them to shipp*: 'betook them. So in Chauc. Mo. 553' [P].
81	*the[n]*: them [MS].
82	*Mikle*: 'mickle, i.e., great' [P].
83	*sprange*: 'sprung, spronge' [P].
89	*honour*: hon [MS], overbar over the *o* and *r*.
94	*with wright & not with wrong*: 'perhaps not with right but w[ith] wrong' [P]. The end of w[*ith*] cropped by binder.
95	*i[n]*: im [MS]. At this point P incorrectly numbers the line 100.
100	*went*: another *&* before this word [MS].
104	a second *&*; either crossed out or superimposed on another letter, with a looped descender, after 'him' [MS].
106	*done*: 'done' [P].
107	*the[y]*: the [MS]. See also lines 115, 133, 151, 201, 219, 263, 330, 386, 395, 462, 465, 469, 471, 507, 545, 566, 573, 581, 582, 591, 594, 787, 884, 886, 1007, 1218, 1233, 1265, 1288, 1290, 1416, 1447, 1469, 1473, 1487, 1488, 1489, 1514, 1516, 1521, 1561, 1562, 1564, 1592, 1647, 1707, 1712, 1737, 1754, 1762, 1788, 1796, 1810, 1811, 1814, 1839, 1846, 1924, 1971, 2072, 2110, 2111, 2131, 2220, 2227, 2231, 2254, 2329, 2337, 2343.
108	*Danes*': 'th' crossed out at beginning of line, possibly eye-slip from the line above [MS]; 'Danes' [P].
111	*strond*: 'Here it signifies the Country in general so in Chauc.' [P].
120	*so[n]e*: some [MS]; *Land*: 'Lond' [P].
121	*To all*: 'That all &c' [P].
123	*blinne*: 'blinn, cessare' [P].
127	*England*: 'Englond' [P].
128	*stond*: 'i.e. time' [P].
133	*the[y] said*: the said [MS]; 'i.e. the Lords said' [P].
140	*the*: they [MS]; 'the' [P]. See also lines 148, 241, 252, 582, 868, 936, 950, 1475, 1524, 1527, 1756 [second instance], 1788, 1881, 2269.
142	*nay wold*: 'ne wold, i.e. would not.' [P].
145	*all in fere*: 'all together' [P].
147	*hendlye*: 'hendly, gently' [P].
148	*d[e]ske*: dske [MS]; 'on the Deis by him they sit, i.e., at the high table' [P].
149	*& [he] bade*: 'He bade' [P].
153	*gone*: barely visible in MS, covered by binding. Reading supplied by HF, although given the final word of 154, there is a case here for 'goone'.
156	*read*: 'cou[n]sel' [P], overbar over the *u*.
167	[*your*]: obscured by bleed-through from verso. Reading supplied by HF.
168	[*all thing*]: obscured by bleed-through from verso. Reading supplied by HF.
174	*slowen*: 'forte flane, an arrow. G. D. Chauc flone arrows. i.e., he doth not know a sword from an arrow [or perhaps slawne, slone, slain. see below ver.194 pag 159. ver. 66' [P]. Percy struck through the first part of his comment with a single diagonal stroke. The reference to page 159, verse 66 is to line 997. Letter crossed out between '194' and pag'.
181	*dole*: 'sorrow, misfortune.' [P].
184	*thinge*: a *k* crossed out before the *g*: the scribe wrote 'thinke' and emended to 'thinge'.
190	*slowen*: 'i.e. slew (slewen)' [P].
203	*slowe*: 'slo, i.e. slaine.' [P].

204	*Ereles*: the *l* changed from an *s* [MS]; 'Erles.' [P].
205	*reede*: 'counsel' [P].
218	*staleworth*: stalelworth [MS]; 'stalworth, brave, stout.' [P].
226	[*The 12 Barrons*]: part in brackets cropped. Reading suggested by HF.
232	*com[m]ons*: 'commons' [P].
236	*2ᵈ parte:*: text in LH margin, with curly bracket encompassing lines 236–44.
239	*tre[a]son*: hole over the *a*; *unde[r]stoode*: undestoode [MS].
241	*the*: they [MS]; 'the' [P]; *childre[n]*: childrem [MS].
245	*moe*: 'moe' [P].
246	*hend*: 'gentle' [P].
249	*accompackement*: an *r* changed to a *c* on the third *c*; 'a compactment i.e., compact.' [P].
262	*ryedey*: first *e* interlined, no caret; 'ready' [P].
271	*assayle*: scribe wrote 'assaye' and inserted a clumsy *l* after the *y*, masking the *e* [MS].
283	*t[h]ey*: hole over the *h*.
284	*[s]aine*: faine [MS]; 'They send to Vort*ime*r to saine' [P].
285	*if he [in] peace*: if he peace [MS].
290	*Englande*: 'Englonde' [P].
298	*boaste*: boalte [MS], scribe began to write an *h* and changed it to a *l*; a loop under the *l* to change it into an *s*.
300	*s[o]lace*: salace [MS].
301	*helde*: 'holde, idem' [P].
306	*liverr*: 'livere, liveray, wages, pay &c. (liverée Fr.). Urry' [P].
325	*Barro[n]*: hole over the *n*.
338	*England*: 'Englonde' [P].
339	*sibb & couthe*: 'sibb, kindred, couthe, acquaint*anc*e' [P].
346	*swarren*: *w* interlined, with caret [MS].
348	*wreake*: 'i.e. revenged' [P].
354	*her*: 'his, or perhaps for their' [P]; *meanye*: 'family, company, retinue.' [P].
361	*shold his*: 'on his' [P].
370	*swithe*: 'soon, presently' [P].
373	Reading supplied by HF: only 'Th' of 'Then' and 'blith' now discernible.
376	*welcomed*: 'welcomed' [P].
377	*seazed*: 'gave possession. a Law-term.' [P].
385	*a Lyte*: 'a little' [P].
386	*smite*: 'smite' [P].
391	*fell*: 'fell' [P].
405	*love*: 'i.e. sake, or perhaps along of' [P].
415	*cursing*: 'cursing i.e., in ~~wickedness, see Chauc.~~ Excommunications' [P].
423	*thoe*: 'i.e. then' [P].
426	*fleemed*: 'fleem. banish, drive away. Urry' [P].
442	*need*: 'need' [P].
447	*That itt be [surlye &] well made*: reading supplied by HF. Only the opening two words may be discerned with confidence, HF noting that after *&* the MS was 'broken away'. It is unclear how much text was available to Furnivall, or whether he reconstructed on the basis of 444.
454	*bore*: 'bare' [P].
455	*arreare*: 'i.e. to rear.' [P].
468	*sped*: 'sped: i.e. did speed' [P]; a letter crossed out after 'sped' in P's gloss.
474	*the[r]e*: thee [MS].
481	*la[n]d*: lamd [MS].
482	*Learned*: 'perhaps Lay' [P].
483	*worke*: 'werke' [P].
489	*England*: 'Englond' [P].
495	*we[re]*: hole in MS over the 're'.
496	*opposed*: 'appose, examine, ask questions. hinc pose. Urry. Jun.' [P].
499	*quell*: 'i.e. kill' [P].

505	*no[e]*: the *e* may be written over the beginnings of an *m* (the next word being 'man') [MS].
509	*witterlye*: 'i.e., certainly. Vid. Chauc.' [P].
511	*knave*: 'i.e. a Male child. So in Chauc.' [P].
514	*sley*: 'slay or slew' [P].
518	[*Thus the sky*]: MS partly missing: reading supplied by HF. The looped *k* is just discernible, but elsewhere in this text the word used is 'skye' (508, 1565, 1572); *there*: immediately between this word and the catchword is a seemingly incomplete scribal mark. Although at first appearing to be the tops of one or two letters, P's comment 'thore: Chaucer.' – recorded in full by HF, although only the first word now visible – is immediately below this mark. Given that there is no bleed-through from the verso, P was clearly writing in empty space; i.e., the mark is of no significance.
522	*lesse*: 'leaze, lease' [P].
523	*Iwis*: 'I wis', added by scribe, with a thinner nib [MS].
536	*sond*: 'sonde, message' [P].
537	*England*: 'Englonde' [P].
538	*stint*: 'i.e., stay, desist.' [P].
554	*a stond dwell*: 'wait a while' [P].
558	*withouten lesse*: 'Lease, Lese, Chauc.' [P].
562	*3.ᵈ parte*:: text in LH margin, with curly bracket encompassing lines 562–69.
568	*of pryde*: 'of pryde' [P].
576	*Our Ladye's will*: 'The Attributes of the deity are here applied to *the* Virgin Mary' [P].
580	*bidden*: 'biden, i.e. bide' [P].
581	*Fell the[y] beene*: 'They been fell, strong' [P].
590	*feendes*: the *s* is vestigial [MS].
594	*w[end]*: hole in MS over '–end'. Reading supplied by HF; [*filed*]: 'filed, i.e. defiled' [P], the word half-obscured by cropping. HF comment: 'There is part left of one letter more than *filed*.'
598	*unde[r]stand*: understand [MS]; cf. line 239.
600	*go[o]d [wo]man*: 'go[o]d' partly obscured by hole; '[wo]man' by damage to MS.
604	*I of told*: 'of those I told' [P].
606	'delend' [P]: nothing has been flagged in this line, but it likely that P viewed the opening *&* as superfluous.
611	*cursse*: the *r* written above the line, no caret [MS].
614	*to grame*: 'grame, grief, vexation, anger, madness. S. Gram, furor. Urry. Here it is a Verb.' [P]. The 'Gr' of 'Gram' is in Anglo-Saxon characters.
623	*rose up*: a *p* between 'rose' and 'up' [MS].
629	*shrift*: 'Confession' [P]; *houzell*: 'received the Eucharis[t]. S. husl. Eucharistia. Lye.' [P]. The *t* of Eucharis[t] cropped.
645	*incomberment*: 'incombrous is used by Chaucer for combersome' [P].
652	*in fere*: 'together' [P].
656	*spousage*: 'spousinge' [P].
659	*qu[i]cke*: qucke [MS]; *dolven*: 'dug, buried. Chauc.' [P].
669	[*Some younge man's body*]: foot of page obscured by damp stains. Reading supplied by HF.
670	*t[hert]o*: page torn between *t* and *o*. Reading supplied by HF.
671	*hett*: 'promis'd' [P].
676	*s[hee]*: hole in MS. HF's reading 'she' at this point is used only once by the scribe in this text, the spelling 'shee' being preferred throughout.
678	*hande*: 'honde' [P].
685	*great*: added in LH margin by the scribe, accompanied by omission mark π.
711	*h[e]*: hole over the *e*.
713	*lem[m]an*: 'Mistress' [P].
718	*opposed*: 'apposed, examined' [P].
726	*Harlotts*: 'Harlot apud Chauc is a loose person of either Sex. Urr[y].' [P].
732	*her selfe*: 'selve' [P].
733	*delfe*: 'delve' [P].

739	*wan hope*: 'wan-hope, despair, so wan-grace is want of grace. wan is privative apud A. S. Gl. ad. G. D.' [P].
742	*sooth be[forne]*: after 'all' the MS deteriorates at the foot of the page. While some words may be construed, the part in brackets is illegible. Reading supplied by HF.
746	*minde*: what appears to be a malformed *e* after the *d*.
750	*s[l]oth*: shoth [MS].
759	*spurred*: 'sperred, sparred, &c. i.e. spar'd, bolted, locked. from Spar a wood bar, or bolt. Urry in Chauc.' [P]. P omitted the second *r* in 'sperred', and inserted it above the line, with caret.
761	*Crosse*: 'croisse q' [P].
768	*dreerye cheere*: 'dreerye cheere' [P].
780	*Chi[d]d*: HF noted that the 'MS. has either *Child* or *Chidd*, with the short stroke of the *d* dotted for *i*'. The sense is clearly 'chidd'; *resse*: 'res, rees, rese, rage ap*u*d Chauce*r*. Urry' [P].
790	*When*: inserted in LH margin by scribe, presumably because he had blotted the first word of the line.
806	*[t]raine*: MS 'traine' altered to 'braine', or possibly vice versa. The original word was probably 'straine'(see Explanatory Note). It is likely that the scribe's lack of familiarity with the term led him to confusion at this point.
807	*cam*: cann [MS].
808	*awaked*: beginnings of a loop over the *w* [MS].
810	*hands*: 'honde' [P].
812	*wende*: 'ween'd' [P].
819	*[bringe]*: bright [MS]; 'bringe' [P].
829	*any*: 'many', the *m* crossed out by scribe [MS].
831	*bo[n]e*: bome [MS].
839	*thy*: written by scribe above 'his', which has been crossed out [MS].
843	*will greater*: 'still – became or to greaten began' [P].
845	*perceived*: 'perceived' [P].
848	*opposed*: 'examined' [P].
850	*against*: a *b* crossed out before this word [MS].
851	*slowe*: 'slo, slaw, slain' [P].
853	*law*: 'lay' [P].
857	*villa[n]ye*: one minim too few in MS.
868	*the*: they [MS]; 'the' [P].
873	*[man]*: omitted in MS.
875	*Selcoth*: 'selcoth, strange, uncommon. Gl. ad G. Doug.' [P].
880	*nay shall*: 'ne shall' [P].
885	*th[ou goe], & free*: text missing at foot of page. Reading supplied by HF.
888	*[hee]*: shee [MS]; *[him]*: her [MS].
899	*& all*: 'that all' [P].
901	*a-know*: 'acknow, confess, acknowledge. Urry.' [P].
906	*served for to spilt*: 'deserved to be spil[t]' [P], the *t* cropped.
907	*wom[be]*: letters obscured by bleed-through; *gilt*: 'guilt' [P].
909	*to dead*: 'to the dead, vid. Part 4.' [P].
918	*doome*: 'doome' [P].
920	*The*: they [MS]; 'the' [P].
928	*thin[g]e*: thinke [MS]; 'thinge' [P]. See note to line 12, above.
932	*4^{d} parte:*: text in LH margin, with curly bracket encompassing lines 932–39.
934	*lase*: 'Lese, loss, lying. Urry' [P].
940	*[any]*: my [MS].
948	*yare*: 'yare, acutus, Lye: ready. Urry.' [P].
950	*The*: they [MS]; 'the' [P]; *lesse*: 'Lese:' [P].
956	*midwiffe*: the *w* is written over an *f* [MS].
957	*belive*: 'instantly, forthwith' [P].
959	*benison*: 'benediction' [P].
962	*Christendome*: 'at (his baptism)' [P].

967	[*l*]*ore*: bore [MS]; 'lore, q.' [P].
970	*can*: 'gan – Laine (lay)' [P].
977	*his*: this [MS], with heavy downward stroke crossing out opening letter; 'his' [P]; *cheere*: 'chere, Countenance, Visage, Mien. G. ad G. D. [P]; 'syer' crossed out before 'cheere'. See Explanatory Note.
985	*shal be*: the scribe began to write 'shab' and then corrected his mistake.
990	*lodlye*: 'hideous' [P].
997	*slone*: 'slone, slay' [P].
1018	*the 3*: 'these three' [P].
1024	*withouten*: 'without … So in Ch[auc.].' [P]. Gloss partly obscured by stain. Reading supplied by HF.
1028	*neithe*[*r*]: neithe [MS].
1029	*deeme in noe wise*: 'deme, inter alia. judicare.' [P].
1047	*was*: a *b* crossed out before the *w*. The scribe probably began to write 'but'.
1064	*quicke*: quiche, the *h* altered to *k* by scribe [MS].
1066	*br*[*in*]*g*: hole in MS. Reading supplied by HF.
1069	*guiltt*: 'guilt' [P].
1084	*had*: 'thro' [P]; *foode*: 'fewd. Qu.' [P].
1089	*I* interlined, with caret [MS].
1105	*Say*[*n*]*d*: sayd [MS]; 'Send' [P].
1112	*Bela*[*m*]*ye*: Belanye [MS]; 'forté, Belamy, Good friend. apud Chaucer.' [P].
1132	*Ja*[*m*]*e*: Jane [MS].
1138	*mis*[*e*]*begott*: reading supplied by HF, although the size of the hole in the MS implies more than one letter missing.
1139	*I pray thee, God …*: 'I pray God, the Devill thee' [P], written in large faint pencil.
1140	*sha*[*l*]*t*: shast [MS].
1141	*with*: 'with' [P]; *m*[*e*]: my [MS]; 'me' [P]; *shent*: scribe wrote 'brent' and changed the *b* to an *s*, and the *r* to an *h*. Eye-slip from the line above.
1143	*right* [*&*] *skill*: right skill [MS].
1150	[*be*]*gotten*: forgotten [MS]; 'begotten' [P]. Eye-slip from line below.
1174	*hee*: shee [MS]; 'Hee' [P]; *goeth*: 'goeth' [P].
1175	*sooth*: 'true' [P].
1192	*itt sooth*: 'it's sooth' [P].
1202	'It should be five, Vid. Infra. p. 164, Part 5, ver. 185' [P]. This refers to line 1392.
1208	*5*ᵈ *parte*: text in LH margin, with curly bracket encompassing lines 1208–15.
1210	*messenger*: 'messengers' [P].
1211	*Vortiger*: 'Vortiger's' [P].
1218	*stead*: 'place' [P].
1221	*srow*: 'cursed shrow' [P]; *fr*[*o*]*e*: free [MS].
1249	*h*[*i*]*s*: hs [MS]: malformed, although dot for *i* present.
1252	*priv*[*i*]*tye*: privtye [MS].
1268	*wentt*: the *w* written over an indecipherable letter [MS].
1295	*course*: 'corse' [P], written in pencil in LH margin; holes over 'mett', 'course' and 'thith[er] ward'.
1296	*befor*[*n*]*e*: one minim too few in MS.
1323	*hands*: 'hand' [P].
1328	*throw*: 'throw, a Cast, a stroke. Chaucer uses it as the Fr. do coup, for a short space. Urry' [P].
1337	*ti*[*m*]*e*: tine [MS].
1351	*hee*: sheen [MS]: 'Viz, the Chamberlaine' [P]. 'Viz' is written over another word, possibly 'Hee'.
1369	*forlaine*: 'forlyne, fornicari, adulterari. Chaucer. forliȝȝan. Sax. eod[.] sensu. Lye.' [P].
1374	*whome*: 'home' [P].
1379	*shee be take*: 'Hee (the king.) or Shee, i.e. the ~~queen~~ Chamberlaine be taken & confined' [P]. P understandably mistook the subject at this point for the Queen, instead of the chamberlain.

1388 [w]e: he [MS]; 'we' [P].
1390 Land: 'Londe' [P].
1399 What: w'hat [MS].
1402 mentt: 'ment, meant.' [P]; hang: 'hong' [P].
1406 [s]ayne: fayne [MS].
1415 [h]all: all [MS]; 'Hall q' [P].
1416 stonde: 'time' [P].
1427 Certaine: capital C written over an f [MS].
1450 steede: 'place' [P]; by-deene: 'by deene, bedene, instantly, forthwith' [P].
1452 6ᵈ parte:: text in LH margin, with curly bracket encompassing lines 1452–59.
1465 there fould: 'do fold.' [P].
1466 white as Milke reeme: & crossed out after 'white' [MS]; 'milk creame. forte milk or creame' [P].
1472 strenght of their blast: the lower parts of these words cropped; reading taken from HF.
1475 the: they [MS]: 'delend.' [P]; workemen: the r added above the line, no caret.
1489 done: the d written over a long-tailed s: the scribe probably began to write 'soe done'.
1501 unryde: 'forte unrude, horrible, hideous. See p. 387. v. 171. Vid. Gloss. to Gawain Douglas.' [P].
1515 agrise: 'agrise, affright, attack, sett upon. A. S. aȝrisan. horrere. Gl. ad G. d.' [P]. P wrote 'agrisan' using a long-tailed r, the s being above the line over a second (deleted) long-tailed r.
1516 ryssden: ss written over a d. HF suggested the other way round, but 'risen' is clearly preferable to 'ridden'. The inclusion of a d may therefore be an error.
1523 battele: 'battayle' [P].
1524 the: they [MS]; 'the' [P].
1527 the: they [MS]: 'the' [P].
1531 ri[n]ge: one minim only on n.
1534 downe: 'downe, Collis. A. S. dun. Collis, Mons. Jun.' [P].
1535 verome: 'forte venome' [P].
1542 wh[i]te: whte [MS].
1552 younge: 'King' deleted, 'younge' written to the side: eye-slip from line below.
1561 Lorne: 'lost, undone. Urry's Chauce[r]' [P].
1567 lote: 'lote, vet. particip. pro alighted.' [P].
1571 shrew: 'shrew. a Villain. Urry ad Chauc.' [P].
1575 blotted letter between 'he' and 'wold': possibly b.
1590 att: 'of' [P].
1596 tokening: t possibly written over a b [MS]. The scribe may have had in mind the verb 'to betoken', as at 1619, 1624, and 1640.
1604–5 Written as one continuous line by scribe, who indicated line break with superscript and subscript carets.
1608 fare: 'way. It. Condition, Welfare. Urry.' [P].
1611 of thy danger: 'out of danger from thee.' [P].
1612 borrowe: 'pledge, Surety.' [P].
1615 In the LH margin, between 1615 and 1616, P has written 'Hiatus' between two lateral converging lines, indicating that Vortiger's reply is lacking.
1624 di[d]st: dist [MS]; fleame: 'bannish' [P].
1630 Land: 'Londe' [P].
1632 wh[i]te: whte [MS].
1641 waxen, & succour found: 'I would read are waxen now with succour strong' [P].
1642 ma[n]y: one minim too few on the n [MS].
1646 and all beene with thee then: 'and when all or all that been' [P]: 'been' deleted and repeated.
1654 trew: the t written over a b; 'Trew, true' [P].
1659 siker: 'firm, sure' [P].
1663 counsell: 'counsayle' [P]. The word badly blotted in MS, the n interlined, without caret.
1670 But me tell: 'but thou me tell' [P].

1672	*wrought*: HF recorded the comment 'reached, seized' by P at this point, but there is no trace of any such annotation in the MS.
1677	*Merlyne*: the *r* inserted above the line, without caret [MS].
1709	[*they*]: he [MS].
1713	*slaine*: 'slone, idem.' [P].
1716	*7ᵈ parte*: text in LH margin, with curly bracket encompassing lines 1716–23.
1749	*nume*: 'turne nume or nome, i.e. took.' [P].
1754	*there*: 'thore' [P].
1757	*he can them rue*: 'they – rue: to pity, lament. Jun.' [P].
1780	*undernome*: 'received, it perceived. Chaucer vid. Urry. Lye' [P].
1788	*the*: the[y] [MS]; 'the' [P].
1809	*slaine*: 'slone, id.' [P].
1832	*him*: 'them, or hem.' [P].
1841	*both syds*: 'either syde. Sic legerem.' [P].
1843	*battele*: 'battayle' [P]. Words at top of page cropped by binder.
1846	*nye*: *n* written over another letter; scribe may have originally started 'soe' with letter *t*.
1852	'*came*' crossed out between '*they*' and '*to*': the scribe began to write '& when they came to the castle' [MS].
1853	*nume*: 'name, i.e., took' [P]. Next to this comment is another by P but deleted with a single diagonal stroke: 'forte they ma'en pro maken, or maden ut ta'en pro taken = Dialect, vor cal.' The last two words are not wholly clear.
1860	*lymes & lythe*: 'lythe, joint. A.S. lið. artus, membru[m], articulus. G. D. Lye.' [P].
1868	*8ᵈ parte*: text in LH margin, with curly bracket encompassing lines 1868–75.
1879	[*n*]*ought*: hole in MS on the *n*.
1880	*him*: interlined by scribe, with caret. [MS].
1882	*deere*: 'dere, Chaucero est lædere, nocere: Lye.' [P].
1887	*came*: hole in MS on the *m*, losing one minim.
1891	*become*: 'became' [P].
1896	*wound*[*r*]*ed*: wounded [MS].
1904	*wishe*: 'wisse, to direct, instruct, teach, show. Gl. ad. Chauc.' [P].
1907	*what*: loop on lower part of the *h*, suggesting that the scribe began to write 'wat' [MS].
1910	*fare*: 'far' [P].
1931	*trusse*: 'to truss, to pack up close together. Johnson.' [P].
1934	'The Name ought to be concealed here from what follows below, ver 105. This sh*ould* be an Error of *the* Transcriber & these 2 Lines corrupt. Fortè the old man.' [P]. Percy evidently did not approve of the reader learning the identity of the 'old man' at this point; *yorne*: 'yerne. presently. quickly. egarly. Gl. ad Chauc.' [P].
1936	indecipherable word crossed out between 'this' and 'worlde', possibly 'worlld', with the *r* inserted above the line [MS].
1940	*nay*: 'ne can' [P].
1949	*here*: 'here' [P].
1976	*&*: 'delend.' [P].
1983	*a*: interlined, with caret. [MS].
1987	*tent*: 'to take tent, to take heed. tent, attention, notice. Gl. ad. G. D.' [P].
1990	*wreake*: 'wroke or wrake' [P].
1991	*with Merlyn speake*: 'where – spoke. or spake' [P].
1994	[*And when*]: letters indistinct at top of page. P's supposition 'When, or And wh[en]' is logical (missing letters cropped); *was*: 'had or delend.' [P].
1998	*As itt were a stout garrison*: 'fortè one of the Garri*so*n.' [P].
2005	*ma*[*n*]*y*: one minim too few on *n* [MS].
2014	*amonge*: interlined, with caret [MS]; co[*m*]*en*: conen [MS], 'come' [P].
2018	*heard*: 'hard' [P].
2021	*win*[*n*]*e*: wime [MS].
2026	*God's sonde*: 'a Message, anything that may be sent. God's sonde. of God's sending. Urry's Chauc.' [P].
2032	*wrath*: 'rath; soon, early. Chaucer. hinc, rather; *prest*: prest, ready. Chaucer. [P].

2036	*is*: 'was' [P].
2038	*will*: 'wolde' [P].
2039	[*U*]*ther*: other [MS]; 'Uther' [P].
2040	'This Poem was probably written about the time of the Crusados, when all Europe so rung of the Sarracens & Mahomed: so that [?they] became [*a* blotted out] general Names [the *s* added afterwards?] for a Pagan & false God or Idol.' [P]
2049	*pight*: 'i.e., pitched, præt. obsolet.' [P].
2051	*to the*: 'the' crossed out before these words [MS].
2052	*to*: letter crossed out before this word, most likely an *s* for the following 'slay'. An eye-slip [MS].
2057	*nought*: 'not' [P].
2063	*cane*: the *e* blotted, possibly by the scribe himself, as a correction [MS].
2070	*evereche*: 'everiche' [P].
2075	*Ifere*: 'together' [P].
2076	*9.d parte*: text in LH margin, with curly bracket encompassing lines 2076–83.
2081	*a*: half-loop over this letter: scribe began to write *h for* 'heardsman'; 'man' of 'heardsman' and final letter of 'hatt' in line below distorted by gauze.
2087	*roade*: 'rade, rode' [P].
2088	*fraine*: 'i.e. freine, ask.' [P]. The word 'fraine' is repeated by P in a bolder hand in the LH margin.
2090	crossed-out letter, possibly *h*, before '*cold*' [MS]; *tythands*: 'tyding' [P].
2091	*his most wininge*: 'most his wonninge' [P].
2094	*eare*: 'ere, before. Gl. ad. G. D.' [P].
2095	*stead*: 'Place' [P].
2096	*ken*: 'conne' [P].
2100	*rathe*: 'soon' [P].
2104	*seekerlye*: 'sickerlye, surely.' [P].
2109	*right*: letter crossed out before this word; scribe began to write 'hand' [MS]; *hand*: 'honde' [P].
2112	*they*: 'they' [P].
2113	*Champyon*: 'legerim Chapmon.' [P].
2124	*a wyle*: 'while' [P].
2127	*man*: 'man' [P].
2131	*a brayd*: 'a starting; braid, arose, awoke, also a Start. Gl. ad. Chauc' [P].
2132	*& by they*: 'by then they' [P]; *had* interlined, with caret [MS].
2137	*monke's*: 'monke' [P].
2138	*gavelocke*: 'a staff. vid. Bailey.' [P].
2141	*hendlye*: 'hendlye' [P].
2152	*othee*: 'othe, oath' [P].
2153	*quante*: 'quaint, strange, odd Gl. ad Chauc.' [P].
2157	*to*: *t* is looped, obscuring the word [MS].
2160	*ine*: 'inne' [P].
2165	*all*: 'delend' [P]. It is not clear which word P was wanting to delete. HF assumed 'all', but the line as it stands makes sense uncorrected.
2174	*as councellour*: 'a counsellere q[u]' [P]. Final letter cropped.
2187	*nume*: 'nume, i.e. took' [P]. P initially wrote 'nunne' or 'runne', before crossing it out in favour of 'nume'.
2193	*yare*: 'ready' [P].
2195	*sythe*: 'time (vices)' [P].
2199	*I you plight*: the 'you' is supplied by scribe, in the LH margin, with his customary π symbol below it, and below the line to indicate the omission.
2203	*rod*: 'rode' [P].
2204	*slaine*: 'slawne' [P]. P wrote 'slawe' and crossed it out before 'slawne'.
2205	*drawne*: 'drawe' crossed out [P].
2209	[*was*]: omitted by scribe, 'was q' with subscript caret added by P at end of line, who also added a caret between 'he' and 'warned'.

2220	*lesse*: 'Lese' [P].
2224	*oste*: 'i.e. host' [P].
2230	*dere*: 'hurt, damage' [P].
2232	*they*: *t* corrected by scribe from an *f*.
2236	*all sworne & some*: 'rather "sworne all and some"'. [P].
2239	*Land*: 'Lond' [P].
2240	*name*: 'i.e., took, from nym, to take.' [P].
2244	*rathe*: 'early soon' [P].
2245	*scathe*: 'Loss, damage, hurt. Gl. ad Chau[c.]' [P].
2246	*manner*: according to HF, P added a final *e* to this word. It is certainly in a lighter ink, but it is a secretary *e*, although slightly askew.
2247	*Listen*: *&* crossed through before this word, by scribe.
2254	*the[y]*: thew [MS]: scribe added a *w* to the end of 'the' (for 'they'), most likely an eye-slip from the opening letter to the following word.
2257	*Malador*. This name is clearly spelled 'Malador' at line 2261, but a final flourish at the end of the word at line 2257 is partially obscured by a small hole in the MS – ?Maladors.
2269	*the*: they [MS]; 'the' [P].
2271	*seas*: possibly 'seat', with the *t* overlaid by an *s*.
2272	*blow*: flow, the *f* changed to a *b* [MS].
2289	*well*: 'better' [P].
2290	*heere*: 'hair' [P].
2292	The top of this line is masked by the mount. Reading supplemented by HF.
2299	*everye-eche*: 'everiche one' [P].
2300	*doughtye*: written by scribe in LH margin, with the π symbol below it and under the line to indicate omission.
2321	*fayne*: 'glad' [P].
2326	*stryde*: 'strive, or striffe.' [P]. Given the rhyme at the end of 2327, most likely a scribal error for the words P glosses.
2340	*then*: 'than' [P].
2354	*understoode*: the *r* written above the line, no caret [MS].
2365	*man*: 'mon' [P].
2369	*asket*: askes, the *s* overwritten by a *t* [MS].
2379	*ffins*: the scribe has written 'ffins' in a larger and thinner hand below and to the right of the end of line 2379.

Kinge Arthurs Death

Marian Trudgill and John Withrington

The Percy Folio ballad *Kinge Arthurs Death* (*KAD*) might more accurately be described as two works that have been fused together. The first part of the ballad (Percy's 'the Legend') is 96 lines long and consists of a first-person narrative account of Arthur's own life and deeds. In 1931, Millican demonstrated the indebtedness of the ballad to Richard Lloyd's *The Nine Worthies*, published in septenary couplets in 1584.[1] Most of Lloyd's text appears, adapted to a greater or lesser extent, in this initial part of the ballad, presented as 4-line stanzas (which are perhaps better suited to the ballad form). While Arthurian material was central to Percy's vision of the *Reliques*, *KAD* does not appear to have played a particularly significant role in that respect. For example, unlike the Arthurian ballad 'King Ryence's Challenge', which is not to be found in PF, it is possible that the hybrid nature of the poem – as evidenced by Percy's decision to separate the text into two parts, marked by a double rule after line 96 – caused him some unease or uncertainty: certainly the frequency of his insertion of parentheses in the text is somewhat unusual.

The PF version, rendered in 4-line ballad stanzas rhyming on the second and fourth lines, omits seven of Lloyd's 32 couplets, including the three penultimate ones, and four are transposed. Three of the omitted couplets merely catalogue more of Arthur's conquests (Lloyd, 1584, 17–18, 21–22, and 23–24) and consequently do not affect the narrative flow. The fourth omitted couplet (Lloyd, 1584, 49–50) describes the battle that ensued after the truce between Arthur and Mordred was agreed, and its absence is not of much significance; the battle is described in greater detail in the second part of the ballad (Percy's 'the Death'), and indeed the lines may have been omitted for this reason. The last three omitted couplets (57–62) describe how Arthur and Mordred killed each other, Arthur's departure to 'Avillion' to be healed, and the mystery surrounding his death. Again, most of this is dealt with in the 'Death' (97–end). Lloyd's final couplet, meanwhile, is moved to the end of the 'Death' and transposed into the third person to match the whole of the second part of the ballad.

As well as omissions, the unknown continuator makes four transpositions of Lloyd's text: two significant, two not. The main transposition is of course the moving of Lloyd's last couplet to the end of the 'Death', noted above. The second is almost equally interesting. The MS version moves the stanza beginning '5 kings of Pavye' (37–40) from its place after Lloyd's couplet beginning 'And *Lucius* the Emperour great of *Rome*' (29–30) to before Lloyd's 'I conquered all *Gallia*' (25–26), and invents a Grecian emperor 'Who after lost his life' (40). This improves Lloyd's rather clumsy sequence, in which lines 29–30 describe Arthur's conquest of Lucius, 31–32 describe the destruction of the 'Five Kings of Painims', and 33–34 return to the subject of Lucius. The other two transpositions are of less significance, but Lloyd's order is perhaps slightly better.

In the 'Death', clearly delineated by the sudden change to the third-person narrative, we are presented with a detailed account of Arthur's final battle and the demise of the Round Table. Here, the ballad bears a close resemblance to the final part of Malory's *Le Morte Darthur* (*LMD*),[2] together with corresponding sections of the stanzaic *Morte Arthur*, with which Malory was of course familiar.

Some striking stylistic differences exist between the two parts, with the 'Death' being markedly more balladic in form. The use of repetition is particularly noteworthy, with several stanzas appearing almost identical in nature. For example, when Lukin first goes to the river and reports back to Arthur (204–11) and is then sent to the river again (216–23), the verbal repetition lends to the poem an increasing sense of drama. A similar effect is generated by the repetition at 165–68 and 181–84, when Arthur laments the death of his knights. The repeated use of the refrain or variant 'Alacke, this was a woefull case/As ever was in Christentye!' (139–40, 147–48) and the words 'Alas/Alacke' serve to contribute to an atmosphere of pathos. Other examples of repetition include the regular use of the phrase, 'I tell you certainlye'. The 'Death' also shares a number of stylistic similarities with other poems in PF, including *KAKC* and 'Fflodden Ffeilde'. A key example is the use of the formula, 'Then bespake him Noble King Arthur/these were the words says hee …' (197–98).

Whether the 'Death' was created as a continuation to the 'Legend', or was already in existence, has been the subject of critical debate (Wilson, 1975, 143 ff.). Percy himself, although unaware of Lloyd's poem, identified a distinction and published the first and second sections of the ballad as two separate poems in his *Reliques*, presenting them as 'King Arthur's Death: A Fragment' (*Reliques*, III, 28–36) and 'The Legend of King Arthur' (*Reliques*, III, 37–41), correctly transposing the PF version of Lloyd's last stanza back to its original position, thus restoring it to a first-person narrative.[3] This distinction was maintained in later editions, for the 'Fragment', with Percy adding 30 lines to the original 154 lines as found in the PF.

Notwithstanding its heterogeneous origins and the sudden switch in the narrative at line 97, some notable artistic adaptations have been made to the inherited texts. These include several points at which separate episodes from Malory's text have been run together into a single episode, with the result that the dramatic tension is intensified. For example, the throwing of Excalibur into the lake and the disappearance of Arthur 'from under the tree' occur simultaneously, as it were, lending to the work an air of mystery. There is also evidence in the 'Death' of a number of verbal borrowings from the 'Legend' (Wilson, 1975, 144–45).

The degree of artistry on display in the ballad leads Hodder to assert that the piece should be 'more appropriately described as a single, composite text'.[4] Indeed, a significant number of the changes that were made suggest that its creator was not necessarily always as careless as may previously have been suggested and possibly that his changes may have been part of a deliberate adaptation on his part, rather than ineptitude. While the indebtedness to printed source material is apparent, and while this makes difficult an assessment of any dialectal contributions, it remains undeniable that the end result has been to make of *KAD* a brisk, fast-moving ballad well suited to recital and performance.

Notes

[1] Charles Bowie Millican, 'The Original of the Ballad "Kinge Arthurs Death" in the Percy Folio MS', *PMLA* 46(4) (1931), pp. 1020–24. Millican prints in full on pp. 1023–24 that part of Lloyd's text which relates to Arthur.

[2] Examples of similarities between *KAD* and *LMD* are provided in the Explanatory Notes. See also Robert H. Wilson, 'Malory and the Ballad "King Arthur's Death"', *Medievalia et Humanistica: Studies in Medieval & Renaissance Culture* 6 (1975), pp. 139–49. Lloyd was quite likely indebted to East's 1578 edition of *LMD* as his source for inspiration.

[3] Unusually, Percy annotated a number of words and phrases in the text of *KAD* by enclosing them within parentheses, probably since they reflected apparent metrical infelicities or linked to his marginal comments. The insertion of three asterisks in the shape of an inverted triangle against the title signals his intention of including the ballad in the *Reliques*.

[4] Karen Hodder, 'Arthur, The Legend of King Arthur, King Arthur's Death', *AE*, 73. Hodder goes on to say of *KAD* that it deserves 'to be considered as a not entirely unsuccessful attempt to integrate inherited romance material by someone who wrote the version preserved in the Percy Folio using both *The Legend* and Malory's *Morte Darthur*'. In the light of this, Millican's description (1931, 1024) of the Folio MS version of Lloyd's text as 'chaos' seems somewhat unjust.

Editions and Related Texts

HF, I, 497–507.

Millican, Charles Bowie, 'The Original of the Ballad "Kinge: Arthurs Death" in the Percy Folio MS', *PMLA* 46(4) (1931), pp. 1020–24.

Further Reading

Donatelli, Joseph M. P., 'The Percy Folio Manuscript: A Seventeenth-Century Context for Medieval Poetry', in P. Beal and J. Griffiths (eds), *English Manuscript Studies, 1100–1700*, vol. 4 (Toronto: University of Toronto Press, 1993), pp. 114–33.

Hodder, Karen, '*Arthur, The Legend of King Arthur, King Arthur's Death*', *AE*, 72–74.

Rogers, Gillian, 'The Percy Folio Manuscript Revisited', in Maldwyn Mills, Jennifer Fellows, and Carol M. Meale (eds), *Romance in Medieval England* (Cambridge: D. S. Brewer, 1991), pp. 39–64.

Wilson, Robert H., 'Malory and the Ballad "King Arthur's Death"', *Medievalia et Humanistica: Studies in Medieval & Renaissance Culture* 6 (1975), pp. 139–49.

Withrington, John, 'The Arthurian Epitaph in Malory's "Morte Darthur"', in Richard Barber (ed.), *Arthurian Literature* 7 (Cambridge: D. S. Brewer, 1987), pp. 103–44.

Kinge Arthurs Death

    Off Bruite his blood in Brittaine borne,   p. 178/f. 89r   *Brutus's blood*
        King Arthur I am to name;   *by name*
    Through Christendome & heathynesse
        Well knowen is my worthy fame.

5   In Jesus Christ I doe beleeve,
        I am a christyan borne;
    The Father, Sone, & Holy Gost,
        One God, I doe adore.

    In the 490 yeere
10   Over Brittaine I did rayne
    After my savior Christ His byrth,   *Christ my saviour's birth*
        What time I did maintaine   p. 179/f. 89v

    The fellowshipp of the Table Round,
        Soe famous in those dayes,
15 Wheratt 100 Noble K*nigh*ts*
        & 30: sitt alwayes,

    Who for their deeds & Martiall feates,
        As bookes done yett record,
    Amongst all Nations
20   Wer feared throwgh the world.

    & in the castle off Tyntagill
        K*ing* Uther mee begate
    Of Agyana, a bewtyous Ladye,*
        & come of his estate.

25 & when I was 15 yeere old,*
        Then was I crowned K*ing*;
    All Brittaine was att an uprore,
        I did to quiett bringe.

    & drove the Saxons from the realme,
30   Who had opprest this Land;
    & then I conquered througe Manly feats*
        All Scottlande with my hands.

    Ireland, Denmarke, Norway,
        These countryes wan I all,
35 Iseland, Gotheland, & Swethland,
        & made their K*ing*s my thrall.

5 Kings of Pavye I did kill,*
    Amidst *tha*t bloody strife;
Besides the Grecian Emperour,
40   Who alsoe Lost his liffe.

I conquered all Gallya,
    *Tha*t now is called France;
& I slew the hardy Froland feild,*
    My honor to advance;

45 & the ugly Gyant Danibus,*
    Soe terrible to vewe,
*Tha*t in St Barnard's Mount did Lye,*
    By force of armes I slew;

& Lucyes the Emperour of Roome,*   *ruin*
50   I brought to deadly wracke;
& a 1000 more of Noble K*nigh*ts
    For feare did turne their backes,

Whose carkasse I did send to Roome,*   *bier*
    Cladd poorlye on a beere;
55 & afterward I past Mountjoye,*
    The next approching yeere.

Then I came to Roome, where I was mett
    Right as a conquerour,
& by all the cardinalls solempnelye*
60   I was crowned an Emperour.

One winter [there] I made abode,
    & then word to me was brought
How Mordred, my sonne, had oppressed the crowne,*
    What treason he had wrought

65 Att home in Brittaine heere w*i*th my Queene;
    Therfore I came w*i*th speede
To Brittaine backe w*i*th all my power,   *avenge*
    To quitt *tha*t traiterous deede;

& when att Sandwiche I did Land,*
70   Where Mordred me w*i*thstoode,
But yett att last I lan[d]ed there,
    W*i*th effusion of Much blood.

Ffor there my nephew S*ir* Gawaine dyed,
    Being wounded on *tha*t sore*

Kinge Arthurs Death   215

75   That Sir Lancelott in fight
         Had given him before.

      Thence chased I Mordred away,*
      Who fledd to London wright;   *right*
      Ffrom London to Winchester
80   & to Corwalle hee tooke his flyght;

      & still I him pursued with speed,
         Till att the Last wee mett,
      Wherby appointed day of fight
         Was agreede & sett;   p. 180/f. 90r

85   Where wee did fight soe Mortallye
         Of live eche other to deprive,
      That of a 100:1000 men*
         Scarce one was left alive.

      There all the Noble chivalrye
90   Of Brittaine tooke their end.
      O, see how fickle is their state
         That doe upon feates depend!

      There all the traiterous men were slaine,
         Not one escapet away;
95   & there dyed all my Vallyant Knights –
         Alas that woefull day!*

      But upon a Monday after Trinity Sonday*
         This battaile foughten cold bee;
      Where ma[n]y a Knight cryed wellaway –
100   Alacke, the more pittye!

      But upon Sunday in the evening then,
         When the King in his bedd did Lye,
      He thought Sir Gawaine to him came,
         & thus to him did say:

105   'Now as you are my unckle deere,
         I pray you be ruled by mee;
      Doe not fight as tomorrow day,
         But put the battelle of if you may,   *delay the battle*

      'For Sir Lancelott is now in France,
110   & many Knights with him full hardye,
      & within this Month here hee wil be,
         Great aide wil be to thee.'

Hee wakened forth of his dreames;
    To his Nobles *that* told hee,
115 How he thought S*i*r Gawaine to him came,
    & these words sayd Certainly.*

& then the[y] gave the K*ing* councell all,
    upon Munday Earlye,
*Tha*t hee shold send one of his heralds of armes,
120   To parle with his sonne if itt might bee.

& 12 knights K*ing* Arthur chose,*
    The best in his companye,
*Tha*t they shold goe to meete his sonne
    To agree if itt cold bee.

125 & the K*ing* charged all his host   *ordered his army*
    In readynesse for to bee,
*Tha*t Noe man shold noe weapons sturr*
    W*i*thout a sword drawne amongst his K*nigh*ts the[y] see;   *Unless*

& Mordred upon the other p*ar*t
130   12 of his K*nigh*ts chose hee,
*Tha*t they shold goe to meete his father
    Betweene these 2 hosts fayre & free.

& Mordred charged his ost*
    In like mannour most certainely,
135 *Tha*t noe man shold noe weapons sturre
    W*i*thout a sword drawne amongst them the[y] see,

For he durst not his father trust,
    Nor the father the sonne certainley,
Alacke, this was a woefull case
140   As ev*er* was in Christentye!   *Christendom*

But when they were mett together there,
    & agreed of all things as itt shold bee,
& a monthe's League then there was*
    Before the battele foughten shold bee,

145 An Adder came forth of Bush,
    Stunge one of K*ing* Arthir's K*nigh*ts below his knee;*
Alacke, this was a woefull chance*
    As ev*er* was in Christentye!

The K*nigh*t he found him wounded there,
150   & see the wild worme there to bee,   *snake*

His sword out of his scabberd he drew;
    Alas, itt was the more pittye!

& when these 2 osts saw the sword drawen,
    The[y] Joyned battell certainlye,
155 Till of a 100:1000: men   p. 181/f. 90v
    Of one side was left but 3.

But all were slaine *tha*t durst abyde,
    But some awaye *tha*t did flee;
K*ing* Arthur upon his owne p*a*rtye
160   Himselfe alive cold be,

& Lukin the Duke of Gloster,*
    & Bedever his Butler certainlye.
The K*ing* looked about him there,*
    & saw his K*nigh*ts all slaine to bee;

165 'Alas!' then sayd Noble K*ing* Arthur
    '*Tha*t *ever* this sight I see;
To see all my good K*nigh*ts lye slaine,
    & the traitor yett alive to bee.

'Loe where he leanes upon his sword hillts,*
170   Amongst his dead men certainlye;
I will goe slay him att this time;
    Nev*er* att better advantage I shall him see.'

'Nay, stay here, my Leege,' then said the Duke,
    'For love & charitye,
175 For wee have the battell woone,
    For yett alive wee are but 3.'   *Even though*

The K*ing* wold not be p*er*swaded then,
    But his horsse then Mounted hee;
His Butler t[hat] helped him to horsse,*
180   His bowells gushed to his knee.

'Alas!' then said noble K*ing* Arthur,
    '*Tha*t this sight I *ever* see;
To see this good k*nigh*t for to be slaine
    For love for to helpe mee!'

185 He put his speare into his rest,
    & att his sonne he ryd feirclye;
& through him there his speare he thrust
    A fatham thorrow his body.

The sonne he felld him wounded there,*
    & knew his death then to bee;
He thrust himselfe upon his speare,
    & gave his father a wound certainlye.

But there dyed S*ir* Mordred,
    Presently upon *tha*t tree;
But or e[r]e the K*ing* returned againe,
    His butler was dead certainlye.

Then bespake him Noble Kin*g* Arthur,
    These were the words sayd hee:
Sayes, 'take my sword Escalberd*
    From my side fayre & free,

'& throw itt into this river heere,
For all the use of weapons I'le deliver uppe,
    Heere underneath this tree.'

The Duke to the river side he went,
    & his sword in threw hee,
& then he kept Escalberd,
    I tell you certainlye;

& then he came to tell the K*ing*;
    The K*ing* said, 'Lukin, what did thou see?'
'Noe thing, my leege,' the[n] sayd the Duke,
    'I tell you certainlye.'

'O, goe againe,' said the K*ing*,
    'For love & charitye,
& throw my sword into *tha*t river,
    *Tha*t neve*r* I doe itt see.'

The Duke to the river side he went,
    & the K*ing*'s scaberd in threw hee;*
& still he kept Escalbard,
    For vertue sake faire & free.

He came againe to tell the K*ing*;
    The K*ing* sayd, 'Lukin, what did thou see?'
'Nothing, my leege,' then sayd the Duke,
    'I tell you certainlye.'

'O, goe againe, Lukin,' said the K*ing*,
    'Or the one of us shall dye.'

i.e., spear

Excalibur

p. 182/f. 91r

>   Then the Duke to the river sid went,*
>   & the K*ing*'s sword then threw hee;
>
>   A hand & an arme did meete *tha*t sword,
>   & flourished 3 times certainlye;
> 230   He came againe to tell the K*ing*,
>   But the K*ing* was gone from under the tree.
>
>   But to what place, he cold not tell,
>   For nev*er* after hee did him see;
>   But he see a barge from the land goe,
> 235   & hearde Ladyes houle & cry certainlye;
>
>   But whether the K*ing* was there or noe,
>   He knew not certainlye.
>   The Duke walked by *tha*t River's side,*
>   Till a chappell there found hee,
>
> 240   & a preist by the aulter side there stood.
>   The Duke kneeled downe there on his knee
>   & prayed the preists, 'for Christ's sake,
>   The rights of the church bestow on mee.'   *rites*
>
>   For many dangerous wounds he had upon him,
> 245   & liklye he was to dye.
>   & there the Duke lived in prayer,
>   Till the time *tha*t hee did dye.
>
>   K*ing* Arthur lived K*ing* 22 yeere,*   *reigned for 22 years*
>   In honor and great fame,
> 250   & thus by death suddenlye
>   Was deprived from the same.
>   ffins.

Explanatory Notes

15–16 *100 Noble K*nights/*& 30*: Lloyd (8) has the more usual number of 150, as does Malory. References to Malory's work are taken from the edition by Sommer.

23 *Agyana*: *KAD* is the only example of this form of 'Ygerna', Arthur's mother. Lloyd has 'Igrayne' (12), as does *LMD*. Robert Ackerman does not provide any other examples of the name as found in PF. See Robert William Ackerman (ed.), *An Index of the Arthurian Names in Middle English* (Stanford, CA: Stanford University Press, 1952).

25–26 This detail originates with Geoffrey of Monmouth's *HRB*.

31–52 Taken from a chronicle source, deriving ultimately from *HRB*.

37 *Pavye*: Presumably, Pavia. Lloyd (31) has 'Painims', i.e., pagans, which makes more sense.

43 *& I slew the hardy Froland feild*: 'And I slew the hardy Froll on the field of battle'.

45	*the ugly Gyant Danibus*: the name first appears in some MSS of Wace's *Roman de Brut*, where the giant is called Dinabuc (Wace, *Wace's Roman de Brut: A History of the British Text and Translation*, ed. Judith Weiss (Exeter: Exeter University Press, 1999), p. 284; line 11,317). Robert Manning calls him Dynabrok (Robert Manning, *The Story of England by Robert Manning of Brunne, A.D. 1338*, 2 vols, ed. Frederick J. Furnivall (London: HMSO, 1887; repr. Cambridge: Cambridge University Press, 2012), vol. 1, line 12,340). He is not named in *HRB* nor in *LMD*, but appears in the Anglo-Norman *Brut* (*The Oldest Anglo-Norman Prose Brut Chronicle*, ed. Julia Marvin (Woodbridge: Boydell Press, 2006), line 11,317). Ackerman lists the various occurrences of the name but asserts that the author of *KAD* or his source 'has mistakenly associated Dinabus with a later exploit of the Roman campaign'.
47	*St Barnard's Mount*: also referred to in the text as Mountjoye, the mountain pass of Great St Bernard, in northern Italy. The more usual name for the site of Arthur's combat against the giant is Mont St Michel, first appearing in *HRB*. It is called 'Mount Bernard' in the *Alliterative Morte Arthure* (*AMA*) (566). After Arthur's defeat of the giant in *LMD* he calls for a church to be built 'on the same hylle in the worship of saynte Mychel' (V, v).
49	*Lucyes the Emperour of Roome*: in *AMA*, *LMD*, and Lloyd he is known as Lucius.
53	*Whose carkasse*: i.e., the Emperor's body.
55	*Mountjoye*: see note to line 47.
59–60	Arthur is crowned Emperor here. For this unusual title for Arthur, see John Withrington, 'King Arthur as Emperor', *Notes & Queries* 233 (1988), pp. 13–15; *cardinalls*: the Senate performs this ceremony in Lloyd (36).
63	*Mordred, my sonne*: the reference here to Mordred's genealogy is of interest in the context of Arthurian romance: in the chronicles, Mordred is referred to as Arthur's nephew (as P himself notes), whereas the romances refer to Mordred as Arthur's son, resulting from an incestuous relationship with his sister, an incident not alluded to in the ballad. Adding 'my sonne' makes the line hypermetrical (see Textual Note to line 86 below).
69	*Sandwiche*: in *HRB*, Arthur lands at Richborough; in *LMD*, Dover.
74	*that sore*: i.e. wound. This refers to the combats before Lancelot's castle of Benwick, prior to Arthur receiving the news of Mordred's treachery. In *LMD*, the dying Gawaine tells Arthur, 'I am smyten upon thold wounde the whiche sir launcelot gaf me' (XXI, ii).
77–80	In *HRB*, Mordred goes to Winchester, then to Cornwall; in *LMD*, he flees first to Canterbury, then agrees to meet Arthur at Salisbury.
87–88	*100:1000 men*: repeated at 155–56, referring to the slaughter of the last battle in Cornwall. This incremental repetition by the second author is part of the pulling together of the two parts of the ballad.
96	Unusually, the scribe did not mark a division here: one might have expected a 'Parte 2d^a', in line with his practice elsewhere. See Textual Note.
97–103	'and this day was assygned on a monday after Trynyte sonday ... Soo vpon Trynyte sonday at nyghte kynge Arthur dremed a wonderful dreme ... So the kynge semed veryly that there came syr Gawayne vnto hym' (*LMD*, XXI, iii).
116	*Certainly*: the first occurrence of this word, used for emphasis, and occurring only in the 'Death' part of *KAD*.
121	*12 knights*. in *LMD*, the number of knights is 14.
127–28	Incremental repetition (see also lines 135–36, 139–40, 147–48).
133–38	'In lyke wyse syr mordred warned his hoost that and ye see ony swerde drawen look that ye come on fyersly & soo slee alle that euer before you stondeth for in no wyse I wyl not truste for thys treatyse' (*LMD*, XXI, iiii).
143	*a monthe's League*: *LMD*'s reading – that the king charged Lucan and Bedyuere 'in ony wyse & they myght take a traytyse for a monthe day wyth Syr mordred' (XXI, iii) – makes it clear that a breathing space or truce was to be negotiated. Lines 143–44 in *KAD* seem to imply that the space of a month is simply an interlude before a final confrontation. It is unclear why the scribe should have thought 'league' an appropriate choice of word at this point.
146	*Stunge one of King Arthir's Knights*: in *LMD*, Malory does not state which side the injured knight belonged to.

147–48	'And kyng Arthur took his hors and sayd allas thys vnhappy day … And neuer was there seen a more doolfuller batiayle in no crysten londe' (*LMD*, XXI, iiii).
161–62	Bedivere and Lucan have reversed their traditional roles here. In *LMD*, it is Lucan who dies as he lifts Arthur, and Bedevere who throws the sword. Lucan, not Bedivere, is normally referred to as the butler, although the latter is so called in *HRB*. It is not clear why Lucan is called the Duke of Gloucester.
163–66	'Thenne the kyng loked aboute hym & thenne was he ware of al hys hoost & of al his good knyghtes were lefte no moo on lyue but two knyghtes that one was Syr Lucan de butlere & his broder Syr Bedewre … Alas that euer I shold see thys dolefull day' (*LMD*, XXI, iiii).
169–92	In *LMD*, Sir Mordred is similarly described as leaning upon his sword among a heap of dead men. However, in *LMD*, Arthur is on foot rather than horseback, and Lucan dies slightly after Arthur kills Mordred (*LMD*, XXI, iiii–v).
199	'Escalberd' is possibly a conflation of 'Escalibor' and 'scabbard'. In *LMD*, Arthur commands Bedwere to take 'Excalybur my god swerde and goo with it to yonder water syde and whan thou comest there I charge the throwe my swerde in that water & come ageyn and telle me what thou there seest' (*LMD*, XXI, v).
217	*& the* K*ing's scaberd in threw hee*: Lucan throws his sword in first, then Arthur's scabbard, then Excalibur. In *LMD*, Bedivere hides the sword on his first two visits to the lake, and finally throws in Excalibur.
226–29	'And thenne he threwe the swerde as farre in to the water as he myght & there cam an arme and an hande aboue the water and mette it & caught it and so shoke it thryse and braundysshed' (*LMD*, XXI, v).
238–29	'And so he wente al that nyght and in the mornyng he was ware betwyxte two holtes hore af [sic] a chapel and an ermytage' (*LMD*, XXI, v).
248–51	King *Arthur lived* King *22 yeere*: here the final lines of Lloyd's verse appear, transposed into the third person. It is not clear where this figure comes from. In Lloyd's part of the text, Arthur starts his reign in 490. In *HRB*, Constantinus, son of Cador of Cornwall, and Arthur's heir, is crowned in 542, but *HRB* gives no information about the length of Arthur's reign.

Textual Notes

There is a hole in the MS over the *E* of *KING*[*E*]. Underneath the title, and with no closing bracket, Percy has written 'The former [part] of this Ballad is upon the Plan of Guy & Phillis. (See page 252.)' The word 'part' obliterated by hole, but reading supplied by HF.

In the LH margin, opposite the title: 'A very curious romantic old Balad or rather two. See St. 25'. Starting on a new line: 'NB: The Facts here referred to, may be found related at large in the Old Chronicles, (Especially an old Chronycle Folio black Lettre printed at Antwerp 1493, by Gerard de Lee[w])'. [Percy's reference is to Gerard de Leew's reprint of Caxton's 1480 edition of the *Cronycles of the londe of Englond*, published in Antwerp in 1493.]

1	*Bruite his blood*: 'Brutus' blood, rather Bruty's' [P].
2	*to*: '**by**' [P].
3	'NB. In this & the following, I made many corrections, wh*ich* I did not think it necessary to enumerate. P.'
6	*borne*: '(bore is used in G.D. for borne passim' [P]. RH bracket lost through cropping.
7	*Gost*: a half-loop over the *g* [MS].
16	*30*: *sitt*: 'sat' [P].
19	*Amongst all Nations*: 'other' in margin, with caret between 'all' and 'Nations' [P].
21	*Tyntagill*: 'Tyntagel' [P].
23	*Agyana*: 'It is Igerne in the Old Chronicles' [P]; *Ladye*: 'Dame' [P].
25	*when*: inserted above the line, with caret [MS].
28	*quietl*: thick vertical stroke stretches from first *t* up to 'was' in line above.
31–32	'All Scot*l*and then thro' manly feats I conquer'd with my hands. Sic Legerim' [P].
32	*hands*: 'hand' [P].

33	*Ireland, Denmarke, Norway*: 'and' inserted after 'Denmarke', with caret [P].
37	*Pavye*: 'Pavye' [P].
43	*Froland feild*: 'Froll in field. – Froll, or Frolle according. to the old Chronicles, was a Roman Knight. governor of France.' [P].
45	*Danibus*: 'called Dynabus in the Chronicles.' [P].
49	*&*: '& delend.' [P].
57	*Roome*: 'Rome' [P].
60	*an*: amended by P by enclosing within parentheses.
61	[*there*] *I made*: 'I made' [MS]; 'there I made' [P].
62	*&*: amended by P by enclosing within parentheses.
63	*my sonne*: amended by P by enclosing within parentheses; 'In the chronicles &c. he is called his Nephew.' [P]; *had oppressed*: 'per' [P].
65	*heere*: amended by P by enclosing within parentheses.
68	*quitt*: 'i.e. requite' [P].
70	*Where*: 'There' [P]; *withstoode*: as HF noted, there is a dip-stroke between the *d* and the *e*.
71–72	Both these lines are affected by bleed-through from the title on the reverse side of this folio, and by holes over the words 'landed' and 'blood'.
74–76	*sore*: 'shore' [P in the RH margin]. P evidently then changed his mind, adding in the LH margin, 'in that sore [the] which Sir Lancelot in fight [Had], &c.'. The words '[the]' and '[Had]' are no longer visible because of the cropping of the MS, although HF seem to have been able to read them.
75–76	Written as one line in MS, separated by a vertical line (suggesting that it was originally committed in error).
78	*wright*: 'right' [P].
79	*Winchester*: the word 'and' appears faintly after 'Winchester', in Percy's hand. Since P added parentheses to *&* at the beginning of the following line, this addition is somewhat puzzling.
80	*&*: amended by P by enclosing within parentheses; *hee*: amended by P by enclosing within parentheses; *flyght*: beginnings of a loop over *g*, suggesting that the scribe started to write letter *h*.
83	*appointed*: 'an appointed' [P].
84	*Was*: 'there was' [P].
85–86	'Where we did fight of mortal life Eche other to deprive' [P]. P's comment features as a couplet in 'The Legend of King Arthur' as printed in the *Reliques* (*Reliques*, III, 41, lines 85–86).
86	*other*: amended by P by enclosing within parentheses; 'life each to' [P]. P's parentheses recognizes that the inclusion of the word 'other' creates a hypermetrical line.
91	*state*: 'states' [MS]. HF transcribed the word as 'state', noting that 'The *e* has a flourish like *s* at the end'. The conclusion of the word, however, is more than a flourish – cf. 'estate' at line 24 and 'feates' at line 92 – and surely prompted Percy to correct to 'state' in the margin.
92	*upon*: 'on' [P]. PF's reading somewhat alters the meaning of this line: knights depend on their prowess in arms; 'fate' implies chance.
94	*escapet away*: beginnings of a loop over the *w* of 'away' [MS].
96	The double rule after this line, indicating the division between the two Parts, is by P, as is the comment in the LH margin, alongside lines 95–96, extending to 101: 'Hitherto the King himself speaks – in what follows, the Poet carries on the Narrative. From the difference of Style & Meter, they should seem to be two different Songs'.
97	*a Monday*: 'The Morn' [P].
98	*foughten*: amended to 'fought(en)' by P.
99	*ma*[*n*]*y*: one minim too few on the *n*.
104	*say*: 'crye' [P].
106	*you*: amended by P by enclosing within parentheses.
107	*day*: amended by P by enclosing within parentheses; 'delend' [P].
108	*But put the battelle of if you may* [MS]: 'but put it off if you may' [P].
110	*with him full*: amended by P by enclosing within parentheses.

112	*wil be*: 'to give' [P].
116	*&*: amended by P by enclosing within parentheses.
117	*the*[*y*]: the [MS]. See also lines 128, 136, 154.
119	*heralds*: herauds, *l* written over the *u*. [MS]; *of armes*: amended by P by enclosing within parentheses.
120	*parle*: 'parle, parly' [P]; *with his sonne*: amended by P by enclosing within parentheses.
126	*for*: amended to '(for)' by P.
128	*Without a sword*: 'unless swordes' [P]; *amongst his Knights*: amended by P by enclosing within parentheses.
136	*amongst*: 'against' [P].
146	*Arthir's*: no dot on the *i*, possibly a minim missing here.
149	*wounded*: scribal π symbol after 'him', signifying an omission, with 'wounded' added in LH margin. See also note to line 244.
153	*the*: they [MS].
172	*advantage*: the *g* blurred.
176	*For yet alive wee are but 3.*: medial dot after *3* [MS]; *For*: this may be eye-slip from previous line, with, e.g., '&' intended; 'Altho alive we' [P], 'fortè delend' [P].
179	*t*[*hat*] *helped him*: thelped [MS], 'helped, or as he helped' [P].
184	*For love*: 'for his love' [P].
189	*felld*: 'felt' [P].
190	*knew*: 'knew' [P]. HF noted a possible reading of *know*; it may be that P felt obliged to confirm his preferred reading in the margin.
194	*tree*: half-loop over *r* [MS].
195	*e*[*r*]*e*: The second letter is indistinct, the scribe having either overwritten or blotted at this point.
197	*Then bespake him*: 'viz. Lukyn Duke of Gloster' [P]. P's gloss shows that he has not recognized the formula: 'Then bespake him … these were the words sayd hee'.
197–203	HF print these lines as a 7-line stanza, but 201–3 are marked off by P as 3-lines. The apparent corruption of the second stanza is likely to stem from the fact that Lloyd's work was written in septenary couplets.
199	*take my sword Escalberd*: 'Caliburn, The sword of King. Arthur was presented A.D. 1191 to Tancred, King. of Sicily, by our King. Richard. I. See Rapin Vol. I'. (Percy's reference is to Paul de Rapin's *L'Histoire d'Angleterre*. Written between 1724 and 1727, it was subsequently translated into English and continued by Nicholas Tindal, and published from 1725 onwards.)
208	*tell*: letter *t* has a looped descender [MS].
210	*the*[*n*]: the [MS]. P placed a cross by this word and wrote 'then' in the margin.
216	*he*: P marked this word with a cross, presumably intending to gloss it.
227	*the*: then [MS].
231	*But the King was gone from under the tree*: 'This is the tradition alluded to by Don Quixote' [P].
235	*Ladyes*: 'By this Word Old English Writers expressed what *the* Romans called Nymphae, &c. summo ulularunt vertice Nymphae. Æn. 4, 168' [P].
240	*aulter*: 'altar' [P].
243	*rights*: 'rites' [P].
244	*wounds*: scribal π symbol after 'dangerous', signifying an omission, with 'wounds' added in LH margin; *upon him*: 'delend.' [P].
248–51	'I take this stanza to belong to the first part.' [P].
249	*fame*: word is blurred in the MS.
251	*ffins*: the scribe has written 'ffins' in a larger and thinner hand below and to the right of the end of line 251; *from*: 'of' [P].

The Grene Knyght

Diane Speed

The Grene Knyght (*GK*), described by HF as 'as infant antiquarian effort' (*Reliques*, I, 57), is generally thought to have been composed in the late fifteenth century. The unique copy in the PF is the end product of a considerable transmission history, evidenced, for example, in the mix of forms in both end-rhyme and mid-line positions. The poet's dialect may have been northern or Midland but cannot be fixed with certainty.[1]

The presentation of the tail-rhyme stanza in the extant text is uneven. The edition published here follows the stanzaic divisions in the Folio, where the 6-line stanza is the norm. Over half the poem, however, has a residual rhyme scheme in which four successive tail lines rhyme, suggesting either that the poem may originally have been written in 12-line stanzas or that the poet was heavily influenced by a 12-line stanza in his immediate model or in other similar poems. The stanzaic divisions as provided present anomalies of three-line stanzas at 49–51 and 444–46 and 9-line stanzas at 58–66 and 459–67; it is not impossible that some lines are missing in these places, but the sense is adequate as it stands. Percy explicitly notes 'some great omission' between 455 and 456, but again the sense is adequate.

The uncertain status of the extant text might be thought to make critical judgements more problematic. In recent years, however, serious criticism has emerged of the text as we have it, taking as its starting point, inevitably, comparison with *Sir Gawain and the Green Knight* (*SGGK*), which tells essentially the same story and shares with *GK* numerous parallels of narrative detail and expression.[2] *GK* has commonly been understood to be a direct descendant of *SGGK*, with or without intermediaries;[3] an alternative suggestion is that they may both share a common original,[4] but it seems plausible that the story would have been better known from *GK* than from its great predecessor, *SGGK*. Perhaps the aural memory of a performance lies behind the original composition of *GK* or forms part of its transmission history.[5] In the end, the exact nature of the relationship between the two extant poems must remain a moot point. More broadly, *GK* may be grouped with other medieval English poems featuring Gawaine, including those in the Percy Folio;[6] notably, the name 'Bredbeddle' appears also in *King Arthur and King Cornwall* (*KAKC*: see pp. 51–70, above), and a variant of the Temptation in the *Carle off Carlile* (see pp. 331–52, below).

GK is very much shorter than *SGGK*. Less space is given to details of character, setting, and incident, and some episodes receive much less attention proportionately: the content of the last three fitts of *SGGK* occupies only the second half of *GK*; the three days of hunting and temptation, which occupy a third of *SGGK*, occupy one day, and a twelfth of *GK*. A pervasive difference in narrative structure concerns the narratorial perspective: in *SGGK*, the story unfolds largely through the eyes of the Arthurian court and Gawaine in particular so that the reader is positioned with them and implicated in the serious issues raised by the action, whereas in *GK* simultaneous actions are related by an omniscient narrator with whom the reader is positioned outside the story, beyond potential implication in whatever issues might be raised.[7] For the reader of *GK*, the evocation of the Golden Age of chivalry is simply an exercise in cheerful nostalgia.

At the same time, the poet's world as portrayed is invested with a distinct familiarity, whether with real life or with popular tales. Among the particular narrative details that differ from those of *SGGK*, the Knight appears not to be green of body (105); he merely has a green horse and green array (80–81); the lady's lace is not green but white (397), and its adoption by Arthur's court bestows a pretty origin on a prominent chivalric order of latter days (501–6); the motive for the challenge is the witch's desire to help her daughter meet the gallant Gawaine (46–48, 61–66); and the Knight's own motive is his desire to see if Gawaine lives up to his reputation for valour (67–72, 133–44), although his challenge is actually directed towards the whole court (134, 136, 143–44), as it is in *SGGK* (285, 291) – nevertheless, it is Gawaine alone who is his quarry. There is no reference to larger narrative patterns of Arthurian legend which resonate with the name 'Morgne la Faye' in *SGGK*, and no profound questioning of the values of the Arthurian world or the real world for which it might stand. All the challenger finally wants is to be part of Arthur's court (489–91), and in the narrative frame the reader is simply presented with 'our' king and queen (16–17, 515). The appearance of a porter (92–108) and a trouble-making but inconsequential Kay (154–62) further locate the poem in the world of popular romance evoked by the very choice of tail-rhyme stanzas as the medium of communication.[8]

Notes

[1] Prof. Michael Benskin, in private correspondence. See also Rhiannon Purdie, *Anglicising Romance: Tail-Rhyme and Genre in Medieval English Literature* (Cambridge: D. S. Brewer, 2008), pp. 190–93.

[2] For parallels, see George Lyman Kittredge, *A Study of Gawain and the Green Knight* (Cambridge, MA: Harvard University Press, 1916), pp. 282–89; *Sir Gawain and the Green Knight*, ed. Sir Israel Gollancz, with Introductory Essays by Mabel Day and Mary S. Serjeantson, EETS OS 210 (London: Oxford University Press, 1940), pp. xxxviii–xxxix. For a discussion, see Gillian Rogers, 'Themes and Variations: Studies in Some English Gawain-Poems', PhD thesis, University of Wales, 1978, 213–51.

[3] See, for example, Madden, 352; HF, II, 56; Kittredge, 1916, 134; Rogers, 1978, 366.

[4] This idea was advanced by J. R. Hulbert ('Syr Gawayn and the Grene Kny3t', *Modern Philology* 13 (1915–16), pp. 433–62 and pp. 689–730) and developed by Gray ('A Note on the Percy Folio *Grene Knight*', in Bonnie Wheeler (ed.), *Arthurian Studies in Honour of P. J. C. Field*, Arthurian Studies LVII (Cambridge: D. S. Brewer, 2004), pp. 166–67).

[5] Diane Speed (ed.), 'The Grene Knight', in *Medieval English Romances*, 3rd ed., 2 vols (Durham: University of Durham, 1993), I, 237. Hahn notes not only that an inventory of books held by

Sir John Paston in the late 1470s included a work called 'The Green Knyghte' (although Hahn believes that Paston 'likely owned a more literary, and literate version' than *GK*), but that the legend was sufficiently popular that in 1575 Captain Cox's repertoire included a performance piece called 'Sir Gawyn', which could well be a version related to *GK* (see Hahn, 309–10) and Introduction, above.

6 See Clinton Machan, 'A Structural Study of the English Gawain Romances', *Neophilologus* 66 (1982), pp. 629–37.

7 See Speed, 1993, I, 200. Matthews points out that the narrator's frequent asseverations of truth-telling reinforce the narratorial leading of the reader. David O. Matthews, '"A Shadow of Itself?": Narrative and Ideology in *The Grene Knight*', *Neophilologus* 78 (1994), p. 308.

8 Speed, 1993, I, 199–201. Percy's attention to the significance of the rhyme scheme is evidenced in his efforts to explain unfamiliar words, as in his gloss on 'gate' ('path', 290) as 'way', from Icelandic *gata*, and his mistaken gloss on 'mell' ('speak', 37) as 'meddle', from French *mêler*.

Editions

Hahn, 309–35.

HF, II, 56–77.

Madden, 224–42.

Speed, Diane (ed.), 'The Grene Knight' in *Medieval English Romances*, 3rd ed., 2 vols. (Durham: University of Durham, 1993), I, 236–59; II, 321–30, 348–50.

Further Reading

Gray, Douglas, 'A Note on the Percy Folio *Grene Knight*', in Bonnie Wheeler (ed.), *Arthurian Studies in Honour of P. J. C. Field*, Arthurian Studies LVII (Cambridge: D. S. Brewer, 2004), pp. 165–71.

Hahn, Thomas, and Symons, Dana M., 'Medieval English Romance', in Peter Brown (ed.), *A Companion to Medieval English Literature and Culture c.1350–c.1500* (Malden, MA: Blackwell, 2007), pp. 344–45.

Rogers, Gillian, 'Themes and Variations: Studies in Some English Gawain-Poems', PhD thesis, University of Wales, 1978, pp. 213–51.

—— 'The Grene Knight', in Derek Brewer and Jonathan Gibson (eds), *A Companion to the Gawain-Poet*, Arthurian Studies 38 (Cambridge: D. S. Brewer, 1997), pp. 365–72.

Speed, Diane, '*The Grene Knight*', AE, 199–201.

The Grene Knyght

	List! Wen Arthur he was K*ing*,	p. 203/f. 101v
	He had all att his leadinge	
	The broad Ile of Brittaine;	
	England & Scottland one was,*	
5	And Wales stood in the same case,	
	The truth itt is not to layne.	*conceal*
	He drive allyance out of this Ile;	*foreigners*
	Soe Arthur lived in peace a while,	
	As men of Mickle maine.	*great power*
10	K*nigh*ts strove of their degree,*	
	W*hi*ch of them hyest shold bee:	
	Therof Arthur was not faine.	*displeased*
	Hee made the Round Table for their behove,	*benefit*
	*Tha*t none of them shold sitt above,	
15	But all shold sitt as one,	*on an equal footing*
	The K*ing* himselfe in state royall,	
	Dame Guenever, our queene, w*i*thall,	*likewise*
	Seemlye of body & bone.*	*Lovely*
	Itt fell againe the Christmase	
20	Many came to *tha*t Lord's place,	
	To *tha*t worthye one,	
	W*i*th helme [on] head & brand bright,	*sword*
	All *tha*t tooke order of k*nigh*t;	
	None wold linger att home.	
25	There was noe castle nor mano*u*r free	*noble*
	*Tha*t might harbour *tha*t companye,	*lodge*
	Their puissance was soe great.	*numbers were*
	Their tents up the[y] pight,	*pitched*
	For to lodge there all *tha*t night;	
30	Therto were sett to meate.	*they sat down to their meal*
	Messengers there came [&] went	
	With much victualls, verament,	*provisions; truly*
	Both by way & streete.	
	Wine & wildfowle thither was brought;	
35	W*i*thin they spared nought	
	For gold, & they might itt gett.	*if*
	Now of K*ing* Arthur noe more I mell,*	*speak*
	But of a venterous k*nigh*t I will you tell,	*knight errant*
	*Tha*t dwelled in the west countrye.*	

40	S*ir* Bredbeddle, for sooth, he hett;*	*indeed; was called*
	He was a man of Mickele might	
	& Lo*r*d of great bewtye.	
	He had a lady to [h]is wiffe;	
	He loved her deerlye as his liffe,	
45	Shee was both blyth & blee.*	
	Because S*ir* Gawaine was stiffe in stowre,	*resolute in battle*
	Shee loved him privilye paramour,	*was secretly in love with him*
	& shee nev*er* him see.	*without having seen him*
	Itt was Agostes *tha*t was her mother;*	
50	Itt was witchcraft & noe other	
	*Tha*t shee dealt withall.	*practised*
	Shee cold transpose k*nigh*ts & swaine	*labourers*
	Like as in battaile they were slaine,	
	Wounded both Lim & lightt.*	
55	Shee taught her sonne, the k*nigh*t, alsoe	
	In transposed likenesse he shold goe,	
	Both by fell & frythe.	*moor and woodland*
	Shee said, 'Thou shalt to Arthur's hall,	
	For there great adventures shall befall	
60	That ev*er* saw K*ing* or K*nigh*t.'*	*p. 204/f. 102r*
	All was for her daughter's sake*	
	*Tha*t [the witch] soe sadlye spake	*determinedly*
	To her sonne-in-law, the K*nigh*t,	
	Because S*ir* Gawaine was bold & hardye	
65	& therto full of curtesye,	
	To bring him into her sight.	
	The knight said, 'Soe mote I thee,	*upon my life*
	To Arthur's court will I mee hye,	*hasten*
	For to praise thee right,	*respect your wishes*
70	& to prove Gawaine's points 3,*	*test; qualities*
	& *tha*t be true *tha*t men tell me,	*If*
	By Mary, Most of Might.'	
	Earlye, soone as itt was day,	
	The K*nigh*t dressed him full gay,	
75	Umstrode a full good steede;	*sat astride*
	Helme & hawberke both he hent,	*coat of mail; took*
	A long fauchion, verament,	*curved sword*
	To fend them in his neede.	*defend*

The Grene Knyght 229

	*Tha*t was a Jolly sight to seene,	*see*
80	When horsse & armour was all greene*	
	& weapon *tha*t hee bare.	
	When *tha*t burne was harnisht still,	*man; armed completely*
	His countenance he became right well,	*suited*
	I dare itt safelye sweare.	
85	*Tha*t time att Carleile lay our K*ing*;*	
	Att a Castle of Flatting was his dwelling,	*his, i.e. the Green Knight*
	In the Forrest of Delamore.	*Delamere*
	Forsooth, he rode, the sooth to say;	*truth*
	To Carleile he came on Christmas Day,	
90	Into *tha*t fayre countrye.	
	When he into *tha*t place came,*	
	The porter thought him a Marvelous groome.	*man*
	He saith, 'S*ir*, wither wold yee?'	*where do you want to go?*
	Hee said, 'I am a venterous K*nigh*t,	
95	& of yo*u*r K*ing* wold have sight	
	& other Lo*rd*s *tha*t heere bee.'	
	Noe word to him the porter spake,	
	But left him standing att the gate	
	& went forth, as I weene,	*believe*
100	& kneeled downe before the K*ing*,	
	Saith, 'In life's dayes, old or younge,	
	Such a sight I have not seene,	
	'For yonder att yo*u*r gates right,'	
	He saith, 'hee is a venterous K*night*;	
105	All his vesture is greene!'	
	Then spake the K*ing*, proudest in [p]all,	*most splendidly clothed*
	Saith, 'Bring him into the hall –	
	Let us see what hee doth meane.'	*intend*
	When the Greene K*nigh*t came before the K*ing*,*	
110	He stood in his stirrops strechinge,	
	& spoke with voice cleere,	
	& saith, 'K*ing* Arthur, God save thee,	
	As thou sittest in thy p*r*osperitye,	
	& Maintaine thine honor.	
115	'Why thou wold me nothing but right,	*because; would wish*
	I am come hither, a venterous [Knight],	
	& kayred thorrow countrye farr,	*have ridden*
	To prove poynts in thy pallace	

	*Tha*t longeth to manhood in ev*er*ye case	*pertain*
120	Among thy Lo*rd*s deere.'	
	The K*ing* he [sate] full still	
	Till he had said all his will.	
	Certein thus can he say,	*he said*
	'As I am *t*rue k*nigh*t and K*ing*,	
125	Thou shalt have thy askinge:	
	I will not say th[ee] nay,	
	'Whether thou wilt on foote fighting	*want to fight on foot*
	Or on steed-backe justing,	
	For love of Ladyes gay.	
130	If & thine armor be not fine,*	*suitable*
	I will give thee p*ar*t of mine.'	
	'Godamercy, Lo*rd*!' can he say.	*God reward you*
	'Here I make a challenging	
	Among the Lords both old & younge	
135	*Tha*t worthy beene in weede,	*are; clothing*
	W*hich* of them will take in hand,	*to see which; accept it*
	Hee *that* is both stiffe & stronge	
	& full good att need –	
	'I shall lay my head downe:	p. 205/f. 102v
140	Strike itt of, if he can,	*let him strike it off*
	W*i*th a stroke to garr itt bleed,	*make*
	For this day 12 monthe another at his.*	
	Let me see who will answer this –	
	A knight *tha*t is doughtye of deed;	*brave*
145	'For this day 12 month, the sooth to say,	
	Let him come to me & feicth his praye,	*receive his due*
	Redlye or ev*er* hee blin.	*promptly and without delay*
	Whither to come I shall him tell,	
	The readie way to the Greene Chappell;	*shortest*
150	*Tha*t place I will be in.'	
	The K*ing* att ease sate full still,	
	& all his lords said but litle	
	Till he had said all his will.	
	Upp stood S*i*r Kay, *that* crabbed k*nigh*t,*	*ill-tempered*
155	Spake mightye words *tha*t were of height,	*haughty*
	*Tha*t were both Loud & shrill:	

The Grene Knyght

     'I shall strike his necke in tooe,
     The head away the body froe!'
        The[y] bade him all be still,
160   Saith, 'Kay, of thy dints make noe rouse!*   *blows; boast*
     Thou wottest full litle what thou does –   *know*
        Noe good, but Mickle ill.'

     Eche man wold this deed have done.
     Up start Sir Gawaine soone,   *at once*
165   Upon his knees can kneele.   *knelt*
     He said, '*Tha*t were great villanye   *would be; baseness*
     W*i*thout you put this deede to me,   *if you did not grant*
        My leege, as I have sayd –

     'Remember, I am yo*u*r sister's sonne.'*
170   The K*i*ng said, 'I grant thy boone.   *request*
        But mirth is best att meele!
     Cheere thy guest & give him wine,
     & after dinner to itt fine   *carry it through*
        & sett the buffett well!'

175   Now the Greene K*nigh*t is set att meate,
     See[m]lye served in his seate*
        Beside the Round Table.
     To talke of his welfare, nothing he needs;
     Like a K*nigh*t himselfe he feeds
180   W*i*th long time reasnable.   *for*

     When the dinner it was done,
     The K*i*ng said to S*i*r Gawaine soone,
        W*i*thouten any fable,   *lie*
     He said, '[A]n you will doe this deede,   *if*
185   I pray Jesus be yo*u*r speede;   *grant you success*
        This k*nigh*t is nothing unstable.'   *wavering*

     The Greene K*nigh*t his head downe layd.
     S*i*r Gawaine to the axe he braid,*   *reached out*
        To strike w*i*th eger will.
190   He stroke the necke bone in twaine;
     The blood burst out in eve*r*ye vaine;
        The head from the body fell.

     The Greene K*nigh*t his head up hent;   *took up*
     Into his saddle wightilye he sprent,   *vigorously; leapt*
195   Spake words both Lowd & shrill,
     Saith, 'Gawaine, thinke on thy covenant!   *promise*

This day 12 monthes see thou ne want   *do not fail*
    To come to the Greene Chappell!'

All had great marvell *tha*t the[y] see   *saw*
200 *Tha*t he spake soe merrilye
    & bare his head in his hand.
Forth att the hall dore he rode right,
& *tha*t saw both K*ing* and knight
    And lords *tha*t were in land.

205 W*i*thout the hall dore, the sooth to saine,   *tell*
Hee sett his head upon againe,
    Saies, 'Arthur, have heere my hand!*
Whensoev*er* the K*nig*ht cometh to mee,
A better buffett, sickerlye,   *certainly*
210   I dare him well warr[an]d.'   *guarantee*

The Greene K*nig*ht away went.
All this was done by enchantment   p. 206/f. 103r
    *Tha*t the old witch had wrought.
Sore sicke fell Arthur the K*ing*,
215 & for him made great mourning
    That into such bale was brought.   *dire straits*

The Q*ueen*e shee weeped for his sake.
Sorry was S*i*r Lancelott Dulake,*
    & other were dreery in thought,   *others; sad*
220 Because he was brought into great p*er*ill.
His mightye manhood will not availe*
    *Tha*t before hath freshlye fought.   *boldly*

Sir Gawaine comfort King and Q*ueen*e   *comforted*
& all the doughtye there bedeene;   *together*
225   He bade the[y] shold be still,
Said, 'Of my deede I was nev*er* feard,*   *death*
Nor yett I am nothing adread,
    I swere by S*aint* Michaell;

'For when draweth toward my day,   *it draws*
230 I will dresse me in mine array,   *equip*
    My p*ro*mise to fulfill.
S*i*r,' he saith, 'as I have blis,*
I wott not where the Greene Chappell is;   *know*
    Therfore seeke itt I will.'

235	The royall Cou[r]tt, verament,	
	All rought Sir Gawaine's intent;*	*supported*
	They thought itt was the best.	
	They went forth into the feild,	
	Knights that ware both speare & sheeld;	*wore*
240	The[y] priced forth full prest.	*galloped; swiftly*
	Some chuse them to Justinge,	*set themselves*
	Some to dance, Revell, & sing;	
	Of mirth the[y] wold not rest.	*from*
	All they swo[re] togeth[er] in fere	*as a group*
245	That, and Sir Gawaine overcome were,	*if*
	The[y] wold bren all the West.	*burn*
	Now leave wee the King in his pallace.	
	The Greene Knight come home is	
	To his owne Castle.	
250	This folke frend, when he came home,*	*asked*
	What doughtye deeds he had done;	
	Nothing he wold them tell.	
	Full well hee wist in certaine	*knew*
	That his wiffe loved Sir Gawaine,	
255	That comelye was under kell.	*in her head-covering*
	Listen, Lords, & yee will sitt,	*if*
	& yee shall heere the second fitt,	
	What adventures Sir Gawaine befell!	

2ᵈ parte

	The day is come that Gawaine must gone.*	*leave*
260	Knights & Ladyes waxed wann	*pale*
	That were without in that place.	
	The King himselfe siked ill,	*sighed*
	Ther Queene a swounding almost fell,	*in a faint*
	To that Jorney when he shold passe.	
265	When he was in armour bright,	
	He was one of the goodlyest Knights	
	That ever in Brittaine was borne.	
	They brought Sir Gawaine a steed,*	
	Was dapple-gray & good att need,	
270	I tell withouten scorne.	*jest*
	His bridle was with stones sett,	
	With gold & pearle overfrett	*ornamented all over*
	& stones of great vertue.*	*power*

He was of a furley kind;   *marvellous nature*
275 His stirropps were of silke of Ynd,   *India*
    I tell you this tale for true.

When he rode ov*er* the Mold,   *ground*
His geere glistered as gold   *shone*
    By the way as he rode.
280 Many furleys he there did see;   *marvels*
Fowles by the water did flee
    By brimes & bankes soe broad.   *rivers*

Many furleys there saw hee
Of wolves & wild beasts, sikerlye;*
285   On hunting hee tooke most heede.
Forth he rode, the sooth to tell,
For to seeke the Greene Chappell;
    He wist not wehere, indeed.

As he rode in an eve[n]ing late,   p. 207/f. 103v
290 Riding downe a greene gate,   *path*
    A faire castell saw hee,
*Tha*t seemed a place of Mickle prid[e].   *splendour*
Thitherward S*ir* Gawaine can ryde   *rode*
    To gett some harborrowe.   *lodgings*

295 Thither he came in the twylight.
He was ware of a gentle K*night* –   *noble*
    The L*or*d of the place was hee.
Meekly to h*im* S*ir* Gawaine can speake,   *spoke*
& asked him, 'For K*ing* Arthur's sake,
300   Of harborrowe I pray thee.

'I am a far Labordd Knight;   *travelled*
I pray you lodge me all this night.'
    He sayd him not nay.
Hee tooke him by the arme & led him to the hall;
305 A poore child can hee call,   *lowly servant, stable-hand*
    Saith, 'Dight well this palfrey.'   *look after; saddle-horse*

Into a chamber the[y] went a full great speed.
There the[y] found all things readye att need,
    I dare safelye swere:
310 Fier in chambers burning bright,
Candles in chandlers burning light;
    To supp*er* the[y] went full yare.   *promptly*

The Grene Knyght

      He sent after his Ladye bright
      To come to supp with that gentle Knight,
315   & shee came blythe withall.   *happy to be there*
      Forth shee came then anon,   *at once*
      Her Maids following her eche one   *each one*
        In robes of rich pall.   *cloth*

      As shee sate att her sup[per],
320   Evermore the Ladye clere   *beautiful*
        Sir Gawaine shee looked upon.
      When the supper it was done,
        Shee tooke her Maids, & to her chamber gone.   *went*

      He cheered the Knight and gave him wine,
325   & said, 'Welcome, by Saint Martine!*
        I pray you take itt for none ill:
      One thing, Sir, I wold you pray;
      What you make soe farr this way?   *you are doing*
        The truth you wold me tell.

330   'I am a Knight & soe are yee;
      Your concell, an you will tell mee,   *secret; if*
        Forsooth, keepe itt I will;
      For, if itt be poynt of any dread,   *matter*
      Perchance I may helpe att need,
335   Either lowd or still.'*

      (For his words that were soe smooth,*
      Had Sir Gawaine wist the soothe,   *known*
        All he wold not have told;
      For that was the Greene Knight*
340   That hee was lodged with that night,
        & harbarrowes in his hold.)   *castle*

      He saith, 'As to the Greene Chappell,
      Thitherward, I can you tell,
        Itt is but furlongs 3.
345   The Master of it is a venterous Knight
      & workes by witchcraft day & night,
        With many a great furley.

      'If he worke with never soe much frauce,*
      He is curteous as he sees cause,
350   I tell you, sikerlye.
      You shall abyde & take your rest,
      & I will into yonder forrest   *will go*
        Under the greenwood tree.'

	They plight their truthes to [be leele],	gave their promises; true
355	Either with other for to deale,*	involved
	Whether it were silver or gold.	
	He said, 'We 2 [beholden] wilbe,	agreed
	Whatsoever God sends you & mee	
	To be parted on the Mold.'*	shared when we meet
360	The Greene Knight went on hunting.	
	Sir Gawaine in the castle beinge	
	Lay sleeping in his bed.	
	Up rose the old witche with hast throwe,	p. 208/f. 104r eager
	& to her dauhter can shee goe,	she went
365	& said, 'Be not adread!'	
	To her daughter can shee say,	she said
	'The man that thou hast wisht many a day,	
	Of him thou maist be sped;	successful
	For Sir Gawaine, that curteous Knight,	
370	Is lodged in this hall all night.'	
	Shee brought her to his bedd.	
	Shee saith, 'Gentle Knight, awake,	
	& for this faire Ladie's sake,	
	That hath loved thee soe deere,	
375	Take her bold[l]y in thine armes;	
	There is no[e] man shall doe thee harme.'	who will
	Now beene they both heere.	
	The ladye kissed him times 3,	
	Saith, 'Without I have the love of thee,	unless
380	My life standeth in dere.'	peril
	Sir Gawaine blushed on the Lady Bright,	looked at
	Saith, 'Your husband is a gentle Knight,	
	By Him that bought mee deare.	
	'To me itt were great shame	
385	If I shold [d]oe him any grame	harm
	That hath beene kind to mee;	
	For I have su[ch] a deede to doe	
	That I can neyther rest nor roe	relax
	Att an end till itt bee.'	
390	Then spake that Ladye gay,	
	Saith, 'Tell me some of your Journey;	
	Your succour I may bee.	I may be able to help
	If itt be poynt of any warr,	

The Grene Knyght

There shall noe man doe you noe darr,   *harm*
395   & [yee] wilbe governed by mee;

'For heere I have a lace of silke;
It is as white as any milke*
   & of a great value.'
Shee saith, 'I dare safelye sweare,
400   There shall noe man doe you deere   *harm*
   When you have it upon you.'

Sir Gawaine spake mildlye in the place;
He thanked the Lady & tooke the lace,
   & promised her to come againe.*
405   The Knight in the forrest slew many a hind;
Other venison he cold none find
   But wild bores on the plaine,

Plentye of does & wild swine,
Foxes & other ravine,   *beasts of prey*
410   As I hard true men tell.   *heard*
Sir Gawaine swore sickerlye,   *confidently*
'Home to your owne welcome you bee,
   By Him that harrowes Hell!'

The Greene Knight his venison downe Layd.
415   Then to Sir Gawaine thus hee said,
   'Tell me anon in heght   *out loud*
What noveltyes that you have won,   *new things*
For heer's plenty of venison.'
   Sir Gawaine said full right,

420   Sir Gawaine sware 'By Saint Leonard!
Such as God sends, you shall have part!'
   In his armes he hent the Knight,
& there he kissed him times 3,
Saith, 'Heere is such as God sends mee,
425   By Mary, most of Might.'

Ever privilye he held the Lace;*   *hidden*
That was all the villanye that ever was
   Prooved by Sir Gawaine the gay.   *concerning*
Then to bed soone the[y] went
430   & sleeped there, verament,
   Till morrow itt was day.

Then *Si*r Gawaine, soe curteous & free,
His leave soone taketh hee
 Att the Lady soe gaye.
435 Hee thanked her & tooke the lace,*   *of*
                     p. 209/f. 104v
& rode towards the Chappell apace;   *quickly*
 He knew noe whitt the way.*   *not at all*

Ev*er*more in his thought he had
Whether he shold worke as the Ladye bade,*
440 *Tha*t was soe curteous and sheene.   *beautiful*
The Greene K*nigh*t rode another way;
He transposed him in another array,
 Before as it was greene.

As *Si*r Gawaine rode ov*er* the plaine,
445 He hard one high upon a Mountaine
 A horne blowne full lowde.*

He looked after the Greene Chappell;*   *for*
He saw itt stand under a hi[l]l,
 Covered with euyes about.   *yew trees*
450 He looked after the Greene K*nigh*t;
He hard him wehett a fauchion bright,*   *sharpen*
 *Tha*t the hills rang about.

The K*nigh*t spake w*i*th strong cheere,   *fierce expression*
Said, 'Yee be welcome, S[ir] Gawaine, heere;
455 It behooveth thee to Lowte.'   *bend down*
He stroke & litle perced the skin,*
Unneth the flesh w*i*thin;
 Then *Si*r Gawaine had noe doubt.   *fear*

He saith, 'Thou shontest! Why dost thou soe?'* *flinch*
460 Then *Si*r Gawaine in hart waxed throe,   *heart; angry*
 Upon his feete can stand,   *stood*
& soone he drew out his sword,
& saith, 'Traitor, if thou speake a word,
 Thy liffe is in my hand!
465 I had but one stroke att thee,
& thou hast had another att mee;
 Noe falshood in me thou found.'*

The K*nigh*t said, withouten laine,   *concealing anything*
'I wend I had *Si*r Gawaine slaine,*   *thought*
470 The gentlest K*nigh*t in this land.
Men told me of great renowne,
Of curtesie, thou might have woon the crowne
 Above both free & bound,   *bondmen*

The Grene Knyght

	'& alsoe of great gentrye;	*nobility*
475	& now 3 points be put fro thee,	
	It is the Moe pittye.	*more*
	Sir Gawaine, thou wast not Leele	
	When thou didst the lace conceale	
	That my wiffe gave to thee.	
480	'Ffor wee were [beholden] , thou wist full well,*	
	For thou hadst the halfe dale	*half share*
	Of my venerye.	*spoils from hunting*
	If the lace had never beene wrought,	
	To have slaine thee was never my thought,	*struck*
485	I swere by God, verelye.	*truly*
	'I wist it well my wiffe loved thee.	
	Thou wold doe me noe villanye,*	
	But nicked her with nay.	*denied her request*
	But wilt thou doe as I bidd thee,	*if you are willing to*
490	Take me to Arthur's court with thee;	
	Then were all to my pay.'	*liking*
	Now are the Knights accorded thore.	*there*
	To the castle of Hutton can the[y] fare,*	*they went*
	To lodge there all that night	
495	Earlye on the other day	*next*
	To Arthur's court the[y] tooke the way,	
	With harts blyth & light.	
	All the Court was full faine	
	Alive when they saw Sir Gawaine;	
500	They thanked God abone.	*on high*
	That is the matter & the case*	*reason; cause*
	Why Knights of the Bathe weare the lace	
	Untill they have wonen their shoen,*	*proven themselves*
	Or else a ladye of hye estate	*position*
505	From about his necke shall it take,	
	For the doughtye deeds that hee hath done.	
	It was confirmed by Arthur the K[ing]	
	Thorrow Sir Gawaine's desiringe;	*through*
	The King granted him his boone.	
510	Thus endeth the tale of the Greene Knight.	p. 210/f. 105r
	God, that is soe full of might,	
	To heaven their soules bring	
	That have hard this litle storye,	

	*Tha*t fell sometimes in the west countrye
515	In Arthur's days our King. ffins

Explanatory Notes

4	*one was*: 'were united'; 'was' is probably singular, with a compound subject functioning as a singular entity, or possibly the northern plural form used when not immediately preceded or followed by a personal pronoun subject.
10–11	'Knights, according to their rank, strove to be the best'.
18	*body & bone*: 'in all respects'. Similar doublets expressing the notion of a whole spectrum occur also at 54, 101, 134, 137, 335, 346, and 473.
37–38	A formal *transitio* establishes an explicit parallel between Arthur's court and the castle of the Green Knight; see also lines 247–49. The Knight's world impinges on Arthur's world and threatens its well-being for a time, but any hovering threat is resolved in the end when he seeks membership of Arthur's society, where he will be subordinate to Arthur and a peer of Gawaine.
39	*west countrye*: while in modern times the 'West Country' refers to south-west England, both Delamere and Carlisle are to be found in the north-west of the country, albeit a long ride apart. Lines 244–46 imply that Arthur's court knows that the stranger must have come from 'the West', and the tale concludes with the reminder that the tale was set in the 'west countrye'. It seems likely therefore that the reference to the west country reflects not so much a topographical location as a generalized reference to a wild and dangerous location.
40	Bredbeddle also features in *KAKC*.
45	'She was both cheerful and lovely looking'.
49	*Agostes*: the name does not appear in other Arthurian literature. In *SGGK*, the sorceress is Morgne la Faye.
54	'Wounded in all parts of the body' (*MED lith*, a joint of the body, hence 'bothe in lith and lim', i.e., in all parts of the body, entirely, n,1(f)).
60	'Greater than has ever been seen by king or knight'.
61–66	These lines express the real motive underlying the witch's words at 58–60. At this point Bredbeddle seems to accept what the witch tells him, but it is revealed later that he has known her underlying purpose all along and not regarded it as a serious threat to his own personal happiness (253–55, 486–88). Gawaine's reputation for both prowess (46, 64) and courtesy (65, 369) is the common factor in the two otherwise separate reasons he is sought out: the witch helps her love-struck daughter meet with the man who is possessed of these qualities, and Bredbeddle is content to go along with the scheme because it gives him the opportunity to test Gawaine's reputation (70–72, 471–76).
70	*Gawaine's points 3*: Gawaine's outstanding qualities: prowess, courtesy, and nobility (cf. lines 471–76).
80–81	The fact that the horse is green is a clear indication of magic, but the man himself is not explicitly described as of the same colour: when he appears at Arthur's court and creates a stir, it is said only that his clothes are green (105).
85–90	The subject of these lines is unclear since they could refer to both Arthur and Bredbeddle. The most likely reading is that while Arthur holds the Christmas court at Carlisle in Cumberland, Bredbeddle's usual residence is some distance to the south, in a castle at Flatting in the forest of Delamere, which is in Cheshire. Logic indicates that 'his' (86) and 'he' (88, 89) refer to the Green Knight. Flatting is not clearly identifiable as the specific name or location of his castle. St Clair-Kendall, however, plausibly suggests that Flatting is a scribal error for the Hutton of 493, to which Gawaine and Bredbeddle repair after their encounter at the Chapel, the initial 'F' having been transferred in oral transmission from the end of the preceding word ('of') before a lightly pronounced 'h' at the beginning

	of 'Hatton', pronounced something like 'att'n' (St. Clair-Kendall, 2007, 298—99). See also note to line 493, below).
91–108	The porter is a conventional figure in medieval romance; his presence here makes the Green Knight's arrival at the court somewhat less extraordinary than his unannounced arrival in *SGGK* (132–37). See also *KAKC* (40–77) and *CARLE* (135–172). However, his behaviour is certainly less courteous than one might have expected towards a new arrival.
109–10	It is part of the drama that the Green Knight, like his confident counterpart in *SGGK*, should not have dismounted before coming into the hall.
130–31	The Green Knight has arrived with a helmet, coat of mail, and sword (76–78), but no lance for jousting. Arthur is thus being polite, but also making a practical offer.
142	The Green Knight makes clear that whoever beheads him will need to face a similar stroke in 12 months' time. *12 monthe*: the noun may have the singular form after the numeral or preserve the Old English (unchanged) plural; similarly '12 month' (145), but cf. '12 monthes' (197).
154–62	Kay's traditional role as the 'crabbed' opposite of the 'courteous' Gawaine in English romances is repeated here, but note that in this text he is not merely rebuked by Gawaine but shouted down by the whole court.
160	*Saith*: apparently the southern plural form, but see line 459, where 'saith' clearly applies to the Green Knight alone.
169	In Geoffrey of Monmouth's *HRB*, Gawaine is the son of Arthur's half-sister Anna and King Lot. The tradition that he is Arthur's nephew persists in Arthurian literature, although his mother's name changes, if it is given at all, usually to Morgause. It is not always stated, possibly because the author concerned takes it for granted that everybody knows this fact. In *SGGK*, 356–57 Gawaine also draws attention to his relationship with Arthur as a means of persuading his king to give him the quest,
176–77	The Green Knight sits at a table adjacent to the Round Table itself.
188	*the axe*: this is the only mention of an axe, presumably featured in the poet's source as it is in *SGGK*. At line 77 he is armed with a falchion.
207	*have heere my hand*: presumably a figurative expression, since the king is some distance away inside the hall and the Green Knight is now beyond the doorway.
218	*Dulake*: written thus in the manuscript. That the expression is here regarded as a one-word surname by the compiler-scribe is supported by its appearance elsewhere in the manuscript, e.g., in the tautologous title of 'Sir Lancelott of Dulake' and in line 76 of the ballad 'The Fall of Princes' (HF, III, 172).
221–22	The shift to the future tense may indicate either that these lines are the direct address of the narrator to the audience or that they are the free indirect thought of the court.
226–31	Cf. Gawaine's similar declaration in *TG*, 42–47.
232	*as I have blis*: literally, 'so may I gain the joy (of heaven)'.
236	*rought*: HF suggested 'reach, took in' and glossed as 'approved', while Hahn has 'understood'. The sense is surely from *MED recchen*, to care or be concerned (whether sth. happens) … v,3: the Court, while concerned for Gawaine's safety, nevertheless approves of and supports his decision. It is the right thing to do.
250–52	The implication is that no one in the castle other than Agostes has reason to think he has been engaged in other than normal chivalric activities.
259–64	The scribe has bracketed these lines and labelled them '2^{d} Parte'.
268–75	As well as this scene being reminiscent of Gawaine's arming in *SGGK*, there is a very similar description of the Queen's horse and gear in *Thomas of Erceldoune* (40ff.). See Ingeborg Nixon (ed.), *Thomas of Erceldoune, Parts 1–2* (Copenhagen: Publications of the Department of English, University of Copenhagen, 1980–83).
273	Precious stones were believed to have particular powers or 'virtues' associated with their physical qualities: see, for example, Joan Evans and Mary S. Serjeantson (eds), *English Medieval Lapidaries*, EETS OS 190 (London: Oxford University Press, 1933).
284	This line echoes Gawaine's experiences in *SGGK*, where he fights wolves and woodwoses (720–23).

325	*Saint Martine*: probably Martin, the fourth-century Bishop of Tours and founder of monasticism in Gaul. Accounts of his early life depict him particularly as a military saint and an example of knightly generosity. See David Hugh Farmer, *The Oxford Dictionary of Saints* (Oxford: Oxford University Press, 2011).
335	'Whatever the circumstances'.
336–38	The elliptical effect of these lines arises from the blending of two ideas: (i) 'because he spoke so smoothly, Sir Gawaine revealed everything', and (ii) 'if Sir Gawaine had known the truth, he would not have revealed everything'. It is not clear why Gawaine would have kept silent had he known his host's identity: he is not travelling in disguise, and he is intending to keep his appointment.
339	*the Greene Knight*: this identifying term is used of the host in the narrator's voice also at lines 360, 414, and 441, before he again assumes a green appearance (442–43).
348	*frauce*: probably meaning 'noise'. P suggests a connection with *frais*, 'to make a noise, crash'. *OED* records the obsolete verb *frais*, to creak, make a grating noise (Scottish, early sixteenth century). *A Dictionary of the Older Scottish Tongue* cites an example dating from *c*.1661, where the definition is 'to exaggerate; to make an outcry or fuss about': *Dictionaries of the Scots Language*, https://dsl.ac.uk (accessed July 2023). The earliest known use of the corresponding noun *fraise*, a 'fuss', commotion (*OED*, n,3) is by the Scottish poet Allan Ramsay, author of *The Tea-Table Miscellany*, in his 1725 play *Gentle Shepherd*, although *OED* also records 'Frace-maker' from 1683.
355	'In dealing with each other'.
359	*on the Mold*: literally 'on the ground', a conventional tag.
397	That the lace is white foreshadows its adoption by the Knights of the Bath (501–6); it is not green, as in *SGGK*, and is therefore less pointedly connected with the Green Knight and the conspiracy in which he takes part.
404	Gawaine promises to return from his perilous appointment, leaving tantalizingly ambiguous the state of his feelings for the lady.
426–28	Gawaine has agreed to share his winnings with his host (354–59), and he refers to the three kisses he has given him as his share (422–44). It is thus difficult to perceive any 'villanye' in his actions with regard to this agreement. Subsequently, however, the Knight says explicitly that Gawaine has done wrong to conceal the lace (477–79) and implies that in so doing he did not keep his side of the agreement (480–82). In *SGGK*, Gawaine is clearly at fault by withholding the girdle because the agreement has been to exchange winnings (1105–11).
435	Gawaine has already taken the lace from the lady (403); here, presumably, he takes the lace from where he has kept it overnight.
437	Gawaine has been given only a general idea of where the Chapel lies (342–44).
439	Gawaine debates whether or not to use the lace as protection against the Green Knight. There may also be sexual innuendo here.
446	Madden suggested that three lines are missing after line 446. The sense does not fail, however, either before or after lines 444–46: the sudden blast of the horn is the more dramatic for coming at the end of a stanza, and Gawaine's responsive peering for its source is the logical beginning of the next stanza. The assonance of the tail rhyme 'lowde' with the tail rhymes of each of the next two stanzas might suggest a 9-line stanza 444–52 followed by a normal 6-line stanza with the same tail rhyme, but this is not necessary.
447–49	The Chapel appears green to the approaching rider because it is set into the foot of a hill and largely covered from view by surrounding yew trees, though visible as it rises from amongst them. Yews are familiar in churchyards and would be appropriately ominous in this narrative, symbolic both of sadness, being associated with bows and death, and of immortality, being evergreen and very long-lived, here perhaps suggestive of the death that must occur ahead of eternal life. See 'Yew', in Camilla Lockwood (ed.), *Brewer's Dictionary of Phrase and Fable*, 18th ed. (Edinburgh: Chambers Harran, 2009), p.1451.
451	*a fauchion*: the kind of weapon the Green Knight brought to Arthur's court (77). In the absence of any mention of an axe here (in contrast to *SGGK*, 2223), it may be implied that he uses this sword to strike Gawaine; cf. note to line 188, above.
456–57	'He struck, and slightly cut the skin, but scarcely pierced the flesh beneath'.

459–67	*thou shontest*: as in *SGGK*, the Green Knight accuses Gawaine of flinching from the blow. In return, Gawaine accuses him of being a traitor, because he believes he will strike again, although the Green Knight has said nothing about a further blow. See *SGGK*, 2265–87 and Gillian Rogers, 'The Grene Knight', in Derek Brewer and Jonathan Gibson (eds), *A Companion to the Gawain-Poet*, Arthurian Studies 38 (Cambridge: D. S. Brewer, 1997), p. 368.
467	*Noe falshood*: Gawaine can honestly say this, since the bargain was to share the winnings, not to exchange them, and he might reasonably have thought that his share was the three kisses he gave his host from his wife. Madden suggested that three lines are missing after this line. The sense does not fail, however: Gawaine has protested his innocence, but the Knight proceeds without further ado to counter Gawaine's argument by saying that, although he had thought he was dealing with the noblest of men, Gawaine has actually failed at three points.
469–79	The grounds for Gawaine's good reputation are his prowess ('renowne', 471, connotes success in fighting), courtesy (472), and nobility (470, 474). He is now said to have failed in all three areas through the single wrong action of concealing the lace. See note to lines 426–28, above.
480	'As you know full well, we had a bargain'.
487–88	Gawaine has avoided the 'villanye' of allowing himself to be seduced by his host's lady, while yet committing 'villanye' in respect of his agreement with his host.
493	*the castle of Hutton*: evidently the home of the Green Knight, almost certainly identifiable with the castle of Flatting in the Forest of Delamere (see note to lines 85–90, above), just three furlongs from the chapel (344). Hutton has been variously identified by Hahn (354), probably with Hatton in Cheshire, seven miles north of Delamere Forest and a Stanley stronghold; less probably, by Madden, with Hutton in Inglewood Forest in Cumbria, north of Carlisle, with which Gawaine is associated in other romances; and by Anne Wilson (*Traditional Romance and Tale: How Stories Mean* (Ipswich: Brewer, 1976), pp. 308–16) as Hooten in the Cheshire Wirral, another Stanley stronghold (Edward Wilson, 'Sir Gawain and the Green Knight and the Stanley Family of Stanley, Storeton, and Hooton', *Review of English Studies* 30 (1979), pp. 314–15). HF's (II, 76) suggested Hutton Manor House in Somerset seems too far away.
501–9	This derivation of the Order of the Bath from Arthurian times is not found elsewhere. It lends a retrospective importance to the poem as a supposedly historical document; it may also suggest an interest on the poet's part in a particular Knight of the Bath, perhaps someone whose patronage he sought. The Order was said to have been founded by Henry IV at his coronation in 1399, and the present Order is supposedly a revival of the earlier one. In both cases, Knights wore a lace or knot of white silk on the left shoulder. In the earlier case, the lace was to be worn until removed by the prince or a noble lady after the Knight had performed a significant act of chivalry. See the Somerset Herald's account in HF, II, 57; see also Charles Boutell, *Boutell's Heraldry*, rev. J. P. Brooke-Little (London: Frederick Warne, 1978), p. 196.
503	*wonen their shoen*: literally, 'won their shoes'; cf. 'won their spurs'.

Textual Notes

Although Percy did not reproduce this poem in the *Reliques*, he does pay close attention to it within the manuscript. Among his useful contributions is the gloss on '*gate*' ('path', 290) as 'way', from Icelandic *gata*; among his mistakes is the gloss on '*mell*' ('speak', 37) as 'meddle', from French *mêler*. His addition of 'in 2 Parts.' after the title, to which he must have returned after finding '2nd Parte' as a heading halfway through the text, indicates an attentive reading of the text. He also added the following two introductory notes: in the LH margin, against the title: 'A curious Adventure of Sir Gawaine. explaining a Custome used by the Knights of the Bath'; in the RH margin, just below the title: 'NB. See a Fragment. p. 29 wherein is mention of a Green Knight & decapitation p. 29. 31' (P originally put 32 and changed it to the correct page number, 31, and is a reference to *KAKC*).

1	*Wen*: 'when' [P].
6	*not to layne*: 'without layne, i.e. without lying. – or with*out*. altering the line (<u>only dele</u>[te] <u>it is</u>) it is, "Not to conceal the truth."' [P].
7	*drive allyance*: '[d]rave aliens' [P]; the *d* has been cropped.
9	*men*: 'man' [P]. P's suggestion fits the context better. The line is more likely to refer to Arthur (8) than to 'knights' (10).
10	*strove*: stronge [MS]; 'Kni*gh*ts. strove of (about) &c' [P]. P's suggested 'strove' makes more sense. It is possible that the PF scribe, or a predecessor, mistook the letter *u/v* for *n* when copying, and unconsciously wrote 'stronge' at this point.
15	*as one*: 'at one' [P].
22	[*on*]: & [MS].
28	*the*[*y*]: the [MS] (see also lines 159, 199, 225, 240, 246, 307, 308, 312, 429, 493, 496); *pight*: 'pitched, or put.' [P].
31	[*&*] *went*: went [MS]; 'and went' [P].
37	*mell*: 'mell, meddle. fr. mêler. Urry' [P].
38	*I will you tell*: 'I tell' [P]. P put light square brackets round 'will you', and glossed 'I tell', presumably because he thought it scanned better – or possibly that it was more poetic.
40	*hett*: 'hight, was called' [P].
43	[*h*]*is*: wis [MS].
45	*blyth & blee*: 'so bright of blee. <u>blee</u> is, colour, Complexion. bleo S. Color Urry' [P]. P's 'bright of blee' (i.e., fair of face) is plausible. It could be, however, that the original intention was that she was both 'blyth' (i.e., cheerful) and of a [fair] 'blee' (i.e., complexion).
47	*paramour*: 'I wo*u*ld. read par amour' [P].
48	*&*: 'and yet' [P].
49–51	Three lines may be missing from this three-line stanza, either before 49 or after 51.
54	*Wounded*: 'and wound' [P]; *lightt*: 'lythe, a joint, a limb, a nerve – . Sax. lið, artus. Urry.' [P].
56	*he shold goe*: 'to go' [P].
58	Madden suggested that three lines might be absent from this 9-line stanza after 60 (i.e., that the 9-liner might originally have been two 6-liners), but there seems to be no break in the sense here.
62	[*the witch*]: they wh*i*ch [MS]. Madden ingeniously suggested 'That the witch soe sadly spake', and the description of the mother as a witch in line 213 supports such a reading.
68	*mee*: scribal π symbol after 'I', signifying an omission, with 'mee', added in LH margin.
73	*as*: interlined by scribe, with caret [MS].
75	*Umstrode*: 'and strode, i.e. bestrode' [P].
79	*that*: 'th*a*t, i.e. it' [P], a deletion by P is unreadable.
87	*Delamore*: 'Delamere' [P].
88	*Forsooth*: 'for soe hee' [P].
90	*fayre countrye*: 'countrye faire' [P]
91	*came*: 'come or was come' [P].
104	*hee is*: 'there is' [P].
106	[*p*]*all*: 'first or formost of all' [P]. Madden emended to 'proudest in pall', i.e., 'most splendid in fine clothing': see also line 318 and *LD*, 1955: 'Tho thou bee proude in pall'. *MED pal*, a fine cloth; a type of fine cloth, ?satin; fine clothing, n.
114	*honor*: 'honnere' [P].
116	[*Knight*]: '[Knight]' added by P at end of line.
117	*farr*: 'farre, or perhaps faire' [P].
121	[*sate*]: sayd [MS]; 'satt' [P]. *still*: 'quietly' [P], followed by an indecipherable word deleted.
123	*Certein thus can*: 'Certes then gan' [P].
126	*say th*[*ee*] *nay*: say thy nay [MS], preceded by 'see' deleted; 'say thee nay' [P].
127	*wilt*: 'wilt bee' [P].
128	*on steed-backe*: the *o* of '*on*' altered from an *i* [MS]; 'on steed-back, i.e. on horse-back' [P].
131	*mine*: 'mine' [P], perhaps having read *m* as a different letter: the first minim is unusually high [MS].

136	*hand*: 'hond' [P].
140	*can*: 'con' [P].
144	*A knight*: 'perhaps To a *Knigh*t.' [P].
146	*feicth*: the first letter is almost certainly an *f*, and the phrase may be understood with reference to *MED fecchen*, to go after, get, and return with (someone, something) to a person or place, v. However, HF read this word as *seicth*, presumably from the verb 'to seek'. For *praye*, *MED prei(e*, booty, spoil, plunder; an object obtained by pillage, a piece of stolen property; also *fig*, n,2. The line can probably best be glossed as 'receive his due': with somewhat black humour, Gawaine should come and receive the blow that will be his due reward.
147	*Redlye*: Rudley [MS]; 'redlye, i.e. readily. Vid. G. D.' [P]. *blin*: 'blin, linger, delay.' [P].
152	*litle*: 'littell' [P].
160	*Saith*: '[i.]e. they say;' [P]; *rouse*: 'praise, extolling. boast – Jun. perhaps roust, noise. G. Doug.' [P].
161	*what*: 'that' [P]; *does*: 'doest' [P].
176	*See[m]lye*: seenley [MS], with scribal omission mark π over the *n*.
178	*talke*: final letter added by P.
180	*reasnable*: 'resonable' [P].
184	*[A]n*: on [MS]; 'an' [P].
193	*hent*: 'took' [P].
194	*wightilye*: 'actively' [P].
206	*upon*: 'up on' [P].
210	*warr[an]d*: latter part of word indistinct, but could open with *h*; 'warrand' [P].
224	*bedeene*: 'immediately' [P].
226	*feard*: 'fraid' [P].
235	*royall Cou[r]tt*: 'royall Couett' [MS]; 'royall Courtt' [P].
239	*both*: letter *t* possibly written over a *d*.
240	*priced*: 'pricked' [P]; *prest*: 'ready' [P].
244	*swo[re] togeth[er]*: *re* and *er* obliterated by holes in MS.
250	*This folke frend*: 'His folke freyn'd, i.e. inquired' [P]; *frend*: 'foul fiend' crossed out, 'ask' [P].
256	*Lords*: 'Lordings' [P].
259	*2ᵈ parte*: text in LH margin, with curly bracket encompassing lines 259–64.
266	*one of the goodlyest Knights* [MS]: the failure of rhyme in the manuscript indicates a failure on the part of the scribe to recognize a common ME idiom in which the pronoun 'one' is used pleonastically with the superlative.
274	*furley*: 'ferlie. wonder, wonderful. Sax. ferlic repentinus, horrendus. Gl. ad G. D.' [P].
289	*eve[n]ing*: eveing [MS].
290	*gate*: 'Gate, way. Isl. Gata, via. Gl. ad G. D.' [P].
291	*saw hee*: 'hee saw. or saw he "there"' [P].
292	*prid[e]*: missing *e* [MS] supplied by P.
294	*harborrowe*: 'harburee or harbere Lodging. Urry' [P].
304	*by the arme*: enclosed in square brackets by P. (The line seems too long, but may be read with the expected four stresses.)
311	*chandlers*: 'candlestickes' [P].
312	*yare*: 'yare. acutus. ready eager, nimble.' [P].
318	*pall*: 'any rich or fine Cloth, but properly purple: taken from the Robe worn by Bishops.' [P].
319	*att her sup[per]*: the 'tt' and *h* partially lost, the *per* abbreviation lost, through holes in MS. Reading supplied by HF.
323	'Shee tooke her Maids, & to her chamber will gone' [MS]; 'will' struck through by scribe.
339	*For*: 'for all' [P].
341	*harbarrowes*: 'harberow'd lodged' [P].
347	*furley*: 'wonder' [P].
348	*frauce*: 'perhaps frais, to make a noise, crash G. ad G. D.' [P].
351	*You*: omitted by scribe and then inserted in margin.
354	*truthes*: 'trothes' [P]; *[be leele]*: 'beleeve' [MS]; 'be leil' [P], P signalling the gloss not with his usual caret, but with the symbol ‡. See note to line 477 below.

357	[*beholden*]: both [MS]. There is obviously a past participle missing here, and 'both' may be the scribe's rendering of a partially obscured form as an instinctive response immediately following '2', though grammatically redundant and unnecessarily emphasizing there were two parties to the agreement.
363	*with hast throwe*: 'tho, then' [P].
375	*bold*[*l*]*y*: second *l* blotted [MS], supplied by HF.
376	*no*[*e*]: hole in MS, M emends silently.
380	*dere*: 'Dere, lædere nocere Lye' [P].
385	[*d*]*oe*: *do* blotted [MS]; *grame*: 'Grame, Chaucer. Grief, sorrow, vexation, anger, Madness. trouble, affliction. S. GRam furor Urry' [P].
387	*su*[*ch*]: hole in MS at this point. Reading supplied by HF.
391	*some*: 'Sir' [P].
395	[*yee*]: supplied by M.
400	*deere*: 'hurt, vid. Supra.' [P].
401	*upon you*: 'on you.' [P]. As HF notes, evidence of part of a *p* or *&* between 'it' and 'upon'.
412	*Home to your owne*: 'to your own home welcome &c.' [P].
423	*times*: the MS may read 'tines' at this point. To the right is a large penciled '3' in the margin. The writing does not appear to be P's. Possibly a note by HF to remind the reader that the character in the MS is a number, and not a yogh?
428	*by*: 'on' [P].
432	*soe*: interlined by scribe with caret [MS].
437	*whitt*: letter *h* deleted before word [MS].
445	*one high*: 'on high' [P].
448	*hi*[*l*]*l*: hole in MS.
449	*euyes*: 'I suppose Ivyes or, perhaps Eughes. i, e Yews.' [P]. The plural form makes 'ivyes' unlikely, as the plural would normally refer to different kinds of ivy. Again, while ivy might well cover the wall of a chapel, as of any building, yew trees are particularly familiar around church buildings; see Explanatory Note to lines 447–49.
451	*wehett*: Scribal π symbol indicating correction, with 'whett', added in LH margin. Unreadable word struck out in text. Possibly *feitch*, in that the scribe was unconsciously thinking of an alliterative pairing with 'fauchion'?
455–56	In the LH Margin, between 455 and 456, P has written: 'Some great omission' between two lateral converging lines.
457	Although it is possible to understand 'perced' at 456 as preceding 'the flesh', the line is distinctly short and another verb may be missing; alternatively, an '&' may be missing at the beginning of the line.
460	*in hart*: marginal scribal correction, with caret [MS]. *throe*: MS holed; 'forte idem ac Thra apud G. Dougl*as*. ferox acer, audax vel poti[us] pertinax. Vide Lye.' [P]. Reading supplied by HF.
464	*hand*: 'hond' [P].
470	*land*: 'Londe' [P].
473	*bound*: 'bond' [P].
475	*3 points*: 'perhaps these points, q. d. thou hast forfeited these qualitie[s]' [P]; *s* no longer visible, supplied by HF.
477	*Leele*: 'i.e., loyal: honourable, true.' [P].
480	[*beholden*]: both [MS], as at 357.
482	*venerye*: preceded by 'veretye', struck out [MS]; 'venison, or rather hunting. So in Chauc Fr. Venerie. Urry' [P].
491	*pay*: 'content, liking.' [P].
492	*thore*: 'there' [P].
498	*the*: interlined above the line by scribe, with caret.
500	*abone*: 'aboone, above, idem.' [P]; MS *n* could equally be read as *u*, i.e., *v*. However, 'abone' roughly rhymes with 'shoen' at 503.
501	*the matter*: 'the' interlined by scribe with caret [MS].
509	*him his boone*: lower part of these words no longer visible. Reading supplied by HF.
515	*ffins*: the scribe has written 'ffins' in a larger and thinner hand at the end of this line to signify the end of the piece.

Boy and Mantle

Raluca Radulescu

The ballad *Boy and Mantle* (*BM*), described by Child as 'An exceedingly good piece of minstrelsy' (I, 257), is – apart from Malory's version, which was adapted from the Prose *Tristan* – one of only two examples in English Arthurian romance of the theme of testing a woman's fidelity by means of a magic object. It comes approximately halfway through the Folio, from p. 284/f. 140r to p. 287/f. 141v, and consists of 194 lines in, predominantly, 4-line stanzas, rhyming *abab*, with seven 6-liners, rhyming, more or less, *abcbdb*. According to Melissa Furrow, the spelling and scribal language show signs of a Northern origin as, for example, *tane* for *taken*, *shreeven* for *shriven*, *knive* for *knife*.[1] Furrow points to signs that it was influenced by the alliterative long line (for example, lines 53–54) and some inexact rhymes (for example, *greene/beseeme* (42/44) and *king/wronge* (132/134)), and considers that the original was possibly written in the north or the North Midlands, 'perhaps in the latter half of the fifteenth century', but that it has, like most of the Folio texts, undergone a certain amount of modernization in the interim (1985, 298).

In the medieval literature of Europe there are many Arthurian examples of this form of chastity test. Some deal with a mantle, some with a drinking-horn. The mantle test occurs in *Le Lai du Cort Mantel* (*c*.1200), also known as *Le Mantel Mautaillié* – a text that is preserved in five manuscripts and was printed in either 1577 or 1578 – in which the telltale sign of infidelity is the shortness of the mantle when donned by unfaithful wives. The test also appears in Raoul de Houdenc's *La Vengeance Raguidel* (*c*.1220–30); in reported form in Sir Thomas Gray of Heton's *Scalacronica* (Cambridge, Corpus Christi College, MS 133), written in Anglo-Norman and begun in 1355; and in German in Ulrich von Zatzikhoven's *Lanzelet* (*c*.1200–3). There are two interesting Scandinavian versions: the Old Norse *Möttuls Saga*, derived from *Mantel*, written in prose between 1217 and 1263 for King Hákon Hákonarson, now extant only in Icelandic copies of the original translation; and the fourteenth-century Old Icelandic *Skikkju Rímur* ('Mantle Rhymes'), a three-part ballad in 4-line stanzas based on *Möttuls Saga*. This contains two parallels to *BM*: the variable colours of the mantle, and the 'old knight' (here King Felix the Old), and his wife, who have been married for two hundred years.[2] Carados is the hero of most versions of both the mantle and the horn tests, although there are many variants of the name.[3]

The earliest known example of the horn test is Robert Biket's *Le Lai du Cor* (Bodl. MS Digby 86), an Anglo-Norman poem of *c*.1200. The *First Continuation* of Chrétien de Troyes's *Perceval* (late twelfth- or early thirteenth-century), of which there are three distinct redactions, includes the virtually self-contained narrative of *Carados*, in which the tester is the hero's father. Other versions of the horn test occur in Heinrich von dem Türlin's *Diu Crône* (*c*.1215–20), which substitutes a tankard for the horn, and where both men and women are tested, and in the fourteenth-century *La Tavola Ritonda*, in which, like the Prose *Tristan*, from which it derives, the test takes place in King Mark's court in Cornwall, although it was originally intended for Arthur's, and nobody is the winner. The only other English example is the fifteenth-century humorous tale *Sir Corneus*, in which the fabliau element is very strong (Furrow, 1985, 271–91).

BM is the only version to include three tests – not only the mantle and the horn but also the boar's head, which may only be carved by the knife of a man whose wife is perfectly faithful to him. Both the two latter tests are for the men, while the mantle tests only the women. Nevertheless, the purpose of each is to test the women's fidelity to their husbands or lovers, and, like most of the other versions of this motif, the tests cause great mirth among the men and great shame and humiliation among the women. The mantle test is the only one recounted in any detail, the boar's head test being disposed of rather perfunctorily in six stanzas, and the two 6-line stanzas of the horn test seemingly tacked on at the last minute. A further 6-line stanza sums up the whole very concisely. The boar's head test is unique to *BM*, although there is a tantalizing reference to such a challenge in the thirteenth-century poem *Annot and John*, preserved in the Harley Lyrics (BL MS Harley 2253, *c*.1340), written in the North-West or North Midlands, in which the besotted John compares his beloved, variously, to jewels, flowers, birds, spices, and famous heroines and heroes, among whom is Caradoc. Annot, says John, 'Cud ase Cradoc in court carf þe brede'.[4] *Annot and John* also includes in its lists the Welsh heroine, Tegau Eurvron [Gold-Breast], the wife of Caradawc Vreichvras. Tegau appears in a fifteenth-century triad as one of the 'Three Chaste Wives of the Island of Britain' (NLW, MS Peniarth 47), in a sixteenth-century version of the list of the 'Thirteen Treasures of the Island of Britain' as the possessor of a chastity-testing mantle, and in another sixteenth-century manuscript as the possessor of a cup and a carving-knife, neither of which, however, seems to have been used as a test.[5] Percy, in his note to *BM* at the end of volume III of the *Reliques*, cited the belief of his Welsh correspondent, Evan Evans, that the story was taken 'from what is related in some of the old Welsh MSS, of Tegan Earfron, one of King Arthur's mistresses. She is said to have possessed a mantle that would not fit any immodest or incontinent woman'.[6]

Together with *MSG*, *BM* was a key text for Percy, who, in February 1759, sent 'very large Transcripts' of these ballads, with others, to his friend and (he hoped) future collaborator, William Shenstone, for his comments (*Letters*, VII, 22). The two ballads were the first two items to be printed off for the *Reliques*, *BM* occupying pp. 1–11, and the first half of *MSG*, pp. 12–16 of the sheet (Sheet B), and together they formed the first two items in what began as volume I, but which later became volume III, after the change of dedication. Unusually, Percy printed the manuscript version of *BM* almost verbatim, pronouncing that he believed it to be 'more ancient, than it will appear to be at first sight; the transcriber of that manuscript having reduced the orthography and style in many instances to the standard of his own times' (*Reliques*, III, 1). Not, apparently, perceiving any irony in that last statement, Percy then inserted, at the end of the volume, a version of *BM* aimed at 'such readers, as have no relish for pure antiquity'. This version, 'as revised and altered by a modern hand', constituted the work of Shenstone and Percy, which, while following the main outlines and incorporating some lines from the Folio version, dresses up the sparseness of the original in language more consonant with Percy's idea (greatly influenced by Shenstone) of what he believed would reflect the tastes of a contemporary audience. Thus Percy transposes the horn and boar's head tests and inserts them into the middle of the mantle test, between Craddocke's wife's success and Guenever's violent denunciation of her.[7]

As a ballad, *BM* works well; its swift movement and brisk telling, with no extraneous details, make for lively entertainment, although it would possibly not be a prime favourite with contemporary women, because of its markedly anti-feminist slant, common to all its predecessors, an anti-feminism primarily aimed at Guenever, whose reputation for infidelity was of long standing. A feature that strongly suggests that the story of the mantle test was originally a stand-alone ballad is the quite complex, carefully wrought structural patterning of incremental repetitions that runs through it, punctuating the action. This sense of structure is largely absent from the brief boar's head test, although it does manage one instance of incremental repetition at 157–60 (possibly two, if Percy's extra couplet between 152 and 153 is accepted), and the horn test, although wittily recounted, leaves little room for structure. The composite nature of the ballad contributes to its charm, although it leaves open some intriguing questions, such as the role of the Boy, which is ambiguous, for he appears at first to be simply a messenger, but he himself initiates the boar's head test by killing the boar and bringing its head back to be cut up. Is the boar a magical beast, or does the Boy make it so? The ballad, then, seems rather to be a compendium of chastity-testing tales than a single unified one, with a strong impression of summary from 151 onward (where there is a break after the Boy's accusation of Guenever), as if the poet was thereafter simply remembering fragments of similar testing tales. The effect is to delay the denouement of the mantle test until the final 6-line stanza, where all three tales are neatly tied together.

Notes

[1] Melissa M. Furrow (ed.), *Ten Fifteenth-Century Comic Poems*, Garland Medieval Texts 13 (New York: Garland, 1985), pp. 296–99.

[2] For a brief discussion of the Arthurian portion of *Scalacronica*, see Richard Moll, *Before Malory: Reading Arthur in Later Medieval England* (Toronto: University of Toronto Press, 2003), pp. 50–52. Marianne Kalinke provides a useful summary of the theme of chastity tests in an Arthurian context ('Chastity Tests', in Norris J. Lacy (ed.), *The New Arthurian Encyclopedia* (Chicago: St James Press, 1991), pp. 81–83), while Burgess and Brook include a detailed discussion of sources

and analogues in respect of *Le Lai du Cort Mantel*, together with a translation of the lai as an Appendix (Glynn S. Burgess and Leslie C. Brook (eds and trans.), *The Lay of Mantel*, French Arthurian Literature V (Cambridge: D. S. Brewer, 2013), pp. 18–25).

[3] Child, I, 264n. As evidence of Arthur's existence, Caxton, in his Preface to *LMD*, states that Cradoc's mantle and Gawaine's skull may be viewed in Dover.

[4] Thorlac Turville-Petre (ed.), *Alliterative Poetry of the Later Middle Ages: An Anthology* (London: Routledge, 1989), p. 16. This episode had thus been associated with Caradoc for at least a century, possibly two, before *BM* is assumed to have been written.

[5] See Rachel Bromwich (ed.), *Trioedd Ynys Prydein* (Cardiff: University of Wales Press, 2006), pp. 183, 260.

[6] *Reliques*, III, 323. Percy's words are taken directly from Evans's letter of 13 January 1764 (*Letters*, V, 60).

[7] 'The incidents of the MANTLE and the KNIFE have not, that I can recollect, been borrowed from any other writer' (*Reliques*, III, 1). Percy suggested to Warton in May 1761 that Spenser was indebted to *BM* for the episode of Florimel's girdle in the *Faerie Queene* (see *Letters*, III, 6, 10), and noted that the trial of the horn also features in *LMD*.

Editions and Related Texts

Child, I, 257–74.

Furrow, Melissa M. (ed.), *Ten Fifteenth-Century Comic Poems*, Garland Medieval Texts 13 (New York: Garland, 1985), pp. 293–311.

HF, II, 301–11.

Further Reading

Burgess, Glynn S., and Brook, Leslie C. (eds and trans.), *The Lay of Mantel*, French Arthurian Literature V (Cambridge: D. S. Brewer, 2013).

Kalinke, Marianne E., 'Chastity Tests', in Norris J. Lacy (ed.), *The New Arthurian Encyclopedia* (Chicago: St James Press, 1991), pp. 81–83.

Rogers, Gillian, '*The Boy and Mantle* and *Sir Corneus*', *AE*, 219–21.

Boy and Mantle

  In the third day of May*   *p. 284/f. 140r*
    To Carleile did come
  A kind curteous child,   *youth of gentle birth*
    That cold much of wisdome.   *possessed*

5 A kirtle & a Mantle
    This Child had uppon,
  With brauches and ringes   *brooches*
    Full richelye bedone.   *adorned*

  He had a sute of silke,
10   About his middle drawne;
  Without he cold of curtesye*
    He thought itt much shame.

  'God speed thee, King Arthur
    Sitting att thy meate!
15 & the goodly Queene Guenever!
    I canott her forgett.

  'I tell you Lords, in this hall,
    I hett you all he[ed]e,*   *p. 285/f. 140r*
  Except you be the more surer,
20   Is you for to dread.'

  He plucked out of his potewer,*   *purse*
    & longer wold not dwell,
  He pulled forth a pretty mantle,
    Betweene 2 nut-shells.

25 'Have thou here, King Arthur,*
    Have thou heere of mee;   *Take this mantle from me*
  Give itt to thy comely queene
    Shapen as itt is alreadye.   *just as it is*

  'Itt shall never become that wiffe
30   That hath once done amisse.'
  Then every Knight in the King's court
    Began to care for his wiffe.*

  Forth came dame Guenever,*
    To the mantle shee her biled;*
35 The Ladye shee was newfangle,   *fond of novelty*
    But yett shee was affrayd.

When shee had taken the Mantle,*
    Shee stoode as she had beene madd:
It was from the top to the toe
40   As sheeres had itt shread.   *shredded it*

One while was itt gaule,*   *red*
    Another while was itt greene,
Another while was itt wadded;*   *blue*
    Ill itt did her beseeme.

45 Another while was it blacke
    & bore the worst hue;
'By my troth,' qu*o*th *Ki*ng Arthur,*
    'I thinke thou be not true.'

Shee threw downe the mantle*
50   *Tha*t bright was of blee,   *brightly coloured*
Fast with a rudd redd   *scarlet-faced*
    To her chamber can shee flee.

Shee curst the weaver & the walker*
    That clothe *tha*t had wrought,
55 & bade a vengeance on his crowne   *head*
    *Tha*t hither hath itt brought.

'I had rather be in a wood
    Under a greene tree,
Then in *Ki*ng Arthur's court
60   Shamed for to bee.'

Kay called forth his ladye
    & bade her come neere;
Saies, 'Madam, & thou be guiltye,*   *if*
    I pray thee, hold thee there.'   *stay where you are*

65 Forth came his Ladye*
    Shortlye & anon;
Boldlye to the Mantle
    Then is shee gone.

When shee had tane the Mantle*   *taken*
70   & cast it her about,
Then was shee bare
    All above the Buttocckes*

Then every Knight*
    *Tha*t was in the King's court

75 Talked, lauged, & showted
  Full oft att *tha*t sport.

 Shee threw downe the mantle
  *Tha*t bright was of blee;
 Ffast with a red rudd
80   To her chamber can shee flee.

 Forth came an old K*nigh*t
  Pattering ore a creede   *mumbling a prayer*
 & he p*ro*ferred to this litle boy
  20 markes to his meede,   *reward*

85 & all the time of the Christmasse
  Willignglye to feede;
 For why this Mantle might*
  Doe his wiffe some need.

 When shee had tane the mantle*   p. 286/f. 141r
90   Of cloth *tha*t was made,
 Shee had no more left on her
  But a tassell and a threed.
 Then every K*nigh*t in the K*ing*'s court
  Bade evill might shee speed.   *wished her bad luck*

95 Shee threw downe the Mantle
  *Tha*t bright was of blee,
 & fast w*i*th a redd rudd
  To her chamber can shee flee.

 Craddocke called forth his Ladye,
100   & bade her come in;
 Saith, 'Winne this mantle, Ladye,*   *without any fuss*
  w*i*th a litle dinne;

 'Winne this mantle, Ladye,
  & it shal be thine,
105 If thou never did amisse
  Since thou wast mine.'

 Forth came Craddocke's Ladye
  Shortlye & anon,
 But boldlye to the Mantle
110   Then is shee gone.

 When shee had tane the mantle
  & cast itt her about,

Upp att her great toe
    Itt began to crinkle & crowt. *pucker up*
115 Shee said, 'Bowe downe, Mantle,
    & shame me not for nought;

'Once I did amisse,
    I tell you certainlye,
When I kist Craddocke's mouth*
120   Under a greene tree,
'When I kist Craddocke's mouth
    Before he marryed mee.'

When shee had her shreeven,* *confessed*
    & her sines shee had tolde, *sins*
125 The mantle stoode about her
    Right as shee wold, *just as she wanted*

Seemelye of coulour, *Pleasing*
    Glittering like gold.
Then every K*nigh*t in Arthur's court
130   Did her behold.

Then spake dame Guenever
    To Arthur our King,
'She hath tane yonder mantle
    Not w*i*th wright but w*i*th wronge!*

135 'See you not yonder woman
    *Tha*t maketh herselfe soe cleare?*
I have seene tane out of her bedd
    Of men fiveteeene,

'Preists, Clarkes & wedded men
140   From her by-deene,* *indeed*
Yett shee taketh the mantle
    & maketh herselfe cleane!'

Then spake the litle boy
    *Tha*t kept the mantle in hold;
145 Sayes, 'K*ing*, Chasten thy wiffe,
    Of her words shee is to bold.

'Shee is a bitch & a witch*
    & a whore bold!
King, in thy owne hall
150   Thou art a Cuchold!'*

BOY AND MANTLE

A litle boy stoode
    Lookeing over a dore
He was ware of a wyld bore*
    Wold have werryed a man.   *attacked*

155 He pulld forth a wood kniffe,*
    Fast thither *tha*t he ran;
He brought in the bore's head,*
    & quitted him like a man.   *acquitted himself*

He brought in the bore's head,
160   And was wonderous bold;
He said there was nev*er* a Cuchold's kniffe   p. 287/f. 141v
    'Carve itt that cold.'

Some rubbed their k[n]ives
    Uppon a whetstone;
165 Some threw them under the table
    & said they had none.

K*ing* Arthus & the Child
    Stood looking them upon;
All their k[n]ives' edges
170   Turned backe againe.   *Slid off again*

Craddoccke had a litle knive
    Of Iron & of steele;
He birtled the bore's head   *cut up*
    Wonderous weele,   *Wondrously well*
175 *Tha*t every K*nigh*t in the K*ing*'s court
    Had a morssell.

The litle boy had a horne
    Of red gold *tha*t ronge;   *rang*
He said, 'There was noe Cuckolde
180   Shall drinke of my horne,
But he shold itt sheede   *spill*
    Either behind or beforne.'

Some shedd on their shoulder,   *spilled*
    & so[m]e on their knee;
185 He *tha*t cold not hitt his mouth
    Put it in his eye;
& he *tha*t was a Cuckold,
    Every man might him see.

	Craddoccke wan the horne		*won*
190	& the bore's head;		
	His ladye wan the mantle		
	Unto her meede.		*As her reward*
	Everye such a lovely Ladye,		
	God send her well to speede!	ffins	*prosper*

Explanatory Notes

1   The third of May seems generally to have been regarded as a day of ill-omen. It was also celebrated in the liturgy as the feast of the Invention of the True Cross, i.e., the day that Saint Helena discovered the True Cross and threw down the statue of Venus, regarded not only as the goddess of love, but also as the goddess of lechery (D. W. 'Chaucerian Tragedy', *ELH* 19(1) (1952), pp. 1–37). It would thus be an appropriate day for a revelation of marital infidelity. However, most of the analogues place this event at Pentecost.

11–12   'He would have thought it shameful not to have known his manners'.

18–20   'I command you all to pay attention. Unless you are very sure of yourselves, you should be afraid'.

21   *potewer*: according to *OED potewer*, apparently a scribal variant of pautner, n² [*pautener*, a small bag; a pouch, a purse]. *OED* cites only *BM* and another text in the PF, *Sir Degree* (HF, III 47, line 866, 'poteuere') as examples.

25–26   The first, brief, example of incremental repetition. See also notes to lines 37, 49–52, 65–68, 73–74, 101–4, 119–22, 153–58, 157–60.

32   *wiffe*. This word introduces an additional stress to the line and fails to rhyme with line 30 ('amisse'), most likely because the scribe unconsciously had in mind line 29 – 'Itt shall never become *that* wiffe'– and repeated the word in question as a result. In a marginal note, P corrected the line to read '(began to care for his:)' and incorporated that reading into the version printed in the 1765 *Reliques* (III, 4).

33–38   *Forth came*: this formula introduces three of the four victims to be tested (the Old Knight's wife being the exception). The wording of Guenever's donning of the mantle differs in detail from that of the other two (Kay's wife at 65–70 and Craddocke's wife at 107–12), which are virtually identical. This is the first of several sequences of effective incremental repetition running throughout the ballad.

34   *biled*: 'she was led to the mantle' (*MED bileden*, to guide or instruct, v,1). There is, however, no 'was' in the line. HF have 'biled', with a note: 'Query the *le* in the MS', possibly on the assumption that the word was 'bid'.

37   Another of the repetitions punctuating the action: see also lines 69 (Kay's wife), 89 (the old knight's wife), and 111 (Craddocke's wife).

41   *gaule*: 'goules', i.e. 'gules', the heraldic term for red.

43   *wadded*: 'woaded'. *OED woad*, to dye, colour, or stain … with woad, v,1; that is, the mantle turned blue.

47–48   Arthur's comment is remarkably mild, as it is in *Sir Corneus*. Compare his violent reaction in Biket's *Cor*, when he tries to stab the queen, but is held back by his knights, and his angry revenge on Cornwall for his revelation of his sojourn in Guenever's bower (for *KAKC*, see above).

49–52   This stanza is repeated twice more, at 77–80 (Kay's wife) and 95–98 (the old knight's wife), another of the sequences of repetition.

53   *walker*: fuller. To full cloth is to scour and beat it, treating it with fuller's earth to achieve a smooth texture.

63   Typically, the churlish Kay assumes his lady to be guilty even before she attempts the test.

65–68   This stanza is repeated, except for the name, at 107–10.

69	*tane*: MED taken, v: chiefly North and North-East Midlands. Also occurring at 89 and 111. Cf. the form taken at 37.
72	*Buttocckes*: For the 1765 *Reliques* Percy substituted the line with 'Before all the rout', most likely to avoid any hint of impropriety. For line 76 of the version of *BM* 'As revised and altered by a modern hand', i.e., Shenstone, asterisks were employed to calm those of a nervous disposition: 'And left her b**side bare'.
73–74	A sequence of incremental repetition that continues with 93–94, 129–30, and 175–76. These repetitions form a progressive 'punctuation mark' separating each episode.
87–88	'Because trying on this mantle might satisfy his wife's need'. The old knight is perhaps trying to bribe the Boy, so that he will allow the mantle to fit her.
89–94	In PF, a stanza-division is made after line 92 of this 6-line stanza, i.e., creating a 4-line stanza followed by a 2-line stanza. The rhyme at 90 ('made') breaks the *-eede* sequence which begins at 82, and continues to 94.
101–4	More incremental repetition in Craddocke's summons to his wife.
119–22	Another instance of incremental repetition.
123	*shreeven*: shriven. An action usually performed by a priest, after the penitent has confessed his or her sins. Here, Craddocke's lady appears to have shriven herself. Compare Gawain's 'lay' confession to Bercilak in *SGGK*, 2377–88.
134	*wright*: a scribal error, brought about by the word's closeness to 'wronge' in the same line (cf. *MER*, 94 and *KAD*, 78, where the same error occurs).
136	'who claims to be so pure'. The scribe uses the word 'cleare' here, but 'cleane' at 142; both can mean 'pure', but 'cleare' in this line breaks the *-eene* rhyme running through both stanzas (135–42).
140	*by-deene*: OED bedene, adv., a word of constant occurrence in northern Middle English verse, but of uncertain origin … often used without any appreciable force, as a rhyme word, or to fill up the measure.
147	*bitch*: OED bitch, an unpleasant or despicable woman; *spec*. (originally) a lewd or lascivious woman, (later) a malicious or spiteful woman, n,1, II 3a.
150	*Cuchold*: spelt thus also at 161, although the scribe reverts to the more normal spelling, 'cuckold(e)' at 179 and 187.
153–58	There are stanza-markings before 153 and after 158, making a 6-line stanza rhyming man/ran/man; there was obviously no gap in the scribe's exemplar. See Textual Notes for P's insertion of two lines between 152 and 153, making a 4-line stanza in place of 151–52. P's second inserted line creates another instance of incremental repetition with the line 'He was ware of a wyld bore'.
155	*a wood kniffe*: quite possibly a mistake for 'good'.
157–60	Another example of incremental repetition.

Textual Notes

7	*brauches*: 'brooches' [P].
18	*he[ed]e*: heate [MS]; 'heed Qu.' [P]; letter *h* crossed out after 'all'.
21	*potewer*: 'See pag. 382 ver. 98.' [P]. P's reference is to *Sir Degree*.
25	*Arthur*: Arthure [MS, with *e* crossed out].
29	*y^t* crossed out before *Itt*.
31	*Knight*: 'K^t', squeezed in between 'every' and 'in' by scribe, interlined with caret [MS].
32	*wiffe*: '(began to care for his:)' [P].
34	*her biled*: the *e* blotted in MS. P has put a cross by 'her', but does not comment, possibly because he felt that the word should be 'was' but failed to note it. It is also possible that the scribe did not understand the word 'biled'; *to*: has been added in the LH margin by the scribe.
35	*newfangle*: 'newfangle, is fond of a new thing: catching at Novelty ab. A.S. fanȝan apprehendere capere. Corrite – i e. hinc fang. Gloss. ad G. D.' [P].
36	blotted letter *y* after *But* [MS].
38	*stoode*: sttoode [MS].
40	*shread*: 'i.e. divided' [P].
41	*gaule*: 'gule Qu.' [P].

50	*blee*: 'colour Complexion. bleoh idem Saxon.' [P].
51	*rudd*: 'complexion' [P].
52	*chamber*: the 'be' blotted; *flee*: last *e* blotted [MS]; 'flee.' [P].
53	*walker*: 'i.e. Fuller Jun.' [P].
82	In LH Margin: 'patter, obscuro murmure, humilibus q*ue* susurris hypocritarum instar coram populo preculas fundere. Junius. They say in Shropshire to pather, i.e. to make a noise, as when one rubs the feet ag*ain*st the ground, and scratches' [P]; *a creede*: 'a creede. Qu.' [P].
83	*proferred*: 'proferred see f. 190 Line 2^d.' [P]. P's reference is to *Chevy Chase* (HF, II, 138).
114	*crowt*: 'to crinkle, to go in & out, to run in flexures. from Krinckelen belg. Johnson.' [P].
123	*shreeven*: 'i.e. confessed. Shrive, fateri confiteri. Hinc Shrove tide. Jun.' [P].
134	*wright*: 'right' [P].
136	*cleare*: 'cleane' [P].
151	*A litle*: 'The little boy.' [P].
152	*Lookeing*: cf. the *ke* formation in 'maketh' in 142. In the right margin, between 152 and 153, P inserted the following couplet: 'And there as he was Lookin[g]/He was ware of a wyld Bore Qu.' Below this, in faint pencil: 'Bore. Quaere'.
162	*Carve*: 'carve' [P].
163	*k[n]ives*: kives [MS].
168	*them upon*: 'upon them Qu.' [P].
169	*k[n]ives*: kives [MS]; *edges*: the *d* malformed, the last letter partly obscured by an overwritten letter [MS].
173	*birtled*: 'birtled, or britled' [P]. *OED* brittle, (*Hunting*) to cut up (a deer or boar), v,1. The *l* and the *e* have been metathesized by the scribe.
184	*so[m]e*: one minim too few on the *m* [MS].
194	*ffins*: the scribe has written 'ffins' at the end of the line to signify the end of the piece.

Libius Disconius

Maldwyn Mills and John Withrington

Libius Disconius (*LD*)[1] is a late version of a fourteenth-century romance, composed in the London region. It must have been very popular, since no fewer than five medieval copies of it have survived,[2] at least one later print of it must also have existed,[3] and self-evidently it was still popular enough in the mid-seventeenth century for the PF scribe to have access not just to a version of the text, but to copy out its 2,241 lines.[4] Its lively and varied subject matter would have counted for something here. Like its twelfth-century French counterpart, *Le Bel Inconnu* (*BI*),[5] it tells of a young man of obscure birth whom Arthur names, makes a knight, and then agrees to send on a dangerous mission (made known to Arthur and his court by two messengers, Hellen and the dwarf Teddelyne), to rescue the captive Lady of Sinadowne, i.e., Segontium in North Wales. In between his departure from court and the achievement of this mission he fights with a succession of knights and giants, as well as with a small army of vassals bent on avenging a wrong he had done their lord (1063–314). It could serve as a textbook example of the Arthurian 'romance of adventures'.

Percy himself was enthusiastic about *LD*, both for its supposed pedigree and for its own merits. Two years after he had written to Warton, expressing his belief that Chaucer had been inspired by *MSG* to write 'The Wife of Bath's Tale', Percy wrote to Lord Hailes, linking *LD* to Chaucer's 'Tale of Sir Thopas', saying of PF that it contained

> an infinite farrago of ancient Songs, Ballads, Metrical Romances, Legends in verse and poems of the low and popular kind:– Some pretty correct, others extremely mutilated and inaccurate .– There is more than one piece in it, quoted by Chaucer as very popular, if not ancient even in his time [*Percy then quotes from 'Sir Thopas', including the line referring to 'Sir Libeaux and Blandamoure'*] ... Now the Romance of Sir Libeaux (in my MS. Sir Lybyus) and Blandamoure is found very correct in my Collection. (8 September 1763; *Letters*, IV, 54–55)[6]

In his 'Essay on the Ancient Metrical Romances', Percy provides a detailed summary to demonstrate the skill of the medieval romance authors 'in distributing and conducting their fable', which gives it something like exemplary status as a romance.[7] What is more unexpected, however, is that he should at the same time praise it for its epic qualities:

If an Epic Poem may be defined, 'A fable related by a poet, to excite admiration and inspire virtue, by representing the action of some one heroe, favoured by heaven, who executes a great design, spite of all the obstacles that oppose him:' I know not why we should withhold the name of EPIC POEM from the piece which I am about to analyse.[8]

Percy also presents *LD* as 'Epic' in a marginal note at the head of the text itself, albeit in rather different terms: 'This Piece may be considered perhaps as one of the first rude Attempts towards the Epic or Narrative Poem in Europe since the Roman Times. ... The Hero is one. The great action to which everything tends is one: there is little interruption of episode'.[9]

Here 'little interruption of episode' is what surprises, given the number and scale of the adventures that punctuate the hero's journey from Arthur's court to his arrival at Sinadowne. But most of these are not really unconnected with this, his explicit goal. Most obviously, because four of them end by mentioning it (487–89, 757–89, 1060–62, and 1567–72), and because his success in all of them (together with Hellen's occasional praise and apologies) make it increasingly likely that he will be equal to whatever awaits him there.[10] Most important of all is the fact that while all of these adventures come as a surprise to Libius, the majority are far from being so to his two guides, who are able to give him precise information about where they are and who his opponent will be.[11] Which can only imply that the combats themselves take place along a route that was fixed and (presumably) already travelled along by the guides. In consequence, we can read these adventures as the component parts of a single, very large adventure (Percy's 'great design'), to which events at Sinadowne form the predetermined climax.

In PF itself, these limits are marked out by the division of the text into nine parts, of which only the second (which joins together the combats with William de la Braunche and with his cousins), and the eighth and ninth (which split into two parts the combat with Mabam and Iron) could have been defined differently. A surprising feature is that the story breaks off before Libius can marry the Lady after he has rescued and transformed her (in marked contrast to all the medieval versions). This abrupt ending greatly offended HF (though not, apparently, Percy himself),[12] but seems much less likely to have been deliberate than the product of a defective source-text. But, however accidental, it has its own aptness to this particular story. By making Arthur's court the hero's point of final return, as well as first departure, it confirms the status of *LD* as a – perhaps even, the – supremely Arthurian romance of adventures.[13] However, when Percy turns from the poem's apparent antiquity and structure to its style, he is much less indulgent than before: 'If the execution, particularly as to the diction and sentiments, were but equal to the plan, it would be a capital performance; but this is such as might be expected in rude and ignorant times, and in a barbarous unpolished language' (*Reliques*, III, xvi).

'Barbarous' seems excessive, but 'unpolished' conveys quite well the general texture of this late version of the romance, in which a long and complex process of transmission has often affected the language, making the versification irregular, and the phrasing less meaningful.[14] Compare, for example, the different accounts which

C^{15} and PF give of the stanza in which the guides tell the Lady's steward of the hero's prowess on the way there (the rhyme-words of the tail-lines are set in bold):

Anon that mayde Elene	Then mayd Ellen anon-rightes
Was fette with kny3tes ten	Was feitched forth with 5 Knights
Be-fore Syr **Lambard**;	Beffore Sir **Lamberd**.
Sche and þe dwerk y-mene	Shee & the dwarffe bydeene
Tolde seuen dedes kene	Told of 6 battells keene
Þat he dede **dydyr-ward**,	That he had done **thitherward**.
And how that Syr Lybeauus	The[y] sayd that Sir Lybius then
Fau3t with fele schrewys	Had fought with strong men
And for no deth ne **spared**.	& beene in stowers **hardye**.
Lambard was glad and blyþe	Then they were glad & blythe
And þonkede fele sy[th]e	& thanked God alsoe s[w]ithe
God and Seynt **Edward**.	That he were soe **mightye**.
C (1663–74)	PF (1771–82)

As can be seen from *C*, the stanza was originally of 12 lines, rhyming *aabaabccbddb*, with both couplet- and tail-lines of broadly equal weight. In PF, the couplet-lines contain four main stresses as often as three; the stanza rhymes *aabccb* in its first half, and alteration of two of the tail-rhyme words produces two stanzas of 6 lines in place of one of 12. Such short stanzas are very common in PF, and others of 3, 9, and 18 lines can be found. Sometimes, too, the alteration of the tail-lines will disrupt the original close relationship of metrical form to narrative content.[16] The most striking example of this comes between lines 133 and 294, which begins with two 6-line stanzas describing the dwarf Teddelyne on his arrival at Arthur's court, and ends with another two in which Libius requests, and the king provides, a blessing on his mission. Into both the earlier and the later of these stanza pairs, three extra lines have been inserted, with the first three upsetting, and the second three restoring, this close relationship. In between, these points fall seriously out of step with each other to make the progress of the narrative at once more jerky and less logical than before.[17]

But not all the innovations of PF are negative. They also give proof of a real concern with intelligibility; sometimes by making more up to date the vocabulary of the original; sometimes by making good significant gaps in the narrative itself. The first is mostly to be seen in the substitution of new words and phrases for old;[18] the second is the (less frequent) insertion of longer passages. (The two most important of the latter come near the end of the story.) The first clears up the fate of Iron, the less imposing of the two enchanters, who even in the best of the medieval texts was never decisively shown to have been killed, like his fellow Mabam, by Libius.[19] In PF, however, this is quite clearly shown, in an interpolated passage (2101–24), which follows nine lines (corresponding to *L* 2049–57)[20] that express the hero's fear of what Iron may still do to him. In this new passage, Libius finds and beheads Iron, and then returns to the hall to search for the Lady herself. The last three lines of the original stanza, expressing his worries about Iron, are then (as 2122–24) rather neatly made to express his fears for the safety of the Lady instead.

She becomes even more prominent in the second major insertion of material in PF, made just after she has offered to marry him. In the medieval texts, in his eagerness to return to the castle to tell Lamberd of his victory over the enchanters, he had ignored the fact that her restoration to human form had left her naked.[21] In PF, however, the interpolation of 2185–99 shows him to be at once (very practically) aware of her needs, and (very chivalrously) deferential to her wishes. He has come a long way from his woodland origins.

Notes

[1] That is, 'The Fair Unknown'. His real name is Ging(g)laine (lines 7, 13, and 32).

[2] An indefinite number of lost intermediate copies are also implied by the extreme textual diversity of the surviving texts. The Ashmole copy (*A*) stands particularly close to PF in its first half.

[3] For these lost prints, see HF, II, 414 and M. Kaluza (ed.), *Lybeaus Desconus*, Altenglische Bibliothek 5 (Leipzig: O.R. Reisland, 1890), pp. x–xi. Both note references to 'Lib(b)ius' in Skelton's *Philip Sparrow* (?1505) and in Henry Crosse's *Vertue's Commonwealth* (1603), that were made in (very) brief lists of romance heroes: I am grateful to Dr J. L. Fellows for supplying me with a facsimile of the second of these. Kaluza also noted that in both of these lists the spelling of the hero's name is closer to that of PF than to any found in the medieval texts. See also Explanatory Note to line 198 [M. M.].

[4] As a heroic figure, Libius is referenced in English texts spanning the fifteenth and sixteenth centuries, for example in *The Wedding of Sir Gawain and Dame Ragnell* (for which see pp. 99–113 above), *LMD*, and *CARLE* (line 33). The author of the related *Syre Gawene* and the *Carle of Carelyle* seemingly thought that *Syr Lebyus Dyskoniis* and *syr Ferr Vnkowpe* were separate characters (lines 55 and 61: see pp. 331–34 below). The name 'Sir Lybyus Dysconyus' also appears on the thirteenth-century Round Table at Winchester.

[5] Only a single copy of *Le Bel Inconnu* has survived. Its first half is made up of the same episodes as LD (although not always in the same order) and gives roughly the same names to a number of the hero's opponents. But while the name *Ging(g)laine* never appears in *LD* after 32, *Guingla(i)n(s)* is used throughout the whole of the second half of *BI* (3233–6264). *LD*, 706 makes reference to a 'French booke' as its source, as does *C* at 222 (equiv. *LD*, 261) and 2122 (where PF is defective), and *L* at 245 and 2196.

[6] Percy's letter implies that, at the time, he construed Chaucer's reference to 'Libeaux and Blandamoure' as meaning two separate people. This may explain his extended musing in his marginal note to *LD*, 129.

[7] *Reliques*, III, xii–xvi. For Chaucer's allusions to Libius in 'Sir Thopas', see Joanne. A. Charbonneau, 'Sir Thopas', in Robert Correale and Mary Hamel (eds), *Sources and Analogues of The Canterbury Tales*, 2 vols (Cambridge: D. S. Brewer, 2005), II, 649–714.

[8] *Reliques*, III, xiii. Percy notes that this definition is taken from the 'Discours sur la Poesie Epique' prefaced to Fénelon's *Télémaque*, a preface written by Andrew Michael Ramsay for the 1717 edition of this work.

[9] This note is reproduced in full on p. 323 below. In a briefer note on f. 72v/p.145, *MER* had also been labelled 'epic'. Like *LD*, this text is divided into nine parts and has as its climax the restoration of the true heir to a throne, but both the territory usurped and the fighting needed to win it back are on an enormously greater scale than in *LD*.

[10] See lines 481–83 and 522–24. Both the Lady and the dwarf, however, will later reproach him for other failings: she for his lust (1546–54), the dwarf for his rashness (883–88). This second lapse, and his behaviour in 19–21, are the only points at which *LD* comes close to the Middle English *Percyvelle*, that other forest-bred romance hero, for whom see *AE*, 136–41.

[11] At Arthur's court, the dwarf had given him warning that he would have to fight a number of 'battells' before meeting with the Lady, together with details of the setting of the first of these (202–7). But it is left to Lamberd, the steward of the Lady of Sinadon, to tell him that the Lady's captivity is the work of enchanters (1795–1833).

[12] 'It is so very wrong of the copier or translator to have broken off the story without giving the wedding between Lybius and his love' (HF, II, 497). As in the medieval texts, the Lady had herself already proposed marriage to him (2179–81), but without any immediate response.

[13] Not that either Arthur or his court have been forgotten in this romance: a number of episodes end with Libius sending them proofs of his victories (415–29, 574–88, 745–47, 1036–41, 1270–75, and 1303–11), and sometimes go on to describe how both king and court then reward or praise him (748–50, 1042–53, and 1312–14).

[14] See, e.g., Explanatory Notes to lines 723 and 1388.

[15] See 'Manuscripts and Sigla', below. This 'older copy … preserved in the Cotton Library' is noted by Percy (III, xviii), who draws attention to its 'innumerable variations'. Furnivall sets out a large number of its variant details in the footnotes to the text in HF.

[16] For the variant forms of the tail-rhyme stanza, see Maldwyn Mills, 'The Percy Folio Text of *Libius Disconius*', in S. Watanabe and Y. Hosoya (eds), *A Festschrift in Honour of Mitsunori Imai to Celebrate His Seventieth Birthday* (Tokyo: Shohakusha, 2009), pp. 79–92. Rhiannon Purdie provides an excellent summary of *LD*'s provenance, rhyme scheme, and existing MSS, supporting the view that *LD* originated in the London area ('though neither Essex nor Kent can be positively ruled out'), and ascribes to it a date of before *c*.1380 (Rhiannon Purdie, *Anglicising Romance: Tail-Rhyme and Genre in Medieval English Literature* (Cambridge: D. S. Brewer, 2008), pp. 211–14).

[17] This is most strikingly apparent in the 12-line stanzas at lines 223–34, 235–46, and 247–58.

[18] For example, at the cost of the rhyme, the modernizing of 'ying' to 'young' at lines 106, 958, 1078, and 2123. See also Explanatory Notes 1192–93.

[19] See Maldwyn Mills, 'A Medieval Reviser at Work', *Medium Aevum* 32 (1963), pp. 11–23.

[20] See 'Manuscripts and Sigla', below.

[21] In the earlier texts, the provision of clothing is first mentioned after two stanzas in which the hero returns to Lamberd to tell of his victory: see *C* 2068–76.

Manuscripts and Sigla

Analogues of PF have survived in five other MSS.

London, Lincoln's Inn MS 150 (fragmentary; *c*.1400) (*H*)

London, BL MS Cotton Caligula A.ii (*c*.1450–60) (*C*)

Naples, Biblioteca Nazionale, MS XIII.B.29 (dated 1457) (*N*)

London, Lambeth Palace, MS 306 (*c*.1460) (*L*)

Oxford, Bodl. MS Ashmole 61 (*c*.1490) (*A*)

Editions

HF, II, 404–99.

Kaluza, M. (ed.) *Lybeaus Desconus*, Altenglische Bibliothek 5 (Leipzig: O. R. Reisland, 1890): edited text, with variants from all 6 MSS.

Mills, Maldwyn (ed.), *Lybeaus Desconus*, EETS OS 261 (Oxford: Oxford University Press, 1969). MSS *C* and *L* in parallel, noting variants from the other three MSS as well as PF. A useful summary of readings unique to PF is at pp. 291–302.

Salisbury, Eve, and Weldon, James (eds), *Lybeaus Desconus* (Kalamazoo, MI: Medieval Institute Publications, 2013): MSS *L* and *N*, https://d.lib.rochester.edu/teams/publication/salisbury-and-weldon-lybeaus-desconus (accessed July 2023)

Further Reading

Horobin, Simon, and Wiggins, Alison, 'Reconsidering Lincoln's Inn MS 150', *Medium Aevum* 77(1) (2008), pp. 30–53.

Luttrell, Claude, '*Le Conte du Graal* and Precursors of Perceval', *Bibliographical Bulletin of the International Arthurian Society* 46 (1994), pp. 291–323.

Mehl, Dieter, *The Middle English Romances of the Thirteenth and Fourteenth Centuries* (London: Routledge & Kegan Paul, 1968).

Mills, Maldwyn, 'A Medieval Reviser at Work', *Medium Aevum* 32 (1963), pp. 11–23.

—— 'The Percy Folio Text of *Libius Disconius*', in S. Watanabe and Y. Hosoya (eds), *A Festschrift in Honour of Mitsunori Imai to Celebrate His Seventieth Birthday* (Tokyo: Shohakusha, 2009), pp. 79–92.

Renaut de Beaujeu, *Le Bel Inconnu*, ed. M. Perret and I. Weill, Champion classiques, série moyen âge 4 (Paris: Champion, 2003).

Weldon, James, '"Naked as She Was Bore": Naked Disenchantment in *Lybeaus Desconus*', *Parergon* ns 24(1) (2007), pp. 67–99.

—— 'Lybeaus Desconus', in S. Echard and R. A. Rouse (eds), *The Encyclopedia of Medieval Literature in Britain*, 3 vols (Chichester: John Wiley & Sons, 2017), III, 212–16.

Libius Disconius

    Jesus Christ, Christen Kinge,   *p. 317/f. 156v*
    & his mother, *tha*t sweete thing,
        Helpe them att their neede
    *Tha*t will listen to my tale:
5   Of a knight I will you tell,
        A doughtye man of deede.
    His name was cleped Ginglaine –   *called*
    Gotten he was of Sir Gawaine   *Begotten*
        Under a forrest side;   *edge*
10 A better knight, *w*ithout fable,   *truly*
    W*i*th Arthur att the Round Table   *p. 318/f. 157r*
        Yee heard never of read.

    Gingglaine was faire & bright,
    An hardye man and a wight,   *bold*
15   Bastard thoe hee were;
    His mother kept him w*i*th all her might   *guarded*
    Ffor he shold not of noe armed K*nigh*t
        Have a sight in noe mannere:
    But he was soe savage   *Because*
20 And lightlye wold doe outrage   *readily*
        To his fellowes in fere,   *To all men he met with*
    His mother kept him close   *hidden*
    Ffor dread of wicked losse,   *evil report*
        As hend child and deere.   *noble*

25 Ffor hee was soe faire & wise
    His mother cleped him 'Beufise'   *called; 'Fair Son'*
        & none other name,
    & himselfe was not soe wise
    *Tha*t hee asked not, iwis,   *indeed*
30   What hee hight of his dame.   *was called; mother*
    Soe itt beffell upon a day
    Gingglaine went to play
        Wild deere to hunt for game,   *beasts; sport*
    & as he went over the Lay   *open country*
35 He spyed a knight was stout & gay   *bold; dashing*
    *Tha*t soone he made full tame.*   *overpowered*

    Then he did on *tha*t K*nigh*t's weede   *armour*
    And himselfe therin yeede   *went*
        Into *tha*t rich armoure;
40 & when he had done that deede
    To Glasenbury swithe hee yeede,   *Glastonbury; quickly*
        There Lay K*i*ng Arthur;

  & when he came into the hall
  Amonge the Lords and Ladyes all
45   He grett them with honore,   *greeted*
  And said, 'King Arthur, my Lord,
  Suffer me to speake a word,   *Allow*
   I pray you par amoure.   *as you love me*

  'I am a child uncouthe,   *youth; unknown*
50 Come I am out of the south,
   & wold be made a knight;
  14 yeere old I am
  & of warre well I cann: *And I know all about fighting*
   Therfore grant me my right!'
55 Then said Arthur the King strong
  To the child that was soe younge,
   'Tell me what thou hight;   *are called*
  For never sithe I was borne   *since*
  Sawe I never heere beforne,
60   Noe child soe faire of sight.'

  The child said, 'By Saint Jame,
  I wott not what is my name: *don't know*
   I am the more unwise!   *greater fool*
  But when I dwelled att home
65 My mother, in her game,   *jestingly*
   Cleped mee 'Beaufise'.
  Then said Arthur the King,
  'This is a wonderous thing,
   By God & by Saint Denise!
70 That thou wold be a Knight
  & wott nott what thou hight,
   & art soe faire and wise.

  'Now I will give thee a name,
  Heere amonge all you in same,   *together*
75   For thou art soe faire and free;   *noble*
  I say, by God & by Saint Jame,
  Soe cleped thee never thy dame,
   What woman that ever shee bee!
  Call yee him all thus:
80 Lybius Disconius,
   Ffor the love of mee.
  Looke yee call him this name,
  Both in ernest & in game,*
   Certes, soe hight shall hee!'

85	King Arthur anon-right	*at once*
	With a sword faire & bright,	
	Trulye that same day,	
	Dubbed that Child a knight	
	And gave him armes bright,	*p. 319/f. 157v*
90	Fforsooth as I you say;	*Truly*
	Hee gave to him in that ilke	*at the same (time)*
	A rich sheeld all over gilte	*covered with gold*
	With a griffon soe gay,*	*(painted) griffin; bright*
	& tooke him to Sir Gawaine	*entrusted*
95	Ffor to teach him on the plaine	
	Of every prince's play.	*sport*

	When hee was made a knight,	
	Of [a] boone he asked right	*at once*
	& said, 'My Lord soe free,	
100	In my hart I wold be glad	
	The first battell if I had	*combat*
	That men asked of thee.'	
	Then said Arthur the King,	
	'I grant thee thine askinge,	
105	Whatt battell that ever itt bee;	
	But ever methinke thou art to young	
	Ffor to doe a good fighting,	
	By ought that I can see.'	*anything*

	When he had him thus told,	
110	Dukes, Erles and Barons bold	
	Washed and went to meate;	
	Of wild foule and venison,	
	As lords of great renowne,	
	Inoughe they had to eate;	
115	They had not sitten not a stoure,	*but a while*
	Well the space of halfe an hower,	*Fully*
	Talking att their meate,	
	There came a damsell att that tyde	*time*
	& a dwarffe by her side,	
120	All sweating for heate.	

	The maiden's name was Hellen,	
	Sent shee was unto the King,	
	A Ladye's messenger.	
	The maiden was ware & wise,	*alert; discreet*
125	& cold doe hir message att device:	*properly*
	Shee was not to fere.	*She had no equal*
	The maid was faire and sheene,	*bright*

Shee was cladd all in greene
 & furred with Blaundemere;* *white fur*
130 Her saddle was overgilte
 & well bordered with silke,
 & white was her distere.* *steed*

The dwarfe was cladd with scarlett fine*
 & fured well with good Erm[i]ne,
135 Stout he was & keene; *Sturdy; bold*
Amonge all christen kind
Such another might no man fi[n]d:
 His cercott was of greene;* *surcoat*

His haire was yellow as flower on mold, *earth*
140 To his girdle hang shining as gold;
 The sooth to tell in veretye. *To tell the absolute truth*
All his shoone with gold were dight, *shoes; adorned*
All as gay as any knight:
 There sseemed no povertye. *was no sign of*

145 Teddelyne was his name;
Wide sprang of him the [f]ame,
 East, west, North, & south.
Much he cold of game & glee, *knew about; music*
Ffiddle, crowde, and sowtrye,*
150 He was a merry man of mouth; *speech*

Harpe, ribble, & sautrye, *fiddle*
He cold much of Minstrelsye; *was very skilled*
 He was a good Jestoure, *story-teller*
There was none such in noe country.
155 A Jolly man forsooth was hee
 With Ladyes in their bower.

Then he bade maid Hellen
Ffor to tell her tale by deene *at once*
 & kneele before the King;
160 The maid kneeled in the hall
Among the Lords & Ladyes all,
 & said, 'My Lord, without Leasing, *truly*

'There is a strong case toward;* p. 320/f. 158r
There [is] none such, nor soe hard,
165 Nor of soe much dolour: *sorrow*
[M]y Lady of Sinadone*
Is brought to strong prison,
 That was of great valoure; *worth*

Shee prayes you of a Knight
170 Ffor to win her in fight
    With joy & much honor.'
Up rose *tha*t younge Knight, — *sprang*
In his hart he was full light, — *eager*
    & said, 'My lord Arthur,

175 'My covenant is to have *tha*t fight*
Ffor to winne *tha*t Lady bright,
    If thou be true of word.'
The King said, 'W*i*thout othe, — *I admit*
Thereof thou saiest soothe,
180   Thereto I beare record; — *witness*

'God thee give strenght & might
Ffor to winne *tha*t Ladye bright
    W*i*th sheeld & w*i*th speare dint.' — *blow*
Then began the maid to say,
185 & said, 'Alas *tha*t ilke day — *very*
    *Tha*t I was hither sent!'
Shee said, 'This word will spring wyde: — *speech; travel*
S*i*r King, lost is all thy pride,
    And all thy deeds is shent; — *disgraced*
190 When thou sendest a child
*Tha*t is wittlesse & wild
    To deale doughtilie w*i*th dint: — *sturdy blows*
Thou hast K*nigh*ts of mickle maine: — *great might*
S*i*r Percivall & S*i*r Gawaine,
195   Ffull wise in Turnament.' — *Very experienced*
Tho the dwarffe w*i*th great error — *anger*
Went unto King Arthur
    & said, 'S*i*r, verament,* — *truly*

'This child to be a warryour,
200 Or to doe such a Labor, — *perform; task*
    Itt is not worth one farthing!
Or hee *tha*t Ladye may see — *Before*
Hee shall have battells 5 or three, — *combats*
    Trulye w*i*thout any Leasinge! — *falsehood*
205 Att the Bridge of Perill
Beside the Adventurous Chappell:
    There is the first begining.' — *There will be his starting point at once*
S*i*r Lybius anon answered,
    & said, 'I was never affeard
210 Ffor no man's threatninge;

	'Somewhat have I lerd	*learned*
	Ffor to play with a swerd	*To fight*
	There men hath beene slowe;	*Where; slain*
	The man *tha*t fleethe for a threat,	
215	Other by way or by streete,	*Whether*
	I wold he were to-draw!	*torn apart*
	I will the battell undertake;	
	I ne will never forsake,	*give (it) up*
	Ffor such is Arthur's Lawe.'	*Custom*
220	The made answered alsoe snell,	*at once*
	& said, '*Tha*t beseemeth thee well!	*suits*
	Whosoe looketh on thee may know	
	'Thou ne durst, for thy berde,	
	Abyid the wind of my swerde,*	*Withstand; rush*
225	By ought *tha*t I can see.'	*From all*
	Then said *tha*t dwarffe in *tha*t stond,	*time*
	'Dead men *tha*t lyen on the ground	
	Of thee affrayd may bee!	
	But, betweene ernest & game,	*jest*
230	I counsell thee goe souke thy dame*	
	& winne there the degree.'	*prize*
	The king answered anon right	
	& said, 'Thou gettest noe other K*nigh*t,	
	By God *tha*t sitteth in Trinytee!	
235	'[I]f thou thinke he bee not wight,	*strong (enough)*
	Goe and gett thee another Knight	p. 321/f. 158v
	*Tha*t is of more powere.'	
	The maid for ire still did thinke,	*silently brooded*
	Shee wold neither eate nor d[r]inke	
240	Ffor all *tha*t there were;	
	Shee sate still, wi*th*out fable,	
	Till they had uncovered the table,	
	She and the dwarffe in fere.	*together*
	K*ing* Arthur in *tha*t stond	*then*
245	Comanded of the Table Round	
	4 knights in fere,	
	Of the best *tha*t might be found,	
	In armes hole & sound	*undamaged*
	To arme *tha*t child full right;	
250	& said, 'through the might o[f] Christ,	
	*Tha*t in flome Jordan was baptiste,	*river*
	He shold doe *tha*t he hight,	*had promised*
	& become a Champyon	

Libius Disconius

255	To the Lady of Sinadon,
	    & fell her foemen in fight'.
	 To arme him they were faine,
	 Sir Percivall & Sir Gawaine,
	    & arrayed him like a knight;
		glad
		
		 equipped

260	The 3ᵈ was Sir Agravaine,
	 & the 4ᵗʰ was Sir Ewaine,
	    Them right for to behold.
	 They cast on him right good silke:
	 A sercote as white as a[n]y milke
	    That was worth 20ˡˡ of golde;
		
		 accurately
		
		 £20

265	Alsoe an hawberke faire & bright, Which was full richelye dight With nayles good and fine.	*coat of mail* *made* *rivets*

270	Sir Gawaine, his owne fathere,
	 Hange about his necke there
	    A sheeld with a griffon,
	 & a helme that was full riche,
	 In all the Land there was none such,
	    Sir Percivall sett on his crowne.
		
		 head

275	Sir Agravaine brought him a speare
	 That was good everywhere
	    & of a fell fashion;
	 Sir Ewaine brought him a steede
	 That was good in every neede
	    & as feirce as any Lyon.
		
		 deadly contrivance
		
		 danger

280	Sir Lybyus on his steede gan springe & rode forth unto the king, & said, 'Lord of renowne,	*leaped*

285	'Give me your blessinge
	 Without any Letting.
	    My will is forth me to wend.'
	 The King his hand upp did lifft
	 & his blessing to him gave right,
	    As a king curteou[s] & hende;
		
		 delay
		 wish; set out
		 raised
		
		 gracious

290	& said, 'God, that is of might, & his mother Marry bright, That is flowre of all women,	 *most excellent*
	'Give thee gracce for to gone Ffor to gett the overhand of thy fone & speed thee in thy journey. Amen!'	 *better; enemies* *prosper*

2ᵈ parte

295	Sir Lybius now rideth on his way,	
	& soe did that faire may,	*maiden*
	The dwarffe alsoe rode them beside.	
	Till itt beffell upon the 3ᵈ day,	
	Upon the Knight all the way	
300	Ffast they gan to chide,	*complained*
	& said, 'Lorell and Caitive!	*scoundrel and wretch!*
	Tho thow were such five	*five like you*
	Lost is all thy pride!	
	This way keepeth a Knight	*is guarded by*
305	That with every man will fight:	
	His name springeth wyde!	*fame; spreads*

His name is William de la Braunche,
His warres may noe man staunche,   *attacks; withstand*
He is a warryour of great pride;
310 Both through hart & hanch*   *p. 322/f. 159r*
Swithe hee will thee Launche
All that to him rides.'

Then said Sir Lybius,
'I will not Lett this nor thus   *I will not hold back for any reason*
315 To play with him a fitt;
Ffor any thing that may betide,
I will against him ryde
To looke if that he can sitt.'   *To see if he knows how to stay in the saddle*

The[y] rode on then all 3
320 Upon a faire Causye   *causeway*
Beside the Adventurous Chappell.
A knight anon they can see,   *at once*
With armes bright of blee,   *colour*
Upon the Bridge of Perrill;

325 He bore a sheeld all of greene
With 3 Lyons of gold sheene,   *bright*
Right rich and precyous.
Well ar[m]ed was that Knight:
As he shold goe to fight,
330 As itt was his use.   *custom*

When he saw Sir Lybius with sight,
Anon he went to him aright   *At once; directly*
& said to him there:
'Who passeth here by day or night,

LIBIUS DISCONIUS

335 Certe[s] with me must fight,
　　Or leave his harnesse here.' — *armour*
　Then answered Sir Libyus
　& said, 'Ffor the love of Jesus,
　　Lett us passe now here:
340 Wee be farr froe our freind — *from*
　& have farr for to wend, — *travel*
　　I and this mayden in fere.' — *together*

　Sir William answered thoe — *then*
　& said, 'Thou shalt not scape soe,
345 　Soe God give me good rest!
　Thow & I will, or wee goe, — *before; part*
　Deale stroakes betweene us tow
　　A litle here by west.' — *to the*
　Sir Libyus sayd, 'Now I see
350 That itt will none other bee:
　　Goe forth and doe thy best!
　Take thy course with thy shafft, — *lance*
　If thou can well thy crafft, — *know; business*
　　Ffor I ame here all prest.' — *ready*

355 Then noe longer they wold abyde — *delay*
　But the one to the other gan ryde
　　With greatt randoun; — *speed*
　Sir Libyus there in that tyde — *then*
　Smote Sir William on his side
360 　With a speare felon; — *deadly*
　But Sir William sate soe fast
　That his stirropps all to-brast: — *broke in pieces*
　　He leaned on his arsowne. — *saddle bow*
　Sir Lybius made him stoupe: — *lean (back)*
365 He smote him over the horse croupe — *hindquarters, crupper*
　　In the feeld a-downe. — *To the ground*

　His horsse ran from him away:
　Sir William not long Lay,
　　But start anon upright, — *at once*
370 And said, 'Sir, by my fay, — *faith*
　Never beffore this day
　　I found none soe wight; — *valiant*

　'Now is my horsse gone away:
　Ffight on [foot] I thee pray
375 　As thou art a Knight worthye.'
　Then sayd Sir Lybius,

'By the [love] of Sweete Jesus,
　　Therto full ready [am I].*

Then together they went as tyte　　　　　　　　　　*quickly*
380　& with their swords they gan smite;
　　They fought wonderous Longe!
Stroakes together they lett flinge　　　　p. 323/f. 159v　*fly*
That the fyer out gan springe
　　Ffrom of their helmes strong;

385　But Sir William d[e] la Braunche
To Sir Lybius gan he launche,*
　　& smote on his sheild soe fast
That one cantell fell to the ground,　　　　　　　　　*corner*
& Sir Lybius, att that sonde,*
390　　In his hart was agast.

Then Sir Lybius, with all his might,
Defended him anon- right
　　Was warryour wight & slye.　　　　　　　　*powerful; crafty*

Coyfe & crest downe right　　　　　　　　　　*Hood (of mail)*
395　He made to fly with great might
　　Of Sir William's helme on hye,　　　　　　　*From; at once*
With the point of his sword
He cut of Sir William's berd
　　And touched him full nye.　　　　　　　　*very closely*
400　Sir William smote Sir Lybius thoe
As that his sword brast in tow　　　　　　　　　　　*So*
　　That many men might see with eye.

Then Sir William began to crye,　　　　　　　　　*shout out*
& sayd, 'Ffor the Love of Marrye,
405　　On live let mee weelde!　　　　　　*Let me go on living!*
Itt were great villanye
Ffor to make a Knight dye
　　Weponlesse in the feeld!'

Then spake Sir Lybius
410　& sayd, 'By the [love] of Jesus,
　　Of liffe gettest thou no space　　　　　*thou lives no longer*
But if thou will sweare anon,　　　　　　　　　　*unless*
Or thou out of the felld gone,　　　　　　　　　　*Before*
　　Here before my face,

415	'& on knees kneele downe,	
	& swere by my sword browne	*shining*
	That thou shalt to Arthur wend,	
	& say, 'Lord of great renowne,	
	I am in battell overthrowne;	
420	A knight me hither doth send	
	That men cleped thus:	
	'Sir Lybius Disconius',	
	Unknowen knight and hend.'	*chivalrous*
	Sir William mett him on his knee,*	
425	& the othe there made hee,	*swore*
	& forward gan he wend.	*he went forth*
	Thus departed all the rout:	*separated; group*
	Sir William to Arthur's court	
	He tooke the ready way.	*direct*
430	A sorry case there gan fall:	*came about*
	3 knights, proud and tall,	
	Sir William mett that day;	
	The 3 Knights, all in fere,	*all of them*
	Were his eme's sonnes deere:	*cousins*
435	Stout they were and gay.	
	When they saw Sir William bleed	
	& alway hanged downe his head,	
	They rode to him with great array.*	
	& said, 'Cozen Will[iam]!	
440	Who hath done to you this shame,	
	& why bleedest thou soe long?'	
	Hee said, 'Sirs, by Saint Jame!	
	One that is not to blame:	
	A stout Knight & a stronge;	
445	Sir Lybius Disconius hee hight:	*is called*
	To fell his enemyes in fight	
	He is not farr to Learne!	*has nothing to learn*
	A dwarfe rydeth with him in fere,	*company*
	As he was his Squier:	
450	They ride away full yarne.	*quickly*
	'But one thing greeveth me sore:	
	That he hath made me sweare,	
	On his sord soe bright,	
	That I shold never more,	
455	Till I come to King Arthur,	
	Stint by day nor night	p. 324/f. 160r
	And alsoe to him I ame yeelde	*surrendered*

      As overcome in the feelde,
         By power of his might;
460 Nor against him for to beare
      Neither sheeld nor speare:
         Thus I have him hight.'   *promised*

      Then said the K*nigh*ts 3,
      'Well avenged shalt thou bee,
465   Certes w*i*thout fayle;
      Ffor hee one against us 3,   *alone*
      Hee is not worthe a flee
         Ffor to hold battell!
      Goe forth & keepe thine othe,
470 Tho*ugh* thou be never soe wroth:
         Wee will him assayle;
      Or he this forrest passe,   *Before*
      Wee will his armour unlace,   *take apart*
         Tho itt were double maile!'

475 Theroff wist nothing *tha*t wight   *knew; man*
      S*i*r Lybius, *tha*t gentle K*nigh*t,
         But rode a well good pace.   *briskly*
      He & that maiden bright
      Made together *tha*t night
480   Game & great solace.   *Sport; pleasure*

      Shee cryed him mercye   *begged*
      Ffor shee had spoken him villanye: *insulted him*
         Shee prayed him to forgive her *tha*t tyde.   *time*
      The dwarffe was their squier
485 & served them both in fere   *together*
         Off all *tha*t they had need.

      On the morrow, when itt was day,
      Fforthe the[y] rode on their way
         Towards Sinadowne;
490 Then they sa[w]e in their way   *saw*
      3 K*nigh*ts stout and gay
         Came ryding from Caerleon.
      To him they sayd anon-right,
      'Traitor, turne againe and fight: *back*
495   Thou shalt lose thy renowne!
      & *tha*t maide, faire & bright,
      Wee will her lead att [n]ight
         Herby unto a towne.'   *To a village close at hand*

	Sir Lybius to them gan crye:	*shouted*
500	'Ffor to fight I am all readye	
	Against you all in same!'	*together*
	A[s] prince proude of pride	
	He rode against them *that* tyde,	*then*
	With mirth, sport and game.	
505	The Eldest brother then beere	*thrust*
	To S*ir* Lybius with a Spere:	*At*
	S*ir* Baner was his name.	
	S*ir* Lybius rode att him anon	*at once*
	& brake in tow his thigh bone	
510	& lett him Lye there lame.	
	The K*nigh*t mercy gan crye,	*begged*
	When S*ir* Lybius, certainly,	
	Had smitten hym downe.	
	The dwarffe *tha*t hight Teodline	
515	Took his horsse by the raine:	
	He lept into the arsoone.	*saddle*
	He rode anon *wi*th that	
	Unto the mayd where shee sate,	
	Soe fayre of fashyon.	*in appearance*
520	Then laughed *that* Maiden bright,	
	& said, 'Fforssooth, this young Knight	
	Is a full good Champyon!'	
	The 2*d* brother, he beheld	
	How [h]is brother lay in the feild,	
525	& had lost strenght & might;	
	He smote S*ir* Lybius in *tha*t tyde	*time*
	On the sheeld, with much pride,	
	With his speere full right.	
	S*ir* Lybius away gan beare	p. 325/f. 160v
530	With his good speare	
	The helme of *that* knight;	
	The youngest brother then gan ride,	
	& hitt Sir Lybius in *tha*t tyde,	
	As a man of much might.	
535	& said to him then anon,	
	'S*ir*, thou art, by St John,	
	A fell Champyowne!	*fierce*
	By God *that* sitteth in Trinitye,	
	Ffight I will with thee –	
540	I hope to beare thee downe.'	*expect*
	As warryour out of witt	*enraged*

On Sir Lybius then hee hitt
    With a fell fauchyon;*   *keen sword*
  Soe stifflye his stroakes hee sett,   *hard; laid on*
545 That through helme & basenett*
    He carved Sir Lybius' crowne.

Sir Lybius was served in that stead,   *paid back there*
  When hee felled on his head   *felt*
    That the sword had drawn blood!
550 About his head the sword he waved
  All that hee hitt, forsoothe, hee cleaved   *cut through*
    As warryour wight and good.
  Sir Lybius said swithe thoe,   *angrily then*
  'One to fight against 2
555   Is nothing good !'
  Ffast they hewed then on him
  With stroakes great and grim:
    Against them he stifflye stood.   *firmly*

  &, through God's grace,
560 He smote the eldest in that place
    Upon the right arme thoe;   *then*
  Hee hitt him soe in that place,
  To see itt was a wonderous case: *thing*
    His right arme fell him froe.
565 The youngest saw that sight
  & thought hee had noe might
    To fight against his foe;
  To Sir Lybius hee did up yeeld
  His good Speare & sheeld:
570   Mercy he cryed him thoe.   *begged; then*

  Anon Sir Lybius said, 'Nay,
  Thou shalt not passe th[u]s away,   *so escape*
    By Him that bought mankind!
  But thou & thy brethren twayne,
575 Plight your trothes without Layine   *delay*
    That yee will to King Arthur wende,
  & say, "Lord of great renowne,
  In battaill wee be overcome:
    A Knight us hither hath send
580 Ffor to yeeld thee tower & townne,   *castle*
  & to bee att thy bandowne,   *disposal*
    Evermore withouten end."

	'& but if you will doe soe	*unless*
	Certes I will you sloe,	*kill*
585	As I am true Knight.'	
	Anon they sware to him thoe	
	*Tha*t they wold to Arthur goe;	
	Their trothes anon the[y] plight.	
	S*ir* Lybius & that faire May	
590	Rode forth on the way,	
	Thither as they had hight,	*sworn to do*
	Till itt beffell on the 3.ᵈ day	
	The[y] fell together in game & pley,	*came; sport*
	Hee and *tha*t Maiden bright.	
595	They rode forthe on west	
	Into a wyde forrest,	
	& might come to noe towne;	
	The[y] ne wist what was best,	*didn't know*
	Ffor there they must needs rest,	
600	& there they light a-downe;	*dismounted*
	Amonge the greene eves	*edges (of forest)*
	They made a lodge [& bower with] leaves,	
	W*i*th swords bright and browne:	*shining*
	S*ir* Lybius & that maiden bright	p. 326/f. 161r
605	Dwelled there all night,	
	*Tha*t was soe faire off fashyon.*	*shape*
	Then the dwarffe began to wake	*kept watch*
	Ffor noe theeves shold take	*So that*
	Away their horsses w*i*th guile;	
610	Then for feare he began to quake:	
	A great fyer hee saw make,	*made*
	Ffrom them but a mile.	
	'Arise,' he said, 'worthy K*nigh*t:	
	To horsse *tha*t wee were dight,	*ride; ready*
615	Ffor doubt of more perill!	*fear of*
	Certes I heere a great bost,	*outcry*
	Alsoe I smell a savor of rost,	*roast meat*
	By God & by Saint Gyle!'	

3.ᵈ part

	S*ir* Lybius was stout & gay,	*bold; dashing*
620	& leapt upon his palffrey	
	& tooke his sheeld & speare,	
	& rode forth full fast:	
	2 gyants hee found at Last,	
	[Who] strong & stout were.	

625	The one was blacke as any sole,	*dirt*
	The other as red as fyerye cole,	
	& foule bothe they were.	
	The blacke Gyant held in h[i]s arme	
	A faire mayd by the barme,*	
630	Bright as rose on bryar.	
	The red Gyant full yarne,	*eagerly*
	Swythe about can turne	*Vigorously*
	A wild bore on a spitt;	
	Ffaire the fyer gan berne:	
635	The maid cryed full yerne	*violently*
	For men shold itt witt.	
	Shee said, 'Alas & ever away,	
	*Tha*t ever I abode this day,	
	W*i*th 2 devills for to sitt!	
640	Helpe, Mary, *tha*t is soe mild,	
	For the love of th[y] child,	
	*Tha*t I be not forgett!'	
	S*i*r Lybius said, 'By Saint Jame!	
	Ff[or] to bring *tha*t maid from shame,	
645	Itt were full great price;	*achievement*
	But for to fight w*i*th both in [s]ame	*together*
	It is no child's game,	
	They be soe grim and grise.'	*fearsome*
	He tooke his course w*i*th his shaft	*rode (at him)*
650	As a man *tha*t cold his crafft,	*knew; business*
	& he rode by right assise;	*in the proper way*
	The blacke he smote all soe smart	*so fiercely*
	Through the liver, long & hart	*lung*
	*Tha*t he might never rise.	
655	Then fled *tha*t maiden sheene,	*fair*
	& thanke[d] Marye, Heaven's Queene,	
	*Tha*t succour had her sent.	
	Then came mayd Ellen	
	& [the dwarffe by]dene	*as well*
660	& by the hand her hent,	*took*
	& went into the greaves	*wood*
	& lodged them under the leaves	
	In a good entent;	*friendship*
	& shee besought Jesus	
665	Ffor to helpe S*i*r Lybius,	
	*Tha*t hee was not shent.	*disgraced*

Libius Disconius

	The red Gyant smote thore	
	Att Sir Lybius with the bore,	
	As a woolfe that were woode;	*maddened*
670	His Dints he sett soe sore	*laid on*
	That Sir Lybius horsse, therfore,	
	Downe to the ground yode.	*Fell*
	Then Sir Lybius, with feirce hart,	
	Out of his saddle swythe he start,	*quickly; leaped*
675	As spartle doth out of fyer;	*spark*
	Feir[c]ely as any Lyon	
	He fought with hys fawchyon	
	To quitt the Gyant his hyer.	*pay; wages*
	The Gyant's spitt, sickerlye,	*truly*
680	Was more then a cowletree*	
	That he rosted on the bore;	
	He laid on Sir Lybius fast,	p. 327/f. 161v *hard*
	All the while the spitt did last,	*As long as*
	Ever more and more.	
685	The bore was soe hott then,	
	That on Sir Lybius the grease ran,	
	Right fast thore;	
	The gyant was stiffe & stronge	*stalwart*
	(15 foote he was Longe):	
690	Hee smote Sir Lybius full sore.	
	Ever still the gyant smote	*Constantly*
	Att Sir Lybius, well I wott,	*know*
	Till the spitt brast in towe;	*broke*
	Then, as man that was wrath,	
695	Ffor a Trunchyon forth he goth*	
	To fight aga[i]nst his foe;	
	& with the End of that spitt	
	Sir Lybius sword in 3 he hitt.	
	Then was Sir Lybius wonderous woe!	
700	Or he againe his staffe up caught,	*Before; lifted*
	Sir Lybius a stroke him rought	*dealt*
	That his right arme fell him froe.	
	The Gyant fell to the ground	
	& Sir Lybius in that stond	*then*
705	Smote of his head thoe.	
	In a French booke itt is found.	
	To the other he went in that stond	
	& served him right soe.	*in the same way*

He tooke up the heads then
710 & bare them to *that* faire maiden
  *Tha*t he had woone in fight.
The maid was glad & blythe
And thanked God often sithe   *many times*
  *Tha*t ever he was made a K*nigh*t.

715 Sir Lybius said, 'Gentle dame,
Tell me now what is your name
  & where *that* you were borne.'
'S*ir*,' she said, 'by S*ain*t Jame,
My father is of rich fame,   *great*
720 & dwelleth here beforne;   *close at hand*
He is a Lo*r*d of much might,
An Erle & a Noble Knight,
  His name is S[ir] Arthore;*
& my name is Vylett,
725 *Tha*t the Gyant had besett   *besieged*
  For the Castle [y]ore.   *earlier*

'As I went on my demeaning*
Tonight in the eveni[n]ge,
  None evill then I thought,
730 The gyant, without leasing,   *truly*
Out of bush he gan spring
  & to the fyer me brought;
Of him I had beene shent,   *disgraced*
But *tha*t God me succour sent
735 *Tha*t all this world hath wrought!
S*ir* k*nigh*t, God yeeld thee thy meed,   *grant; reward*
Ffor us *that* on the roode did bleed   *cross*
  & w*i*th his blood us bought.'

W*i*thout any more talking,
740 To their horsses they gan spring   *On; leapt*
 & rode forth all in same,   *together*
& told the Erle in every thing,   *detail*
How he wan in fighting   *rescued*
  His Daughter from woe & shame.
745 Then were these heads sent
Unto K*ing* Arthur for a present,
  W*i*th much mirth & game,   *sport*
*Tha*t in Arthur's court arose
Of S*ir* Lybius great Losse   *praise*
750 & a right good name.   *reputation*

	The Erle, for *tha*t good deede,	
	Gave Sir Lybius for his meede	*reward*
	Sheeld and armour bright,	
	& alsoe a noble steede	
755	*Tha*t was good in everye need,	
	In travayle & in fight.	*hardship*
	Now S*ir* Lybius and his May	
	Tooke their leave & rode their way	
	Thither as they had hight;	*promised*

4:d parte

760	Then they saw in a parke	p. 328/f. 162r
	A Castle stiffe & starke	*powerful; strong*
	*Tha*t was full marvelouslye dight:	*fashioned*
	Wrought itt was w*i*th lime & stone:	*Built*
	Such a one saw he never none,	
765	With towers stiffe & stout.	*sturdy; strong*
	S*ir* Lybius said, 'Soe have I blis,	
	Worthy dwelling here itt is	*(A) suitable*
	To them *tha*t stood in doubt!'	*danger*
	Then laughed *tha*t Maiden bright	
770	& sayd, 'Here dwelleth a K*nigh*t,	
	The best *tha*t here is about:	
	Who soe will w*i*th him fight,	
	Be he baron or be he knight,	
	He maketh him to loute.	*submit*
775	'Soe well he loveth his Leman,	*mistress*
	*Tha*t is soe faire a woman	
	& a worthy in weede,	*dress*
	Who soe bringeth a fairer then,	
	A joly fawcon as white as swan*	*gyrfalcon*
780	He shall have to his meede;	*reward*
	& if shee be not soe bright	
	W*i*th S*ir* Gefferon he must fight,	
	& if he may not speed	*prosper*
	His [head] shall be from him take	
785	& sett full hye upon a stake,	
	Trulye w*i*thouten dread,	*doubt*
	'The sooth you may see and heere:	*truth; hear*
	There is on every corner	
	A head or tow full right.'	
790	S*ir* Lybius sayd alsoe soone,	*at once*

	'By God & by S*ai*nt John,	
	W*i*th S*i*r Gefferon will I fight	
	& chalenge the Jolly fawcon,	*lay claim to*
	& say *tha*t I have one in the towne:	
795	A lemman alsoe bright!	*as beautiful*
	'& if hee will her see	
	Then I will bri[n]g thee,	
	Be itt [by day or] night.'	
	The dwarffe sayd, 'By Sweete Jesus!	
800	Gentle S*i*r Lybyus Disconiys,	
	Thou puttest thee in great p*er*ill:	
	S*i*r Giffron La Fraudeus*	*the Trickster*
	In fighting he hath an use	*practice*
	Knights for to beguile.'	*deceive*
805	S*i*r Lybius answered and sware	
	& said, 'Therof I have no care,	
	By God & by S*ai*nt Gyle!	
	I will see him in the face	
	Or I passe out of this place,	*Before*
810	Ffor all his subtulle wile!'	*cunning trickery*
	W*i*thout any more questyon,	*debate*
	The[y] dwelled still in the towne	*quietly*
	All night there in peace;	
	On the morrow he made him readie	
815	Ffor to winne him the Masterye,	*victory*
	Certe[s] w*i*thouten Lease:	*lie*
	He armed him full sure	*securely*
	In the sayd Armor	
	*Tha*t [Erle] Arthur's was,	
820	& his horsse began he to stryde:	*he mounted*
	The dwarffe rod by his syde	
	To *tha*t strong palace.	
	S*i*r Gyffron la Ffraudeus	
	Rose up, as itt was his use,	*custom*
825	In the morrow tyde,	*at dawn*
	Ffor to honor sweete Jesus:	
	Then he was ware of S*i*r Lybius,	
	As a prince of much pryde.	*great splendour*
	Ffast he rode into *tha*t place.	
830	Sir Jeffron marvailed att *tha*t case	*action*
	& loud to him did crye	

Libius Disconius

  With voyce loud and shrill:
  'Comest thou for good or ill?
   Tell me now on hye!'   *quickly*

835 Sir Lybius said alsoe tyte,   p.329/f. 162v *at once*
  'Certes I have greate delight
   With thee for to fight:

  Thou [sayst] great despite,   *insult*
  Thou hast a Le[mm]an, none so whyte,   *fair*
840   By day or by night;
  As I have one in the towne
  Ffairer of fashion   *shape*
   Ffor to see with sight;
  Therfore thy Jolly fawcowne
845 To King Arthur with the crowne
   Bring I will by right!'

  Sir Geffron said alsoe right,
  'Where shall wee see that sight
   Whether the fairer bee?'   *Which (of them)*
850 Sir Lybius said, 'Wee will full right
  In Cardigan see that sight,
   There all men may itt see;   *Where*
  In the middes of that Markett   *market place*
  There shall they both be sett
855   To looke on them soe free,
  & if my Leman be browne,*   *less attractive*
  Ffor thy Jolly fawcowne
   Just I will with thee.'   *joust*

  Sir Geffron said alsoe then,
860 'I wold faine as any man,   *as gladly*
   Today att yondertyde;*
  All this I grant thee well,
  & out of this Castell
   To Cardigan I will ryde.'*
865 Their gloves were there up yold,   *raised*
  That forward to hold,   *agreement; uphold*
   As princes proud in pryde;
  Sir Lybius wold no longer bli[nn]   *delay*
  But rode againe to his inn   *lodging*
870   & wold no longer abyde.

  He said to maid Ellen
  That was soe bright & sheene,   *fair*
   'Looke thou make thee bowne!   *get ready*

	I thee say, by *Saint* Quintin,	
875	S*i*r Gefferon's Leman I will winn:	*defeat*
	Today shee will come to towne;	
	In the midds of this cytye	
	*Tha*t men may you see,	
	& of you bothe the fashion,	*appearance*
880	& if thou be not soe bright	
	W*i*th S*i*r Geffron I shall fight	*must*
	To winne the Jollye fawcowne.'	
	The dwarffe answered, 'Forthy,	*Indeed*
	*Tha*t thou doest a deed hardye	*rash*
885	For any man borne!	
	Thou wilt doe by no man's read,	*act; advice*
	For thou f[a]rest in thy child head	*behaves; folly*
	As a man *tha*t wold be lorne;	*lost*
	& therfore I thee pray	
890	To wend forth on thy way,	
	& come not him beforne.'	
	S*i*r Lybius said, '*Tha*t were great shame:	
	I had lever w*i*th great grame	*rather; torment*
	W*i*th wild horsses to be torne.'	
895	Maid Ellen, faire and free,	
	Made hast sickerlye	*truly*
	Her for to attyre	*dress*
	In Kei[r]cheys *tha*t were white,	*headcloths*
	For to doe all his delight,	*pleasure*
900	With good gold wyer.	*thread*
	A vyolett mantle, the sooth to say,	
	Ffurred well with gryse gay	*grey fur*
	Shee cast about her Lyer;	*body*
	The stones shee had about her mold	*head*
905	Were p*re*cyous & sett with gold:	
	The best in *tha*t shire.	
	S*i*r Lybius sett *tha*t faire May	*maiden*
	On a right good Palffrey,	
	& rode forth all three;	
910	Every man to other gan say,	
	'Heere cometh a faire May.	
	And lovelye for to see!'	p. 330/f. 163r
	Into the Markett hee rode	
	& boldly there abode	
915	In the [m]iddes of *tha*t citye.	
	Anon the[y] saw Geffron come ryde	*Then*

  & 2 squiers by his side
   & namore meanye.   *no other attendants*

  He bare a sheelde of greene,
920 Richelye itt was to be seene,   *It was splendid of appearance*
   Of gold was the bordure;
  Dight itt was with flowers   *Adorned*
  & alsoe with rich colours,
   Like as itt were an Emperour.   *As if*
925 The squires did with him ryde:
  The one bare by his side
   3 shafts good & stoure;   *strong*
  The other bare his head upon*
  A gentle Jolly fawcon,
930 That was laid to wager.

  & after did a Lady ryde,
  Ffaire & bright, of Much pryde,
   Cladd in purple pall.   *satin*
  The people came farr & wyde
935 To see that Ladye in that tyde,   *then*
   How gentle shee was and small.   *refined*
  Her mantle was of purple fine,
  Well furred with good Armine: *ermine*
   Itt was rich and royall;
940 A sercotte sett about her necke soe sweete,   *tunic*
  With dyamond & with Margarett   *pearls*
   & many a rich Emerall.

  Her colour was as the rose red,
  Her haire that was on her head
945 As gold wyer itt shone bright;
  Her browes were alsoe silke spread,   *like*
  Ffaire bent in lenght & bread,   *curved*
   Her nose was faire and right;   *straight*
  Her eyen gray as any glasse:
950 Milke white was her face,
   The[y] said that sawe that sight;
  Her body gentle and small,
  Her beautye for to tell all
   Noe man with tounge might.

955 Unto the Markett men gan bring
  2 Chaires for to sitt in,
   Their bewtye for to descrye;   *compare*
  Then said both old & younge,

	Fforssooth, without Leasing,	*falsehood*
960	Betweene them was partye:	*dispute*
	Geffron's Leman was faire & cleere	*bright*
	As ever was any rose on bryer,	
	Fforsooth without Lye;	
	Maid Ellen the Messenger	
965	Seemed to her but a Launderer	*washerwoman*
	In her nurserye.	*upbringing*
	Then said Sir Geffron la Fraudeus,	
	'Sir Knight, by sweet Jesus,	
	Thy head thou hast forlore!'	*forfeited*
970	'Nay,'said Sir Lybius,	
	'That was never my use!	*way*
	Just I will therfore.	*I will joust to decide the matter*
	'& if thou beare me downe,	
	Take my head on thy fawchyon,	*sword*
975	& home with thee itt lead;	
	& if I beare downe thee,	
	The Jerffaucon shall goe with mee,	
	Maugre thy head indeed!	*In spite of anything you can do!*
	'What needeth us more to chyde?	*argue*
980	But into the saddle let us glyde	*leap*
	To prove our mastery!'	*powers*
	Either smote on others sheeld the while	*constantly*
	With crownackles that were of steele,*	
	With great envye.	*enmity*
985	Then their speares brake assunder:	
	The dints fared as the thunder	*were like*
	That cometh out of the skye;	
	Trumpetts & tabours,	
	Herawdyes & good desoures,*	
990	Their stroakes for to descrye.	p.331/f. 163v *record*
	Geffron then began to speake:	
	'Bring me a spere that will not breke,	
	A shaft with one crownall,	
	Ffor this young fe[r]ley freke	*amazing man*
995	Sitteth in his saddle steke	*as firmly*
	As stone in Castle wall!	
	I shall make him to stoope	*fall backwards*
	Swithe over his saddle croope,	*Right; crupper*
	& give him a great fall;	
1000	Tho he were as wight a warryour	*powerful*

As Alexander or Arthur,
    Sir Lancelott or Sir Percivall!'

    Then the Knights both tow
    Rode together swithe thoe,   *vigorously*
1005   With great ren[d]owne;*   *At great speed/violence*
    Sir Lybius smote Sir Geffron soe
    That his sheild fell him froe   *from*
        Into the feeld againe;   *back*
    Then laughed all that was there,
1010   & said, without more,   *at once*
        Duke, Erle or Barron:
    That the[y] saw never a Knight,
    Ne noe man abide might   *endure*
        A course of Sir Geffron.   *bout*

1015 Another course gan the[y] ryde:
    Sir Geffron was aggreeved that tyde   *angered then*
        Ffor hee might not speede;   *succeed*
    He rode againe alsoe tyte,   *at once*
    & Sir Lybius he ga[n] smite
1020   As a doughtye man of deed.

    Sir Lybius smote him soe fast
    That Sir Geffron soone he cast
        Him and his horsse a-downe;
    Sir Jeffron's backe bone he brake,
1025 That the folkes hard itt cracke: *heard*
        Lost was his renowne!
    Then they all said, lesse & more,   *lowly; noble*
    That Sir Geffrons had Lore   *forfeited*
        The white Gerffawcon;
1030 The people came Sir Lybius before
    & went with him, lesse & more,
        Anon into the towne.
    & Sir Geffron from the feeld
    Was borne home on his sheild,
1035   With care & rueffull mone;   *sorrow and lamentation*
    The gerffawcon sent was
    By a knight that hight Chaudas
        To bring to Arthur with the crowne.

    & rote to him all that dead,   *a full account of that exploit*
1040 & with him he gan to leade
        The fawcon that Sir Lybius wan;
    When the King had heard itt read,

He said to his knights in that stead,   *place*
   'Sir Lybius well warr can: *fight*
1045 He hath me sent, with honor,
That he hath done battells 4   *combats*
   Since that he began;
I will him send off my treasure
Ffor to spend to his honor,
1050   As falleth for such a man.'   *is proper*

A 100ˡⁱ ready prest   *£100; promptly*
Of floryins to spend with the best
   He sent to Cardigan towne;
Then Sir Lybius held a feast
1055 That lasted 40 dayes att Least,
   With Lords of renowne;
&, att the 6: weeke end,
Hee tooke his leave for to wend   *leave*
   Of duke, Erle and Barron.

5ᵈ parte

1060 Sir Lybius and his faire May
Rode forth on their way
   Towards Sinadon.
Then as they rod, in a throwe,   *short time*
Hornes heard they lowd blowe,
1065   & ho[u]nds of great game;   *very sportive*

The dwarffe said in that throwe,   *moment*
'That horne I well know,
   Many yeeres agone: *past*

That horne bloweth Sir Ortes de Lile,
1070 That served my ladye a while,   p. 332/f. 164r   *once*
   Seemlye in her hall,   *Graciously*
& when shee was taken with guile,
He fled from that perill
   West into Worrall.'*   *The Wirral*

1075 But as they rode talking,
They saw a ratch run[n]inge   *hound*
   Overthwart the way;   *Across*
Then said both old & young   *all of them*
Ffrom the[ir] first begining   *day of birth*
1080   They saw never none soe gay: *bright*
Hee was of all couloures

That men may see on flowers
    Betweene Midsummer & May
The Mayd sayd, alsoe soone,   *at once*
1085 'Soe faire a ratch I never saw none,
    Nor pleasanter to my pay: *more to my liking*

'Wolde to God that I him ought!'   *owned*
Sir Lybius anon him caught
    And gave him to maid Elen;
1090 They rode forth all rightes   *straight ahead*
And told of fighting with Knights
    For ladyes bright & sheene.   *fair*
They had ridden but a while,
Not the space of [a] Mile
1095   Into that forest greene,
Then they saw a hind sterke*   *sturdy*
And 2 greyhounds that were like
    The ratch that I of meane.   *speak*

The[y] hunted still under the Lind   *trees*
1100 To see the course of that hind   *running*
    Under the forest side.   *edge*
There beside dwelled that Knight   *close at hand*
That Sir Otes de Lile hight,   *was called*
    A man of much pride;

1105 He was cladd all in Inde   *blue cloth*
& fast pursued after the hind
    Upon a bay distere;   *war-horse*
Loude he gan his horne blow
For the hunters sholde itt know,   *recognize*
1110   And know where he were.
As he rode by that woode right   *straight along*
There he saw that younge Knight
    & alsoe that faire May;
The dwarffe rode by his side:
1115 Sir Otes bade they shold abyde –   *halt*
    They Ledd his ratch away.

'Ffreinds,' he said, why doe you soe?
Let my ratch from you goe –
    Good for you itt were!
1120 I say to you, without Lye,
This ratch has beene my,   *mine*
    All out this 7 yeere.   *For wholly*

	Sir Lybius said anon tho,	*at once*
	'I tooke him with my hands 2,	
1125	And with me shall he abyde!	
	I gave him to this maid hend	*fair*
	That with me dothe wend,	*travels*
	Riding by my side.'	
	Then said Sir Otes de Lile,	
1130	'Thou puttest thee in great perill	
	To be slaine if thou abide!'	
	Sir Lybius said in that while,	
	'I give right nought of thy wile,	*craft*
	Churle, tho thou chyde!'*	*threaten*

1135	Then spake Sir Otes de Lile	
	& said, 'Thy words be vile –	
	Churle was never my name!	
	I say to thee, without fayle,	
	The countesse of Carlile,	
1140	Certes was my dame;	*Truly; mother*
	& if I [w]ere armed now	
	As well as art thou,	
	Wee wold fight in same	*together*
	Or thou my ratch from me reve	*take away*
1145	We wold play, ere itt were eve,	
	A wonderous strong game!'	*very dangerous*

	Sir Lybius said, alsoe prest,	*at once*
	'Goe forth & doe thy best:	
	Thy ratch with mee shall wend!'	p.333/f. 164v *must go*

1150	They rode on right west	
	Througe a deepe forrest,	
	Then as the dwarffe them kend;	*guided*
	Sir Otes de Lile in that stower	*then*
	Rode home into his Tower,	
1155	& for his friends sent;	
	& told them, anon rights,	
	How one of Arthur's Knights	
	Shamely had him shent,	*humiliated*

	And had his ratche away I-nome	*snatched*
1160	Then the[y] sayd, all and so[m]e,	*all together*
	'That thee[f]e shall soone be tane,	*villain; captured*
	& never home shall hee come,	
	Tho he were as grim a groome	*man*
	As ever was Sir Gawaine!'*	

1165	They dight them to armes	*armed themselves*
	With gleaves and gysarmes	*swords; axes*
	As they wold warr on take;	*start fighting*
	Knights and squiers	
	Leapt on their disteres	
1170	For their Lord's sake.	
	Upon a hill, trulye,	
	Sir Lybius they can espye,	*caught sight of*
	Ryding a well good pace;	
	To him gan they loud crye	*shouted*
1175	& said, 'Thou shalt dye	
	Ffor thy great trespas!'	*crime*
	Sir Lybius againe beheld	*behind him*
	How full was the feild,	
	For many people there was;	
1180	He said to Maid Ellen,	
	'Ffor this ratch, I weene,	*believe*
	To us commeth a careffull case.	*sorrowful fate*
	'I rede that yee withdraw	*advise*
	Yonder into the wood's wawe*	*edge*
1185	Your heads for to hyde;	
	Ffor here upon this plaine,	
	Tho I shold be slaine,	
	The battell I will abyde!'	
	Into the forrest the[y] rode,	
1190	And Sir Lybius there abode	*awaited*
	Of him what may betyde.	*happen to*
	Then the[y] smote at him with crossebowes,*	
	With speare, & with bowes Turkoys:	*Turkish*
	That made him wounds wyde.	
1195	Sir Lybius with his horsse ran	
	& bare downe horsse and man,	*knocked*
	Ffor nothing wold he spare.	
	Every man said then	
	That hee was the feend Sathan	
1200	That wold mankind forfare;	*destroy*
	Ffor he that Sir Lybius raught	*hit*
	His death wound there he caught,	
	& smote them downe bydeene.	*together*
	But anon he was beset	*soon, hemmed in*
1205	As a fish in a nett,	
	With groomes fell and keene.	*By fierce and bold vassals*

	For 12 knights, verelye,	*truly*
	He saw come ryding redylye	*all prepared*
	In armes faire & bright.	
1210	All the day they had rest,	
	For the[y] thought in the forrest	*intended*
	To s[l]ee Sir Lybius that Knight.	
	In a sweate they were all 12*	
	(One was the Lord himselfe,	
1215	In the ryme to read right).	
	They smote att him all att once,	
	Ffor they thought to breake his bones	
	& fell him downe in fight.	
	Ffast together can the[y] ding,	*dealt blows*
1220	& round the[m] stroakes he gan flinge	*let fly*
	Among them all in fere;	*together*
	Fforsooth without leasing,	*falsehood*
	The sparkells out gan springe	
	Of sheeld and her[n]esse cleere.	*bright armour*
1225	Sir Lybius slew of them 3,	
	& 4 away gan flee	
	And wold not come him nere.	p. 334/f. 165r *closer*
	The Lord abode in that stoure,	*stood firm; conflict*
	& soe did his sonnes 4,	
1230	To sell their lives deere.	
	Then they gave stroakes rive,	*numerous*
	He one against them 5,	
	& fought as they were wood.	*mad*
	Nye downe they gan him bring;	*Almost*
1235	As the water of a Spring	
	Of him ran the bloode!	
	His sword brake by the hilte,	
	Then was he neere spilt	*almost done for*
	He was full madd of moode.	*enraged*
1240	The Lord a stroake on him sett	*laid*
	Through helme and Basnett,	
	In the skull itt stoode.	*stayed*
	Then in a swoone he lowted lowe;	*stooped*
	He leaned on his saddle bow	
1245	As a man that was nye slake.	*almost exhausted*
	His 4 sonnes were all abowne	
	Ffor to perish his Acton,*	
	Double Maile and plate;	
	But as he gan to smert	*feel pain*

Libius Disconius

1250	Againe he plucked up his hart,	*courage*
	As the Ki[n]de of his estate,	*As was natural to one like him*
	& soone he hent in his fist	*seized*
	An axe *tha*t hanged on his sadle crest –	*bow*
	Almost itt was too late!	
1255	Then he fought as a K*nigh*t.	
	Their horsses fell downe right –	
	He slew att stroakes 3.	*struck down*
	& when the Lo*rd* saw the fight,	
	Of his horsse adowne gan light,	*dismounted*
1260	Away hee fast gan flee.	
	S*i*r Lybius noe longer abode,	
	But after him fast he rode	
	& under a chest[en] tre	*chestnut*
	There he had him killed,*	
1265	But the Lo*rd* him yeelded	
	Att his will for to bee,	
	& for to yeeld him his stent:	*(fixed) payment*
	Treasure, Land and rent,	
	Castle, hall & tower.	
1270	S*i*r Lybius consented therto	
	[In] forward *tha*t he wold goe	*On condition*
	Unto King Arthur,	
	& say, 'Lord of great renowne,	
	In battell I am overthrown	
1275	& sent thee to honor!'	
	The Lo*rd* granted theretill	*to that*
	Ffor to doe all his will.	
	They went home to his tower,	
	& anon Maiden Ellen	
1280	W*i*th knights fiveteene	
	Was feitched into the Castle.	
	Shee & the dwarffe bydeene	*between them*
	Told of his deeds Keene,	*bold*
	& how *tha*t itt befell	
1285	That hee had pr*es*ents 4	
	Sent unto King Arthur,	
	*Tha*t he had woone full well.	
	The Lo*rd* was glad & blythe,	
	& thanked God often sithe,	*many times*
1290	& alsoe S*ain*t Michall	

  *Tha*t such a noble Knight
  Shold for that Ladye fight,
   *Tha*t was soe faire and free.   *noble*
  In the towne dwelled [that] K*nigh*t;
1295 Att the full fortnight
   S*i*r Lybyus there gan bee,

  & did heale him of his wounds,
  Bothe hole and sound,
   By the 6 weekes' end.
1300 Then S*i*r Lybius and his May   *maiden*
  Rode forthe on their way
   To Sinadon to wend.
  & alsoe the Lord of *tha*t tower   *castle*
  Went unto K*ing* Arthur
1305 & prisoner him did yeeld,
  & told how a K*nigh*t younge
  In fighting had him woone   p. 335/f. 165v
   & overcome him in the feeld;

  & said, 'Lo*r*d of great renowne,
1310 I am in battell brought adowne
   W*i*th a K*nigh*t soe bolde!'
  K*ing* Arthur had good game,   *great delight*
  & soe had they all in same   *together*
   *Tha*t heard that tale soe told.

6.^d parte:

1315 Now let us rest a while
  Of S*i*r Otes de Lile,
   & tell wee other tales.
  S*i*r Lybius rode many a mile,
  Sa[w]e adventures many & vile,*
1320   In England & in Wales,

  Till itt beffell in the monthe of June,
  When the fenell hangeth in the towne,
   All greene in seemlye manner;   *attractively*
  The midsu[mm]er day is faire & long,
1325 Merry is the foules' songe,   *birds'*
   The notes of birds on bryar.

  S*i*r Lybius then gan ryde
  Along by a river side,
   & saw a faire Citye,
1330 W*i*th pavillyons of much pride,   *tents; splendour*

LIBIUS DISCONIUS

      & a castle faire & wyde,
          And gates g[r]eat plentye.   *numerous*
      He asked fast what itt hight.   *eagerly; was called*
      The maid said, anon right,   *at once*
1335   'S*i*r I will tell thee:
          Men clepeth itt Ile Dore.   *call*
      There hath beene slaine K*nigh*ts more
          Then beene in this countrye

      'Ffor a Ladye *tha*t is of price –   *excellent*
1340 Her coulour is red as rose on rise.   *branch*
          All this cuntry is in doubt,   *fear*
      Ffor a Gyant *tha*t hight Maugys
      (There is noe more such theeves)   *evil doers*
         *Tha*t Lady hee lyeth about.   *besieges*
1345 He is heathen, as blacke as pitch,
          Now there be no more such,   *none like him*
            Of deeds strong & stout;   *bold*
      What K*nigh*t *tha*t passeth this brigg,
      His armes he must downe ligg,   *lay*
1350   & to the gyant Lout.   *bow down*

      'He is 20 foote of lenght,
      & much more of strenght
          Then other K*nigh*ts five.
      S*i*r Lybius, now bethinke thee –   *consider*
1355 Hee is more grim*m*er for to see
          Then anyone alive;

      'He beareth haires on his brow
      Like the bristles of a sow;
          His head is great & stout,   *bold*
1360 Eche arme is the lenght of an ell,*
      His fists beene great & fell,   *forbidding*
          Dints for to drive about.'   *Blows; strike around*

      S*i*r Lybius said, 'Maiden hend,
      On our way wee will wend
1365   Ffor all his stroakes ill!   *evil*
      If God will me grace send,
      Or this day come to an end,   *Before*
          I hope him for to spill.   *destroy*
      Tho I be young & lite   *slight*
1370 I will him sore smyte,
          & let God doe his will!
      I beseech God almight

>   That I may soe with him fight
>   That g[i]ant for to kill.'
>
> 1375 Then they rode forth all 3
>   Unto that faire cytye,
>   Men call itt Ile Dore;
>   Anon Maugy can they see
>   Upon a bridge of tree, — *wood*
> 1380   As grimm as any bore.
>
>   His sheild was blake as ter,*
>   His paytrill & his crouper,
>   3 maum[m]etts therein were,
>   The[y] were gaylye gilt with gold; — *brightly*
> 1385 & a spere in his hand he did hold
>   & alsoe his sword in fere. — *as well*
>
>   He cryed to him in despite — *scorn*
>   & said, 'Ffellow I thee quite!* — *defy*
>   Now what thou art mee tell,
> 1390 & turne againe alsoe tyte, — *And go back as quickly as possible*
>   Ffor thine owne proffitt, — *good*
>   If thou love thy selfe well.'
>
>   Sir Lybius said, anon-right, — *immediately*
>   'King Arthur made me a Knight.
> 1395   Unto him I made my vow
>   That I shold never turne my backe
>   Ffor noe such devill in blacke.
>   Goe make thee readye now!'
>
>   Now Sir Lybius & Maugys
> 1400 O[n] horsses proud of price — *excellent*
>   Together they rode full right.
>   Both Lords & Ladyes there
>   Lay on pount tornere*
>   To see that seemlye sight, — *pleasing*
> 1405 & prayed to God, loud & still,
>   If that itt were His will,
>   To helpe that Cristyan knight;
>   & the vile Gyaunt
>   That beleeveth in Termagant*
> 1410   That he might dye in fight.
>
>   Theire speres brake assunder,
>   Their stroakes fared as the [th]under, — *were like*
>   The peeces gan out spring.

	Every man had great wonder	
1415	That Sir Lybius had not beene under	*down*
	Att the first begininge.	*From the very*
	Anon they drew sords bothe,	
	As men that were full wrothe	
	Together gan they dinge.	*struck blows*
1420	Sir Lybius smote Maugyes thoe	
	That his sheild fell him froe –	
	In the feild he gan itt fling.	*hurl*
	Maugyes gan smite in that stead	*there*
	Sir Lybius horse on the head	
1425	& dashed out his braine;	
	His horsse fell downe dyinge.	
	Sir Lybius sayd nothing,	
	But start up againe.	*leaped*
	An axe in his hand he hent anon	*seized promptly*
1430	That hunge on his sadle arson,	*saddlebow*
	& smote a stroake of maine	*might*
	Through Maugis horsse swire,	*neck*
	Carved him throug[h] long and liver,*	*lung*
	& quitt him well againe.	*paid him back*
1435	Descrive the stroakes cold no man	
	That were given betwene them then –	
	To bedd peace was no boote thoe!	*It was useless to ask for a truce!*
	Deepe wounds there they caught,	
	Ffor they both sore fought,	
1440	& either was other's foe.	*each of them*
	Ffro the hower of prime*	
	Till itt was evensong time	
	They fought together thoe.	
	Sir Lybius thirsted then sore	
1445	& sayd, 'Maugyes, thine ore!	*mercy*
	To drinke lett me goe,	
	'& I will grant to thee	
	What love thou biddest mee,	*favour, ask*
	Such happe if thee betyde.	*chance*
1450	Great shame itt wold bee	
	A Knight for thirst shold dye,	
	& to thee litle pryde.'	*honour*
	Maugies granted him his will	
	Ffor to drinke his fill,	
1455	Without any more despite.	*opposition*
	As Sir Lybius lay over the banke,	

Through his helme he dranke;
   Maugyes gan him smite

That into the river he goes.
1460 But up anon he rose;
   Wonderffull he was dight,*   *bit*
With his armour every deale!
'Now by Saint Micaheel,
   I am twise as light!   *nimble*
1465 What, weenest thow, feend fere,*
That I unchristened were?
   Or thou saw itt with sight?   *Before*
I shall, for thy baptise,   p. 337/f. 166v
Well qu[i]tte thee thy service,   *repay*
1470   By the grace of God almight!'
A new battell there began.
Either fast to other ran   *Each of them*
   & stroakes gave with might.

There was many a gentleman
1475 And alsoe Ladyes as white as swan,
   They prayed all for the Knight!

But Maugis anon in the feild
Carved assunder Sir Lybius' sheild,   *Cut to pieces*
   With stroakes of armes great.
1480 Then Sir Lybius rann away,
Thither where Maugis' sheild Lay,
   & up he can itt gett,   *lifted*

& ran againe to hi[m].
With stroakes great and grim,
1485   Together they did assayle,   *attacked*
There beside the watter brim[m]e,   *edge*
Till itt waxed wonderous dimm,   *dark*
   Betweene them lasted that battell.
Sir Lybius was warryour wight,   *valiant*
1490 & smote a stroke of much might
   Through hawberke, plate, and maile.
Hee smote of by the shoolder bone
His right ar[me] soone and anon,   *promptly*
   Into the feild without faile.

1495 When the gyant that gan see,
That he shold slaine bee,
   Hee fled with much maine.   *vigorously*
Sir Lybius after him gan hye,   *rushed*

& wit&h strong stroakes mightye
1500   Smote his backe in twaine.
Thus was the Gyant dead.
Sir Lybius smote of his head,
      Then was the people faine.   *delighted*
Sir Lybius bare the head to the towne;
1505 The[y] mett him with a faire procession,
      The people came him againe.   *towards*

A Ladye white as the Lyllye flower,
Hight Madam de Armoroure,*   *Called*
      Received that gentle Knight,
1510 & thanked him, in that stoure,   *combat*
That hee wold her succour
      Against that feend to fight.

Into the chamber shee him ledd
& in purple & pall shee him cledd,   *dressed*
1515   & in rich royall weede;   *clothing*
& proffered him, with honor,
Ffor to be lord of towne & tower
      & her owne selfe, to meede.   *as a reward*

Sir Lybius frened her in hast,*   *courted*
1520 & love to her anon he cast,
      Ffor shee was faire & sheene.   *bright*
Alas, that hee had not beene chast!
Ffor afterwards, att the Last,
      Shee did him betray & teene.   *harm*

1525 12 monthes and more
Sir Lybius tarryed thore,
      & his mayden with renowne,*
That he might never outscape   *escape*
Ffor to helpe & for to wrake   *avenge*
1530   The Ladye of Sinadone.

Ffor that faire Lady
[C]old more of Sorcery   *Knew; about*
      Then such other five;
Shee made him great melodye
1535 Of all manner of minstrelsye
      That any man cold discreeve.   *imagine*
When he looked on her face
Him thought, certainlye, that hee was
      In paradice alive,

1540	With fantasye and fayrye –	*With illusions and enchantment*
	& shee bleared his eye	*deluded him*
	With false sorcerye.	
	Till itt beffell, upon a day,	
	He mett with Ellen *that* may	
1545	Betwene the Castle & the tower.	*Between the castle walls and keep*

7ᵈ parte

	Then unto him shee gan say,	p. 338/f. 167r
	'Thou art false of thy fay	*faith*
	Unto King Arthur!	
	Ffor the love of that Ladye	
1550	That can soe much curtesye*	
	Thou doest thee dishonor!	
	My Ladye of Sinadon	
	May long lye in prison,	
	& *tha*t is great dolour.'	
1555	Sir Lybius hard her speake –	
	Him thought his hart wold breake	
	Ffor sorrow & for shame.	
	Att a posterne there beside	*rear gateway*
	By night they gan out ryde	
1560	Ffrom *tha*t gentle dame.	
	Hee tooke with him his good steede,	
	His sheeld & his best weede,	*armour*
	& rode forth all in same;	*together*
	& the steward, stout in fere,	*bold companion*
1565	He made him his Squier,*	
	Sir Geffelett was his name.	
	They rode forth on their way	
	But lightly on their Journey,	*easily*
	On bay horsses and browne,	
1570	Till itt beffell upon a day	
	They saw a Citye faire and gay,	
	Men call itt Sinadowne,	
	With a Castle hye & wyde,	
	And pavillyons of much pride	
1575	*Tha*t were of faire fashyon.	*splendidly made*
	Then said Sir Lybius,	
	'I have great wonder of an use'	*custom*
	*Tha*t he saw in the towne.	

	They gathered dirt & mire full fast	*sewage*
1580	Which beffore was out cast,	*discharged*
	They gathered in, iwis.	*truly*
	Sir Lybius said in hast,	
	'Tell me now, mayd chast,	
	What betokeneth this?	*means*
1585	They take in all their hore	*filth*
	That was cast out beffore –	
	Methinke they doe amisse!'	
	Then sayd Mayd Ellen,	
	'Sir Lybius, without Leasing,	*falsehood*
1590	I will tell thee why itt is.	
	'There is no K[night] soe well arrayed,*	*finely dressed*
	Tho he had before payd,	
	That there shold take ostell,	*lodging*
	Ffor a dread of a steward	
1595	That men call Sir Lamberd;	
	He is the Constable of the Castle.	*chief officer*
	But ride into the Castle gate	
	& aske thine inne theratt,	*lodging*
	Both faire and well,	
1600	And or he bidd thee nede,*	
	Justing he will thee bedd,	
	By God & by Saint Michaell!	
	'& if he beare thee downe	
	His trumpetts shal be bowne	*trumpeters; ready*
1605	Their beaugles for to blow.	
	Then over all this towne,	
	Both mayd & garsowne	*serving boy*
	But dirt on thee shall throwe,	
	&, but thou thither wend,	*turn away from there*
1610	Unto thy live's end	
	Cowarde thou shalt be know,	
	& soe may King Arthur	
	Losse all his great honor	
	For thy deeds slowe.'	*tardy*
1615	Sir Lybius sayd, 'That were despite!	*would be humiliating*
	Thither I will goe full tyte,	*immediately*
	If I be man on live!	
	Ffor to doe Arthur's delight	*pleasure*
	& to make that Lady quite*	*avenge*
1620	To him I will drive.	*hasten*

	Sir Geffelett make the ready	
	& lett us now goe hastilye,	
	Anon *tha*t wee were bowne.'	*At once; ready*
	They rode forth on their gate	*way*
1625	Till they ca[m]e to the Castle gate,	
	That was of g[r]eat renowne,	p. 339/f. 167v
	& there they asked Ostell,	*lodging*
	In *tha*t faire Castell,	
	Ffor a venturous knight.	*Questing*
1630	The porter faire & well,	
	Lett them in full snell,	*quickly*
	& asked anon right,	*at once*
	'Who is yo*u*r governor?'	*lord*
	They sayd, ' King Arthur,	
1635	A man of much might.	
	To be a king he is worthye,	
	He is the flower of Chivalrye,	
	His fone to fell in fight.'	*enemies*
	The porter went, without fable,	*truly*
1640	To his lord the Constable,	
	& this tale him told:	
	'S*i*r, w*i*thout any fable,	
	Of Arthur's Round Table	
	Be comen 2 knights bold.	
1645	The one is armed full sure	*securely*
	W*i*th rich & royall armoure,	
	With 3 Lyons of gold.'	
	The lo*rd* was gladd & blythe,	
	& said to them, full swythe,	*at once*
1650	Just with them hee wold.	
	'Bidd them make them yare	*ready*
	Into the feeld forto fare,	
	W*i*thout the Castle gate.'	*Outside*
	The porter wold not stent,	*linger*
1655	But even anon went	*directly*
	To them lightlye att the yate,	*swiftly*
	& sayd, anon-rightes,	
	'Yee adventurous knights,	
	Ffor nothing *tha*t yee Lett!	*hold back*
1660	Looke yo*u*r sheelds be good & strong,	
	& your speres good and long,	
	Sheild, plate & Basnett,	

	'& ryde you into the feild.	
	My Lord, with speare and sheild,	
1665	Anon with you will play.'	joust
	Sir Lybius spake words bold	
	& said, 'This tale is well told	
	& pleasant to my pay!'	liking
	Into the feld the[y] rode	
1670	& boldlye there abode	
	In their best array.	gear
	S[ir] Lamberd armed full weele	
	Both in Iron and in steele	
	That was both stout & gay.	tough; shining
1675	His sheeld was sure & fine,	strong; splendid
	3 bores' heads was therin,	
	As blacke as brond brent;	charcoal
	The bordure was of rich armin –	
	There was none soe quent a ginn	elegant; device
1680	From Carlile into Kent –	
	& of the same paynture	decoration
	Was his paytrell & his armoure.	(horse's) breast plate
	In lande where ever he went,	
	2 squiers with him did ryde	
1685	& bore 3 speares by his side	
	To deale with doughtye dint.	blow
	Then that stout stewered	
	That hight Sir Lamberd	
	Armed him full well & bright,	quickly
1690	& rode into the feild ward.	towards the field
	Ffeircely as any Libbard,	leopard
	There abode him that knight.	Where
	Him tooke a speare of great shape;	massive
	He thought he came to Late,	
1695	When he him saw with sight!	
	Soone he rode to him that stond	time
	With a speare that was round,	
	As a man of much might.	
	Either smote on other's shield	Each (of them)
1700	That the peeces fell in the feild	
	Of theire speares long;	
	Every man to other tolde,	
	'That younge Knight is full bold.'	
	To him with a speare he flounge.	Rushed

1705	Sir Lamberd did stifflye ssitt;	*firmly*
	He was wrath out of his witt	*frenzied*
	Ffor Ire and for teene,	p. 340/f. 168r *wrath*
	& sayd, 'Bring me a speare,	
	Ffor this Knight is not to Lere,	*needs no teaching*
1710	Soone itt shal be seene!'	
	Then they tooke shaftes round	
	With crownalls sharpe ground,	*lance-heads*
	& fast together did run.	
	Either proved other in that stond	*Each strove; time*
1715	To give either there death's wound,	
	With harts as feirce as any Lyon.	
	Lamberd smote Sir Lybius thoe	
	That his sheeld fell him froe	
	Into the feild a-downe;	
1720	Sir Lamberd him soe hitt	
	That unnethes hee might sett	*hardly; sit*
	Upright in his arsow[n]e,	*saddle*
	His shaft brake with great power.	
	Sir Lybius hitt him on the visor,	
1725	That of went his helme bright.	*So that*
	The pesanye, ventayle & gorgere*	
	With the helme flew forth in fere,	*together*
	& Sir Lamberd upright	*leaning backwards*
	Sate rocki[n]g in his sadle,	
1730	As a chyld in a cradle,	
	Without maine & might.	*any strength*
	Every man tooke other by the lappe,*	
	& laughed and gan their hands clappe,	
	Barron, Burgesse and Knight.	
1735	Sir Lamberd, he thought to sitt bett.	*more firmly*
	Another helme he made to fett	*had brought*
	& a shaft full meete,	*suitable*
	& when they together mett	
	Either other on their helmes sett	*brought down*
1740	Strokes grim & great.	
	Then Sir Lamberd's speare brast,	*shattered*
	& Sir Lybius sate soe fast	
	In the saddle there hee sett,	
	That the Constable Sir Lamberd	

1745	Ffell of his horsse backwerd,	
	Soe sore they there mett!	*painfully*
	Sir Lamberd was ashamed sore.	
	Sir Lybius asked if he wold more.	*wanted*
	He answered and said, 'Nay!	
1750	Ffor sithe that ever I was bore	*since, born*
	Saw I never here beffore	
	None ryde soe to my pay!	*liking*
	By the faith that I am in,	
	Thou art come of Sir Gawayine's kin,*	
1755	Thou art soe stout and gay.	
	If thou wilt fight for my ladye	
	Welcome thou art to mee,	
	By my troth I say!'	*faith*
	Sir Lybius sayd, 'Sikerlye,	*Truly*
1760	I will fight for my Ladye,	
	I promised soe to King Arthur;	
	But I ne wott how ne why	*don't know*
	Who does her that villanye,	
	Ne what is her dolor;	
1765	But this maid that is her mesenger	
	Certes has brought me here,	*Indeed*
	Her for to succour.'	
	Sir Lamberd said in that stond,	*then*
	'Welcome, Sir Knight of the Table Round,	
1770	Into my strong tower!'	
	Then mayd Ellen anon-rightes	*at once*
	Was feitched forth with 5 Knights	
	Beffore Sir Lamberd.	
	Shee & the dwarffe bydeene	*together*
1775	Told of 6 battells keene	*bitter*
	That he had done thitherward.	*on the way there*
	The[y] sayd that Sir Lybius then	
	Had fought with strong men	
	& beene in stowers hardye.	*fierce combats*
1780	Then they were glad & blythe	*cheerful*
	& thanked God alsoe s[w]ithe	*at once*
	That he were soe mightye.	
	They welcomed him with mild cheere,	
	& sett them to supper	
1785	With much mirth and game.	
	Sir Lybius & Sir Lamberd in fere	*together*

	Of ancyents *tha*t beffore were	*knights of old*
	Talked both i[n] same.	*together*
	*Si*r Lybius sayd, 'W*i*thout fable,	p. 341/f. 168v *Truly*
1790	Tell me now, *Si*r Constable,	
	What is the K*nigh*t's name	
	*Tha*t hath put in prison	
	My Ladye of Sinadon,	
	*Tha*t is soe gentle a dame?'	
1795	*Si*r Lamberd said, 'Soe mote I gone,	*may live*
	K*nigh*ts there beene none	
	*Tha*t dare her away Lead.	
	2 clarkes beene her fone,	*scholars; enemies*
	Ffull false in body & in bone,	
1800	*Tha*t hath done this deede.	
	They be men of Masterye	*great learning*
	Their artes for to reade of Sorcerye;	*to speak of*
	Mabam the[y] hight one in deede,	*is called*
	& Iron hight the other, verelye,	
1805	Cla[r]ckes of Nigromancye,	*Students; black magic*
	Of them wee have great dread!	
	'This Mabam & Irowne	
	Have made in the towne*	
	A palace of quent gin;	*cunningly contrived*
1810	There is no Erle ne barron	
	*Tha*t has hart as Lyon	
	That dare come therin.	
	Itt is all of the faierye	*enchantment*
	Wrought by Nigromancye,	
1815	*Tha*t wonder it is to winne.	*That makes it most difficult to conquer*
	There they keepe in prison	
	My Ladye of Sinadowne,	
	*Tha*t is of K*nigh*t's kinn.	*family*
	'Oftentimes wee [hear] her crye,	
1820	Ffor to see her w*i*th eye,	
	Therto we have no might!	
	This Mabam & Iron, trulye,	
	Had sworene to death, trulye,	
	Her death for to dight,	*bring about*
1825	But if shee grant until	*Unless; agree*
	Ffor to do Mabam's will	
	& give him all her right	*that is hers*
	Of all *tha*t Dukedome fayre	

Therof is my ladye heyre,
1830   *Tha*t is soe much off might.

'Shee is soe meeke & soe faire,
Therfore wee be in dispayre
    Ffor the dolour that shee's in.'
Then sayd S*i*r Lybius,
1835 'Through the helpe of Jesus,
    That Ladye I will winne,   *rescue*

'& Mabam & Iron,
Smite of, there anon,   *at once*
    Theire heads in *tha*t stoure,   *fight*
1840 & wine that Lady bright,
& bring her to her right
    W*i*th joy & much honor.'

Then there was no more tales to tell
In *tha*t strong Castle.
1845   To supp & make good cheere,   *[But] to*
The Barrons & urgesse all
Came to *tha*t seemlye hall   *splendid*
    Ffor to listen and heare

How S*i*r Lybius had wrought,
1850 & if the K*nigh*t were ought,   *valiant*
    His talking for to harke.
They found them sitting in fere,
Talking att their supper,
    Of K*nigh*ts stout and starke.   *bold; strong*

1855 & after, they went to rest,
& tooke their likei[n]g as them list,   *pleasure; wished*
    In *tha*t Castell all night.

8*ᵈ* parte

On the morrow, anon-right,   *at once*
S*i*r Lybius was armed bright;
1860   Ffresh he was to fight.

S*i*r Lamberd led him algate   *all the way*
Right unto the Castle yate,   *As far as*
    Open they were full right.
No man durst him neere bringe,   *closer*
1865 Fforsooth w*i*thout Leasing,   *falsehood*
    Barron, Burgess ne K*nigh*t,   *freeman*

	But turned home againe:	
	Sir Gefflett, his owne swaine	*squire*
	Wold with him ryde,	
1870	But Sir Lybius, for certaine,	
	Sayd he shold backe agai[n]e	p. 342/f. 169r *must*
	And att home abyde;	
	Sir Gefflett againe gan ryde	*back*
	With Sir Lamberd for to abyde,	*remain*
1875	& to Jesu Christ they cryed	
	Ffor to send them tydings gladd	
	Of them *tha*t long had	
	Destroyed their welthes wyde.	*possessions*
	Sir Lybius, Knight curteous,	
1880	Rode into *tha*t proud palace	
	& att the hall he light.	*dismounted*
	Trumpetts, hornes & shaumes, ywis,	*pipes*
	He found beffore the hye dese;	*dais*
	He heard & saw with sight	
1885	A fayre fyer there was, stout & stowre,	*full; fierce*
	In the midds of the flore,	
	Brening faire and bright.	*Blazing*
	Then further in hee yeed	*went*
	& tooke with him his steede	
1890	*Tha*t helped him to fight.	
	Ffurthermore he began to passe	*Further in*
	& beheld then everye place	
	All about the hall;	
	Of nothing, more ne lesse,	
1895	He saw no body *tha*t there was	
	But minstrells cladde in pall:	*fine cloth*
	With harpe, fidle and [r]ote,*	
	And alsoe with Organ note,	
	Great mirth they made all;	
1900	And alsoe fiddle and sautrye.*	*psaltery*
	Soe much of minstrelsye	
	Ne sa[w] he never in hall.	
	Before every man stood	
	A torch fayre and good,	
1905	Brening full bright.	
	Sir Lybius Evermore yode	*kept on going*
	Ffor to witt, with Egar mood,	*bold spirit*
	Who shold with him fight.	
	Hee went into all the corners	

LIBIUS DISCONIUS 311

1910 & beheld the pillars
 [That seemelye] were to sight,
Of Jasper fine & Cristall;
All was flourished in the hall –   *adorned*
 Itt was full faire and bright.

1915 The dores were all of brasse,
& the windowes of faire glasse,
 [With] ymagyrye itt was drive.   *Filled with pictures (of stained glass)*
The hall well painted was,
Noe fairer in noe place,
1920 Marvelous for to descrive.

Hee sett him on the hye dese,
Then the minstrells were in peace   *stopped playing*
 That made the mirth soe gay;
The torches that were soe bright
1925 Were quenched anon-right,   *went out suddenly*
 & the minstrells were all away.

The dores & the windowes all
The[y] bett together in the hall   *slammed*
 As itt were strokes of thunder!
1930 The stones in the Castle wall
About him downe gan fall –
 Thereof he had great wonder.
The earth began to quake
& the dese for to shake
1935 That was him there unnder;   *underneath*
The hall began for to breake
And soe did the wall eke,   *as well*
 As they shold fall assunder.   *in pieces*

As he sate thus dismayd,
1940 He held himselfe betrayd.
 Then horses heard hee nay.
To himselfe then he sayd,
'Now I am the better apayd,   *pleased*
 For yett I hope to play!'   *fight*
1945 Hee looked forth into the feild,*
Saw there, with speare and sheild
 Men of armes tway   *two*
In purple & pale armoure,*
Well harnished, in that stoure,   *adorned*
1950 With great garlands gay.   *bright*

	The one came ryding into the hall	p. 343/f. 169v
	& to him thus gan call,	
	'Sir K*nigh*t adventurous!	
	Such a case there is befall,	*situation*
1955	Tho thou bee proude in pall	*finely dressed*
	Ffight thou must w*i*th us!	

'I hold thee quent of ginne   *very cunning*
If thou my Ladye wi[nn]e
    *Tha*t is in prison.'
1960 S*i*r Lybius sayd, anon-right,
    'All fresh I am for to fight,
        W*i*th the helpe of Godde's sonne!'

S*i*r Lybyus, w*i*th good hert,   *boldly*
Ffast into the saddle he start.   *leaped*
1965   In his hand a speare he hent,   *gripped*
& feircly he rode him till   *towards*
His enemyes for to spill,   *destroy*
    Ffor *tha*t was his entent.
But when they had together mett
1970 Either on other's helme sett   *Each*
    W*i*th speares doughtye dent.   *blow*
Mabam his speare all to-brast,   *shattered*
Then was Mabam evill agast,   *terrified*
    & held him shameffully shent.   *dishonoured*

1975 & with *tha*t stroke felowne   *deadly*
S*i*r Lybius bare him downe   *knocked*
    Over his horsse tayle,
Ffor Mabam's saddle arsowne   *bow*
Brake therewith and fell downe
1980   Into the feild, w*i*thout fayle.
Well nye he had him slone,   *killed*
But then came ryding Iron
    In a good hawberke of mayle;
All fresh he was to fight,
1985 & thought he wold, anon-right,   *at once*
    S*i*r Lybius assayle.

S*i*r Lybius was of him ware   *saw him*
& speare unto him bare
    & left his brother still.
1990 Such a stroke he gave hime thore
    *Tha*t his hauberke all to-tore;   *tore in pieces*
    That liked him full ill!   *pleased*
Their speares brake in 2 –

Libius Disconius

	Swords gan they draw tho	
1995	W*i*th hart grim and grill,	*angry*
	& stifflye gan to other fight;	*boldly*
	Either on Other proved their might	*Each*
	Eche other for to spill.	*destroy*
	Then together gan they hew.	
2000	Mabam, the more shrew,	*greater villain*
	Up he rose againe.	
	He heard, & alsoe knew	*realized*
	Iron gave strokes few;	
	Therof he was not faine;	*happy*
2005	But to him he went full right	*directly*
	Ffor to helpe Iron to fight	
	And avenge him on his enemye.	
	Tho he were never soe wroth,	
	S*i*r Lybius fought against them both	
2010	And kept himselfe manlye.	*defended*
	When Mabam saw Iron*	
	He fought as a Lyon	
	The k*nigh*t to slay w*i*th wreake.	*in revenge*
	Beffore his farder arsowne,*	*front saddle bow*
2015	Soone he carved then downe	*Promptly*
	S*i*r Lybius steed's necke.	
	S*i*r Lybius was a worthy warryour	
	& smote a 2 his t[h]ye in that stoure,	*in two*
	Skine, bone and blood.	
2020	Then helped him not his clergye,	*learning*
	Neither his false Sorcerye,	*Nor*
	But downe he fell w*i*th sorry moode.	*heart*
	S*i*r Lybius of his horsse alight	
	W*i*th Mabam for to fight,	
2025	In the feild both in fere.	*together*
	Strong stroakes they gave w*i*th might,	
	Tha*t* spa[r]keles sprang out full bright	
	Ffrom helme and harnesse cleere	*shining*
	As either fast on other bett,	*struck*
2030	Both their swords mett,	
	As yee may now heare.	p.344/f. 170r
	Mabam, *that* was the more shrew,	
	The sword of S*i*r Lybius he did hew	
	In 2 quite and cleare.	*cleanly*

2035	Then Sir Lybius was ashamed	
	& in his hart evi[l] agramed,	*fiercely angry*
	Ffor he had Lost his sword,	
	& his steed was lamed,	
	& he shold be defamed	
2040	To King Arthur his lord.	
	To Iron lithelye he ran	*nimbly*
	& hent up his sword then,	*lifted*
	That sharpe [e]dge had & hard,	
	& ran to Mabam right	
2045	& fast on him gan fight,	*vigorously*
	& like a madman he fared.	*acted*
	But ever then fought Mabam	
	As he had beene a wyld man,	
	Sir Lybius for to sloe.	
2050	But Sir Lybius carved downe	
	His sheild with that fawchowne	*(curved) sword*
	That he tooke Iron froe.	
	True tale for to be told,	
	The left hand with the sheild,	
2055	Away he smote thoe.	
	Then sayd Mabam him till,	*to him*
	'Sir, thy stroakes beene ill!	*deadly*
	Gentle Knight now hoe!	*stop!*
	'& I will yeeld me to thee,	
2060	In love and in Loyaltye,	
	Att thine owne will,	*On; terms*
	& alsoe that Lady free,	
	That is in my posstee,	*power*
	Take her I will thee till.	*Give; to you*
2065	Ff[o]r through that sh[r]ueed dint	*evil blow*
	My hand I have tint –	*lost*
	The veinim will me spill!	*destroy*
	Fforsooth, without othe,	*Truly I admit*
	I venomed them both,	
2070	Our enemyes for to kill.'	
	Sir Lybius sayd, 'By my thrifft,	*fortune*
	I will not have of thy gift	
	Ffor all this world to w[i]nn!	
	Therfore lay on stroakes swythe!	*At once*
2075	The one shall cut the other blythe	*speedily*
	The head of by the Chi[n]!'	

Libius Disconius

	Then *Si*r Lybius and Mabam	
	Ffought together fast then,	
	& lett for nothing againe,	*left off*
2080	*Tha*t *Si*r Lybius, *tha*t good K*nigh*t,	
	Carved his helme downe right	
	& his head in twayne.	

9ᵈ parte

	Now is Mabam slaine,	
	& to Irom he went againe	
2085	W*i*th sword drawne to fight;	
	Ffor to have Cloven his braine,	*split*
	I tell you for certaine,	
	He went to him full right;	

	But when he came there,	
2090	Away he was bore,	*carried*
	Into what place he [n]ist.	*knew not where*

	He sought him, for the nones,	*indeed*
	Wyde in many woones;	*places*
	To fight more him List.	*He wanted to*

2095	As he stood & him bethought	*considered*
	*Tha*t itt wold be deere bought	
	That he was from him fare,	*had got away*
	Ffor he wold w*i*th sorcerye	
	Doe much torment[r]ye,	
2100	& *tha*t was much care.	

	He tooke his sword hastilye,	
	& rode upon a hill hye,	
	& looked round about.	
	Then he was ware of [a] valley;	*caught sight of*
2105	Thitherward he tooke the way	
	As a sterne K*nigh*t and stout.	

	As he rode by a river side,	
	He was ware of him *tha*t tyde	[*Iron*]; *then*
	Upon the river brimm.	*bank*
2110	He rode to him full hot	p. 345/f. 170v
	& of his head he smote,	
	Ffast by the Chinn,	*Right*

  & when he had him slaine,
  Ffast hee tooke the way againe
2115   For to have *tha*t lady gent.
  As soone as he did thither come,
  Of his horsse he light downe
    And into the hall hee went

  & sought *tha*t ladye faire and hend,   *gracious*
2120 But he cold her not find,
    Therfor he sighed full sore.
  Still he sate mourni[n]g   *motionless*
  Ffor *tha*t Ladye faire & young;
   For her was all his care;
2125 He ne wist what he doe might,   *didn't know*
  But still he sate & sore he sight,   *sighed*
   Of Joy hee was full bare.   *bereft*

  But as he sate in *tha*t hall
  He heard a window in the wall,
2130   Ffaire itt gan unheld;   *opened*
  Great [wonder] there withall
  In his hart gan fall.
   As he sate & beheld,

  A worme out gan pace   *dragon; came*
2135 W*i*th a woman's face,
   *Tha*t was younge & nothing old.   *not at all*
  The worme's tayle & her winges
  Shone fayre in all thinges,   *every way*
   & gay for to beholde.

2140 Grislye great was her taile,   *Horribly*
  The clawes large w*i*thout fayle;
   Lothelye was her bodye.
  S*i*r Lybius swett for heate
  There sate in his seate,
2145   As all had beene affire him by. *As if everything near him were ablaze*

  Then was S*i*r Lybius evill agast   *terrified*
  & thought his body wold brast.   *burst*
   Then shee neighed him nere,   *drew closer to*
  &, or S*i*r Lybius itt wist,   *before; knew*
2150 The worme w*i*th mouth him Kist
   & colled about his lyre.   *wound; body*

Libius Disconius

&, after that kissing,
The worme's tayle and her wing
   Ffell away her froe; — *from*
2155 She was faire in all thing,
A woman without Leasing — *truly*
   Fairer he saw never or thoe. — *before that*
Shee stood upp alsoe naked — *as*
As Christ had her shaped. — *created*
2160   Then was Sir Lybius woe!
Shee sayd, 'God that on the rood gan bleed, — *cross*
Sir knight, quitt thee thy meede, — *give; reward*
   Ffor thou my fone wold sloe. — *enemies*

'Thou hast slaine now, full right,
2165 2 clarkes wicked of might
   That wrought by the feende. — *worked*
East, west, north, and south,
They were masters of their mouth; — *at casting spells*
   Many a man they have shend. — *destroyed*

2170 'Through their inchantment
To a worme the[y] had me meant,*
   [In] woe to wrapp me in,
Till I had k[i]ssed Sir Gawaine,
That is a noble Knight certaine,
2175   Or some man of his kinn.

Ffor thou hast saved my liffe,
Castles 50 a[n]d five
   Take to thee I will, — *Bestow upon*
& my selfe to be thy wiffe,
2180 Right without striffe, — *dispute*
   If itt be your will.'

Then was he glad & blythe — *joyful*
& thanked God often sythe — *many times*
   That him that grace had sent — p. 346/f. 171ʳ
2185 & sayd, 'My L[adye] faire & free,
All my love I leave with thee,
   By God omnipotent!

I will goe, my Lady bright,
To the castle gate full right, — *directly*
2190   Thither for to wend,
Ffor to feitch your geere — *clothes*
That yee were wont to weare,
   & them I will you send.

'Alsoe, if itt be yo*ur* will,
2195 I pray you to abyde still
  Till I co[m]e againe.'   *return*
'S*ir*,' shee said, 'I you pray,
Wend forth on your way,
  Therof I am faine.'   *glad*

2200 S*ir* Lybius to the castle rode
There the people him abode.
  To Jesu Chr[i]st gan they crye,
Ffor to send them tydings glad
Of them *that* Long had
2205   Done them tormentrye.
S*ir* Lybius is to the Castle come,
& to S*ir* Lamberd he told anon,
  And alsoe the Barronye,
How S*ir* Mabam was slaine,
2210 & S*ir* Iron, both twayine,
  By the helpe of mild Marye.

When *that* K*nigh*t soe keene   *bold*
Had told how itt had beene,
  To them all bydeene,   *together*
2215 A rich robe good & fine,
Well furred w*i*th good Ermine,
  He sent *that* Ladye sheene;   *bright*

Kerchers and garlands rich   *circlets*
He sent to her priviliche:
2220   *That* mayd he wold home bring.

& when shee was readye dight   *made ready*
Thither they went, anon-right,
  Both old and young,

& all the folke of Sinadowne,
2225 W*i*th a faire procession
  The Ladye home they fett.   *escorted*
& when they were come to towne,
Of p*re*cyous gold a rich crowne
  There on her head the[y] sett.

2230 They were glad and blythe
& thanked God often sithe,
  That from woe them had brought.
All the Lor*ds* of dignitye

	Did him homage and fealtye,
2235	As of right they ought.
	They dwelled 7 dayes in the tower There *Sir* Lamberd was governor, W*i*th mirth, joy and game; & then they rode w*i*th honor
2240	Unto King Arthur, The knights all in same. ffins

Explanatory Notes

36	Percy sees in this action 'marks of [the hero's] courage' (*Reliques*, III, xiii), but in the medieval texts the knight is already dead when Lybius finds him. This would have given additional point to the dwarf's later taunt: 'Dead men *tha*t lyen on the ground/Of thee affrayd may bee!' (227–28).
83	*in ernest & in game* represents a word-pattern common in this romance: see, for example, 1027, 'lesse & more', and 1405, 'loud & still'.
93	In two English Arthurian romances the griffin was associated with Gawaine's coat of arms – i.e., *The Awntyrs off Arthure* (508–9) and the alliterative *Morte Arthure* (3869) – which may explain the award of this particular shield to Libius Disconius. For other devices associated with Gawaine, see Gerard J. Brault, *Early Blazon: Heraldic Terminology in the Twelfth and Thirteenth Centuries with Special Reference to Arthurian Heraldry* (Woodbridge: Boydell, 1997), pp. 38–43. However, at line 1647, Libius' coat of arms is described as '3 lyons of gold', a device that would have resonated with a medieval audience ('it is a highly plausible conjecture that Henry [II] bore one or more lions on his shield and that the tinctures were those which became firmly established in the Royal Arms of England (*gules, three leopards or*) with King Richard I' (Brault, 1997, 21)). William de la Braunche's device also comprises three lions – 326, *C* 284 and *L* 307 – but on a green background.
129	Percy's letter to Lord Hailes of 8 September 1763 implies that at the time Percy construed Chaucer's reference to 'Libeaux and Blaindamore' as meaning two separate people. At the time of publication of the *Reliques* in 1765, it would seem that this interpretation was still in his mind: 'As for *Blandamoure*, no Romance with this title has been discovered; but as the word occurs in that of *Libeaux*, 'tis possible Chaucer's memory deceived him' (*Reliques*, III, xviii). His extensive annotations in the MS of *LD* at this point indicate, however, that at a later date he considered the possibility that Chaucer was deliberately confusing the proper name 'Blandamore' with the noun 'Blaundemere': 'This word comes in so oddly, that I c[oul]d almost be tempted to think that Chaucer in his burlesque Romance of Sir Thopas might allude to it sportively … But after all perhaps this construction is too forced'.
132	Although found in all the texts, 'distere' (a steed fit for a knight) is less appropriate for Hellen than 'palffrey' (*OED palfrey*, a horse for ordinary riding … *esp. a small saddle horse for a woman*, n). That the hero's horse is called a palfrey at 620, as opposed to the 'destrer' may be the result of the need to rhyme with the preceding line.
133–56	It is odd that the dwarf is described in such detail, while Libius has to make do with a mere nine lines (13–21). Compare the lengthy description of the relatively obscure Sir Ironside in *CARLE*, 37–60. (See *CARLE* Explanatory Notes 37 ff. and 55, which point out that Ironside's heraldic device of a griffin hints at a confusion in sources between this knight and Gawaine.)
138	In *C* 126 the dwarf wears a surcoat that is 'overt', i.e., open. 'Of greene' suggests a misreading of 'overt' as 'o(f) vert', possibly as a result of an aural transmission error.

149	A crowde was an instrument of Celtic origin resembling a violin, with between three and six strings; the 'sowtrye' was a kind of dulcimer, played by plucking the strings.
163	'A desperate situation is at hand'.
166	*Lady* is the title given to this character throughout, and 'dukedome' the word applied to her territory at 1828.
175	'It was agreed that I should be given that combat'.
198	*Sir, verament* is not to be found in any of the earlier texts, but it appears in the account given of the opening scenes of the story found in Copland's *The Squyr of Lowe Degre* of *c.*1560 (line 629), itself based upon a text printed by Wynkyn de Worde *c.*1520. This supports the case made for the existence of an early print of *LD*. Copland's print and *LD* are reproduced as 'The Squire of Low Degree' in Erik Kooper (ed.), *Sentimental and Humorous Romances* (Kalamazoo, MI: Medieval Institute Publications, 2006), pp. 127–79.
224	While it might make more sense here for Hellen to refer to 'thy' sword, as opposed to 'my' sword, P's gloss – i.e., that Hellen is mocking Libius – is surely right. Note also her reference to the 14-year-old's 'beard' at 223.
230	'I recommend you go back to be suckled by your mother': the insult as to the hero's youthful inexperience is clear.
310–12	'He will swiftly pierce through heart and haunch all those who ride against him' (*MED launchen*, to pierce … wound (with a spear); strike … slash (with a sword); cut off … thrust, penetrate, v,1). Cf. line 386.
378	P's marginal comment 'am I' fits better than the MS reading.
386	The sense is that William aggressively attacks Libius, the slash of his sword being powerful enough to hack off a part of Libius' shield.
389	P at this point suggested 'stounde' instead of 'sonde', defining it as perhaps 'time, moment, space', and this reading is supported by *C* 347. HF retained 'sonde', glossing it as 'message', a plausibly ironic use of the word (*MED sonde*, message, communication, n,2(a)).
424	'Sir William acknowledged him on bended knee'.
438	If 'array' is meant, the sense would be that they rode to Sir William in the 'disposition of men in martial order, a display of military force' (*OED array*, n,2). However, at this point, *C* 396 and *L* 416 have 'de-ray' and 'deraye' respectively, i.e., 'impetuosity, ferocity, violence in battle' (*MED deraie*, n,1(c)).
543	A falchion is a sword with a curved blade.
545	A basinet is a close-fitting helmet worn under a much larger helm.
606	This line refers back to 602; i.e., their temporary shelter was well made.
629	*MED* notes that 'barme' can mean 'lap', and 'in (on) barme' 'at (one's) bosom or in (someone's) arms' (*barm*, n,1(a, b)). The sense seems to be that the giant is clutching the maid closely to his chest.
680	*cowletree* is an obsolete form of 'cowl-staff', i.e., 'a stout stick used to carry a "cowl", being thrust through the two handles of it; a pole or staff used to carry burdens, supported on the shoulders of two bearers … a familiar household requisite, and a ready weapon' (*OED cowl-staff*, n(a). *OED cowl*, a tub or similar large vessel for water, n,2a). The spit used by the giant to roast a boar is even longer than such a staff.
695	Having broken the spit in two, the giant retains one half to use as a truncheon.
723	Only in PF is the girl's father named Sir Arthore at this point; in *C* 660 and *L* 690 the Earl is called 'Antore' and 'Anctour' respectively. Presumably the source used by the PF scribe either consciously or unconsciously used the more familiar name of 'Arthur' at this point.
727	None of the senses given for 'demeaning' in *OED* and *MED* seems appropriate here. P's observation that the word probably meant 'going a walking' is probably closest to the intention.
779	The prize is similarly described at 793, 844, 857, and 882, but as a jerffaucon (i.e., gyrfalcon) at 977, 1029, and 1036. The former spelling is found throughout the Ashmole manuscript. Kaluza (1890, xxxvi) interpreted this to mean that the author of an earlier

	form of PF had moved from one exemplar to another between 882 and 977. See also Percy's note to line 929.
802	'Fraudeus' as an epithet for Giffron here, and at 823 and 967, is found only in PF. Like the reference to his 'subtulle wile' at 810, it goes with his ability to 'beguile' opponents (802–4). Giffron gives no proof of such cunning in the joust itself.
856	*browne*: *MED broun*, dark, dull, adj.1(a). The sense seems to be not so much brown in colour, but a play by Libius on his words at line 839. Libius invites a comparison between Gyffron's lemman, and his own companion.
861	*yondertyde*: although written as one word in the MS, the sense is surely that of 'yonder tide'– i.e., that place (*MED yonder*, over there, adv.,(a), plus *MED tide*, time, n,(a)) – in place of 'undertide' (morning) in the medieval texts. Sir Geffron readily agrees to Libius' proposal of 850–58.
864	*Cardigan*: Cardigan is not usually associated with the king in Arthurian legend. A more likely location is Carlisle (*L* 830, 'Cardyle'). *C* 813 and 990 has 'Karlof' and 'Cardelof', i.e., Cardiff.
928	The unexpected 'his head upon' corresponds to 'redy boun' ('quite ready') in other texts. However, a simpler explanation is that either the scribe or the source had 'hand' instead of 'head' in mind; i.e., the sense then would be, 'The other bore upon his hand/A gentle gyrfalcon'.
983	*crownackles*: lance-heads with spreading points: the singular form 'crownall' – *OED coronal*, n,3 – is found at line 993. Coronals were particularly used in jousting, where the spreading points would maximize impact at the cost of penetration.
989	*desoures*: would normally mean 'story-tellers' (*OED disour*, n). Here it could denote officials recording the blows struck in the combat (*MED descriven*, to give a verbal or written account, v,1,3).
1005	*ren[d]owne*: the MS 'renowne', i.e., 'distinction' is not impossible, but HF were surely right to prefer 'ren[d]owne', i.e., *MED randoun*, n., 'with great speed or violence'. See line 357 and *MER*, 1820.
1074	The Wirral was a favourite refuge for outlaws, described as a 'wyldrenesse' in *SGGK*, 701.
1096	*sterke*: possibly an attempt to make sense of 'stirke', itself a mistranscription of 'strike', i.e., 'run swiftly' (*MED striken*, v,11).
1134	Otes is outraged at being called a churl (*MED cherl*, a commoner; hence 'cherlish', a boor, a base fellow), retorting hotly that his mother was a Countess. Lines 1153–59 indicate that this insult, and the kidnapping of his hound, has angered him greatly.
1164	Medieval variants of the story have Lancelot's name here, as opposed to Gawaine. While it is possible that the change of name was prompted by the need to rhyme with 1161, the change was surely made in mind with Gawaine's reputation as a particularly English hero, as well as being the father of Libius himself.
1184	*wawe*: *C* and *L* at this point (1112, 1138) read 'schawe' (*OED shaw*, a thicket, small wood, copse or grove; a strip of wood or underwood forming the border of a field, n,1(a, b)). The sense seems to be that Libius advises Ellen to make for the edge of the wood and seek cover.
1192–93	*crossebowes*: translates the 'arblaste' (i.e., arbalest) of the medieval texts. The reference to spears and 'bowes Turkoys' is unique to PF. Turkish bows were renowned for their long range and ability to inflict devastating injuries, particularly at close quarter, hence 1194. (See Adam Karpowicz, 'Ottoman Bows: An Assessment of Draw Weight, Performance and Tactical Use', *Antiquity* 81 (2007), pp. 675–85.) The attribution of the bows to Turks would have added a certain exotic frisson to the narrative (see Lawton, 2003, 173–94).
1213	*In a sweate*: rather than attacking Libius in a state of perspiration, the text is likely to be a mistranscription of 'off sewte (i.e., 'in livery'), as in *C* 1141 and *L* 1167.
1247	'To pierce his padded jacket' (*OED acton*, padded jacket or jerkin worn under armour for protection, n).
1264–65	'He would have killed him, had the lord not yielded'.
1319	'Saw many worthy adventures'. While the modern meaning of 'vile' features at line 1408, *C* 1223 at this point speaks of 'aventurus fyle'. *MED*'s adjectival *fele* (excellent, worthy, proper, good) or possibly 'fele' implying diversity in numbers, would suit the context here.

1360   The ell was of variable length, but in England was usually of 45 inches (114 cm).

1381–83   P provides his own gloss to *ter*, but it is possible that the phrase is simply 'black as tar': *C* and *L* both call the shield as black as pitch (1273, 1335); *paytrill*: is a piece of armour designed to protect the chest of a horse; a *crouper* (crupper) is a strap attached to the rear of a saddle to prevent it sliding forward. Both pieces of equipment are here decorated with *maum[m]etts*, i.e. images of Mahomet, supposedly worshipped as a god by 'Saracens' such as Maugys. See also the note to line 1409.

1388   The usual meaning for *quite* ('pay back', 'reply to', 'punish') can hardly apply here, as Libius has not yet spoken or acted. However, at *C* 1280 and *L* 1342, Maugys calls Libius that fellow in 'white'. It is possible that PF's reading may ultimately derive from a northern dialectical form of this word.

1403   HF suggested that *pount tornere* might be the name of the bridge, but at this point *C* 1295 refers to 'pomet tours' (i.e., 'ornate towers'), while *C* and *L* both refer to lords and ladies who 'leyn out/laynen in' their towers. Whether a bridge or tower, the sense is of people leaning over a wall to watch the action.

1409   Termagant is a Saracen god; his association with Mahomet in medieval literature is noted by Percy in his endnote to 'King Estmere' (*Reliques*, I, 60).

1433   *throug[h] long and liver*: although possibly influenced by 653, having cut through the horse's neck, Libius achieves the anatomically challenging feat of continuing the blow through the animal's lung and heart. It is possible that the reading here derives ultimately from the phrase 'bon & lyre' (i.e., bone and flesh), present in *C* and *L* at this point.

1441   *hower of prime*: could be any time between 6 a.m. and 9 a.m.

1461–62   'He, like every bit of his armour, was in a fine state!'

1465–66   'What, you devil's companion, did you think that I had not been christened?'

1508   Rather than a name associated with the profession of armourer, a more likely explanation is to be found in the name assigned in *C* and *L*, i.e., 'la Dame d'Amour'.

1519   Although the spelling is unusual, *frened* can only mean 'sought her favour' (*MED frainen*, v,5).

1527   'And his mayden of renowne'.

1550   Rather than accuse the lady of an excess of 'curtesye', a more likely charge is that of sorcery (see line 1532), as happens at *C* 1442 and *L* 1504.

1565–66   There is a difference of status between Libius and Geffelett in that the latter is named as the knight's squire but assigned a knightly title too. Lamberd's porter seemingly refers to them as equals at 1644 and 1658.

1591–93   *payd*: unlikely to mean that money has changed hands. A more likely explanation is *MED paien*, to be pleased, content, or satisfied; be content or happy (to do sth), 2,a,ppl. In which case these lines can be glossed, 'There is no knight, so finely dressed, would lodge there, no matter how well disposed he was beforehand'.

1600–01   'And before he satisfies your need, he will ask you to joust with him'.

1619   This line suggests that Libius (not unnaturally) regards Lamberd as the oppressor of the Lady. Mabam and Iron, the real villains, are not identified as such (by Lamberd himself) until 1795–806.

1726   Respectively, armour attached to the helmet, extending over the neck and upper chest; chain mail for the lower face, neck, upper chest; armour protecting the throat.

1732   *lappe*: could mean a fold of cloth in any part of a garment, and *C* 1624 has 'hod', i.e., hood. The sense seems to be that people clutch at each other in their excitement.

1754   This is the first time that any character in the romance has guessed what the reader was told as early as line 8.

1808–9   Here *towne* must be the walled settlement adjoining the castle in which Lamberd entertains Libius. The proximity of the enchanters' palace to the latter is vividly conveyed at 1819–21.

1897   [r]*ote*: a kind of stringed instrument, 'with a soundboard, and either bowed or plucked' (*OED*, n,2).

1900   'psaltery': also a kind of stringed instrument, 'with a sounding board or box, similar to the dulcimer but played by plucking the strings with the fingers or a plectrum' (*OED*, n).

1945	*feild*: may mean either 'field of combat' or (more literally) the open country made visible by the collapse of the hall in lines 1930–38.
1948	*In purple & pale armoure*: *MED purple pal*, rich linen dyed purple; royal or imperial clothing, adj.(a). See also line 1955.
2011	It should be Iron seeing Mabam, as both *C* 1891 and *L* 1965 record.
2014–16	These lines, even more than the 'lamed' of 2038, make it odd that Libius should still be able to ride this horse at lines 2102 and 2200.
2171–72	P glossed *meant* as 'mingled, mixed', and while this is certainly possible, and could refer to the combination of human face on beastly body, more likely is the current meaning, i.e., intention (*OED mean*, to intend, v,1). At this point, *C* and *L* have respectively 'y-went' and 'went' (2027, 2104), i.e., changed or transformed. It is possible accordingly that the scribe unconsciously followed the initial letter of the preceding word – 'me' – when transcribing 'went'. The opening word of the next line in the MS – 'Ne' – makes no sense at all. *C* and *L* both commence their following lines with 'In' (2028, 2105). The meaning of these two lines in PF accordingly can be glossed, 'They intended me to become a dragon, in woe to wrap me in'.

Textual Notes

Percy's writing is rather faint at this point, and the MS has crumbled away at the edges. Where indistinct or missing, the following transcriptions are supplemented by those of HF.

P has written 'In Nine Parts' after the title. In the LH margin, opposite the title, there is:

> This Piece may be considered perhaps as one of the first rude Attempts towards the Epic or Narrative Poem in Europe since the Roman Times. Nor is it deffective in the most essential Parts of Epic Poetry: The Hero is one. The great action to which everything tends is one: there is little interruption of episode; & it [be]gins nearer the [Eve]nt than most [of that a]ge.

To the right of the opening line on the RH side: 'This appears to be more ancient than the Time of Chaucer. See The Rhyme of S*i*r Thopas quoted below, St. 22ᵈ. – N.B. The Rhyme of Sir Thopas seems to be intended in Imitation of this old Piece. – N.B. This is a Translation from *th*e French. [Vid. p. 327] st. 15.'

25	*Ffor*: '[And] for, i.e. because' [P].
26	*Beufise*: 'Beau-vise' [P].
30	*What hee hight*: 'what he was called; wh*a*t his Name was. See St. 11.' [P].
41	*swithe*: 'prompte, Jun.' [P].
45	*grett*: 'did greet' [P].
48	*par amoure*: 'par-amour or perhaps pour-amour. it is not here a compound word signifying <u>Mistress</u>; but is a Phrase equivalent to that [in] St. 14, lin. 3.' [P]: 'in' is missing from Percy's comment.
64	*home*: 'hame, idem' [P].
79	*thus*: thius [MS]; 'thus' [P].
80	*Lybius Disconius*: 'Le beaux Desconus, i.e. the fair unknown' [P].
96	*play*: HF thought that a final letter *a* had been obscured by a blot. The letter *e* seems more likely.
97	*a*: inserted above line, with caret.
98	[*a*]: the [MS]; 'Other boone or another boone or One other Dᵒ' [P].
107	*good*: followed by 'thing' deleted [MS].
125	*att device*: 'i.e. Will, Pleasure. See Chaucer. Gloss.' [P].
129	*Blaundemere*: written lengthwise by Percy, in the RH margin, extending upward to top of page: 'This word comes in so oddly, that I c[oul]d almost be tempted to think that Chaucer in his burlesque Romance of Sir Thopas might allude to it sportively, as thus: … Sir Libeaux and his [at this point P deleted and underlined the last word with four dots, inserting "(or his)" to the right] Blaundemere Scilʳ. the Blaundemere Furr mentioned in his Romance &c. — But after all [the next few words are scribbled out and unreadable]

perhaps this construction is too forced. N.B. It might be the other Version which Chaucer alludes to'. Percy continues his commentary, written mostly lengthwise in the LH margin, extending to opposite line 144: 'See Chaucer's Rhyme of Sir Thopas, where this word seems to be mistaken, viz.:

>Men speken of Romaunces of Pris,
>Of Hornechild and of Ipotis
>Of Bevis & Sir Gie
>Of Sir Libeaux and Blaindamoure
>But Sir Thopas bereth the flowre
>Of rich Chivalrie.'

132   *distere*: 'apud Chauc*er*. Destrer, a War-horse, or Led Horse. Vid Gloss' [P].
134   *Erm[i]ne*: Ermne [MS].
137   *fi[n]d*: fimd [MS].
138   *cercott*: 'Surcoat, A Gown & Hood of *the* same – an upper Coat, Ch. Gloss' [P].
140   *hang*: 'hung' [P].
142   *All*: 'als, also.' [P].
146   *[f]ame*: same [MS]; 'fame' [P].
151   *ribble*: 'ribble, a fiddle or guittern, Gl. Ch.' [P].
164   [*is*]: omitted [MS].
166   [*M*]*y*: ny [MS].
169   *you of*: 'of you' [P].
179   *saiest*: sayest [P].
189   *is shent*: 'are shent, i.e. disgraced' [P].
196   *Tho*: 'then' [P].
202   *Or*: 'i.e. before' [P].
211   *lerd*: 'lered, i.e. learned. See Ch. Gl.' [P].
213   *There*: 'Where – have been slaw, Qu.' [P].
215   *Other*: 'i.e. "either". So they still speak in Shropshire.' [P]
220   *made*: 'The Maid.' [P]; *snell*: 'snel, i.e. presently, immediately. See Gl. ad Ch.' [P].
224   *Abyid*: 'abyde' [P]; *my*: 'perhaps any: or perhaps she taunts him, as not a Match for a Woman' [P]
230   *souke*: 'souke, i.e. suck, Chauc.' [P].
235   [*I*]*f*: Lower part of these letters missing.
239   *d[r]inke*: dinke [MS].
248   *hole*: 'whole' [P].
250   [*o*]*f*: o [MS].
251   *flome*: 'i.e. River; Ital. fiume' [P].
252   *hight*: 'i.e. promised, engaged' [P].
256   *faine*: 'glad' [P].
263   *a[n]y*: one minim too few in the MS.
270   *griffon*: 'griffyne, qu.' [P].
288   *curteou[s]*: curteour [MS].
294   *Amen*: deleted word immediately preceding, most likely 'amen'. It is possible that the scribe felt that this word, concluding as it does the first part of the text, and given its spiritual status, should commence with an initial capital.
295   *2ᵈ parte*: text in LH margin, with curly bracket encompassing lines 295–303.
301   *Lorell*: 'Lewd, base fellow, Homo perditus Lye' [P]
308   *staunche*: 'stop, stay, resist' [P].
311   *Swithe*: 'soon' [P].
312   *All*: 'and all *that* – ride, qu.' [P].
319   *The[y]*: The [MS]. See also 488, 588, 593, 598, 812, 916, 951, 1012, 1015, 1099, 1160, 1189, 1192, 1211, 1219, 1384, 1505, 1669, 1777, 1803, 1928, 2171, 2229.
328   *ar[m]ed*: arned [MS].
335   *Certe[s]*: Certer [MS]; 'certes' [P].
342   *in fere*: 'together' [P].
353   *can*: 'con' [P].

354	*prest*: 'i.e. ready.' [P].
357	*randoun*: 'Apud. G. Doug. Randoun: The swift Course, Flight or Motion of any thing. Fr. randon, idem. Gl. G. D' [P].
360	*felon*: 'fel, felon, feloun, wicked, also cruel, fierce. Gl. Chauc.' [P].
370	*my*: my in [MS].
374	[*foot*] omitted [MS]; 'on [foot] I &c'. [P].
377	*love*: leave [MS]. See also 410. At 2186 the scribe correctly uses both words in the same line.
378	[*am I*]: I am [MS]; 'am I' [P].
383	*the*: they [MS].
385	*d*[*e*]: do [MS].
388	*cantell*: 'cantle, a Piece, a part. Gl. Ch.' [P].
389	*sonde*: 'Perhaps Stounde, time, moment, space' [P]
393	*Was*: 'as, qu.' [P].
396	MS: 'he' crossed out before 'Of' – most likely an eye-slip from the opening word of the preceding line.
401	*As*: 'That his, &c' [P].
402	*That many men*: 'As men, &c' [P].
405	*On live*: 'i.e., alive' [P]
410	[*love*]: leave [MS].
434	*Were*: where [MS]; *eme's*: 'eme, Uncle. See Jun. eame. See Gl. Ad Chauc. &c.' [P].
439	*Will*[*iam*]: Will [MS], followed by scribal deleted 'Who hath done to'; i.e., the scribe mistakenly carried on writing the following line.
450	*yarne*: 'yerne, inter al. nimble, Ch. Gl.' [P].
458	*in*: 'into' [MS].
468	*battell*: 'battayle' [P].
470	*Though*: 'Tho:' [MS].
490	*sawe*: 'saw' [P]. HF is surely correct in that the scribe originally wrote either 'say' or 'saye', and then overwrote the letter *w*.
497	[*n*]*ight*: might [MS].
501	*in same*: 'i.e. all together; it seems a contraction of the Fr. ensemble. See G. D. Gl. <u>alsame</u>, sub. verb, same' [P].
502	*As*: A [MS]; 'As, q.' [P].
516	*arsoone*: 'Fr. Arçon, a saddle bow. Per Meton. <u>Saddle</u>' [P].
524	[*h*]*is*: is [MS].
545	*basenett*: 'helmet or head-piece, Fr. D°. Galea' [P].
548	*felled*: 'felt' [P].
558	*Against*: 'gainst' [P].
572	*th*[*u*]*s*: this [MS].
581	*bandowne*: 'Fr. bandon, "A son bandon," i.e. at his will and Pleasure. Gl. G. Doug.' [P].
601	*eves*: 'eaves, Metaph. from a house building' [P]
602	[*& bower with*]: with bower & [MS].
616	*bost*: 'burst, report, like the discharge of a gun: It is still called <u>bost</u> in Shropsh.' [P].
619	*3^{d} part*: text in LH margin, with curly bracket encompassing lines 619–24.
620	Followed by deleted '& rode forth full fast' [MS]. The scribe mistakenly skipped a line and, on realizing his mistake, was forced to delete it.
624	[*Who*]: omitted from MS. P's comment 'Who' is faint but signalled by a caret at the opening of this line.
628	*h*[*i*]*s*: hus [MS]. As HF noted, there is a dot over the *u* of 'hus', suggesting that the scribe may have realized his error.
629	*barme*: 'Sinus, gremium' [P].
630	*bryar*: 'brere, so in Chauc.' [P].
635	*cryed*: 'cryed' [P]. The last letter in the MS overlaps with the downstroke of the opening letter of 'gan' in the line above. That, and the indistinct opening two letters to 'cryed' may have prompted Percy to include this gloss as an aide-memoire to the word in question.
641	*th*[*y*]: the [MS]; 'perhaps thy' [P].

644	*Ff*[*or*]: ffea [MS]; 'for' [P].
646	[*s*]*ame*: shame [MS]. The scribe most likely had the end of 644 in mind at this point; 'i.e. together, ensemble, Fr.' [P].
648	*grise*: 'id. ac grisly, horrid, horrible' [P].
653	*long*: 'lung' [P].
656	*thanke*[*d*]: thanke [MS]; *d* added by Percy.
659	*&* [*the dwarffe by*]*dene*: and by the dwarffe dene [MS]; 'and the Dwarf by-dene' [P]
661	*greaves*: 'i.e, Groves, Bushes. So in Chauc.' [P].
667	*thore*: 'i.e. there, metri gratiâ. so in Chauc.' [P].
672	*yode*: 'went' [P].
675	*spartle*: 'sparkle' [P].
676	*Feir*[*c*]*ely*: Feirely [MS].
707	*stond*: 'stound' [P].
723	*S*[*ir*]: S [MS].
724	*Vylett*: 'Vilett, Violette' [P].
726	[*y*]*ore*: ore [MS].
727	*on my demeaning*: 'probably going a walking, demener, the same as promener, qu.' [P].
728	*eveni*[*n*]*ge*: evenige [MS].
760	*4ᵈ parte*: text in LH margin, with curly bracket encompassing lines 760–65.
761	*starke*: 'i.e. strong' [P].
784	[*head*]: omitted [MS]; 'his [head] shall' [P].
788	*corner*: Percy has added an *e* to the end of this word.
795	*alsoe*: 'al soe' [P].
797	*bri*[*n*]*g*: One mimim too few in the MS.
798	[*by day or*] *night*: day or by night [MS]; 'by day or night, or del[et]e by' [P].
800	*Lybyus*: Lybyius [MS]. One minim too many after the second *u*.
812	*The*[*y*]: the [MS]; 'they' [P].
816	*Certe*[*s*]: Certer [MS].
819	[*Erle*]: King [MS]; 'sir Arthores, or K*nigh*t Ar[thor]es' [P].
838	[*sayst*]: hast [MS].
839	*Le*[*mm*]*an*: lennan [MS].
861	*yondertyde*: 'fortè ondertyde' [P].
868	*bli*[*nn*]: blim [MS].
883	*Forthy*: 'for thy, therefore, according to Gl. Ch. & G. D., here it should seem to be forthwith' [P].
884	*hardye*: 'hardye, qu.' [P].
887	*f*[*a*]*rest*: fforest [MS].
893	*grame*: 'i.e. grief, sorrow, vexation, anger; madness: trouble, affliction, Gl. ad Chauc.' [P].
898	*Kei*[*r*]*cheys*: Keicheys [MS]; 'Kercheffs, qu.' [P].
908	*On*: One [MS]; *right*: added by scribe in left hand margin, signalled by a caret [MS].
915	[*m*]*iddes*: niddes [MS].
918	*meanye*: 'attendants' [P].
921	*bordure*: 'bordure' [P].
924	*itt*: 'hee' [P].
925	*The*: 'Two' [P].
927	*stoure*: 'Idem ac sture, ingens, crassus, Lye' [P]. There are two-and-a half partly deleted lines to the right of this gloss, beginning 'idem stoure' and ending 'G. D. and Chaucer'. [P].
929	*Jolly fawcon*: 'I w*ou*ld read Ier-faucon. See St. 37 below' [P]. P is referring here to 973–78.
936	*gentle*: 'forte, gimp' [P].
960	*partye*: 'partye' [P]; 'This Line in a Parenthesis' [P].
962	*bryer*: 'brere' [P].
965	*Launderer*: 'i.e. Launderess, Laundress' [P].
969	*forlore*: 'lost' [P].
983	*crownackles*: 'This seems to be the same as Crownall, st. 40. both seem to signify the heads of *th*e spears' [P].

994	*fe[r]ley*: ffeley [MS].
995	*steke*: 'steke for stuck, rhithmi gratia' [P].
1005	*ren[d]owne*: renowne [MS].
1006	*smote*: smote [P].
1007	*ff* deleted after *fell* [MS].
1008	*againe*; 'I would read adowne. see below, st. 45' [P].
1019	*ga[n]*: gam [MS].
1029	*Gerffawcon*: Gerffaucon [MS]. One minim too few in the *w*.
1034	*borne*: 'borne' [P].
1037	*Chaudas*: 'There was one Chandos a herald, whose book is preserved in Worcester College Library, Oxon' [P].
1039	'He wrote, sic legerim'.[P]; *dead*: 'deed' [P].
1050	*falleth*: 'fitteth, qu.' [P].
1051	*ready prest*: 'ready, speedy' [P].
1060	*5ᵈ parte*: text in LH margin, with curly bracket encompassing lines 1060–68.
1063	*a throwe*: 'a short space, sed vid. infra, perhaps in a row' [P].
1065	*ho[u]nds*: hoinds [MS]; 'hounds' [P].
1066	*throwe*: 'a cast, a stroke. It. short space. Chauc. Gl.' [P].
1076	*ratch*: 'Ratches, Genus Canum: Bracones. Lye. Jun.' [P]; *run[n]inge*; runinge [MS].
1079	*the[ir]*: the [MS].
1086	*pay*: 'satisfaction, liking' [P].
1087	*ought*: 'owned, possest' [P].
1094	*[a]*: omitted [MS].
1096	*hind sterke*: 'stout Hind' [P].
1099	*Lind*: 'properly a Teil or Lime tree, but in these ballads it seems to be used for Trees in general' [P].
1105	*Inde*: 'i.e. azure or blue as used by Lydg. – black according to Sp. Gl. ad Ch. [P].
1115	*they*: the [MS].
1126	*hend*: 'gentle, kind' [P].
1134	*Churle*: 'Churle' [P].
1141	*[w]ere*: vere [MS].
1144	*reve*: 'bereave, take away' [P].
1150	'th' deleted after *right* [MS].
1152	*kend*: 'taught, made known. Gl. Ch.' [P].
1159	*I-nome*: 'y-nome, taken. Sax niman, to take, hinc nim. Lye' [P].
1160	*so[m]e*: sone [MS]; 'some' [P].
1161	*thee[ſ]e*: theese [MS].
1166	*gleaves*: 'gleave, a sword, cutlace, Fr. glaive' [P]; *gysarmes*: 'gysarme, a halbert or Bill. Sh' [P].
1184	*wawe*: 'wawe is used in Chaucer for a wave, but that can hardly be the sense here' [P].
1193	*bowes Turkoys*: 'i.e. longbowes. Fr Turquois, Turkish, such as the Turks use. Gl. ad G. D.' [P].
1200	*forfare*: 'perdere, perire. A.-S. forfaran, Lye' [P].
1206	*groomes*: 'men' [P].
1211	*the[y]*: the [MS].
1212	*s[l]ee*: see [MS].
1215	*the*: they [MS].
1220	*the[m]*: they [MS].
1224	*her[n]esse*: heriesse [MS]: one minim too few in the MS; 'harnayse' [P].
1231	*gave*: 'gan' [P]; *rive*: 'rive, To thrust, stab, to rend, &c. Gl. ad Ch.' [P].
1246	*abowne*: 'ready' [P].
1247	*Acton*: 'Fr. Hocqueton' [P].
1251	*Ki[n]de*: kimde [MS].
1263	*chest[en]*: chest of [MS]; 'a chesten tree, i.e. a Chesnut Tree. Sic legerim. vid. Gl. ad Chauc.' [P].
1267	*his stent*: 'his stint, apud Salopienses, signifies his measure, his quantity, his share [P].

1271	[*In*]: him [MS].
1294	[*that*]: a [MS].
1296	Lybyus: Lybyius [MS]. One minim too many after second *u*.
1315	*6ͩ parte:*: text in LH margin, with curly bracket encompassing lines 1315–23.
1319	*sa[w]e*: there appears to be an additional minim after the *w*. The stroke is unclear since it merges into the *y* of 'Lybius' above.
1323	*manner*. P adds an *e* at the end of this word.
1324	*midsu[mm]er*: midsuner [MS]. One minim too few, the scribe using an overbar on a letter *n* instead of an *m* at this point.
1326	*bryar*: 'briere' [P].
1332	*g[r]eat*: geat [MS].
1340	*rise*: 'sprig, twig, shrub, Jun. Lye' [P].
1355	*grimmer*: grimmner [MS]. Scribal π above this word.
1369	*lite*: 'lite, little.' [P].
1374	*g[i]ant*: grant [MS]; 'giant qu.' [P].
1381	*as ter*: 'perhaps as Aster, Haster, or Aster is a word still used in Shrops[hire] signifying the back of the chimney. "as black as the Haster" is a common Expression with the͞m' [P]. The last four letters of 'Shropshire' lost through cropping.
1382	*paytrill*: 'Poitrel, peytrel, antilena: The breast-armour for a horse. Jun.' [P].
1383	*maum[m]etts*: maumnnetts [MS], one minim too many in the MS.; 'Mammet, a puppet, an Image, a false god. Jun.' [P].
1387	2 deleted letters before *cryed* [MS].
1400	*O[n]*: of [MS] 'On Horses' [P].
1412	[*th*]*under*. 'thu' blotted [MS].
1430	*arson*: 'arçon. Fr. i.e. saddle bow' [P].
1432	*swire*: 'swire, swere, the neck. Gl. ad Ch.' [P].
1433	*throug[h]*: through [MS]; 'through lung' [P]; *liver*: P adds a final *e* to 'liver'.
1436	three letters blotted before 'were' [MS].
1437	'It was no boot then to bid [propose] peace' [P].
1465	*thow*: cf. lines 302 and 346. HF read this as 'thout', but it seems likely that on the final stroke of the *w* the scribe unintentionally ran up, then on into the opening 'ff' of the succeeding word; *fere*: some three letters blotted out before 'fere' – possibly an aborted attempt at the word [MS].
1466	*unchristened*: 'unchristened' [P].
1469	*qu[i]tte*: qutte [MS].
1483	*hi[m]*: hinn [MS]. One minim too many in the MS.
1486	*brim[m]e*: brimne [MS]. One minim too few in the MS.
1488	*battell*: 'battayle' [P].
1491	*hawberke*: 'coat of mail: <u>thro' plate & mail</u> is used both by Milton & Spencer.' [P].
1493	*ar[me]*: last two letters blotted [MS].
1495	*the gyant*: inserted in left-hand margin by scribe, signalled by a caret [MS].
1503	*faine*: 'glad' [P].
1519	*frened*: 'asked' [P]. Immediately above P initially wrote 'answered', and then struck through in favour of 'asked'.
1524	*betray & teene*: 'enrage, vex, grieve. Gl. ad G. D.' [P]. In left-hand margin: 'N.B. This does not appear from anything which follows in this Ballad: unless it be her detaining him by her enchantments in these stanzas' [P].
1526	*thore*: 'there: so in Chauc.' [P].
1529	*wrake*: 'wreak, i.e. revenge' [P].
1532	[*C*]*old*: Told [MS].
1546	*7ͩ parte*: text in LH margin, with curly bracket encompassing lines 1546–51.
1547	*fay*: 'faith' [P].
1577	*I have*: 'He had (or)' [P]; *use*: 'use' [P]. This latter word is unclear in the MS, P signalling the gloss not with his usual caret, but with the symbol ‡.
1578	*he saw*: 'I see' [P].
1585	*hore*: 'Sax. horh, fimus, scruta, phlegma. limus, Bens. Voc.' [P].

1591	K[night]: K: [MS]. The scribe uses this abbreviation elsewhere to indicate 'king' (e.g., 1761 and 2040), but 'Knight' is clearly preferable to HF's 'King'. The equivalent lines in C (1482) and L (1545) both have 'knight' at this point.
1593	ostell: 'Fr. hostel, hospitium, Domus' [P].
1604	trumpetts: 'Trumpetters' [P].
1605	beaugles: 'bugles, hunting horns. from bugle, a wild bull, Lye' [P].
1607	garsowne: 'Fr. Garçon, Boy' [P].
1625	ca[m]e: cane [MS].
1626	g[r]eat: geat [MS].
1651	yare: 'ready, Sax. Gearwe' [P].
1652	feeld: it appears that the scribe originally wrote the word 'castle', probably resulting from an eye skip to the following line. He then deleted the offending word, using the π symbol underneath to flag that the correct word was written in the LH margin.
1654	stent: 'stint, stop' [P].
1668	pay: 'liking' [P].
1672	S[ir]: 'S' [MS]
1677	brond brent: 'i.e. burnt brand' [P].
1679	quent: 'quent, queint' [P]; ginn: 'ginne, trick, contrivance' [P].
1707	teene: 'anger, madness, vexation' [P].
1721	unnethes: 'scarcely' [P].
1722	arsow[n]e: arsowme [MS]. One minim too many in the MS; 'saddle' [P].
1726	ventayle: 'ventail, The Part of the Helmet which lifts up. Johns. [P]; gorgere: 'id. ac Gorget. The Piece of Armour which defends the throat. Johns.' [P].
1729	rocki[n]g: rockimg [MS]. One minim too many in the MS.
1736	fett: 'fett, fetch' [P].
1744	the: they [MS].
1755	Thou: a letter at the end of this word has seemingly been blotted out. The scribe may have started to write 'thow'.
1781	s[w]ithe: sithe [MS].
1788	i[n]: im [MS]. One minim too many in the MS.
1805	Cla[r]ckes: Clackes [MS]; 'Clarkes' [P].
1809	quent: 'curious contrivance' [P].
1811	hart followed by blotted ha [MS].
1815	it: heavily blotted [MS].
1819	[hear]: omitted [MS].
1820	A blotted w after 'see' [MS].
1827	him: hiim. One minim too many in MS.
1838	of: followed by deleted anon [MS].
1843	Then: heavily smeared blot at end of word, with en written above line [MS].
1856	likei[n]g: likeng [MS]. One minim too few in MS.
1860	8ᵈ parte: text in LH margin, with curly bracket encompassing lines 1858–66.
1861	algate: 'at all events, by all means' [P].
1868	swaine: 'youth, servant. Jun.' [P].
1871	agai[n]e: agane [MS]. One minim too few in MS.
1875	they: 'sc. the People' [P].
1882	shaumes: 'Shaumes, a Psaltery; a Musical Instrument like a Harp. Chau. Gl.' [P]; ywis: y-wis [P].
1883	dese: 'Dese, Deis. The High table' [P].
1897	[r]ote: note [MS].
1900	sautrye: 'a Psaltery: vid. Supra' [P].
1902	sa[w]: say [MS]; 'saw' [P].
1906	yode: 'went' [P].
1907	witt: 'know' [P].
1911	[That seemelye] written at the end of 1910.
1912	Jasper: 'jasper' [P].
1917	[With]: that [MS].
1928	The[y] bett: 'They beat' [P].

1935	*there unnder*: 'there under' [P]. Although HF interpreted this as 'there vnner', the two words are conjoined by a bold downward stroke, possibly implying a *t*. The scribe may have thought he was writing 'thereto', then continued it into the opening letter *u*.
1946	*sheild*: sheiild [MS]. One minim too many in MS.
1956	*must*: in left margin; blotted 'might' in text [MS], scribe using the π symbol to flag that the correct word was written in the LH margin.
1957	*quent of ginne*: 'clever of contrivance' [P].
1958	*wi[nn]e*: wime [MS]. One minim too few in the MS.
1975	*stroke felowne*: 'felon stroke, i.e. a murderous stroke' [P].
1995	*grill*: 'idem ac grisly. Gl. ad Ch.' [P].
2000	*shrew*: 'shrew, apud Chaucer est, a Villaine; here it seems to signify shrewd, cunning, artful' [P].
2018	*t[h]ye*: conjoined before the letter *h* is the beginning of a previous attempt at the letter.
2019	*Ski[n]e*: skime [MS]. One minim too many in the MS.
2027	*spa[r]keles*: spaakeles [MS].
2029	*bett*: 'did beat' [P].
2036	*evi[l]*: evis [MS]; *agramed*: 'agramed, displeased, grieved, Gl. ad Chauc. rather (agramed) angered. A.-S.Gram. Furor. Lye.' [P].
2041	*lithelye*: 'lithely, gently (nimbly)' [P].
2043	*[e]dge*: eidge [MS].
2053	*told*: 'teld, <u>rhythmi gratiâ</u>' [P].
2058	*now hoe*: 'i.e. now stop' [P].
2063	*posstee*: 'posté, apud Chauc. est Power. Vid. Gl.' [P].
2065	*Ffor*: ffror [MS]; *sh[r]ueed*: shueed [MS].
2066	*tint*: 'lost' [P].
2073	*w[i]nn*: wnn [MS]. One minim too few in the MS.
2076	*Chin*: Chim [MS]. One minim too many in the MS.
2083	*9ᵃ parte*: text in LH margin, with curly bracket encompassing lines 2083–91.
2089	*there*: 'thore' [P].
2091	*[n]ist*: list [MS].
2092	*for the nones*: 'the nones, or nonce, on purpose; de industria. Jun. purposely' [P].
2093	*woones*: 'wone, a house, habitation' [P].
2099	*torment[r]ye*: tormenteye [MS].
2104	*[a]*: omitted [MS].
2117	*horsse*: beginning of *s* above *r* [MS].
2121	*sore*: 'sair. Scotice' [P].
2122	*mourni[n]g*: mournig [MS].
2131	*[wonder]*: omitted [MS]; 'fear or dread' [P].
2142	*Lothelye*: 'i.e. loathsome' [P].
2151	*lyre*: 'apud Scot. flesh. Apud Chauc. lere is the Complexion or Air of *the* face' [P]
2171	*meant*: 'this word signifies mingled, mixed, ap*u*d G. Doug. Chauc. &c' [P].
2172	*[In]*: 'ne' [MS].
2173	*k[i]ssed*: kssed [MS].
2176	*Ffor*: 'because' [P].
2177	*a[n]d*: amd [MS].
2183	*sythe*: 'Time – also since, afterwards, Gl. Chauc.' [P].
2185	*L[adye]*: Lord [MS], 'Ladye' [P] .
2196	*co[m]e*: cone [MS]. One minim too few in the MS.
2198	*on your way*: the scribe began to repeat 'I you pray' from the preceding line and got as far as 'I you p'. On realizing his mistake, he erroneously retained *I* and inserted 'on' above the line, added *r* above the line to 'you', and partly overwrote the *p* with 'way'.
2202	*Chr[i]st*: chrst [MS].
2208	*the Barronye*: 'i.e. The Barrons collectively' [P].
2219	*priviliche*: 'i.e. privily' [P].
2225	Blotted *th(e)* at head of line [MS].
2241	*ffins*: the scribe has written 'ffins' in a larger and thinner hand at the end of this line to signify the end of the piece.

Carle off Carlile

Gillian Rogers and John Withrington

The *Carle off Carlile* (*CARLE*) was most likely composed sometime between 1500 and 1550, and is uniquely preserved on ff. 223r–226v (pp. 448–55) of the PF. The dialect is that of the north/North Midlands, and is mostly written in four-stress couplets, derived ultimately from a tail-rhyme version.[1] Our witness for that is the northern romance, *Syre Gawene and the Carle of Carelyle* (*Carelyle*), preserved uniquely on ff. 12–26 of NLW MS Brogyntyn II.1 (formerly MS Porkington 10) of *c.*1470,[2] and containing 660 lines in a basic 12-line tail-rhyme stanza, rhyming *aabccbddbeeb*. The similarities between the two versions, both in terms of plot and shared lines, make it evident that both derive from a common original; that this was in tail-rhyme rather than in couplets is indicated by the fact that the *CARLE*-poet frequently takes a tail-rhyme line also present in *Carelyle* and invents a second line to make up his couplet. As Auvo Kurvinen points out, such lines do not contain new matter but consist of 'fillers' or padding.[3]

The tale is, in essence, an Imperious Host exemplum with additional features, in which the prospective guest is warned in advance about the dangers of lodging with the Host. He ignores the warning and is lavishly and hospitably entertained and comfortably lodged. In some versions he is offered his host's bed and his wife for the night, a motif known as Sex Hospitality.[4] Next morning, as he takes his leave, he remembers the warning and asks why he has not been beaten. His host replies that the visitor had the courtesy to allow him to be master in his own hall. This basic pattern is sometimes varied to include three guests, only one of whom escapes a beating.[5] A further adaptation is to include tests of the guests' courtesy and obedience, a situation particularly suited to the character of Gawaine, who, in these late Middle English romances, is the epitome of courtesy, seen as an active and positive virtue rather than a superficial politeness. The function of his courtesy, as the key to the resolution of the situation, is more strongly emphasized in *CARLE* than *Carelyle*, even in situations which run contrary to the very idea of the courtesy due from a guest to his host, most startlingly, perhaps, in the scene in which the Carle bids him 'of curtesye/Gett into this bed with this faire Ladye' (335–36), the lady in question being the Carle's wife, an injunction repeated later when Gawaine is ordered into bed with the Carle's daughter (353–54).[6]

The story follows the same pattern in both versions, although the order of certain episodes varies, and the motivation behind the Host's activities is radically different, the antagonist of *Carelyle* having sworn an oath to kill all visitors who do not obey his every command, and his *CARLE* counterpart being enchanted, like the Turk in *TG*, by 'nigromance' and requiring decapitation to disenchant him.

Gawaine himself is the hero of four of the many analogues, of which the Old French *Le Chevalier à l'épée* (written before 1210) and *Hunbaut* (written in the second half of the thirteenth century) are the best known, and in both of which his testing concerns the Host's daughter. In the former, which of all the analogues has the most in common with the *Carle*-poems, his host requires him to make love to his daughter and will brook no refusal, as a result of which Gawaine spends an uncomfortable night trying to avoid the attentions of a sword hanging above the pair's bed, riding off with her as his bride the following morning, having rejected the offer of gold and silver, and the host's castle. The sword is the means by which the host has killed more than 20 guests, seeking to find the best knight of the world. In *Hunbaut*, Gawaine, requested to kiss the host's daughter just once, kisses her four times, and is lucky to escape with his life. He does, however, spend the night with the daughter, who comes to him when all is quiet.[7]

A strong influence on both the *Carl* versions is the closely related tale-type, *The King and Beggar*, in which a person of humble rank entertains a stranger who is, unknown to him, a king, and teaches him a lesson in manners, that is, that a guest must allow his host to be 'lord of his own'; he must allow him to dictate what goes on in his own hall. In *CARLE*, this is a lesson that Gawaine does not need to be taught; he articulates the principle as early as line 126, before he has actually met the Carle. His variations on a related formula, expressing the guest's complete obedience to his host's every whim (302, 396), reinforce the message. Disenchantment by Decapitation, which has nothing to do with the Beheading Game as we see it in *SGGK* and *GK*, is not an essential part of an Imperious Host tale, and *Carelyle* works reasonably well as a modified example of such a tale, having its own internal logic of cause and effect, although the Carle, not being enchanted, does, of course, remain a grotesque giant at the end of it.[8] The introduction of the Disenchantment motif turns *CARLE* into a different kind of tale, much more akin to folk-tale than is *Carelyle*, but retaining exactly the same elements of the basic plot. In some ways it makes a more satisfactory denouement, seeming to exonerate the Carle from any blame for his actions, than does the renunciation of a vow made 20 years before. But of course the heaps of dead men's bones remain in both versions, to cast their shadow over the happy endings.[9]

The decapitation scene's resemblance to the similar scene in *TG* (268 ff.), however, strongly suggests that one of these borrowed from the other. The order of events in *CARLE* is very confused, giving rise to the suspicion that it is an interpolation, perhaps provoked by the poet's dissatisfaction at the idea of a vow being the Carle's motivation for all that killing.[10] In *TG*, as far as we can ascertain, the decapitation arises naturally, in a logical sequence; after the tests have been successfully accomplished and after the King of Man and all his giant minions have been disposed of, the Turk is free to ask Gawaine to perform this last act for him, the wished-for outcome of all his striving. It seems more likely that the *CARLE*-poet borrowed this from *TG*, written at approximately the same time, than that *TG*, eclectic as it is, borrowed from *CARLE*.

Contemporary and later audiences would surely have perceived this tale as burlesque: all the chief characters – Gawaine, Kay, Baldwin, and Arthur himself – are subjected to the autocratic, arbitrary behaviour of a grotesque mind-reading ogre-figure, who demands instant obedience to his every whim, and who exacts a swift revenge on those whose idea of the courtesy due to a host does not match up to his own. Kay and Baldwin come in for some particularly rough treatment. Arthur, whose only contribution to events is to call a hunt and to praise his host's feast, is commanded to enjoy himself, and even Gawaine, the perfectly courteous and obedient hero, is treated for the most part with tolerant contempt by his Imperious Host.[11]

Notes

[1] 'The earliest possible date of composition would be about 1500. Metrical and linguistic evidence shows, however, that part of the romance probably belongs to the ME period. This suggests that an older romance was rehandled about 1500, or in the course of the sixteenth century. The subject and its treatment favour a date before 1550 rather than after' (Auvo Kurvinen (ed.), *Sir Gawain and The Carl of Carlisle: In Two Versions* (Helsinki: Suomalaisen Tiedeakatemia, 1951), p. 63. Kurvinen provides an excellent discussion of *CARLE*'s language, versification, and vocabulary on pp. 55–63. See also Explanatory Note to line 269, below).

[2] See Daniel Huws, 'MS Porkington 10 and its Scribes', in Jennifer Fellows et al. (eds), *Romance Reading on the Book: Essays on Medieval Narrative Presented to Maldwyn Mills* (Cardiff: University of Wales Press, 1996), p. 202. See also Rhiannon Purdie, *Anglicising Romance: Tail-Rhyme and Genre in Medieval English Literature* (Cambridge: D. S. Brewer, 2008), pp. 187–89.

[3] Kurvinen, 1951, 64–70; see also Gillian Rogers, 'Folk Romance', *AE*, 197–224, 353n23. For example, *Carelyle*'s 3-line unit (43–45), listing the names of four more knights joining the hunt, ends with the tail-line 'The kny3t of armus grene'. *CARLE* retains that line but adds another to rhyme with it: 'And alsoe Sir Gawaine the sheene' (27–28). There are frequent non-rhymes, often the result of modernization: for example, 'there/more' (33–34).

[4] Stith Thompson, *Motif Index of Folk Literature: A Classification of Narrative Elements in Folktales, Ballads, Fables, Mediaeval Romances, Exempla, Fabliaux, Jest-Books and Local Legends*, 6 vols (Copenhagen: Rosenkilde and Bagger, 1955–57), 5, 373–74, T281: 'Host gives his wife (daughter) to his guest as bed companion'. For a summary of the many analogues to this situation, see Gillian Rogers, 'Themes and Variations: Studies in Some English Gawain-Poems', PhD thesis, University of Wales, 1978, 319 ff.

[5] As in Etienne de Bourbon's *De Tribus Militibus*, BL MS Add. 16589, f. 88, col. 2 (late thirteenth-century), given in full in George Lyman Kittredge, *A Study of Gawain and the Green Knight* (Cambridge, MA: Harvard University Press, 1916), pp. 271–72.

[6] The Carle locks them in with a silver key, thereby stressing the obligatory nature of this liaison (355–60).

[7] See *Le Chevalier à l'épée*, in R. C. Johnston and D. D. R. Owen (eds), *Two Old French Gauvain Romances: (Le Chevalier à l'épée & La Mule sans frein)* (Edinburgh: Scottish Academic Press, 1972) and M. Winters, *'The Romance of Hunbaut': An Arthurian Poem of the Thirteenth Century* (Leiden: E. J. Brill, 1984). The third analogue of which Gawaine is the hero is an anonymous Italian canzone, or morale, of the fourteenth century, while the fourth is an anonymous sixteenth-century Latin prose exemplum in BL Harleian MS 3938, f. 121, printed by Kittredge (1916, 96–97. See Rogers, 1978, 319–45, for a discussion of the Imperious Host topos).

[8] Grotesque giants with normal-sized beautiful daughters are by no means uncommon, however. In *Kulwych and Olwen*, for instance, Olwen's father is the giant Yspaddaden Pen Kawr. In the *Brut*

Tysilio and the BL MS Cotton Cleopatra B. V. version of the *Brut y Brenhinedd*, Guenevere is said to be the daughter of the giant Govran, or Ogvren.

[9] *Carleyle*'s version, which includes the vow to kill all who disobey the host, can be seen as an example of the 'Evil Custom of the Castle', which it is the hero's task to overthrow. The Carle's tirade against Arthur and his knights would then fit into place as part of the general hatred of his fellow men that inspired the vow. In *CARLE*, on the other hand, the Carle's vendetta against Arthur's knights highlights the absurdity of an enchanted person waging war against the very people upon whom he depends for his disenchantment (405–8), and further reinforces the idea that Disenchantment by Decapitation is an insertion into this essentially Imperious Host tale.

[10] Thus: (a) The Carle takes Gawaine to see the dead men's bones; (b) Gawaine goes to take his leave; (c) the Carle insists on dining first; and (d) only then does he ask Gawaine to behead him.

[11] Nonetheless, Gawaine fulfils his customary role in these English Gawaine-romances of reconciling good and evil by means of drawing his erstwhile opponents into the circle of the Round Table.

Editions

Hahn, 373–91.

HF, III, 275–94.

Kurvinen, Auvo (ed.), *Sir Gawain and The Carl of Carlisle: In Two Versions* (Helsinki: Suomalaisen Tiedeakatemia, 1951). A useful edition, with *Carelyle* and *CARLE* printed in parallel.

Madden, 256–74.

Further Reading

Brandsen, T., 'Sir Gawain and the Carl of Carlisle', *Neophilologus* 81 (1997), pp. 299–307.

Kittredge, George Lyman, *A Study of Gawain and the Green Knight* (Cambridge, MA: Harvard University Press, 1916).

Pollack, Sean, 'Border States: Parody, Sovereignty, and Hybrid Identity in *The Carl of Carlisle*', *Arthuriana* 19 (2009), pp. 10–26.

Ramsey, Lee, 'The Monstrous Churl and Other Arthurian Themes', in *Chivalric Romances: Popular Literature in Medieval England* (Bloomington: Indiana University Press, 1983), pp. 200–08.

Rogers, Gillian, 'Themes and Variations: Studies in Some English Gawain-Poems', PhD thesis, University of Wales, 1978.

—— , '*Syre Gawene and the Carle of Carelyle* and *The Carle off Carlile*', *AE*, 204–7.

Shimomura, Sachi, *Odd Bodies and Visible Ends in Medieval Literature* (Basingstoke: Palgrave Macmillan, 2006), pp. 72–84.

Thompson, Raymond H., '"Muse on Þi Mirrour …": The Challenge of the Outlandish Stranger in the English Arthurian Verse Romances', *Folklore* 87(2) (1976), pp. 201–8.

Carle off Carlile

		p. 448/f. 223r
	Listen to me a litle stond,	*for a little while*
	Yee shall heare of one *that* was sober & sound.	*prudent; strong*
	Hee was meeke as maid in bower,	
	Stiffe & strong in every stoure.	*valiant; battle*
5	Certes, w*i*thouten fable,	*truly*
	He was one of the Round Table.	
	The K*nigh*t's name was S*i*r Gawaine,	
	That much worshipp wan in Brittaine.	*honour won*
	The Ile of Brittaine called is*	
10	Both England & Scottand, Iwis.	*indeed*
	Wales is an angle to *that* Ile,	
	Where K*ing* Arthur sojorned a while,	
	W*i*th him 24 K*nigh*ts told,	*in all*
	Besids Barrons & dukes bold.	
15	The K*ing* to his Bishopp gan say,	*did say*
	'Wee will have a Masse today,	p. 449/f. 223v
	Bishopp Bodwim shall itt done.	
	After, to the f[or]rest wee will gone,	
	Ffor now itt's grass time of the yeere*,	*deer-hunting season*
20	Barrons bold shall breake the deere.'	*cut up*
	Ffaine theroff was S*i*r Marrocke,*	*pleased*
	Soe was S*i*r Kay, the K*nigh*t stout.	*arrogant*
	Ffaine was S*i*r Lancelott Dulake,	
	Soe was S*i*r Percivall, I undertake.	
25	Ffaine was S*i*r Ewaine,	
	& S*i*r Lott of Lothaine,	
	Soe was the K*nigh*t of armes greene,*	
	& alsoe S*i*r Gawaine the sheene.	*noble*
	S*i*r Gawaine was steward in Arthur's hall,*	
30	Hee was the curteous K*nigh*t amongst them all.	
	K*ing* Arthur & his Cozen Mordred,*	
	& other K*nigh*ts withouten Lett.	*truly, indeed*
	S*i*r Lybius Disconyus was there	
	W*i*th proud archers lesse & more.	
35	Blanch Faire & S*i*r Ironside,*	
	& many K*nigh*ts *that* day can ryde.	
	& Ironside, as I weene,*	*as I think*
	Gate the Knight of armour greene –	*fathered*
	Certes, as I understand –	
40	Of a faire Lady of Blaunch Land.	
	Hee cold more of honor in warr	*knew*
	Then all the K*nigh*ts *that* with Arthur weare.	*were*
	Burning dragons he slew in Land,	
	& wilde beasts, as I understand.	

45	Wilde beares he slew *that* stond,	*at that time*
	A hardyer K*nigh*t was never found.	
	He was called in his dayes	
	One of K*ing* Arthur's fellowes.	
	Why was hee called Ironsyde?	
50	Ffor ever armed wold hee ryde;	
	Hee wold allwais armes beare,	
	Ffor Gyants & hee were ever att warr.	
	Dapple-coulour was his steede,*	
	His armour and his other weede.	*garments*
55	Azure of gold he bare,*	
	With a Griffon lesse or more,	
	& a difference of a Molatt*	*five-pointed star*
	He bare in his crest Allgate.	*always*
	Wheresoever he went, East nor west,	
60	He nev*er* forsooke man nor beast.	
	Beagles keenely away the[y] ran,	*eagerly*
	The K*ing* followed affter w*i*th many a man.	
	The grayhounds out of the Leashe,	
	They drew downe the deere of grasse.	*fat deer*
65	Ffine tents in the feild were sett,	*pitched*
	A merry sort there were mett	
	Of comely k*nigh*ts of kind.	*knights noble by nature*
	Uppon the bent there can they lead,*	
	& by noone of the same day,	
70	A 100.ᵈ harts on the ground the[y] lay.	
	Then S*i*r Gawaine & S*i*r Kay,*	
	& Bishopp Bodwin, as I heard say,	
	After a redd deere the[y] rode,	
	Into a forrest wyde & brode.	
75	A thicke mist fell them among*	
	*Tha*t ca[u]sed them all to goe wronge.	
	Great moane made then S*i*r Kay	
	*Tha*t they shold loose the hart *tha*t day;	
	*Tha*t red hart wold not dwell.	*stay*
80	Hearken what adventures them beffell.	
	Ffull sore the[y] were adread	
	Ere the[y] any Lodginge had.	
	Then spake S*i*r Gawaine,	
	'This Labour wee have had in vaine.	
85	This red hart is out of sight,	
	Wee meete w*i*th him no more this night.	
	I reede wee of our horsses do light	*I advise; dismount*
	& lodge wee heere all this night.	
	Truly itt is best, as thinketh mee,	*p. 450/f. 224r*
90	To Lodge low under this tree.'	
	'Nay,' said Kay, 'goe wee hence anon,	

	Ffor I will lodge whersoere I come;	
	For there dare no man warne me	*deny me (entrance)*
	Of whatt estate soever hee bee.'	
95	'Yes,' said the Bishopp, '*tha*t wott I well.*	*know*
	Here dwelleth a Carle in a Castele,	
	The Carle of Carlile is his name,*	
	I know itt well, by St. Jame.	
	Was there ne*ve*r man yett soe bold	
100	*Tha*t durst lodge within his hold,	
	But & if hee scape w*i*th his liffe away,*	
	Hee ruleth him well, I you say.'	
	Then said Kay, 'All in fere*	*all together*
	To goe thither is my desire.	
105	Ffor & the Carle be never soe bolde,*	
	I thinke to lodge w*i*thin his hold,	
	Ffor if he jangle & make itt stout,	*argues; behaves violently*
	I shall beate the Carle all about,	
	& I shall make his bigging bare	*dwelling*
110	& doe to him mickle Care.	*much*
	& I shall beate [him], as I thinke,	
	Till he both sweate & stinke.'*	
	Then said the Bishopp, 'So mote I fare,	*as I hope to prosper*
	Att his bidding I wil be yare.'	*ready*
115	Gawaine said, 'Lett be thy bostlye fare,*	*boastful behaviour*
	Ffor thou dost ever waken care.	
	If thou scape w*i*th thy liffe away,	
	Thou ruleth thee well, I dare say.'	
	Then said Kay, '*Tha*t pleaseth mee.	
120	Thither Let us ryde all three.	
	Such as hee bakes, such shall hee brew;*	
	Such as hee shapes, such shall hee sew;	
	Such as he breweth, such shall he drinke.'	
	'*Tha*t is contrary,' said Gawaine, 'as I thinke,*	
125	But if any faire speeche will he gaine,	*win him over*
	Wee shall make him Lord w*i*thin his owne.	
	If noe faire speech will avayle,	
	Then to karp on Kay wee will not faile.'*	
	Then said the Bishopp, '*Tha*t senteth mee.	*I agree*
130	Thither lett us ryde all three.'	
	When they came to the Carle's gate,	
	A hammer they found hanging theratt.	
	Gawaine hent the hammer in his hand	*took hold of*
	And curteouslye on the gates dange.*	*knocked*
135	Fforth came the porter, with still fare,	*quietly*
	Saying, 'Who is soe bold to knocke there?'	
	Gawaine answered him curteouslye,	
	'Man,' hee said, 'that is I.	

	Wee be 2 Knights of Arthur's inn,*	
140	& a Bishopp, no moe to min.*	
	Wee have rydden all day in the forrest still,	*silent*
	Till horsse & man beene like to spill.	*perish*
	Ffor Arthur's sake, that is our Kinge,	
	Wee desire my Lord of a night's Lodginge*	
145	& harbarrow till the day att Morne,	*shelter*
	That wee may scape away without scorne.'	*escape; disgrace*
	Then spake the crabbed Knight, Sir Kay,	*ill-tempered*
	'Porter, our errand I reede the[e] say,	*advise you to*
	Or else the Castle gate wee shall breake	
150	& the Keyes thereof to Arthur take.'	
	The Porter sayd with words throe,*	
	'There's no man alive that dares doe soe!	
	[I]f a 100ᵈ such as thou his death had sworne,	
	Yett he wold ryde on hunting to-morne.'	
155	Then answered Gawai[n]e, that was curteous aye,*	
	'Porter, our errand I pray thee say.'	
	'Yes,' said the Porter, 'withouten fayle,	
	I shall say your errand full well.'	
	As soone as the Porter the Carle see,	
160	Hee kneeled downe upon his knee.	
	'Yonder beene 2 Knights of Arthur's in,	p. 451/f. 224v
	& a Bishopp, no more to myn.	
	They have roden all day in the forrest still	
	That horsse [&] man is like to spill.	
165	They desire you, for Arthir's sake, their King,	
	To grant them one night's Lodginge,	
	& herberrow till the day att Morne,	
	That they may scape away without scorne.'	
	'Noe thing gree[v]es me,' sayd the Carle, 'without doubt,*	
170	But that the Knights stand soe long without.'	*outside*
	With that, the Porter opened the gates wyde	
	& the Knights rode in that tyde.	*time*
	Their steeds into the stable are tane,	*taken*
	The Knights into the hall are gone.	
175	Heere the Carle sate in his chaire on hye	
	With his legg cast over the other knee.	
	His mouth was wyde & his beard was gray,	
	His lockes on his shoulders lay.	
	Betweene his browes, certaine,	
180	Itt was large there a spann,	*broad; hand-span*
	With 2 great eyen brening as fyer.	*burning*
	Lord, hee was a Lodlye syer!*	*loathsome, fearsome*
	Over his sholders he bare a bread*	*beard*
	3 taylor's yards, as clarkes doe reede.*	
185	His fingars were like to teddar-stakes,	*tethering-posts*

& his hands like breads *that* wives may bake.
50 Cubitts he was in height,*
Lo*rd*, he was a Lothesome wight!   *creature*
When S*ir* Gawaine *tha*t Carle see,
190   He halched him f[u]ll curteouslye,*   *greeted*
& saith, 'Carle of Ca[r]lile, God save thee,*
As thou sitteth in thy p*ro*speritye.'
The Carle said, 'As Christ me save,*
Yee shall be welcome for Arthur's sake.
195   Yet is itt not my p*ar*t to doe soe,
Ffor Arthur hath beene ever my foe.
He hath beaten my K*nigh*ts & done them bale,   *harm*
& sen[t] them wounded to my owne hall.
Yett, the truth to tell, I will not Leane,   *lie*
200   I have quitt him the same againe.'   *repaid*
'*Tha*t is a kind of a knave,' said Kay, 'w*i*thout Leasing,   *lying*
Soe to revile a Noble King.'
Gawaine heard & made answere,
'Kay, thou sayst more then meete weere.'   *fitting*
205   With *tha*t, they went further into the hall,*
Where bords were spredd & covered w*i*th pall,   *fine cloth*
& 4 welpes of great Ire
They found Lying by the fire.
There was a beare *tha*t did rome,   *roamed about*
210   & a bore *tha*t did whett his tushes fome;   *foaming tusks*
Alsoe a bull *tha*t did rore,
& a Lyon *tha*t did both gape & rore.*
The Lyon did both gape and gren.   *snarl*
'O peace, whelpes!' said the Carle then.
215   Ffor *tha*t word *tha*t the Carle did speake,
The 4 whelpes under the bord did creepe.
Downe came a Lady faire & free,*   *noble*
& sett her on the Carle's knee.
One whiles shee harped, another whiles song,
220   Both of Paramours & lovinge amonge.
'Well were *tha*t man,' said Gawaine, '*tha*t ere were borne,
That might Lye with *tha*t Lady till day att morne.'
'*Tha*t were great shame,' said the Carle free,
'*Tha*t thou sholdest doe me such villanye.'   *dishonour me so*
225   'S*ir*,' said Gawaine, 'I sayd nought.'
'No, man,' said the Carle, 'more thou thought.'
Then start Kay to the flore,*   *jumped up*
& said hee wold see how his palfrey fore.   *fared*
Both corne & hay he found Lyand,
230   & the Carle's palfrey by his steed did stand.
Kay tooke the Carle's palfrey by the necke,
& soone hee thrust him out att the hecke.*   *stable door*

	Thus Kay put the Carle's fole out,	
	& on his backe he sett a clout.	
235	Then the Carle himselfe hee stood there by,	
	And sayd, 'This buffett, man, thou shalt ab[u]y.'	*pay for*
	The Carle raught Kay such a rapp,	p. 452/f. 225r *dealt*
	Tha*t* backward he fell flatt.	
	Had itt not beene for a feald of straw,*	*bale*
240	Ka[y]e's backe had gone in 2.	
	Then said Kay, '& thow were w*i*thout thy hold,	*if; outside; castle*
	Man, this buffett sho*l*d be deere sold!'*	
	'What!' sayd the Carle, 'dost thou menace me?	
	I swere by all soules sicerlye,	*certainly*
245	Man, I swere further thore,	*with regard to this*
	If I heere any malice more,	
	Ffor this one word *tha*t thou hast spoken,	
	Itt is but ernest thou hast gotten.'	*a foretaste*
	Then went Kay into the hall,	
250	& the Bishopp to him can call,	
	Saith, 'Brother Kay, where you have beene?'	
	'To Looke my palfrey, as I weene.'	*see to*
	Then said the Bishopp, 'Itt falleth me	*it occurs to me*
	Tha*t* my palfrey I must see.'	
255	Both corne & hay he found Lyand,	
	& the Carle's palffrey, as I understand.	
	The Bishopp tooke the Carle's horsse by the necke,	
	& soone hee thrust him out att the hecke.	
	Thus he turned the Carle's fole out,	
260	& on his backe he sett a clout.	
	Sais, 'Wend forth fole, in the Devill's way!	*go*
	Who made thee soe bold w*i*th my palfrey?'	
	The Carle himselfe he stood thereby:	
	'Man, this buffett thou shalt abuy.'	
265	He hitt the Bishopp upon the crowne,	*head*
	Tha*t* his miter & he fell downe.	
	'Mercy!' said the Bishopp, 'I am a clarke!*	
	Somewhatt I can of Chr[i]st's werke.'	*know something of*
	He saith, 'By the Clergye I sett nothing,*	
270	Nor yett by thy Miter, nor by thy ringe!	
	It fitteth a clarke to be curteous & free,	*befits*
	By the con[n]ing of his clergy.'	*knowledge; (clerical) office*
	With *tha*t, the Bishopp went into the hall,	
	& S*ir* Gawaine to him can call,	
275	Saith, 'Brother Bishopp, where have you beene?'	
	'To looke my palfrey, as I weene.'	
	Then sayd S*ir* Gawaine, 'It falleth mee	
	Tha*t* my palfreye I must needs see.'	
	Corne & hay he found enoughe Lyand,	

280	& the Carle's fole by his did stand.	
	The Carle's fole had beene forth in the raine,*	
	Therof Sir Gawaine was not faine.	
	Hee tooke his mantle that was of greene	
	& covered the fole, as I weene,	
285	Sayth, 'Stand up fole, & eate thy meate,	
	Thy Master payeth for all that wee heere gett.'	
	The Carle himselfe stood there by,	
	& thanked him of his curtesye.*	
	The Carle tooke Gawaine by the hand	
290	& both together in the hall they wend.	
	The Carle called for a bowle of wine,	
	& soone they settled them to dine.	
	70 bowles in that bowle were,*	
	He was not weake that did itt beare.	
295	Then the Carle sett itt to his Chin,	
	& said, 'To you I will begin.'	
	15 gallons he dranke that tyde,	
	& raught to his men on every side.	*gave (the bowl)*
	Then the Carle said to them anon,	
300	'Sirrs, to supper gett you gone.'	
	Gawaine answered the Carle then,	
	'Sir, att your bidding wee will be ben.'*	
	'If you be bayne att my bidding,	
	You honor me, without Leasinge.'	
305	They washed all & went to meate,	
	& dranke the wine that was soe sweete.	
	The Carle said to Gawaine anon,*	
	'A long speare see thou take in thy hand,	
	Att the buttrye dore take thou thy race,*	
310	& marke me well in middest the face.'	*take aim at*
	'A', thought Sir Kay, 'that that were I,*	
	Then his buffett he shold deere a[b]uy!'	
	'Well' quoth the Carle, 'when thou wilt, thou may,	
	When thou wilt thy strenght assay.'	*try*
315	'Well Sir,' said Kay, 'I said nought.'	
	'Noe,' said the Carle, 'but more thou thought.'	p. 453/f. 225v
	Then Gawaine was full glad of that,	
	& a long spere in his hand he gatt,	
	Att the buttery dore he tooke his race	
320	& marked the Carle in the middst the face.	
	The Carle saw Sir Gawaine come in ire,	
	& cast his head under his speare.	*ducked his head*
	Gawaine raught the wall such a rapp,	*gave*
	The fyer flew out & the speare brake.	
325	He stroke a foote into the wall of stone,	
	A bolder Barron was there never none.	

	'Soft!' said the Carle, 'thow was to radd.'*	*Gently; too eager*
	'I did but, S*ir*, as you me bade.'	
	'If thou had hitt me as thou had ment,	
330	Thou had raught me a fell dint.'	*terrible blow*
	The Carle tooke Gawaine by the hand	
	& both into a Chamber they wend.	
	A full faire bed there was spred,	
	The Carle's wiffe therin was laid.	
335	The Carle said, 'Gawaine, of curtesye,*	
	Gett into this bedd w*i*th this faire Ladye.	
	Kisse thou her 3*se* before mine eye,	
	Looke thou doe no other villanye.'	
	The Carle opened the sheetes wyde,	
340	Gawaine gott in by the Ladye's syde.	
	Gawaine over her put his arme,	
	W*i*th *tha*t, his flesh began to warme.	
	Gawaine had thought to have made in fare:	*gone further*
	'Hold!' q*uo*th the Carle, 'man, stopp the[r]e!	
345	Itt were great shame,' q*uo*th the Carle, 'for me,	
	*Tha*t thou sholdest doe me such villanye.	
	But arise up, Gawaine, & goe w*i*th me,	
	I shall bring thee to a fairer Lady then ev*er* was shee.'	
	The Carle tooke Gawaine by the hand,*	
350	Both *in*to another Chamber they wend.	
	A faire bedd there found they spred,	
	& the Carle's daughter therin Laid.	
	Saith, 'Gawaine, now for thy curtesye,	
	Gett thee to bedd to this faire Lady.'	
355	The Carle opened the sheetes wyde,	
	S*i*r Gawaine gott in by the Ladye's side.	
	Gawaine put his arme over *tha*t sweet thing.	
	'Sleepe, daughter,' sais the Carle, 'on my blessing.'	
	The Carle turned his backe & went his way,	
360	& lockt the dore with a silver Kaye.	
	On the other morning when the Carle rose,	
	Unto his daughter's chamber he goes.	
	'Rise up, S*i*r Gawaine, & goe with mee,	
	A marvelous sight I shall lett thee see.'	
365	The Carle tooke him by the hand,	
	& both into another chamber they wend,	
	& there they found ma[n]y a bloody serke	*shirt*
	W*hi*ch were wrought with curyous werke.	*skilful workmanship*
	1500 dead men's bones	
370	They found upon a rooke att once.	*in a heap*
	'Alacke!', q*uo*th Sir Gawaine, 'what have beene here?'*	
	Saith, 'I & my welpes have slaine all there.'	
	Then S*i*r Gawaine, curteous & kind,	

CARLE OFF CARLILE

	He tooke his leave away to wend,	
375	& thanked the Carle & the Ladyes there,	
	Right as they worthy were.*	
	'Nay,' said the Carle, 'wee will first dine,	
	& then thou shalt goe w*i*th blessing mine.'	
	After dinner, the sooth to say,	
380	The Carle tooke Gawaine to a Chamber gay	
	Where were hanginge swords towe.	
	The Carle soone tooke one of tho,	*straightaway*
	& sayd to the K*nigh*t then,	
	'Gawaine, as thou art a man,	
385	Take this sword & stryke of my head.'	
	'Nay,' said Gawaine, 'I had rather be dead!	
	Ffor I had rather suffer pine & woe	*pain*
	Or ever I wold *that* deede doe.'	*Before ever*
	The Carle sayd to S*i*r Gawaine,	
390	'Looke thou doe as I thee saine,	*tell you*
	& therof be not adread,	
	But shortly smite of my head.	
	Ffor if thou wilt not doe itt tyte,*	*quickly*
	Ffor ssooth thy head I will of smyte!'	
395	To the Carle said S*i*r Gawaine,	p. 454/f. 226r
	'S*i*r, your bidding shall be done.'	
	He stroke the head the body froe,	
	& he stood up a man thoe	*then*
	Of the height of S*i*r Gawaine,	
400	The certaine soothe, w*i*thouten Laine.	*truth; lying*
	The Carle sayd, 'Gawaine, God blese thee,	
	Ffor thou hast deliv*er*ed mee!	
	Ffrom all false witchcrafft	
	I am deliv*er*d att the last.	
405	By Nigromance thus was I shapen*	
	Till a K*nigh*t of the Round Table	
	Had, w*i*th a sword, s[m]itten of my head,	
	If he had grace to doe *that* deede.	*God's help*
	Itt is 40 winters agoe	
410	Since I was transformed soe.	
	Since then, none Lodged w*i*thin this wooun*	*dwelling*
	But I & my whelpes driven them downe,	*struck them down*
	&, but if hee did my bidding soone,*	
	I killed him & drew him downe,	
415	Every one but only thee –	
	Christ grant thee of his mercye!	
	He *that* the world made, reward thee this,	
	Ffor all my bale thou hast turned to blisse.	*sorrow*
	Now will I leave *that* Lawe;	*custom*
420	There shall no man for me be slawe.	*slain*

      & I purpose for their sake
      A chantrey in this place to make,
      & 5 preists to sing for aye,
      Untill itt be doomes-day.
425 & Gawaine, for the love of thee,
      Every one shall bee welcome to me.'
      S*i*r Gawaine & the young Lady clere,*   *beautiful*
      The Bishopp weded them in fere.   *together*
      The Carle gave him for his wedding
430 A staffe, miter, & a ringe.
      He gave S*i*r Kay, *tha*t angry K*nigh*t,
      A blood-red steede & a wight.   *powerful*
      He gave his daughter, the sooth to say,
      An ambling white palfrey,
435 The fairest hee was on the mold;   *on earth*
      Her palfrey was charged w*i*th gold.   *laden*
      Shee was soe gorgeous & soe gay,   *finely dressed*
      No man cold tell her array.   *could describe*
      The Carle com[m]anded S*i*r Gawaine to wend,
440 & say unto Arthur our king,*
      & pray him *tha*t hee wold –
      Ffor His love that Judas sold,
      & for His sake *tha*t in Bethlem was borne –
      *Tha*t hee wold dine with him to-morne.
445 Sir Gawaine sayd the Carle unto,*
      'Fforssooth I shall yo*u*r message doe.'
      Then they rode singing by the way
      W*i*th the Ladye *tha*t was gay.
      They were as glad of *tha*t Lady bright
450 As ever was fowle of the day-Lyght.
      They told K*ing* Arthur where they had beene
      & what adventures they had seene.
      'I thanke God,' sayd the K*ing*, 'Cozen Kay,*
      *Tha*t thou didst on live p*ar*t away.'   *escape alive*
455 'Marry,' sayd S*i*r Kay againe,   *To be sure*
      'Of my liffe I may be faine.
      Ffor His love *tha*t was in Bethlem borne,
      You must dine w*i*th the Carle tomorne.'
      In the dawning of the day the[y] rode,
460 A merryer meeting was nev*er* made.*
      When they together were mett,
      Itt was a good thing, I you hett.   *I assure you*
      The trumpetts plaid att the gate   *trumpeters*
      W*i*th tru[m]petts of silver theratt.
465 There [was] all manner of Minstrelsye:
      Harpe, Gyttorne, and sowtrye.   *gittern; psaltery*
      Into the hall the King was fett   *brought*

	& royallye in seat was sett.	
	By then the dinner was readye dight,	*prepared*
470	Tables were covered all on height.	*beautifully set*
	Then to wash they wold not blinn,	*delay*
	& the feast they can beginn.	
	There they were mached arright,	*appropriately paired off*
	Every Lady against a Knight,	*opposite*
475	And Minstrells sate in windowes faire	p. 455/f. 226v
	& playd on their instruments cleere.	
	Minstrells for worshipp att every messe	*course*
	Ffull Lowd they cry 'Largnesse!'*	*largesse*
	The Carle bade the King, 'Doe gladlye,	
480	Ffor heere yee gett great curtesye.'	
	The King said, 'By Saint Michaell,*	
	This dinner Liketh me full well!'	
	He dubd the Carle a Knight, anon,	
	He gave him the county of Carlile soone,	
485	& made him Erle of all that land,	
	& after, Knight of the Table Round.	
	The King said, 'Knight, I tell thee,	
	'Car[l]ile' shall thy name bee.'	
	When the dinner was all done,	
490	Every Knight tooke his leave soone	
	To wend forward soberlye	*quietly*
	Home into their owne countrye.	
	He that made us all with His hand,*	
	Both the sea and the Land,	
495	Grant us all for His sake	
	This false world to forsake.	
	& out of this world, when wee shall wend,	
	To Heaven's blisse our soules bringe.	
	God grant us grace itt may soe bee.	
500	'Amen,' say all, for charitye. ffinis	

Explanatory Notes

9–11 This passage appears in a similar form in *Carelyle* (16–19) and must therefore have stood in the original. A version of the same geography lesson appears in *GK*.

19 *grass time*: *OED grass time*, in the time or season of grease; the time of year when animals are at pasture, n, hence the hunting season; cf. line 64.

21 ff. The list of names in *Carelyle* contains 21 knights. *CARLE*'s list is similar and follows the same order but omits nine.

27 *the Knight of armes greene*: Sir Ironside's son (38).

29–30 *steward in Arthur's hall*: this is a post more usually assigned to Kay as seneschal. That the *CARLE*-poet did not understand this title is shown by 30, where his reference to Gawaine as 'the curteous Knight amongst them all' is an obvious substitute for *Carelyle*'s 'He was master of hem all' (47).

31	'*Cozen Mordred*': in *Carelyle*, he is called Arthur's uncle. Neither version shows an awareness of the father–son/uncle–nephew relationship as depicted in the chronicles.
35	*Blanch Faire*: *Carelyle* has 'Blancheles' at this point, quite possibly a corruption of Brandles/Braundeles, respectively Gawaine's protagonist in *The Jeaste of Sir Gawaine*, and the uncle of two of Gawaine's sons in *LMD*. For *The Jeaste of Sir Gawaine*, see https://d.lib.rochester.edu/teams/text/hahn-sir-gawain-jeaste-of-sir-gawain (accessed July 2023).
37 ff.	*Ironside*: the description assigned here and in *Carelyle* (67 ff.) implies that this figure must have stood in the common original. Elsewhere, Ironside appears only in *LAMBE* (43–44) and as a formidable foe for Gareth in *LMD*. Most of what is said of Ironside could be applied to Gawaine (see Kurvinen, 1951, 107–11; Rogers, 1978, 473–76; Hahn, 107, 389–90), leading to the suspicion that there was some confusion in the common original, and that Gawaine was possibly meant to be the subject of this digression.
53	*Dapple-coulour*: presumably Ironside favoured riding either a piebald or skewbald horse. *Carleyle* makes no such reference to the mount, although it calls Ironside's horse 'Fabele Honde'.
55	*Azure of gold*: 'blue of gold'. Heraldically, this makes no sense. *Carelyle* has 'Of asur for sothe he bare/A gryffyn of golde full feyr' (82–83), i.e., his coat of arms consisted of a blue shield bearing a golden griffin. Griffins as a heraldic device are associated with Gawaine in *The Awntyrs off Arthure* and elsewhere, which further reinforces the idea that Ironside and Gawaine have been confused in this tale.
57	*a difference of a Molatt*: in heraldic terms a molet, or mullet, is a five-pointed star. Used as a 'difference', molets would appear as part of a band across the top of a coat of arms to signify cadency, in this case that the bearer was a third son.
68	'There on the field they began to pursue (the deer)'. Although the MS clearly has 'lead', some editors have favoured 'lend', i.e., 'rest'. However, the context better suits *MED*'s *leden*, of hunters and hounds: ?'to follow (a prey), pursue, v,1,12.
71–72	The choice of the three main characters is possibly symbolic: Kay represents the downside of knighthood, arrogant and bullying, while Gawaine represents the upside, courteous and considerate. Baldwin, who is here as arrogant and bullying as Kay, serves as the anti-clerical focus, as he does in *TG*. The same three characters also appear in *The Avowynge of King Arthur*.
75	*A thicke mist fell them among*: a mist is a frequent precursor of mysterious or Otherworld events, and frequently causes the hero to get lost. *CARLE*'s version is more suggestive of enchantment than that of *Carelyle*, since it clearly states that this mist leads the knights astray, out of Arthur's world.
95–102	We are not told how Baldwin came to know so much about the Carle and his customs. Here he is playing the traditional role of the person who warns the hero what is in store for him should he seek lodging with the Imperious Host. He is the integrator of two roles, which sit uncomfortably cheek by jowl, as the one who warns and as one of the tested knights (see Rogers, 1978, 396).
97	*Carle*: not a 'churl', in that he has a castle, wife, daughter, knights, and is evidently very rich, a fact commented upon by Gawaine as he greets his host (192).
101–2	'If escapes alive, he will be doing well'.
103–12	Baldwin's warning (99–102) provokes a typical reaction from Kay 'the crabbed', which in turn brings forth an equally typical rebuke from Gawaine (115–18); cf. *TG* (19–33) and *MSG* (130–39).
105	'Be the Carle never so bold'.
112	*sweate & stinke*: the usual phrase is 'sweate & swinke', but in this context, 'stinke' is appropriate.
115–18	Note that Gawaine uses the familiar 'thou/thy' to Kay, thus reflecting his anger and contempt. His words at 117–18 are an ironic echo of Baldwin at 99–102, and his comment, 'I dare say' in 118 suggests a certain dryness of tone on his part, particularly in view of his comment at 115–16. His doubts about Kay's courage are confirmed at 315.
121–23	Three proverbs all meaning much the same thing, namely, 'as a man sows, so shall he reap'.

124–26	Gawaine disapproves of Kay's violent speech, and advocates 'faire speech', explicitly stating the principle underlying the Imperious Host tales.
128	'Then we will not fail to speak as Kay suggests'. This addition, which rather spoils the effect of Gawaine's reply, runs contrary to the spirit of the tale.
134	Gawaine's courtesy, more remarked upon in *CARLE* than in *Carelyle*, extends even to the way he knocks at the Carle's gate, here creating a comic effect. In *Carelyle* (178–80), it is Kay who knocks, almost pulling the hammer off the gate in his anger. In *Carelyle*, Gawaine's speech, although courteous, is much briefer, and the porter replies to him at length, warning him that they shall not escape 'wyttout a wellony' (194), while regretting that such knights should come to harm, for his lord 'can no corttessye' (193). The *CARLE*-poet omits this warning, although he retains Kay's bullying rejoinder, albeit in different words (147–50).
139–46	Gawaine's request is repeated at 161–68 by the porter to his master. Note that he asks in Arthur's name, thus underlining both his role as Arthur's representative and the fact that the visitors have powerful allies, an implication lacking in *Carelyle*.
140	'And a bishop, to mention no more'.
144	Note Gawaine's assumption that they have arrived at the castle of a nobleman.
151	'The Porter said angrily' (*MED thro*, angry, threatening; fierce, savage, cruel … adj.,1(b)).
155–56	Gawaine's interjection does not occur in *Carelyle*, and so the explicit contrast between Kay's 'crabbed' behaviour and Gawaine's courtesy seen here is absent. Line 156 is identical to 148 except for the significant contrast of Gawaine's 'pray' with Kay's 'reede': while Kay threatens, Gawaine requests.
169–70	The Carle's response to the porter's message is surprisingly mild, impeccably courteous and overtly hospitable. His response in *Carelyle* (220–22) is more ambiguous.
182–88	Note the repetition of this authorial exclamation, with the last word of each line forming a rhyme with its preceding line.
183	*bread*: a case of metathesis for 'beard', which appears to grow over the Carle's shoulders.
184	'The beard was three tailor's yards across the shoulders'. A tailor's yard, or cloth yard, was 36 inches (90 cm) long: a 'cloth-yard shaft' was frequently a poetic name for the arrow of a longbow.
187	*OED cubit*, an ancient measure of length … usually about 18–22 inches (45–55 cm), n,2. As a bare minimum, this would make the Carle implausibly tall at 75 feet (almost 23 metres). In *Carelyle*, he is a more credible 9 tailor's yards (i.e., 27 feet or 8.25 metres) in height (line 259).
190	Again, note the emphasis on Gawaine's courtesy.
191–92	This greeting, almost word for word, also appears in *GK* (112–13), spoken by the Green Knight to Arthur.
193 ff.	Note that the Carle makes them welcome 'for Arthur's sake', despite his anger against him (compare the King of Man's tirade in *TG*, 152–65). Given the Carle's antipathy it is odd that neither Gawaine nor Arthur seems to know of his existence.
205–16	This passage occurs earlier in *Carelyle*, where the 'whelpus' are the first things of which the guests are made terrifyingly aware before they turn their attention to the Carle. This seems the more likely order of events: here, because they have already taken in his grotesque size, the beasts seem tame by comparison.
212	'Opened his mouth and roared'.
217 ff.	At this point, though not in *Carelyle*, the Carle's wife is introduced, although not named. Her status, however, is indicated by the Carle's fierce reaction (223–24) to Gawaine's comment at 221–22. Gawaine's unthinking observation runs counter to his reputation for courtesy, not least since he has just rebuked Kay for rudeness to his host. Gawaine's 'I sayd nought' (225) may indicate an unguarded comment under his breath that the Carle picked up.
227 ff.	The 'foal' test. As happens in many folk-tales, the same test is undergone by three people, one after the other. Two fail, the third succeeds. This eliminating test is one of courtesy, to find the one guest courteous enough to treat the animal well when he thinks he is unobserved, and so, naturally, Kay and Baldwin fail, Kay demonstrating his innately churlish nature and Baldwin shamelessly 'pulling rank' in their subsequent encounters

with the omniscient Carle. The almost word-for-word sequence of repetitions in this passage is an instance of the much sharper structural patterning that underlies *CARLE*. The oddity of this episode as a test of courtesy is that it is based on an act of discourtesy by all three men – would guests really go out just before dinner to check that their host is treating their horses well?

232   *hecke*: the *OED* definition of *heck*, the lower half of a door', n,1(a), makes more sense in the context than does Percy's suggestion, 'cratch'.

239   *feald*: *OED faud* | *fawd*, a bundle, n. In both cases, the reference is to a bundle of straw: the earlier example dates from *c.*1642, i.e. a matter of years before completion of the PF.

242   *sold*: this completes the Carle's metaphor of buying and selling begun in 236.

267–72 The bishop's attempt to assert his authority as a 'clarke' is met by a tirade against the clergy, reminiscent of that of the King of Man in *TG* (154–65). It does not occur in *Carelyle*, where the Carle merely rebukes Baldwin for his lack of courtesy (314–15). That this was a deliberate alteration on the part of the *CARLE*-poet is suggested by his addition of 268 to make up his couplet before he launches the Carle on his tirade.

269   'I don't care a fig for the clergy'. Hahn (391) suggests that this tirade, like that in *TG*, 'seems to reflect a post-Reformation rather than a medieval attitude'. This would perhaps place the writing of both *CARLE* and *TG* around the middle of the sixteenth century or somewhat later.

281–84 An example of the *CARLE*-poet creating two couplets from a three-line tail-rhyme unit. He is obliged to fall back on the weak 'filler', 'as I weene', to make up his second rhyme.

288   This fits better with the concept of Gawaine's courtesy than does the corresponding line in *Carelyle*, where the Carle 'þankyd hym full curtteslye' (353). It is Gawaine's courtesy at issue here, not the Carle's. Similarly, the act of the Carle taking Gawaine by the hand at 289 does not appear in *Carelyle*.

293   Given the Carle's stature and the amount he drinks (297), the sense seems to be that the Carle's bowl holds as much as 70 'ordinary' bowls.

302–3   'We are ready to do as you say'. The alliterative tag 'bidding ... bain' was relatively common: for example, it appears at line 509 of PF's *John de Reeve* ('att your bidding wee will be baine').

307–30 The 'spear' test: only Gawaine is tested from this point on, his actions mirroring exactly the Carle's instructions (318–20), taking on the challenge and doing his utmost to strike him. In *Carelyle*, the Carle reassures Gawaine that he cannot hurt him (389), which seems to negate the point of the test. Note that the Carle, rather unfairly, rebukes Gawaine for the energy he has displayed (327), whereas in *Carelyle*, he congratulates him (401). At 308, the Carle is noticeably more polite than his *Carelyle* counterpart, who says: 'Fellowe, anoun,/Loke my byddynge be well idoun' (382–83).

309   *race*: *MED ras(e*, a charge, an onslaught, attack, n,2(a). The Carle is carefully coaching Gawaine where to stand, in order to deliver the most effective attack against him.

311–12 Kay's longing for revenge for the blow he has sustained is not echoed in *Carelyle*, and further reinforces the churlish portrayal of him here. Kay's rejoinder (315) and the Carle's reply (316) are a repetition of 225–26, with Kay substituted for Gawaine,

327–30 *Soft*: *OED soft*, used either to enjoin silence, or deprecate haste ... sometimes followed by *you*, adv. 7c. *OED* dates the earliest recorded use in this fashion to 1573. Note that the Carle addresses Gawaine with the familiar 'thou', but Gawaine uses the more respectful 'you'. His reply (328) again underlines the basic rule of the Imperious Host game: total obedience to the Host.

335 ff. The Carle's command to Gawaine to get into bed with his wife, kiss her three times, and do no more, is a further test of Gawaine's obedience, which he fails. The injunction to kiss the wife three times, strongly reminiscent of folk-tale, is not echoed in *Carelyle*, where Gawaine is merely told to kiss her (456). However, when Gawaine oversteps the mark, the sharpness of the Carle's rebuke sits oddly with his next, somewhat ungallant, order to Gawaine, to accompany him to 'a fairer lady than ever was shee', i.e., his daughter (348). The *Carelyle* Carle is considerably more good-humoured about it than his *CARLE* counterpart: 'Whoo ther./That game I þe forbede' (467–68).

349–57   This passage is a virtual repetition of 331–40, without the Carle's admonition to Gawaine to confine himself to kissing. Here, the Carle, having seen the pair into bed, leaves them to it with his blessing. The theme of obedience is, however, more marked in *Carleyle*: 'But, Gawen, sethe þou hast do my byddynge,/Som kyndnis I most schewe þe in anny þinge' (469–70).

371   Gawaine's rather feeble reaction to the startling sight of the dead men's bones and the Carle's confession to having slain them strikes a false note, particularly as he immediately goes to take his leave without further ado.

393–96   The juxtaposition of the Carle's threat to cut off Gawaine's head if he refuses to cut off his, and Gawaine's prompt acquiescence, creates a comic effect.

405–19   'I was transformed thus through enchantment'. The Carle seems to be suggesting that his cruel treatment of knights who fail to live up to his standards of obedience is caused by the necromancy that transformed him.

411–14   The Carle here states in its baldest terms the principle underlying the Imperious Host theme.

413   'And unless he obediently did my bidding'. Kurvinen (1951, 187) plausibly suggests that 'soone has probably been substituted for *bowne*'. Restoring 'bowne' would make it rhyme with 'downe' in the following line: *MED bouen*, to be submissive, obedient, deferential, v,1(a).

427–28   In *Carelyle*, the two are not wedded until the end of the feast to which the Carle invites Arthur and his court, which means that the former is already ennobled by the time that the wedding takes place. In *CARLE*, the Carle does not wait for Arthur's sanction of the marriage, but this might be a result of the misplacement of events so evident in this part of the tale.

440   Note the use of the word 'our' here to describe Arthur. *Carelyle* has 'your' at this point (572), thus underlining the Carle's 'outsider' status. This may, of course, simply be a scribal error.

445–46   Gawaine's reply again emphasizes the 'obedience' topos of the tale. *Carelyle*'s version is much feebler: 'Gawen seyde he scholde' (576).

453–58   Arthur's sole concern here seems to be for Kay's safety, not Gawaine's, and it is Kay who issues the Carle's invitation, repeating his message at 443–44 almost verbatim. (Note his imperious 'must'. The Carle had actually asked Gawaine to invite Arthur to dine with him (444).)

460ff.   The splendour of the feast reveals the Carle's great wealth, deepening the mystery of his presence in the forest around Carlisle, apparently unknown to Arthur, but known to Baldwin.

478   *Largnesse*: largesse, a spelling also occurring in *LAMBE* (215).

481–82   The great King Arthur is reduced to praising his dinner. His response underlines the essentially passive role he plays in this tale, present solely to ratify Gawaine's action in bringing this erstwhile hostile stranger into the circle of the court and the Round Table, a function peculiarly Gawaine's own in these late romances.

493–500   *CARLE* devotes these lines to the standard pious endings of such tales. The words '"Amen", say all, for charitye' suggests a plea for a fitting reward from the audience for telling this tale. In comparison, *Carelyle*'s final two lines appear almost as an afterthought. See Sachi Shimomura, *Odd Bodies and Visible Ends in Medieval Literature* (Basingstoke: Palgrave Macmillan, 2006), pp. 80–83 for an interpretation of the final prayer within the context of the poem as a whole.

Textual Notes

In the LH margin, against the title: 'A curious Song of the Marriage of *Sir* Gawaine one of K*ing* Arthur's Knights'. After 'Gawaine', P wrote 'of' and emended it to 'one'. It is odd that Percy, who by then must have read *TG*, *KAKC*, and *GK*, should have found it necessary to explain who Gawaine was, and that the most noteworthy thing about this 'song' was not the Carle or the tests, but Gawaine's almost incidental marriage at the end. This may, however, reflect his interest in *MSG*, and the importance he assigned that piece.

1	Opening word in large bold script, succeeded by colon, with flourish of opening letter extending to opposite second line.
18	f[or]rest: ffairest [MS], traces of an alteration to the r to turn it into an i.
19	yeere: preceded by 'earth', crossed out [MS]. This suggests that the scribe associated 'grass' with 'earth', rather than with 'grease-time'.
30	the curteous: 'most courteous Knight. of all.' [P].
31	Arthur: Arthut [MS], the u followed by the abbreviation for –er, then by a t, overwritten by an r.
38	Gate: 'i.e. begat' [P].
39	'of a ff crossed out after 'understand' [MS]. The scribe mistakenly began to write down the opening words of the following line.
50	hee: second e masked by a descender from above and an ascender from below.
53	Dapple-coulour: 'Dapple-colour'd' [P].
54	his (second occurrence): the scribe began to write 'hit' and emended to 'his'.
57	Molatt: 'i.e. a mullet' [P].
58	Allgate: second l interlined, no caret [MS].
61	the[y]: the [MS]. See also 70, 73, 81, 82, 459.
63	The (first occurrence): they [MS]; 'the' [P]. P is inconsistent in such corrections. See notes to lines 170, 171, 215, 216, 287, 289, 290, 295, 299, 331, 345, 349, 359, 365, 375; leashe: a blotted, 'Leashe' [P].
64	grasse: 'greace' emended to 'grease' [P].
70	the: 'delend.' [P].
72–74	Lines have mirror image of the title of the piece smudged across them, indicating that the leaf was turned while the ink was still wet.
76	ca[u]sed: one minim too few.
103	Then: preceded by 'the' blurred and struck through [MS]; all in fere: 'i.e. together. Perhaps all on fire' [P].
107	itt: 'him' [P].
111	[him]: omitted in MS.
121	Second such: loop above the u [MS]. The scribe possibly began to write 'shall'.
126	owne: 'aine', [P], written larger, in pencil to rhyme with 'gaine' in line above.
140	min: 'min, ming i.e. mention vide v. 162' [P]; scribe has dotted first minim of m [MS].
148	the[e]: the [MS]; 'thou say or thee (to) say' [P].
151	The: badly blotted and replaced in LH margin by scribal 'the'; throe: 'tho i.e. then' [P].
153	[I]f: of [MS]; 'If' [P].
154	hunting: the g written over another letter; to-morne: 'to-morrow' [P].
155	Gawai[n]e: written in large italics; one minim only on the n, but a dot above, indicating intention of an i [MS].
159	as: preceded by a half-finished blotted as. [MS].
161	in: 'inne' [P].
162	a: diagonal stroke over this letter [MS].
164	horsse [&] man: horsseman [MS]; 'horse & man' [P], the h partially cropped.
165	for: the capital A of 'Arthir' is written over a half-formed e at the beginning of this word [MS].
169	gree[v]es: one minim too few [MS].
170	the: they [MS], 'the' [P], P adding a closing '(' to separate his note from his numbering of line 170; without: superscript h emended from a t.
171	the (first occurrence): they [MS]; 'the' [P].
174	gone: 'gane' [P], correcting the rhyme to agree with tane in the preceding line.
176	cast: 'catt' emended to 'cast' [MS].
182	a Lodlye syer: 'a Lodlye Sire i.e. filthy. p. 387' [P]. P is here referring to Death & Liffe (HF, III, 49–75, line 162: '& lodlye to see').
184	reede: the second e corrected, most likely from an a.
185	teddar-stakes: 'The Stakes by which the hair lines are fasten'd to the ground that are tied to horses feet when they graze in ope[n] fields.' [P]. The n of 'open' is partly masked by the mount.

188	*he*: a *w* crossed out before this word; scribe began to write 'was' [MS].
190	*halched*: 'i.e. saluted' [P]; *f[u]ll*: one minim too many on the *u*, masked by descender in the line above [MS].
191	*Ca[r]lile*: 'Callile', emended to 'Carlile' without crossing out the loop of the first *l* [MS]; cf. line 488, below.
193	*save*: 'perhaps take' [P]. Again, Percy shows a concern for rhyme, here, with 'sake' (194). The word is quite clearly 'save' in the MS.
195	*Yet*: 'yet et' [MS].
198	*sen[t]*: 'send' [MS]; 'sent' [P].
199	*Leane*: 'vid. p. 367. St. 4[5]' [P], the 5 partly masked by the mount: reading taken from HF. P's reference is to *John de Reeve*, his gloss at that point reading '*lean*, celare, occultare, ab. Isl. *leine, launa*, occultare. Lye.' (HF, II, 590; line 822).
201	*said*: beginnings of a capital *C*, or a parenthesis, before this word [MS].
215	*the Carle*: they Carle [MS]; 'the Carle' [P].
216	*the bord*: they bord [MS]; 'the bord' [P].
228	*fore*: 'i.e. fared praet. inusita[t]' [P]. Last *t* cropped: reading supplied by HF.
232	*hecke*: 'i.e. Cratch verb. Scot. D^r. Graing[er]' [P – [er] cropped, reading supplied by HF]; 'with a kick', crossed out, the *w* half-masked by the mount [P]; *OED cratch*, a rack or crib to hold fodder for horses and cattle in a stable or a cowshed, n,1(a).
236	*shalt*: an *l* superimposed over a loop, possibly the beginnings of an *h*; *ab[u]y*: blotted and malformed *u*. Possibly scribe began to write 'aby', and changed to 'abuy' [MS]; 'abye' [P].
238	*backward*: the *b* superimposed over a looped letter, possibly the beginnings of an *h*, anticipating the next word, 'he'.
239	*feald*: 'i.e. a truss of Straw D^r. Grainger.' [P].
240	*Ka[y]e's*: *y* preceded by an extra, blotted, minim [MS]; *2*: 'twa' [P].
245	*thore*: 'tho' [P].
246	*more*: 'moe' [P].
252	*as I weene*: 'als I ween, i.e. I also thinke, intend. sed vid. infra 276.' [P].
259	*fole*: foe, with an *l* squeezed in after *o* [MS].
268	*Chr[i]st's*: chrsts [MS].
272	*con[n]ing*: six minims only in MS; 'cunning or conning' [P].
275	'as I weene' crossed out before 'where' [MS]. An eye-slip to next line, suggesting a copying error.
278	*That*: superscript letter crossed out before this word in MS; 'palfreye' corrected from 'palfreaye' [MS].
287	*The Carle*: they Carle [MS]; 'The Carle' [P].
289	*The Carle*: They Carle [MS]; 'the Carle' [P].
290	*the*: they [MS].
291	*Carle*: Carles [MS].
295	*the*: they [MS]; 'the' [P].
299	*the*: they [MS]; 'the' [P].
302	*ben*: 'baine' [P].
308	*hand*: 'hond' [P].
309	*race*: 'place q.' [P], in pencil in a larger hand, cf. also his glosses at 343, 344, 373, 459.
311	*'A', thought*: 'Ah! thought' [P].
312	*ab[u]y*: *aluy* [MS], 'abuy or abye' [P].
313	*when thou wilt, thou may*: 'then thou (yee) may' [P].
314	*strenght*: as elsewhere in the PF, the scribe adopts this idiosyncratic spelling for 'strength'.
331	*The Carle*: they Carle [MS].
335	*Carle*: Carles [MS].
341	*her* interlined, with caret, by scribe.
343	*in fare*: 'free q:' [P], in pencil, in a larger hand.
344	*the[r]e*: thee [MS]; 'there' [P] added, in pencil, in a larger hand.
345	*the Carle*: they Carle [MS].
349	*The* (first occurrence): They [MS]; 'the' [P].
359	*The Carle*: they Carle [MS].

361	*other*: 'on the next m:' [P]; *Carle*: Carles [MS].	
362	*goes*: corrected from 'goos' [MS].	
365	*The Carle*: they Carle [MS].	
367	*ma[n]y*: one minim too few on the *n* [MS].	
369	*men's bones*: mens a bones [MS]; 'men's bones' – dotted *i* changed to an *e* [P].	
370	*rooke*: 'i.e. a ruck, a heap.' [P].	
373	*kind*: 'hend q' [P], in pencil, in larger hand.	
375	*the Carle*: they Carle [MS].	
380	*tooke*: toke, with first, blotted, *o* inserted by scribe [MS].	
385	*stryke*: scribe began to write *th* and changed it to *st*.	
387	*had*: scribe began to write *r* (presumably anticipating 'rather'), and changed it to *h*.	
404	*deliverd*: last *d* inserted between abbreviation mark for *–er* and *att* [MS].	
407	*s[m]itten*: snitten [MS].	
411	*within*: *t* written above the *i* and crossed, without caret [MS]; *wooun*: the *u* is ambiguous: both Kurvinen and Hahn read as 'woonn' (*OED wone*, a place of habitation or abode, dwelling place, n2(1)).	
413	*my*: the beginning of a loop over the *m*; scribe began to write the *b* of *bidding*.	
420	*for*: 'i.e. thro' me' [P].	
429	*him*: 'sc. the bishop' [P].	
430	*a staffe* …: 'a staff, a miter &c.' [P].	
443	*Bethlem*: scribe wrote *Bethelen*, crossed out the middle *e*, and added an extra minim on the *n* to make an *m* (cf. 'Bethlem' at 457).	
450	*day-Lyght*: scribe began to write an *h* after the *y* in *lyght*, and emended it to a *g*.	
454	*on live*: 'i.e. alive' [P].	
459	*rode*: 'rade q' [P], in pencil, in a larger hand, to provide a rhyme for 'made' in the following line.	
464	*tru[m]petts*: trunnpetts [MS]; *theratt*: therott, with *o* emended to *a* [MS].	
465	*There [was] all*: there all [MS].	
467	*was fett*: loop over *w* of *was*; scribe began to write *f* (for *fett*) and emended to *w*.	
470	*covered*: 'covered' [P], possibly glossed by him because the first *e* looks more like a *d*.	
478	*Largnesse*: 'Largesse qu' [P], with the 'qu' crossed out.	
485	*land*: 'Lond' [P].	
488	*Car[l]ile*: Carllile [MS]. As at 191, the scribe has written 'Carllile'. In this case, the second *l* lacks the loop, the scribe perhaps realizing his mistake in the act of writing.	
500	*ffinis*: the scribe has written 'ffinis' in a larger and thinner hand at the end of this line to signify the end of the piece.	

Bibliography

Thomas Percy: Works and Critical Texts

Baatz, Christine, '"A Strange Collection of Trash"? The Re-Evaluation of Medieval Literature in Thomas Percy's *Reliques of Ancient English Poetry* (1765)', in Barbara Korte et al. (eds), *Anthologies of British Poetry: Critical Perspectives from Literary and Cultural Studies* (Rodopi: Amsterdam, 2000), pp. 105–24.

Bate, Walter Jackson, 'Percy's Use of his Folio-Manuscript', *JEGP* 43 (1944), pp. 337–48.

Byrne, Aisling, and Flood, Victoria, 'The Romance of the Stanleys: Regional and National Imaginings in the Percy Folio', *Viator* 46(1) (2015), pp. 327–51.

Churchill, Irving L., 'William Shenstone's Share in the Preparation of Percy's *Reliques*', *PMLA* 51(4) (1936), pp. 960–74.

Davis, Bertram H., 'Thomas Percy, the Reynolds Portrait, and the Northumberland House Fire', *Review of English Studies* NS 33(129) (1982), pp. 23–33.

—— *Thomas Percy: A Scholar-Cleric in the Age of Johnson* (Philadelphia: University of Pennsylvania Press, 1989).

Donatelli, Joseph M. P., 'The Medieval Fictions of Thomas Warton and Thomas Percy', *University of Toronto Quarterly* 60(4) (1991), pp. 435–51.

Donatelli, Joseph, 'The Percy Folio Manuscript: A Seventeenth-Century Context for Medieval Poetry', in P. Beal and J. Griffiths (eds), *English Manuscript Studies, 1100–1700*, vol. 4 (Toronto: University of Toronto Press, 1993), pp. 114–33.

Eisenberg, Daniel (ed.), *Thomas Percy & John Bowle: Cervantine Correspondence* (Exeter: Short Run Press, 1987).

Friedman, Albert B., 'The First Draft of Percy's *Reliques*', *PMLA* 69(5) (1954), pp. 1233–49.

—— 'Percy's Folio Manuscript Revalued', *Journal of English and Germanic Philology* 53 (1954), pp. 524–31.

Garner, Katie, 'Gendering Percy's *Reliques*: Ancient Ballads and the Making of Women's Arthurian Writing', in Karl Fugelso (ed.), *Corporate Medievalism II*, Studies in Medievalism 22 (Cambridge: Boydell & Brewer, D. S. Brewer, 2013), pp. 45–67.

Groom, Nick (ed.), Thomas Percy, *'Reliques of Ancient English Poetry', With a New Introduction by Nick Groom*, 3 vols; facsimile of the 1765 edition, with critical commentary (London: Routledge/Thoemmes Press, 1996).

—— *The Making of Percy's* Reliques (Oxford: Clarendon Press, 1999).

Hales, John W., and Furnivall, Frederick J. (eds), *Bishop Percy's Folio Manuscript: Ballads and Romances*, 3 vols (London: Trübner & Co., 1867–68).

—— *Bishop Percy's Folio Manuscript: Loose and Humorous Songs* (London: Trübner & Co., 1867).

Hodder, Karen, 'Arthur, *The Legend of King Arthur, King Arthur's Death*', in W. R. J. Barron (ed.), *The Arthur of the English: The Arthurian Legend in Medieval English Life and Literature*, Arthurian Literature in the Middle Ages 2 (Cardiff: University of Wales Press, 1999), pp. 72–74.

Lanier, Sidney, *The Boy's Percy, being Old Ballads of War, Adventure and Love* (New York: Charles Scribner's Sons, 1882).

Lawton, David, '*Scottish Field*: Alliterative Verse and Stanley Encomium in the Percy Folio', *Leeds Studies in English* NS 10 (1978), pp. 42–57.

Louis, Cameron (ed.), *The Commonplace Book of Robert Reynes of Acle: An Edition of Tanner MS 407*, Garland Medieval Texts 1 (New York: Garland, 1980).

Mason, J. F. A., 'Bishop Percy's Account of His Own Education', *Notes & Queries* 204 (1959), pp. 404–8.

Matthews, David O., '"A Shadow of Itself?": Narrative and Ideology in *The Grene Knight*', *Neophilologus* 78 (1994), pp. 301–14.

Millican, Charles Bowie, 'The Original of the Ballad "Kinge: Arthurs Death" in the Percy Folio MS', *PMLA* 46(4) (1931), pp. 1020–24.

Mills, Maldwyn, and Rogers, Gillian, 'The Manuscripts of Popular Romance', in Raluca L. Radulescu and Cory James Rushton (eds), *A Companion to Medieval Popular Romance* (Cambridge: D. S. Brewer, 2009), pp. 57–66.

Mills, Maldwyn, Fellows, Jennifer, and Meale, Carol M. (eds), *Romance in Medieval England* (Cambridge: D. S. Brewer, 1991).

Ogburn, Vincent H., 'Thomas Percy's Unfinished Collection', *Ancient English and Scottish Poems*', *ELH* 3(3) (1936), pp. 183–89.

Percy, Thomas, *Reliques of Ancient English Poetry: Consisting of Old Heroic Ballads, Songs, and other Pieces of our earlier Poets (Chiefly of the Lyric Kind.) Together with some few of later Date*, 3 vols (London: J. Dodsley, 1765).

—— '*Reliques of Ancient English Poetry*', With a New Introduction by Nick Groom, 3 vols; facsimile of the 1765 edition, with critical commentary (London: Routledge/Thoemmes Press, 1996).

—— *Reliques of Ancient English Poetry. Consisting of Old Heroic Ballads, Songs, and other Pieces of our earlier Poets, Together with some few of later Date*, 4th ed., 3 vols (London: Printed by John Nichols, for F. and C. Rivington, 1794).

Radulescu, Raluca L., 'Ballad and Popular Romance in the Percy Folio', in Keith Busby and Roger Dalrymple (eds), *Arthurian Literature* 23 (Cambridge: D. S. Brewer, 2006), pp. 68–80.

Rogers, Gillian, 'The Percy Folio Manuscript Revisited', in Maldwyn Mills, Jennifer Fellows, and Carol M. Meale (eds), *Romance in Medieval England* (Cambridge: D. S. Brewer, 1991), pp. 39–64.

—— 'The Grene Knight', in Derek Brewer and Jonathan Gibson (eds), *A Companion to the Gawain-Poet*, Arthurian Studies 38 (Cambridge: D. S. Brewer, 1997), pp. 365–72.

―― '*The Boy and Mantle* and *Sir Corneus*', in W. R. J. Barron (ed.), *The Arthur of the English: The Arthurian Legend in Medieval English Life and Literature*, Arthurian Literature in the Middle Ages 2 (Cardiff: University of Wales Press, 1999), pp. 219–21.

―― '*King Arthur and King Cornwall*', in W. R. J. Barron (ed.), *The Arthur of the English: The Arthurian Legend in Medieval English Life and Literature*, Arthurian Literature in the Middle Ages 2 (Cardiff: University of Wales Press, 1999), pp. 215–19.

――, '*Syre Gawene and the Carle of Carelyle* and *The Carle off Carlile*', in W. R. J. Barron (ed.), *The Arthur of the English: The Arthurian Legend in Medieval English Life and Literature*, Arthurian Literature in the Middle Ages 2 (Cardiff: University of Wales Press, 1999), pp. 204–7.

Shepard, Leslie, 'The Finding of the Percy Folio Manuscript: A Claim of Prior Discovery', *Notes & Queries* 212 (1967), pp. 415–16.

St Clair-Kendall, S. G., 'Narrative Form and Mediaeval Continuity in the Percy Folio Manuscript: A Study of Selected Poems', PhD thesis, University of Sydney, 1988; rev. 2007 (paginated continuously), https://ses.library.usyd.edu.au/bitstream/handle/2123/6143/clair-kendall-thesis-1988.pdf (accessed July 2023).

Sutherland, Kathryn, 'The Native Poet: The Influence of Percy's Minstrel from Beattie to Wordsworth', *Review of English Studies* 33(132) (1982), pp. 414–33.

Taylor, Andrew, 'Performing the Percy Folio', in Jacqueline Jenkins and Julie Sanders (eds), *Editing, Performance, Texts: New Practices in Medieval and Early Modern English Drama* (London: Palgrave Macmillan, 2014), pp. 70–89.

Tuttle, Donald Reuel, '*Christabel* Sources in Percy's *Reliques* and the Gothic Romance', *PMLA* 53(2) (1938), pp. 445–74.

Wilson, Robert H., 'Malory and the Ballad "King Arthur's Death"', *Medievalia et Humanistica: Studies in Medieval & Renaissance Culture* 6 (1975), pp. 139–49.

Thomas Percy: Letters

Anderson, W. E. K. (ed.), *The Correspondence of Thomas Percy & Robert Anderson*, *The Percy Letters*, vol. IX (New Haven, CT: Yale University Press, 1988).

Brooks, Cleanth (ed.), *The Correspondence of Thomas Percy & Richard Farmer*, *The Percy Letters*, vol. II (Baton Rouge: Louisiana State University Press, 1946).

―― (ed.), *The Correspondence of Thomas Percy & William Shenstone*, *The Percy Letters*, vol. VII (New Haven, CT: Yale University Press, 1977).

Falconer, A. F. (ed.), *The Correspondence of Thomas Percy & David Dalrymple, Lord Hailes*, *The Percy Letters*, vol. IV (Baton Rouge: Louisiana State University Press, 1954).

―― (ed.), *The Correspondence of Thomas Percy & George Paton*, *The Percy Letters*, vol. VI (New Haven, CT: Yale University Press, 1961).

Lewis, Aneirin (ed.), *The Correspondence of Thomas Percy & Evan Evans*, *The Percy Letters*, vol. V (Baton Rouge: Louisiana State University Press, 1957).

Robinson, M. G., and Dennis, Leah (eds), *The Correspondence of Thomas Percy & Thomas Warton*, *The Percy Letters*, vol. III (Baton Rouge: Louisiana State University Press, 1951).

Tillotson, Arthur (ed.), *The Correspondence of Thomas Percy & Edmond Malone*, The Percy Letters, vol. I (Baton Rouge: Louisiana State University Press, 1944).

Wood, Harriet Harvey (ed.), *The Correspondence of Thomas Percy & John Pinkerton*, The Percy Letters, vol. VIII (New Haven, CT: Yale University Press, 1985).

Reference and General Criticism

Anon., *Marlyn* (London: Wynkyn de Worde, 1510), available at www.proquest.com.

—— 'The noble acts newly found, of Arthur of the table round to the tune of Flying Fame'. Broadsheet published in London *c.*1620, by W.I. (ESTC S2568).

—— *A Collection of Old Ballads. Corrected from the best and most Ancient Copies Extant. With Introductions Historical, Critical, or Humorous. Illustrated with Copper Plates*, 3 vols (London: J. Roberts and D. Leach, 1723–25).

—— *The Tragedy of Tragedies; or the Life and Death of Tom Thumb the Great. As it is Acted at the Theatre in the Hay-Market. With the Annotations of H. Scriblerus Secundus* (London: J. Roberts, 1731; facsimile repr. London: Scolar Press, 1973).

Ackerman, Robert William (ed.), *An Index of the Arthurian Names in Middle English* (Stanford, CA: Stanford University Press, 1952).

Anglo, Sydney, 'The *British History* in Early Tudor Propaganda', *Bulletin of the John Rylands Library* 44(1) (1961), pp. 17–48.

Baker, T. F. T. (ed.), *A History of the County of Middlesex*, Victoria History of the Counties of England (gen. ed. C. R. Elrington), vol. 8, *Islington and Stoke Newington Parishes* (London: Oxford University Press for the Institute of Historical Research, 1985).

Barber, Richard, 'Malory's *Le Morte Darthur* and Court Culture under Edward IV', in James P. Carley and Felicity Riddy (eds), *Arthurian Literature* 12 (Cambridge: D. S. Brewer, 1993), pp. 133–55.

Barrett Jr, Robert W., *Against All England: Regional Identity and Cheshire Writing, 1195–1656* (Notre Dame, IN: University of Notre Dame Press, 2009).

Barron, W. J. R. (ed.), *The Arthur of the English: The Arthurian Legend in Medieval English Life and Literature*, Arthurian Literature in the Middle Ages 2 (Cardiff: University of Wales Press, 1999).

Bäuml, Franz H., 'Varieties and Consequences of Medieval Literacy and Illiteracy', *Speculum* 55(2) (1980), pp. 237–65.

Bawcutt, Priscilla, '*Sir Lamwell* in Scotland', in Rhiannon Purdie and Nicola Royan (eds), *The Scots and Medieval Arthurian Legend*, Arthurian Studies LXI (Cambridge: D. S. Brewer, 2005), pp. 83–93.

Bellamy, J. G., *The Law of Treason in England in the Later Middle Ages* (Cambridge: Cambridge University Press, 1970).

Biddle, Martin, *King Arthur's Round Table: An Archaeological Investigation* (Woodbridge: Boydell, 2000).

Boffey, Julia, and Meale, Carol M., 'Selecting the Text: Rawlinson C. 86 and Some Other Books for London Readers', in Felicity Riddy (ed.), *Regionalism in Late Medieval Manuscripts and Texts: Essays Celebrating the Publication of* A Linguistic Atlas of Late Medieval English' (Cambridge: D. S. Brewer, 1991), pp. 143–69.

Bongaerts, Theo (ed.), *Correspondence of Thomas Blount (1618–1679): A Recusant Antiquary; His Letters to Anthony Wood and Other Restoration Antiquaries* (Amsterdam: Holland University Press, 1978).

Boutell, Charles, *Boutell's Heraldry*, rev. J. P. Brooke-Little (London: Frederick Warne, 1978).

Brandsen, T., 'Sir Gawain and the Carl of Carlisle', *Neophilologus* 81 (1997), pp. 299–307.

Brault, Gerard J., *Early Blazon: Heraldic Terminology in the Twelfth and Thirteenth Centuries with Special Reference to Arthurian Heraldry* (Woodbridge: Boydell, 1997).

Brinkley, Roberta Florence, *Arthurian Legend in the Seventeenth Century*, Johns Hopkins Monographs in Literary History III (Baltimore, MD: Johns Hopkins University Press, 1932).

Bromwich, Rachel (ed.), *Trioedd Ynys Prydein: The Triads of the Island of Britain* (Cardiff: University of Wales Press, 2006).

Brown, Mary Ellen, 'Child's Ballads and the Broadside Conundrum', in Patricia Fumerton, Anita Guerrini, and Kris McAbee (eds), *Ballads and Broadsides in Britain, 1500–1800* (Farnham: Ashgate, 2010), pp. 57–72.

Burgess, Glynn S., and Brook, Leslie C. (eds and trans.), *The Lay of Mantel*, French Arthurian Literature V (Cambridge: D. S. Brewer, 2013).

Burgess, Glynn S., and Cobby, Anne Elizabeth (eds), *'The Pilgrimage of Charlemagne'* and *'Aucassin and Nicolette'* (Abingdon: Routledge, 2019).

Burnley, David, 'Of Arthour and of Merlin', in W. R. J. Barron (ed.), *The Arthur of the English: The Arthurian Legend in Medieval English Life and Literature*, Arthurian Literature in the Middle Ages 2 (Cardiff: University of Wales Press, 1999), pp. 83–90.

Calkin, Siobhain Bly, 'Violence, Saracens, and English Identity in *Of Arthour and Merlin*', *Arthuriana* 14 (2004), pp. 17–36.

Carley, James P. (ed.), *Glastonbury and the Arthurian Tradition*, Arthurian Studies 44 (Cambridge: D. S. Brewer, 2001).

Charbonneau, Joanne A., 'Sir Thopas', in Robert M. Correale and Mary Hamel (eds), *Sources and Analogues of The Canterbury Tales*, 2 vols (Cambridge: D. S. Brewer, 2005), II, 649–714.

Chestre, Thomas, *Sir Launfal*, ed. A. J. Bliss (London: Thomas Nelson, 1960).

Child, Francis James (ed.), *The English and Scottish Popular Ballads*, 5 vols (Boston: Houghton, Mifflin, 1882–98; repr. Cambridge: Cambridge University Press, 2014, online 2015).

Clifton, Nicole, 'Modern Readers of the Romance "Of Arthour and Merlin"', *Arthuriana* 24(2) (2014), pp. 71–91.

Cooper, Helen, 'Romance after Bosworth', in Evelyn Mullally and John Thompson (eds), *The Court and Cultural Diversity: Selected Papers from the Eighth Triennial Meeting of the International Courtly Literature Society* (Cambridge: D. S. Brewer, 1997), pp. 149–57.

—— 'Milton's King Arthur', *Review of English Studies* 65(269) (2014), pp. 252–65.

Coote, Lesley A., *Prophecy and Public Affairs in Later Medieval England* (York: York Medieval Press, 2000).

Cross, Tom Peete, *Motif Index of Early Irish Literature* (Bloomington: Indiana University Press, 1952).

Curnow, Demelza Jayne, 'Five Case Studies on the Transmission of Popular Middle English Verse Romances', PhD thesis, University of Bristol, 2002.

Dalrymple, Roger, *Language and Piety in Middle English Romance* (Cambridge: D. S. Brewer, 2000).

Davis, J. W., '*Le Pèlerinage de Charlemagne* and *King Arthur and King Cornwall*: A Study in the Evolution of a Tale', PhD thesis, Indiana University, 1973, pp. 379–80.

Davis, Norman (ed.), *Paston Letters and Papers of the Fifteenth Century*, 2 vols, EETS SS 20, 21 (Oxford: Oxford University Press, 2004).

De, Esha Niyogi, 'From Theater to Ritual: A Study of the Revesby Mummers' Play', in W. F. H. Nicolaisen (ed.), *Oral Tradition in the Middle Ages* (Binghampton, NY: Medieval & Renaissance Texts & Studies, 1995), pp. 115–27.

Dean, Christopher, *Arthur of England: English Attitudes to King Arthur and the Knights of the Round Table in the Middle Ages and the Renaissance* (Toronto: University of Toronto Press, 1987).

Deloney, Thomas, *The Garland of Good Will* (London: Edward Brewster and Robert Bird, 1628).

—— *The Works of Thomas Deloney: Edited from the Earliest Extant Editions & Broadsides with an Introduction and Notes by Francis Oscar Mann* (Oxford: Clarendon Press, 1912).

Dibdin, T. F., *The Bibliographical Decameron; or, Ten Days Pleasant Discourse upon Illuminated Manuscripts, and Subjects Connected with Early Engravings, Typography, and Bibliography*, 3 vols (London: Shakespeare Press, 1817).

Dyche, Thomas, *A New General English Dictionary*, rev. William Pardon (London: Catherine & Richard Ware, 1765).

Echard, Siân (ed.), *The Arthur of Medieval Latin Literature: The Development and Dissemination of the Arthurian Legend in Medieval Latin* (Cardiff: University of Wales Press, 2011).

—— 'Malory in Print', in Megan G. Leitch and Cory James Rushton (eds.), *A New Companion to Malory*, Arthurian Studies LXXXVII (Cambridge: D. S. Brewer, 2019), 96–121.

Eisner, Sigmund, *A Tale of Wonder: A Source Study of The Wife of Bath's Tale* (Wexford: John English, 1957).

Evans, Joan, and Serjeantson, Mary S. (eds), *English Medieval Lapidaries*, EETS OS 190 (London: Oxford University Press, 1933).

Fairer, David, 'The Origins of Warton's *History of English Poetry*', *Review of English Studies* NS 32(125) (1981), pp. 37–63.

Farmer, David Hugh, *The Oxford Dictionary of Saints* (Oxford: Oxford University Press, 2011).

Feylde, Thomas, *Controversy between a Lover and a Jay* (London: Wynkyn de Worde, 1527), available at www.proquest.com (accessed July 2023).

Field, P. J. C., 'What Women Really Want: The Genesis of Chaucer's Wife of Bath's Tale', in Elizabeth Archibald and David F. Johnson (eds), *Arthurian Literature 27* (Cambridge: D. S. Brewer, 2010), pp. 59–85.

—— 'Malory and *The Wedding of Sir Gawen and Dame Ragnell*', *Archiv für das Studium der neueren Sprachen und Literaturen* 219 (1982), pp. 374–81.

Fielding, Henry, *The Tragedy of Tragedies; or the Life and Death of Tom Thumb the Great. As it is Acted at the Theatre in the Hay-Market. With the Annnotations of H. Scriblerus Secundus* (London: J. Roberts, 1731; facsimile repr. Ilkley and London: Scolar Press, 1973).

Flood, Victoria E., 'Exile and Return: The Development of Political Prophecy on the Borders of England, *c.*1136–1450s', DPhil. thesis, University of York, 2013.

—— *Prophecy, Politics and Place in Medieval England: From Geoffrey of Monmouth to Thomas of Erceldoune* (Cambridge: D. S. Brewer, 2016).

Fowler, David C., *A Literary History of the Popular Ballad* (Durham, NC: Duke University Press, 1968).

Fox, Adam, *Oral and Literate Culture in England, 1500–1700* (Oxford: Clarendon Press, 2000).

Friedman, Albert B., Review of David C. Fowler's *A Literary History of the Popular Ballad*, *Speculum* 45(1) (1970), pp. 127–29.

Fumerton, Patricia, 'Remembering by Dismembering: Databases, Archiving, and the Recollection of Seventeenth-Century Broadside Ballads', in Patricia Fumerton, Anita Guerrini, and Kris McAbee (eds), *Ballads and Broadsides in Britain, 1500–1800* (Farnham: Ashgate, 2010), pp. 13–34.

Fumerton, Patricia, and Guerrini, Anita, 'Introduction: Straws in the Wind', in Patricia Fumerton, Anita Guerrini, and Kris McAbee (eds), *Ballads and Broadsides in Britain, 1500–1800* (Farnham: Ashgate, 2010), pp. 1–9.

Fumerton, Patricia, Guerrini, Anita, and McAbee, Kris (eds), *Ballads and Broadsides in Britain, 1500–1800* (Farnham: Ashgate, 2010).

Furnivall, F. J. (ed.), *Robert Laneham's Letter: Describing a Part of the Entertainment unto Queen Elizabeth at the Castle of Kenilworth in 1575* (London: Chatto & Windus, 1907).

Furrow, Melissa M. (ed.), *Ten Fifteenth-Century Comic Poems*, Garland Medieval Texts 13 (New York: Garland, 1985).

Fuwa, Yuri, 'Paving the Way for the Arthurian Revival: William Caxton and Sir Thomas Malory's King Arthur in the Eighteenth Century', *Journal of the International Arthurian Society* 5(1) (2017), pp. 59–72.

Garbáty, Thomas J., 'Rhyme, Romance, Ballads, Burlesque, and the Confluence of Form', in Robert F. Yeager (ed.), *Fifteenth-Century Studies: Recent Essays* (Hamden, CT: Archon, 1984), pp. 283–301.

Geoffrey of Monmouth, *Life of Merlin: Geoffrey of Monmouth Vita Merlini, Edited with Introduction, Facing Translation, Textual Commentary, Name Notes Index and Translations of the Lailoken Tales, by Basil Clarke* (Cardiff: University of Wales Press, 1973).

Gollancz, Sir Israel (ed.), *Sir Gawain and the Green Knight*, with Introductory Essays by Mabel Day and Mary S. Serjeantson, EETS OS 210 (London: Oxford University Press, 1940).

Goodrich, Peter H., *Merlin: A Casebook* (New York: Routledge, 2003).

Gordon, Ian Alistair, *Shenstone's Miscellany, 1759–1763* (Oxford: Clarendon Press, 1952).

Gray, Douglas, 'A Note on the Percy Folio *Grene Knight*', in Bonnie Wheeler (ed.), *Arthurian Studies in Honour of P. J. C. Field*, Arthurian Studies LVII (Cambridge: D. S. Brewer, 2004), pp. 165–71.

Griffith, David, '*The Turke and Gowin*', in W. R. J. Barron (ed.), *The Arthur of the English: The Arthurian Legend in Medieval English Life and Literature*, Arthurian Literature in the Middle Ages 2 (Cardiff: University of Wales Press, 1999), pp. 201–3.

Grosart, Alexander Balloch (ed.), *Robert Chester's 'Love's Martyr, Or, Rosalins Complaint', With Its Supplement, 'Diverse Poeticall Essaies on the Turtle and the Phoenix'* (London: Trübner, 1878; repr. Cambridge: Cambridge University Press, 2014).

Hahn, Thomas, 'Gawain and Popular Chivalric Romance in Britain', in Roberta L. Krueger (ed.), *The Cambridge Companion to Medieval Romance* (Cambridge: Cambridge University Press, 2000), pp. 218–34.

—— (ed.), *Sir Gawain: Eleven Romances and Tales* (Kalamazoo, MI: Western Michigan University, 1995), https://d.lib.rochester.edu/teams/publication/hahn-sir-gawain (accessed July 2023).

Hahn, Thomas, and Symons, Dana M., 'Medieval English Romance', in Peter Brown (ed.), *A Companion to Medieval English Literature and Culture c.1350–c.1500* (Malden, MA: Blackwell, 2007), pp. 344–45.

Hastings, Selina, *Sir Gawain and the Loathly Lady*, by Selina Hastings, with Illustrations by Juan Wijngaard (London: Walker Books, 1985).

Hodder, Karen, 'Henry Lovelich's *History of the Holy* Grail'Holy , in W. R. J. Barron (ed.), *The Arthur of the English: The Arthurian Legend in Medieval English Life and Literature*, Arthurian Literature in the Middle Ages 2 (Cardiff: University of Wales Press, 1999), pp. 78–83.

Holland, William E., 'Formulaic Diction and the Descent of a Middle English Romance', *Speculum* 48 (1973), pp. 89–109.

Horobin, Simon, and Wiggins, Alison, 'Reconsidering Lincoln's Inn MS 150', *Medium Aevum* 77(1) (2008), pp. 30–53.

Hulbert, J. R., 'Syr Gawayn and the Grene Kny3t', *Modern Philology* 13 (1915–16), pp. 433–62 and pp. 689–730.

Hume, David, *The History of England, from the Invasion of Julius Cæsar to the Revolution in 1688 in Six Volumes* (London: A. Millar, 1762).

Huws, Daniel, 'MS Porkington 10 and its Scribes', in Jennifer Fellows et al. (eds), *Romance Reading on the Book: Essays on Medieval Narrative Presented to Maldwyn Mills* (Cardiff: University of Wales Press, 1996), pp. 188–207.

Jansen, Sharon L., *Political Protest and Prophecy under Henry VIII* (Woodbridge: Boydell & Brewer, 1991).

Jarman, A. O. H., 'The Merlin Legend and the Welsh Tradition of Prophecy', in Rachel Bromwich, A. O. H. Jarman, and Brynley F. Roberts (eds), *The Arthur of the Welsh:*

The Arthurian Legend in Medieval Welsh Literature (Cardiff: University of Wales Press, 1991), pp. 117–45.

Johnson, Lesley, and Williams, Elizabeth (eds), *Sir Orfeo and Sir Launfal* (Leeds: University of Leeds, School of English, 1984).

Johnston, R. C., and Owen, D. D. R. (eds), *Two Old French Gauvain Romances: (Le Chevalier à l'épée & La Mule sans frein)* (Edinburgh: Scottish Academic Press, 1972).

Johnson, Samuel, *A Dictionary of the English Language* (London: J. & P. Knapton, 1755).

Johnston, Arthur, *Enchanted Ground: The Study of Medieval Romance in the Eighteenth Century* (London: Athlone Press, 1964).

Jost, Jean E., 'The Role of Violence in "Adventure": "The Ballad of King Arthur and the King of Cornwall" and "The Turke and Gowin"', *Arthurian Interpretations* 2(2) (1988), pp. 47–57.

Kalinke, Marianne E., 'Chastity Tests', in Norris J. Lacy (ed.), *The New Arthurian Encyclopedia* (Chicago: St James Press, 1991), pp. 81–83.

Kaluza, M. (ed.), *Lybeaus Desconus*, Altenglische Bibliothek 5 (Leipzig: O. R. Reisland, 1890).

Karpowicz, Adam, 'Ottoman Bows: An Assessment of Draw Weight, Performance and Tactical Use', *Antiquity* 81 (2007), pp. 675–85.

King, Andrew, 'Dead Butchers and Fiend-like Queens: Literary and Political History in *The Misfortunes of Arthur* and *Macbeth*', in Rhiannon Purdie and Nicola Royan (eds), *The Scots and Medieval Arthurian Legend*, Arthurian Studies LXI (Cambridge: D. S. Brewer, 2005), pp. 121–34.

Kittredge, George Lyman, *A Study of Gawain and the Green Knight* (Cambridge, MA: Harvard University Press, 1916).

Kooper, Erik (ed.), 'The Squire of Low Degree', in *Sentimental and Humorous Romances* (Kalamazoo, MI: Medieval Institute Publications, 2006), pp. 127–79.

Kurvinen, Auvo (ed.), *Sir Gawain and The Carl of Carlisle: In Two Versions* (Helsinki: Suomalaisen Tiedeakatemia, 1951).

Laskaya, Anne, and Salisbury, Eve (eds), *The Middle English Breton Lays* (Kalamazoo, MI: Medieval Institute Publications, 1995), https://d.lib.rochester.edu/teams/text/laskaya-and-salisbury-middle-english-breton-lays-sir-launfal-introduction (accessed July 2023).

Lawlis, Merritt E., 'Shakespeare, Deloney, and the Earliest Text of the Arthur Ballad', *Harvard Library Bulletin* 10 (1956), pp. 130–35.

Lawton, David, 'History and Legend: The Exile and the Turk', in Patricia Clare Ingham and Michelle R. Warren (eds), *Postcolonial Moves: Medieval through Modern* (Basingstoke: Palgrave Macmillan, 2003), pp. 173–94.

Leech, Mary, 'Why Dame Ragnell Had to Die: Feminine Usurpation of Masculine Authority in "The Wedding of Sir Gawain and Dame Ragnell"', in S. Elizabeth Passmore and Susan B. Carter (eds), *The English 'Loathly Lady' Tales* (Kalamazoo, MI: Medieval Institute Publications, 2007), pp. 213–34.

Lindahl, Carl, 'The Oral Undertones of Late Medieval Romance', in W. F. H. Nicolaisen (ed.), *Oral Tradition in the Middle Ages* (Binghampton, NY: Medieval & Renaissance Texts & Studies, 1995), pp. 59–75.

Lloyd, Richard, *A brief discourse of the most renowned actes and right valiant conquests of those puissant princes, called the nine worthies wherein is declared their seuverall proportions and dispositions, and what armes euerie one gaue, as also in what time ech of them liued, and how at the length they ended their liues* (London: R. Warde, 1584).

Lumby, J. R. (ed.), *Bernardus de Cura Rei Famuliaris, with Some Early Scottish Prophecies*, EETS OS 42 (London: Oxford University Press, 1870).

Lupack, Alan (ed.), *Lancelot of the Laik* and *Sir Tristrem* (Kalamazoo, MI: Medieval Institute Publications, 1994), https://d.lib.rochester.edu/teams/publication/lupack-lancelot-of-the-laik-and-sir-tristrem (accessed July 2023).

Luttrell, Claude, '*Le Conte du Graal* and Precursors of Perceval', *Bibliographical Bulletin of the International Arthurian Society* 46 (1994), pp. 291–323.

Lyle, E. B., '"*The Turk and* Gawain" as a Source of *Thomas of Erceldoune*', *Forum for Modern Language Studies* 6(1) (1970), pp. 98–102.

—— '*Sir Landevale* and the Fairy-Mistress Theme in *Thomas of Ercedoune*', *Medium Aevum* 42 (1973), pp. 244–50.

MacCracken, Henry Noble (ed.), *The Minor Poems of John Lydgate. Part I. The Lydgate Canon, Religious Poems*, EETS ES 107 (London: Oxford University Press, 1911; repr. 2006).

McDonald, Nicola (ed.), *Pulp Fictions of Medieval England: Essays in Popular Romance* (Manchester: Manchester University Press, 2004).

McDowell, Paula, 'Mediating Media Past and Present: Towards a Genealogy of "Print Culture" and "Oral Tradition"', in Clifford Siskin and William Warner (eds), *This is Enlightenment* (Chicago: University of Chicago Press, 2010), pp. 229–46.

—— '"The Art of Printing was Fatal": Print Commerce and the Idea of Oral Tradition in Long Eighteenth-Century Ballad Discourse', in Patricia Fumerton, Anita Guerrini, and Kris McAbee (eds), *Ballads and Broadsides in Britain, 1500–1800* (Farnham: Ashgate, 2010), pp. 35–56.

McGillivray, Murray, *Memorization in the Transmission of the Middle English Romances* (London: Routledge, 1990).

Machan, Clinton, 'A Structural Study of the English Gawain Romances', *Neophilologus* 66 (1982), pp. 629–37.

McPherson, James, *Fragments of Ancient Poetry, collected in the Highlands of Scotland, and translated from the Galic or Erse Language* (Edinburgh: G. Hamilton and J. Balfour, 1760).

Macrae-Gibson, O. D. (ed.), *Of Arthour and of Merlin*, 2 vols, EETS OS 268, 279 (Oxford: Oxford University Press, 1973, 1979).

Madden, Sir Frederic (ed.), *Syr Gawayne: A Collection of Ancient Romance-Poems, by Scotish and English Authors, Relating to that Celebrated Knight of the Round Table, with an Introduction, Notes, and a Glossary* (London: Richard and John Taylor, 1839), pp. 275–87, https://archive.org/details/syrgawaynecoll6100maddouft/page/n5/mode/2up (accessed July 2023).

Malory, Sir Thomas, *Le Morte Darthur by Syr Thomas Malory, reprinted and ed. H Oskar Sommer* (London: David Nutt, 1889–91), https://quod.lib.umich.edu/cgi/t/text/text-idx?c=cme;idno=MaloryWks2 (accessed July 2023).

—— *Le Morte Darthur*, ed. P. J. C. Field, Arthurian Studies LXXX, 2 vols (Cambridge: D. S. Brewer, 2013).

Manning, Robert, *The Story of England by Robert Manning of Brunne, A.D. 1338*, 2 vols, ed. Frederick J. Furnivall (London: HMSO, 1887; repr. Cambridge: Cambridge University Press, 2012).

Maynadier, G. H., *The Wife of Bath's Tale: Its Sources and Analogues* (London: David Nutt, 1901).

Marvin, Julia (ed.), *The Oldest Anglo-Norman Prose Brut Chronicle*, ed. Julia Marvin (Woodbridge: Boydell Press, 2006).

Mead, William Edward (ed.), *The Famous Historie of Chinon of England by Christopher Middleton*, EETS OS 165 (London: Oxford University Press, 1925).

Mehl, Dieter, *The Middle English Romances of the Thirteenth and Fourteenth Centuries* (London: Routledge & Kegan Paul, 1968).

Merriman, James Douglas, *The Flower of Kings: A Study of the Arthurian Legend in England between 1485 and 1835* (Lawrence: University Press of Kansas, 1973).

Michelsson, Elisabeth, *Appropriating King Arthur: The Arthurian Legend in English Drama and Entertainments, 1485–1625* (Uppsala: Uppsala University, 1999), pp. 244–75.

Middleton, Roger, 'Chrétien de Troyes at Auction: Nicolas-Joseph Foucault and Other Eighteenth-Century Collectors', in Peter Damian-Grint (ed.), *Medievalism and 'manière gothique' in Enlightenment France* (Oxford: Voltaire Foundation, 2008), pp. 261–83.

Mills, Maldwyn, 'A Medieval Reviser at Work', *Medium Aevum* 32 (1963), pp. 11–23.

—— (ed.) *Lybeaus Desconus*, EETS OS 261 (Oxford: Oxford University Press, 1969).

—— 'The Percy Folio Text of *Libius Disconius*', in S. Watanabe and Y. Hosoya (eds), *A Festschrift in Honour of Mitsunori Imai to Celebrate His Seventieth Birthday* (Tokyo: Shohakusha, 2009), pp. 79–92.

Milton, John, *The history of Britain, that part especially now call'd England from the first traditional beginning, continu'd to the Norman conquest* (London: James Allestry, 1670), https://quod.lib.umich.edu/e/eebo/A50902.0001.001?view=toc (accessed July 2023).

Moll, Richard, *Before Malory: Reading Arthur in Later Medieval England* (Toronto: University of Toronto Press, 2003).

Moore, A. W., *The Folk Lore of the Isle of Man* (London: David Nutt, 1891).

Moore, Samuel, 'Patrons of Letters in Norfolk and Suffolk, c.1450', *PMLA* 27(2) (1912), pp. 188–207; *PMLA* 28(1) (1913), pp. 79–105.

Morris, Brian, and Withington, Eleanor (eds), *The Poems of John Cleveland* (Oxford: Clarendon Press, 1967).

Moschenska, Joe, 'A New Plot', *Times Literary Supplement*, 18 March 2016.

Nastali, Daniel P., and Boardman, Phillip C., *The Arthurian Annals: The Tradition in English from 1250 to 2000*, 2 vols (Oxford: Oxford University Press, 2004).

Nichols, John, *Illustrations of the Literary History of the Eighteenth Century: Consisting of Authentic Memoirs and Original Letters of Eminent Persons, and Intended as a Sequel to the 'Literary Anecdotes'*, 8 vols (London: John Nichols and Son, 1817–58).

Niles, John D., 'On the Logic of *Le Pèlerinage de Charlemagne*', *Neuphilologische Mitteilungen* 81(2) (1980), pp. 208–16.

Nixon, Ingeborg (ed.), *Thomas of Erceldoune, Parts 1–2* (Copenhagen: Publications of the Department of English, University of Copenhagen, 1980–83).

Norris, Ralph, 'Sir Thomas Malory and *The Wedding of Sir Gawain and Dame Ragnell* Reconsidered', *Arthuriana* 19 (2009), pp. 82–102.

Oberempt, Kenneth J., 'Lord Berners' "Arthur of Lytell Brytayne": Its Date of Composition and French Source', *Neuphilologische Mittelungen* 77(2) (1976), pp. 241–52.

Parins, Marylyn (ed.), *Sir Thomas Malory: The Critical Heritage* (London: Routledge, 1987).

Passmore, S. Elizabeth, and Carter, Susan B. (eds), *The English 'Loathly Lady' Tales: Boundaries, Traditions, Motifs* (Kalamazoo, MI: Medieval Institute Publications, 2007).

Pearsall, Derek, *Old English and Middle English Poetry* (London: Routledge & Kegan Paul, 1977).

—— 'Middle English Romance and its Audiences', in M.-J. Arn, H. Wirtjes, and H. Jansen (eds), *Historical & Editorial Studies in Medieval & Early Modern English for Johan Gerritsen* (Groningen: Wolters-Noordhoff, 1985), pp. 38–39.

Pollack, Sean, 'Border States: Parody, Sovereignty, and Hybrid Identity in *The Carl of Carlisle*', *Arthuriana* 19 (2009), pp. 10–26.

Preston, Michael J., 'The Revesby Sword Play', *Journal of American Folklore* 85(335) (1972), pp. 51–57.

Purdie, Rhiannon, *Anglicising Romance: Tail-Rhyme and Genre in Medieval English Literature* (Cambridge: D. S. Brewer, 2008).

Putter, Ad, 'Middle English Romance and the Oral Tradition', in Karl Reichl (ed.), *Medieval Oral Literature* (Berlin: De Gruyter, 2011), pp. 335–52.

—— 'The Singing of Middle English Romance: Stanza Forms and *Contrafacta*', in Ad Putter and Judith A. Jefferson (eds), *The Transmission of Medieval Romance: Metres, Manuscripts and Early Prints* (Cambridge: D. S. Brewer, 2018), pp. 69–90.

Radulescu, Raluca L., and Rushton, Cory James (eds), *A Companion to Medieval Popular Romance* (Cambridge: D. S. Brewer, 2009).

Ramsay, Allan, *The Tea-Table Miscellany: or, a Collection of Choice Songs, Scots and English*, 4 vols (London: A. Millar, 1740).

Ramsey, Lee, 'The Monstrous Churl and Other Arthurian Themes', in *Chivalric Romances: Popular Literature in Medieval England* (Bloomington: Indiana University Press, 1983), pp. 200–08.

Reeve, Michael D. (ed.), and Wright, Neil (trans.), *The History of the Kings of Britain: An Edition and Translation of the* De gestis Britonum (Historia Regum Brittanniae) (Woodbridge: Boydell Press, 2007).

Renaut de Beaujeu, *Le Bel Inconnu*, ed. M. Perret and I. Weill, Champion classiques, série moyen âge 4 (Paris: Champion, 2003).

Ritson, Joseph, *Observations on the Three First Volumes of the History of English Poetry*, 3 vols (London: J. Stockdale & R. Faulder, 1782).

—— *Ancient Songs, from the Reign of King Henry the Third, to the Revolution* (London: J. Johnson, 1790).

—— *Ancient Engleish Metrical Romanceës*, 3 vols (London: G. & W. Nicol, 1802).

Robertson, D. W., 'Chaucerian Tragedy', *ELH* 19(1) (1952), pp. 1–37.

Rogers, Gillian, 'Themes and Variations: Studies in Some English Gawain-Poems', PhD thesis, University of Wales, 1978.

—— 'Folk Romance', in W. R. J. Barron (ed.), *The Arthur of the English: The Arthurian Legend in Medieval English Life and Literature*, Arthurian Literature in the Middle Ages 2 (Cardiff: University of Wales Press, 1999), pp. 197–224.

—— '*King Arthur and King Cornwall*', in W. R. J. Barron (ed.), *The Arthur of the English: The Arthurian Legend in Medieval English Life and Literature*, Arthurian Literature in the Middle Ages 2 (Cardiff: University of Wales Press, 1999), pp. 215–19.

Rollins, Hyder E., 'The Black-Letter Broadside Ballad', *PMLA* 34(2) (1919), pp. 258–339.

Rossi, Carla, 'A Clue to the Fate of the Lost MS. Royal 16 E VIII, a Copy of the *Voyage de Charlemagne*', *Romania* 126(501–2) (2008), pp. 245–52.

Rutter, Russell, 'William Caxton and Literary Patronage', *Studies in Philology* 84 (1987), pp. 440–70.

Salisbury, Eve, and Weldon, James (eds), *Lybeaus Desconus* (Kalamazoo, MI: Medieval Institute Publications, 2013), https://d.lib.rochester.edu/teams/publication/salisbury-and-weldon-lybeaus-desconus (accessed July 2023).

Sánchez-Marti, Jordi, 'The Printed History of the Middle English Verse Romances', *Modern Philology* 107 (2009), pp. 1–31.

Schwegler, Robert A., 'The Arthur Ballad: From Malory to Deloney to Shakespeare', *Essays in Literature* 5(1) (1978), pp. 3–13.

Scott, David, 'William Patten and the Authorship of "Robert Laneham's Letter" (1575)', *English Literary Renaissance* 7(3) (1977), pp. 297–306.

Shepherd, Stephen H. A., *Middle English Romances: Authoritative Texts, Sources and Backgrounds, Criticism* (New York: W. W. Norton & Co., 1995), pp. 380–87.

—— 'No Poet Has His Travesty Alone: *The Weddynge of Sir Gawen and Dame Ragnell*', in Jennifer Fellows et al. (eds), *Romance Reading on the Book: Essays on Medieval Literature Presented to Maldwyn Mills* (Cardiff: University of Wales Press, 1996), pp. 112–28.

Shimomura, Sachi, *Odd Bodies and Visible Ends in Medieval Literature* (Basingstoke: Palgrave Macmillan, 2006), pp. 72–84.

Simpson, Roger, 'St George and the Pendragon', in Richard Utz and Tom Shippey (eds), *Medievalism in the Modern World: Essays in Honour of Leslie J. Workman* (Turnhout: Brepols, 1982), pp. 131–53.

Sklar, Elizabeth, 'Arthour and Merlin: The Englishing of Arthur', *Michigan Academician* 8 (1975), pp. 49–57.

Smith, David Nichol, 'Warton's History of English Poetry', *Proceedings of the British Academy* 15 (1929).

Smith, Margaret M. (ed.), *Index of English Literary Manuscripts*, vol. 3, *1700–1800. Part 2: John Gay–Ambrose Philips, with a First-Line Index to Parts 1 and 2* (London: Mansell, 1989).

Speed, Diane (ed.), 'The Grene Knight', in *Medieval English Romances*, 3rd ed., 2 vols (Durham: University of Durham, 1993), I, 236–59; II, 321–30, 348–50.

Spence, Lewis, *The Fairy Tradition in Britain* (London: Rider & Co., 1948).

Sponsler, Claire (ed.), John Lydgate, *Mummings and Entertainments* (Kalamazoo, MI: Medieval Institute Publications, 2010), https://d.lib.rochester.edu/teams/text/sponsler-lydgate-mummings-and-entertainments-introduction (accessed July 2023).

—— *The Queen's Dumb Shows: John Lydgate and the Making of Early Theater* (Philadelphia: University of Pennsylvania Press, 2014).

Stévanovitch, Colette, 'Enquiries into the Textual History of the Seventeenth-Century *Sir Lambewell* (London, British Library Additional 27897)', in Leo Carruthers et al. (eds), *Palimpsests and the Literary Imagination of Medieval England: Collected Essays* (New York: Palgrave Macmillan, 2011), pp. 193–204.

Stokes, Myra, '*Lanval* to *Sir Launfal*: A Story Becomes Popular', in Ad Putter and Jane Gilbert (eds), *The Spirit of Medieval English Popular Romance* (Harlow: Longman, 2000), pp. 56–77.

Sturlson, Snorri, *Edda*, trans. and ed. Anthony Faulkes (London: Dent, 1987).

Taylor, Andrew, 'The Myth of the Minstrel Manuscript', *Speculum* 66 (1991), pp. 43–73.

Temple, William, *An Introduction to the History of England* (London: Richard Simpson, Ralph Simpson, 1695).

Thompson, Raymond H., '"Muse on Þi Mirrour …": The Challenge of the Outlandish Stranger in the English Arthurian Verse Romances', *Folklore* 87(2) (1976), pp. 201–8.

Thompson, Stith, *Motif Index of Folk Literature: A Classification of Narrative Elements in Folktales, Ballads, Fables, Mediaeval Romances, Exempla, Fabliaux, Jest-Books and Local Legends*, 6 vols (Copenhagen: Rosenkilde and Bagger, 1955–57).

Turville-Petre, Thorlac (ed.), *Alliterative Poetry of the Later Middle Ages: An Anthology* (London: Routledge, 1989).

Vincent, Nicholas, *The Holy Blood: King Henry III and the Westminster Blood Relic* (Cambridge: Cambridge University Press, 2001).

Wace, *Wace's Roman de Brut: A History of the British Text and Translation*, ed. Judith Weiss (Exeter: Exeter University Press, 1999).

Waldron, George, *A Description of the Isle of Man*, ed. William Harrison (Douglas: The Manx Society, 1865): a reprint of Waldron's 1731 edition, www.isle-of-man.com/manxnotebook/manxsoc/msvol11/p01.htm (accessed July 2023).

Warton, Thomas, *Observations on the Fairie Queene of Spenser* (London: R. and J. Dodsley, 1754), https://quod.lib.umich.edu/e/ecco/004884515.0001.000?view=toc (accessed July 2023).

—— *The History of English Poetry from the Close of the Eleventh to the Commencement of the Eighteenth Century*, 4 vols (London: J. Dodsley et al., 1774–81).

Watt, Tessa, *Cheap Print and Popular Piety, 1550–1640* (Cambridge: Cambridge University Press, 1991).

Webster, K. G. T., 'Arthur and Charlemagne', *Englische Studien* 36 (1906), pp. 357–60.

Weldon, James, '"Naked as She Was Bore": Naked Disenchantment in *Lybeaus Desconus*', *Parergon* ns 24(1) (2007), pp. 67–99.

—— 'Lybeaus Desconus', in S. Echard and R. A. Rouse (eds), *The Encyclopedia of Medieval Literature in Britain*, 3 vols (Chichester: John Wiley & Sons, 2017), III, 212–16.

Whiting, Bartlett Jere, *Proverbs, Sentences, and Proverbial Phrases; from English Writings, Mainly before 1500* (Cambridge, MA: Belknap Press, 1968).

Wiggins, Alison Eve, '*Guy of Warwick*: Study and Transcription', PhD thesis, University of Sheffield, 2000.

Williams, Elizabeth, '*Sir Landevale, Sir Launfal, Sir Lambewell*', in W. R. J. Barron (ed.), *The Arthur of the English: The Arthurian Legend in Medieval English Life and Literature*, Arthurian Literature in the Middle Ages 2 (Cardiff: University of Wales Press, 1999), pp. 130–35.

Williams, Jeanne Myrle Wilson, 'A Critical Edition of "The Turke and Gowin"', PhD thesis, University of Southern Mississippi, 1987.

Wilson, Anne, *Traditional Romance and Tale: How Stories Mean* (Ipswich: D. S. Brewer, 1976).

Wilson, Edward, '*Sir Gawain and the Green Knight* and the Stanley Family of Stanley, Storeton, and Hooton', *Review of English Studies* 30 (1979), pp. 308–16.

Winters, M., '*The Romance of Hunbaut*: An Arthurian Poem of the Thirteenth Century' (Leiden: E. J. Brill, 1984).

Withrington, John, 'The Arthurian Epitaph in Malory's "Morte Darthur"', in Richard Barber (ed.), *Arthurian Literature* 7 (Cambridge: D. S. Brewer, 1987), pp. 103–44.

—— 'The Arthurian Epitaph in Malory's "Morte Darthur"', in James P. Carley (ed.), *Glastonbury and the Arthurian Tradition*, Arthurian Studies 44 (Cambridge: D. S. Brewer, 2001), pp. 211–47.

—— 'King Arthur as Emperor', *Notes & Queries* 233 (1988), pp. 13–15.

—— *The Wedding of Sir Gawain and Dame Ragnell*, Lancaster Modern Spelling Texts (Lancaster: Lancaster University, 1991).

—— '"He Telleth the Number of the Stars; He Calleth Them All By Their Names": The Lesser Knights of Sir Thomas Malory's *Morte Darthur*', *Quondam et Futurus* 3(4) (1993), pp. 17–27.

—— '*The Weddynge of Sir Gawen and Dame Ragnell* and *The Marriage of Sir Gawaine*', in W. R. J. Barron (ed.), *The Arthur of the English: The Arthurian Legend in Medieval English Life and Literature*, Arthurian Literature in the Middle Ages 2 (Cardiff: University of Wales Press, 1999), pp. 207–10.

Withrington, John, and Field, P. J. C., 'The Wife of Bath's Tale', in Robert M. Correale and Mary Hamel (eds), *Sources and Analogues of The Canterbury Tales*, 2 vols (Cambridge: D. S. Brewer, 2005), II, 405–48.

Zaerr, Linda Marie, '*The Weddynge of Sir Gawen and Dame Ragnell*: Performance and Intertextuality in Middle English Popular Romance', in Evelyn Birge Vitz et al. (eds), *Performing Medieval Narrative* (Cambridge: D. S. Brewer, 2005), pp. 193–208.

—— *Performance and the Middle English Romance* (Cambridge: D. S. Brewer, 2012), pp. 181–233.

Index

Please note: citations within Explanatory and Textual notes are not indexed

'The Aegyptian Quene'   7
Allde, Edward   71
'The Ancient Ballad of Chevy Chase'   20, 72
Anderson, Robert   30–31n62
Arthour and Merlin (AM)   141–43
Ascham, Roger   41n20

Bailey, Nathan   16
Bale, John   25n2, 33, 35
Barber, Richard   39–40n3
Berners, Lord Gerald   53n2
Bird, Robert   71
Blackmore, Sir Richard   36
Bliss, A .J.   115, 116n1, 117n5
Blount, Edward   5
Blount, Thomas   5–7
Boardman, Phillip C.   26n6, 42n27, n31, n32, 71, 73n4
Boffey, Julia   114–15, 117n6
Bongaerts, Theo   5–6
Bowle, John   26n8, 42–43n37
Bownd, Nicholas   16–17
Boy and Mantle (BM)   18, 22, 23, 28n33, 38, 39, 43n38, 99, 247–50
   text   251–58
Byrne, Aisling   10n17, 11n18, 17, 37, 80

Camden, William   33, 40n9
Campion, Thomas *Masque at Lord Hays Marriage*   34
The Carle off Carlisle (CARLE)   16, 22, 23, 52, 82n11, n12, 224, 331–34
   text   335–52
Carlisle   41n28, 43n38, 116
Caxton, William   19, 21, 32, 33, 35, 39n3
Cervantes, Miguel de   42
Charles I, King   3
Chaucer, Geoffrey   9, 13, 15, 38, 43n43, 101n3, 101n4, 117n7
   'The Wife of Bath's Tale' (WBT)   21, 22, 30n59, 38, 43n42, 46–47, 99–100, 101n3, 102n8, 259
Chester, Robert   33
Child, Francis James   44, 247
Cleveland, John   3, 10n8
   'Newarke'   2–3, 10n8

Clieveland, William   26n11
Congreve, William, *Love for Love*   6–7
Cooper, Helen   11n17, 39n2
Cobbett, Richard, 'The Distracted Puritan'/'O Noble Festus'   4
Cox, Captain Richard   7, 34, 40n15, 41n23, 102n13, 115, 225–26n5

Dalrymple, David *see* Hailes, Lord
Dalrymple, Roger   23
de Troyes, Chrétien   79, 80, 100
   Perceval   37, 42n36, 82n17, 247–48
Deloney, Thomas   14, 26n6, 71
   The Garland of Good Will   7, 18, 71, 72n1, 73n3
Dibdin, Rev. T. F.   10n7
Dicey, Cluer   17, 37, 42n34
Dodsley, J.   18, 25n1, 42n35
Donatelli, Joseph   7, 10n10, 11n21, n22, 20, 28n31
Douglas, Gavin   9
Dugdale, William   33
Dyche, Thomas   16

Edward I, King   33, 39n3
Edward, Robert   115
Eger and Grime   20, 22
Eisner, Sigmund   100
Elizabeth I, Queen   15, 18, 19, 34
Evans, Evan   37, 43n38, n43, 101n3, 143n2, 248

Fabyan, Robert   32
Farmer, Richard   14, 28n32
Feylde, Thomas *Controversy between a Lover and a Jay*   115, 117n7
Field, P. J. C.   100, 102n15
Fielding, Henry, *Tom Thumb*   32, 36
Flood, Victoria   10n17, 11n18, 37, 80
Fowler, David C.   19
Fox, Adam   40n6
Friedman, Albert B.   19, 29n45
Furnivall, Frederick J.   2, 3, 5, 7, 9n6, 10n7, 11n19, 27n15, 40n15, 41n17, 44
Furrow, Melissa   247

Geoffrey of Monmouth *Historia Regum Britanniae* (HRB)   32, 36, 39n2, 141, 143n2

368

Index

Gower, John
    Confessio Amantis 99, 102n8
    'The Tale of Florent' (FLOR) 30n59, 99–100
Grafton, Richard 32
Grainger, James 42n35
The Grene Knyght (GK) 5, 16, 22, 26n14, 51, 52, 79, 224–26, 332
    text 227–46
Groom, Nick 1, 15, 16, 18, 25n3, 26n10, 38, 39, 42n34, 101n4
Gutteridge, Anne 26n11
Guy and Colebrand 20
Guy of Warwick 13, 22, 29n44

Hahn, Thomas 24, 53n3, 78, 225–26n5
Hailes, Lord (David Dalrymple) 17, 18, 27n23, 37, 259
Hales, John W. 2, 3, 9n9, 27n15, 44
Hardyng, John 32
Harington, John 33
Hodder, Karen 143n3, 211–12
Holland, William E. 144n8
Hughes, Thomas *The Misfortunes of Arthur* 36
Hume, David *History of England* 33
Hurd, Richard *Letters on Chivalry and Romance* 18, 28n32

James I, King 4
Jamieson, Robert 30n62
Johnson, Richard
    A Crown Garland of Goulden Roses 25n7
    The History of Tom Thumb 36
    The Nine Worthies of London 26n7
Johnson, Samuel 1, 13, 14, 16
Jonson, Ben 34
Junius, Franciscus 9

Kaluza, M. 262n3
King Arthur and King Cornwall (KAKC) 16, 28n34, 30n54, 51–54, 82n14, 224
    text 56–70
King Arthur's Death (KAD) 18–19, 21, 22–23, 35, 37, 210–12
    text 213–23
King, John 117n3
Kurvinen, Auvo 331

Laneham, Robert 34, 41n17, 115
Lanier, Sidney 31n63
Laskaya, Anne 117n5
Lawton, David 11n23, 21, 78–79
Le Bel Inconnu 259, 262
Leech, Mary 101
Leland, John 32
Libius Disconius (LD) 6, 16, 20, 24, 30n54, 142, 259–63
    text 265–30
Lilley, William 42n32

Lindahl, Carl 19, 24, 30n59
Lloyd, Richard *The Nine Worthies* 21, 35, 210–11, 212n4
Lovelace, Richard 'To Althea from Prison' 2
Lovelich, Henry 141, 143n3
Lydgate, John 25n2, 29n49, 35, 37, 41n23, 115, 117n7, 117n8
Lye, Reverend Edward 9

McDonald, Nicola 9n5, 21–22, 23, 29n42
McDowell, Paula 17, 27n16
McPherson, James 27n26
Macrae-Gibson, O. D. 141–42, 143–44n7
Malory, Sir Thomas 32, 33, 102n15
    Le Morte Darthur (LMD) 18–19, 21, 33, 35–36, 38, 39–40n3, 41n18, 71–72, 211–12
Marie of France *Lanval* 114–15
The Marriage of Sir Gawaine (MSG) 9, 14, 15, 18, 21, 24, 28n34, 30n55, 31n63, 38, 39, 99–103, 114
    text 104–13
Maynadier, G. H. 100
Meale, Carol M. 114–15, 117n6
Merline (MER) 7–8, 10n10, 16, 20, 24, 141–44
    text 146–209
Merriman, James Douglas 32
Millican, Charles Bowie 21, 210
Milton, John 33
minstrelsy tradition 13, 14–15, 16, 17, 18, 19, 27n26, 28n40, 99
Moore, Samuel 11n23
Murray, James 115
Mychell, John 117n3

Nastali, Daniel P. 26n6, 42n27, n31, n32, 71, 73n4
Nicolson, Bishop William 41n25

Parker, Martin 2–3
Partridge, John 42n33
    Merlinus Liberatus 37
Paston, Sir John 78, 81n5, 225–26n5
Patten, William 41n17
Pearsall, Derek 19, 78
Le Pèlerinage de Charlemagne 51–53, 80, 82n14
Pepys, Samuel 7, 14, 17, 37
Percy, Elizabeth 20
Percy Folio (PF)
    annotations 8–9, 43n42, 44–45, 102n6
    date and provenance 1–3
    Elizabethan secretary script 2, 3
    hash-sign 3
    italic style 3
    manuscript damage 2, 45, 51, 53n1, 99
    medial punctus and virgule 3, 10n11
    presentation of manuscript 3–4, 10n13, 53n3

punctuation   3
scribe/compiler   1–3: assumptions about identity   4–5; links to Lancashire and Cheshire   5, 6; links to Stanley family   5; signs of Northern dialect in writing   3
sources   7–8, 11n22, 26n9, 37
stanza divisions   4
watermarks   2, 3
Percy, Thomas
correspondence with Warton   13, 22, 37–39, 42n37, 101n3, 102n9, 250n7
criticised by Ritson   15, 24–25, 39
dedication to Countess of Northumberland   15, 20, 39
discovery of PF   1, 8–9
disowns *Reliques*   15, 24
education   12n25
library   9, 12n25
publications before *Reliques*   14
Reliques
audience   17–20
authenticity and value   9, 13–15, 39
fourth edition published under nephew's name   15
support from Shenstone, Johnson, Farmer   14
Percy, Thomas (nephew of TP)   15, 24
Pinkerton, John   26n11, 30n62, 42n33
Pitt, Sir Humphrey   1, 2, 5, 21, 51, 71
Pope, Alexander
Peri Bathos   36
The Dunciad   25, 36
Purcell, Henry   36
Purdie, Rhiannon   42n26, 81n1
Putter, Ad   20, 22, 28n40

Radulescu, Raluca L.   19, 28n38
Ramsay, Allan
The Ever Green   17
The Tea-Table Miscellany   17, 28n29
Rastell, John   32
Revell, Edward   6
Revell, Elizabeth   6
Revell family   7
Reynolds, Sir Joshua   9n5
Ritson, Joseph   15, 25, 26n13, 28n40, 30–31n62, 39, 102n7
Rivington, Charles   30n61
'Robin Hood' ballads   4, 13
Robinson, Richard   32
Rogers, Gillian   2, 7, 11n22
Rollins, Hyder E.   10n12, n14
Rowley, William   36, 42n28
Rutter, Russell   39n3

St Clair-Kendall, S. G.   2–3, 8, 9n6, 20
Salisbury, Eve   117n5
Sheale, Richard   29n43

Shenstone, William   1, 13, 14, 16, 17–18, 27n18, 28n30, 37, 38, 43n39, 44, 248–49
Shepard, Leslie   1
Shepherd, Stephen   100
'The Siege of Roune'   1
Sir Gawain and the Green Knight (SGGK)   79–81, 224–25, 332
Sir Lambewell (LAMBE)   2, 10n16, 16, 22–23, 24, 114–18
sources   114–16
text   120–40
Sir Lancelott of Dulake (SLDL)   18, 22–23, 71–73, 114–15
text   75–77
Sir Triamore   7, 20, 41n24, 81n2
Speed, John   33
Spenser, Edmund   26n7, 36, 38
The Faerie Queen   18, 34, 41n18
Stanley family connections   5, 10–11n17, n18
Stanley, Sir John   80
Stanley, Sir Joseph   11n18
Stanley, Venetia   5, 11n19
Stévanovich, Collette   115, 117n10
Strange Histories   7
Sturluson, Snorri   79

Taylor, Andrew   8, 11n24, 40n15
Temple, Sir William   33
Thomas the Rymer (TR)   80
'The Tribe off Banburye'   2
The Turke & Gowin (TG)   5, 16, 21, 22, 51, 52, 78–82, 332–33
text   84–98

Vérard, Antoine   52
Vergil, Polydore, *Anglica Historia*   32

Waldron, George A.   80
Walton, Izaak   20–21
Warner, William   40n7
Warton, Thomas   13, 14, 15, 16, 22, 26n12, 28n31, 34, 35–36, 37–39, 42n37, 46–47, 99, 101n3, 102n9, 259
Observations on the 'Faerie Queene'   18, 37–39, 41n18
Watt, Isaac   16
Watt, Tessa   27n20, 29n43
Webster, K. G. T.   80
The Wedding of Sir Gawaine and Dame Ragnell (WSG)   21–22, 24, 29–30n51, 99–100, 114, 262
Withrington, John   11n24, 29n50, 41n23, 102n16
Wycherley, William   17, 27n25

Yonge, William   1

Zaerr, Linda Marie   22, 23–24, 30n60

Printed and bound by CPI Group (UK) Ltd, Croydon, CR0 4YY
30/06/2024

14521514-0002